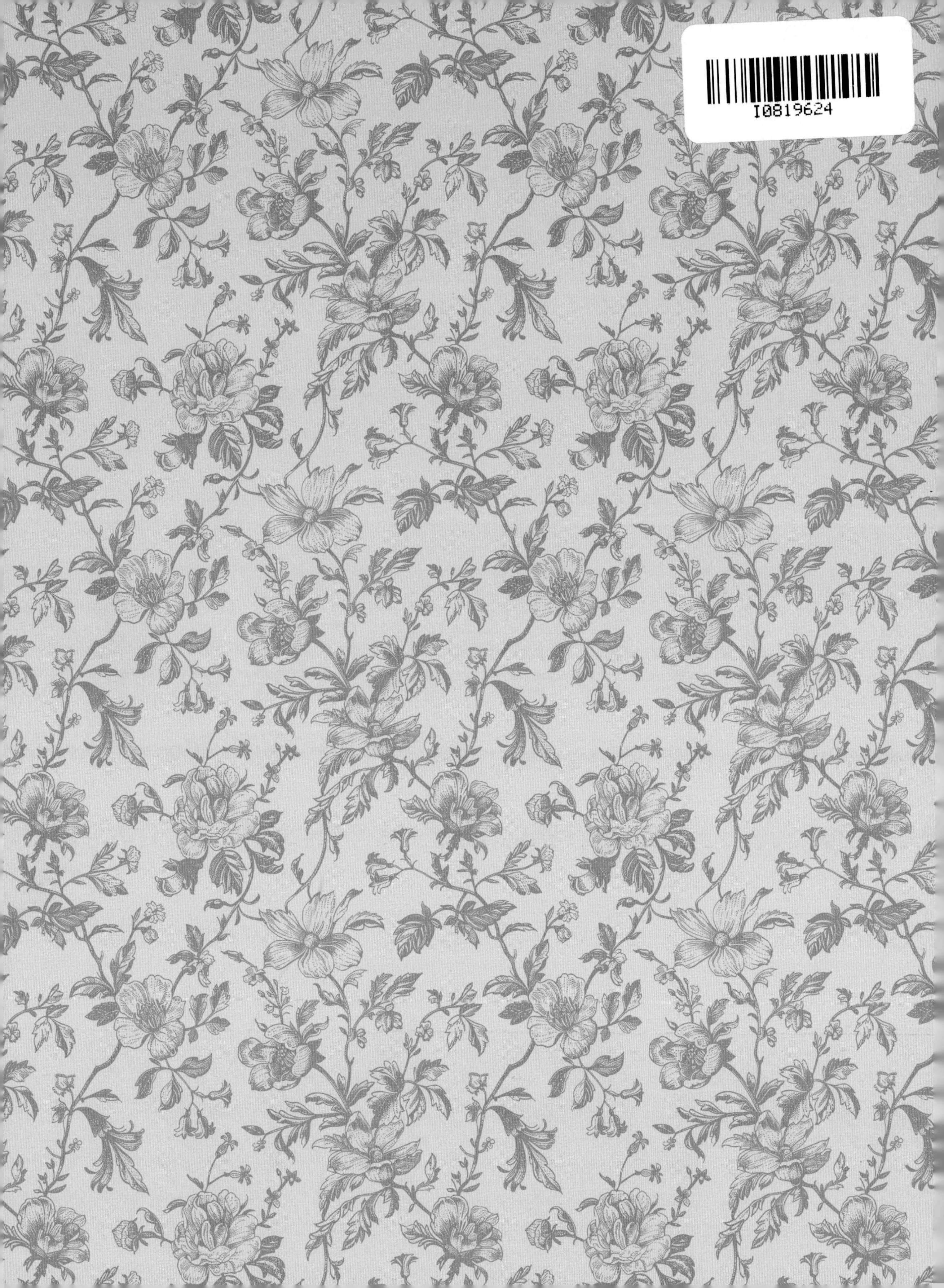
I0819624

Beautiful Blooms

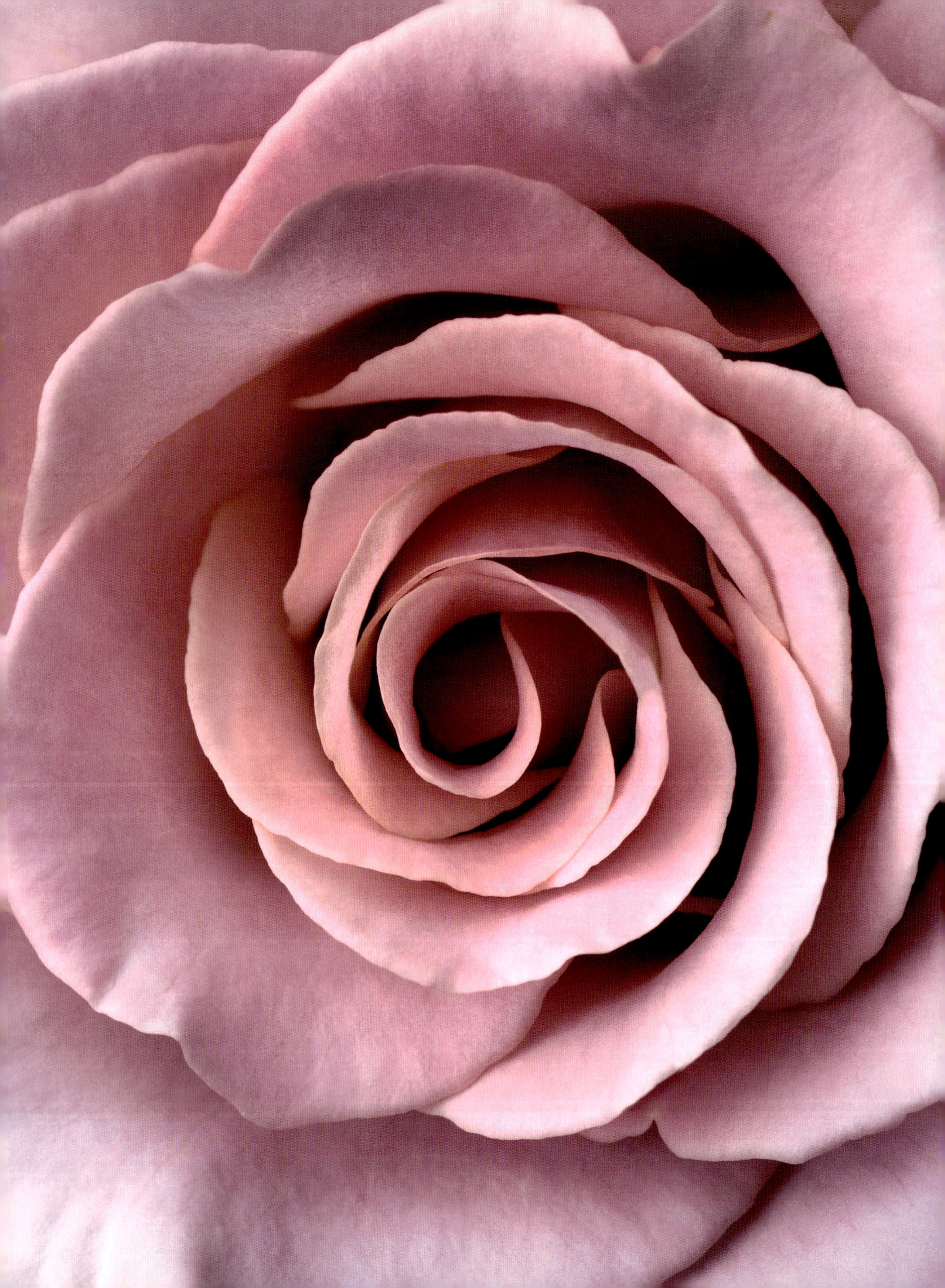

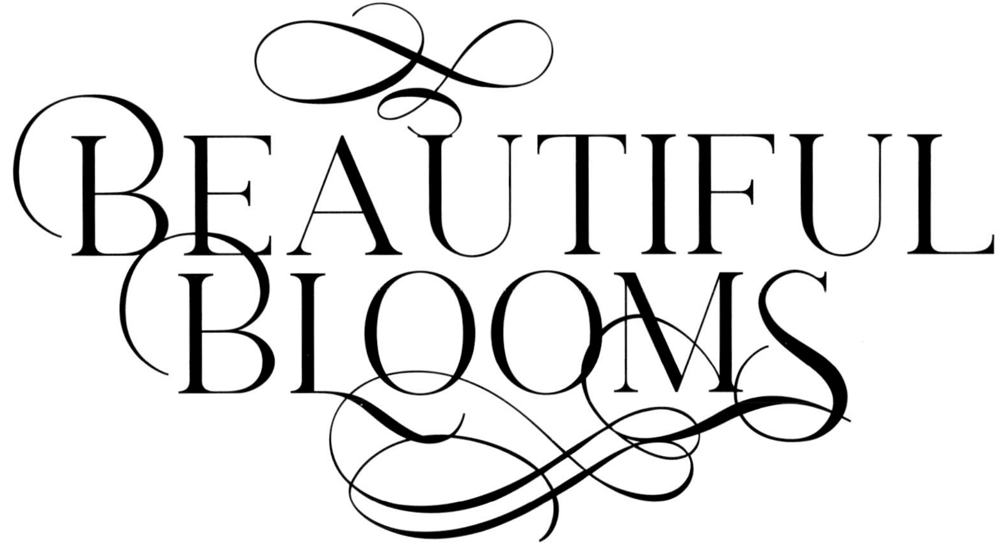

Beautiful Blooms

A Photographic Celebration

Text and Photographs by
GEORGIANNA LANE

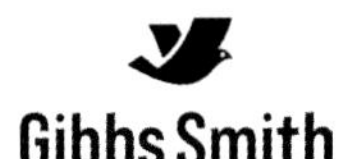
Gibbs Smith

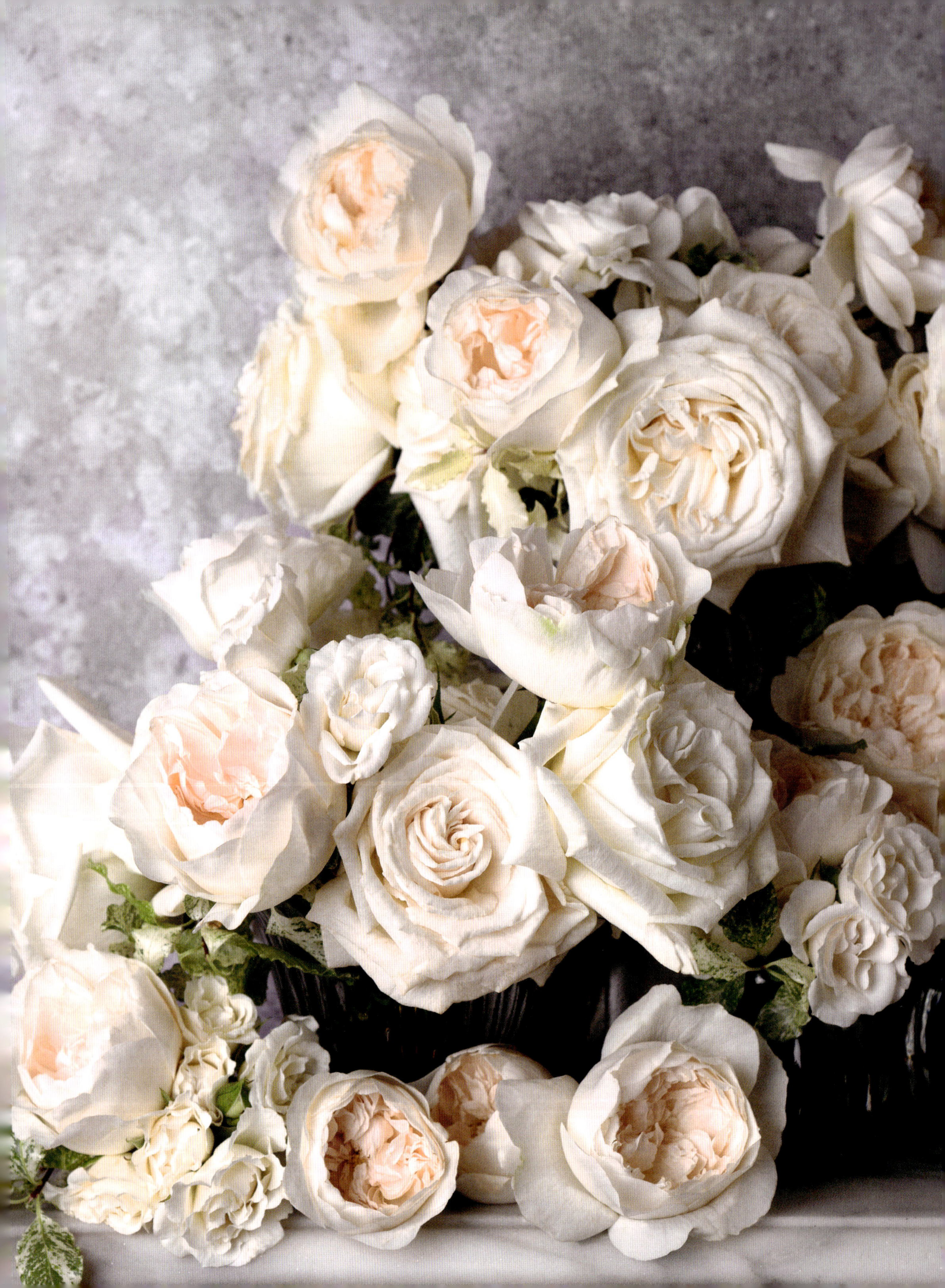

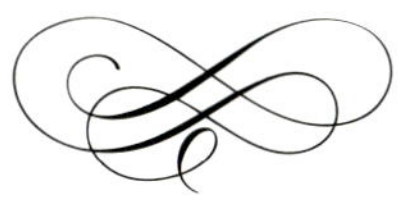

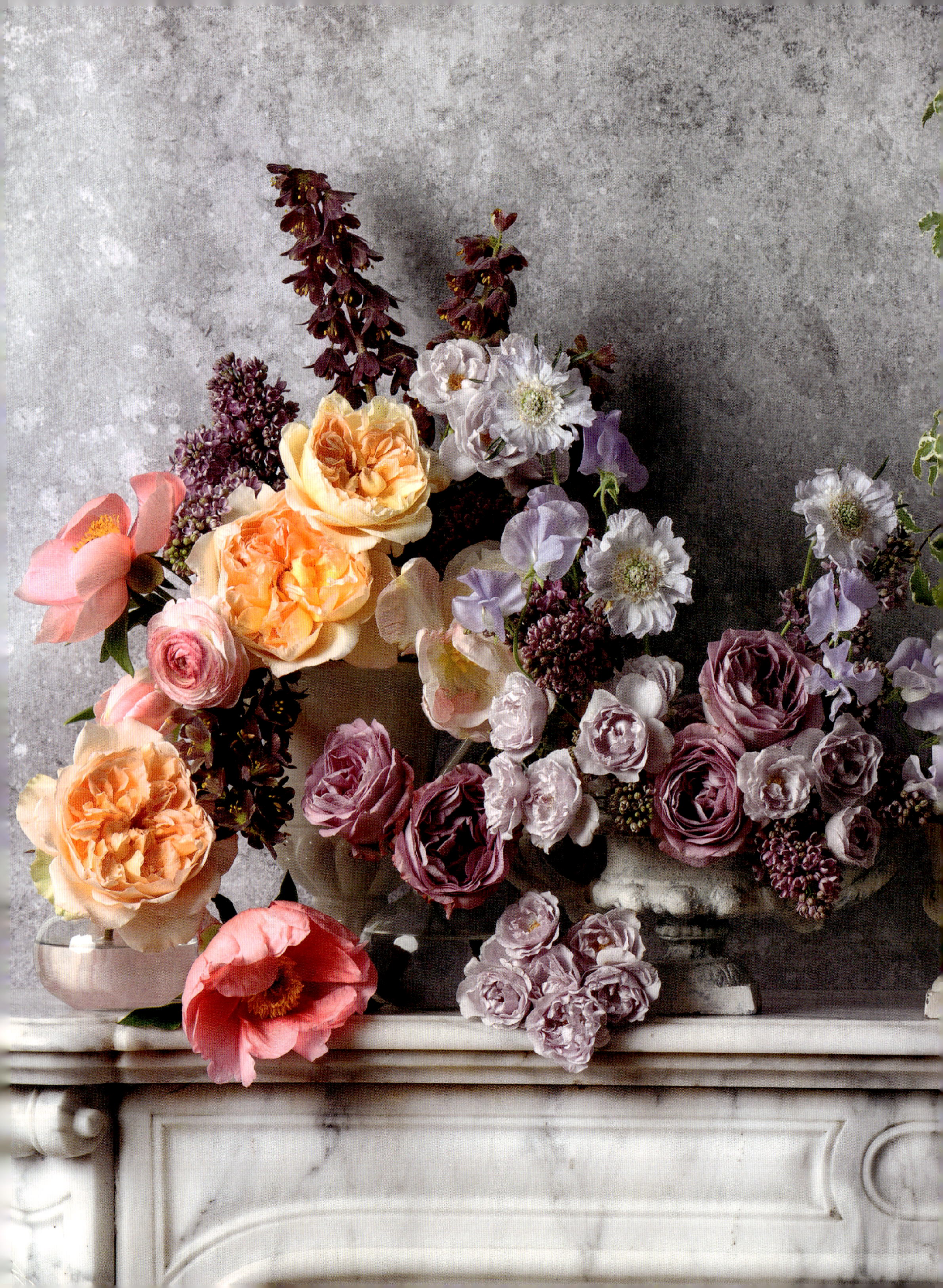

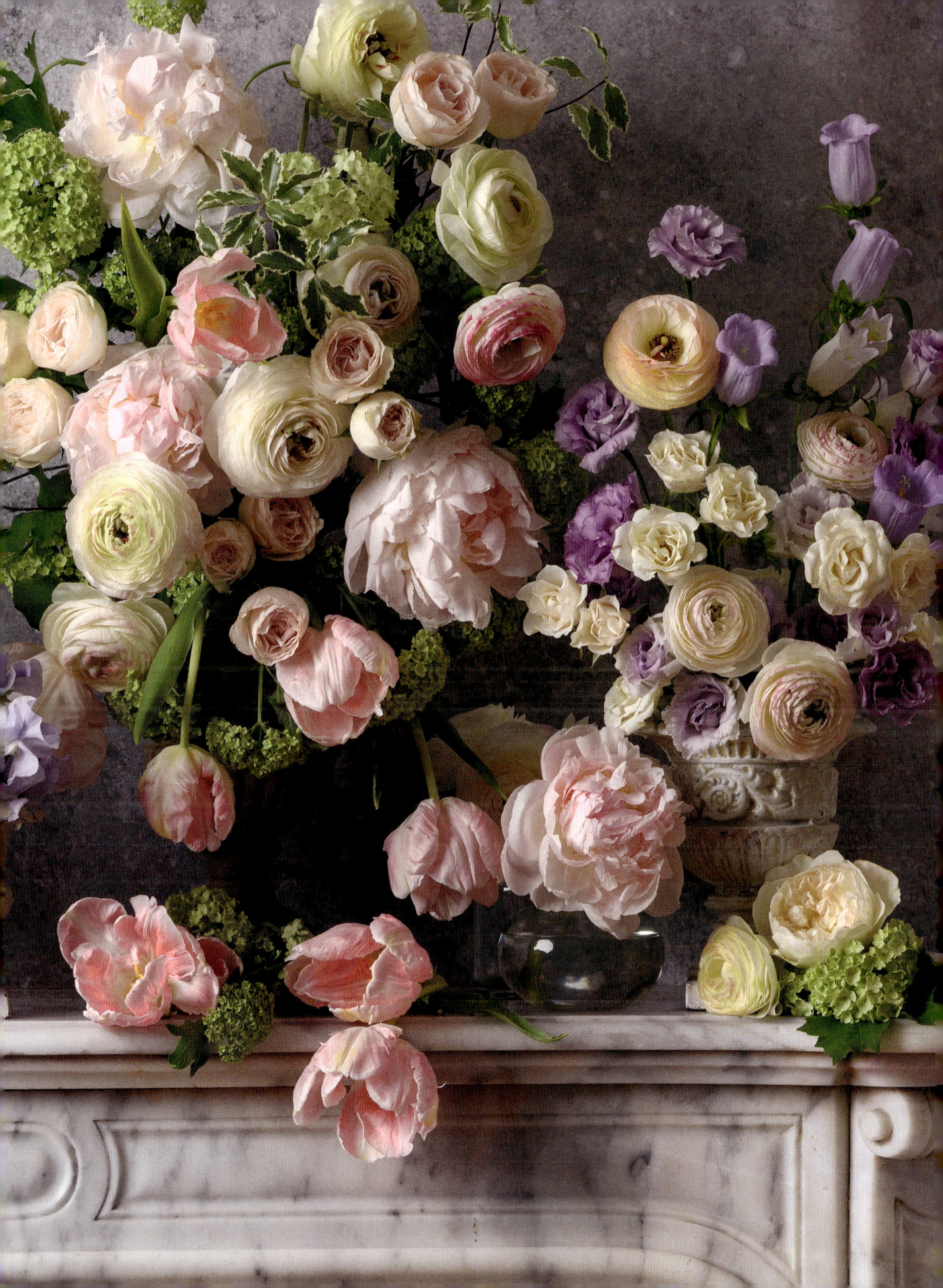

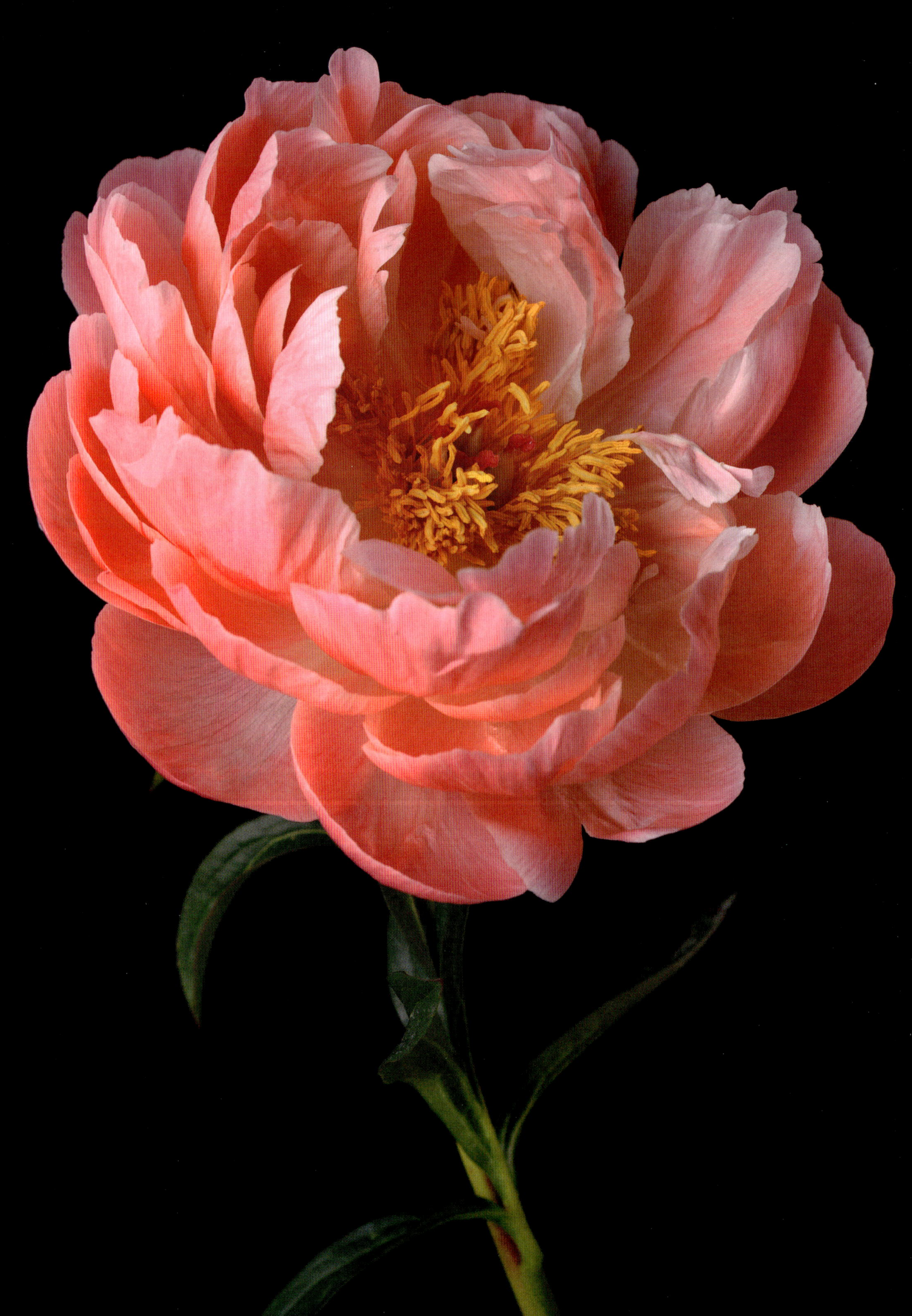

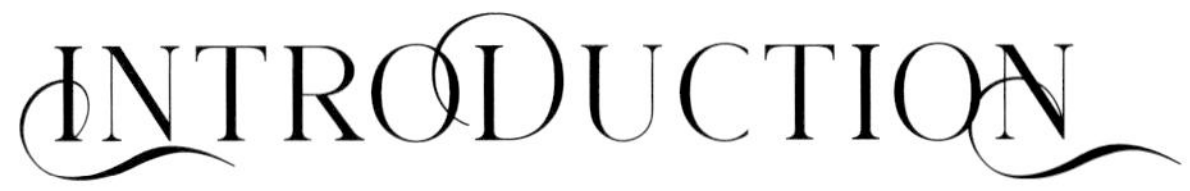

INTRODUCTION

Bloom seeker, blossom hunter, rose chaser, floral sleuth, flower whisperer.

I have been on a quest.

A globetrotting quest that has led from a mountainside rose garden in the Andean foothills to the world's largest collection of peonies at a grand French château, and from a cathedral-like glasshouse on the windswept Cornish coast to rainbow fields of ranunculus in California.

For twenty years, I've undertaken such expeditions in pursuit of elusive, petaled treasures and, like an eighteenth-century botanist, have cradled precious specimens in my hands, shielding them against torrential downpours or relentless sun until they could be lovingly documented.

Into more than a dozen books and tens of thousands of images I have poured my energies and unwavering passion for this endeavor, and always with one goal in heart and mind – to capture in photographs nature's floral glories, so that others might discover their wonders.

This volume has been created so that you may immerse yourself in these marvels and escape to a serene atmosphere of calm and peace, with no agenda beyond reveling in beauty.

Thus, this is not a horticultural encyclopedia, nor a field guide, nor a bouquet-arranging lifestyle manual. Rather, it is a visual celebration of flowering magnificence, an invitation to join the quest, to cross the threshold of the everyday and to enter this enchanted realm.

It is about snow falling on plum blossoms, the hush of hidden gardens and discovering the soul of an iris; it is about noticing the translucence of a poppy, the iridescence of a fading tulip, the poetry of a single rose bud bejeweled with dew.

Taken from my vast photographic library, the floral varieties and locations herein are representative of different phases of my career. The majority of the images have never before been seen. I'm honored to share them, and a bit of each of their stories, with you now.

LEFT: *Paeonia* 'Coral Charm'. May 2015.

EARLY DAYS

My parents were adventurous spirits who instilled in my siblings and me a great sense of the world, a love of travel, of art and of creativity, and a thirst to read, create and dream. On rainy Saturdays, routines were abandoned and we'd be encouraged to linger under the covers with our books and imaginations.

My mother was a highly accomplished musician, my father an international pilot. Both had earned private pilots' licenses by their early twenties and their mutual love of aviation was a uniting force. Flying jaunts over the Primitive Area of Idaho and the landscapes of Nevada and California defined their early relationship.

They were also avid photographers, an activity that we all came to embrace. A camera hung around one's neck was typical attire for any of us at any given moment. In that environment, I began writing and taking photographs at quite a young age, intent on documenting my surroundings.

Amongst the various cameras on hand, I was fascinated by a vintage Kodak Brownie Reflex 20, with its inverted image and flip-open viewfinder. As we lived in a pastoral landscape of apple orchards and rolling hills, the first images I shot were of nature. Framing and focusing through the reflex viewfinder gave me a feeling that I had discovered something extraordinary. I no longer have that camera, but I do still have some of the images taken with it – portals to another time.

In our rural habitat, my awakening to the abundant riches of the floral world began gradually – a vast field of daffodils across the road, apple blossoms tapping softly on my upstairs bedroom window, a curious exploration of the winsome plants at the edge of our woods.

INFLUENCES

Creatively, my first influences were painters and poets. In my early teens, two pivotal discoveries shaped my artistic sensibilities and caused thought-provoking shifts in my perspective.

At age twelve I discovered Shakespeare. His masterful descriptions and lyrical floral metaphors had a singular impact and fueled daydreams of bucolic landscapes, scenes of fairy magic and pastoral frolicking, and a new appreciation for even the most humble of blossoms.

Visually, it was the Impressionists – particularly Monet and Van Gogh – with whom I deeply connected on my first visit to Paris, at age fourteen. Viewing their

RIGHT: Water lilies (*Nymphaeaceae*) at Giverny, France. June 2011.

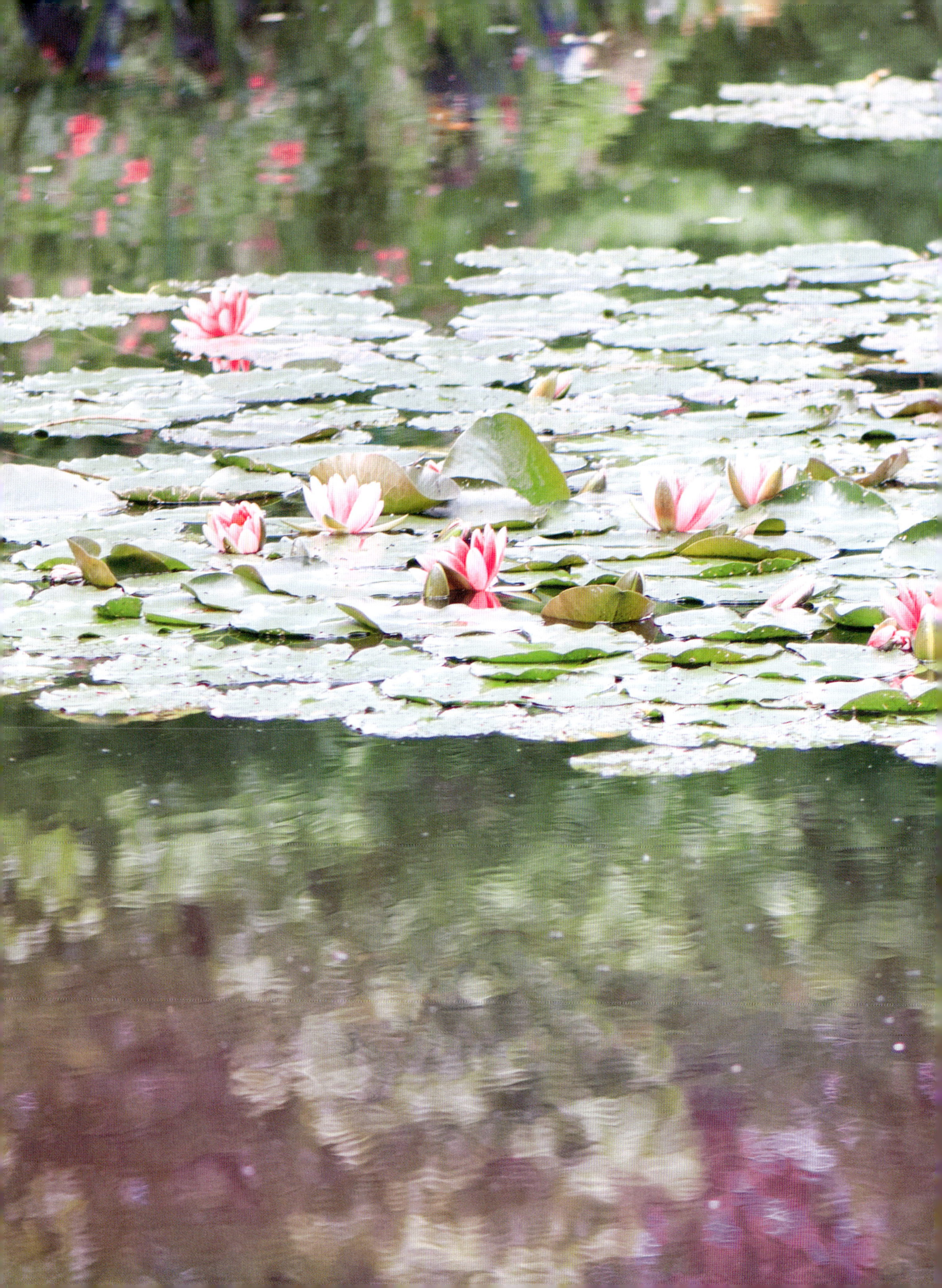

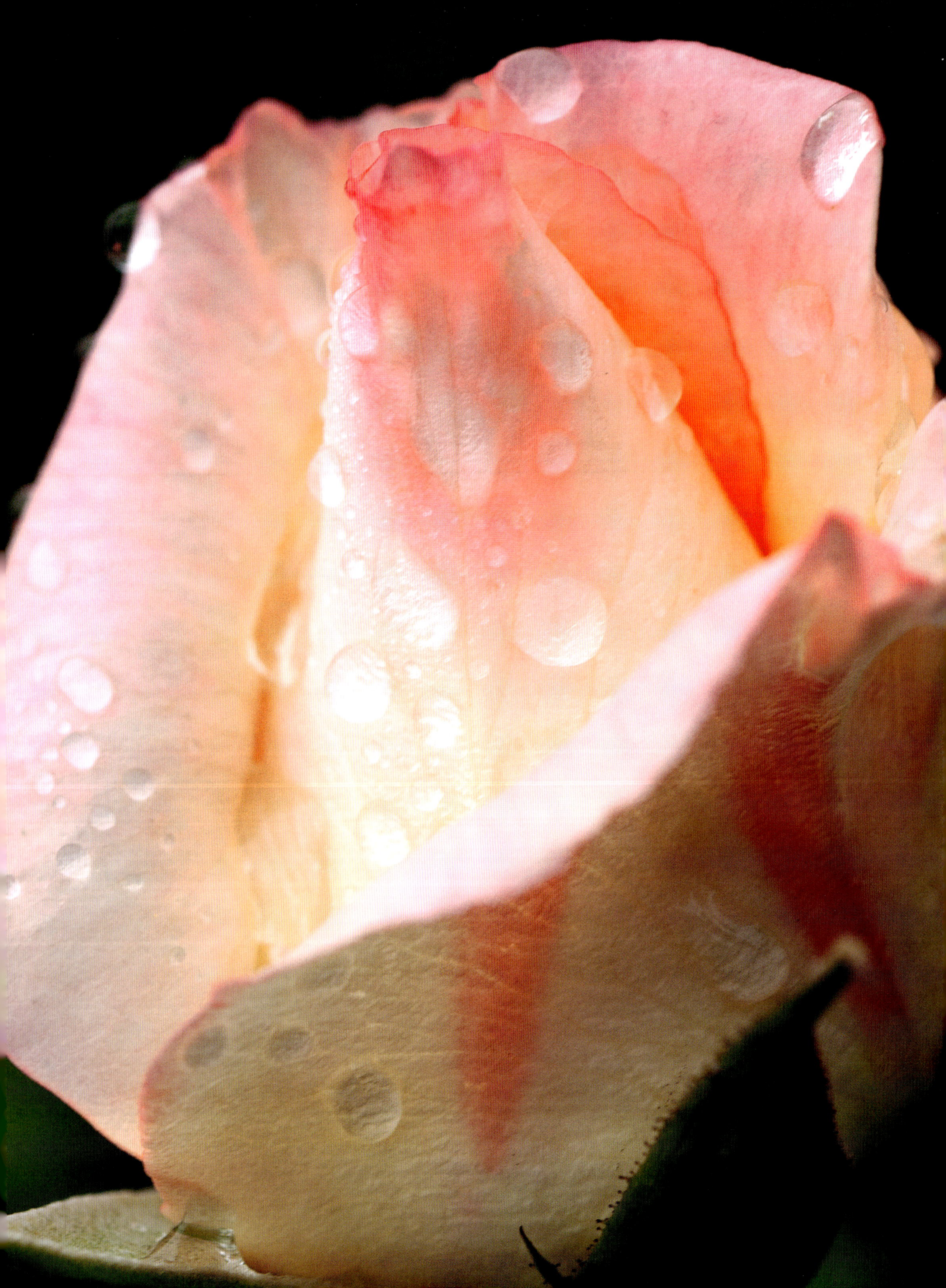

paintings, up close in an intimate museum setting, profoundly affected my own artistic journey. I wholly embraced their romantic vision of an alternate perceived reality, of details left to the imagination and lines blurred literally and figuratively, to create art that expanded perspectives and conceptions.

Later, I studied the Dutch Masters at the Rijksmuseum in Amsterdam and other locations throughout the world, which informed my parallel interest in precisely accurate portraits of individual flowers, a balanced contrast to the dreaminess of the Impressionistic style. In my work I relish the duality of such juxtapositions – the otherworldly and the sharply defined.

In the days just before my father's passing, a local rose garden became a refuge, a place where I could divert my attention from the heavy days of sadness and attempt to grapple with thoughts and feelings too weighty to articulate. Photographing roses there in the early morning became my therapy, moving through the damp grass in the low, slanting sun. One image amongst thousands represents that time to me, that of a flawless bud of *Rosa* 'Diana, Princess of Wales', poignantly glittering with tear-like droplets after a sudden summer shower.

As an adult, I drew much inspiration and knowledge from my former garden, Hillhaven, in the lush Pacific Northwest. When my husband, David, and I purchased the property, I only knew a handful of flowers, but through intensive study – aided by my suddenly useful high-school Latin – I attained an expansive understanding of, and an awakening to, the astounding miracles of the natural world.

We enhanced the garden, already established with numerous species, with hydrangeas, roses, perennials, woodland garden plants and thousands of bulbs.

I never tired of walking amongst them, fingers trailing the tops of beloved plants, with attendant butterflies, moths, ladybugs and dragonflies. And the ever-present birds – the sassy crows and naughty jays, the twittering chickadees and swooping hummingbirds, and my sweet, darling American robins – all sang from dawn until late evening, faithfully keeping me company with a nightly serenade as I deadheaded roses in the gathering twilight.

At Hillhaven I discovered the genuine satisfaction of cutting blooms for the house that we had nurtured and grown ourselves. I am gratified that a number of my bestselling images are of flowers that came from our own leafy paradise.

And now, Paris – where I have lived for many years – exerts a daily and enduring influence. Here, I feel a part of something bigger than myself, something

LEFT: *Rosa* 'Diana, Princess of Wales'. June 2007.

grand and important and exceptional. It is where I feel most inspired. My favorite activity is a solitary early-morning wander through a garden – the Tuileries, Palais Royal and Luxembourg are nearby favorites – when the air is still and cool and the birds are celebrating a new day.

I find nothing more exhilarating as a photographer than having a Parisian park all to myself. Over two decades I have become familiar with the seasonal rhythms and pace of each one, which flowers bloom when and the best vantage points from which to appreciate them.

At dawn in the Tuileries, under the shadow of the Louvre, the Musée d'Orsay and the Jeu de Paume, where I first discovered the Impressionists, I sometimes encounter the ghost of my younger self from that long-ago trip to Paris. We smile and nod in recognition, suspended for that instant in a timeless dimension, acknowledging shared secrets and wishes. I am grateful for her curiosity and intrepid spirit, and I hope she is proud that I have at last fulfilled the heartfelt pledge made with my mother that, one day, I would live in Paris.

LIVING WITH FLOWERS

This enticing world of flowers invites endless explorations into their history, aesthetics, mythology and literary references, all the while revealing fascinating relationships with quantum physics, Fibonacci numbers, fractals and the wavelengths of color. Flowers have been entwined with human culture for millennia, with their own language of meaning and symbolism, and are universally recognized for contributing to emotional well-being.

A flower's fragrance can instantly recall beloved memories, tangible just on the edge of consciousness, elusive but precious. A whiff of lilacs, lily of the valley or sweet peas can whisk us back to a grandmother's embrace, while *Narcissus*, *Hyacinth*, *Daphne* and jasmine allow us to briefly relive an idyllic spring.

As photographic subjects, flowers offer gorgeous, heart-stirring subjects in myriad fascinating forms, colors, shapes and textures, which are combined with a fleeting lifespan, the nature of which engenders in me an urgency to capture every petal and leaf before they are lost upon the winds.

Some feel they are bestowed gifts from the universe, as evidence of the infinite, and who could argue with that?

RIGHT: The Tuileries Garden at dawn, Paris, France. May 2012.

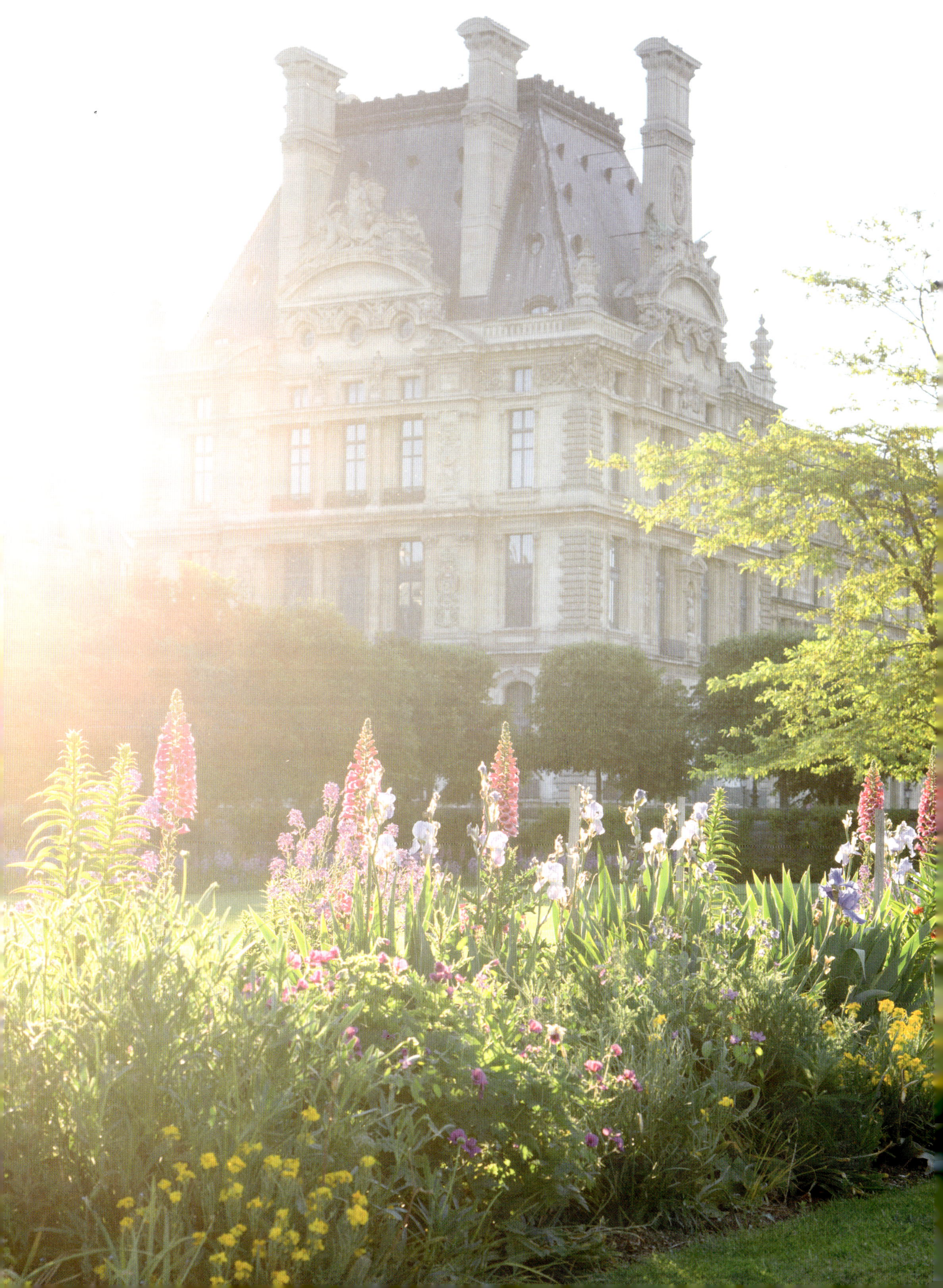

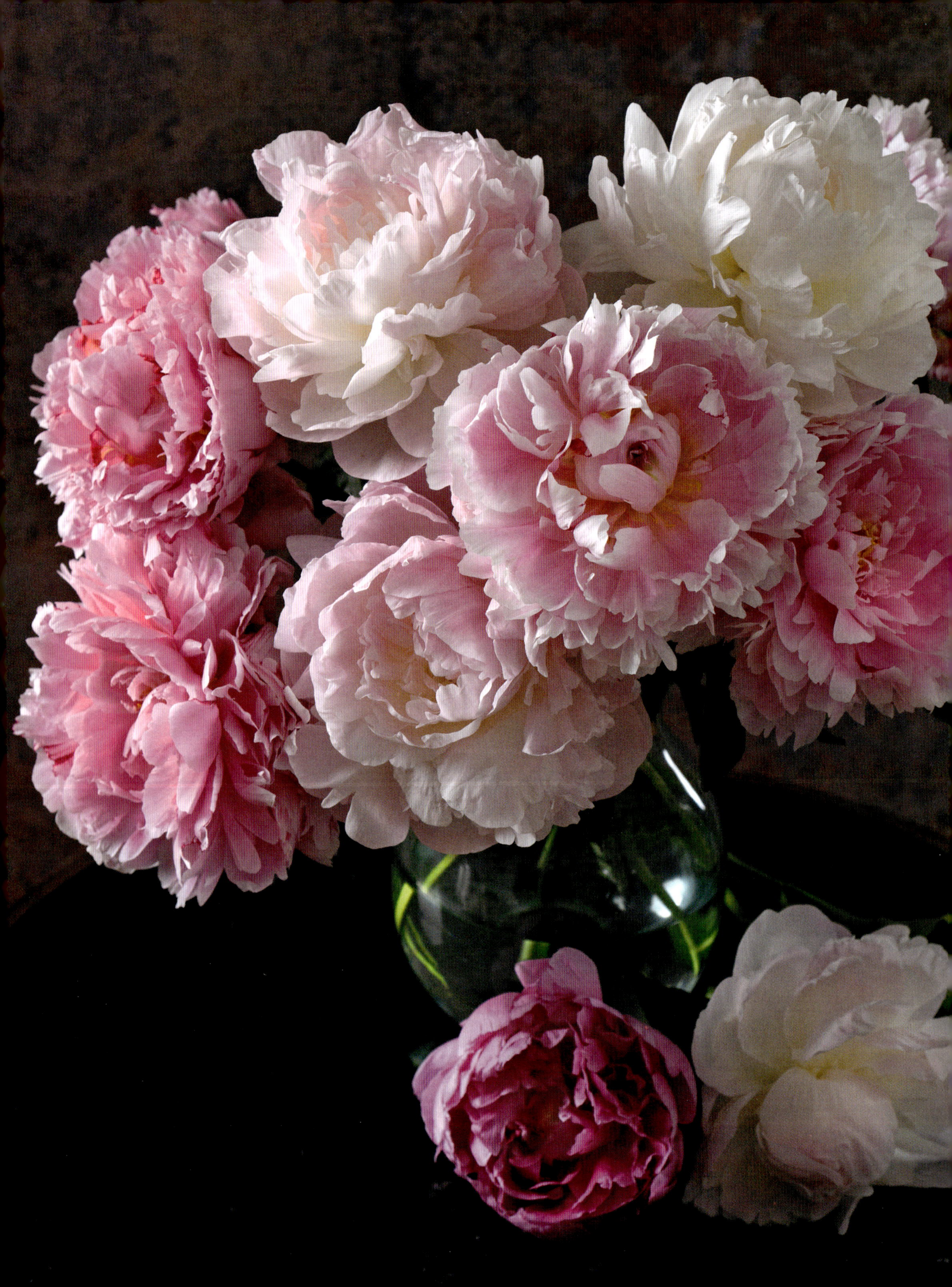

FAVORITE FLOWERS

What defines a favorite flower? Certainly, there are as many answers as there are flowers to inspire them. But after a thorough association with thousands of varieties, I have refined my own, rather lofty, criteria.

To warrant being inked with a flourish onto my exalted list, a flower must present an elegance of form, of pleasing curves or refined symmetry, sculpted without harsh angles or sharpness.

Without question, it must be rendered in an aesthetically pleasing color palette, brushed with pastel prettiness or bedazzled with regal jewel tones that are never garish or crass. Absolutely essential is a transportive fragrance, an enveloping scent that sweetly reminds us of an adored person or place, as if it is a gateway to an earlier time. And if a flower ages gracefully and poetically, gently releasing petals with understated grace, it is sure to capture my heart.

The flowers I love most are the billowy, fragrant, voluptuous, multi-petaled ladies that conjure visions of flouncy petticoats and ruffled collars, of luscious layers of frosting on an extravagant cake. Roses, peonies, iris, double tulips – their very flamboyance elevates them from the crowd and, like debutantes at a grand ball, they pirouette and twirl, slyly flirtatious and fully aware of their irresistible appeal.

I adore flowers that, when cut lavishly for a vase, naturally arrange themselves into a wild tumble of blooms and foliage, requiring no fiddly poking or prodding to be splendidly displayed.

Undoubtedly, roses are my champions – the favorite to grow, to cut, to photograph, and also exuding my favorite scent. With a lengthy flowering season, a painterly spectrum of shades and exhilarating perfume, they will never waver from that pinnacle.

As Shakespeare said, “Of all the flowers, me thinks a rose is best.” Inextricably associated with love, roses are likely the oldest flowers on Earth, dating back 35 million years. With the highest vibrational frequency of the entire plant kingdom, they provide a positive boost like no other. Should I ever be consigned to photograph only roses, that is a challenge I would readily accept.

The two plants on my list that I do forgive for being devoid of scent are hydrangeas and hellebores, because they are so greatly rewarding in other ways.

LEFT: Mixed peonies, Paris, France. June 2025.

Rainbow-hued with clusters of petals larger than my hands, hydrangeas generously give nearly year-round pleasure. I have grown and photographed them for years, including those from our garden that appear on the cover of my book, *Hydrangeas*. At the end of the season they fade into antiqued splendor, adding a burnished glow to the autumn garden.

At winter's end, the shy hellebore flowers emerge from their evergreen leaves, in crimson, lime, magenta and white, impervious to the whimsies of weather, and they soldier on well into April. To fully appreciate the centers of their nodding heads, we planted them on the upward slope outside our kitchen window, giving us an eye-to-eye view of their lovely features.

You may notice, perhaps surprisingly, the absence from my list of certain popular flowers, although I have loved creating books on them. Dahlias are structurally a fascinating photographic subject for me, whose depths I explore with different light and camera angles. And yet, their mostly vivid colors, their lack of discernible aroma and required care eliminate them from my registry. Likewise, ranunculus are wonderful photographic subjects but also are unscented and can be tricky, at least for me, to grow.

MY APPROACH AND PURPOSE

For any artist, their emotional connection to the subject matter drives the intrinsic personal message they wish to impart.

My consuming purpose and intention has always been to create romantic, light-filled, dreamy images with a bit of a magical air, that transport viewers to a place of tranquility and bring moments of grace to their day.

To that end, I strive to make photographs that are not just pretty but that touch a chord, spark a cherished memory or ignite a desire to visit an intriguing locale, even if only virtually.

I approach my work as if I were a painter, carefully composing to eliminate distracting elements, creating a scene that is classic and elegant, and that will be relevant and communicate well into the future, without regard for the latest trends or styles.

And I am continually attempting to create the definitive view of a given flower or place, to accurately create its ideal representation. To do less would be a disservice to nature, to the viewer and, ultimately, to the divine. It is not so much a matter of perfection as it is quantifying their unique essence.

RIGHT: *Rosa* 'Marilyn Monroe', Seattle, Washington, USA. August 2010.

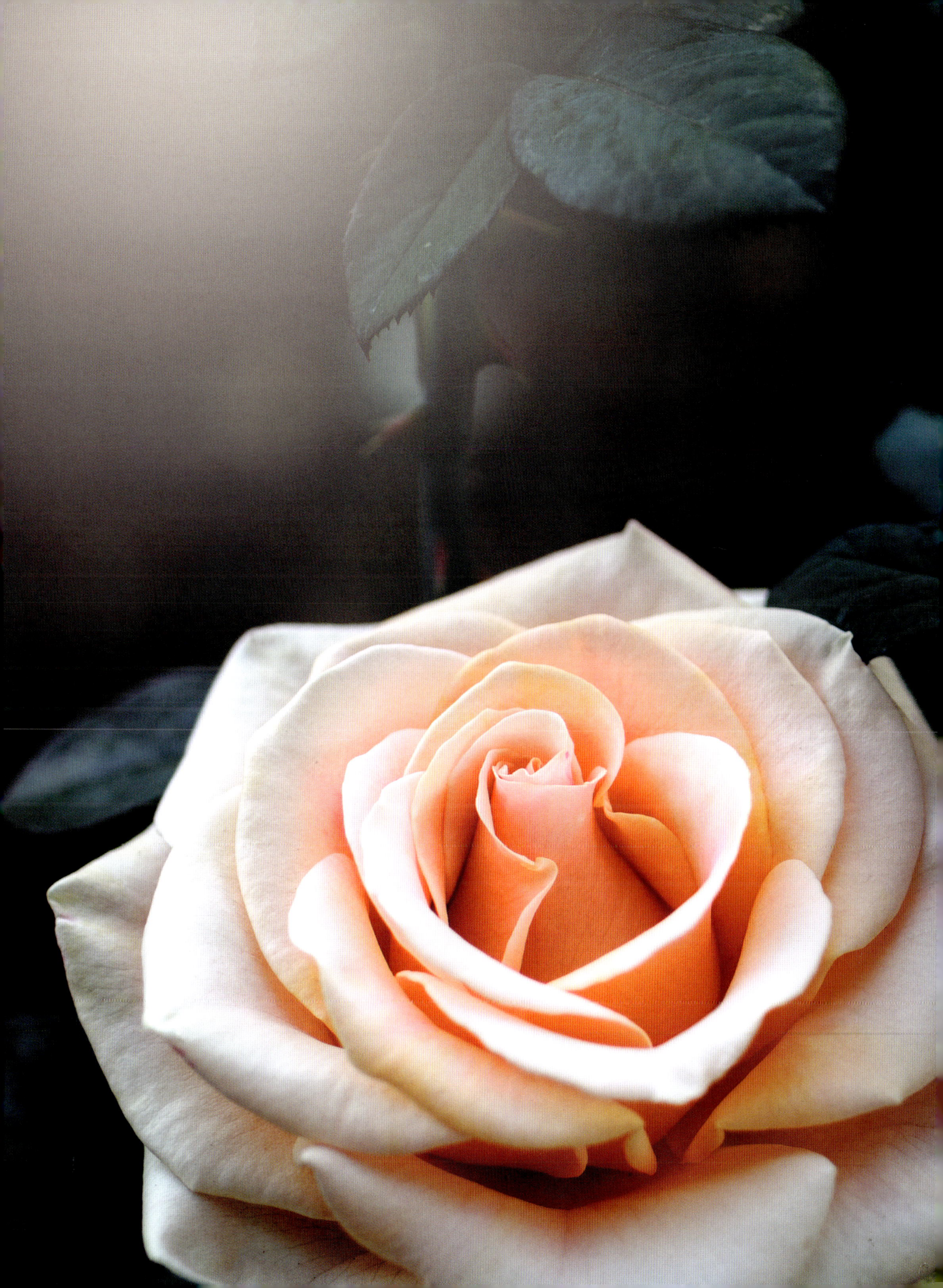

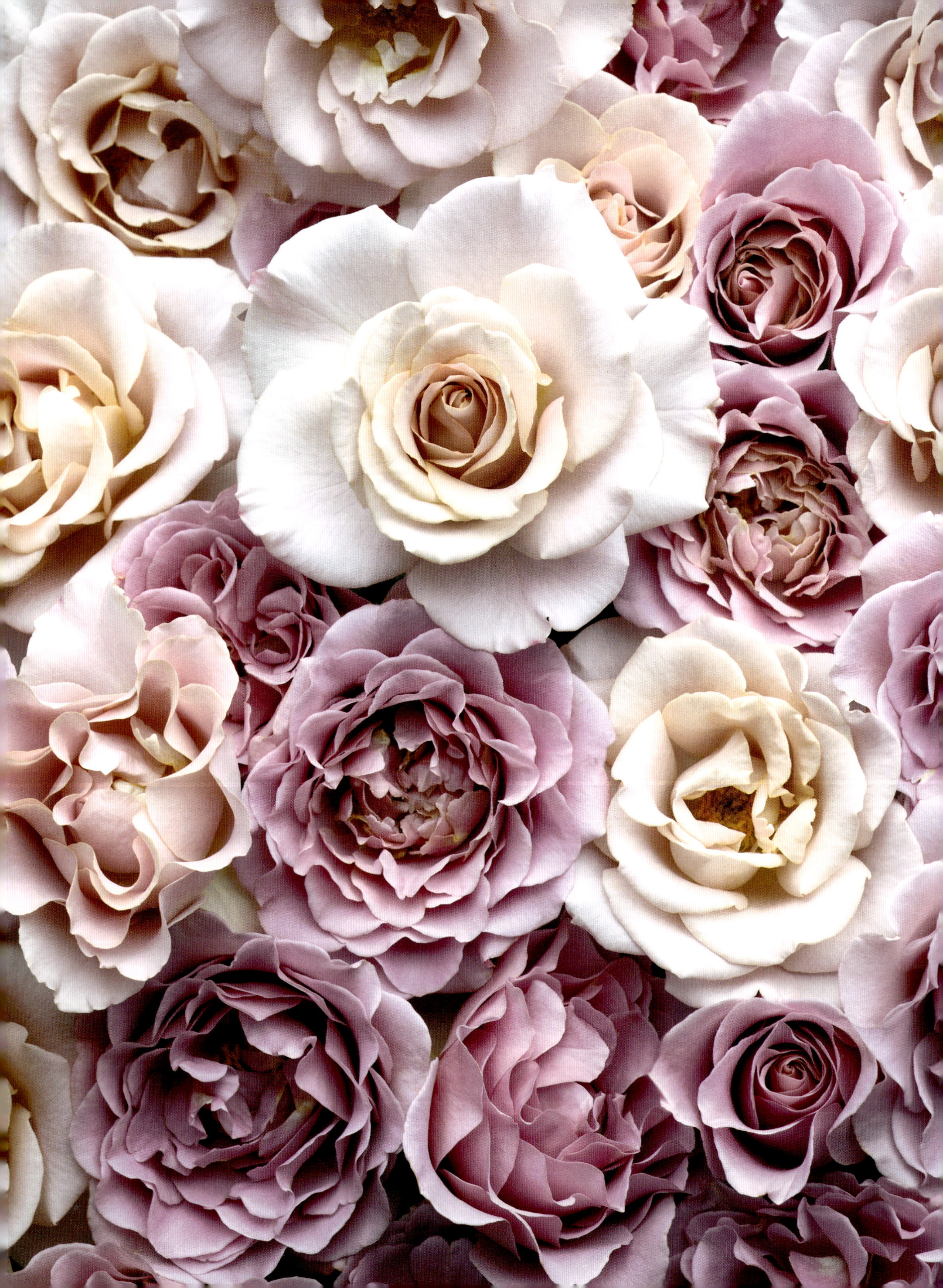

Therefore, I will return to a location repeatedly – day after day, week after week, sometimes year after year – until I feel certain that I have created an image that embodies the quintessential portrayal of that location or flower. There have been times where my diligence has preserved a record of a place that is no longer in existence, which makes me doubly thankful.

Being a professional flower photographer on assignment entails embracing perpetually early starts, adjusting to the ever-present vagaries of weather and developing the ability to disregard physical discomfort until the final frame has been taken of the last bloom.

However, on more relaxed days, unencumbered by schedules, I may not photograph all the flowers that I encounter, but I do try to acknowledge their presence and thank them for existing, for their brief but glorious sojourn in our world. Their accelerated lifespan, with parallels to our own relatively brief existence, allows us to closely observe, in a single bloom, the cycle of life – a microcosm of our own.

Whether in a modest garden or a vast field, I cherish days of meandering, deep in conversation with the flowers, gently coaxing out their enigmatic secrets and the private mysteries tucked between their petals, revealing the exquisite beauty that I humbly dare to capture.

And I remain ever mindful that I'm immensely privileged to preserve their individual personalities and ephemeral grace, even as they poignantly fade before me.

HOW THIS BOOK IS ORGANIZED

Compiling this work, in addition to a full review of my image archives, involved navigating a 20-year-long memory lane of photographic projects. That retrospection led to the realization that revisiting the physical landscapes that I have traversed in my career inevitably meant revisiting the accompanying emotional ones as well.

Equally as indelible as the images captured were the moods evoked by each, and an awareness that an image could bring back not only sights and sounds but the attendant feelings reflecting the current events in my life. Gardens had long been a safe retreat – places of sparkling delight in happy times and healing comfort through difficulties and loss.

Placing myself back in those environments revived a gamut of emotional states: solace, melancholy, uncertainty, serenity, joy, wonder, harmony, grace, grief,

LEFT: *Rosa* 'Stephen Rulo', Seattle, Washington, USA. October 2020.

contentment. Inextricably linked to the images, they suggested to me a framework for this presentation. I choose these days to focus on the positive and uplifting in all things, so I selected for the chapter titles *Wonder, Joy, Reverie, Harmony, Serenity* and *Grace,* as a gradual progression of emotional states that I have experienced through my ongoing personal association with the botanical.

I have curated this collection with a focus on individual portraits and special gardens. The final photographs selected are not sequenced by date or location. Instead of presenting individual images randomly, I've created thematic vignettes or quiet interludes, each devoted to one of the gardens or one type of bloom, to give you more of a sense of it. There are perhaps four to eight pages, complementary in subject and intermingled for balance and interest, offering a gentle progression of mood, color and ambiance.

Thus you are invited on a non-linear but pleasant ramble, moving as a dreamer might effortlessly travel from place to place in an instant.

Each chapter introduction provides insight into the flowers and gardens featured within it. Captions are included where relevant. And yes, you'll find throughout a proliferation of my signature rosy tones and sections heavily festooned with my beloved roses – indulgences for which I do not apologize.

Above all, I am infinitely grateful to have the opportunity to release into the cosmos these examples of many years of my work.

HOPES AND INTENTIONS FOR THE BOOK

I have endeavored in this volume to create a little sanctuary of beauty and inspiration, a haven of respite and reflection, and to imbue each page with positive and uplifting energy. As you embark upon the adventure, I hope that you feel encouraged to delve into and savor these gems of nature and to envision yourself strolling through the misty gardens.

May this book enhance your life and be a continuing source of joy.
Welcome to my world of beautiful blooms.
I am truly happy that you are here.

With love,
Georgianna

PARIS, FRANCE, JULY 2025

RIGHT: Les jardins d'Argences, Normandy, France. June 2011.

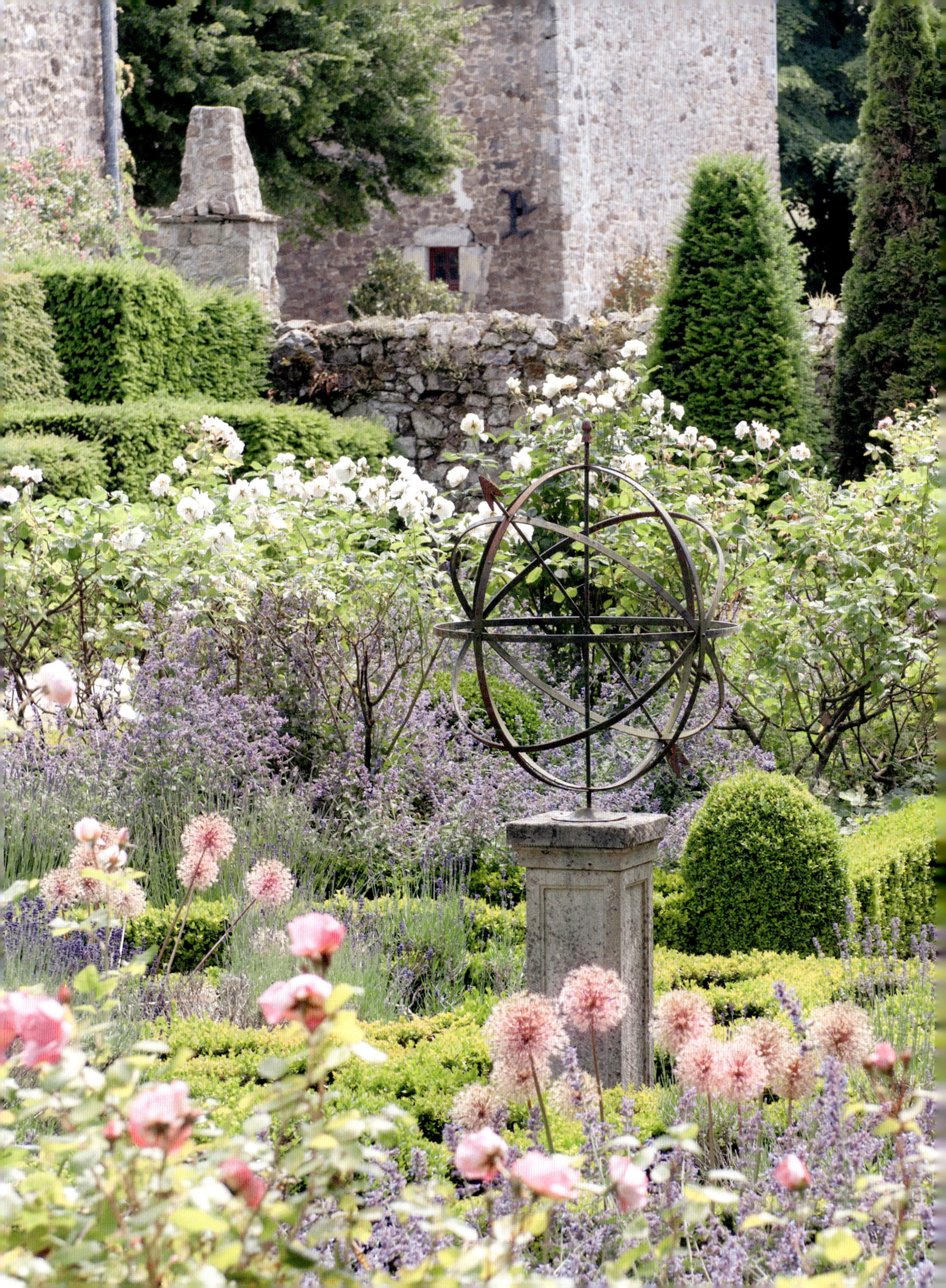

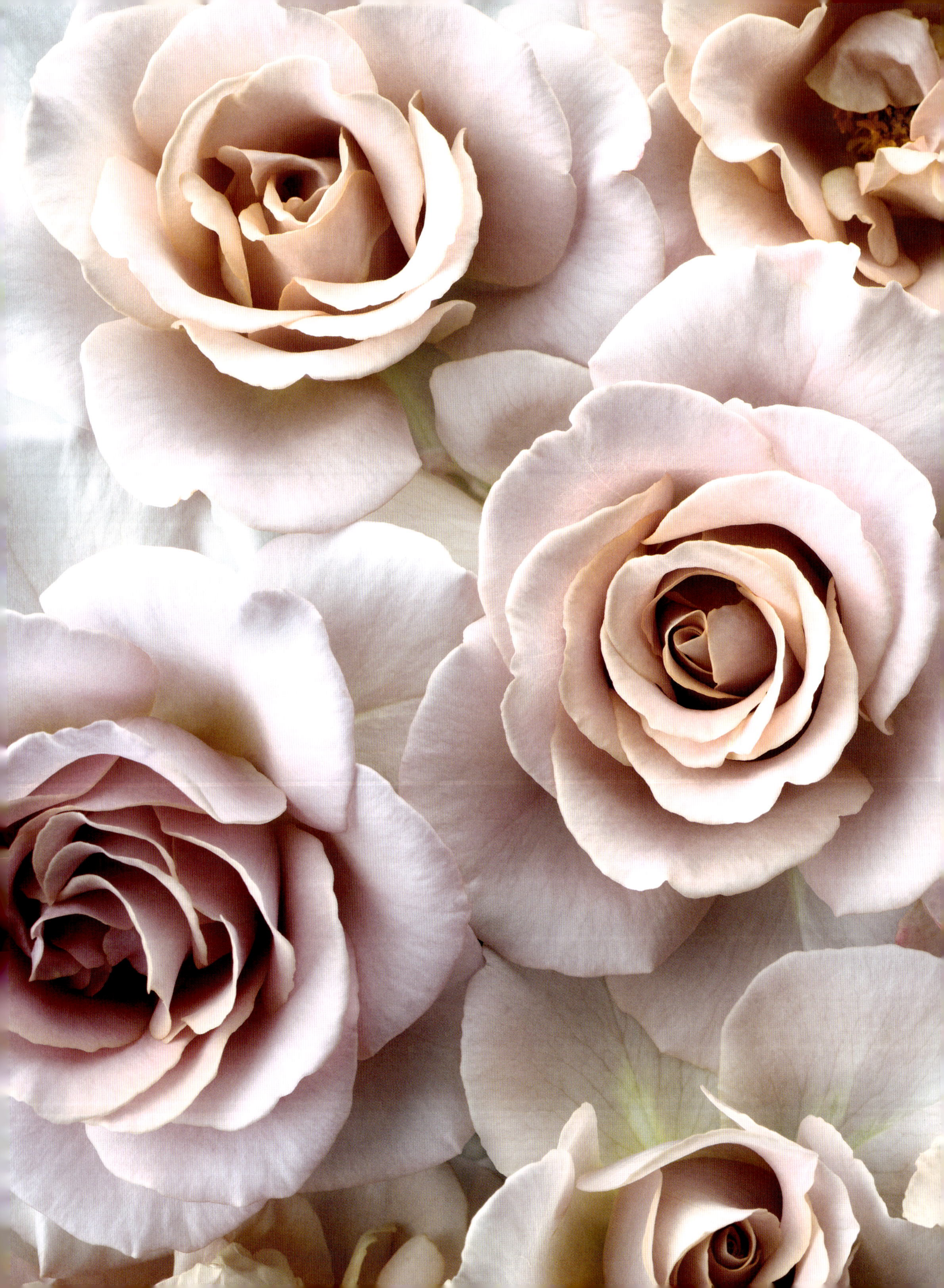

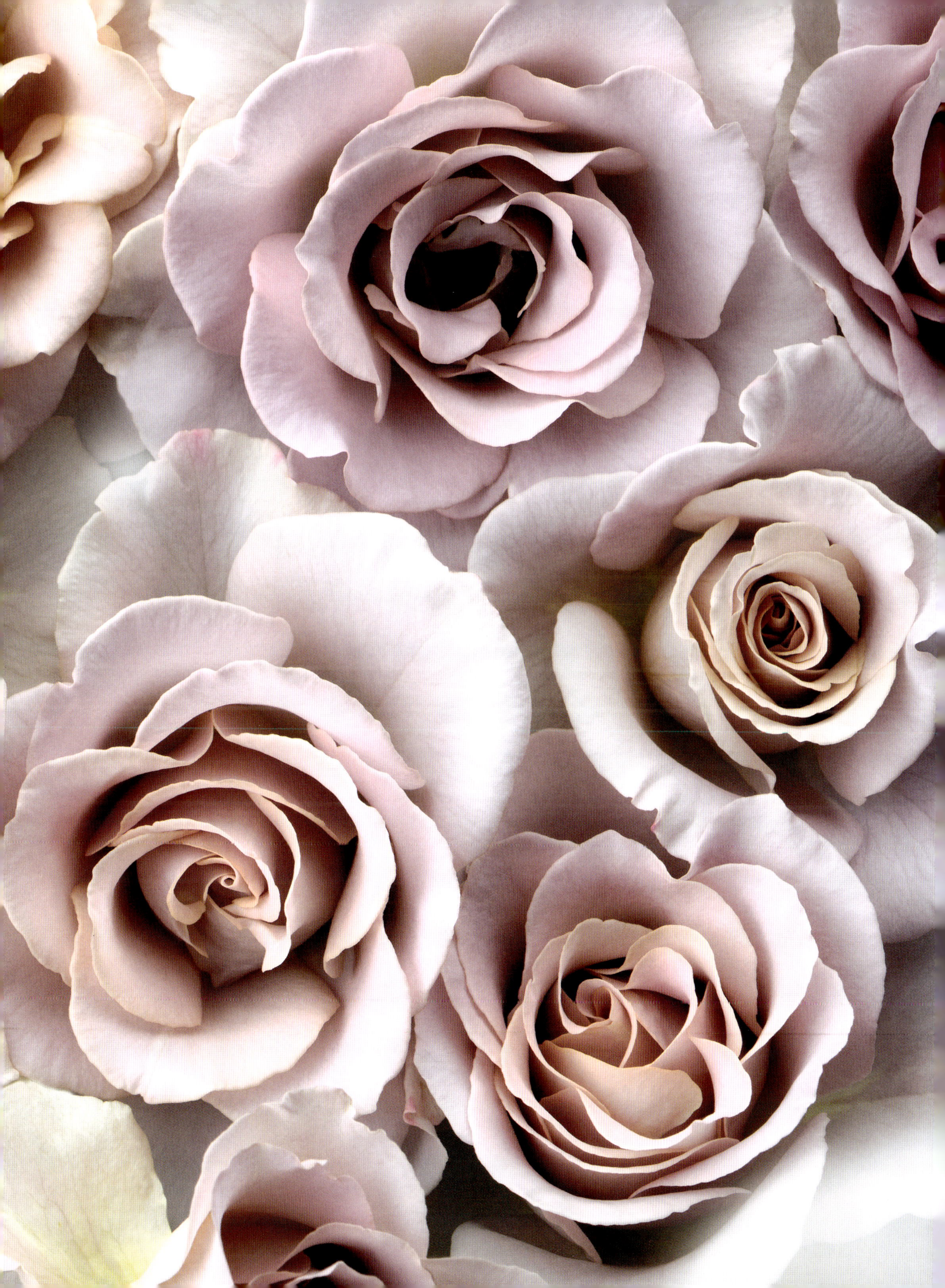

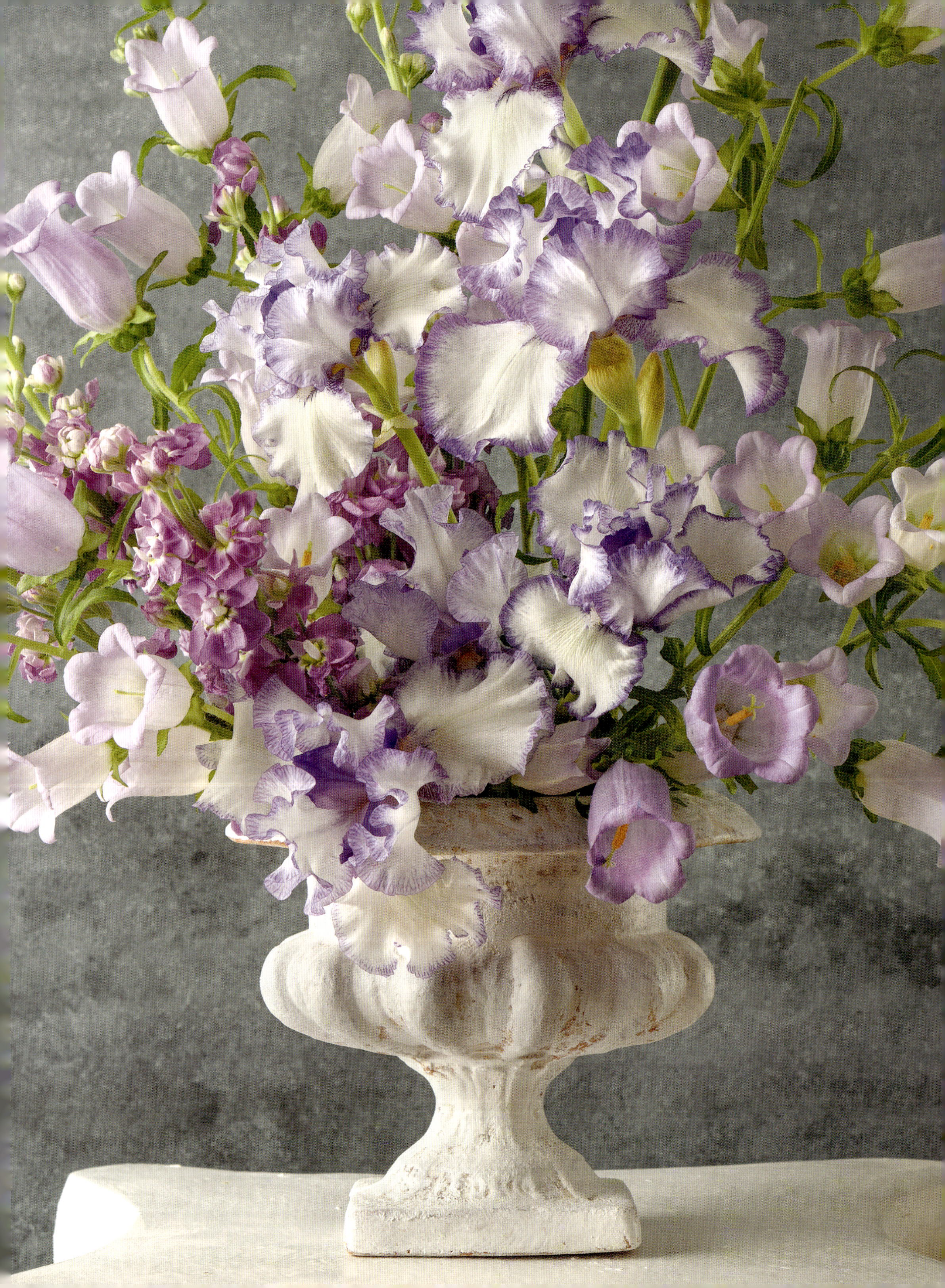

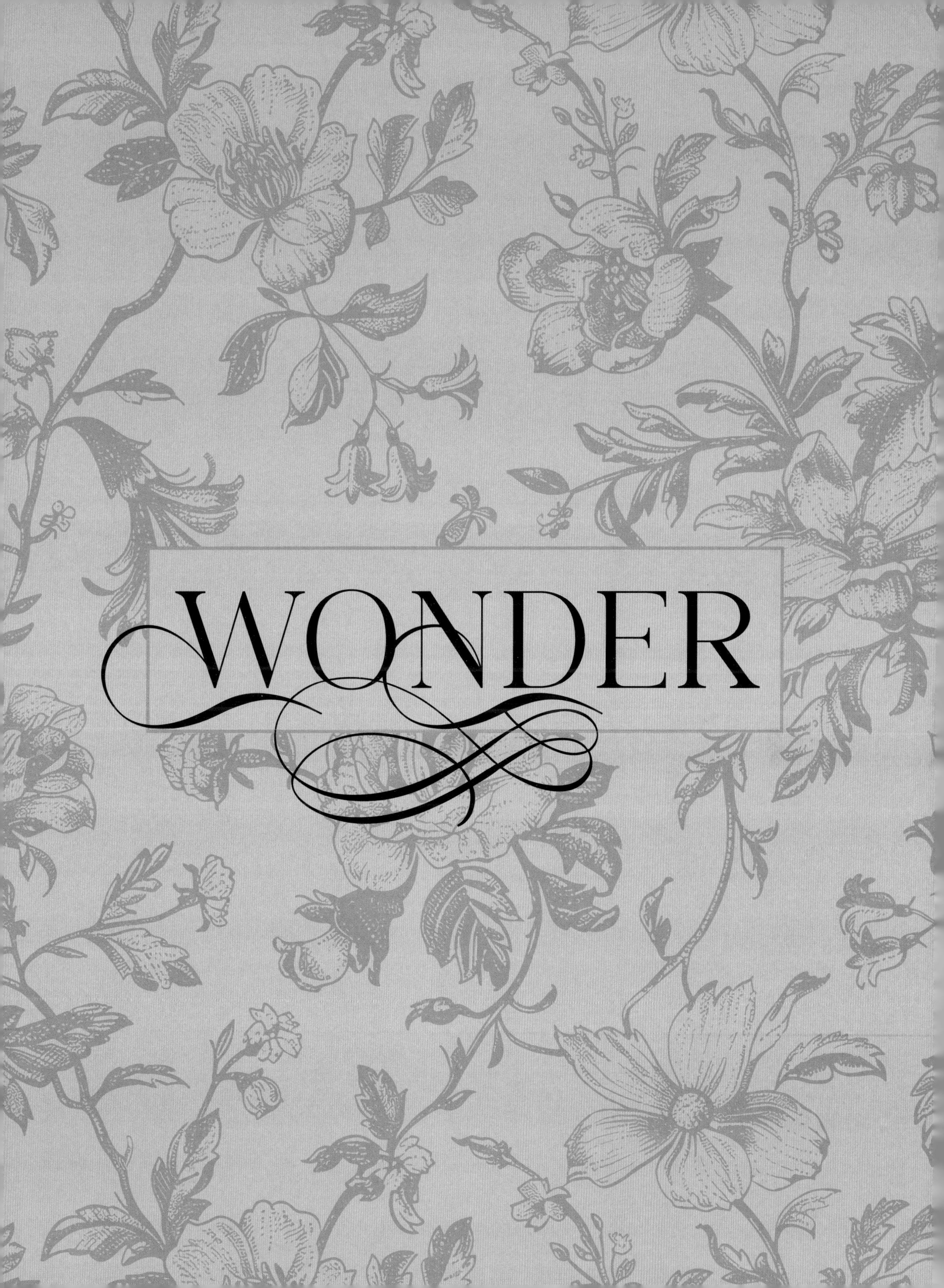

WONDER

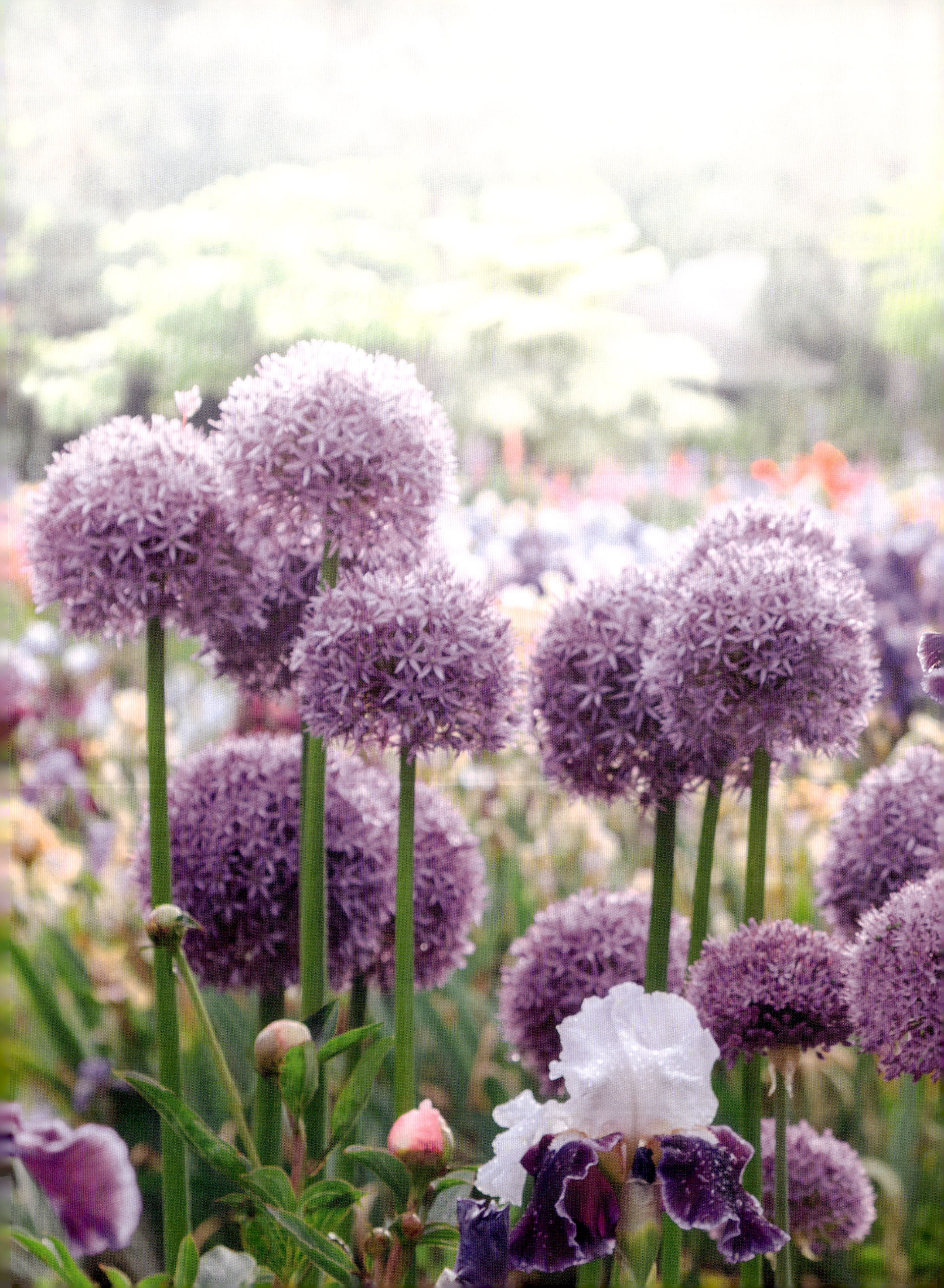

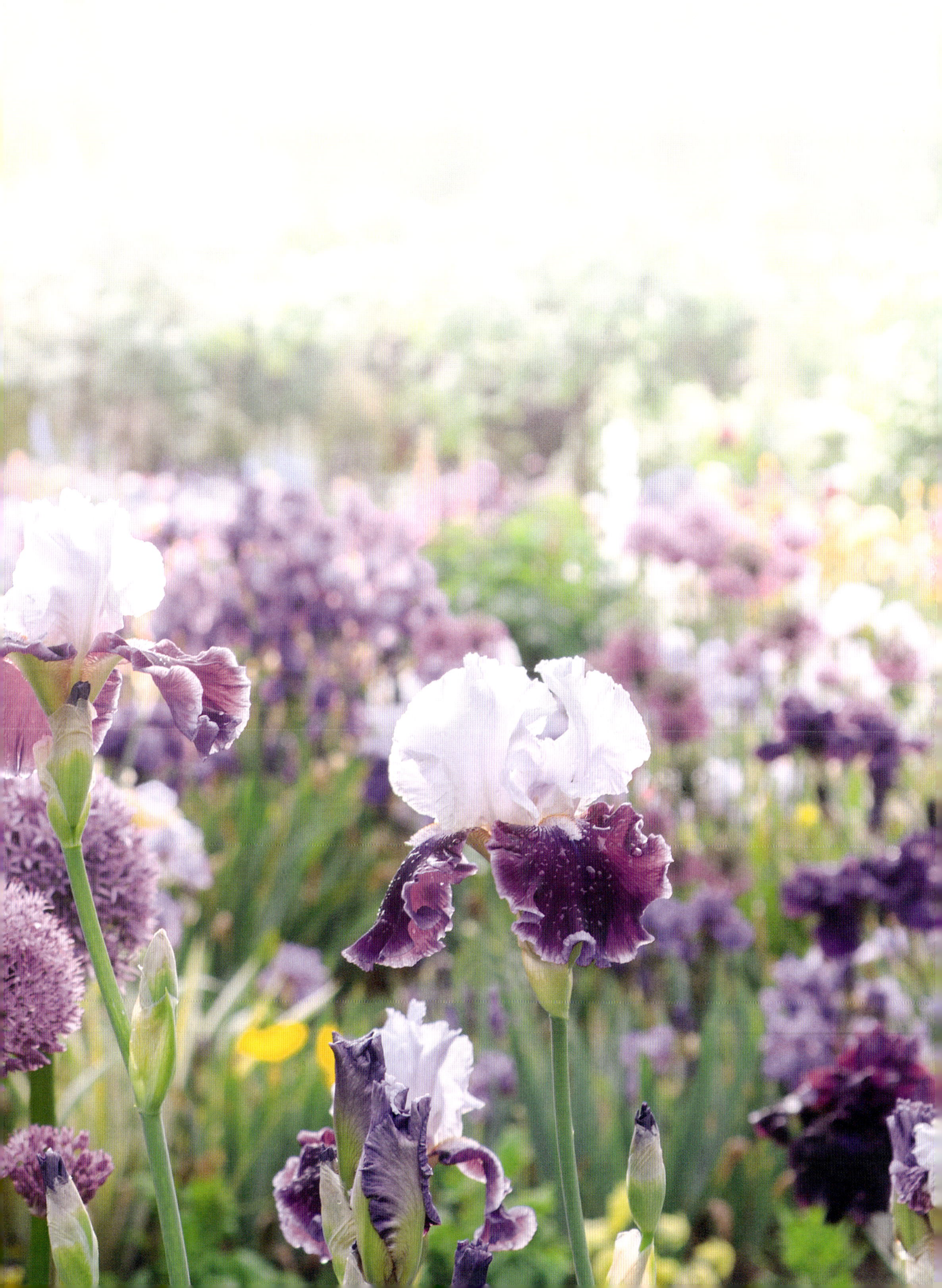

Wonder:
A state of amazement or astonishment at something mysterious or new; curiosity, fascination, surprise.

In the fertile Willamette Valley, south of Portland, Oregon, a magical garden emerges from the river mists each April. I am present at dawn, moving in awe through the plantings, backlit with a shimmering haze. Acres of rippling bearded iris materialize like gossamer scepters, interlaced with sheer poppies, towering lupines, wands of allium and curtains of white wisteria creating an otherworldly tableau that gently coalesces, kaleidoscope-like, before me. Seemingly, the sublime floral spectacle transcends the physical and ascends to the metaphysical, lifting my spirit in a transition towards the eternal.

I experience a *frisson* of excitement, a slightly unsettling shift of perspective, as known realities subtly alter, provoking a sudden questioning of what is true. Heightened perceptions elevate the viewpoint from the mundane to a new level of awareness.

I experience a moment of *wonder*.

And in that state, words retreat into inadequacy, and for me the only tangible proof of this fleeting Elysium lies in a photograph. I reach for my camera, never removing my eyes from the vision before me, willing it to remain until I press the shutter.

This beguiling locale is Schreiner's Iris Gardens. An award-winning, family-owned enterprise with over 100 acres of bearded iris, it has just celebrated its centenary of operation. Of the many gardens I have been fortunate to photograph in my career, it remains a favorite.

Frilly bearded iris are one of the delightful divas of the spring garden, offering a true spectrum of dazzling colors. Unmatched in any other type of flower, they range from pinks and maroons to yellows and golds, and from blues and violets to deep purples. Casting their unique spell, they tilt their heads coquettishly for one to better appreciate their curves and flounces, all crowned with a richly perfumed ruff. Equally charming are the names they bear: 'Pixie Dust', 'Dream of You', 'Enchanted Memory', 'Cherub's Smile', 'Monet's Blue', 'Paint the Sky'.

I am so pleased to share selected highlights from this glorious wonderland.

RIGHT: *Iris* 'Dream of You', Schreiner's Iris Gardens, Salem, Oregon, USA. May 2010.

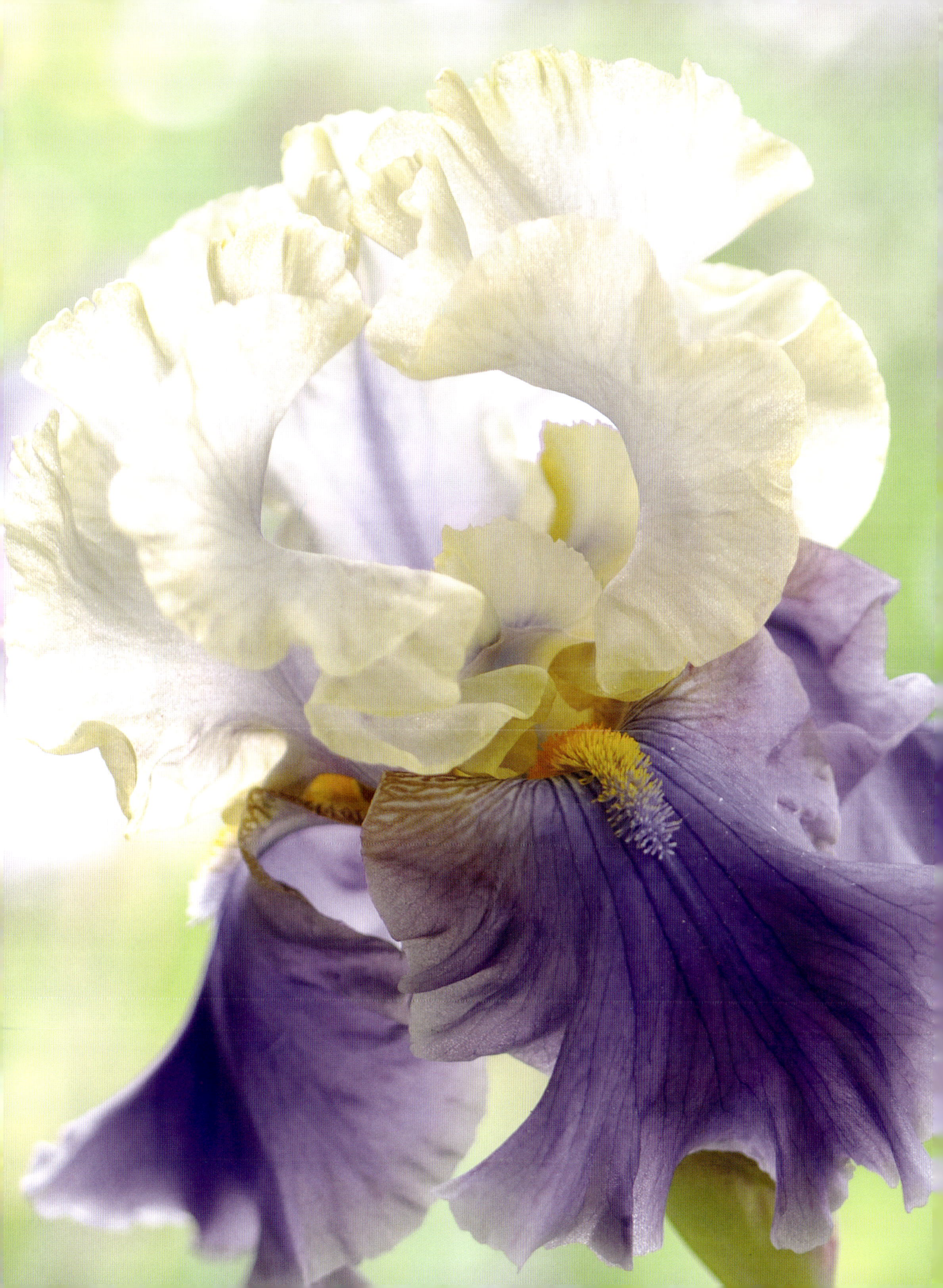

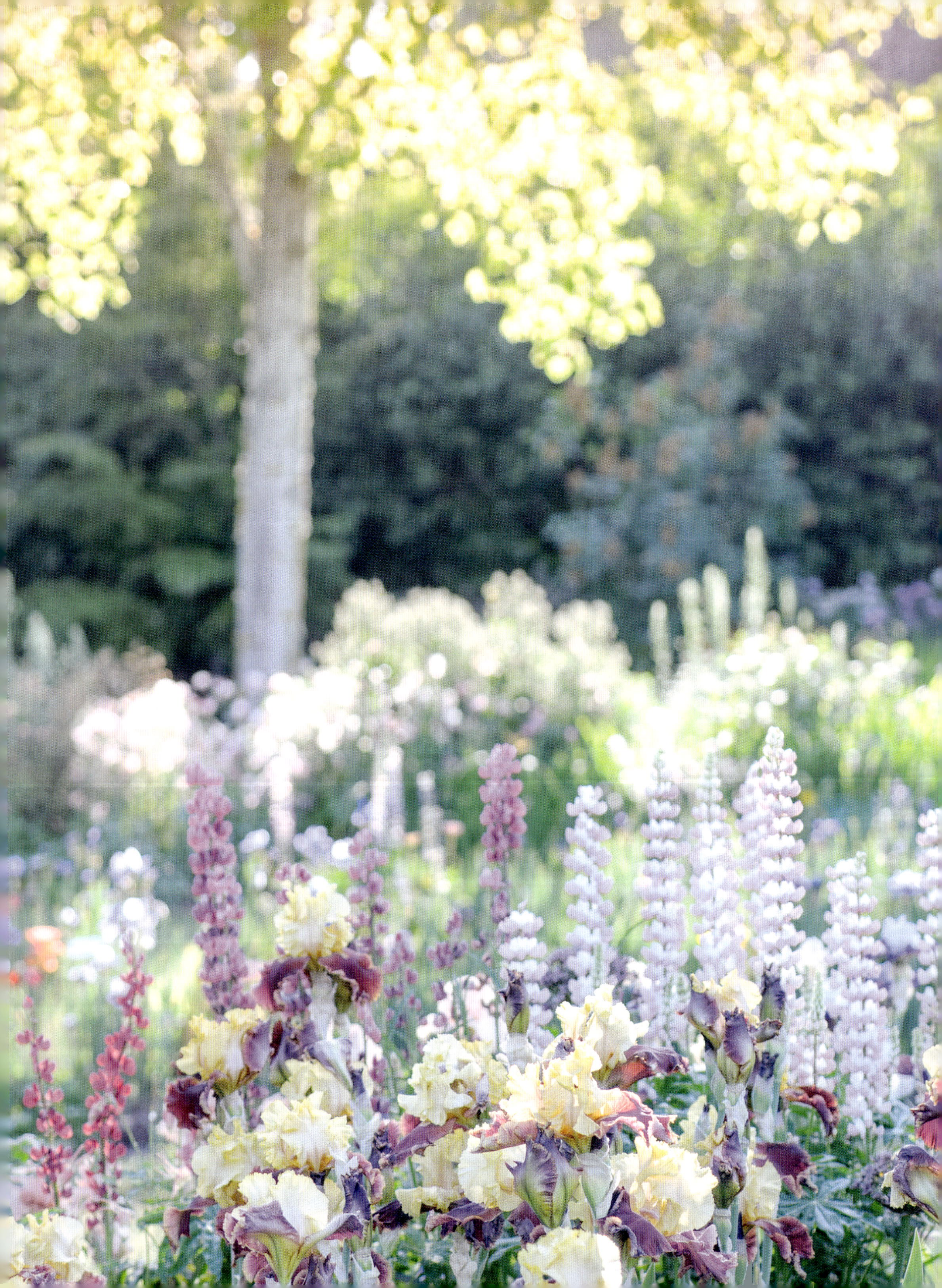

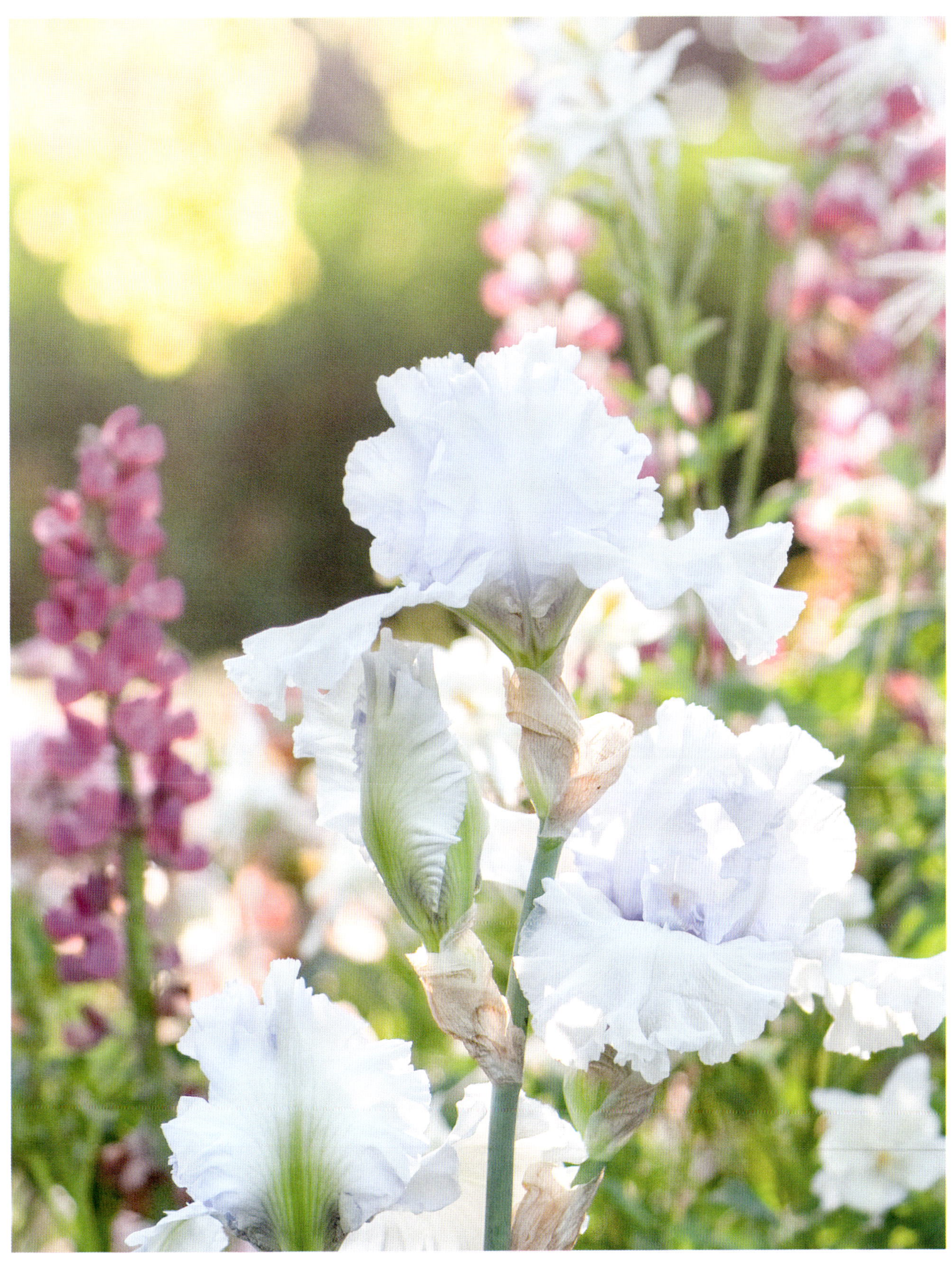

LEFT: Dawn at Schreiner's Iris Gardens, Salem, Oregon, USA. May 2019. ABOVE: *Iris* 'Chinook Winds', Schreiner's Iris Garden. May 2019. OVERLEAF: Allium at Schreiner's Iris Garden.

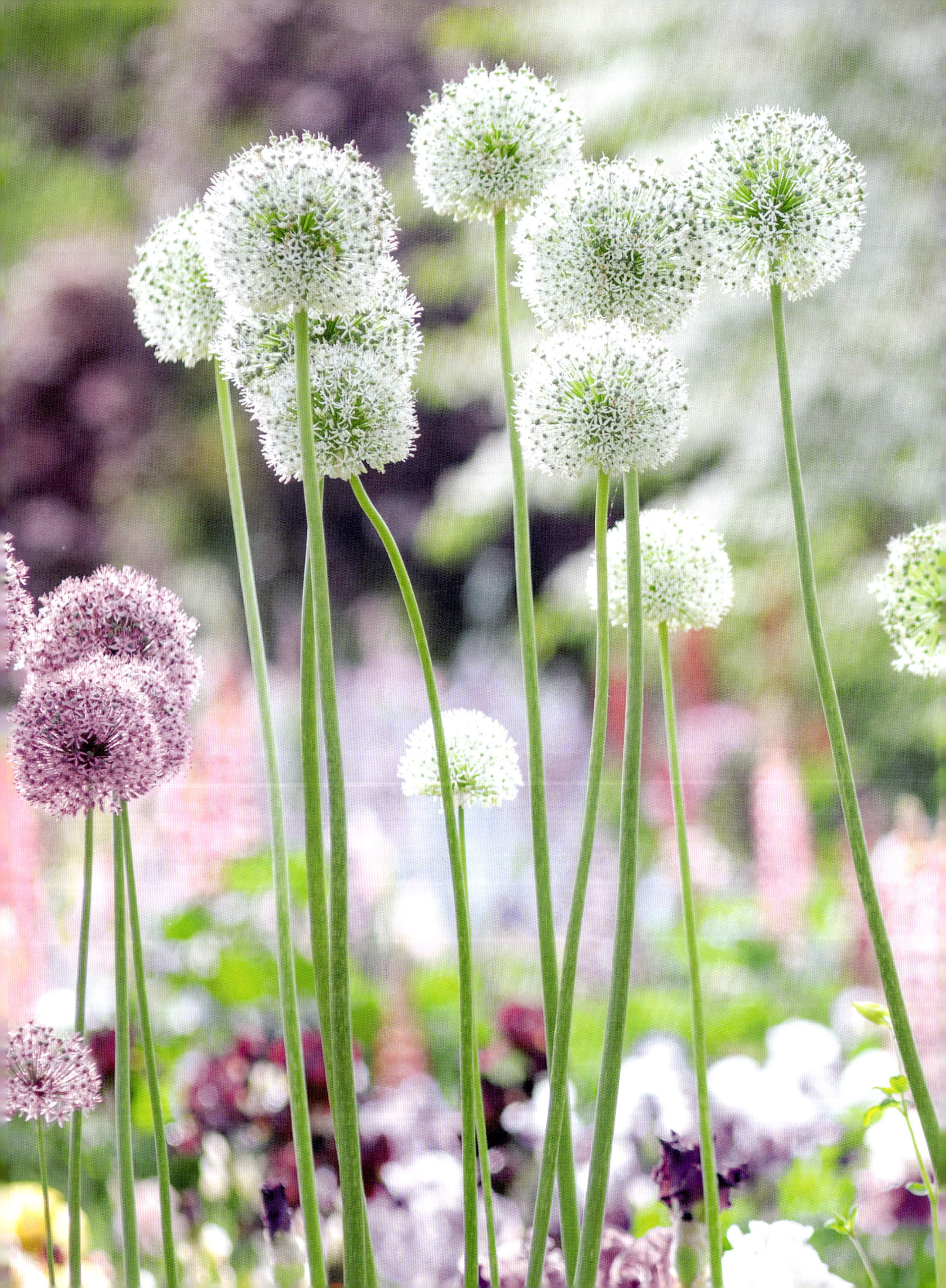

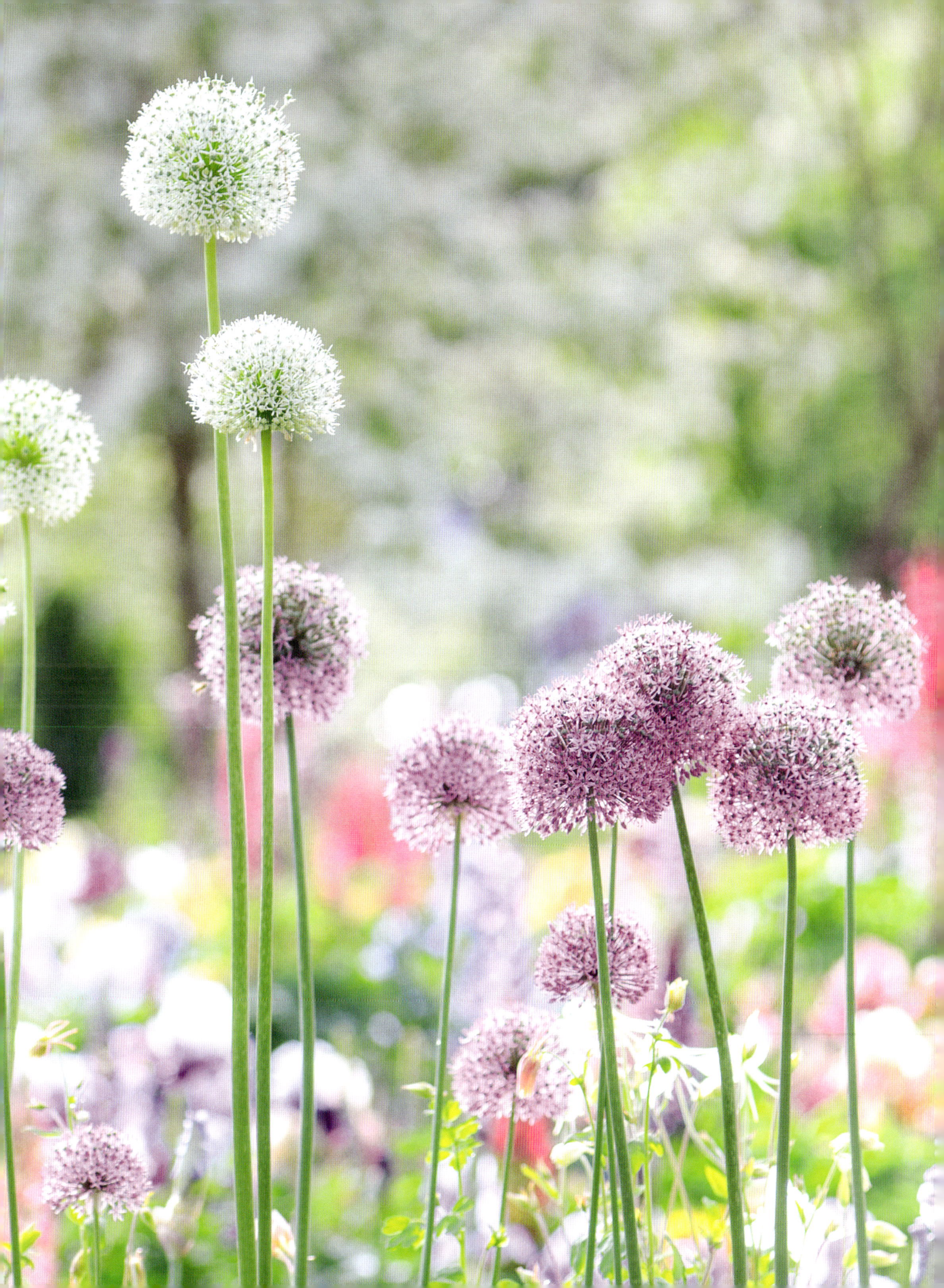

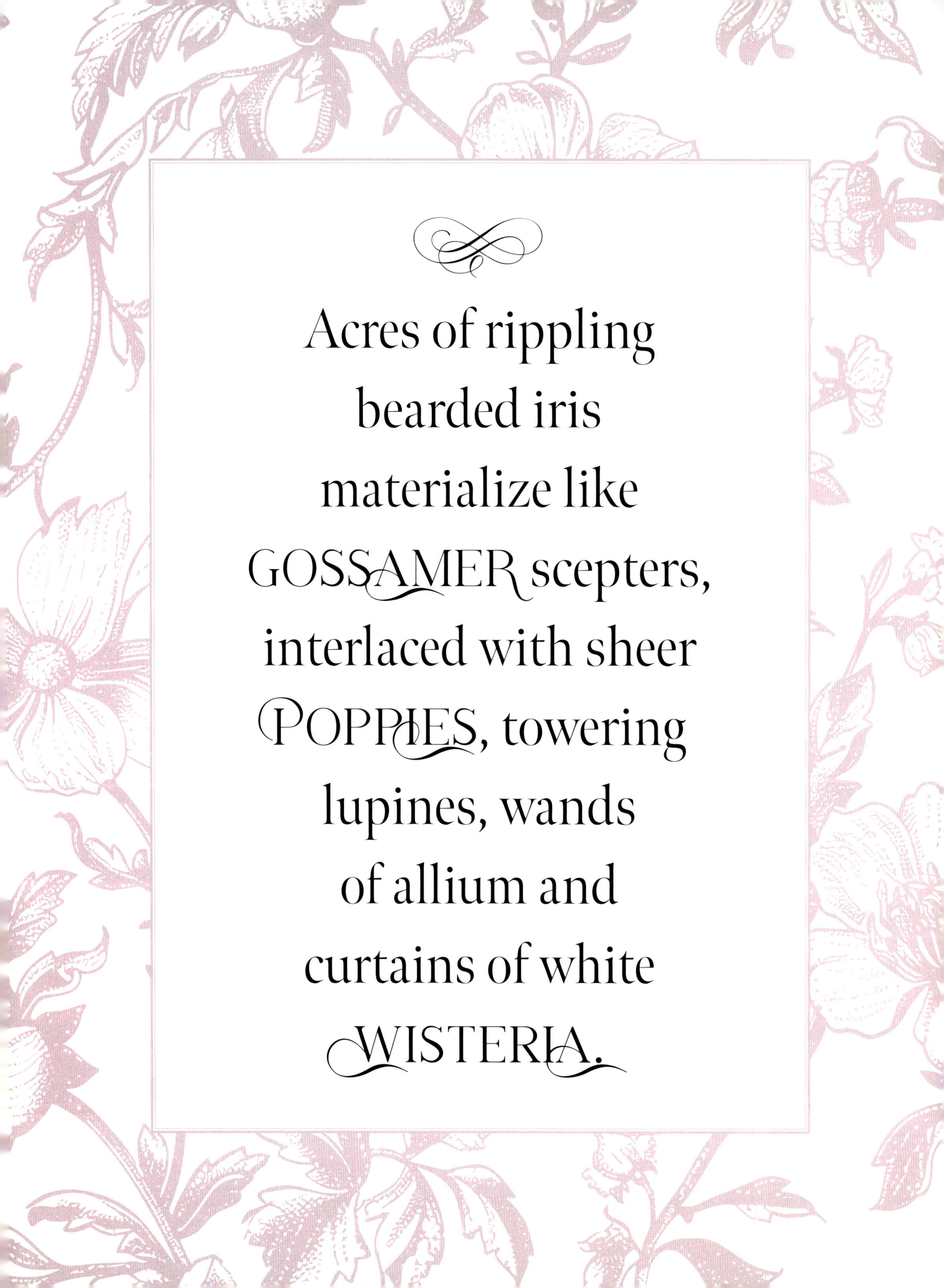

Acres of rippling
bearded iris
materialize like
GOSSAMER scepters,
interlaced with sheer
POPPIES, towering
lupines, wands
of allium and
curtains of white
WISTERIA.

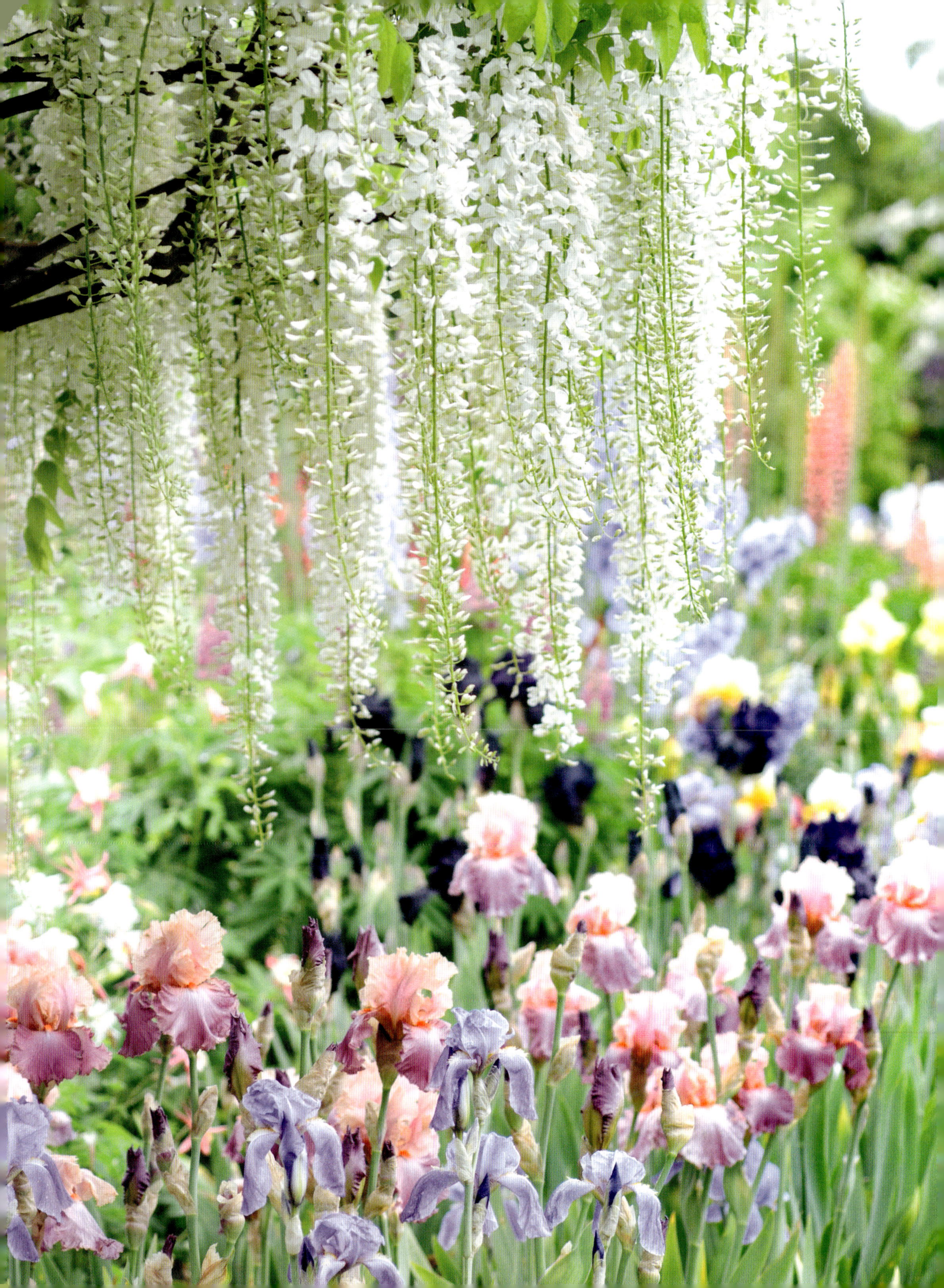

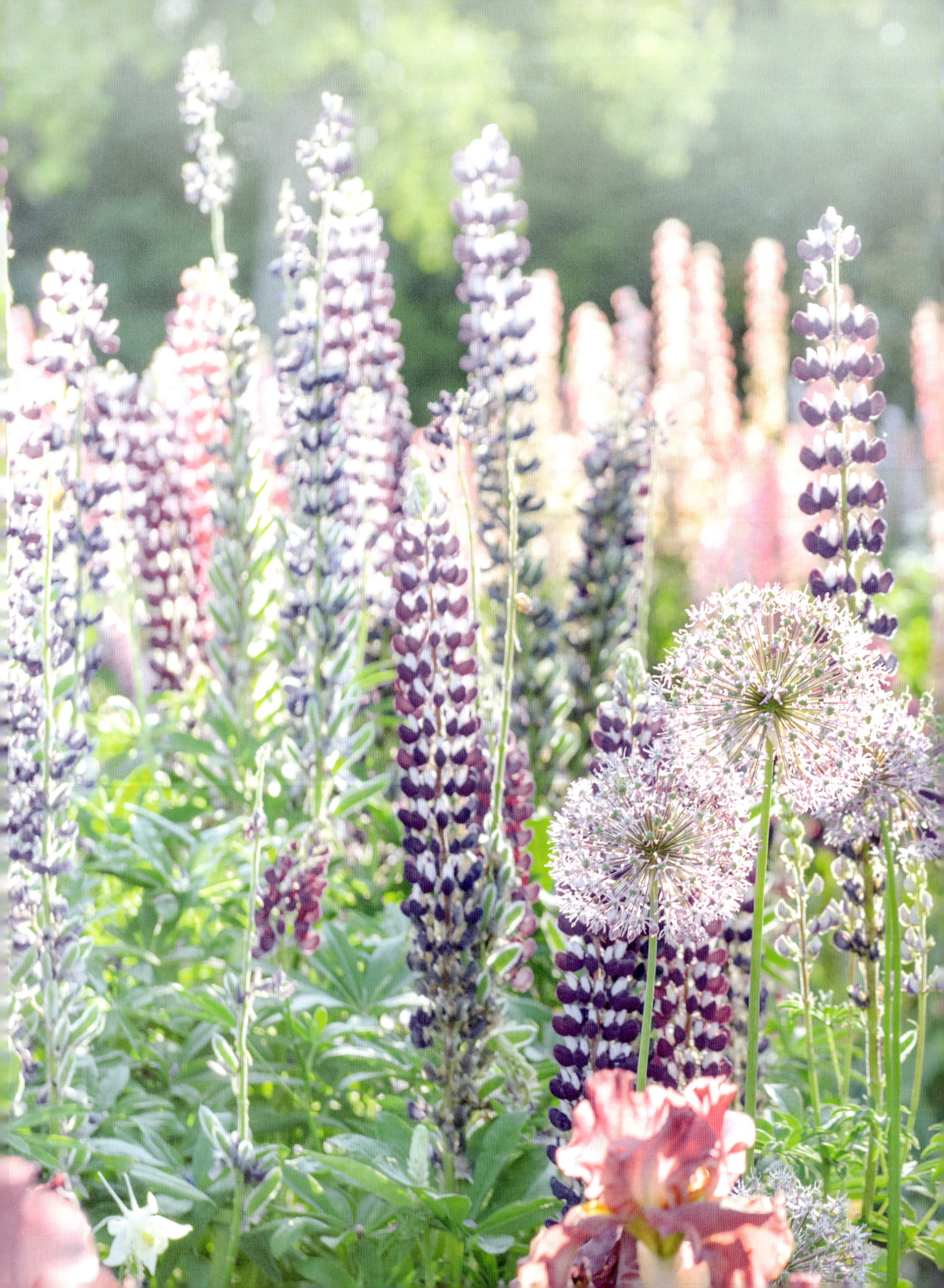

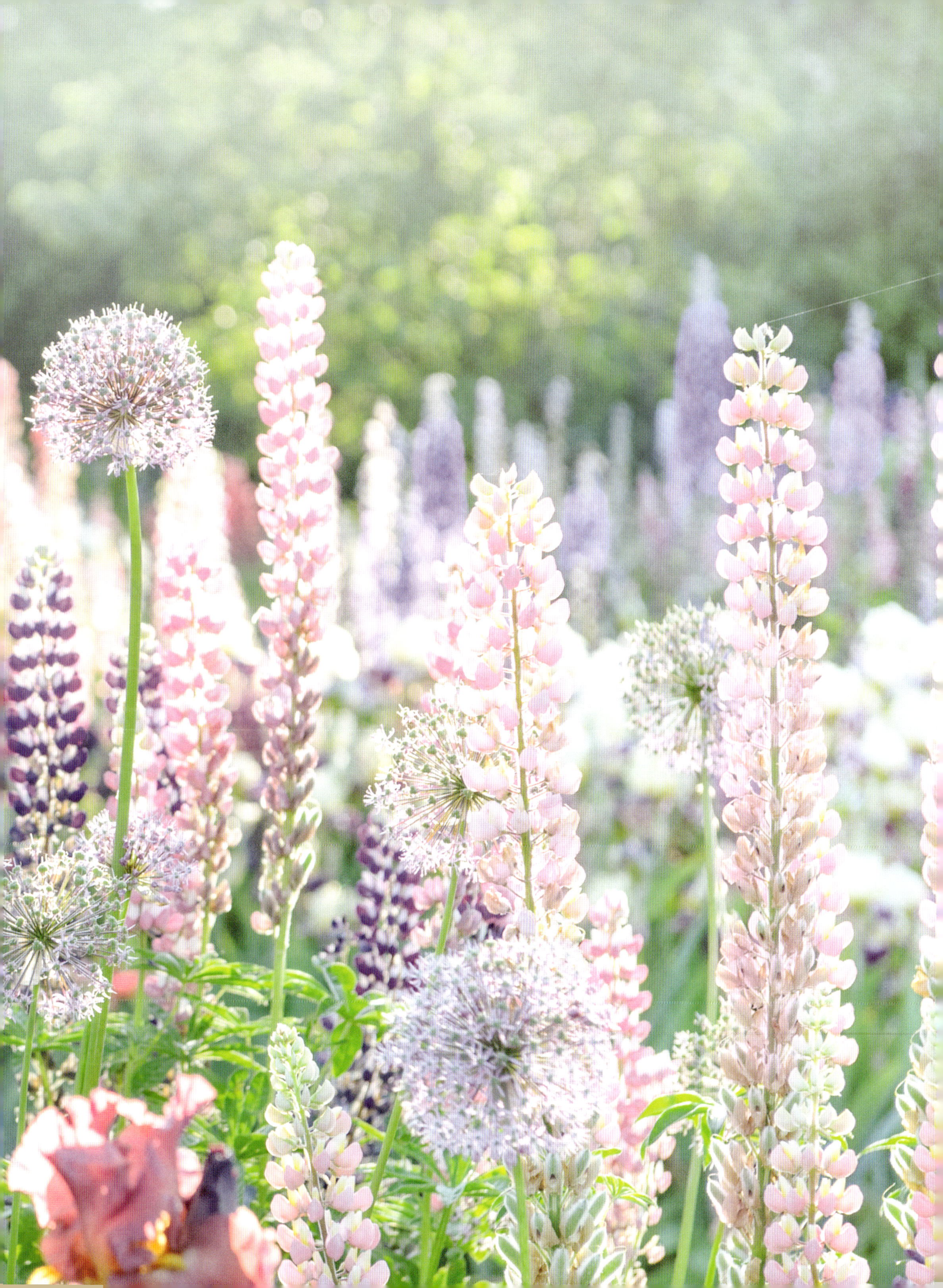

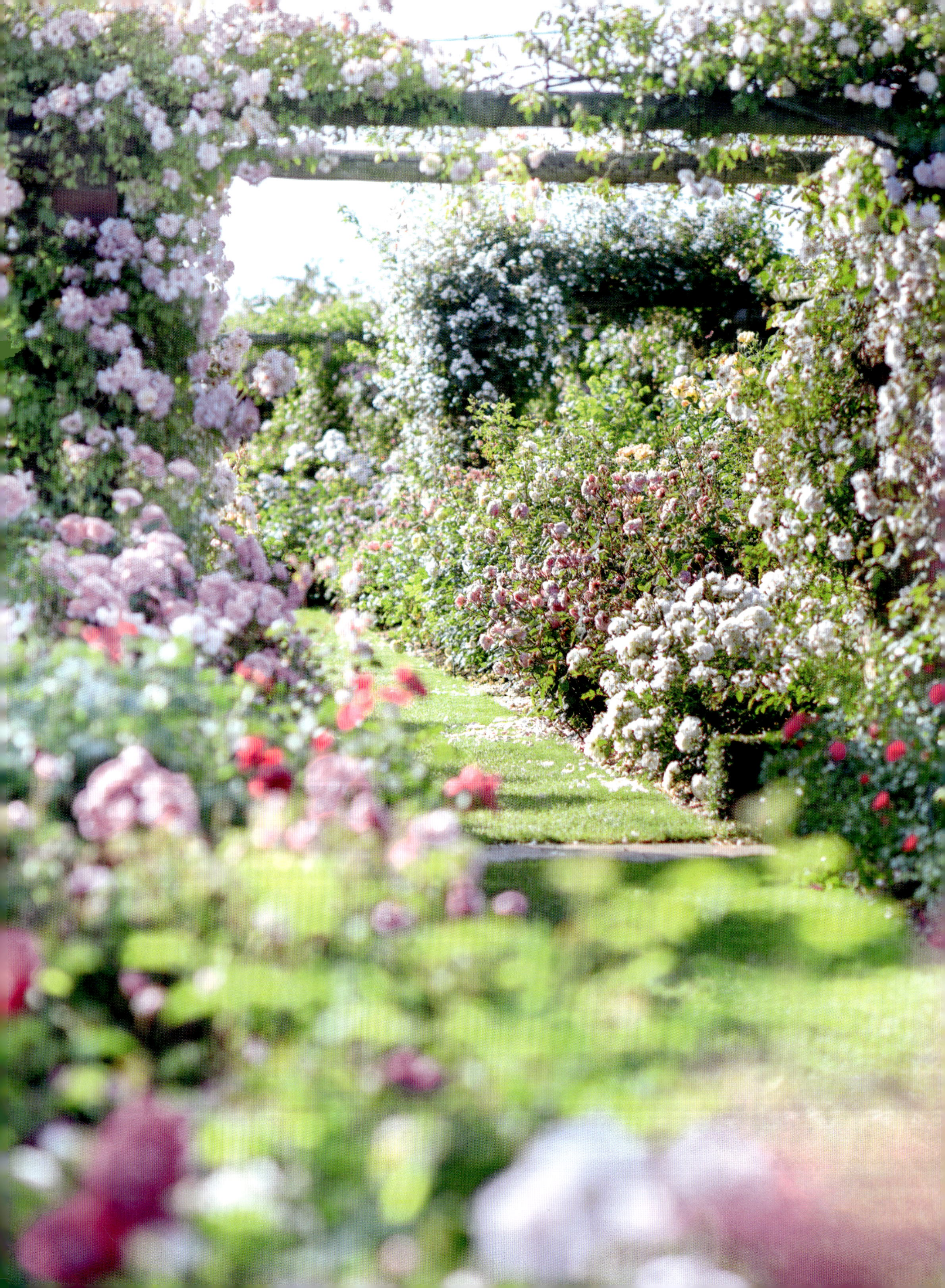

Also showcased in this chapter is a glimpse at my extensive photographic work from the world-famous David Austin Rose Gardens and Plant Centre in Albrighton, in Shropshire, England. Breeders of the most exquisite roses, this is considered one of the finest rose gardens in the world.

In 2015, when I was contracted to photograph my first book, *Vintage Roses,* for Pavilion Books, I traveled to Albrighton. Having been a grower of David Austin English roses for years, they had become my signature photographic subjects. So it was with great anticipation that I arrived at the hallowed source of these magnificent blooms.

There, I was fortunate to work with their Master Rosarian, Michael Marriott, who granted me free run of the entire facility, including the display garden, the breeding areas, the nursery and, a mile or so away, the vast growing fields. Daily, I found myself alone in those fields, amidst 20 acres of David Austin roses, spreading out into the horizon. With gloves and clippers, I ventured into rows overflowing with thigh-high canes of blooms. I cut to my heart's content, filling buckets with *Rosa* 'Queen of Sweden', 'Boscobel', 'Grace' and peachy pink 'A Shropshire Lad', giddy with an abundance that few might ever experience. After loading my car to bursting, I returned to my rented cottage, where I'd set up a mobile studio with lights, backdrops and vintage props sourced from local antique shops. One day, I stood in the fields, with roses as far as I could see in all directions and a huge bundle of cut blooms in my arms, and I remember thinking, "This, *this* is a moment to savor and remember always. It really cannot get better than this."

But it did, in fact, get better. The following year I returned to the Centre and Michael took me to David Austin's private home next door. There, I was introduced to Mr Austin himself and had a once-in-a-lifetime opportunity to present him with a signed copy of my newly published *Vintage Roses*. It was an incredibly special moment for me and a great privilege to meet the man who had brought pleasure to so many all over the world with his acclaimed roses. He was kind and gracious and we took a short stroll together through his own garden, as another visiting photographer snapped a photo of us together in the summer sunshine. Mr Austin was 90 years old at the time and passed away a few years after our meeting. I will never forget this sweet coda to the creation of that book.

LEFT: One of the rose-draped pergolas at the David Austin Rose Gardens, Shropshire, England. July 2015.

EXPLORING THE DAVID AUSTIN ROSE GARDENS

Nothing excites me more than entering a rose garden in late May or June, the thrill of anticipation overtaking all other thoughts. Being granted private access to this sanctuary in particular was indescribable. To push open the white gate in the early morning, well before visitors and most staff arrived, gave me a profound sense of peace and wonderment, of time suspended and cares dissolving in an enveloping sensory cloud of color, scent and texture.

A series of themed sections draw one through arches and trellises, festooned and draped in hundreds of varieties of roses, contrasting in shape, rhythm and mood. The Long Garden forms the main path, with the Renaissance Garden, Victorian Garden and the Lion Garden leading off from it.

I have walked every inch of the brick paths, beneath pergolas dripping with profusely fragrant climbers and ramblers. I've ducked under arbors curtained with tumbling old roses, and encountered the brash peacocks that roam freely. Here exists an unforgettable place of romance and fable, birdsong and dappled sunlight. The roses themselves are miracles of form and hue, each with their distinctive personality and fragrance, often with names invoking English literary, historical and regal associations – Emily Brontë, Roald Dahl, Princess Alexandra, Vanessa Bell and James Galway. Such care goes into the breeding selection of the roses that annually only a handful are newly introduced. Having collected them for many years, I can attest to their captivating qualities. With intoxicating scents, faultless form and densely-packed whorled petals, each astonishes in its own fashion.

Truly, I could have filled this volume with nothing but images of David Austin roses, but I have carefully chosen the selection included here from classic portraits, Dutch Master-inspired arrangements and bundles straight from the field. Several are from my own former garden, Hillhaven, too, a wooded half acre in the verdant Pacific Northwest where I began my education in flowers. Amongst the varieties we grew were *Rosa* 'Lady Emma Hamilton', 'A Shropshire Lad', 'Gentle Hermione', 'Eglantyne' and 'Graham Thomas', and many are featured in *Vintage Roses*.

Working with these flowers on such an intimate basis has been one of the great highlights of my career. I hope the photographs bring some of that magic to you.

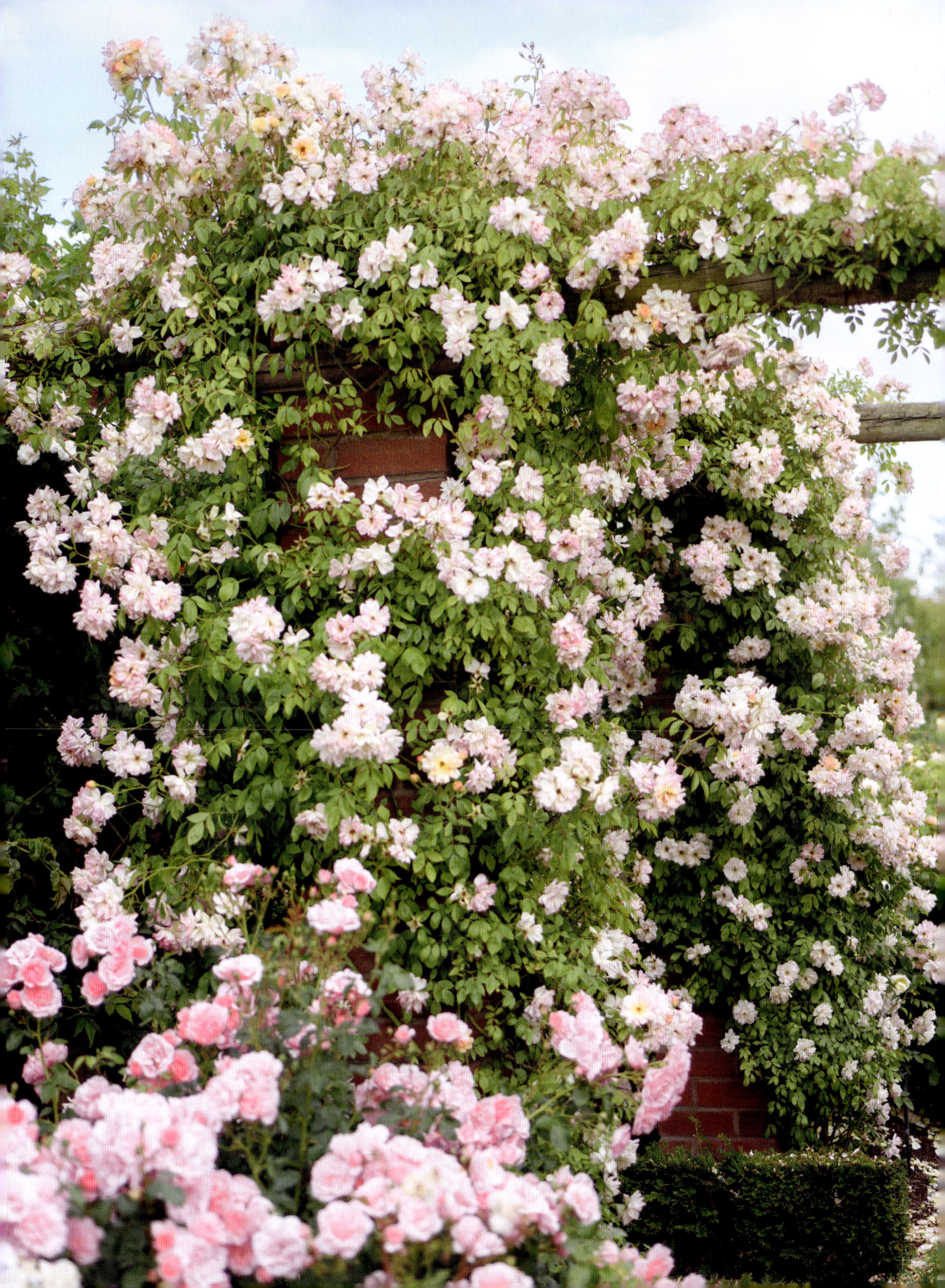

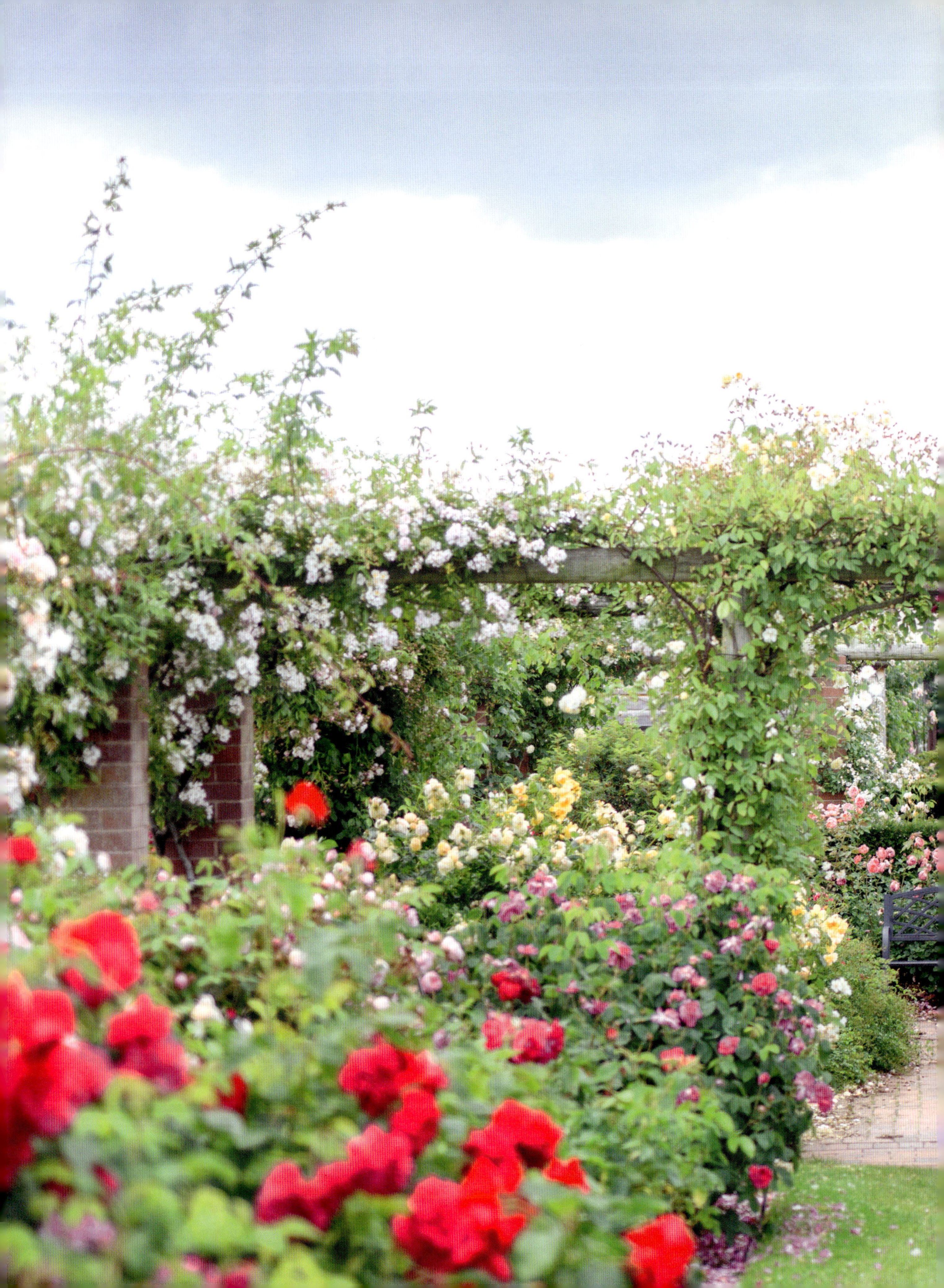

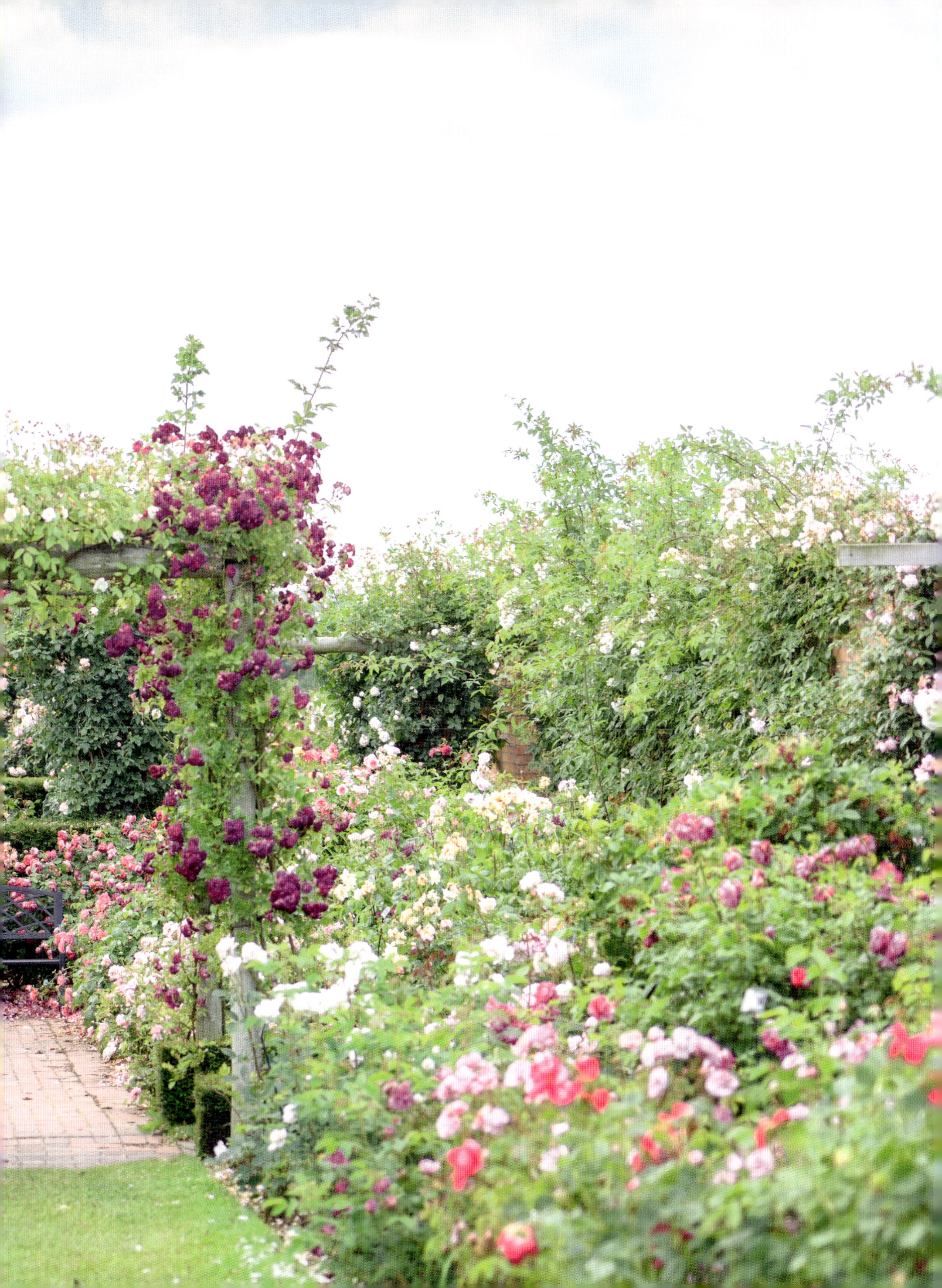

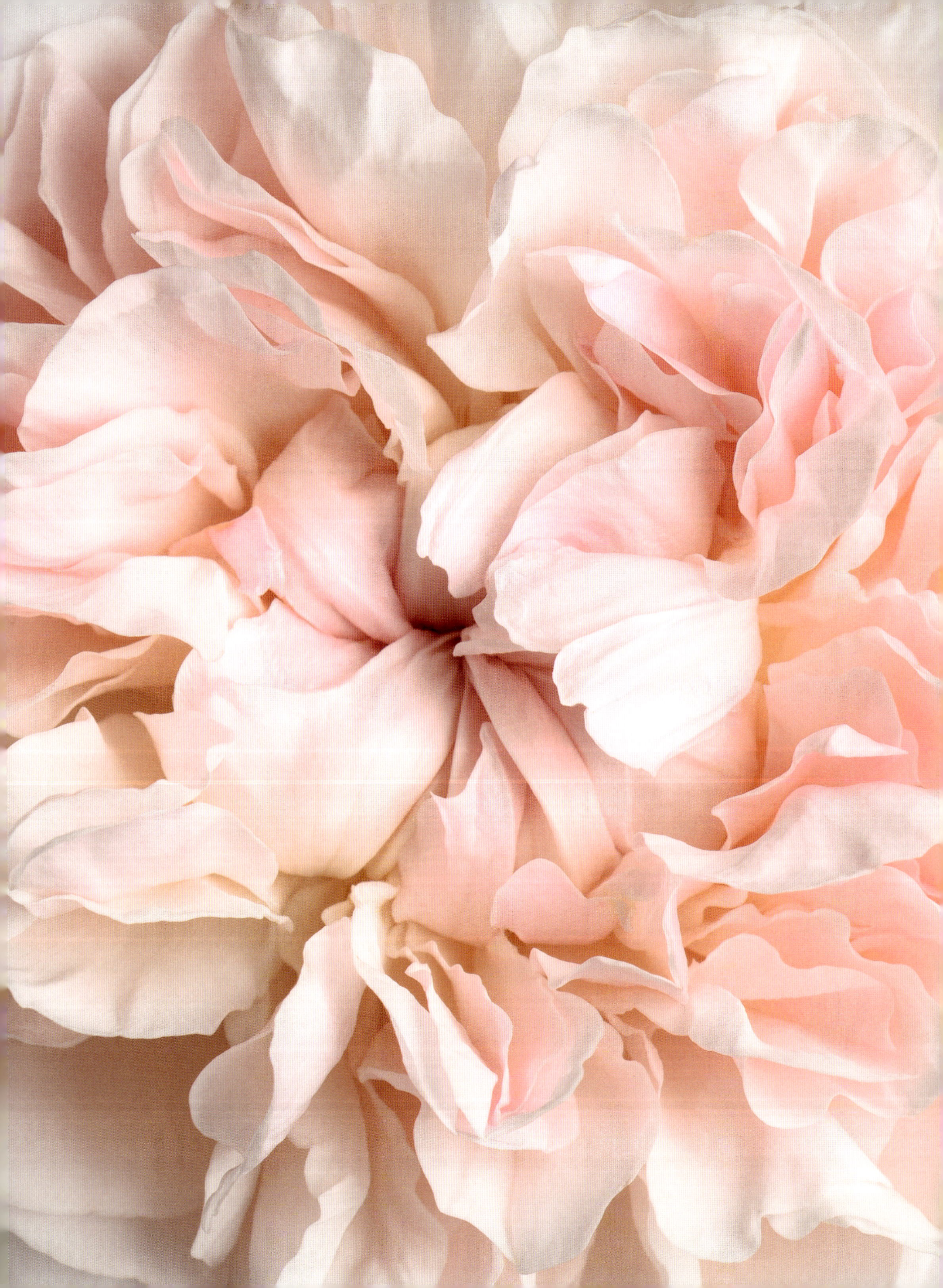

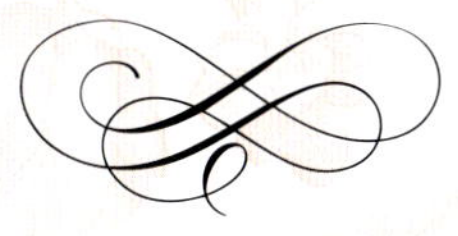

Photographing Roses

David Austin Rose 'Eglantyne'
Hillhaven Garden, Shoreline, Washington, USA

I love words. I love alliteration, nuances of meaning and the satisfaction of crafting the rhythm of a phrase just so. *I strive to continually expand my vocabulary, in both English and in my evolving French. But certain noble subjects defy even the most literate of descriptions, and upending an entire thesaurus of adjectives onto a page will inevitably fail to communicate fully their exquisite reality. Thus it is with roses. The over-100 petals in this David Austin rose 'Eglantyne' from my former garden thwart any attempt at clever metaphor or analogy. No tome of a thousand, or ten thousand, words could ever be adequate. Therefore, I am aware in each moment of what a gift it is to record such a wonder photographically, and to share it with millions across the continents with the click of a button.*

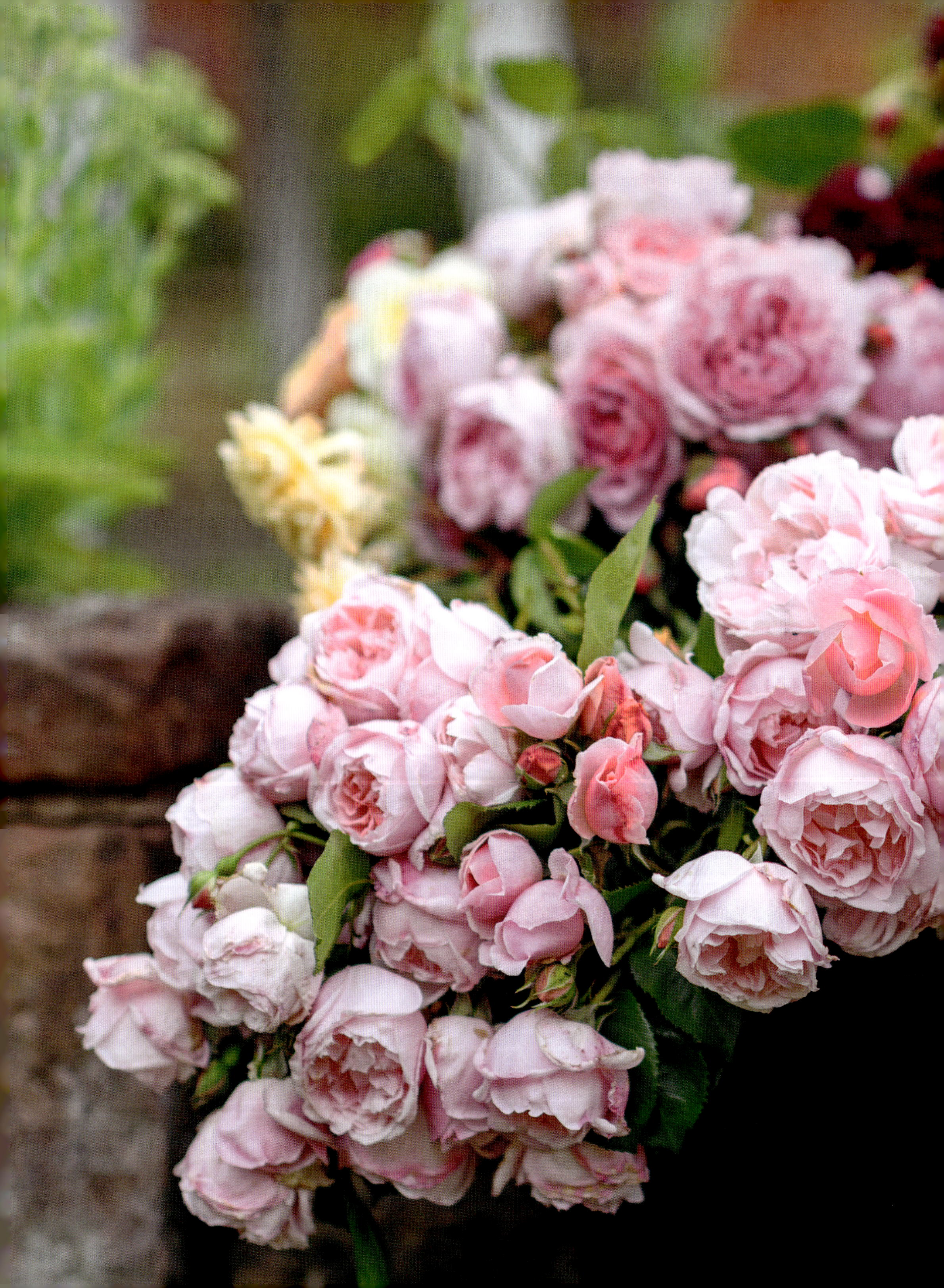

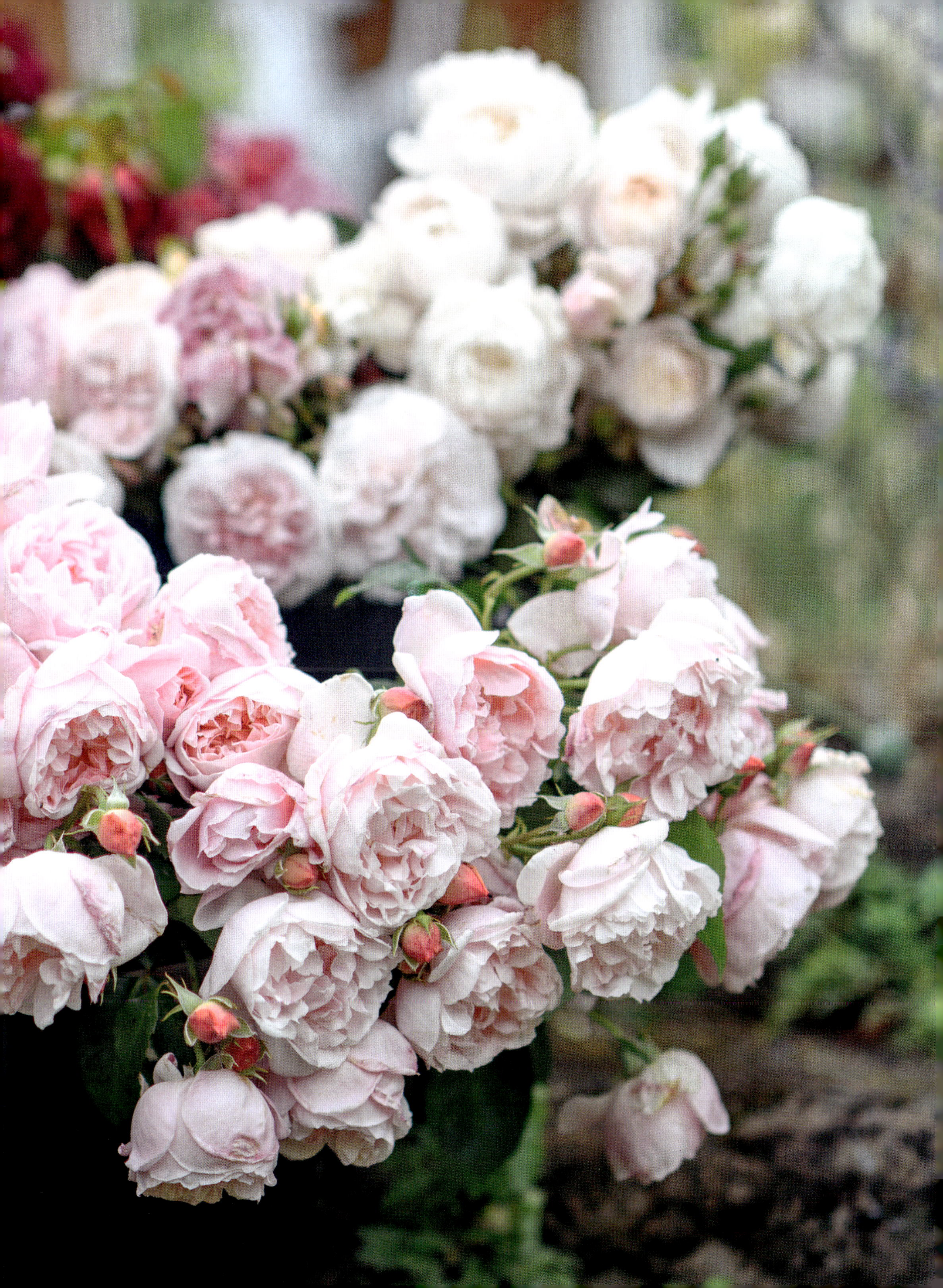

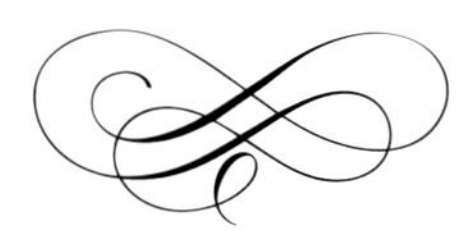

I cut to my HEART'S content, filling buckets with *Rosa* 'Queen of Sweden', 'Boscobel', 'Grace' and peachy pink 'A Shropshire Lad', an ABUNDANCE few might ever experience.

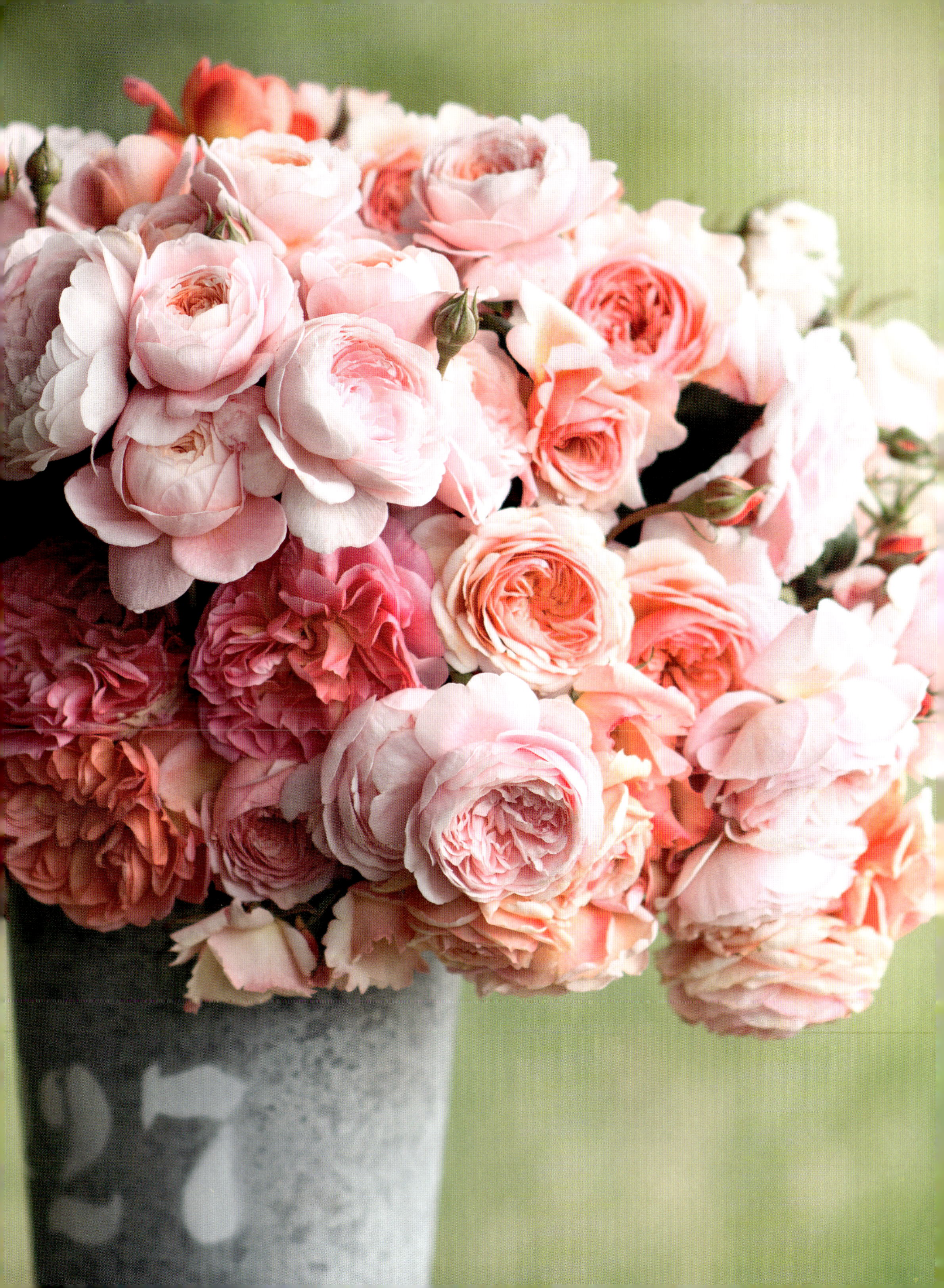

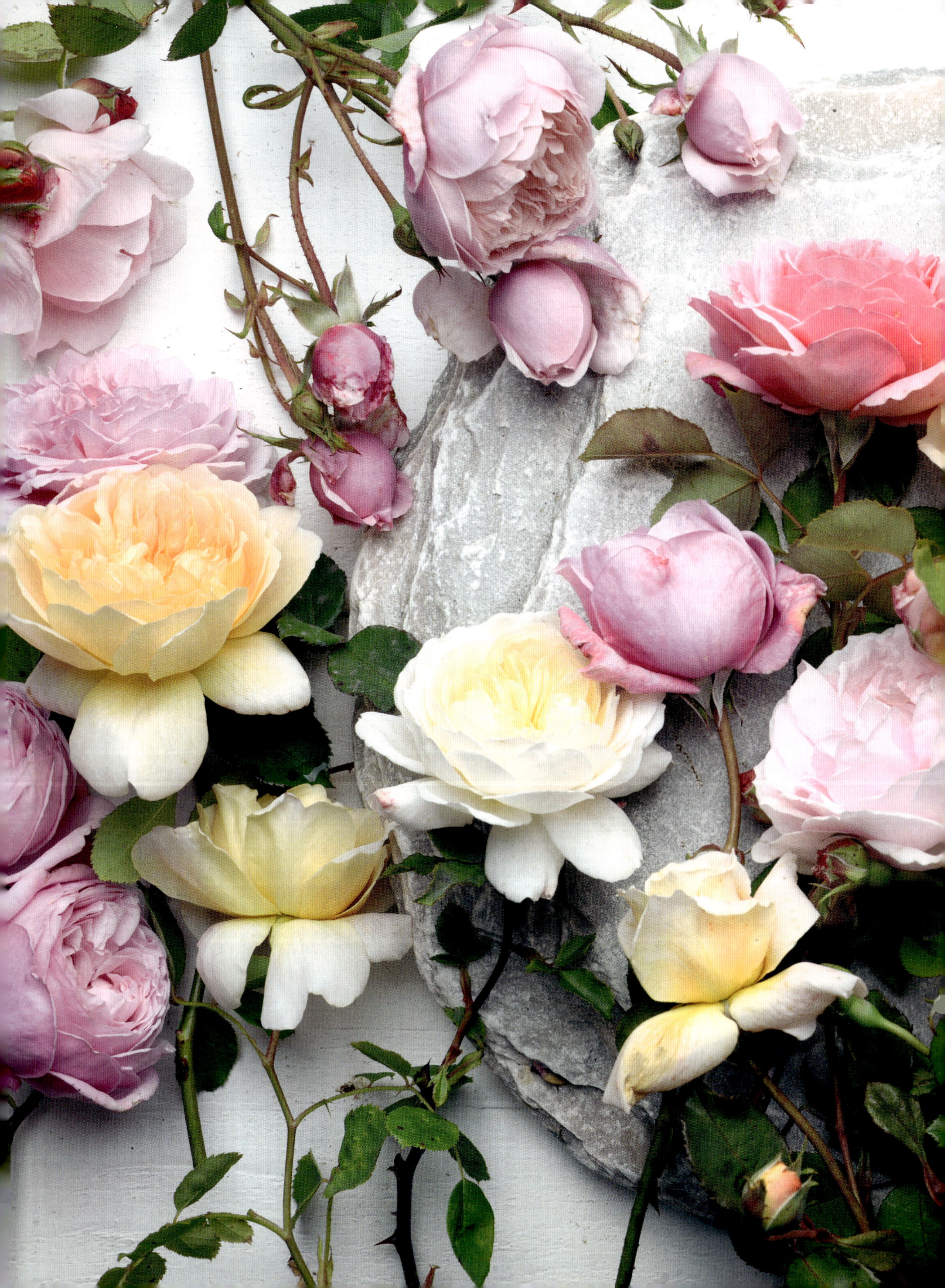

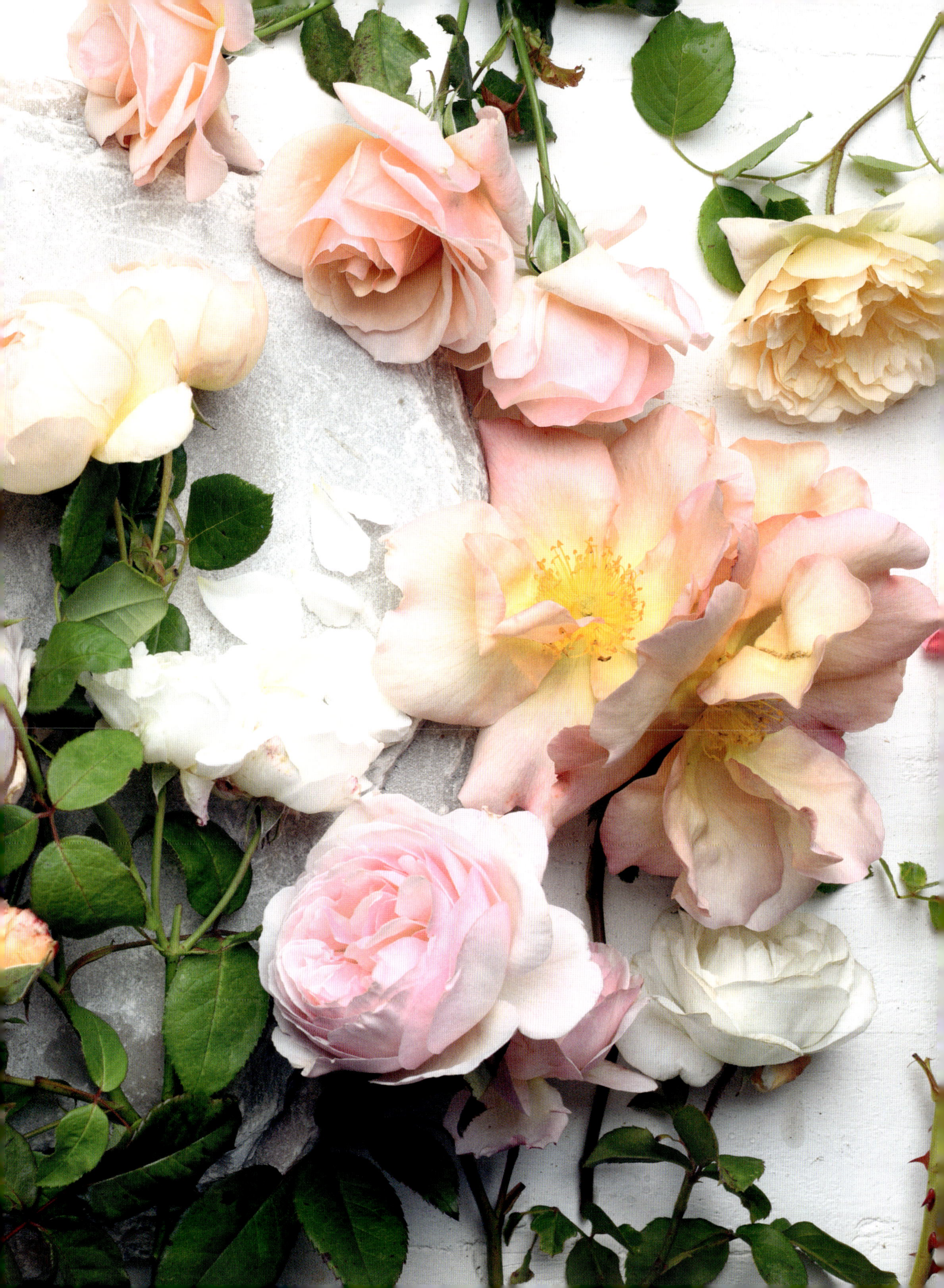

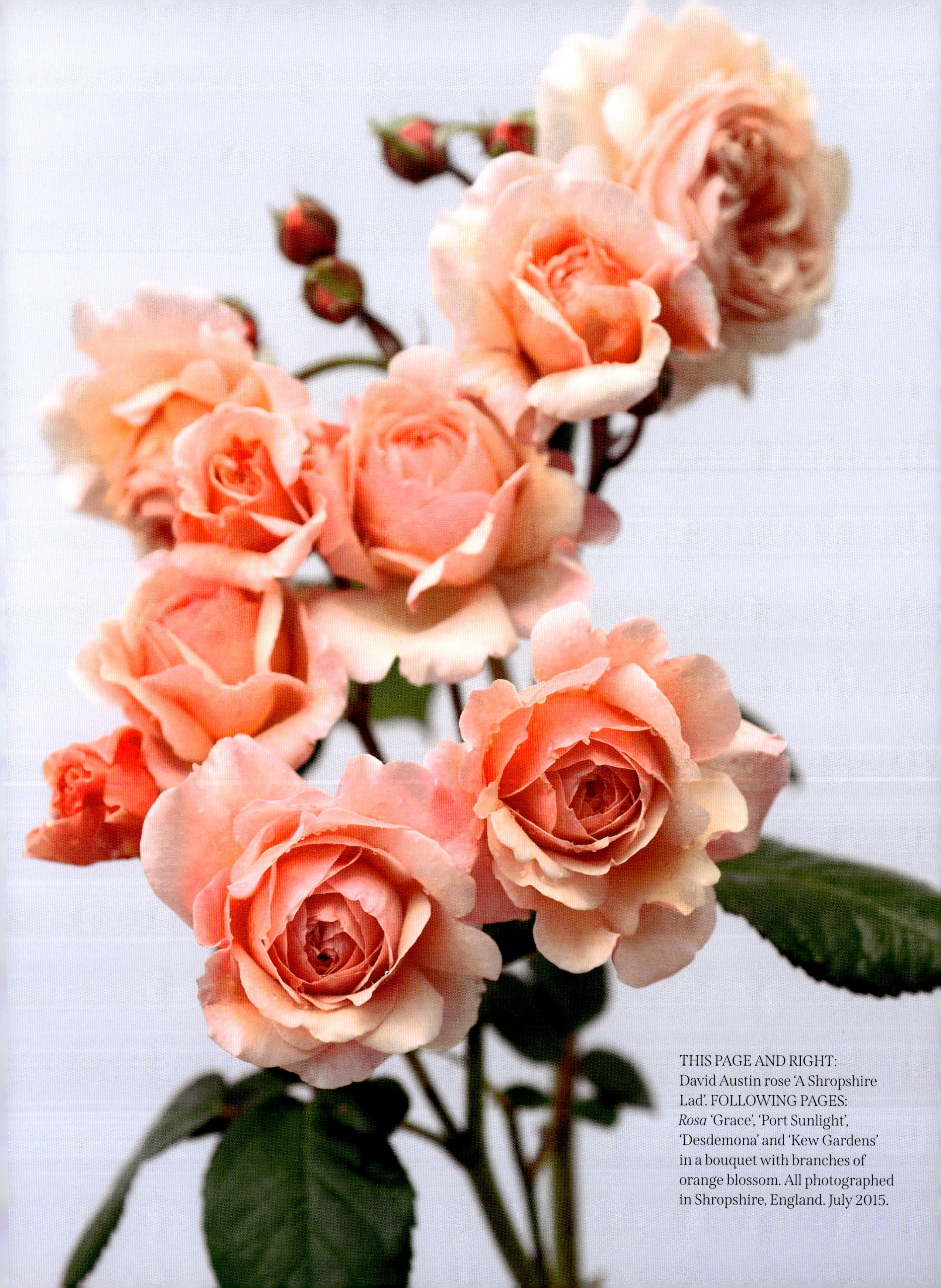

THIS PAGE AND RIGHT: David Austin rose 'A Shropshire Lad'. FOLLOWING PAGES: *Rosa* 'Grace', 'Port Sunlight', 'Desdemona' and 'Kew Gardens' in a bouquet with branches of orange blossom. All photographed in Shropshire, England. July 2015.

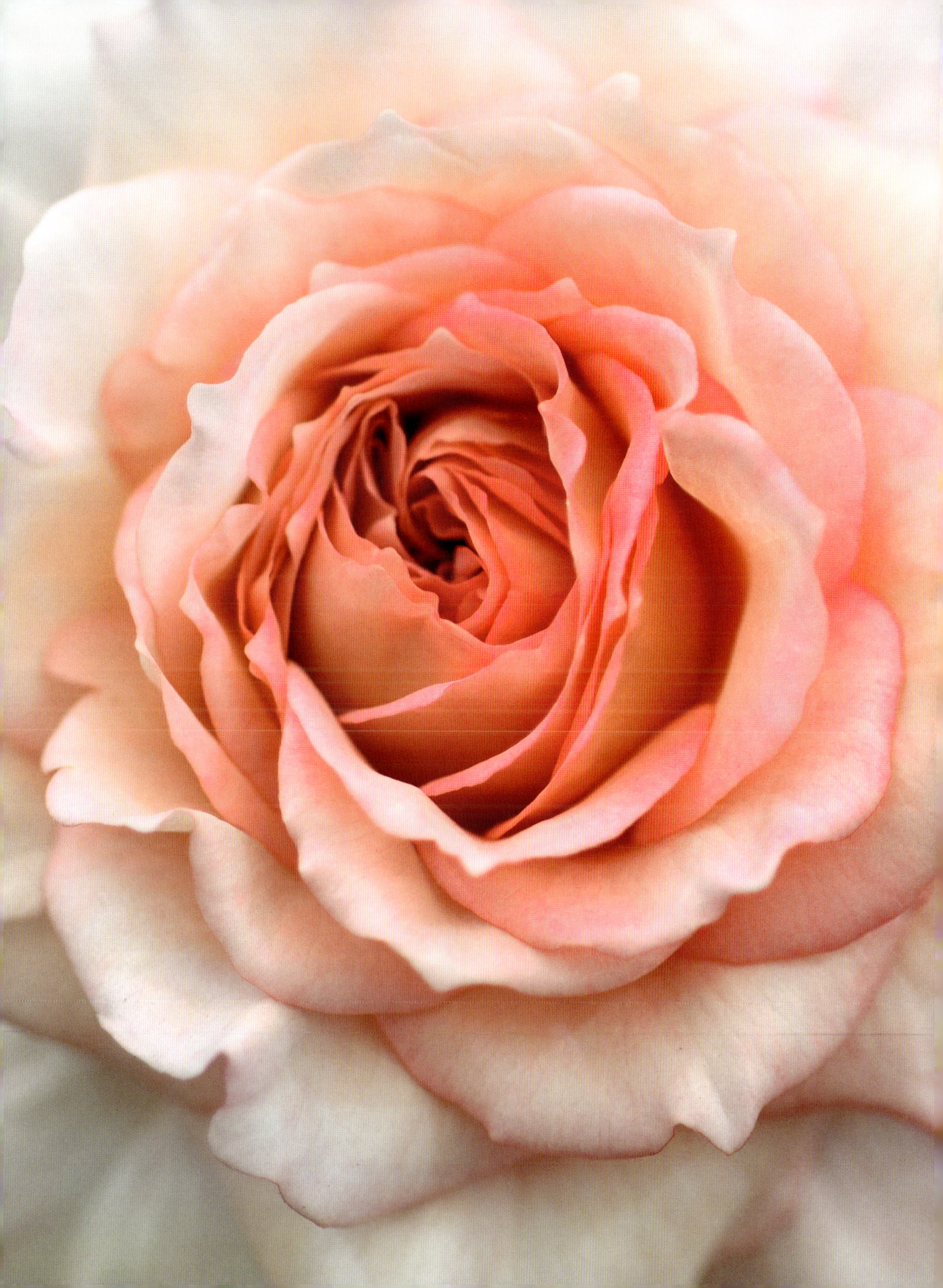

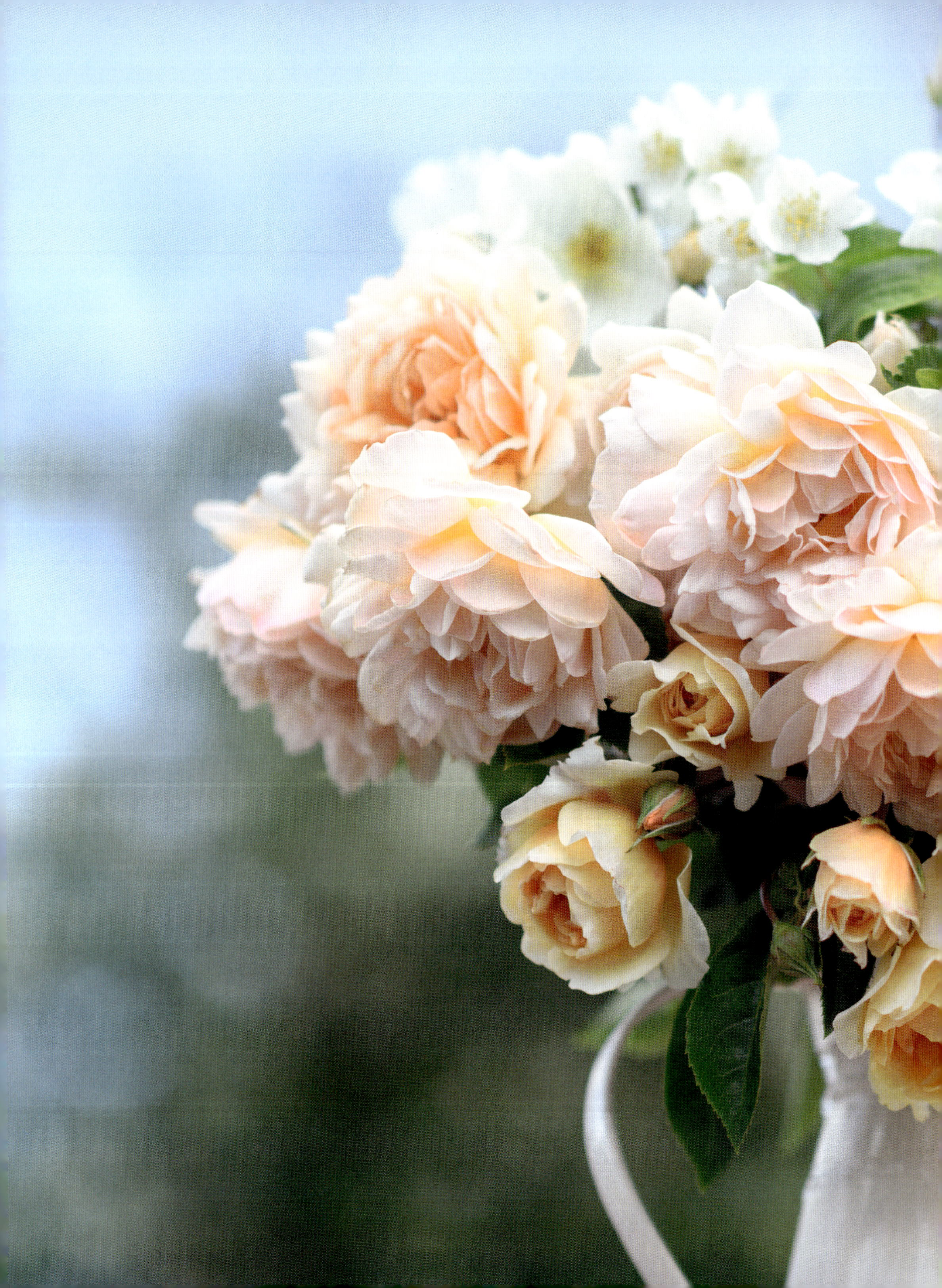

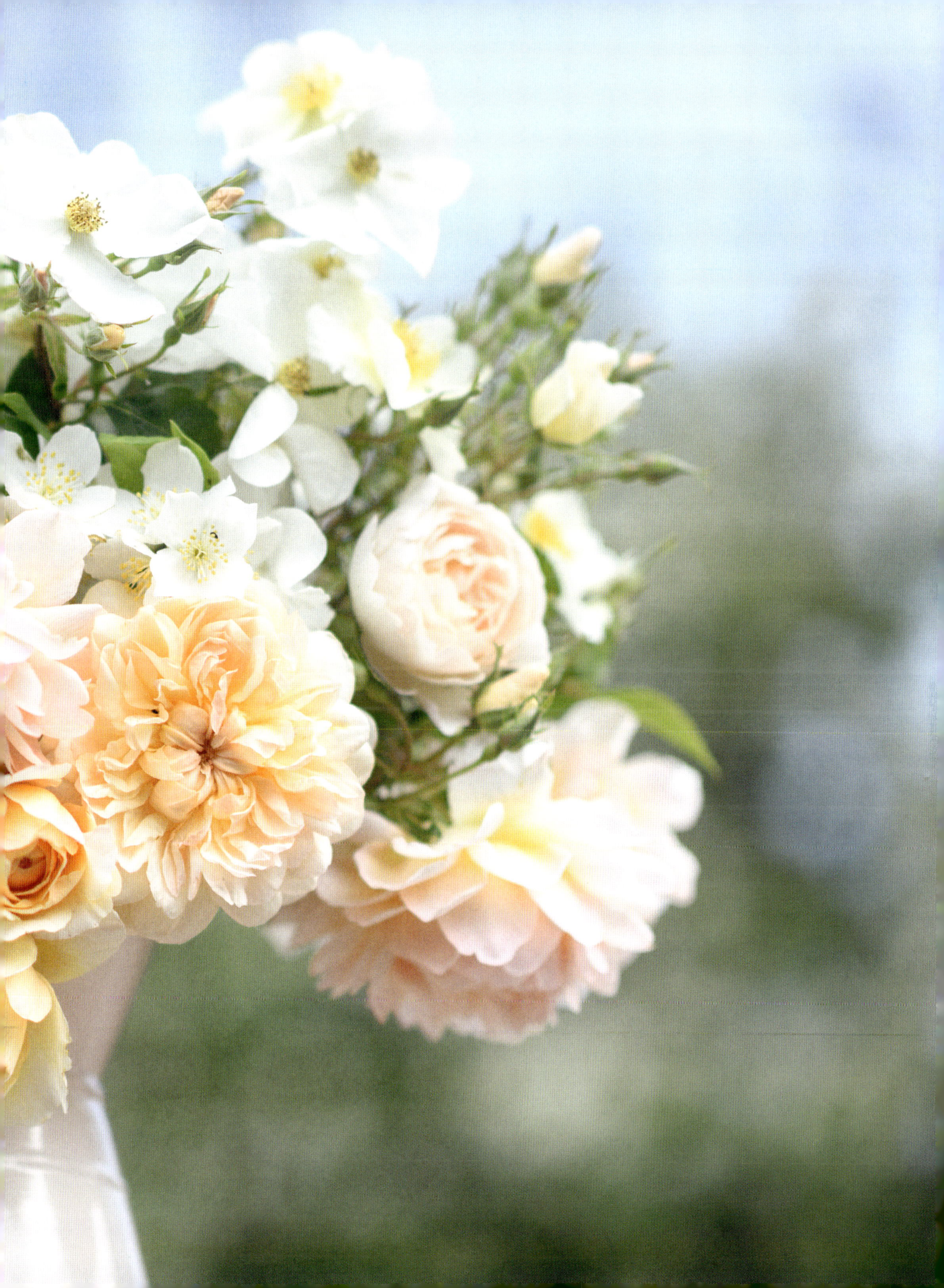

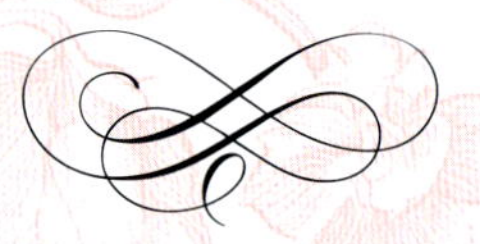

In the Dutch Master Style

Emulating the lighting of the seventeenth- and eighteenth-century Dutch Master still-life painters creates a timeless and romantic style that always produces an impact. Hallmarks of this look include using a light source from above and, commonly, to the left of the subject. The featured flowers are brightly lit but the background is darkened almost to black, with just a few highlighted rims of the blooms in that area showing. It's a technique that is particularly effective with large flowers, such as roses, tulips or peonies, in combination with feathery fronds, trailing leaves and dainty buds, each of which catch a sliver of light to add to the moody atmosphere. These images were created many years ago with David Austin roses and have never before been published.

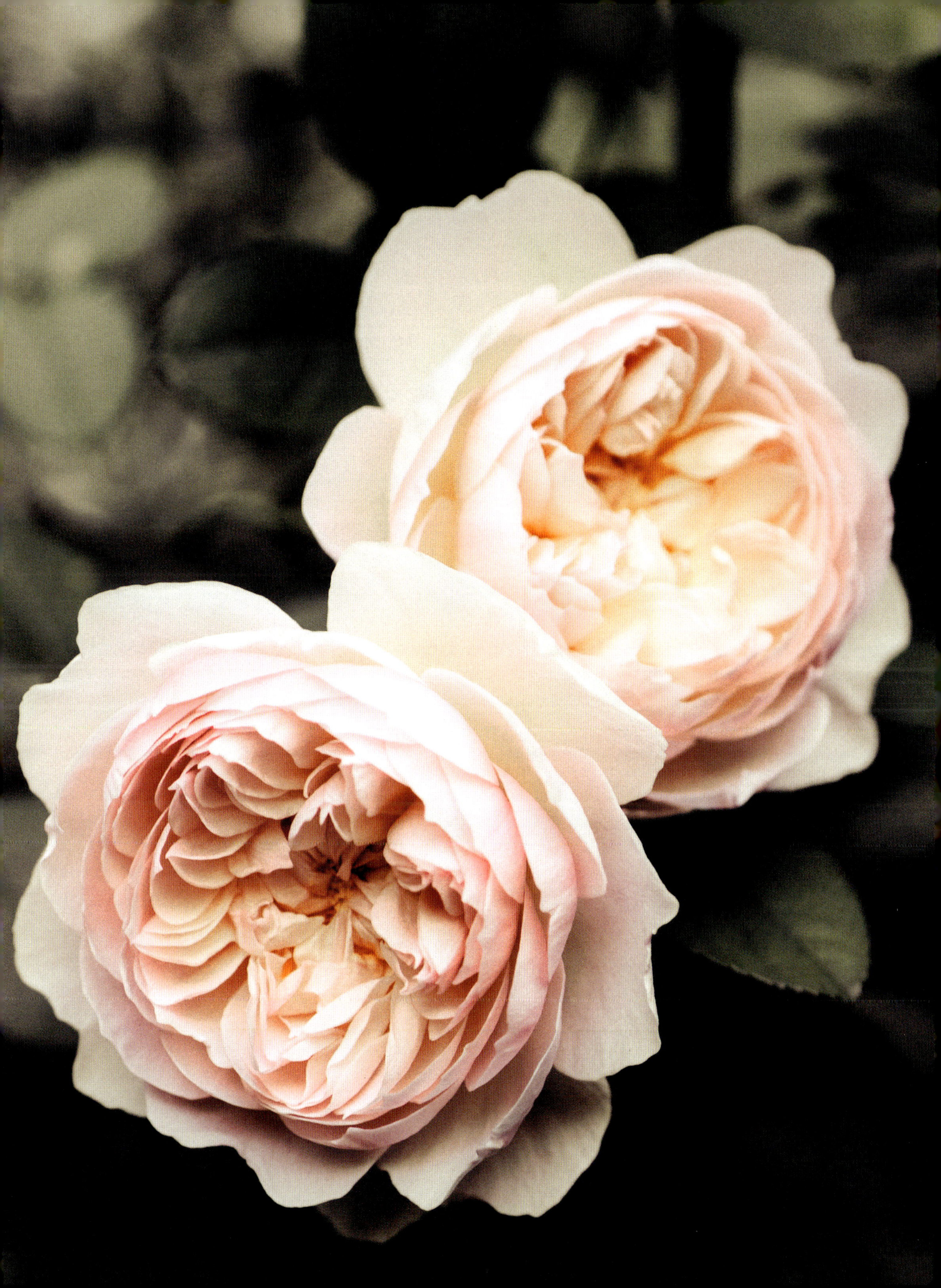

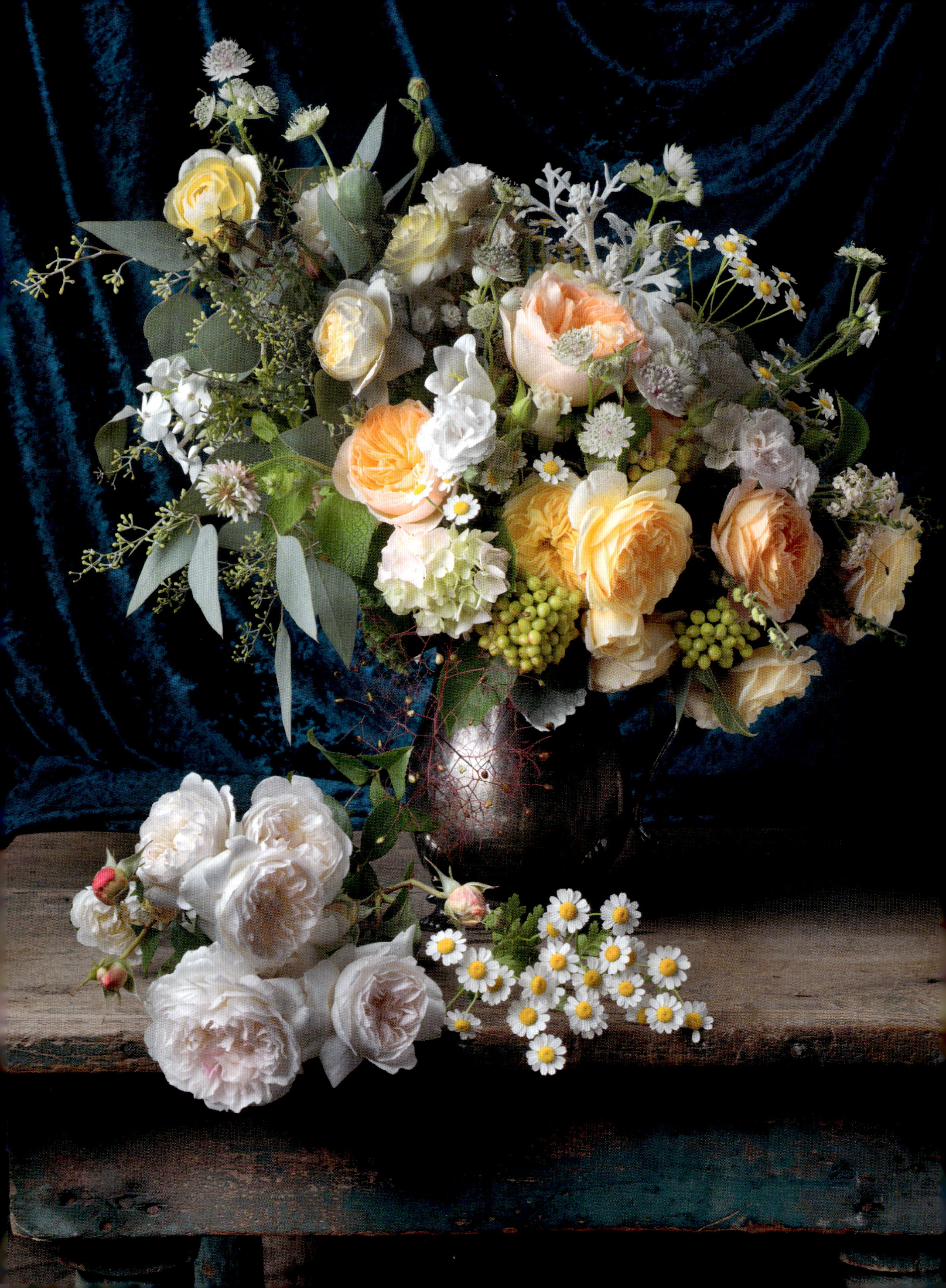

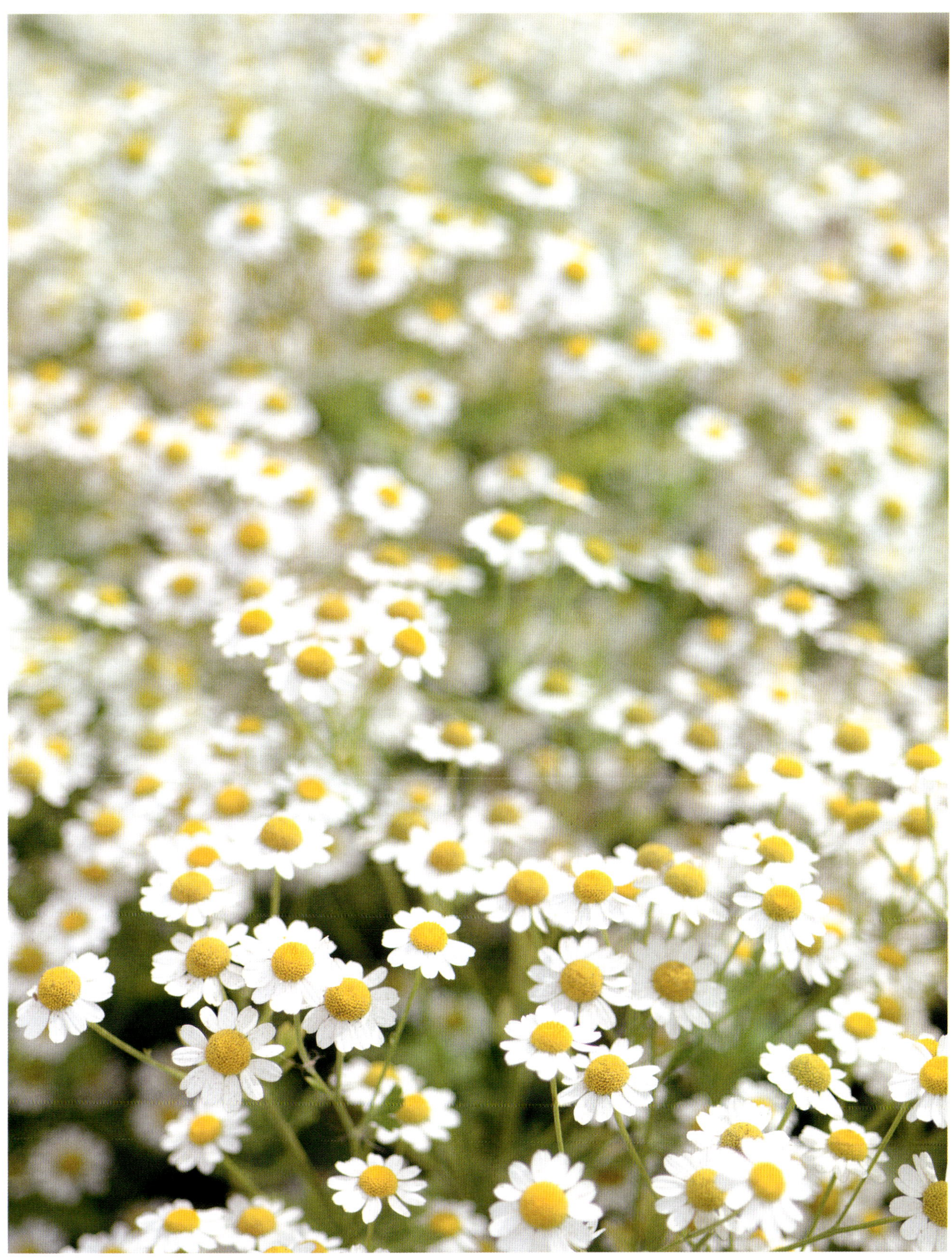

LEFT: David Austin roses 'Port Sunlight', 'Golden Celebration' and 'Tranquillity' in a mixed bouquet with feverfew *(Tanacetum parthenium).* Design by Erin Benzakein, photographed at Floret Farm, Washington, USA. August 2012. ABOVE: A field of feverfew, Washington. July 2014. FOLLOWING PAGES: David Austin roses 'James Galway' and 'Tranquillity'. Photographed at Floret Farm, Washington, USA. August 2012.

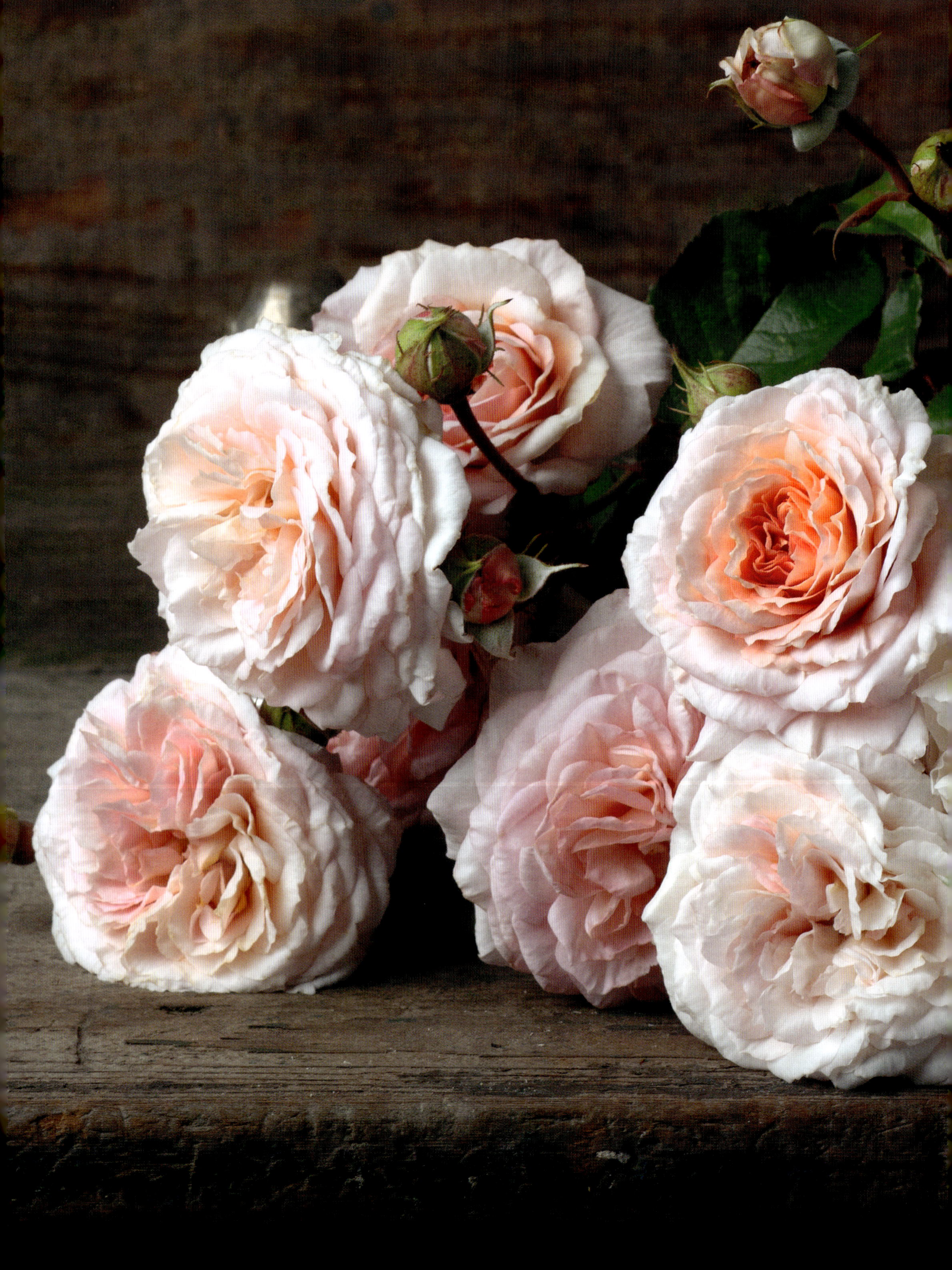

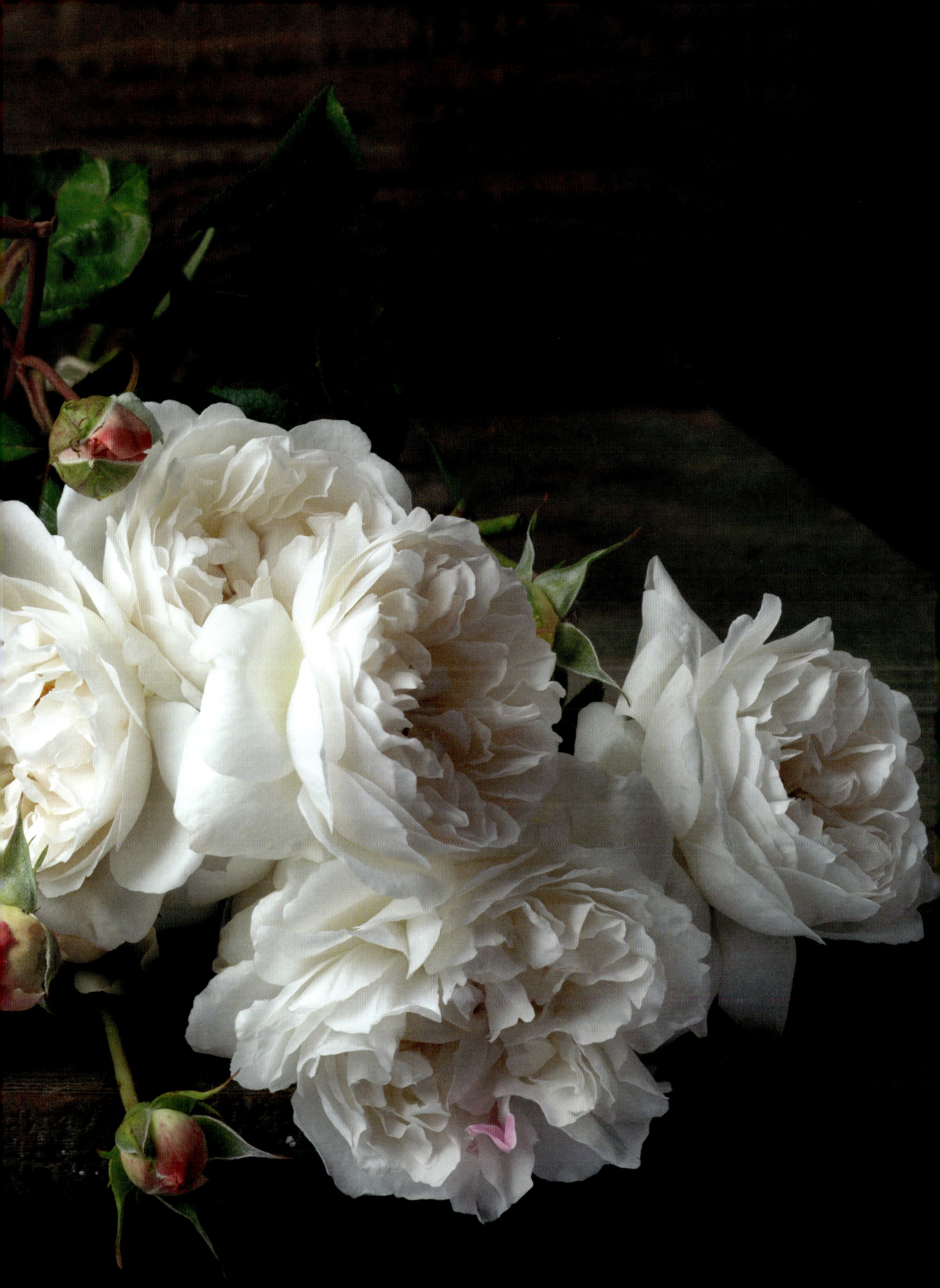

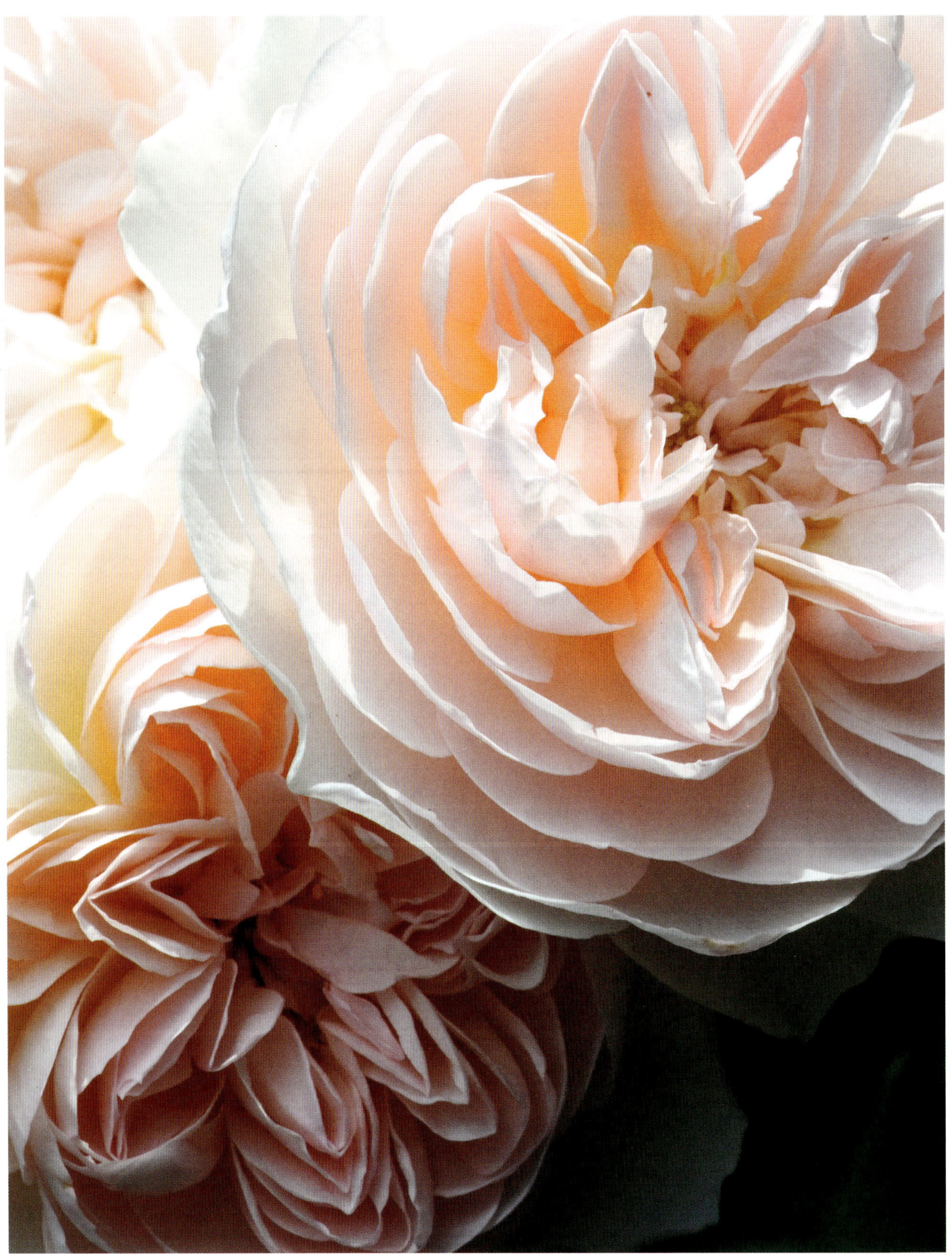

LEFT: David Austin rose 'Gentle Hermione', Hillhaven Garden, Shoreline, Washington, USA. July 2008. RIGHT: David Austin roses 'James Galway' and 'Eglantyne', Hillhaven. July 2012.

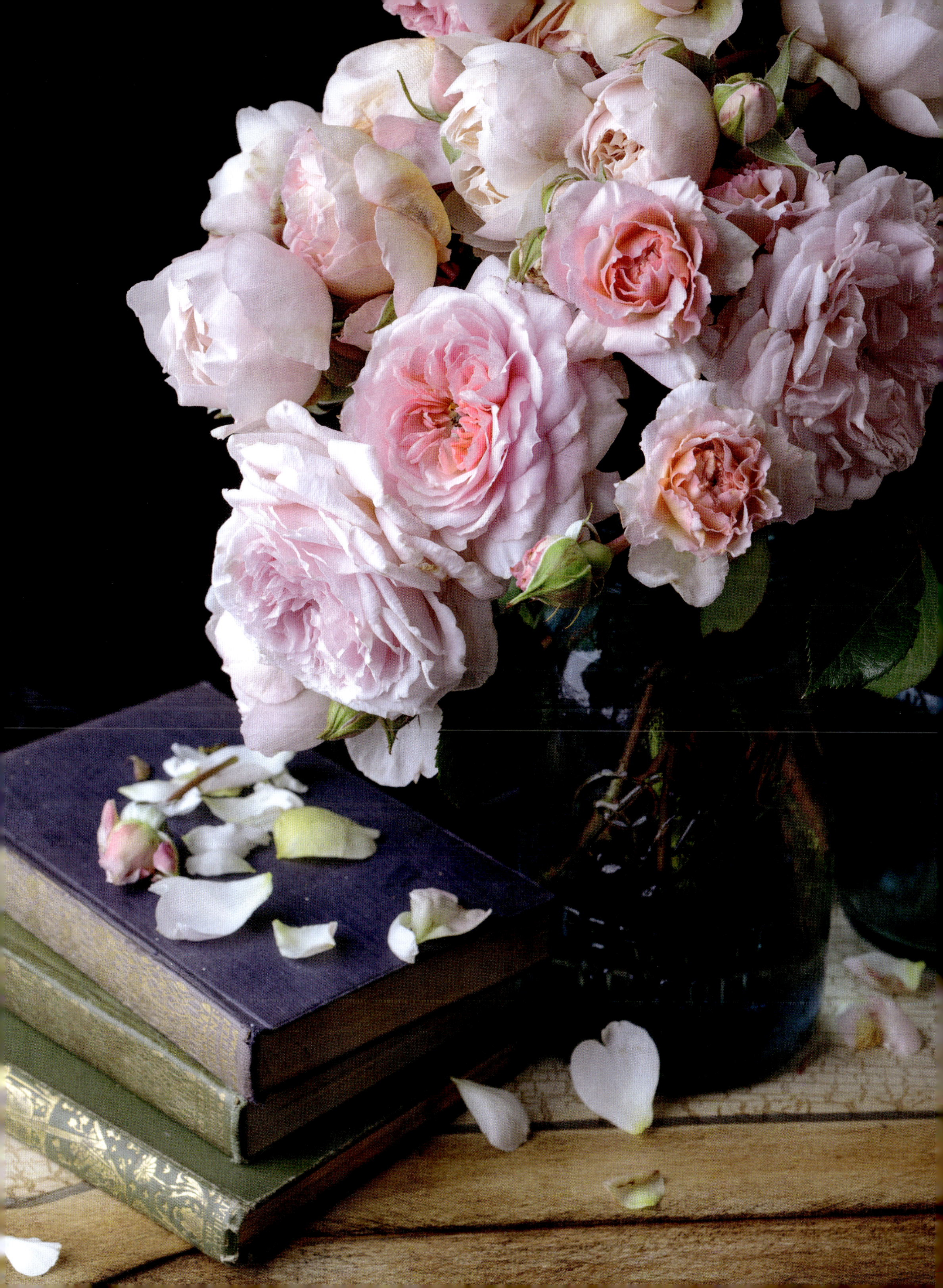

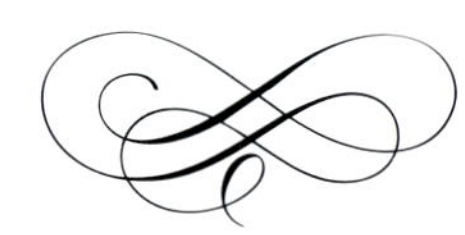

A flower's FRAGRANCE can awaken gossamer wisps of beloved memories, tangible just on the edge of consciousness, elusive but PRECIOUS.

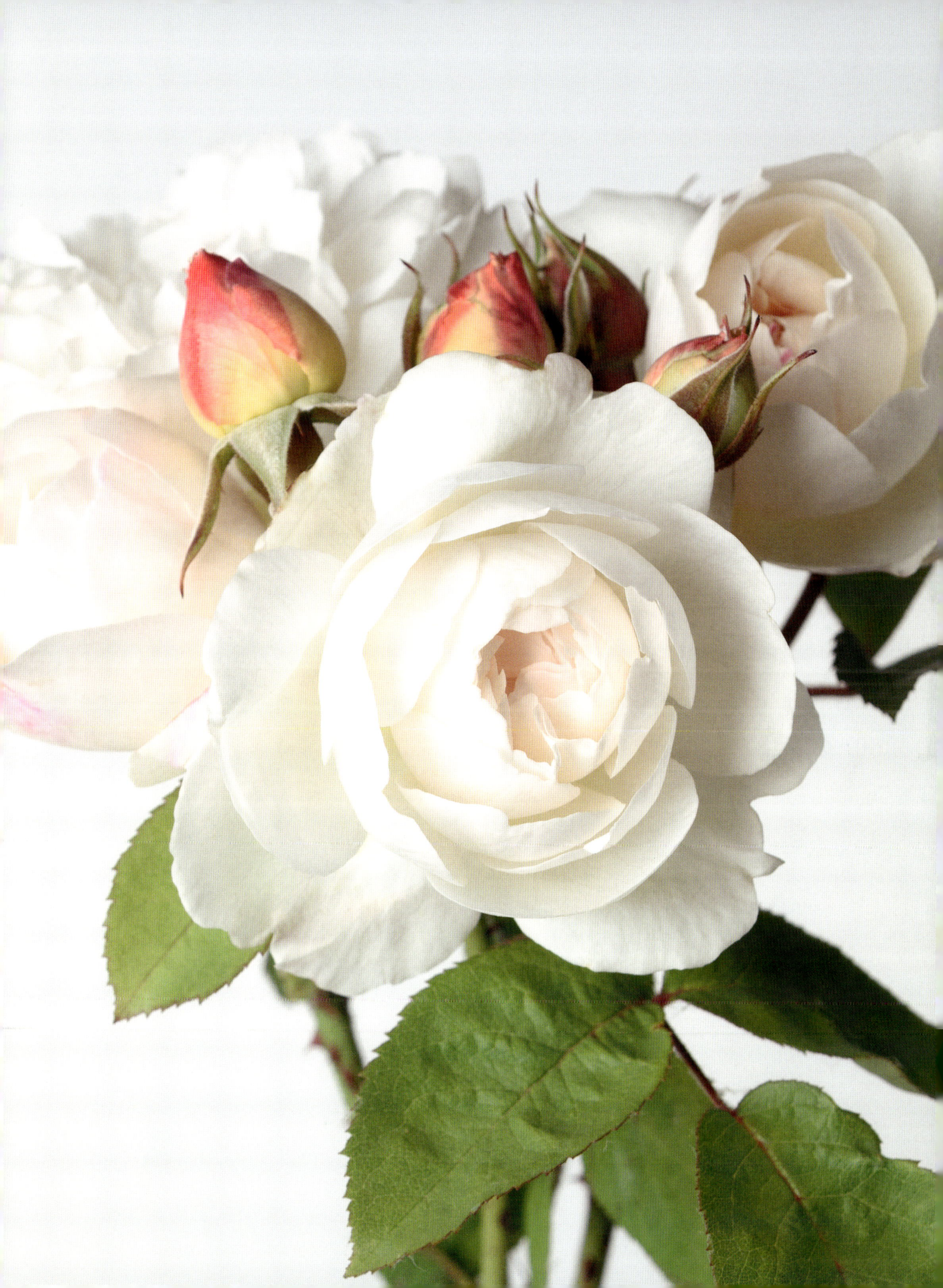

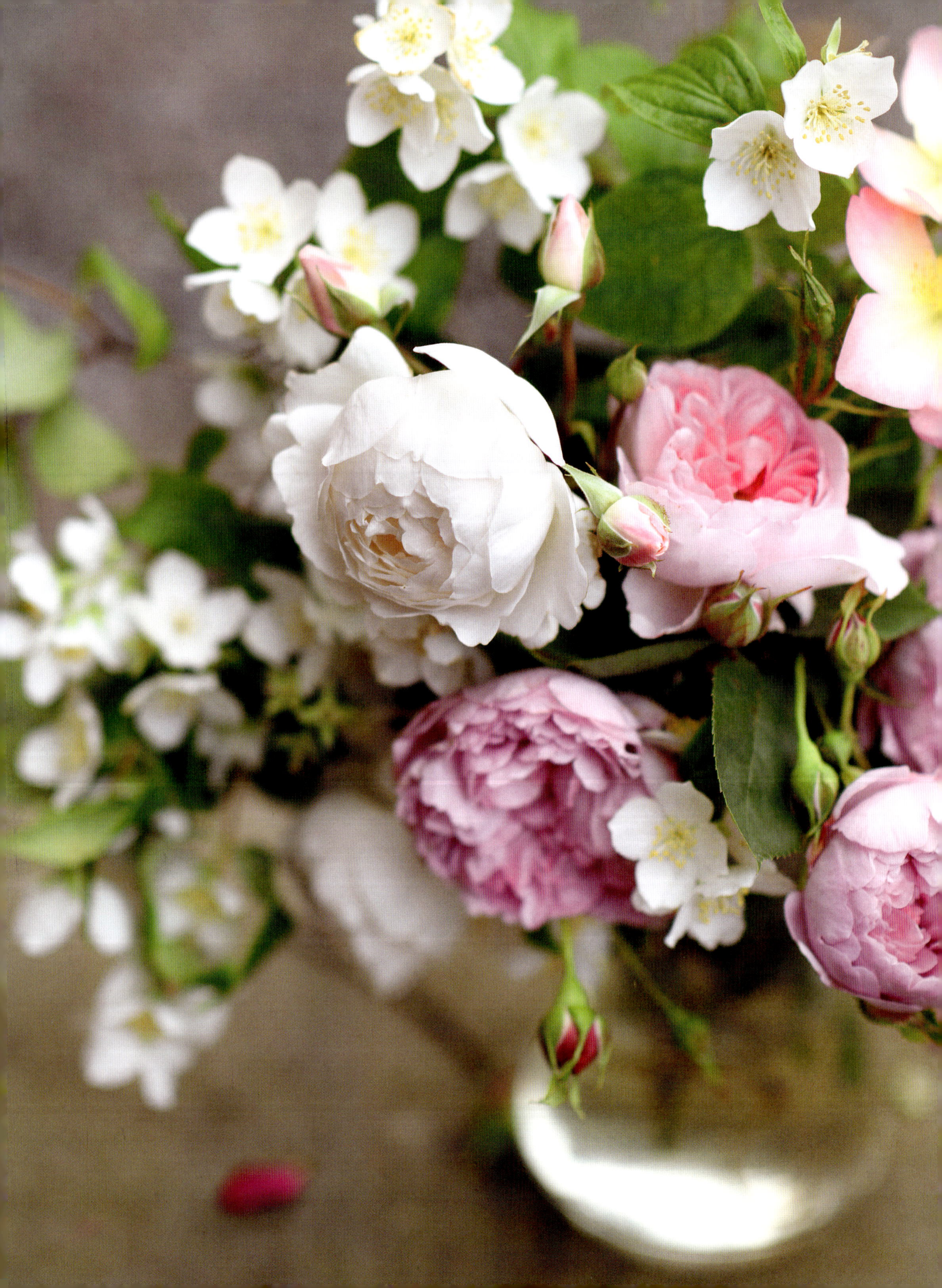

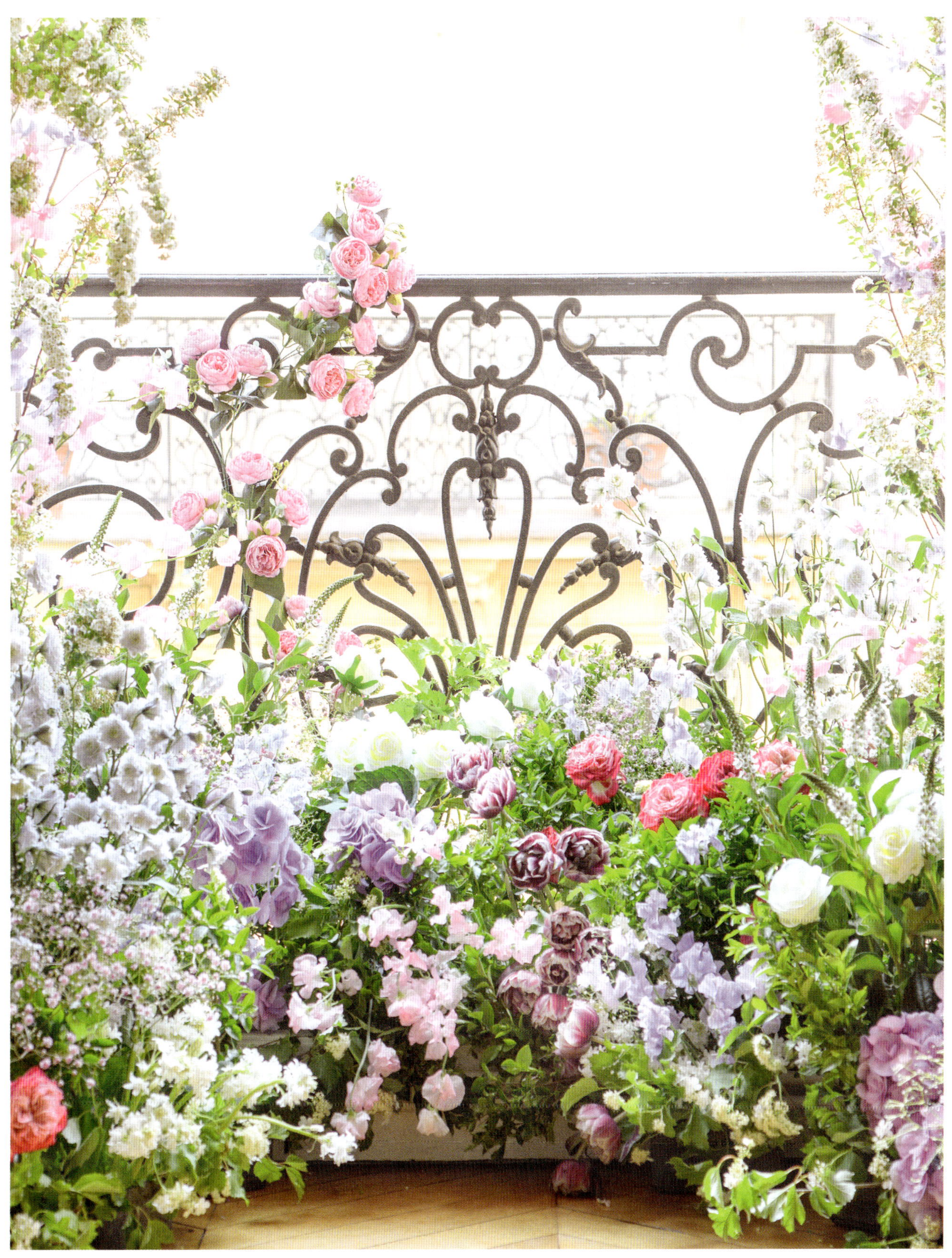

LEFT: David Austin roses 'Desdemona' and 'Charles Rennie MacIntosh', with orange blossom, Shropshire, England. July 2015. RIGHT: Floral display, Paris, France. May 2023. OVERLEAF: The private gate, David Austin Rose Centre, Albrighton, England. July 2015.

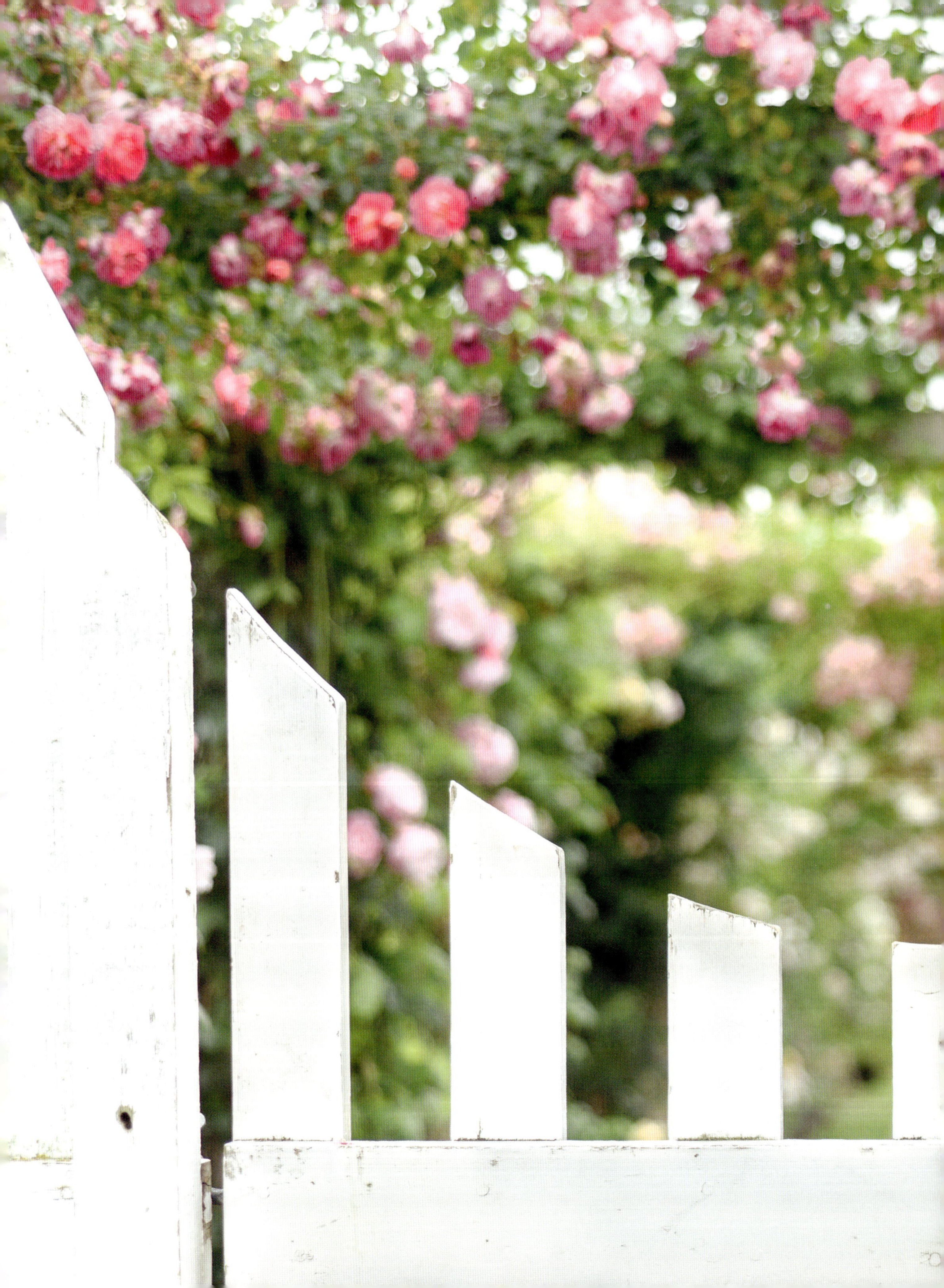

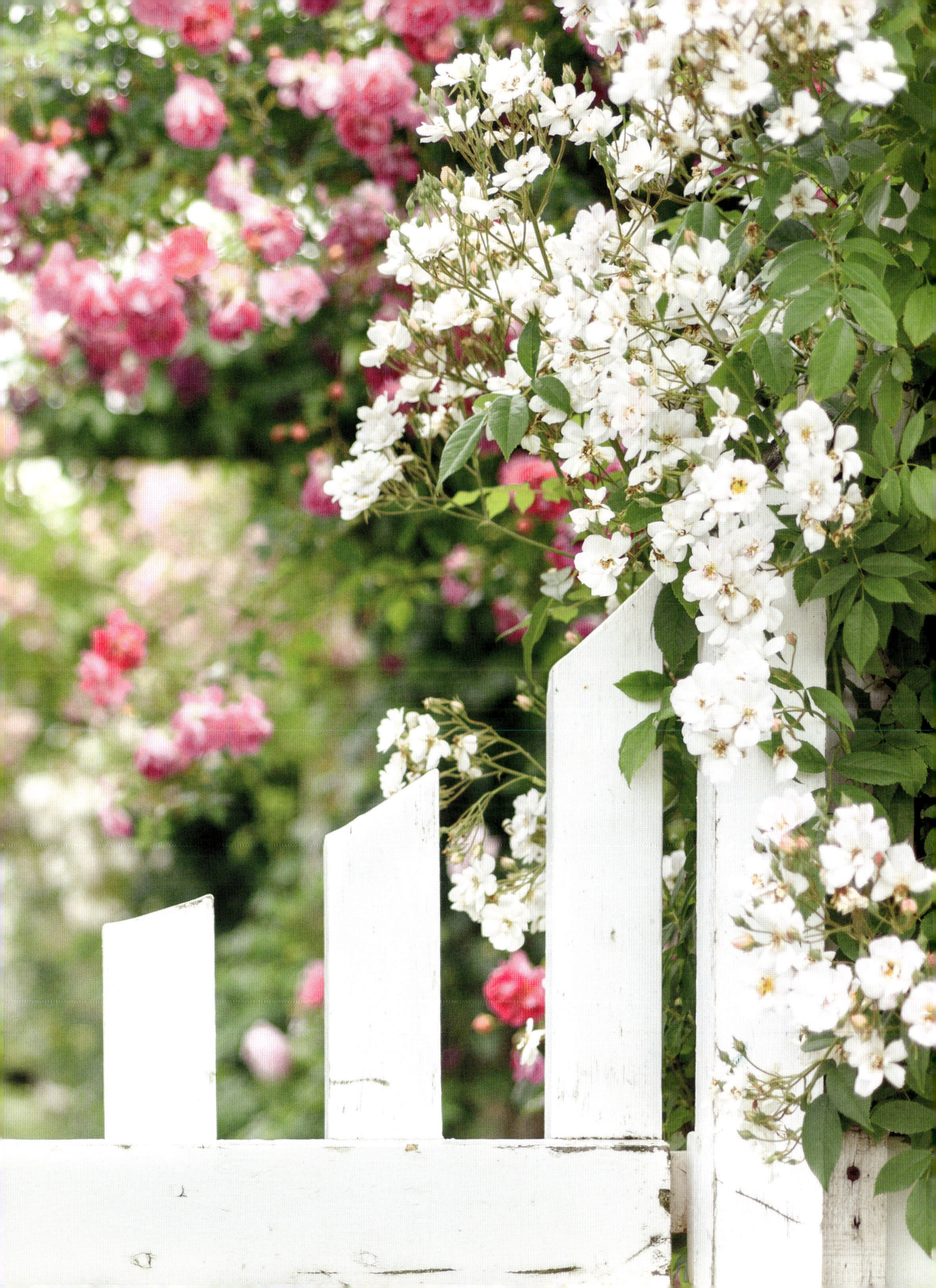

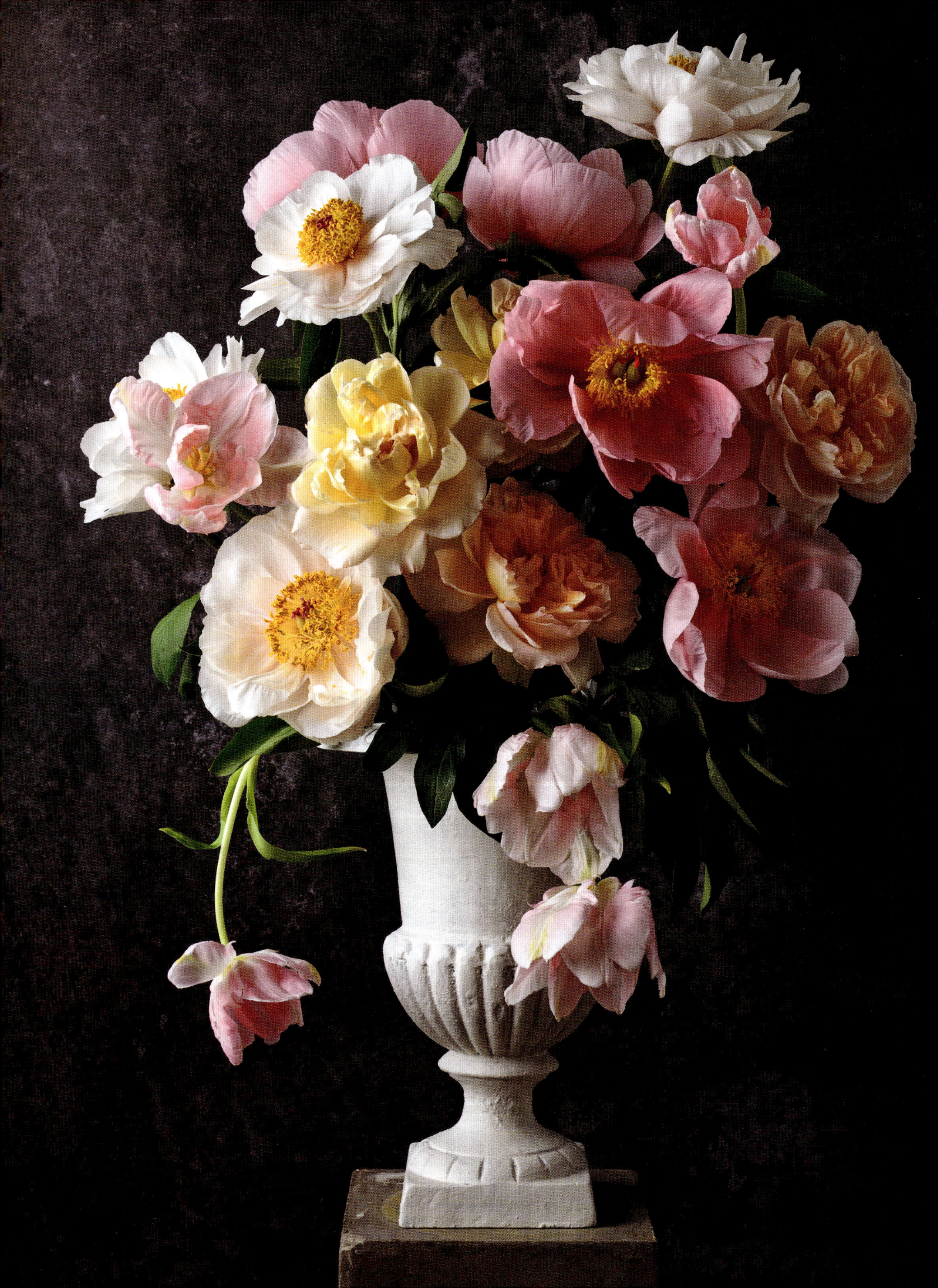

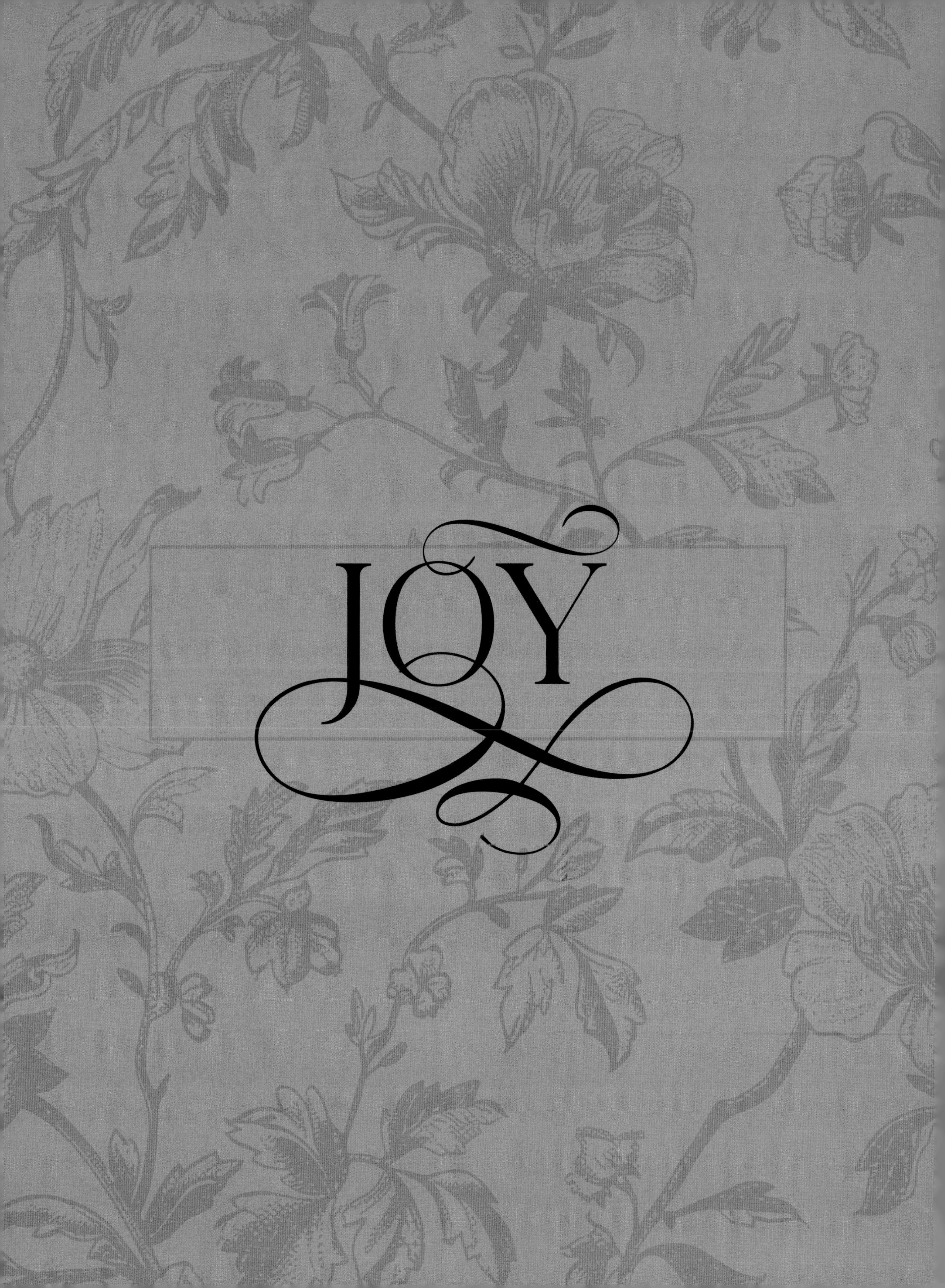
JOY

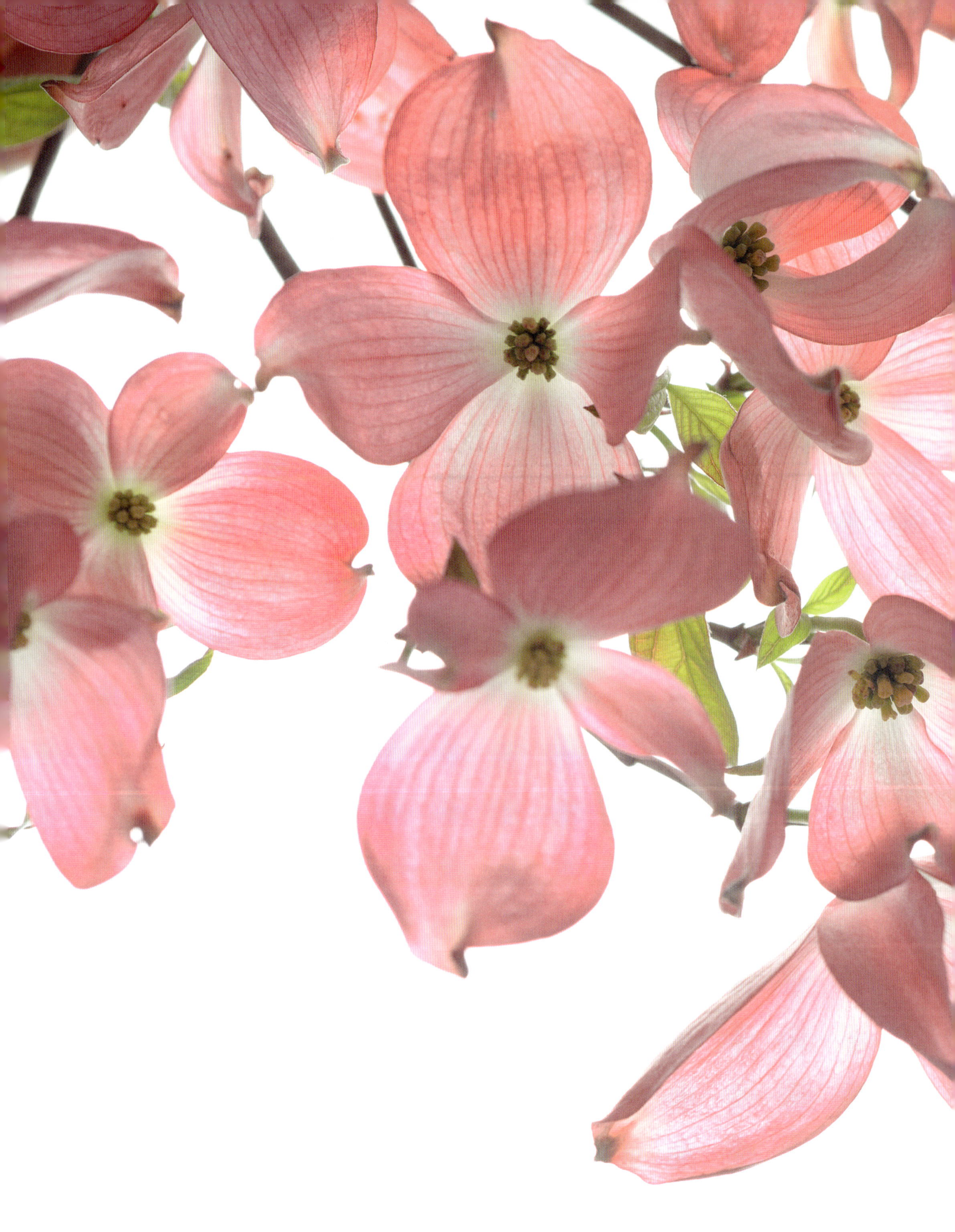

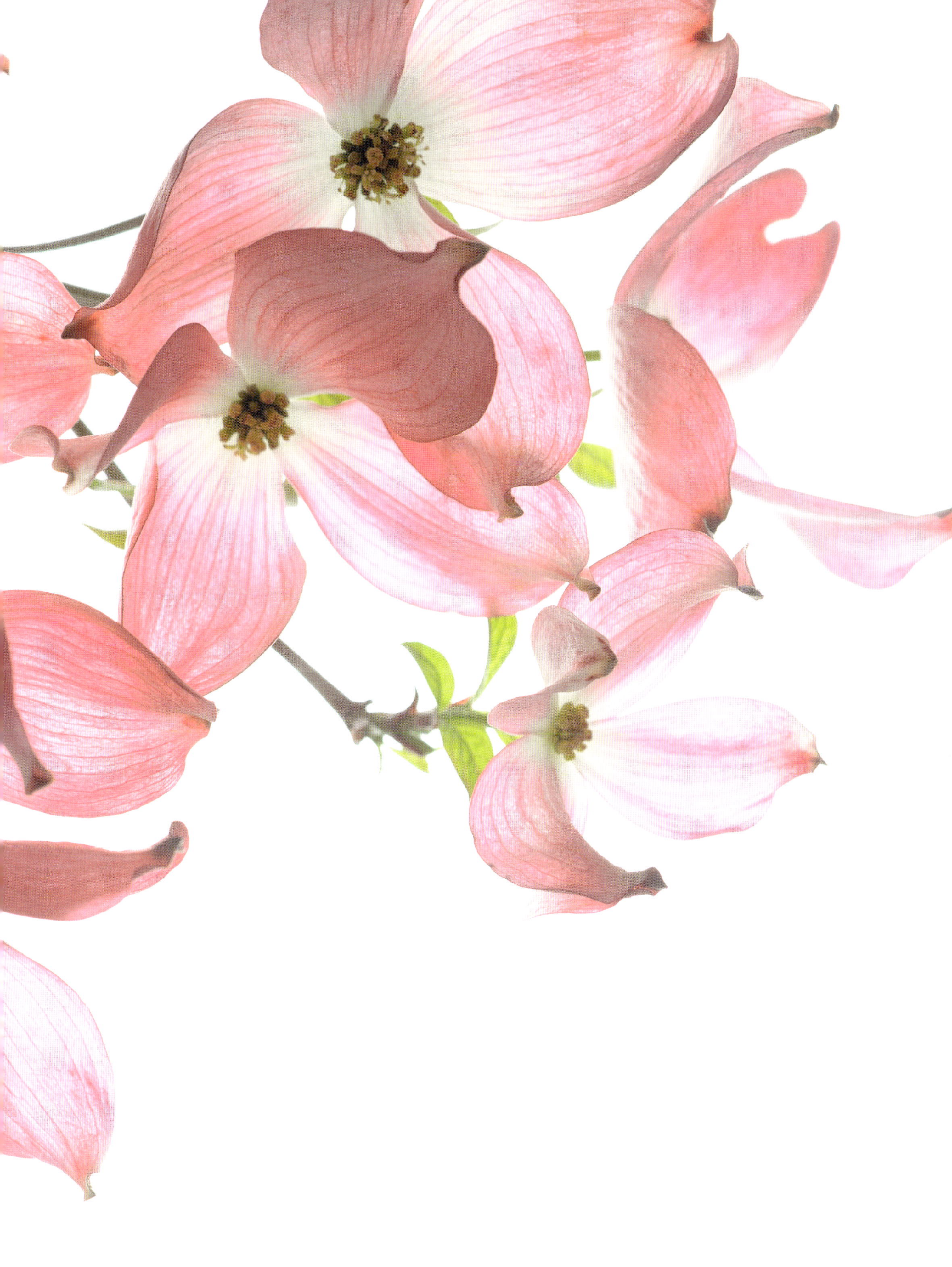

Joy:
A deep feeling of great pleasure and happiness, delight.

Humans have a natural urge to seek joy, to gravitate towards sources of exuberance and uplifting energy, to align themselves with the positive: sunshine, blue skies, dancing, skipping, jumping in exhilaration, the giddiness of the first days of spring.

The floral varieties featured here exemplify these characteristics with bright colors, graceful upward-reaching petals and an insouciant bearing. Deliberately showcased against brilliant-white backgrounds that illuminate the intricacy of their form, they glow with captured light from the sky. The tousled ebullience of dahlias, the perky globes of a field of tulips and the innocent gaiety of a pansy all inject a liveliness and zest into our lives. And who can fail to be cheered at the sight of pretty pink hearts strung across the delicate branch of a bleeding heart plant?

Flowers may be the most universally beloved bringers of joy in existence, transcending political, social and philosophical boundaries. The happiness they spark is unfettered and unrestricted, a purity of emotion that hits directly to the heart. They are instant mood-lifters, smile-bringers and stress-relievers, exuding the positive energy that we crave.

We are drawn to flowers as if magnetically. One only has to observe the awestruck crowds that congregate under a grove of cherry trees in bloom, or that make annual treks to flower fields in their vicinity, twirling with abandon amongst tulips, ranunculus or dahlias.

Throughout my long and in-depth association with flowers, I have personally experienced a continual recharging and witnessed countless scenes of emotional bliss caused by even a single bloom. Frequently, I see first-hand the elation on the faces of visitors to public green spaces as they lean in to inspect the details of an unfamiliar flower or pause rapturously with eyes closed after inhaling the scent of a lily.

But there is science behind our reactions to flowers. In addition to their beauty, fragrance and nurturing presence, it is thought that flowers affect us on a

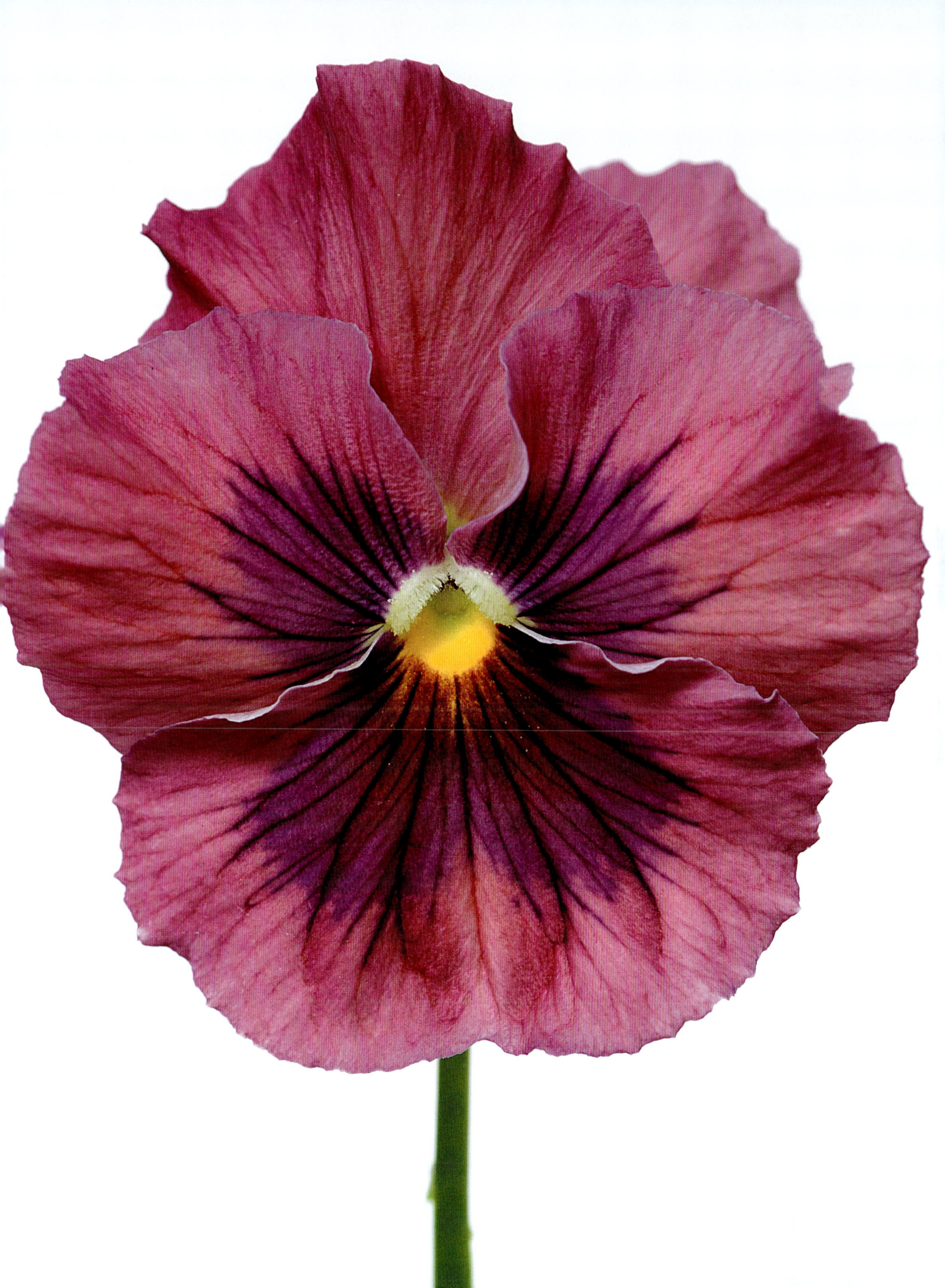

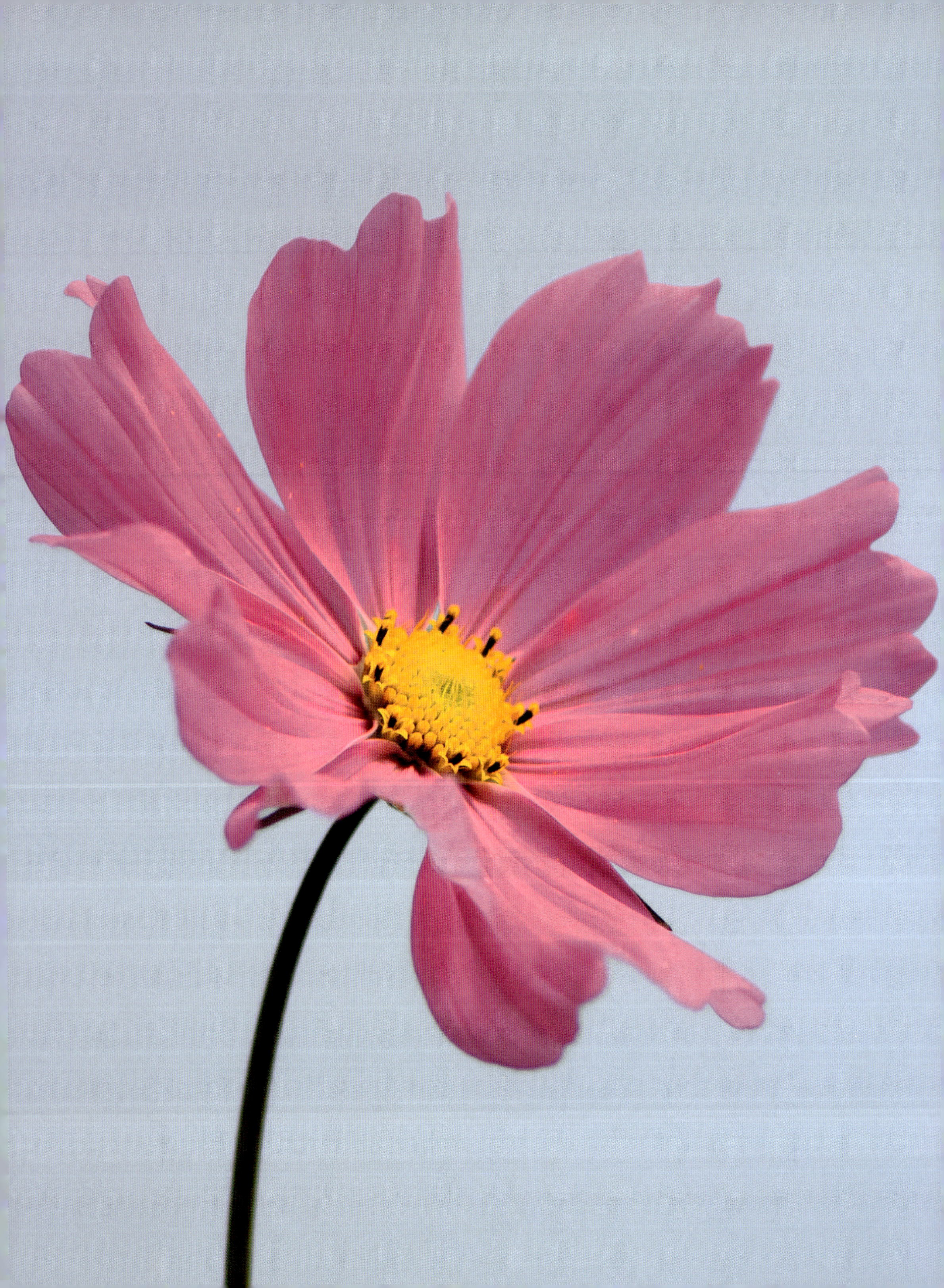

cellular level. Everything in the universe vibrates at its own frequency, and flowers emit a vibrational frequency that is much higher than in the human body, with roses having the highest vibrational frequency of any plant on Earth. This resonance can emanate through an environment, subtly improving mood and outlook.

On another level, flowers provide a necessary visual antidote to our mostly square and rigid man-made environments. Daily, we are surrounded by the geometric and the regimented in our structures and furnishings, yet in nature there exist no straight lines or right angles, and we find the sinuous curves and rounded, undulating forms of flowers to be soothing and relaxing. Whether through feelings of contentment, enthusiasm or jubilation, we need the restorative elixir of a bouquet, a centerpiece or a potted, blooming plant in our surroundings.

Here, our destinations include the Pacific Northwest, Canada, Cornwall, France and the Netherlands, represented by images taken over a period of 15 years.

I have always found tulips great fun to photograph, due to their shapes and beautiful colors. No other flower so resembles a goblet of light, vividly capturing and holding the sun, while offering it gratefully back up to the heavens. In the fertile Skagit Valley of Washington State, USA, the landscape is transformed each April with hundreds of acres of commercially grown tulips, drawing visitors from all over the globe. And in the thoughtfully designed displays at The Butchart Gardens, in Canada, tulips float above pale blue forget-me-nots.

At Keukenhof, the enormous floral display garden in Lisse, outside Amsterdam, the blue river of spiky grape hyacinth winding its way through a woodland in spring is a veritable fairy playground. Its bright hue appears irresistible to all ages of visitors, who cannot help but smile to one another, while children clap in glee at the unexpected sight.

Although not one of my favorites to grow, I fully appreciate how entertaining dahlias are, especially as photographic subjects. Their wild, firework-esque silhouettes and fascinating petal structure ensure they are endlessly captivating. Flower farming and the local flower movement have exploded in popularity over the last ten years – a testament to our intrinsic need for more and more flowers!

LEFT: Cosmos flower (*Cosmos bipinnatus*), Washington, USA. September 2009. OVERLEAF: Field of *Tulipa* 'Rem's Favorite', Skagit Valley, Washington, USA. April 2007.

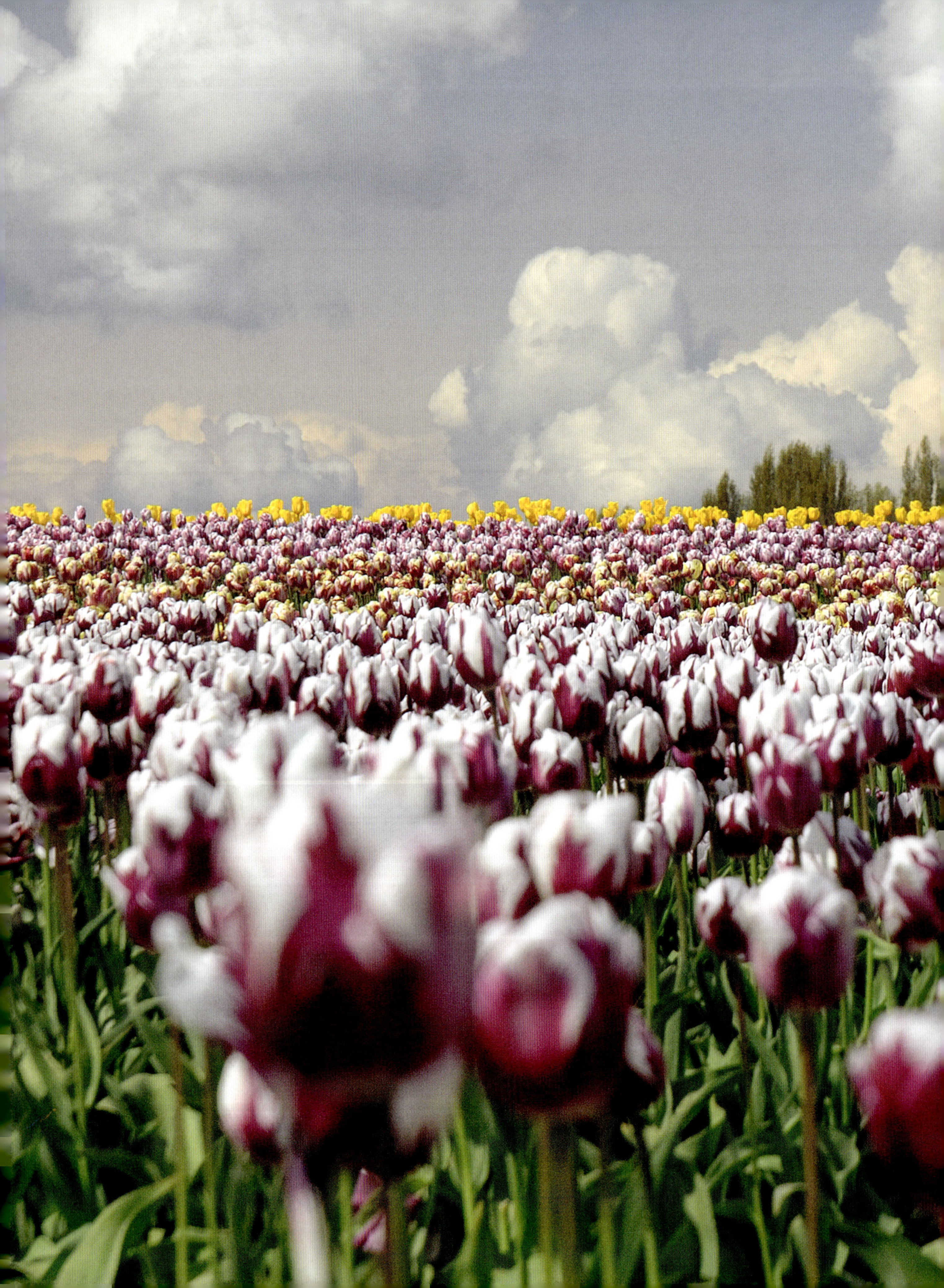

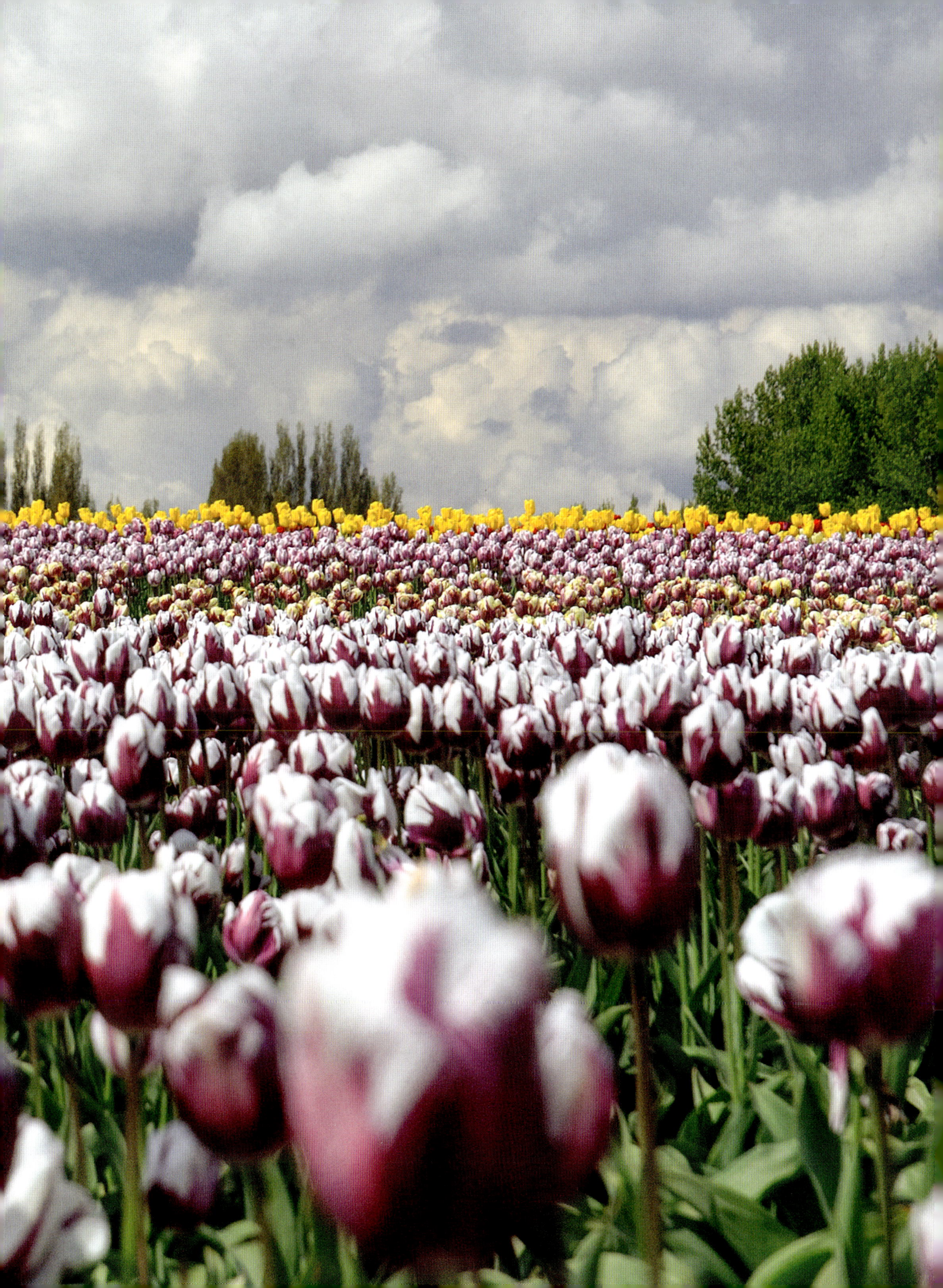

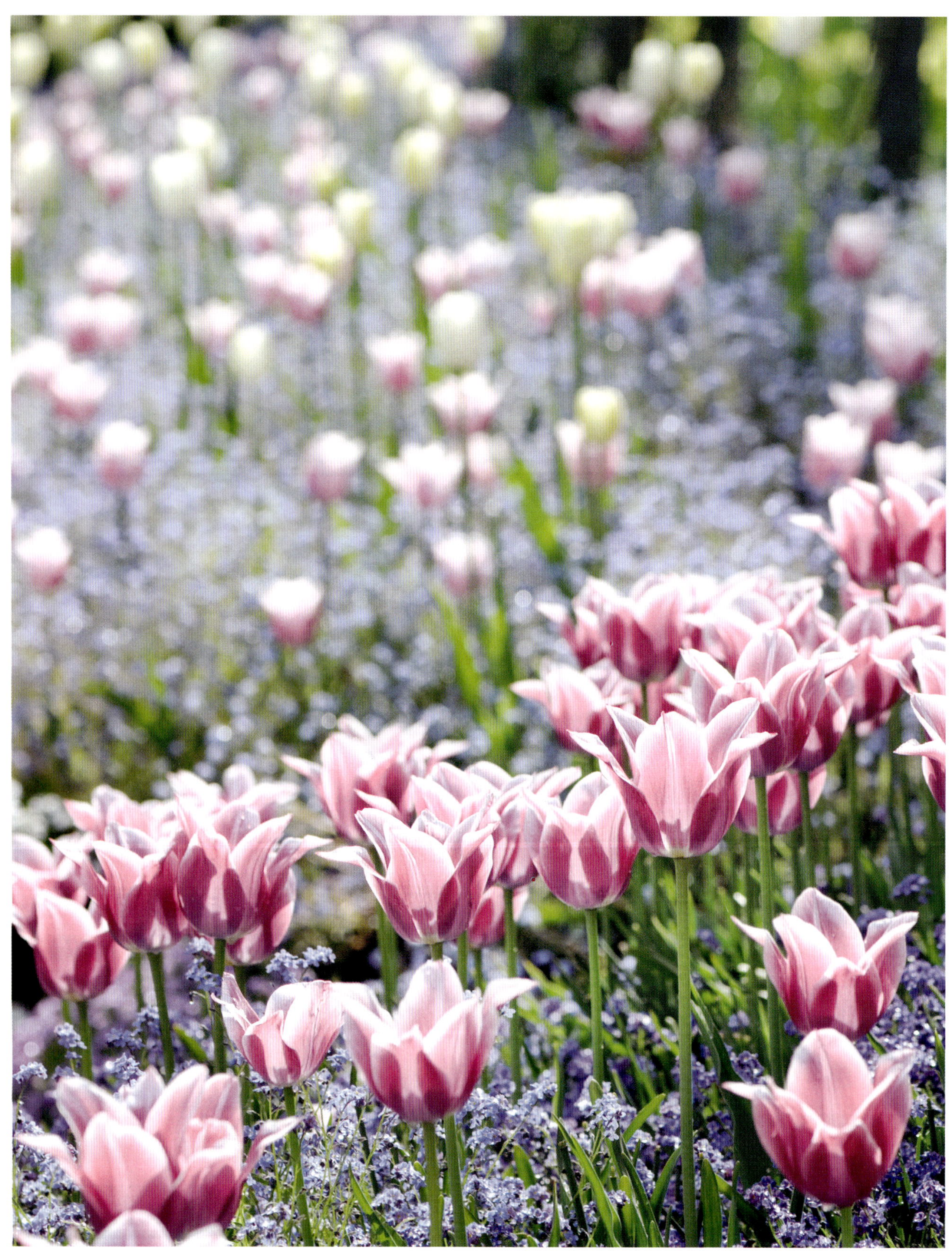

ABOVE AND RIGHT: *Tulipa* 'China Pink', Butchart Gardens. May 2008. OVERLEAF: Bleeding Heart (*Lamprocapnos spectabilis*), Hillhaven Garden, Shoreline, Washington, USA. May 2012.

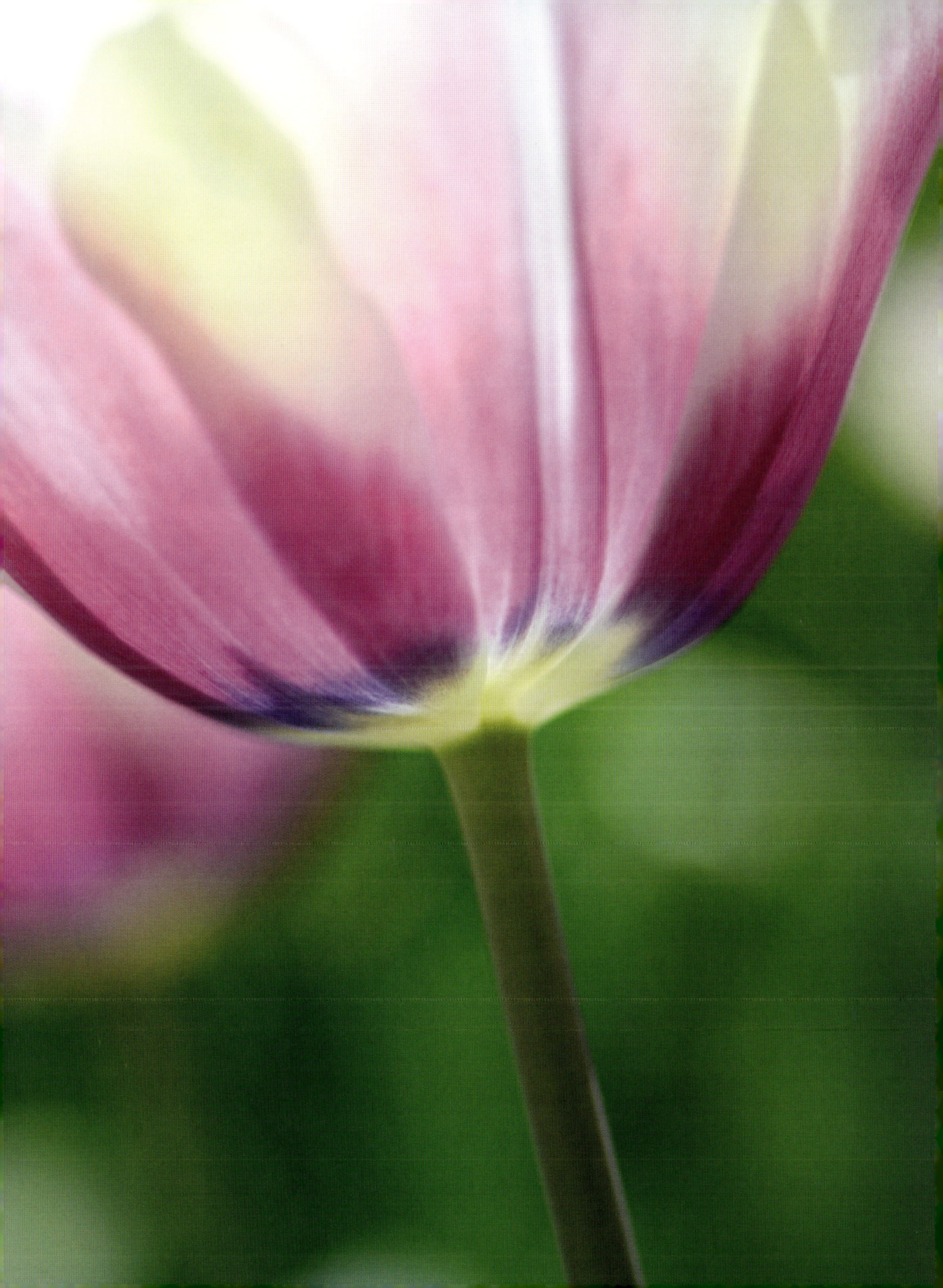

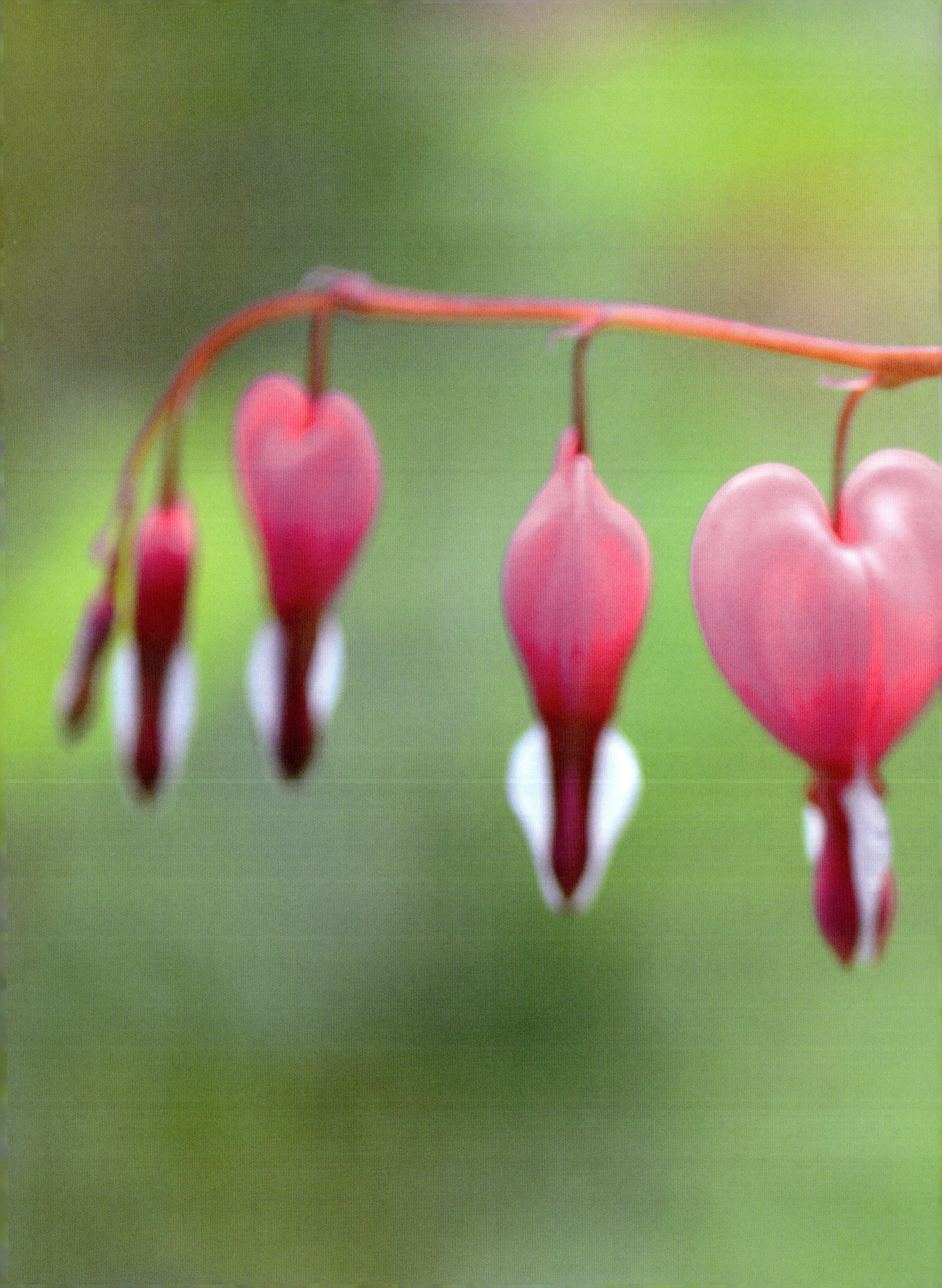

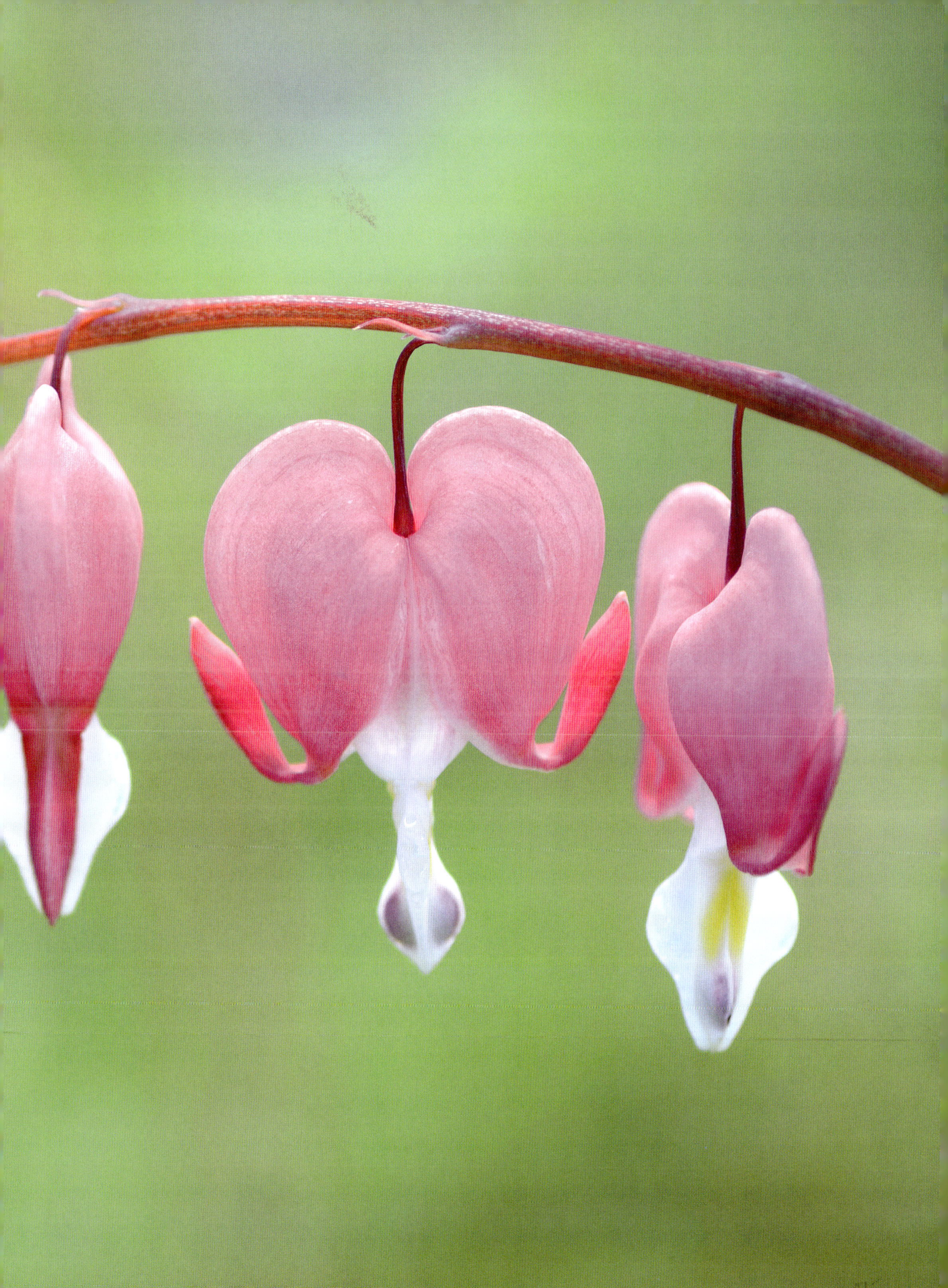

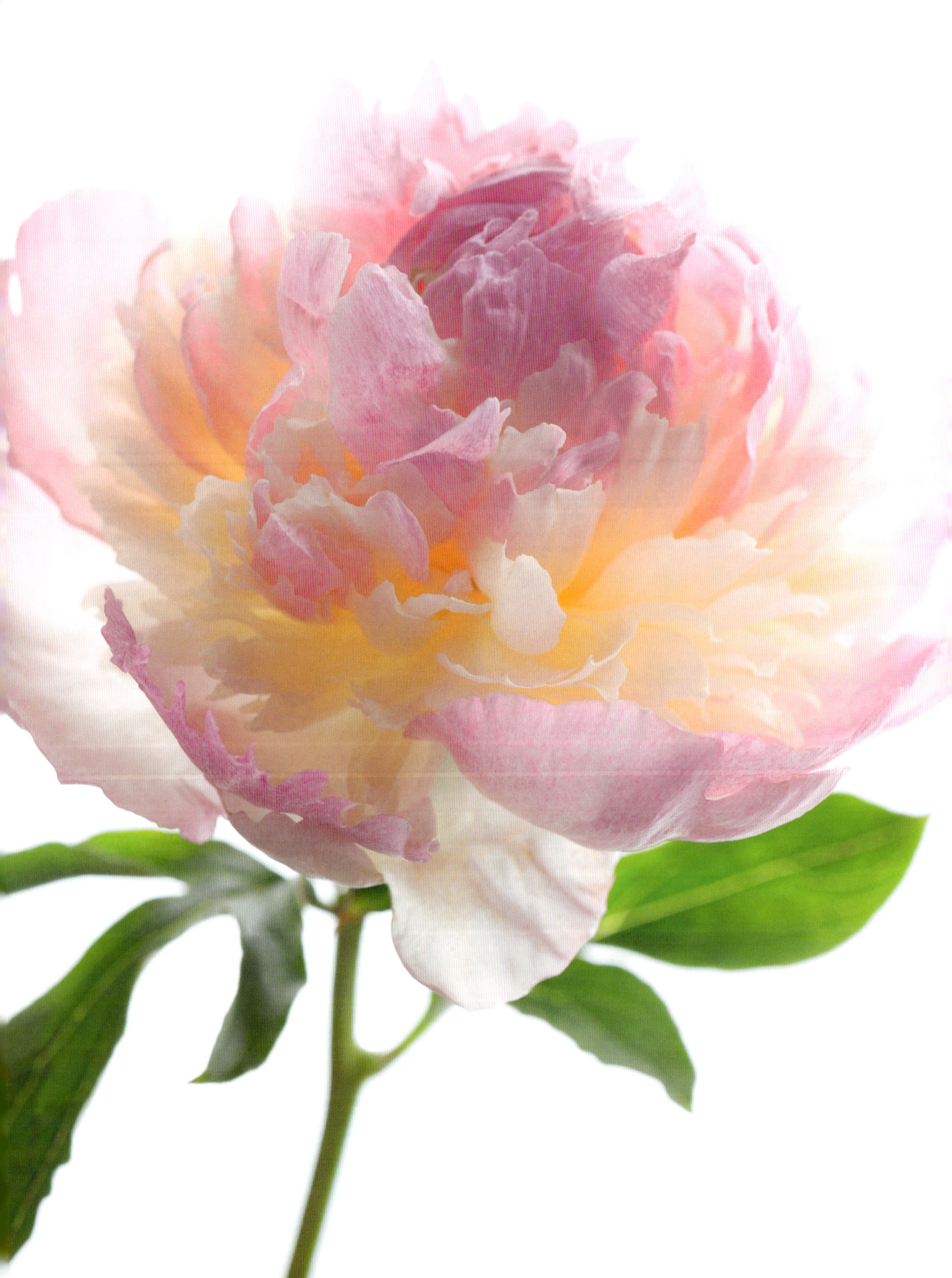

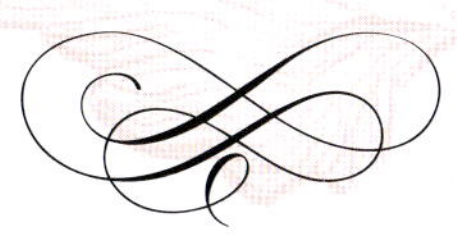

GERALDINE'S PEONIES

Washington, USA
2015-2018

This 'Top Brass' *peony and the field of fluffy white* 'Reine Hortense' *peonies that echo the shapes and color of the early summer clouds (on the following pages) are from a private peony farm in northern Washington, USA, taken under a cerulean sky one June afternoon. The delightful owner welcomed me to her property numerous times over the course of several years. It was there that many important images that appear in one of my most popular books,* Peonies, *were taken. Geraldine and I would spend hours in the fields, discussing the merits of all the varieties and which would earn a spot in the book. At the end of each day, she would insist upon loading my car to the brim with buckets of her freshly cut, organically grown peonies. Such magnanimous abundance was an extravagance that I always remember with gratitude. It is not too dramatic to state that without her enthusiastic spirit, that book would not exist.*

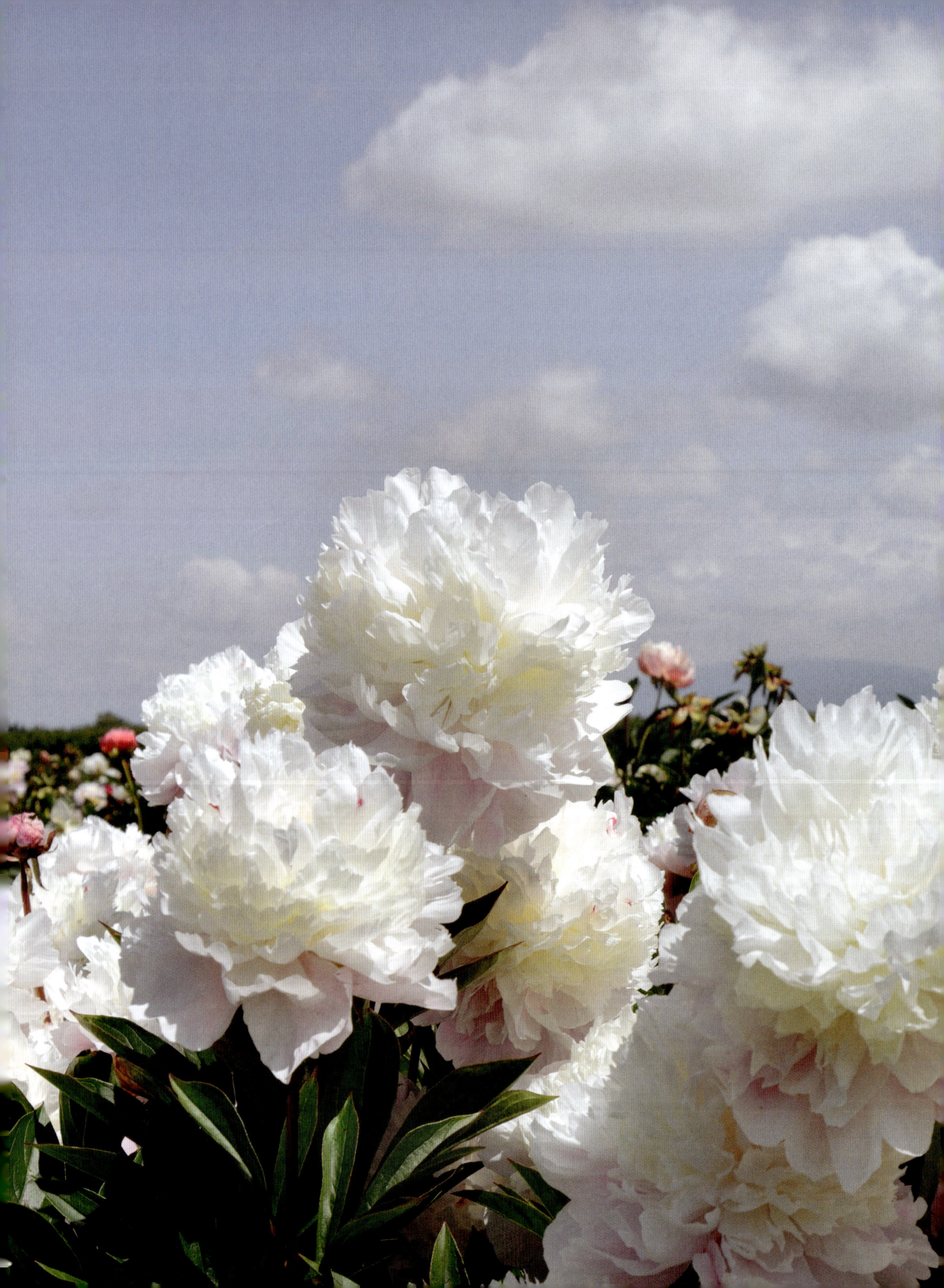

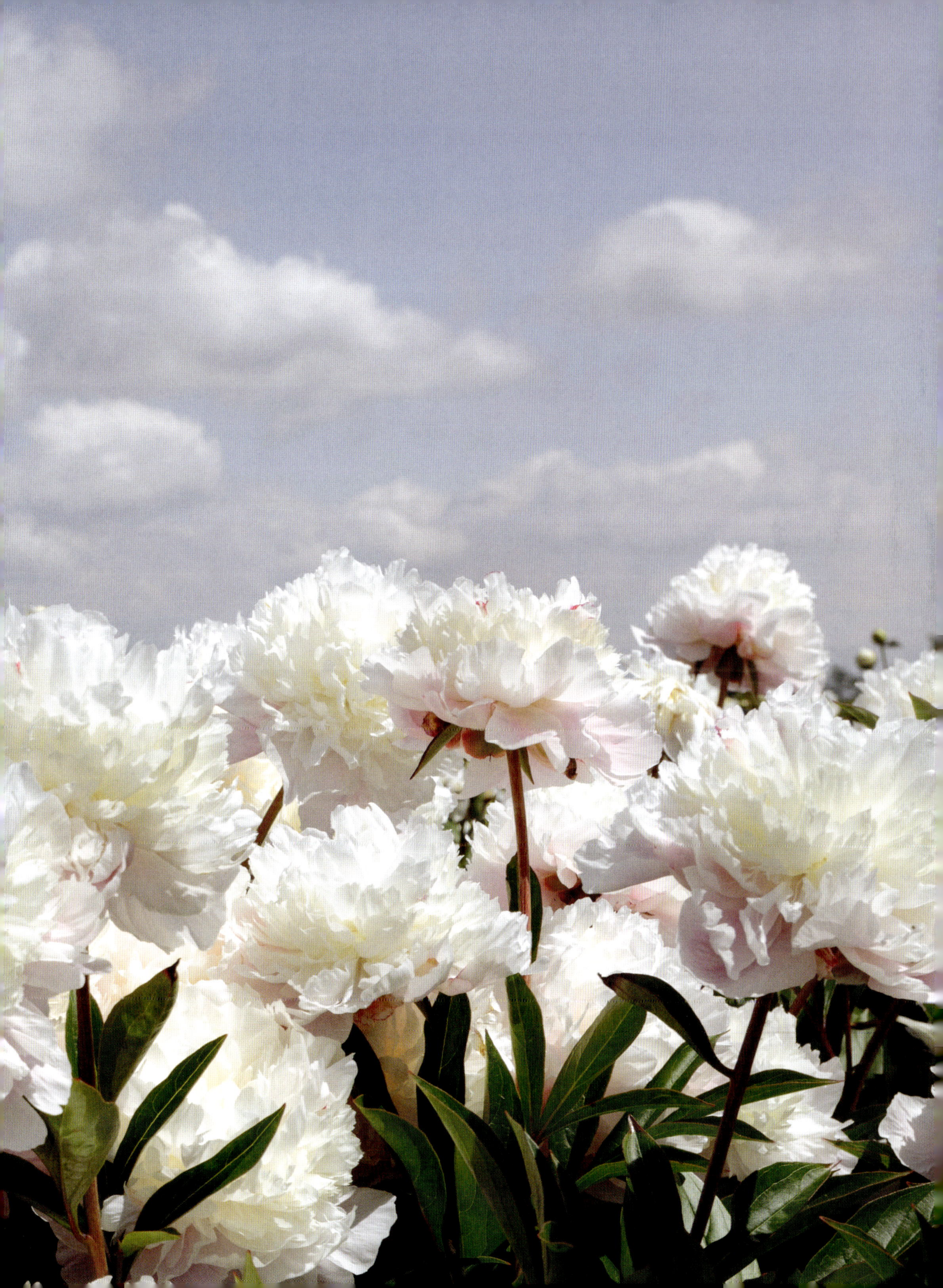

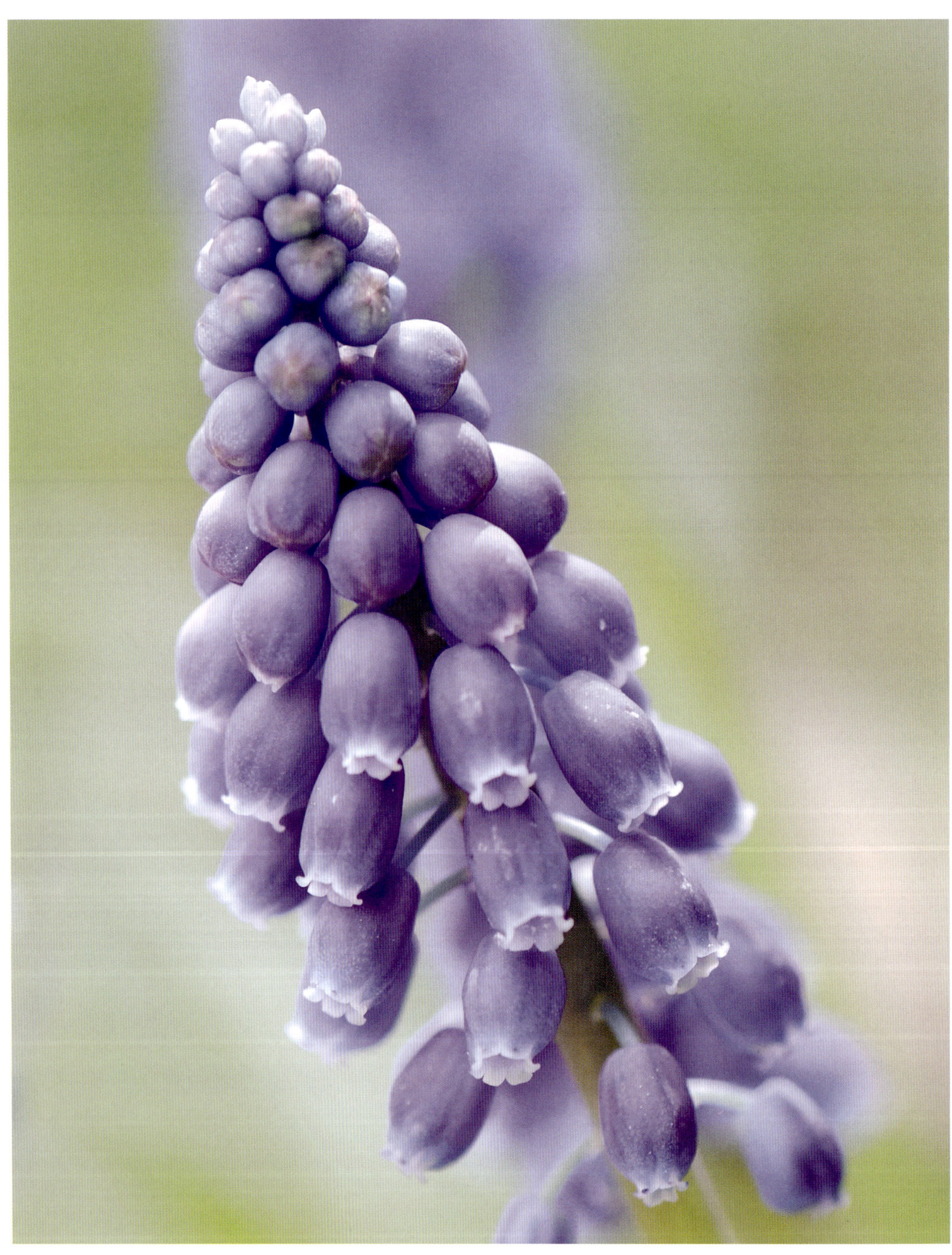

ABOVE: Grape hyacinth (*Muscari*), Hillhaven Garden, Shoreline, Washington, USA. April 2008. RIGHT: River of grape hyacinth at Keukenhof Gardens, Lisse, Netherlands. April 2024. OVERLEAF: Clematis, Amsterdam, Netherlands. May 2012. *Clematis* 'The President', Hillhaven. August 2012.

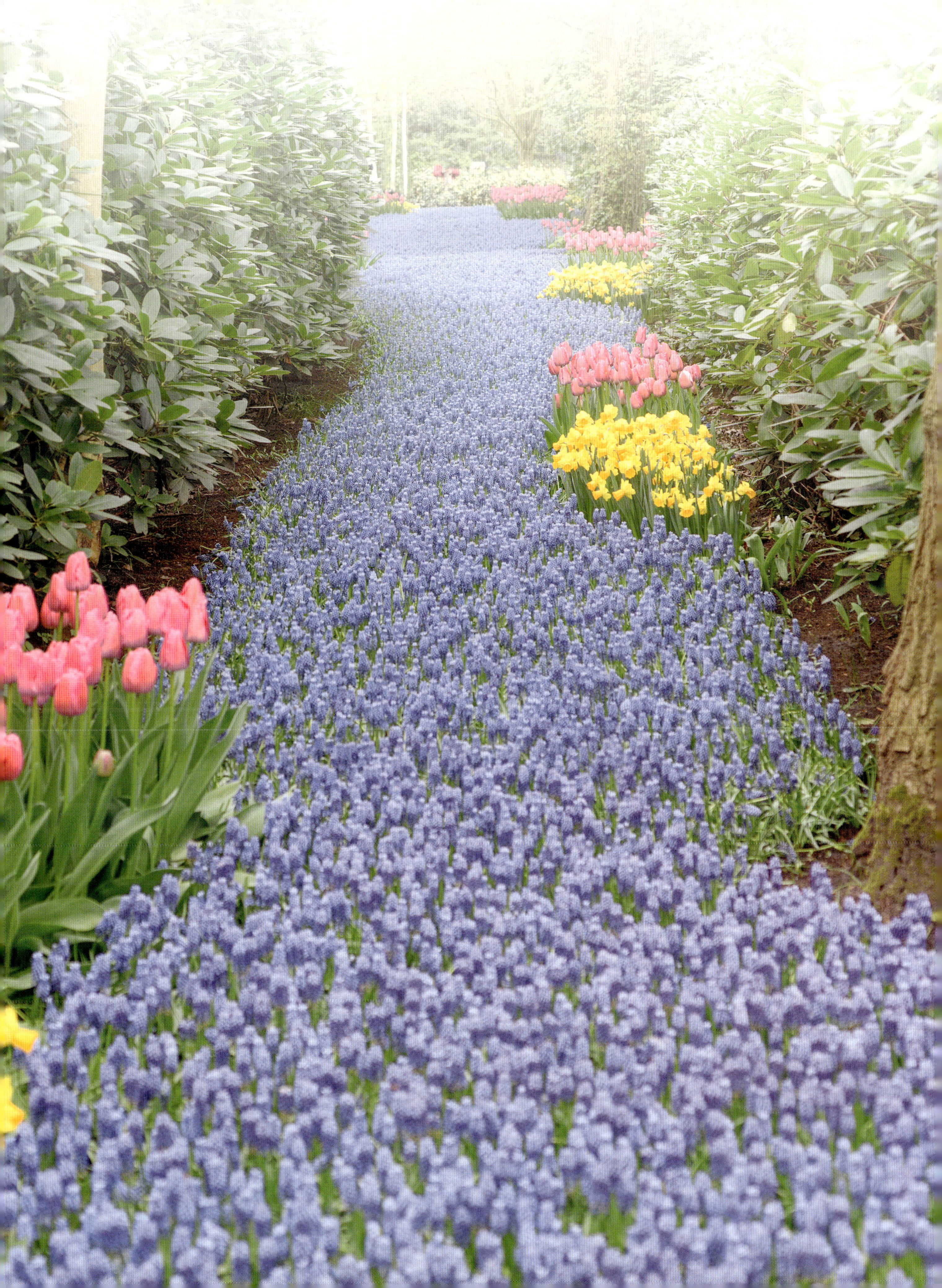

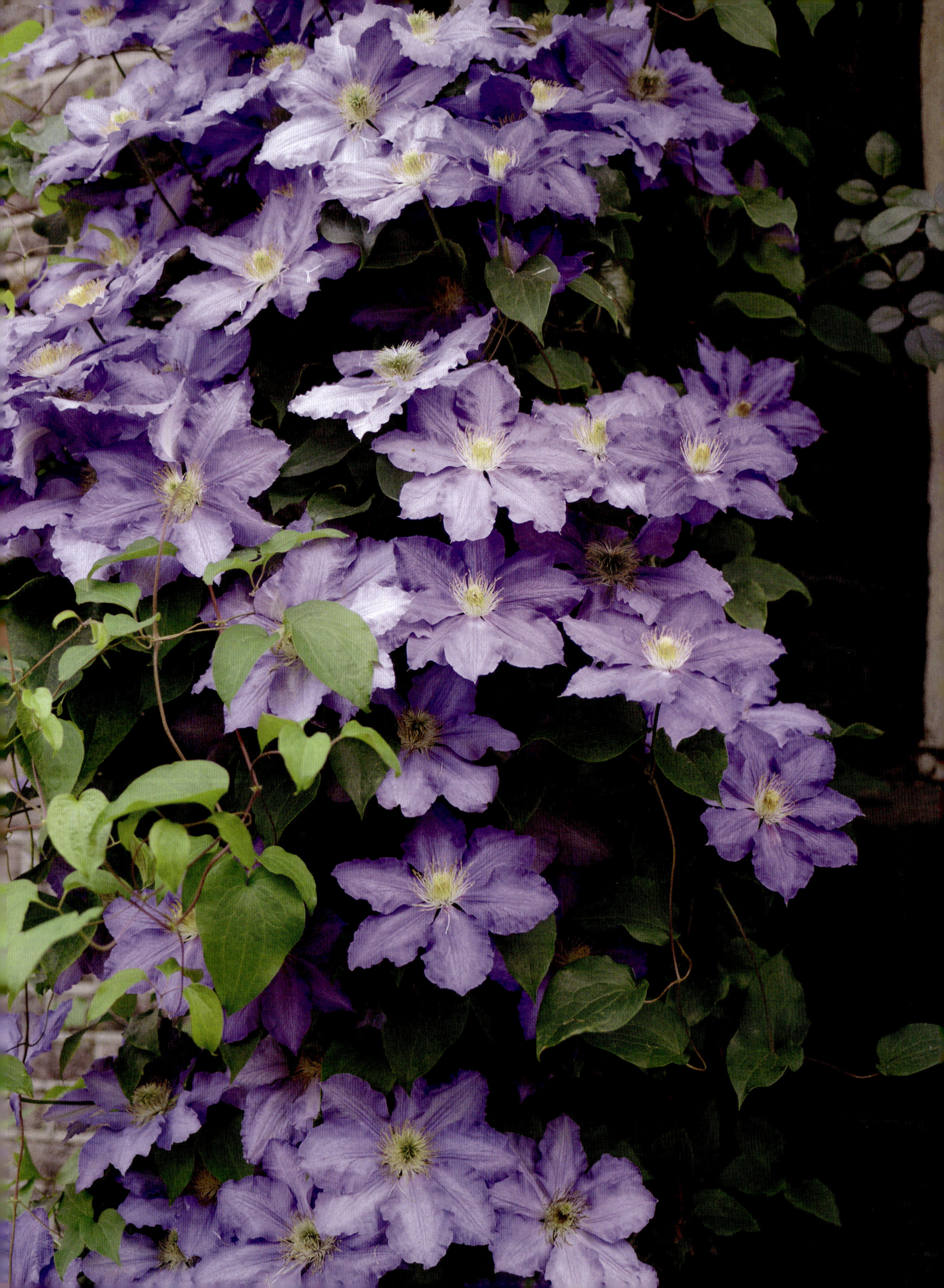

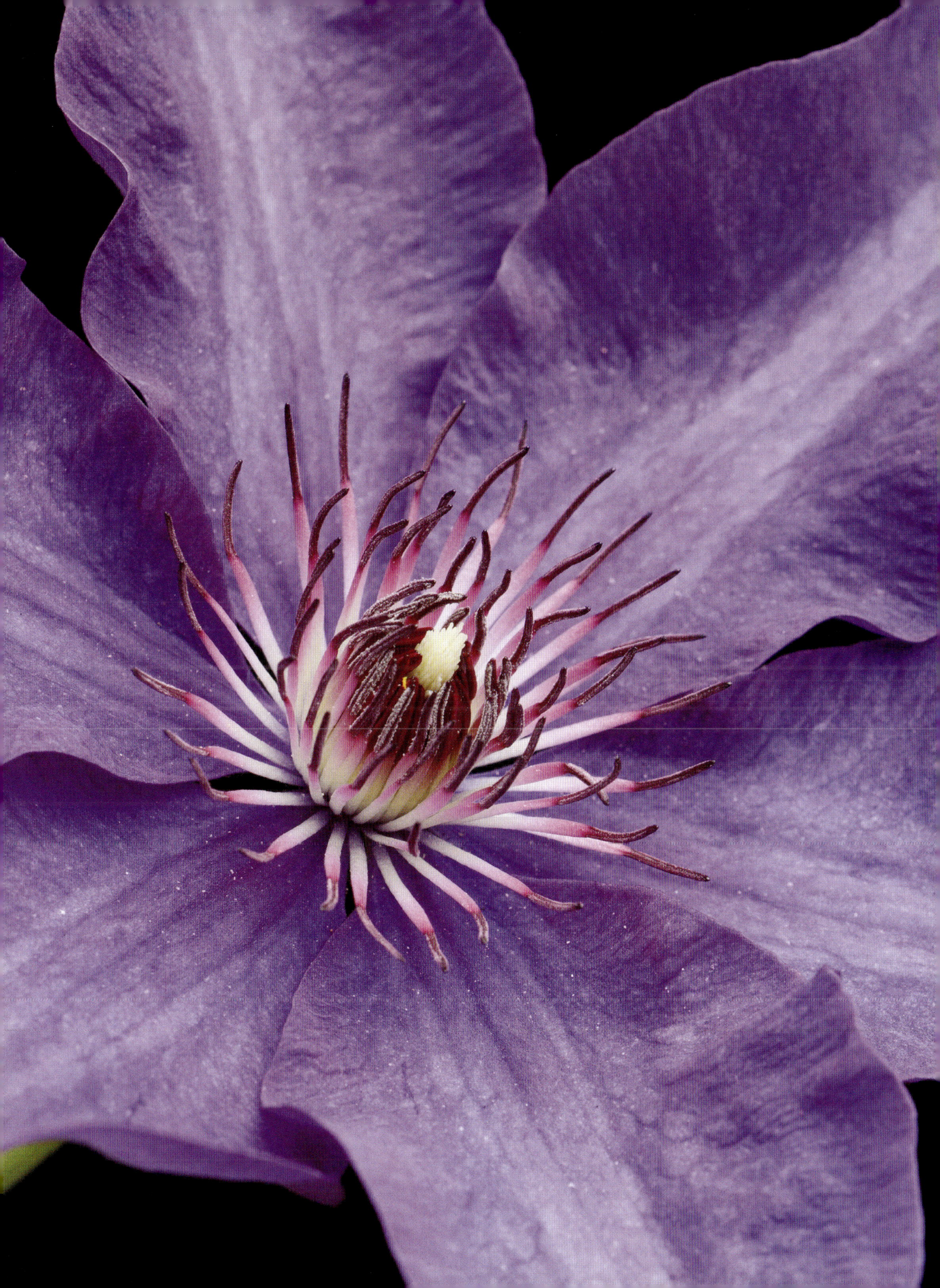

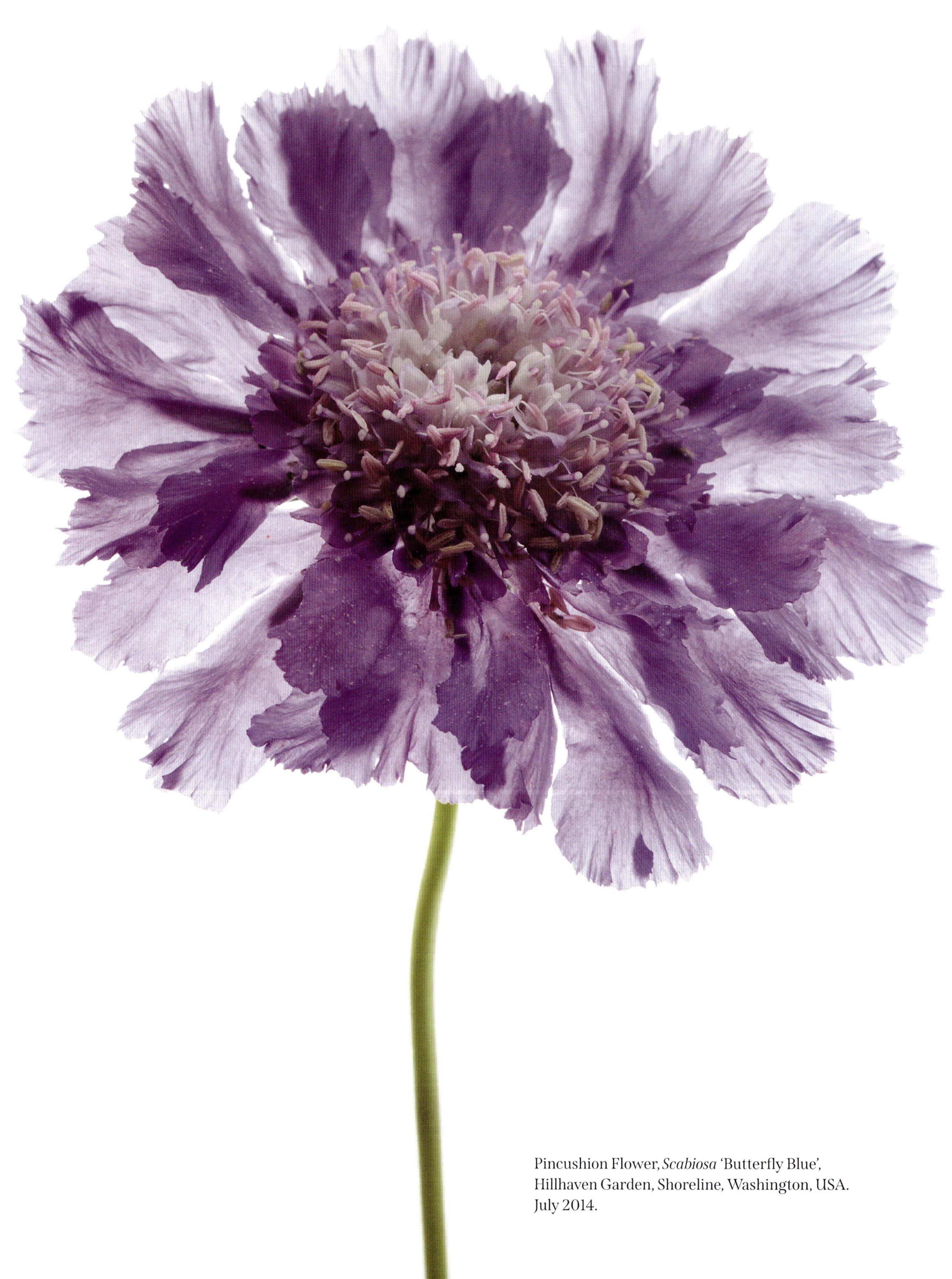

Pincushion Flower, *Scabiosa* 'Butterfly Blue', Hillhaven Garden, Shoreline, Washington, USA. July 2014.

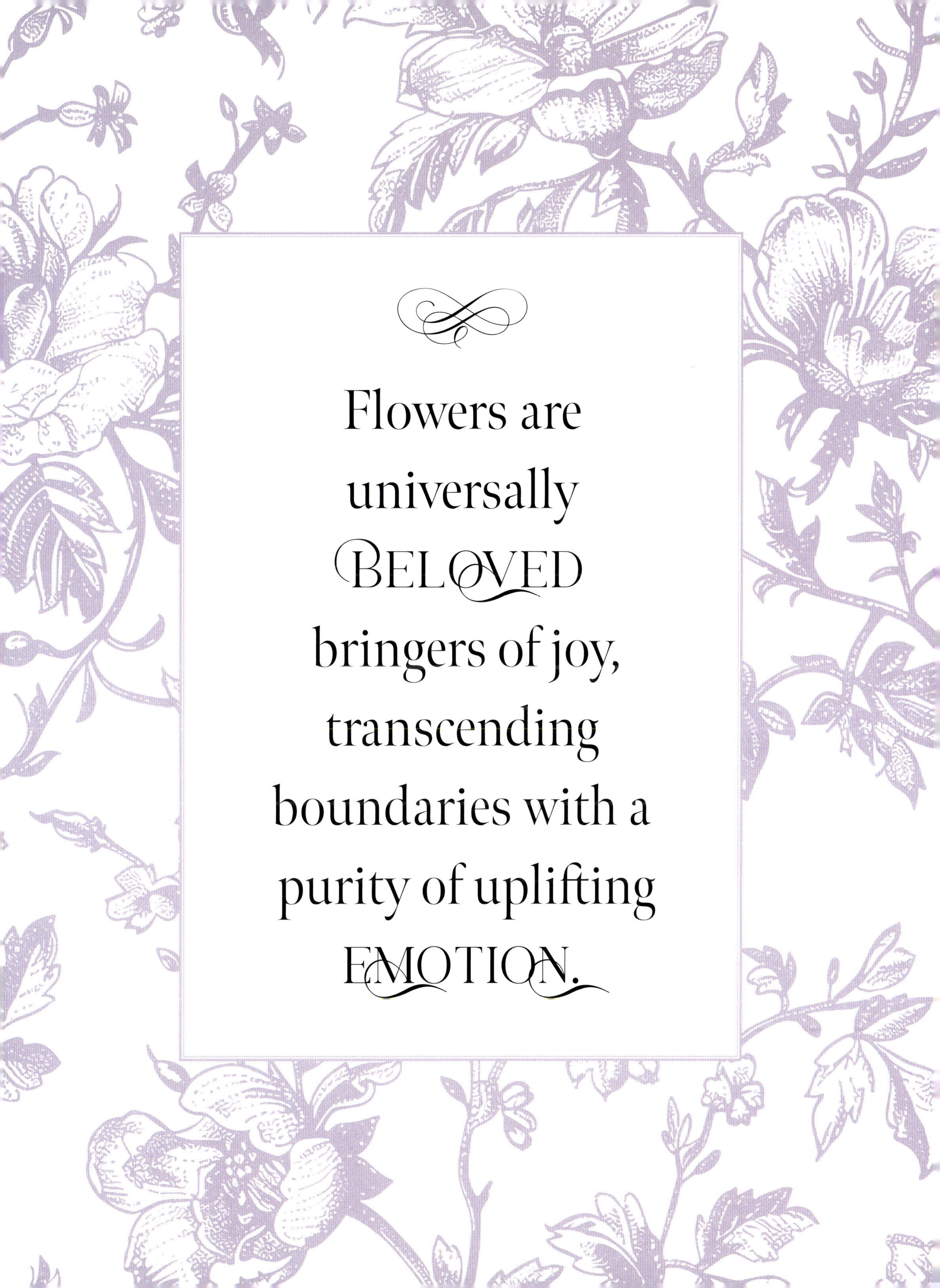

Flowers are universally BELOVED bringers of joy, transcending boundaries with a purity of uplifting EMOTION.

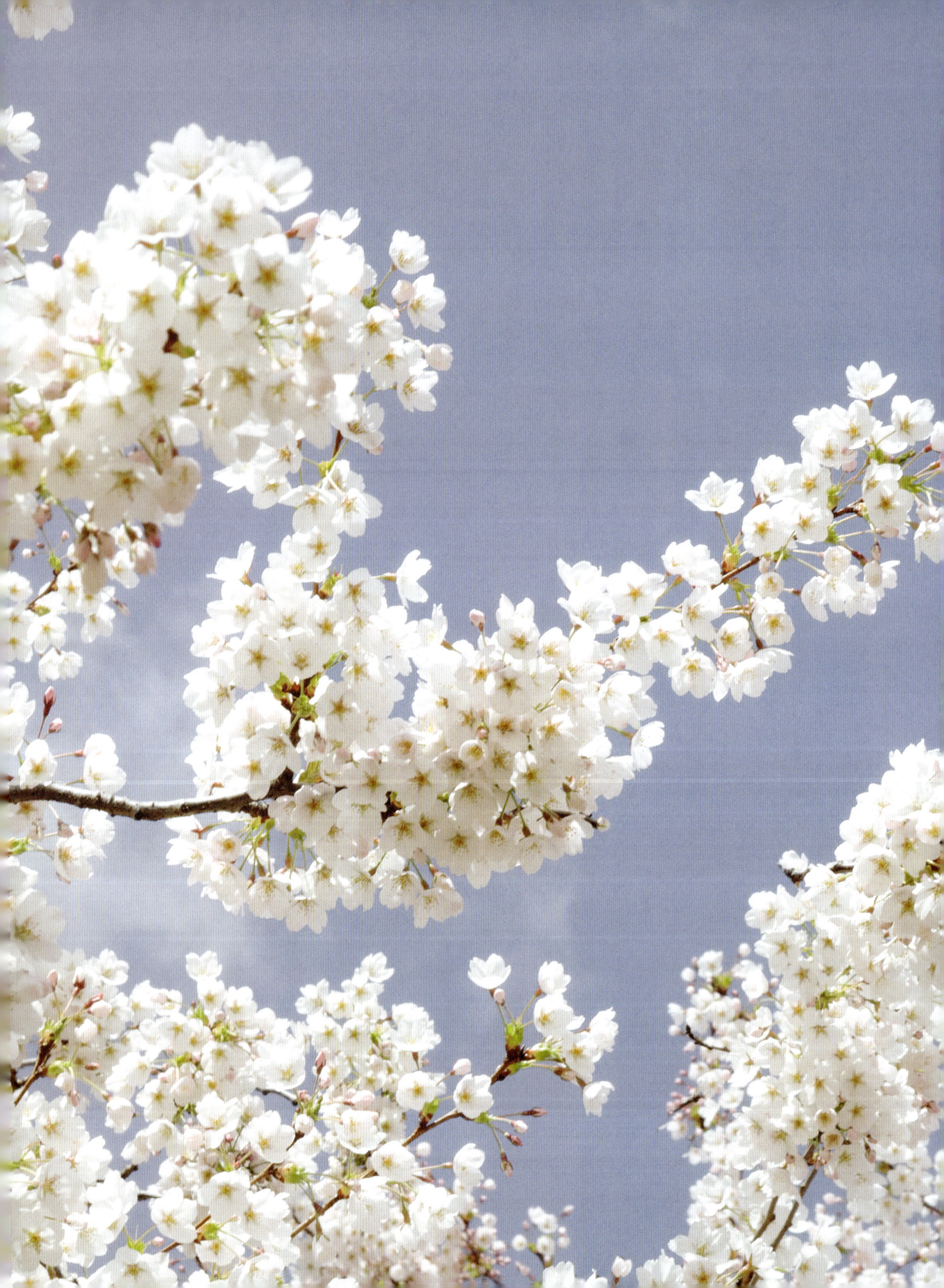

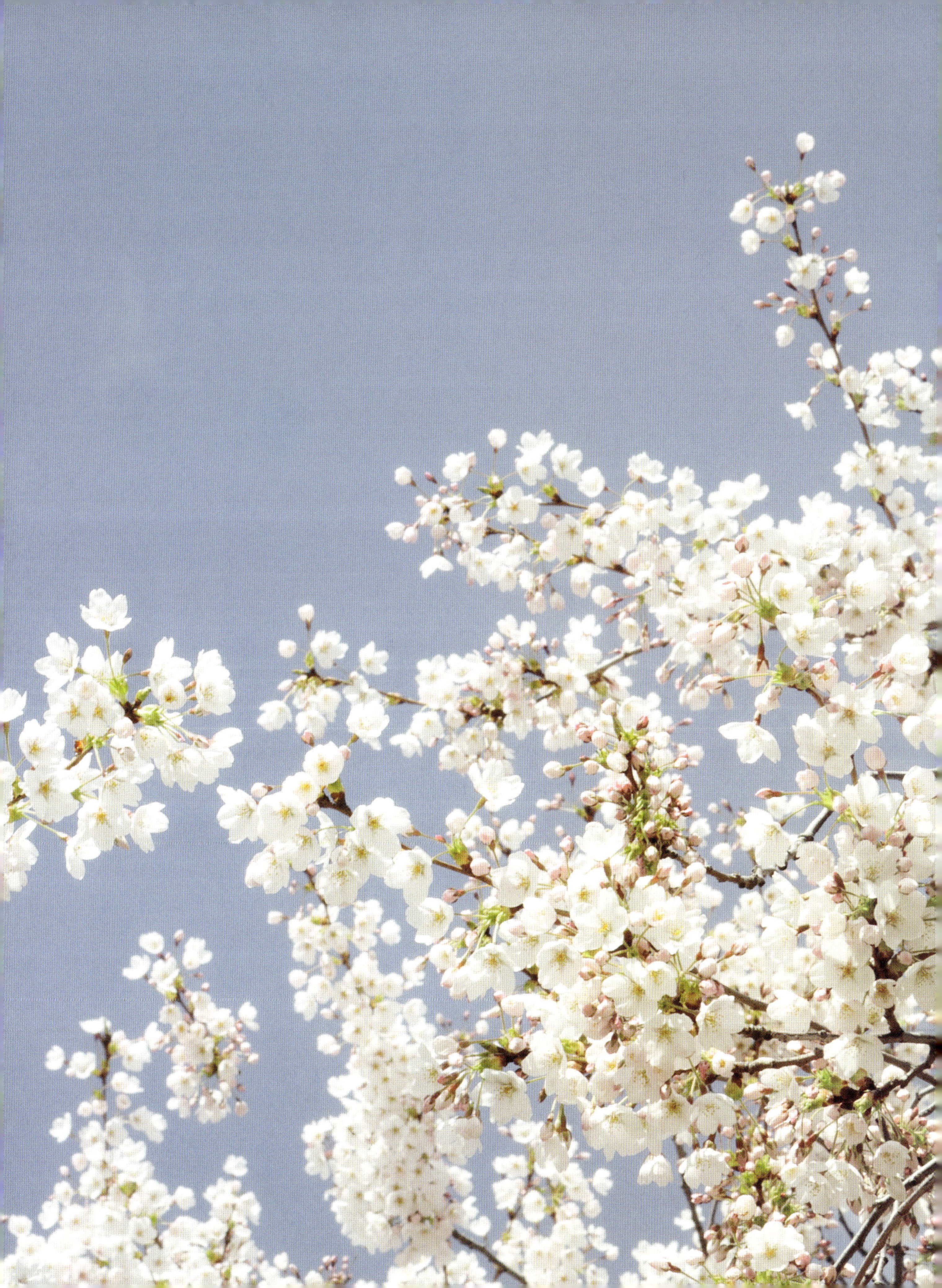

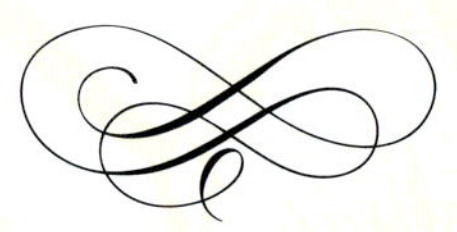

THE DAHLIA CARPET

Cornwall, England
September 2017

The puffy array of dahlias in a tidy arrangement of gentle shades of pinks and creams belies its actual origins. The cuttings were taken from plants growing in the UK National Dahlia Collection in coastal Cornwall, in between lashings of wind and rain, which were then hurriedly transferred to the leaky greenhouse that served as my temporary studio for the book Dahlias. *There, jet-lagged, wet and muddy, I arranged them on a slab of concrete flooring, keeping out the dripping rain from the roof. But those challenges were not what I mulled over at the time. I thought about how pretty they looked together and how beautifully the soft colors and varied textures blended* ensemble, *and about the eventual viewers of the book and the happiness I hoped the image might bring them.*

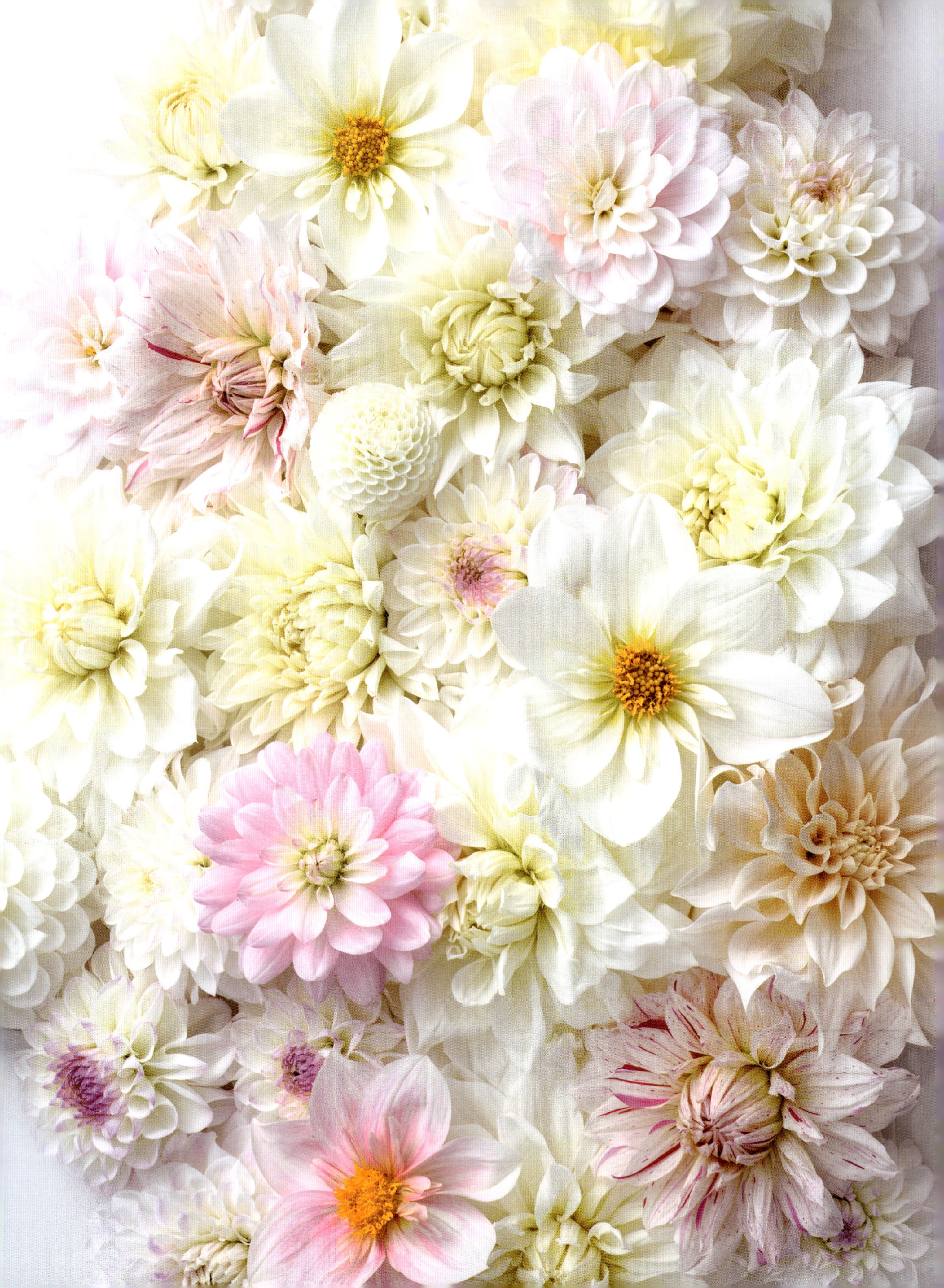

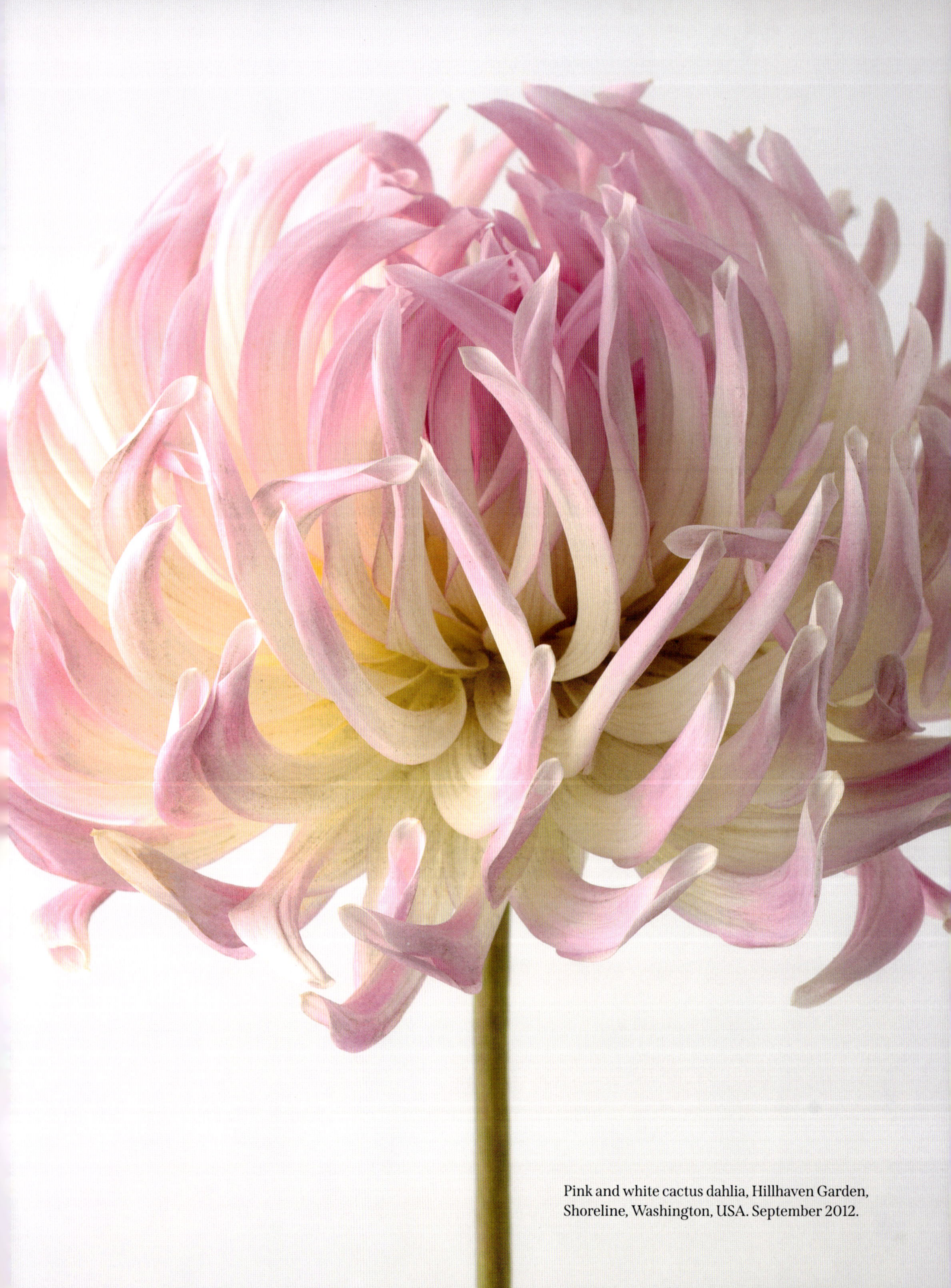

Pink and white cactus dahlia, Hillhaven Garden, Shoreline, Washington, USA. September 2012.

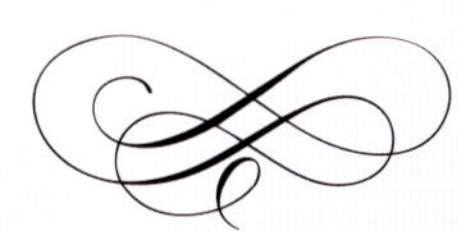

Humans have a NATURAL desire to seek joy, to gravitate towards sources of EXUBERANCE and uplifting energy.

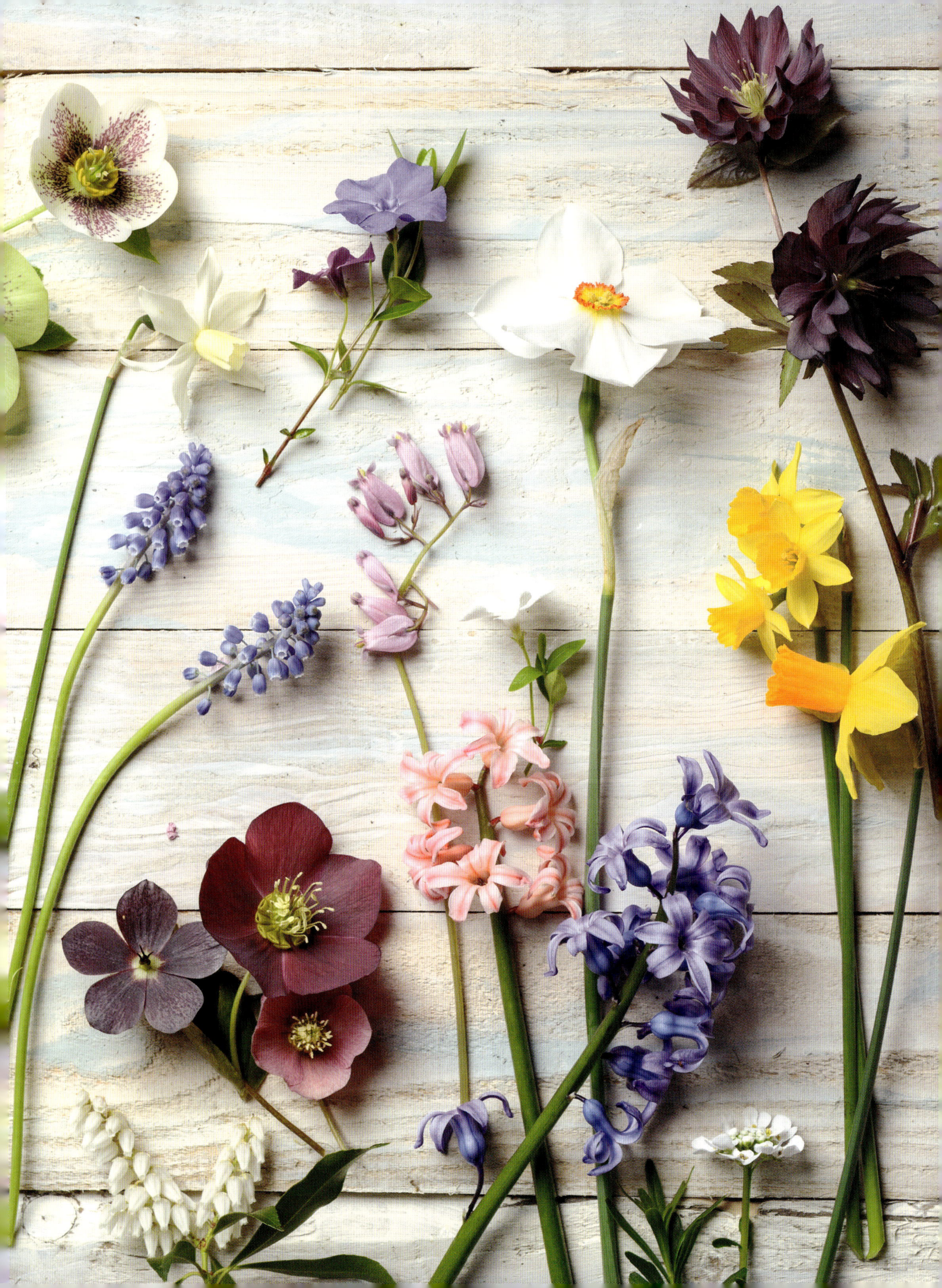

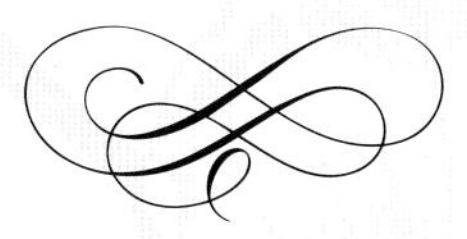

GARDEN JEWELS

Hillhaven Garden, Shoreline, Washington, USA
Spring 2012

From my own garden, Hillhaven, I would regularly cut floral "samplers" – a stem or two of each flower that was gracing the scene on a given day: hellebores, daffodils, Muscari, Hyacinth, *Pacific bleeding heart, periwinkle, peiris, lily of the valley,* Fritillaria. *Arranged in a single bouquet or individually in my antique apothecary bottles, the images provide a snapshot and lasting visual diary entry of the season's treasures, whether spring bulbs from our woodland garden or a rainbow of hydrangea cuttings. Even today, years later, the images still spark a joyful and fond remembrance for those special days.*

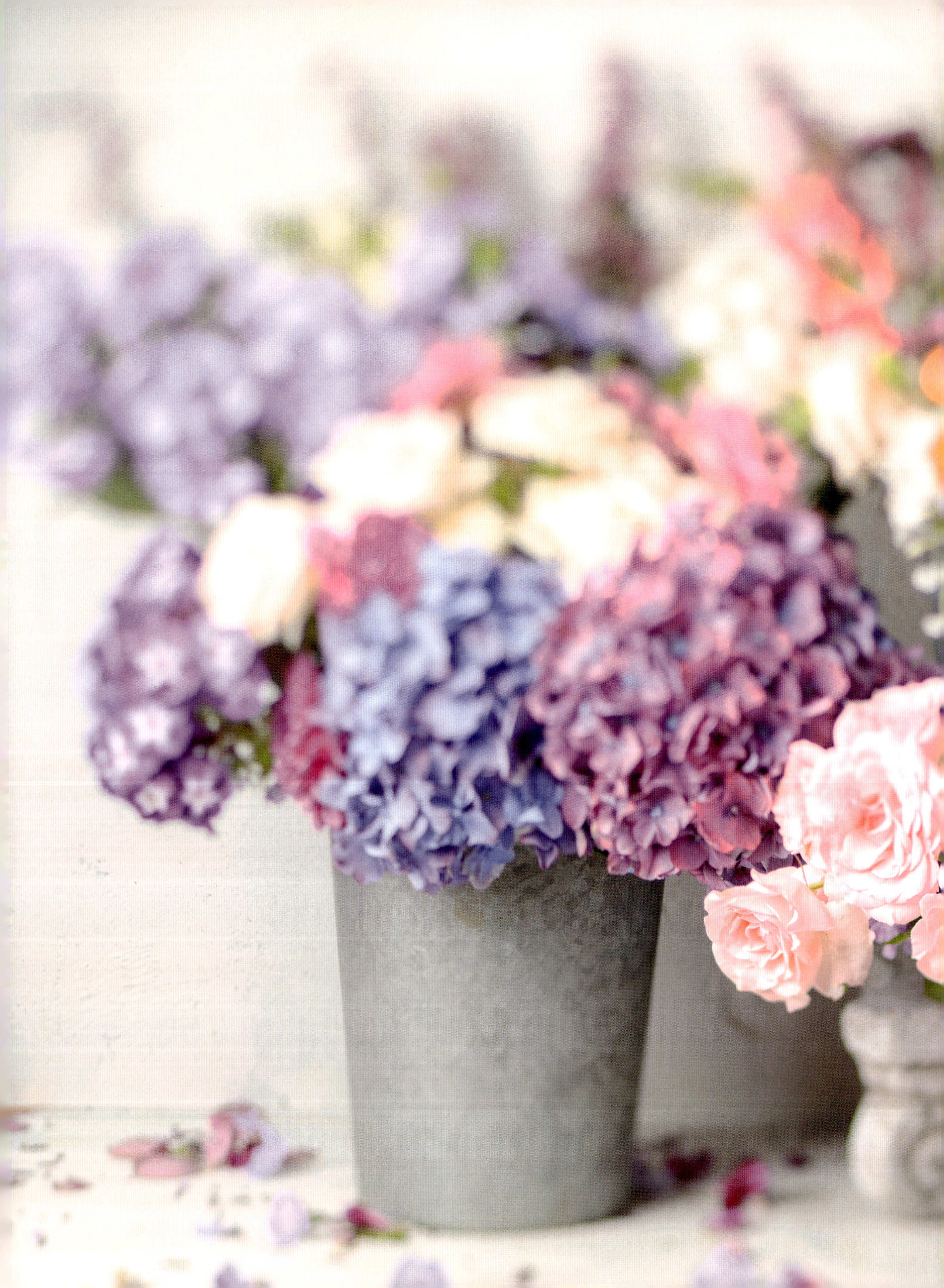

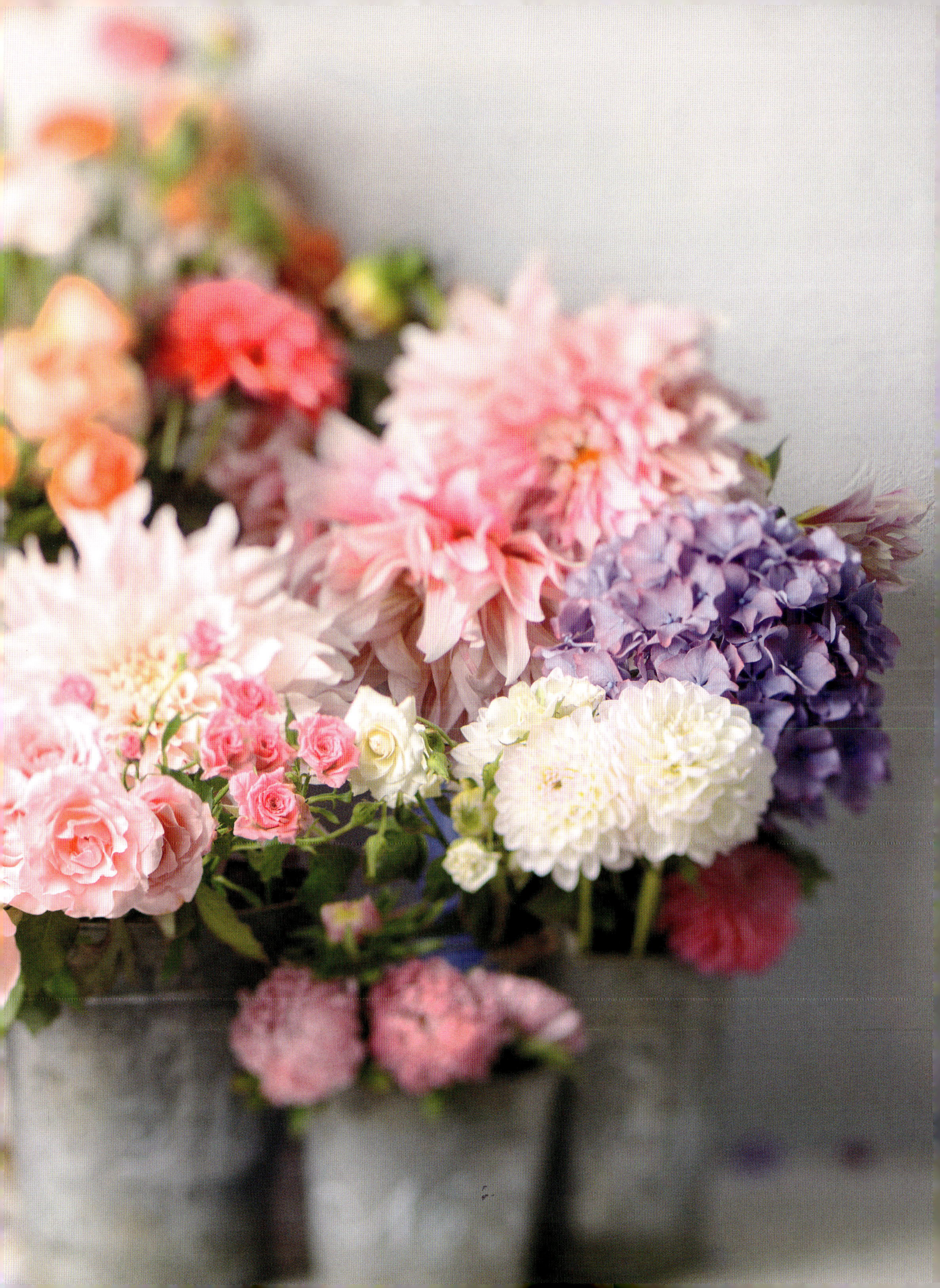

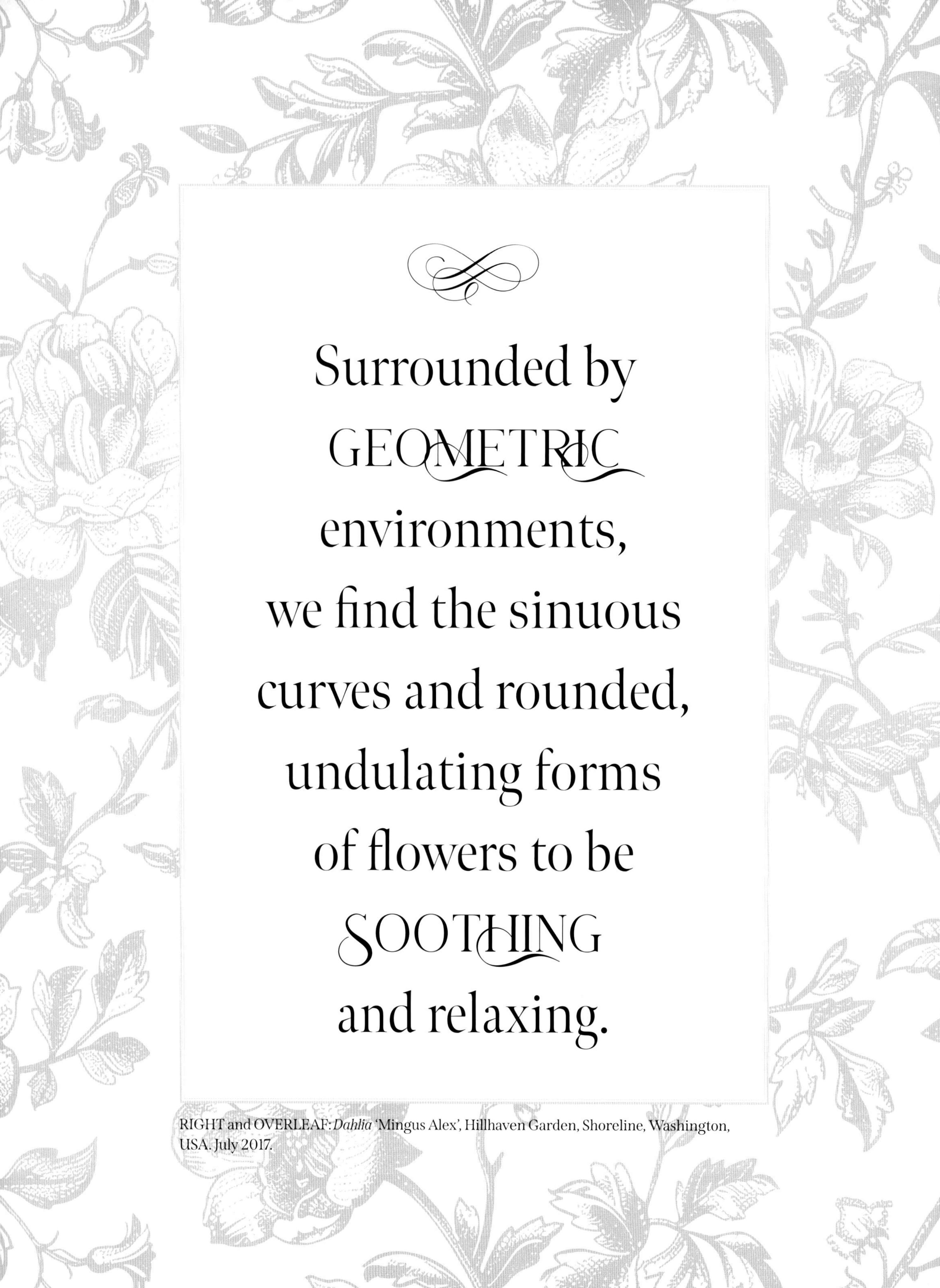

Surrounded by GEOMETRIC environments, we find the sinuous curves and rounded, undulating forms of flowers to be SOOTHING and relaxing.

RIGHT and OVERLEAF: *Dahlia* 'Mingus Alex', Hillhaven Garden, Shoreline, Washington, USA. July 2017.

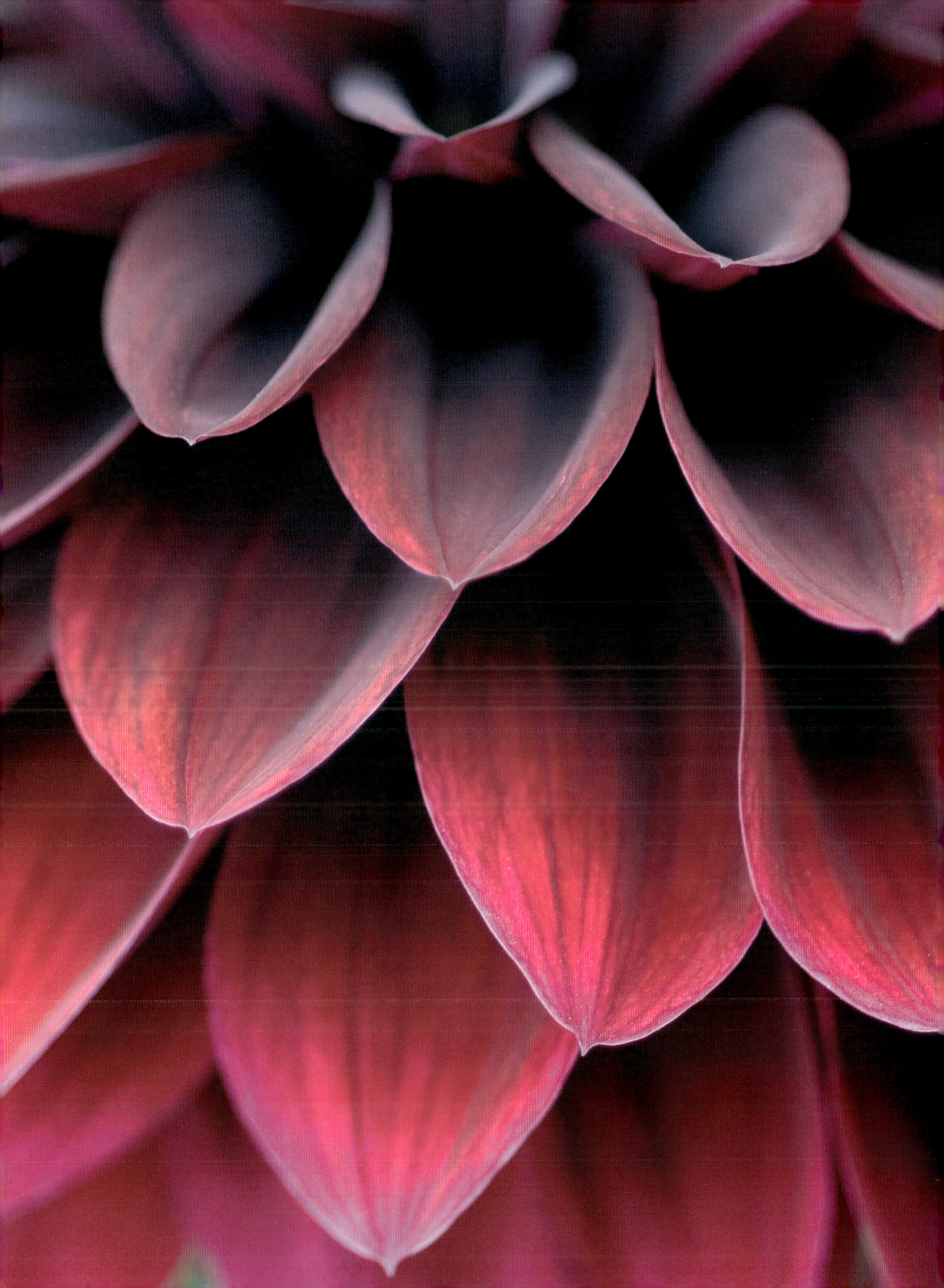

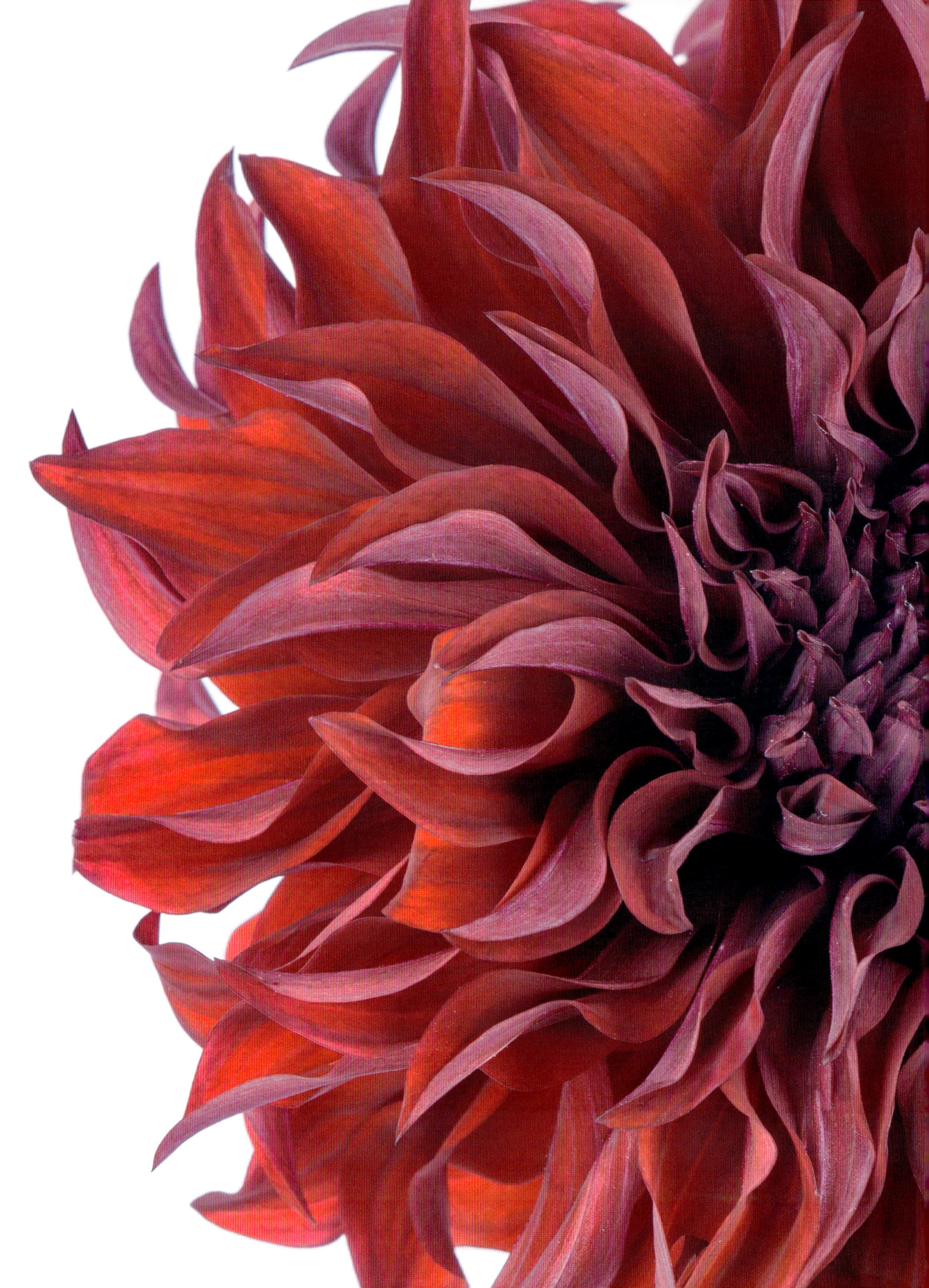

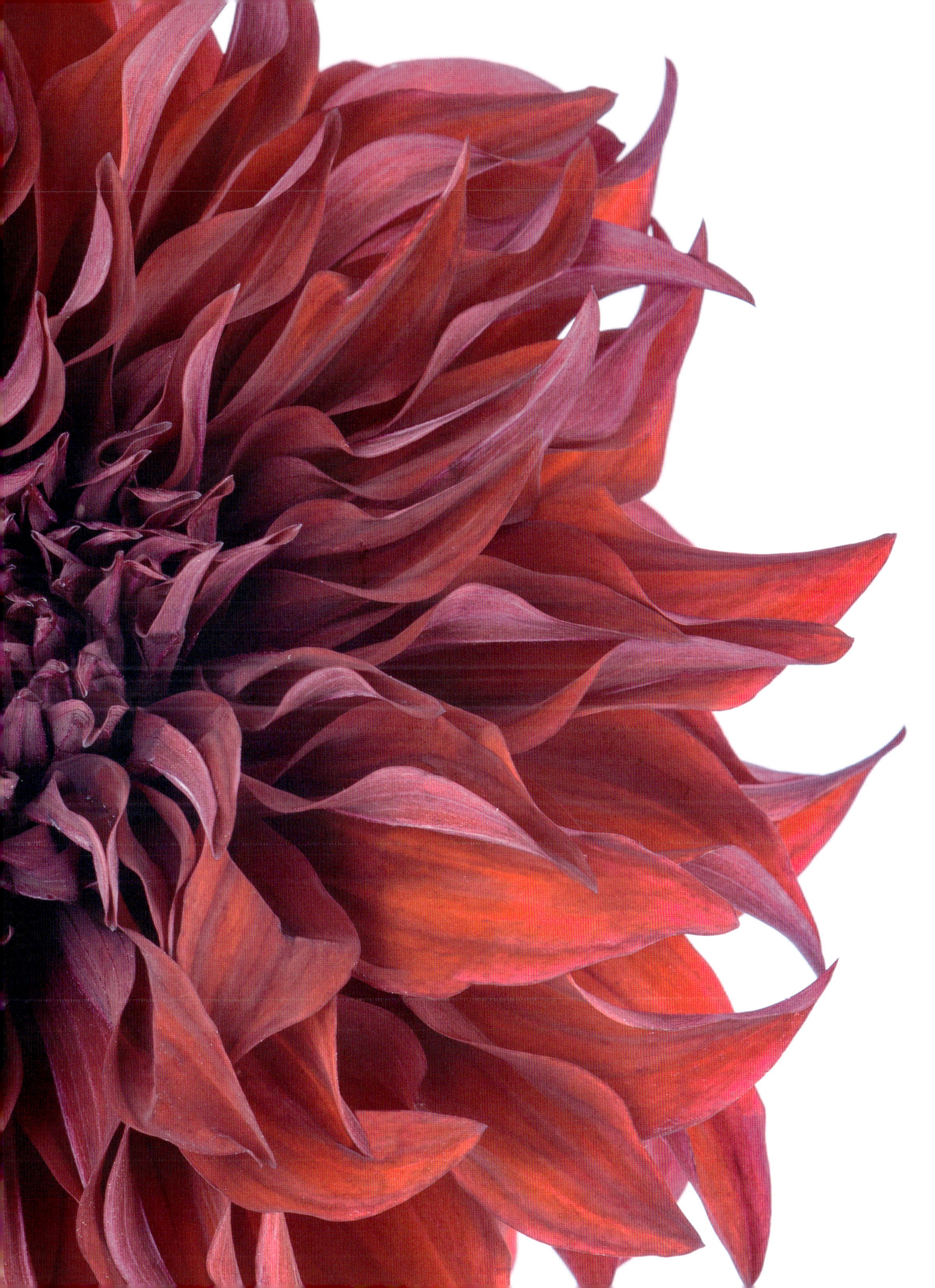

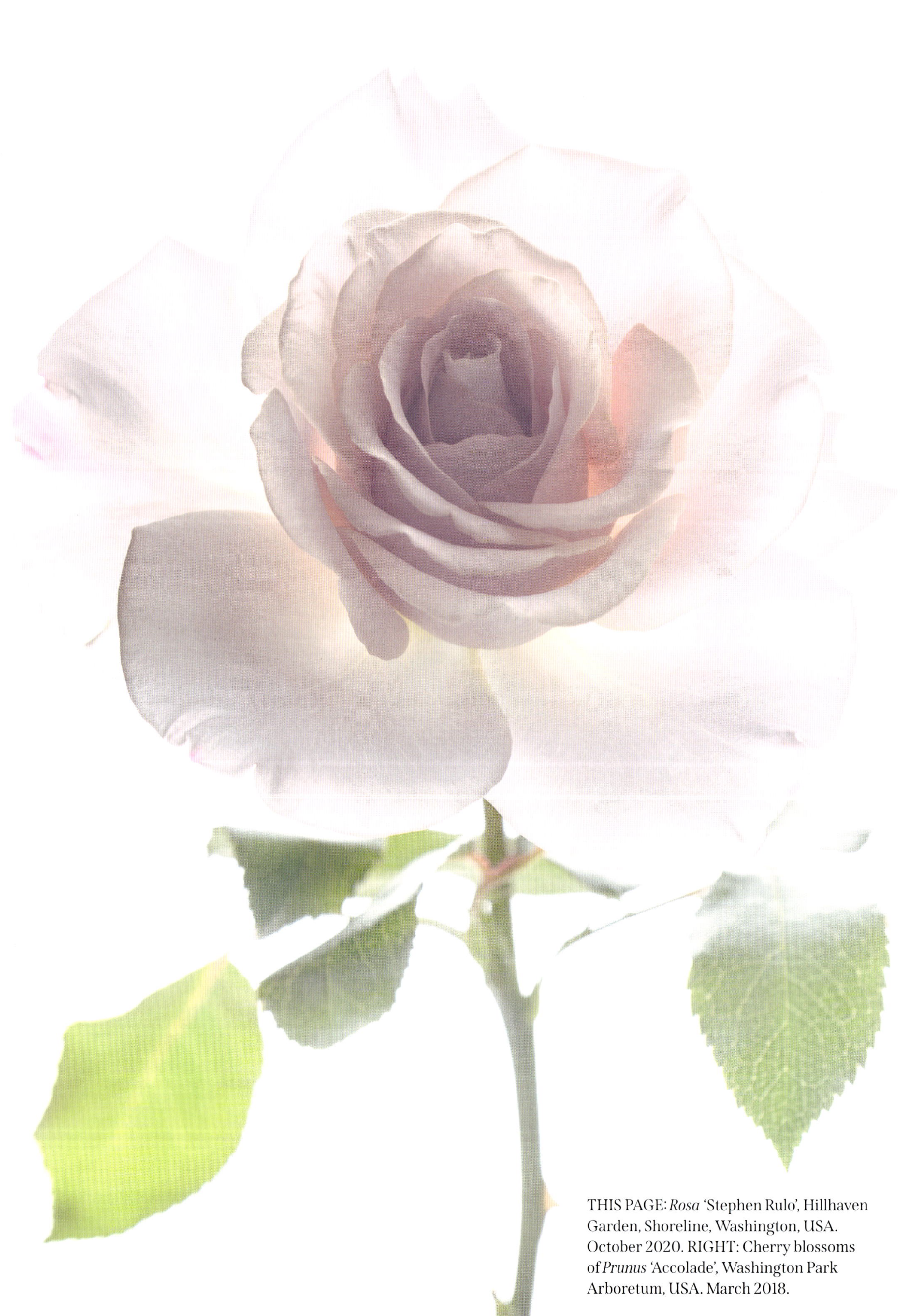

THIS PAGE: *Rosa* 'Stephen Rulo', Hillhaven Garden, Shoreline, Washington, USA. October 2020. RIGHT: Cherry blossoms of *Prunus* 'Accolade', Washington Park Arboretum, USA. March 2018.

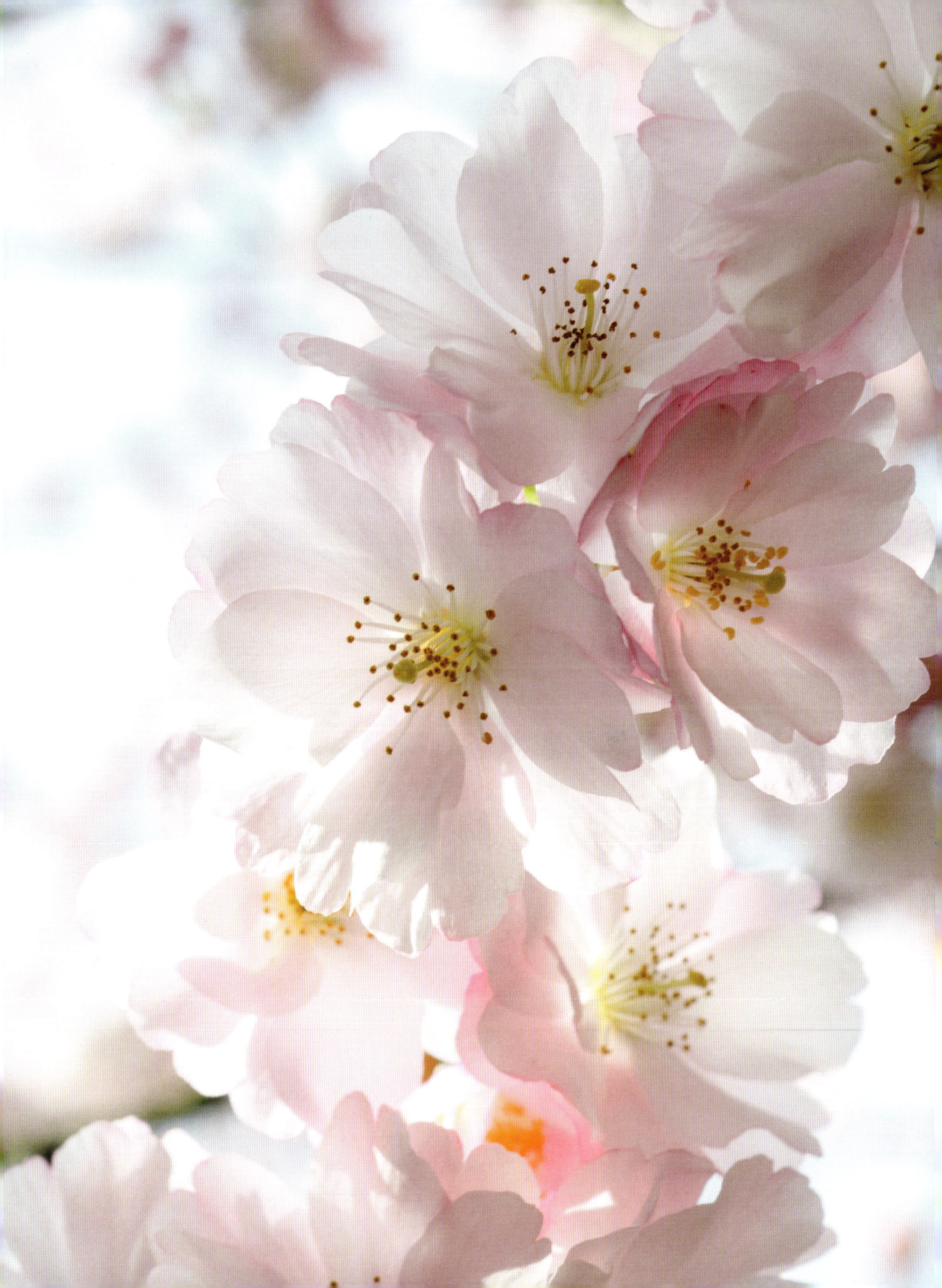

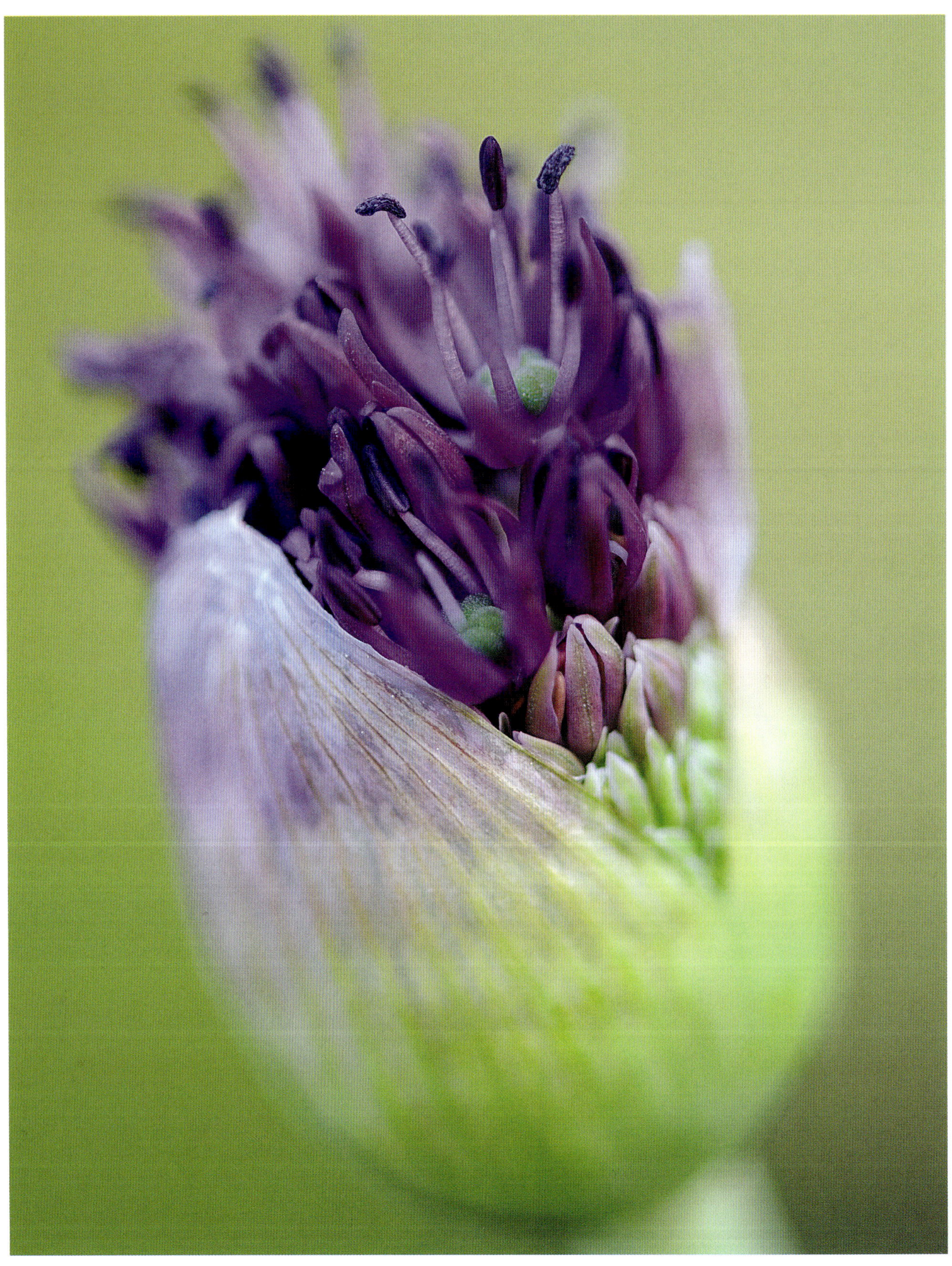

ABOVE: Bud of *Allium hollandicum* 'Purple Sensation', Hillhaven Garden, Shoreline, Washington, USA. May 2008. RIGHT: Bed of *Allium hollandicum* 'Purple Sensation'. May 2008. OVERLEAF: Jardin des Plantes, Paris, France. August 2021.

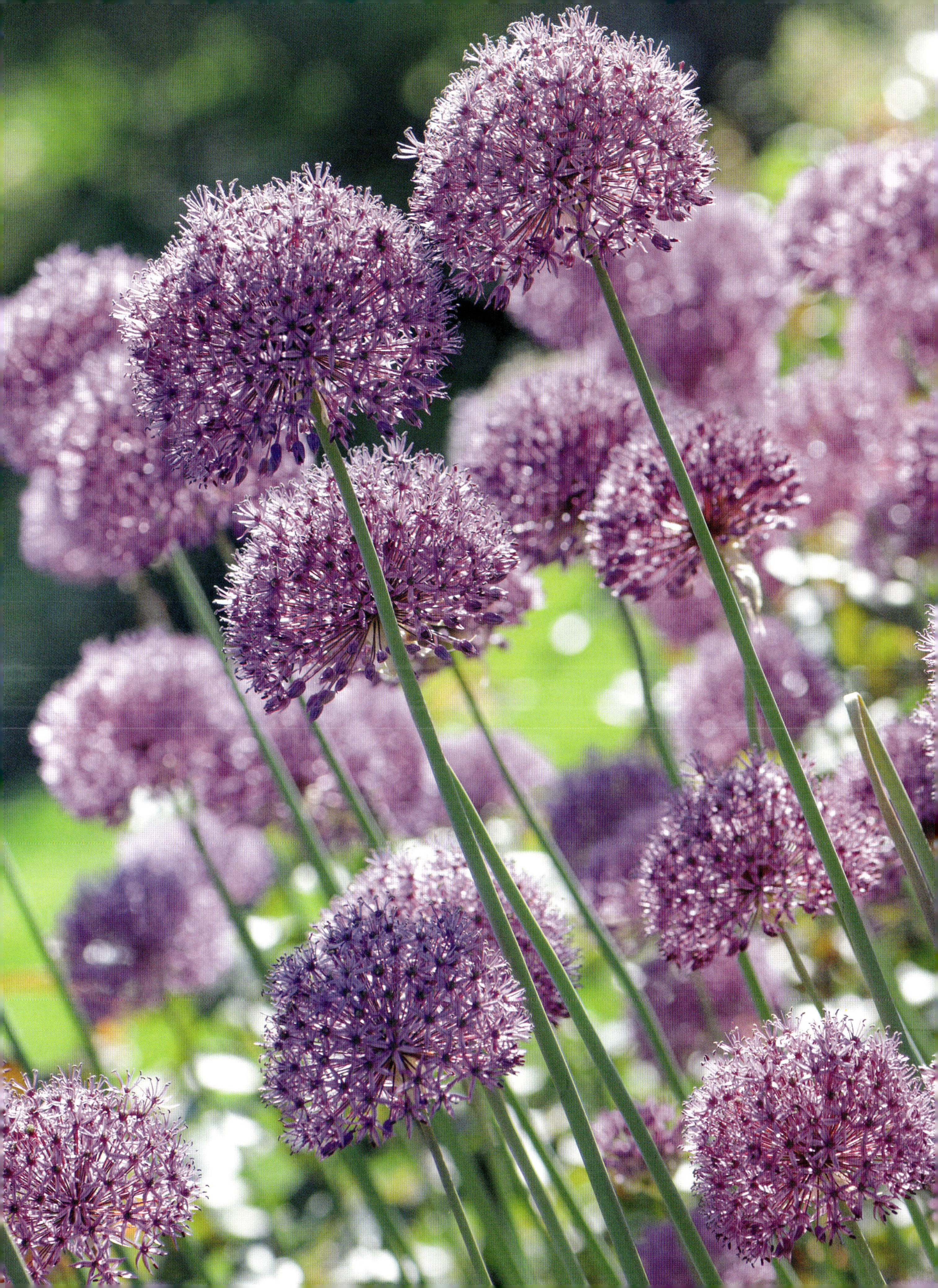

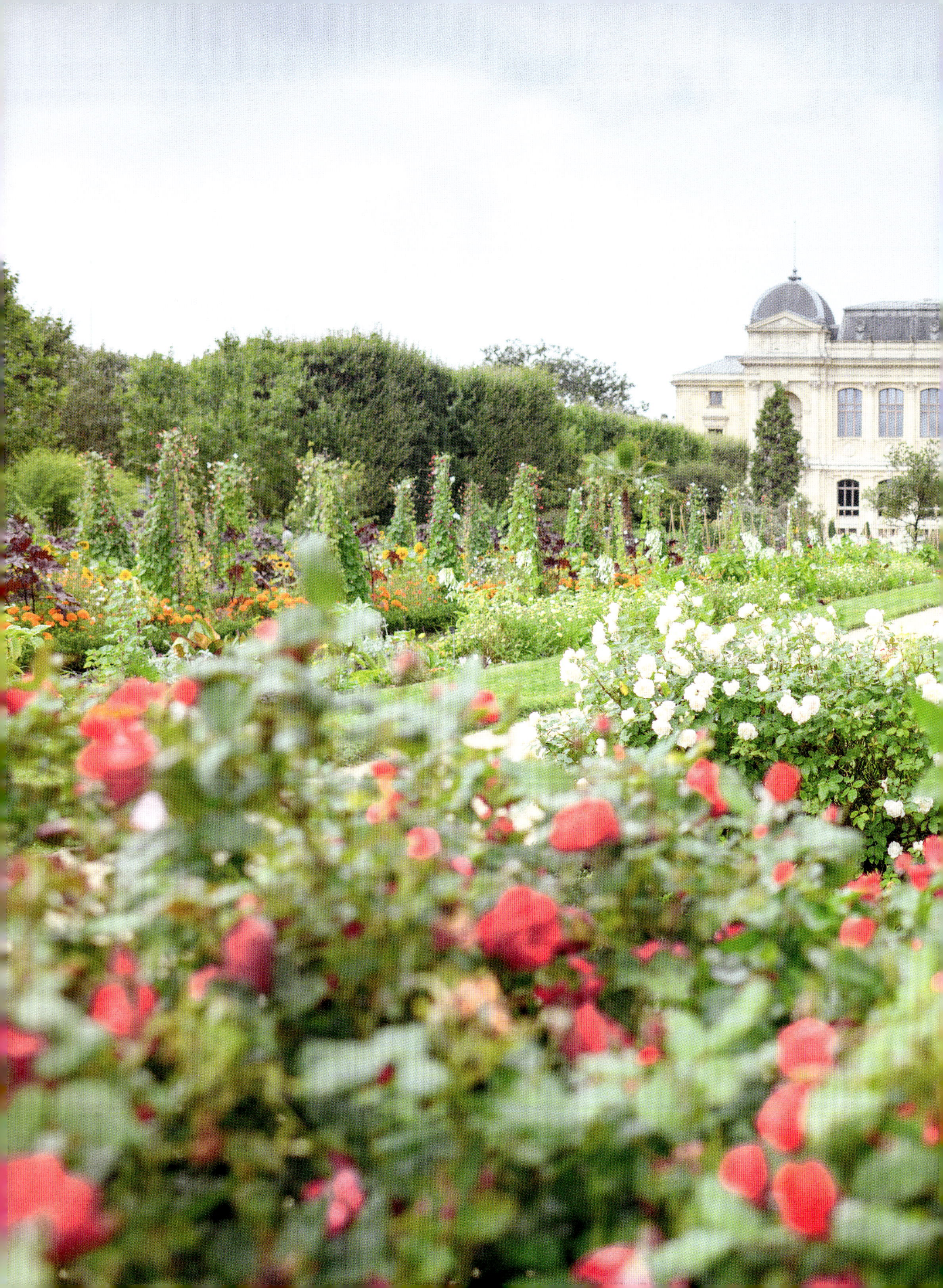

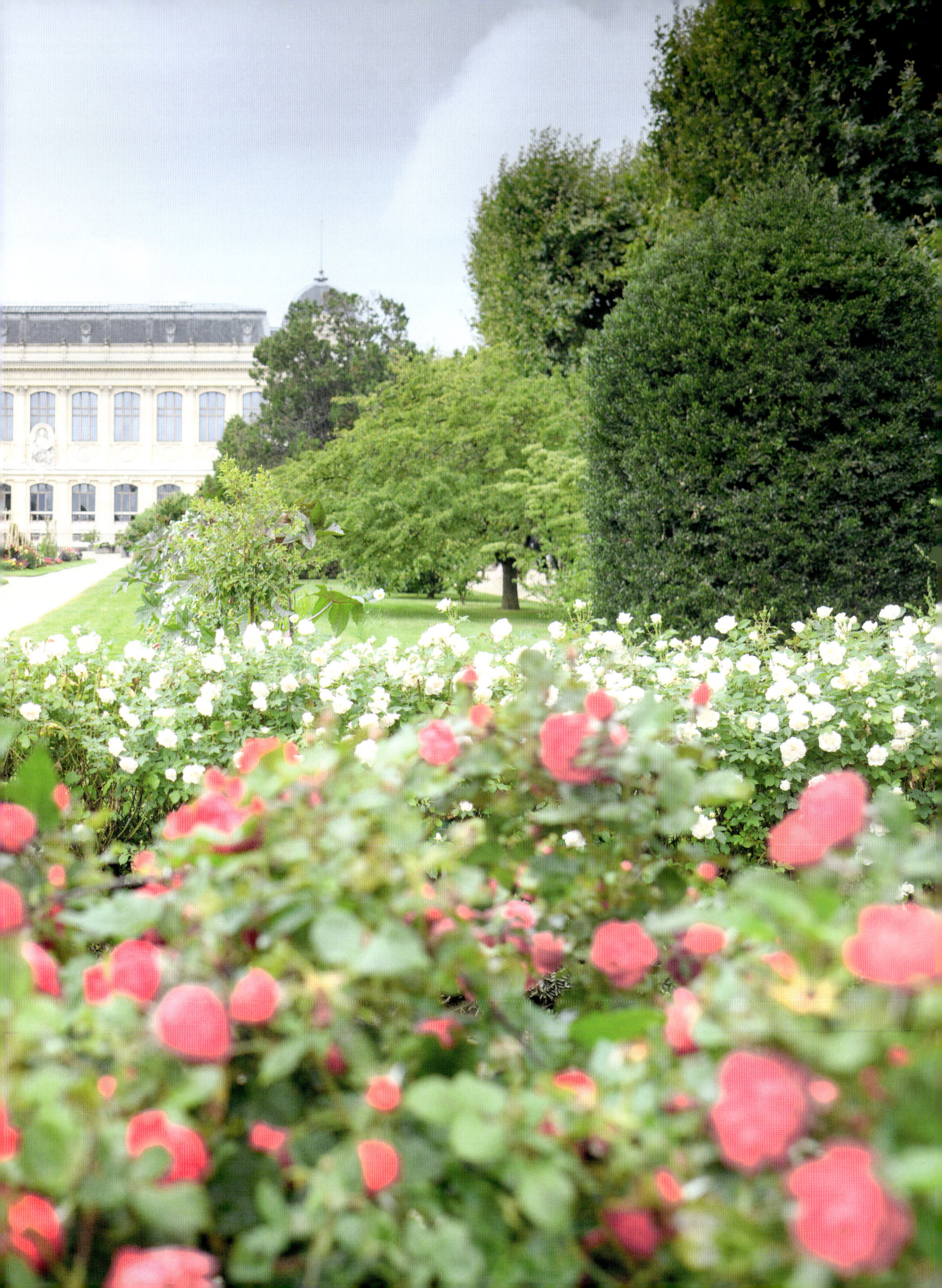

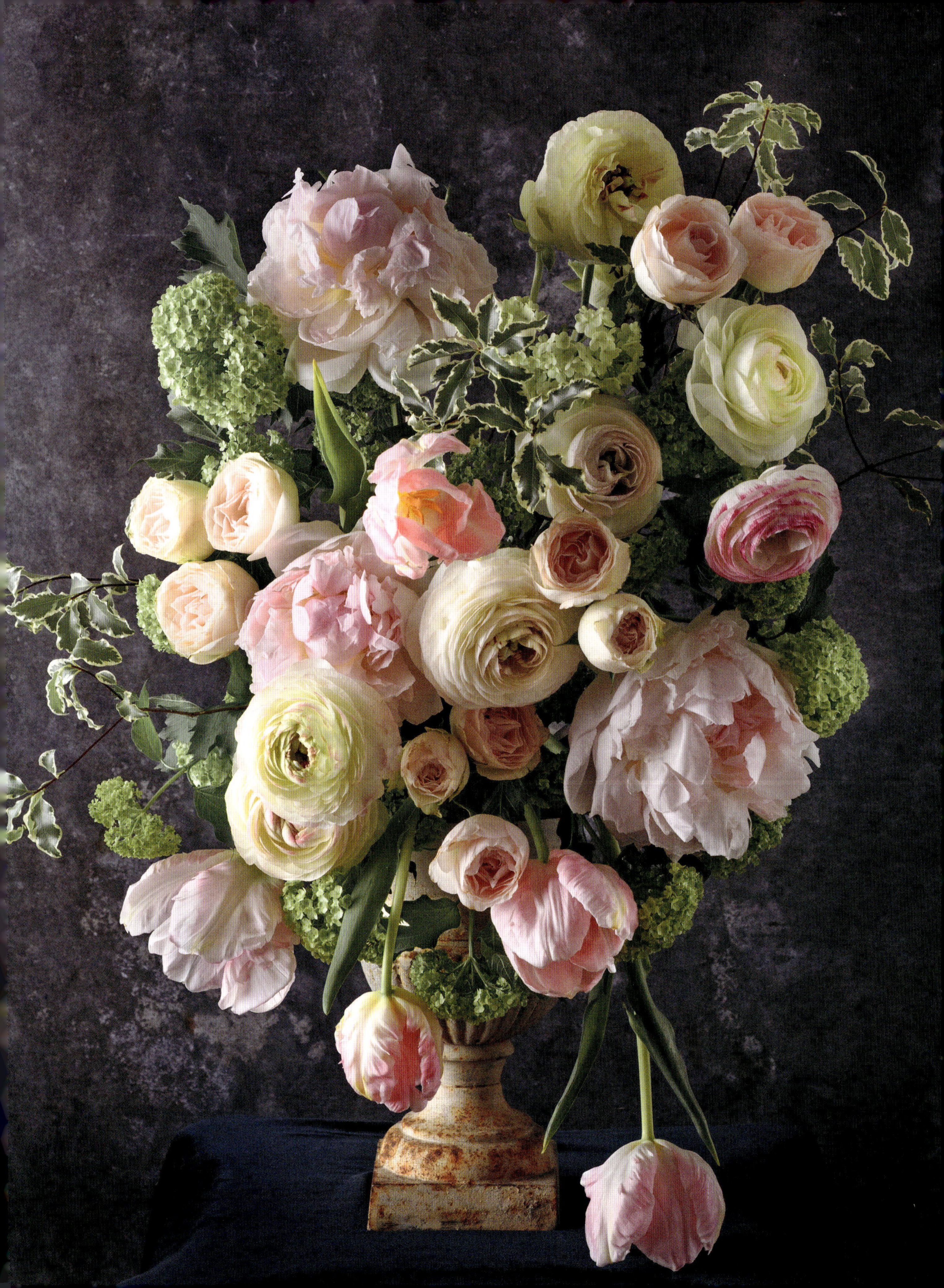

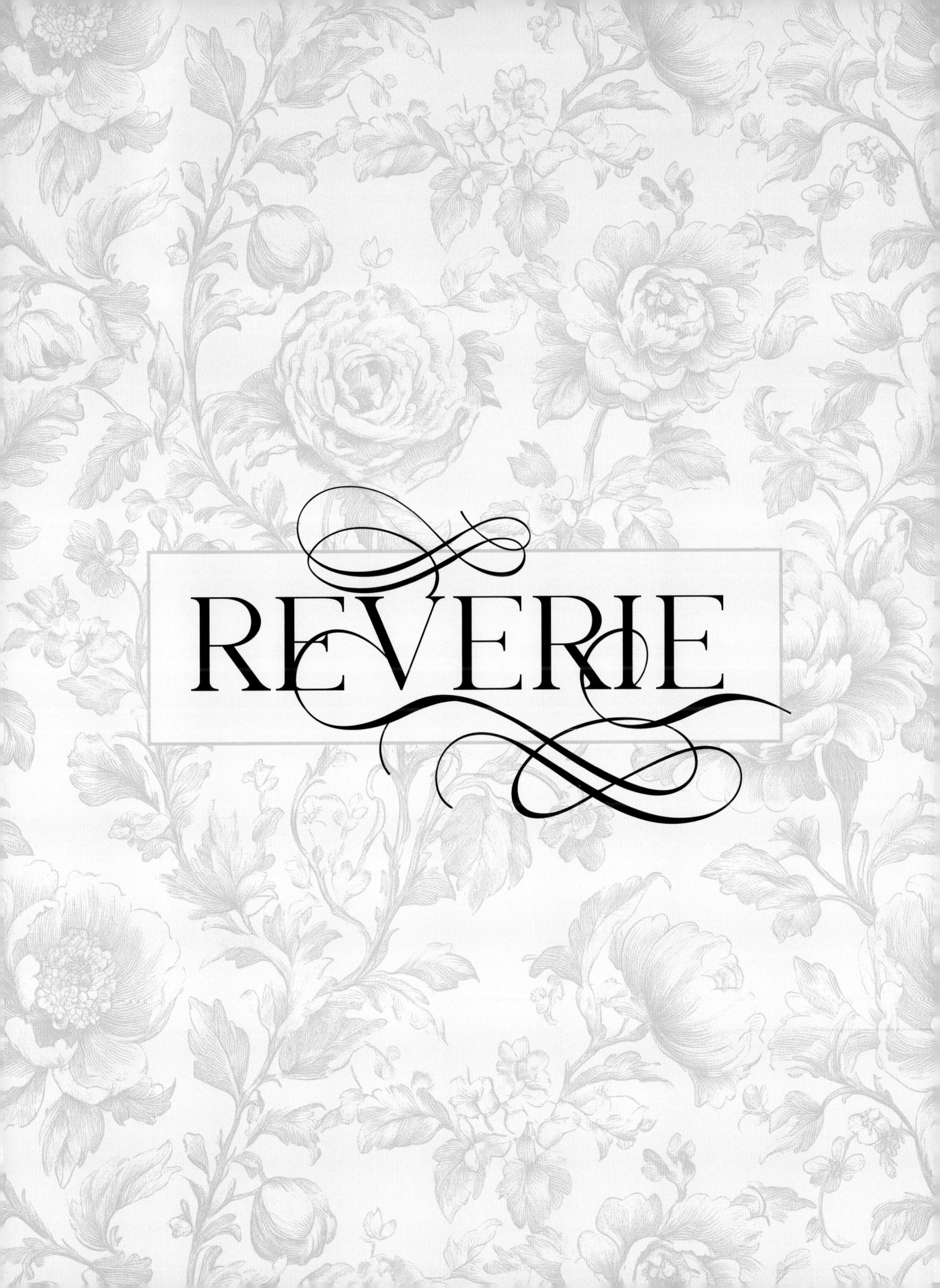
REVERIE

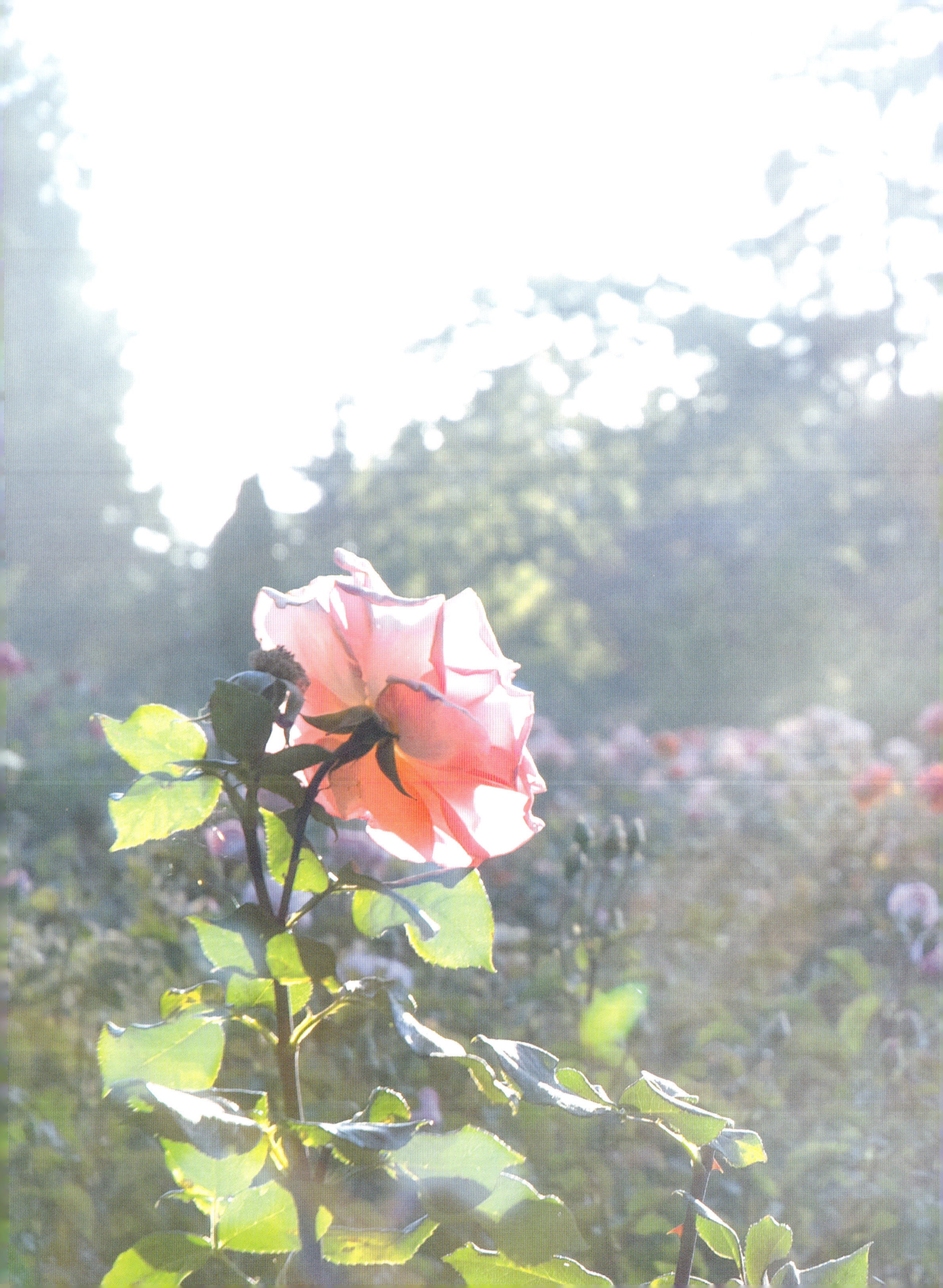

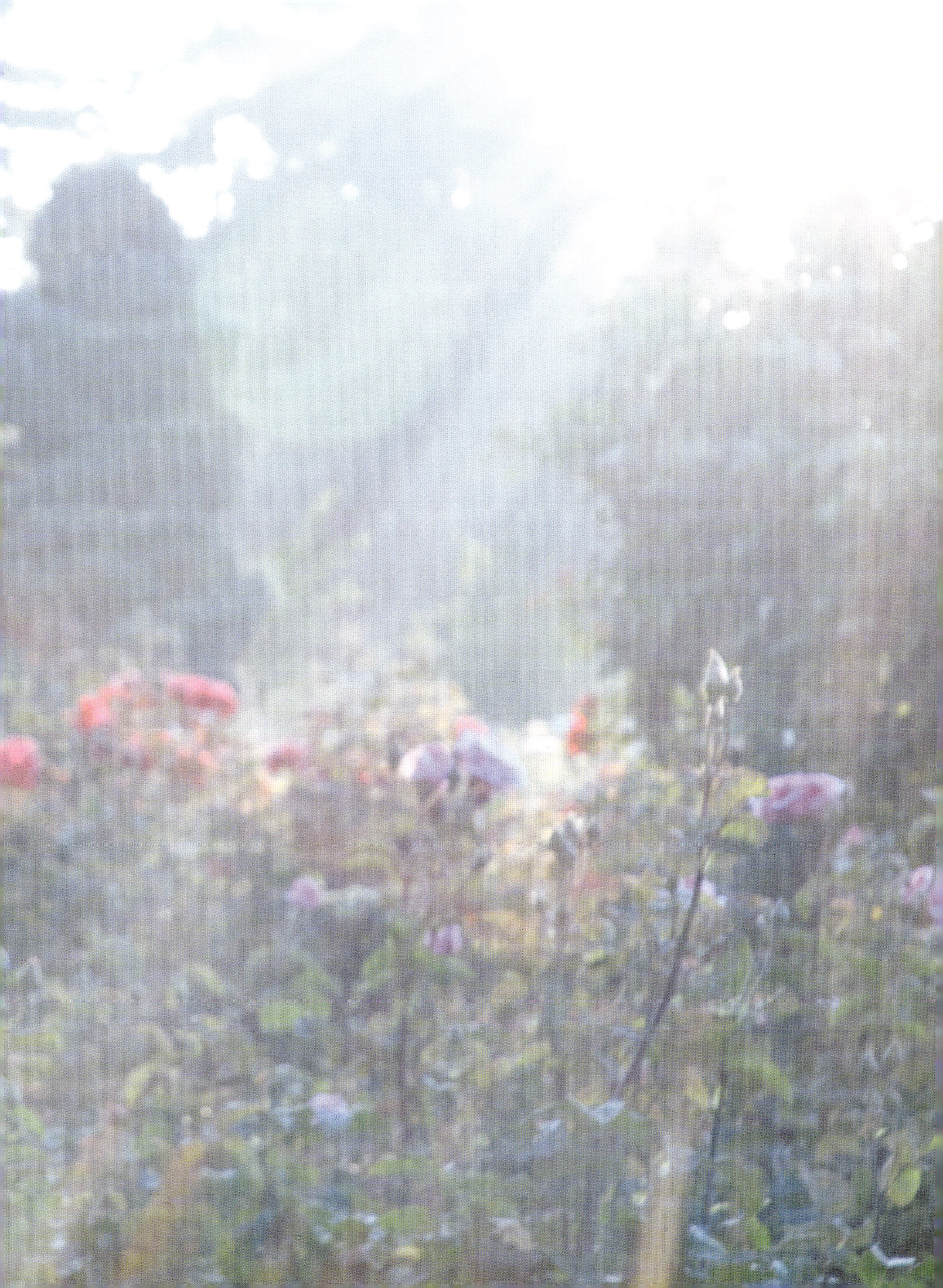

Reverie:
A state of being pleasantly lost in one's thoughts; a daydream.

From the blithe spirit of *Joy*, we enter a state of *Reverie*, following down a converging trail of rose gardens and blossoms, between South America and Europe.

Possibly you have noticed the connections and coincidences, the repeating patterns and interweavings of many of my adventures. Perhaps they are due to my global peregrinations – as evidence that the more we traverse this world, the more we create an ever-developing network of like-minded and curious souls and spirit-enriching places, and that those relationships reverberate across time zones and continents, connecting us all in an eventual embrace.

The framework of this chapter is entwined by a single rose – a distinctly striking rose – flourishing in two different gardens, in two different hemispheres, separated by seven thousand miles but unified in spirit. One public and famous, one hidden and private, blooming in opposite seasons but sharing a kindred visual language of thought-provoking beauty.

Intermingled between the two is an interlude of equally enchanting spring blossoms, undoubtedly one of the most inspiring displays of nature.

THE EDEN ROSE
Also known as Pierre de Ronsard, after the sixteenth-century French poet, the 'Eden' rose has received worldwide acclaim since its introduction in 1985 by Marie-Louise Meilland, of the famous French rose-breeding family. It has been inducted into the Rose Hall of Fame and honored in 2006 as a 'World Rose'. But its accolades aside, it is adored for its refined double blooms, creamy white with magenta edges, that thrive from spring to first frost.

PREVIOUS PAGE: Woodland Park Rose Garden, Seattle, Washington, USA. June 2006
RIGHT: Ranunculus, Hillhaven Garden, Shoreline, Washington, USA. April 2011.

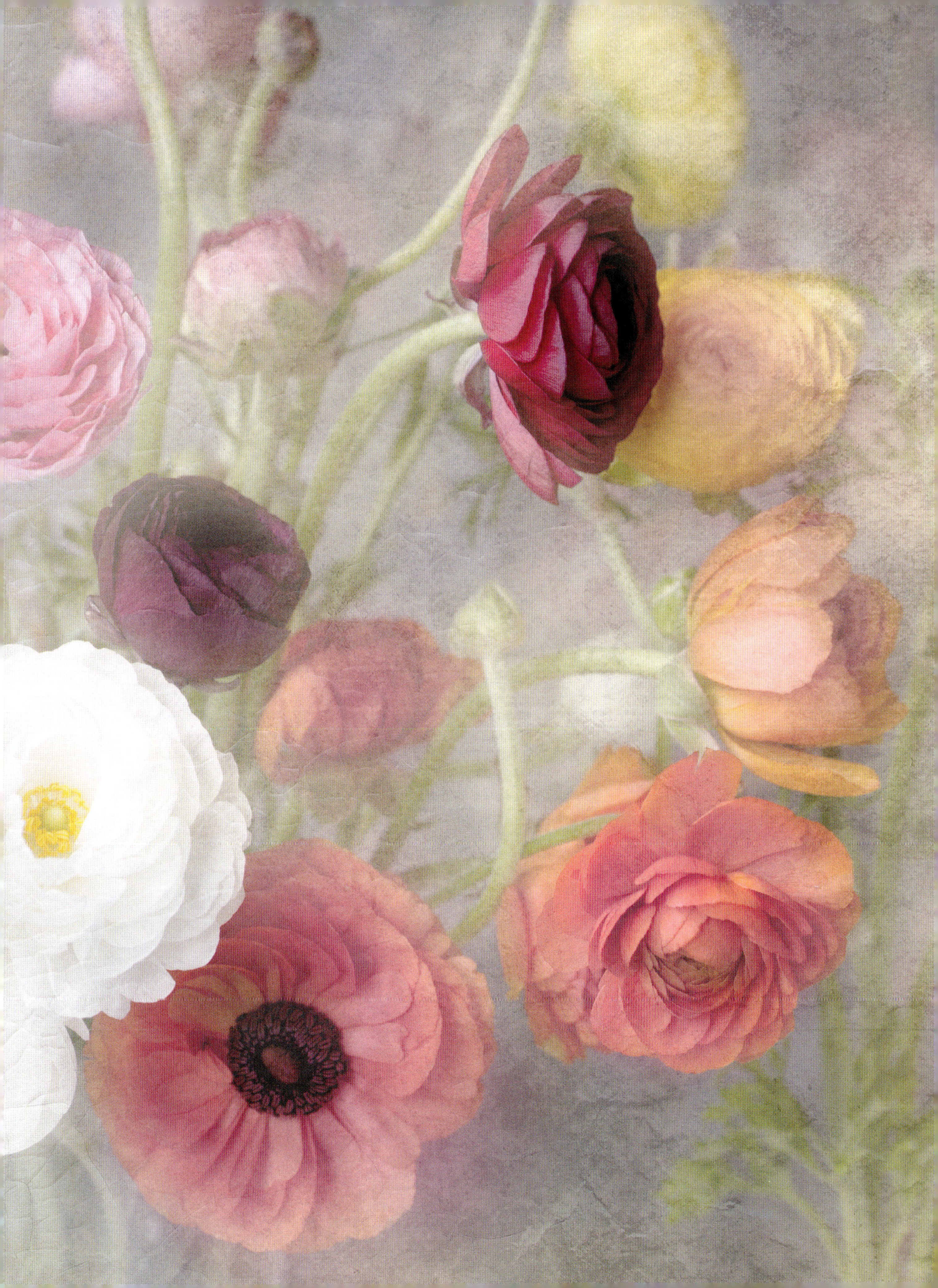

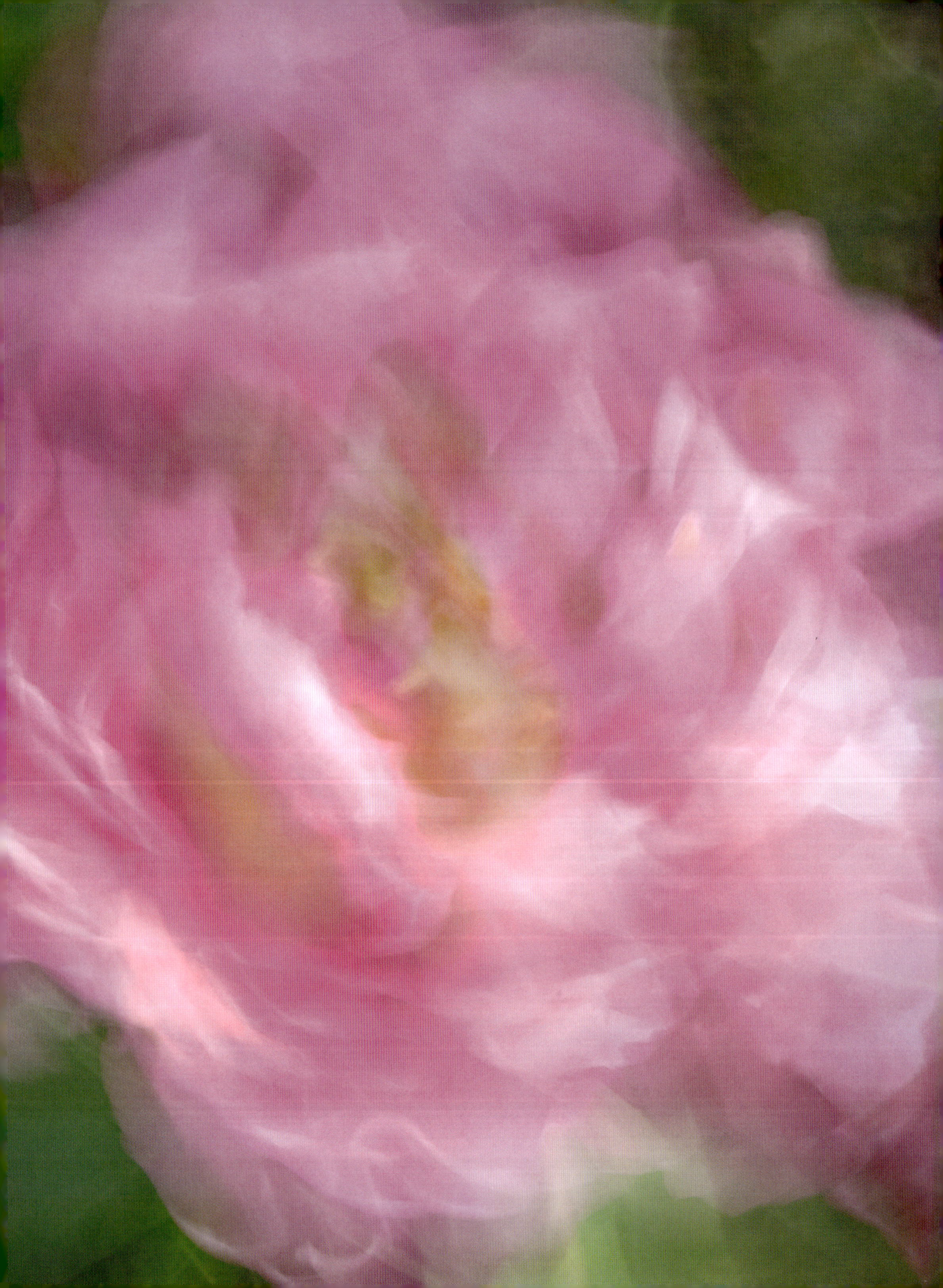

EDEN ROSE AT JARDIN DU PALAIS ROYAL

If there is a singular retreat in all of Paris that I gravitate to almost unconsciously, it assuredly is the Palais Royal garden, an oasis of reflection and inner stillness away from the perpetual bustle of the city.

In all seasons its ordered symmetry is a steadying presence, and a midday walk through its *allées* of plane trees restores my equanimity. An hour in a garden, lost in contemplation, can reacquaint us with our true selves.

The formal, precision architecture is counterbalanced by luxurious plantings, from the annual show of fuchsia magnolias in March to the exuberant wildness of summer roses and the dahlias and windflowers of autumn.

The queens of the late spring garden here are the 'Eden' roses. While the classic Eden Rose (or Pierre de Ronsard) is well represented, many don't realize that the White Eden Rose, also known as Palais Royal, is the most prevalent. This paler version fills and frames the central lawns of the garden. Photographing the roses at their peak is one of my great joys, especially in early morning before the sun crests the top of the buildings, when the shadows are cool and the burbling fountains mask all urban sounds.

BLOSSOMS

Of the spring fruit trees, I am forever enamored with the precious apple blossom, whose delicate bloom of five-cupped petals is surely the sweetest, whether in shades of shell pink or rich magenta.

A much-loved feature of our former garden, Hillhaven, was our pair of Blireana plum trees, always the first to blossom. One year, their early bloom coincided with a late snowstorm, decorating the bright pink flowers with plumes of white. Most springs, I would cut a few branches to bring indoors, mindful of not spoiling the tree's arching shapes. As the blossoms fell one year, I floated them in a pool of water, the better to appreciate their uniformity of form.

LEFT: I once belonged to a photography group called ICM (Intentional Camera Movement). I was quite dedicated to it for several years and spent many a happy time amongst flower fields creating images with a slow shutter while panning or twirling the camera. Most of the blurry results were mixed at best, but the pink tulip here was one of those experiments that was more successful. April 2007.

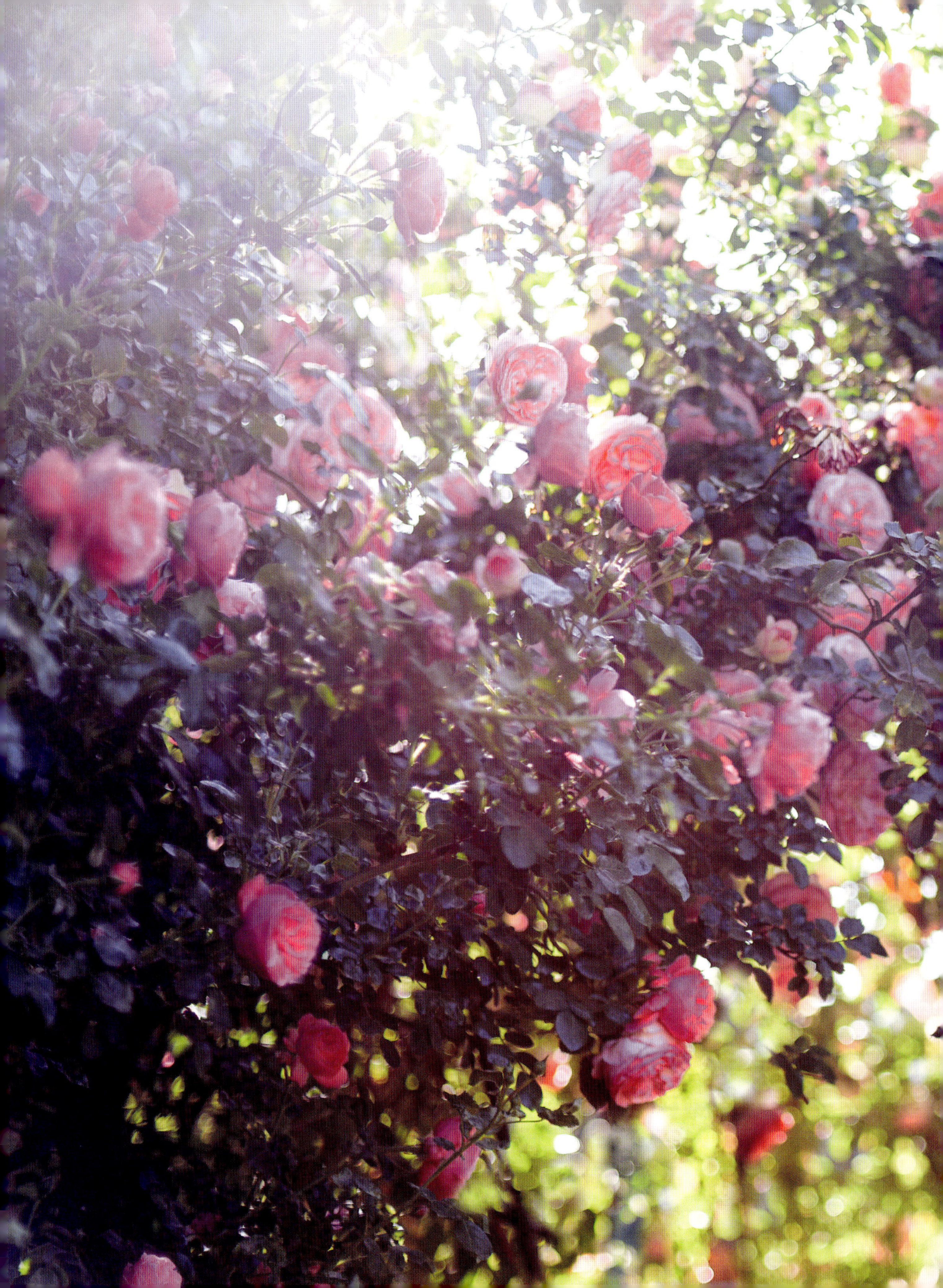

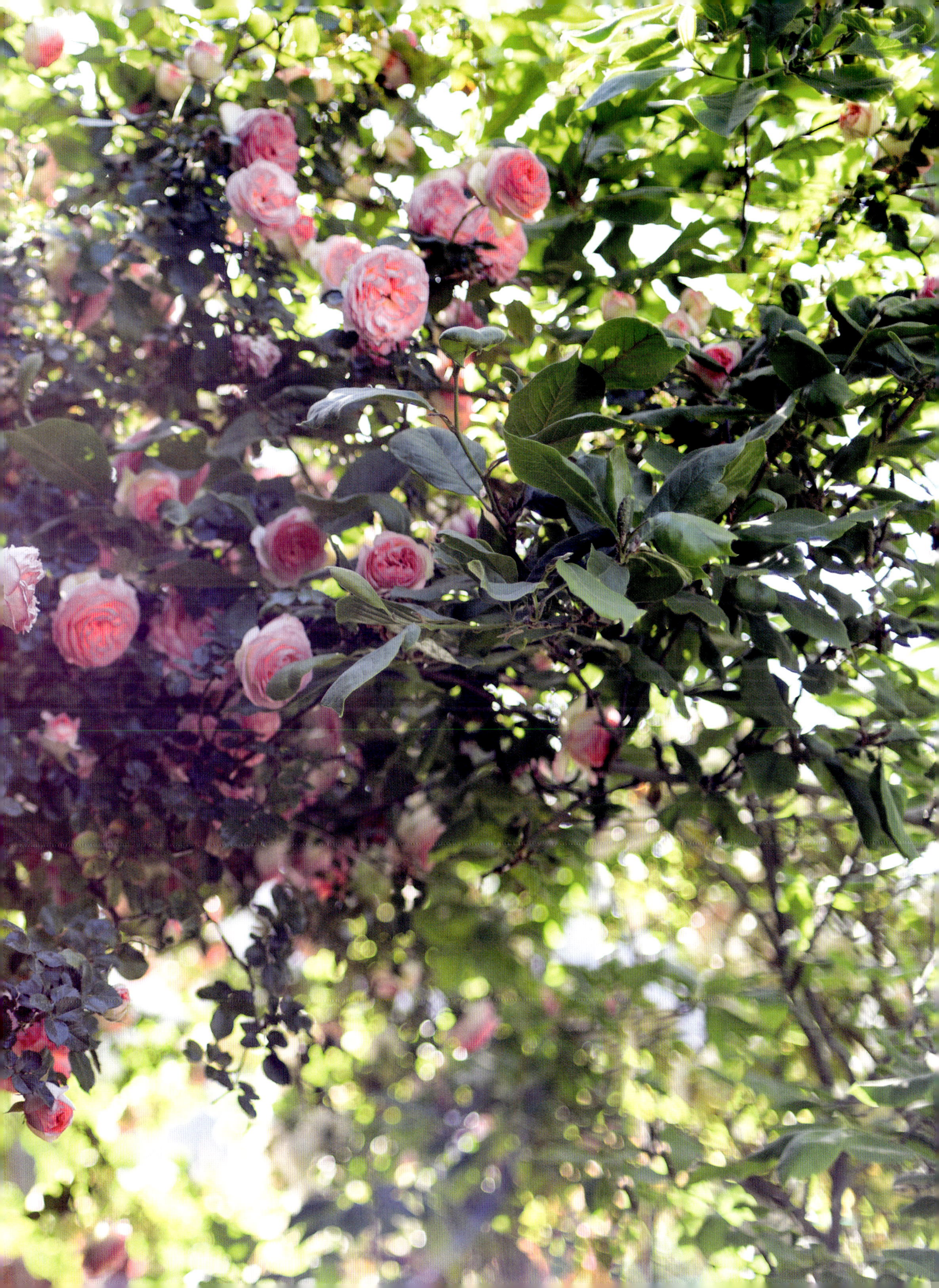

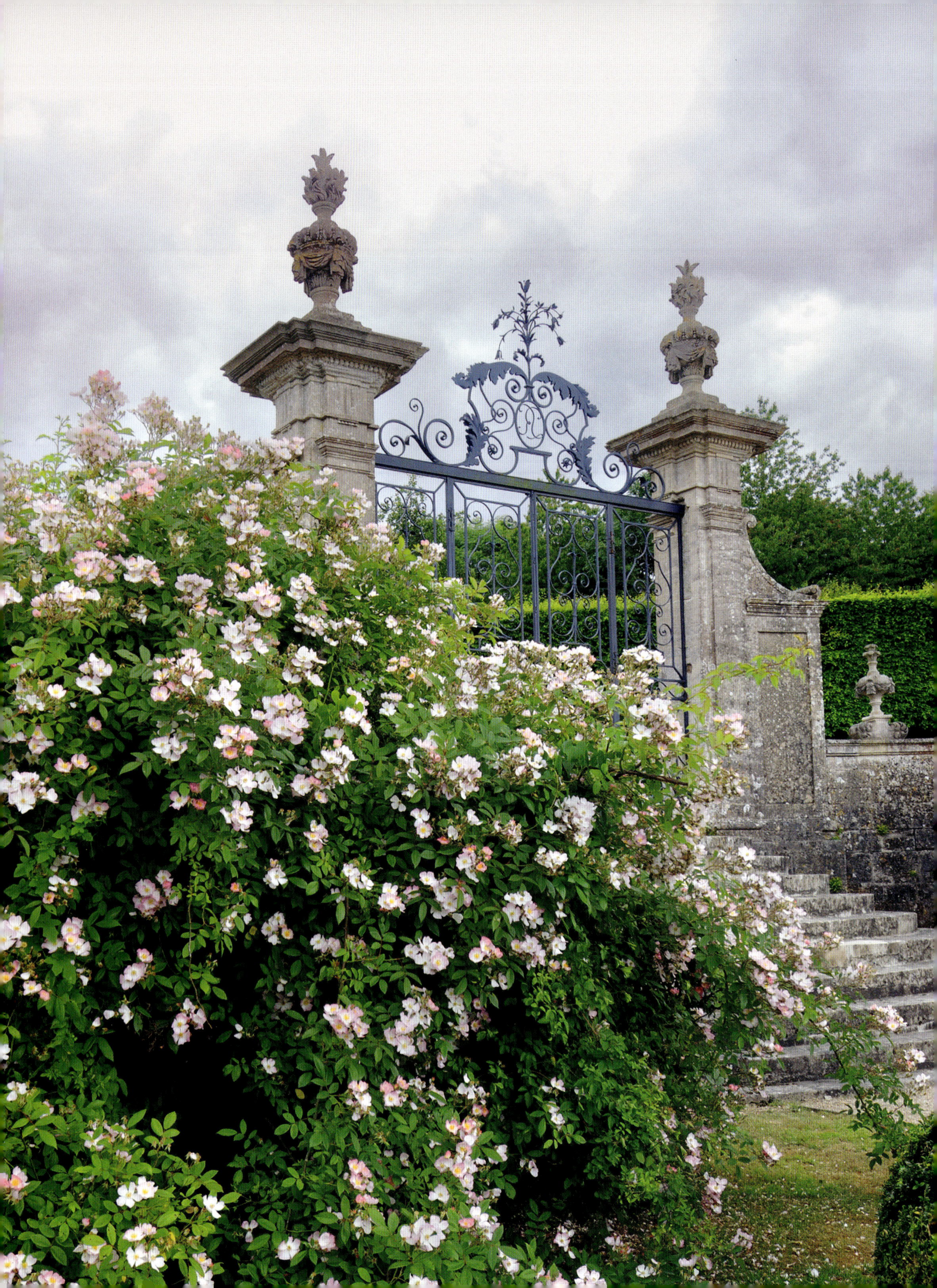

A PARADISE GARDEN IN FRANCE

I continually seek out little-known gardens, and many years ago I discovered the seventeenth-century Jardins du Château de Brécy, near Bayeux, France. Italianate gates and stonework smothered in riots of roses, boxwood parterres, carved lions and conical topiaries represent a labor of love and dedicated restoration. Open at select times in the summer, a visit when in Normandy is well worth the small effort it takes to find it.

SOUTH AMERICAN IDYLL

Traveling as we are in a dream state, we can arrive in an instant to the Andean home of my dear friend Maria Cecilia ('Chichi' to friends and family). Beautifully handcrafted of reclaimed wood, flagstone and colorfully tiled terraces, it is everything you might imagine a Chilean mountain retreat to be. Soaring atriums let in volumes of light, and winding passageways lead to private bedroom suites with lace-strewn beds, each opening onto its own garden and view.

Vintage linens soften the surfaces of the abundant European antiques that somehow wound their way to Santiago flea markets, no doubt via ships that once docked in Valparaiso during its heyday as an international port.

I timed my visits to Chichi's paradise to coincide with peak rose season, which in that part of the southern hemisphere is in early November. At that time, her monumental Eden roses, spilling and tumbling throughout the stone-lined pathways, reached their pinnacle. Upon arriving, I always noticed how the quietude of her garden allowed one's mind to wander in therapeutic contemplation.

After leisurely touring the grounds, we would sit in a courtyard of white iron tables brimming with enameled pitchers of cut roses, while sharing the progress of our spiritual journeys, or silently casting spent blooms into the swimming pool, where they swirled and eddied into artistic clusters. We valued these precious moments spent alone with our thoughts, receptive to the sudden clarity of inspiration.

LEFT and OVERLEAF: Jardins du Château de Brécy, Normandy, France. June 2011.

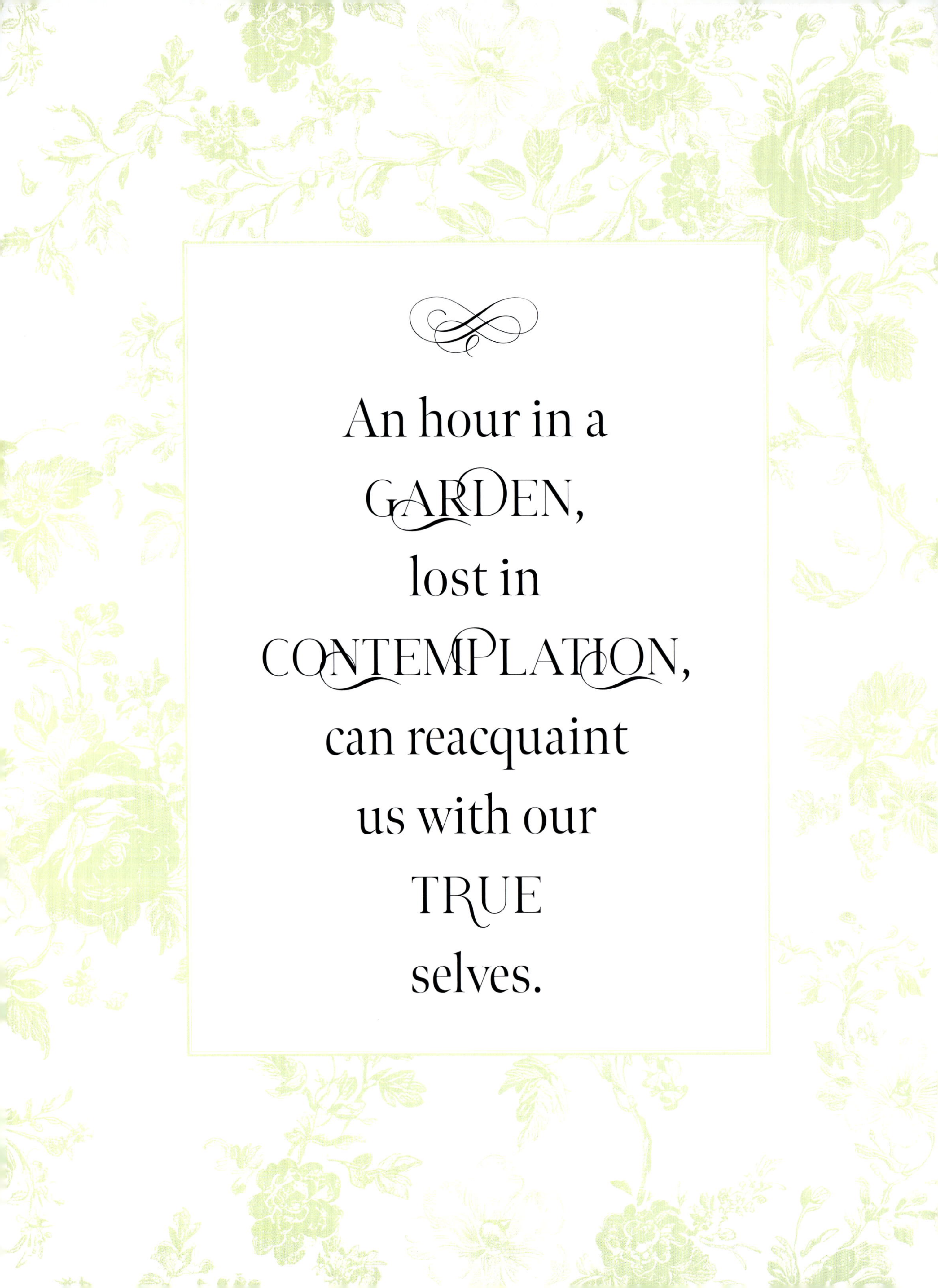
An hour in a
GARDEN,
lost in
CONTEMPLATION,
can reacquaint
us with our
TRUE
selves.

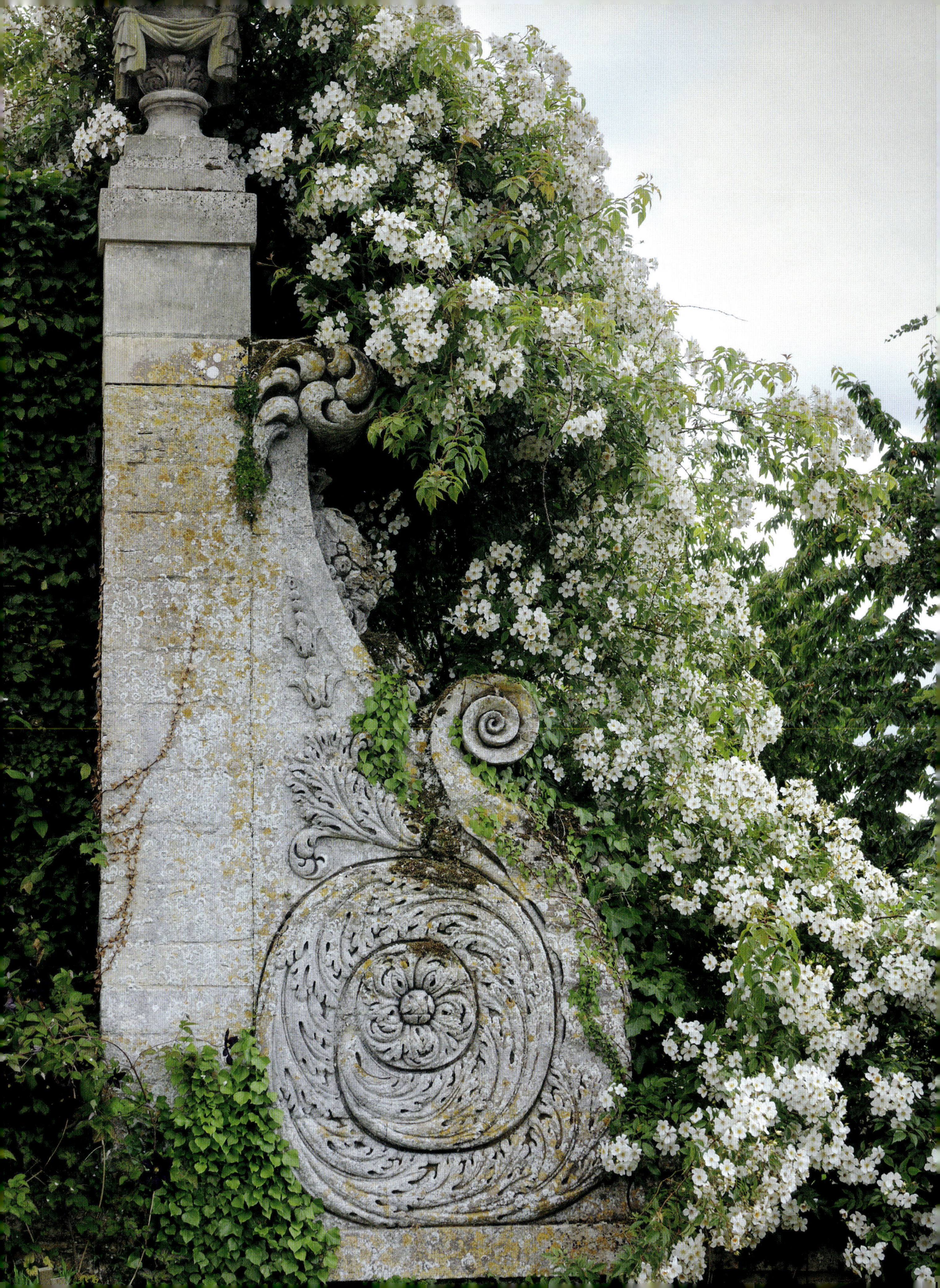

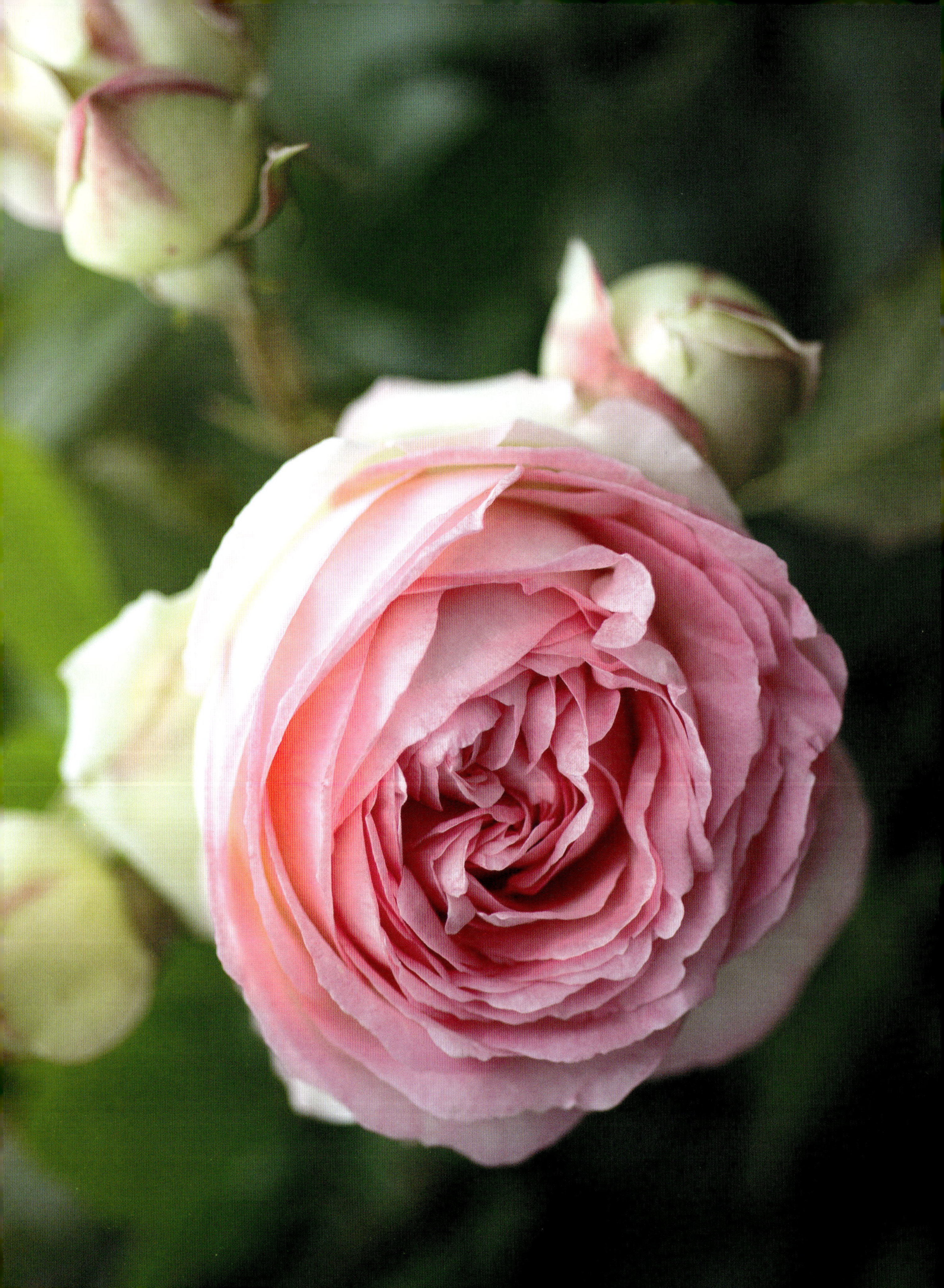

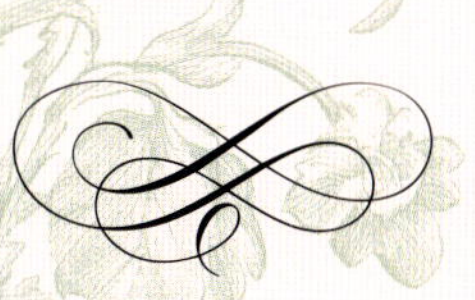

CHICHI'S GARDEN

The Andean Foothills, El Arrayán, Chile
November 2014

I have, earlier in this chapter, described Chichi's resplendent sanctuary garden in South America. Her enormous rose bushes, trained into arching canes, cover the property from its lower reaches well up into the hillside above. The dark pink-edged 'Eden' rose,and the shell-pink 'Ma Maison et Mon Jardin', shown on these pages, dominate the terraces surrounding the house, so laden with blooms that an intricate network of thick metal trellises has been installed to support the weight. Ambling around the vaulted structures, ducking under the cascades of perfume and drifting through a veil of petals, it's as though one has fallen into one of Edward Burne-Jones' Briar Rose *paintings, a Sleeping Beauty dreamland filled with fanciful musings.*

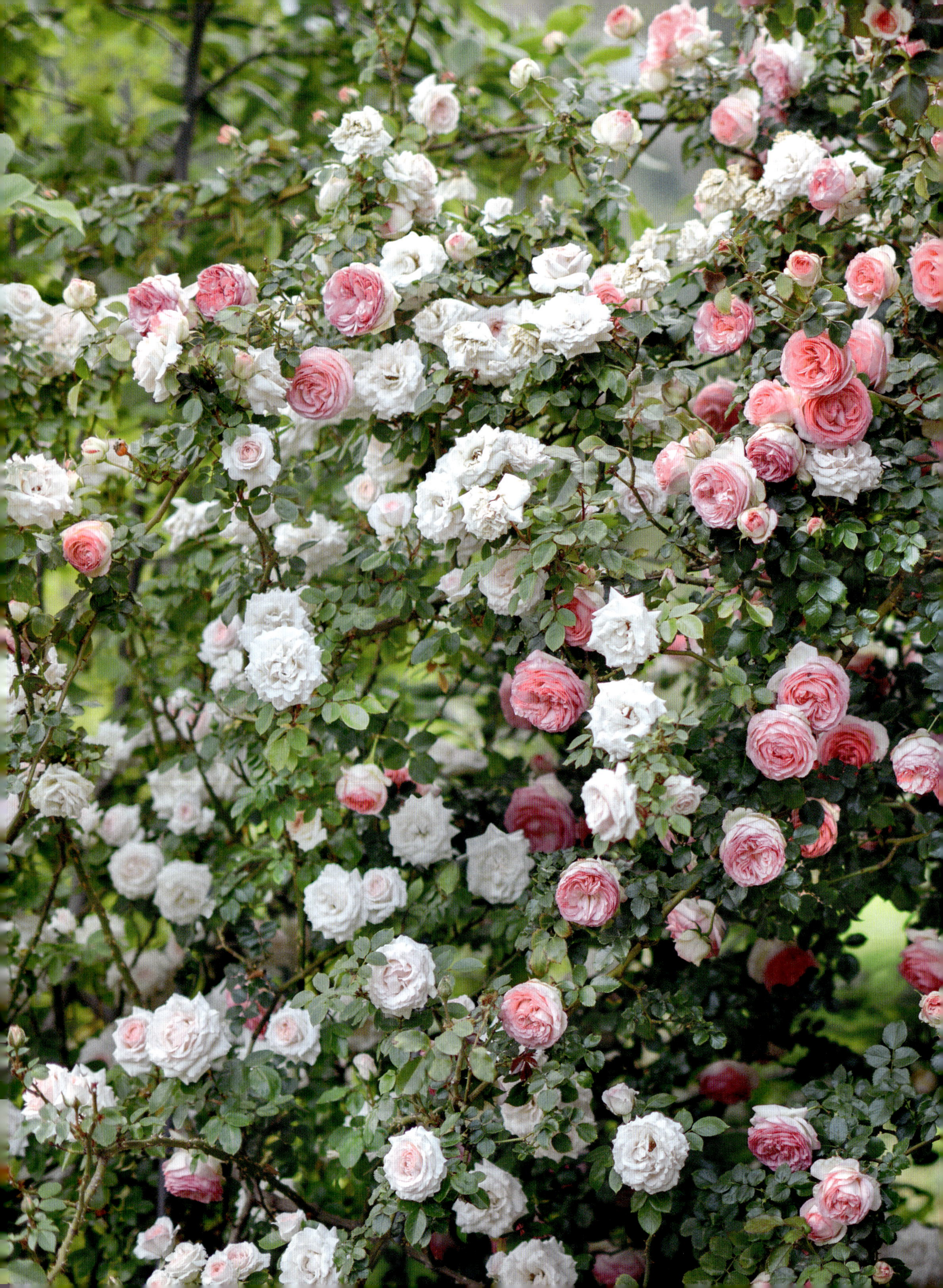

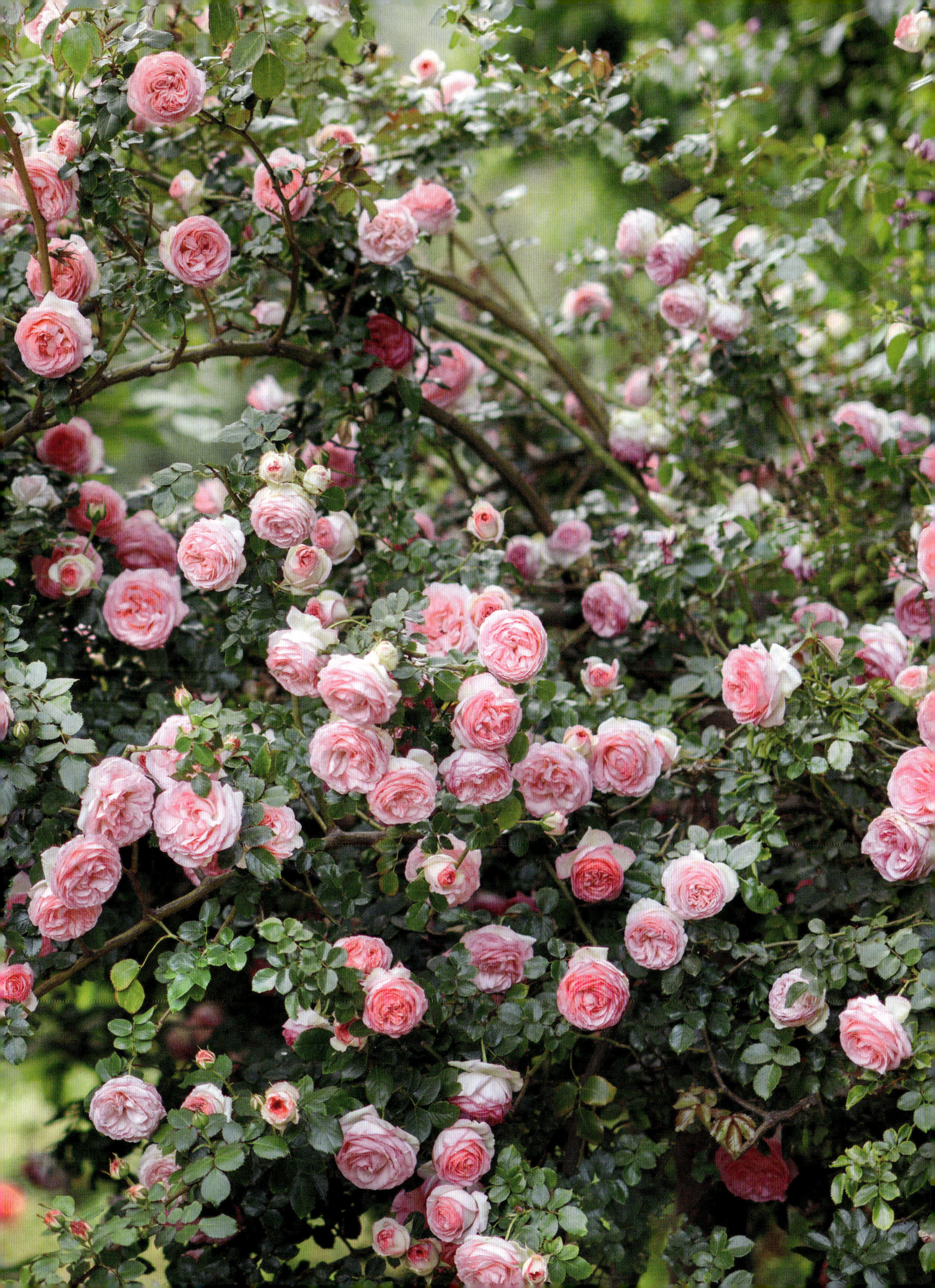

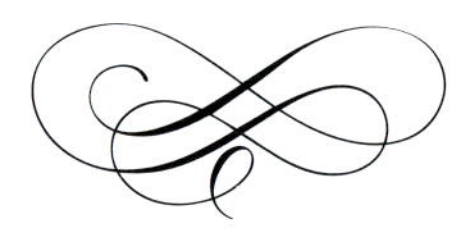

WE valued
these precious
MOMENTS spent
alone with our
THOUGHTS,
receptive to the
sudden clarity of
INSPIRATION.

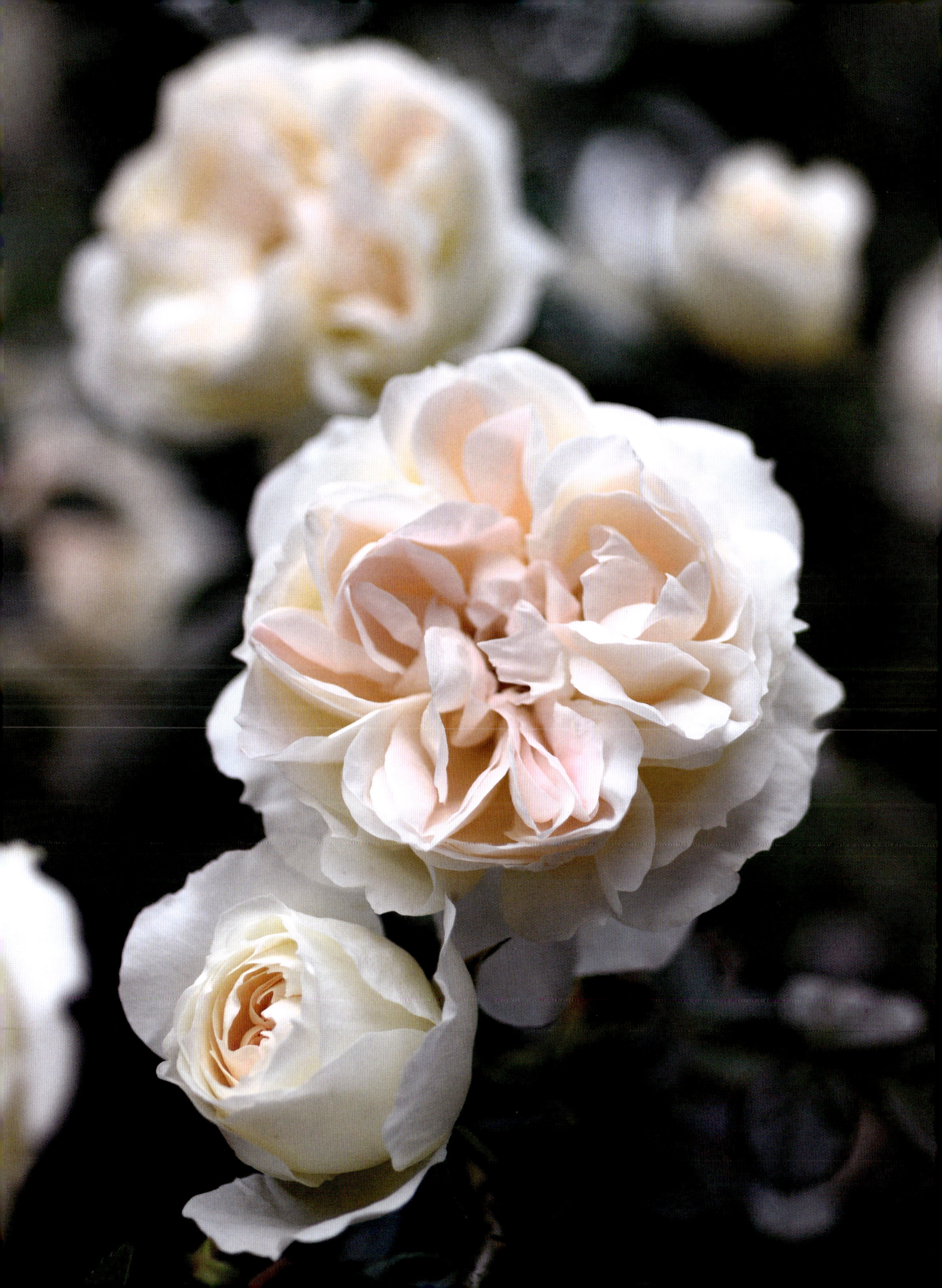

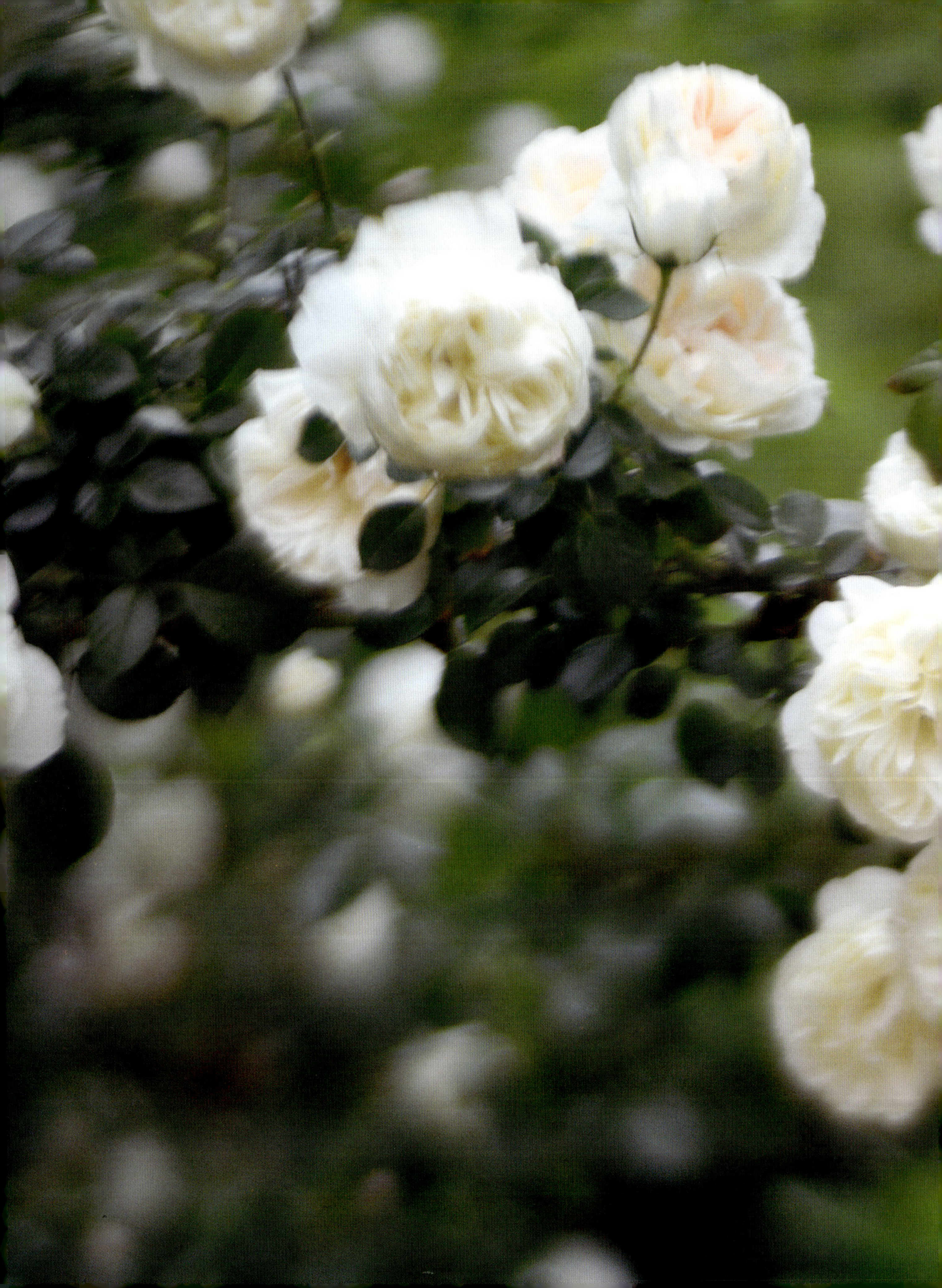

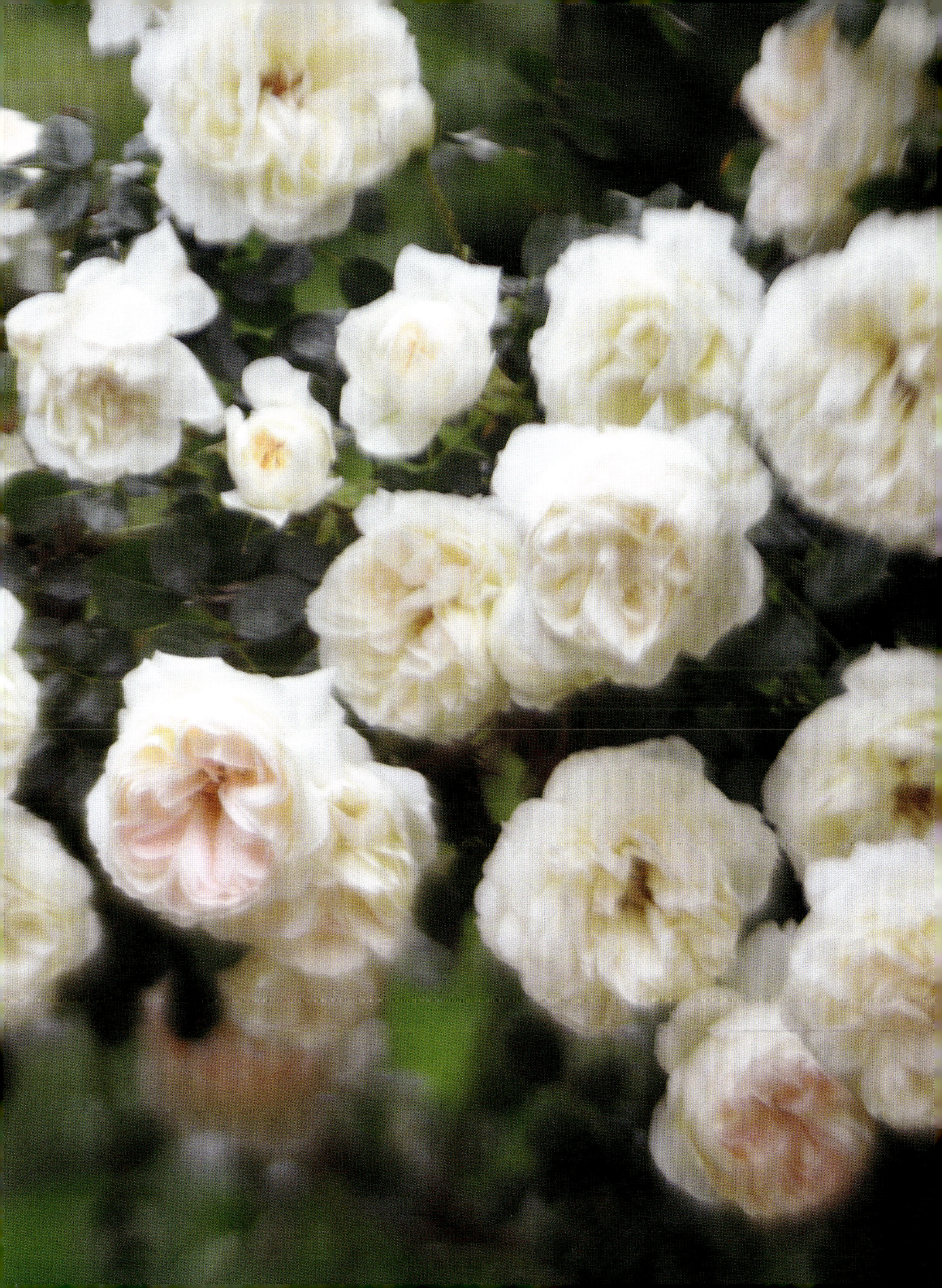

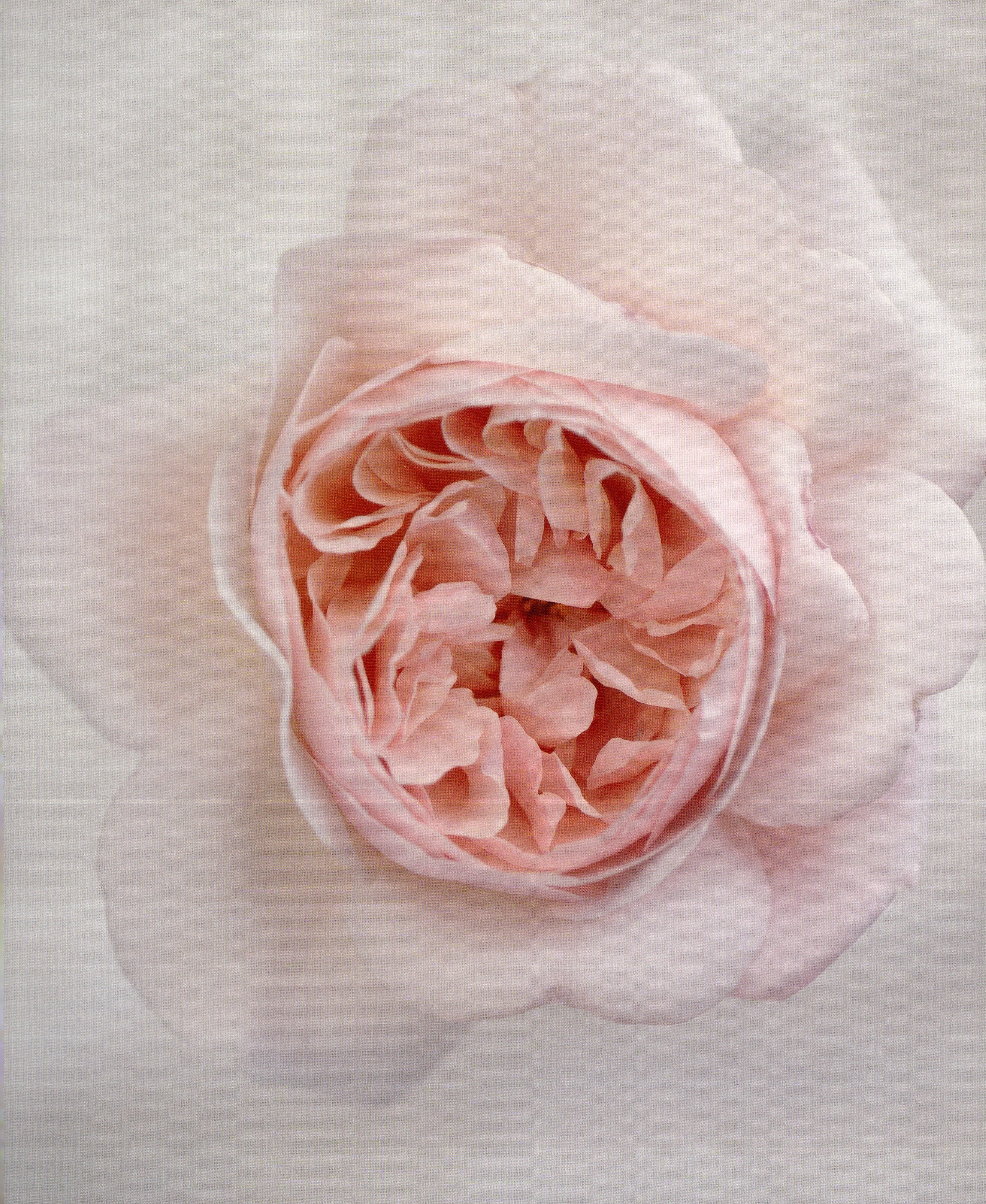

THIS PAGE: David Austin *Rosa* 'A Shropshire Lad', Washington, USA. July 2010. RIGHT: Mixed David Austin white roses falling through a black velvet sky, like stars, Shropshire, England. July 2015.

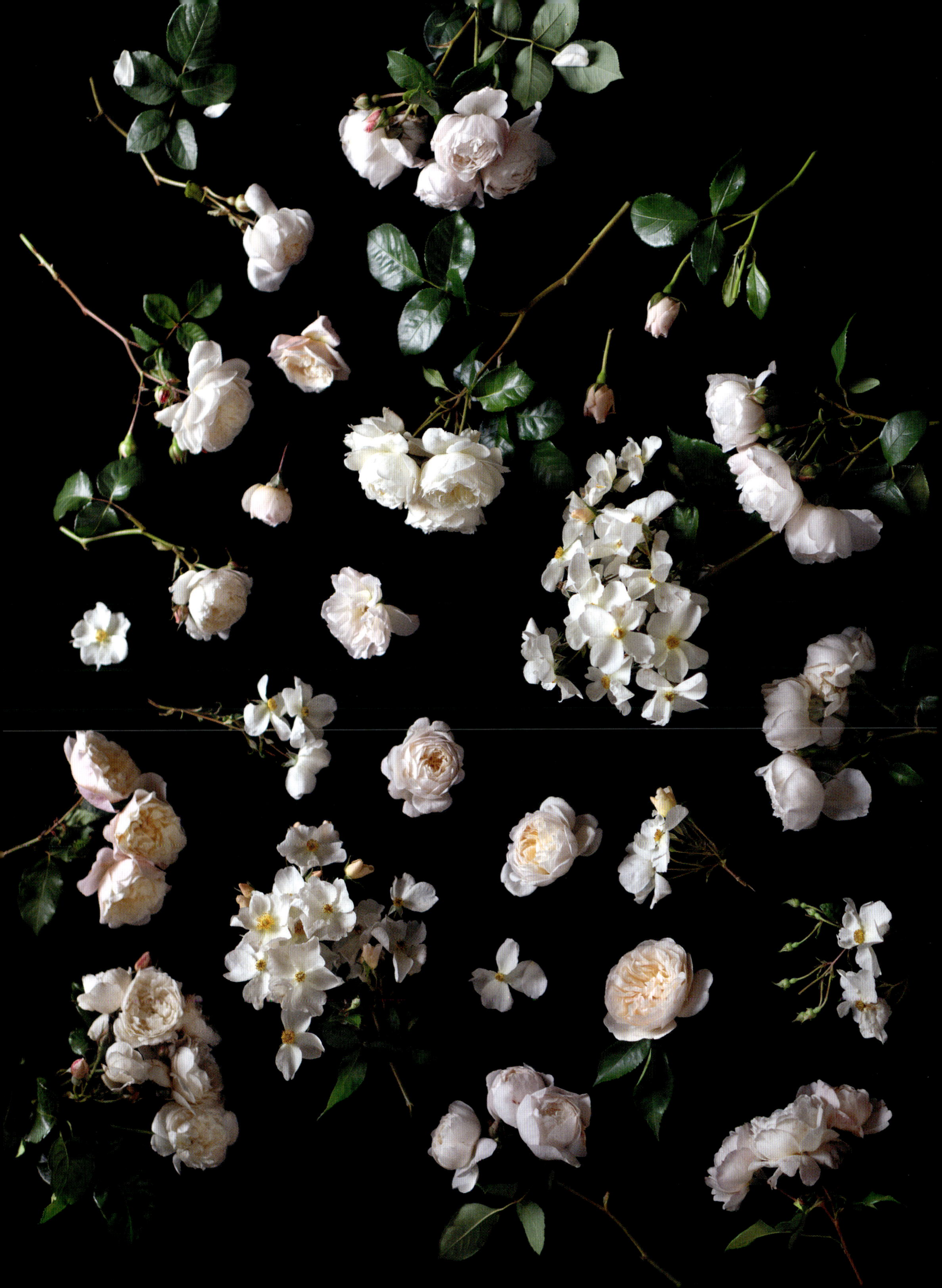

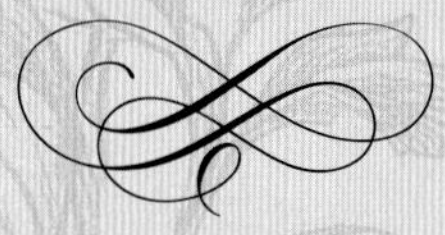

Cherry Blossoms

The English Gardens, The Regent's Park, London, England
April 2019

Timing is the prime consideration in floral photography. Split-second shifts of light can render a scene mythic or mediocre. And though I have taken tens of thousands of images of cherry blossoms around the world, this one remains a favorite.

Daily I returned to this garden during the season, to capture the gentle evolution of the blossoms unfolding. Here, although they are a few days away from peak bloom, I love the atmosphere, with the mist in the distance and the interlacing of the branches fashioning a delicate canopy. As is my habit, I enter at dawn to experience the aura and tranquility of the garden as it exists in its own dimension.

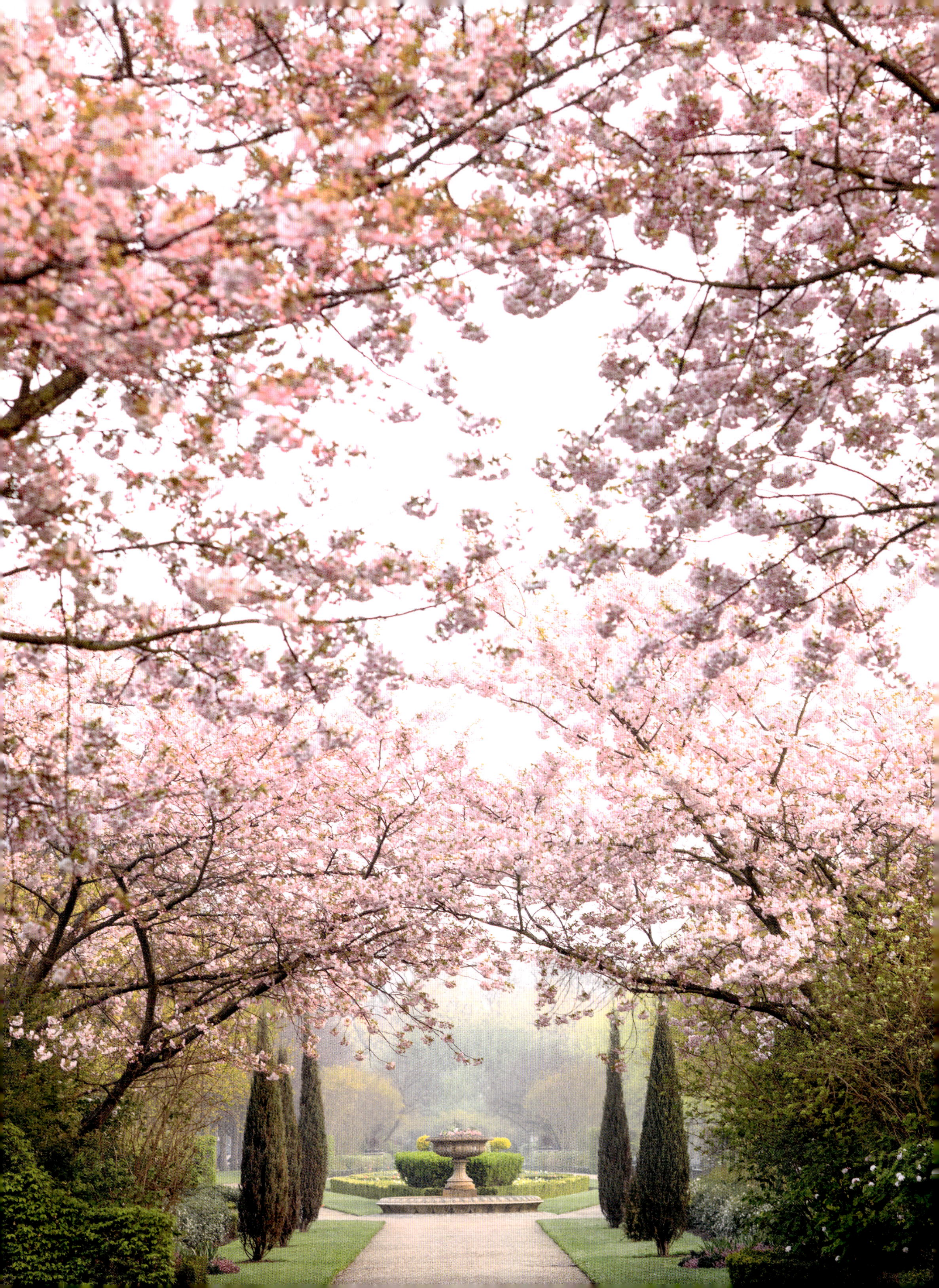

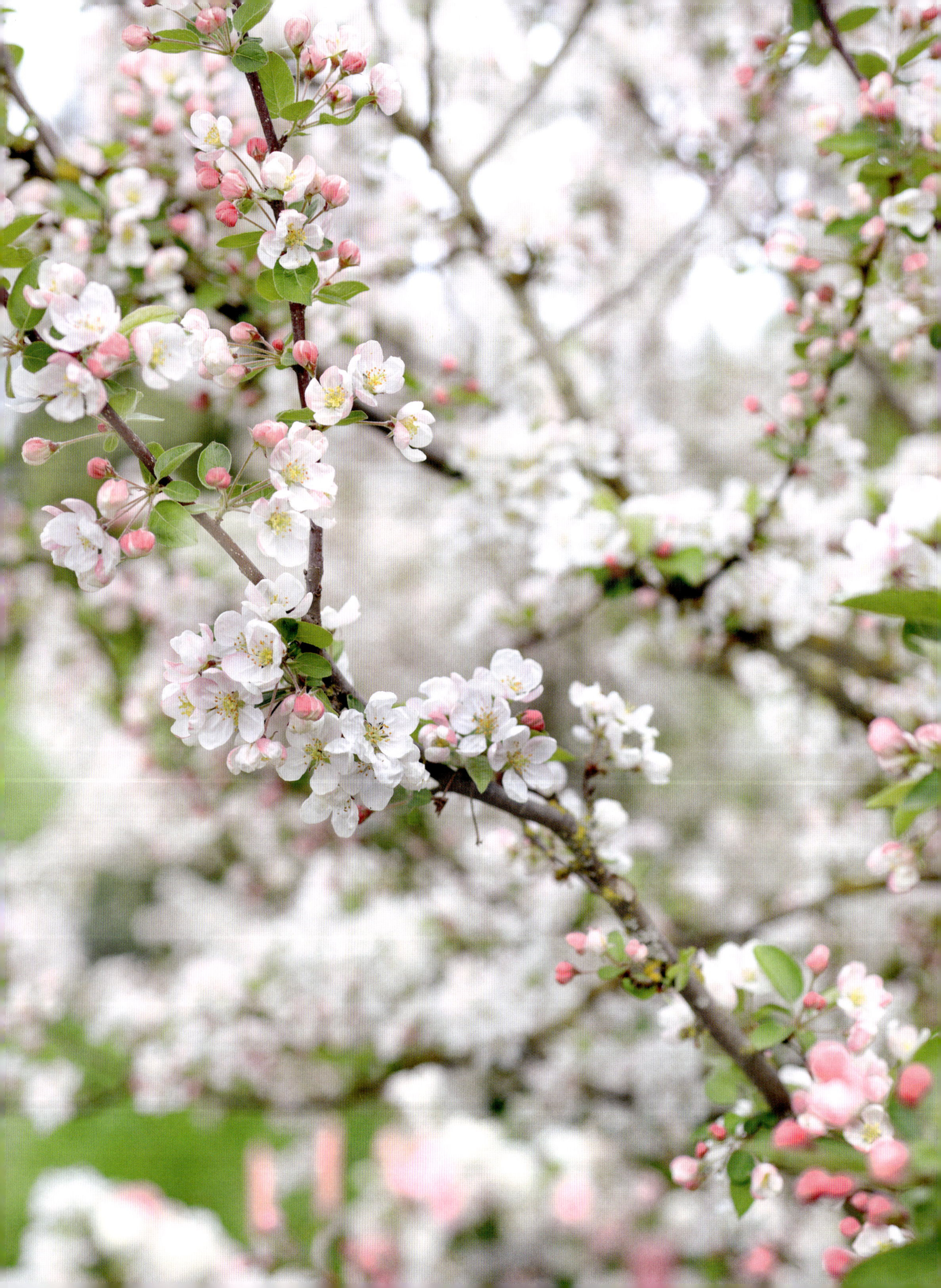

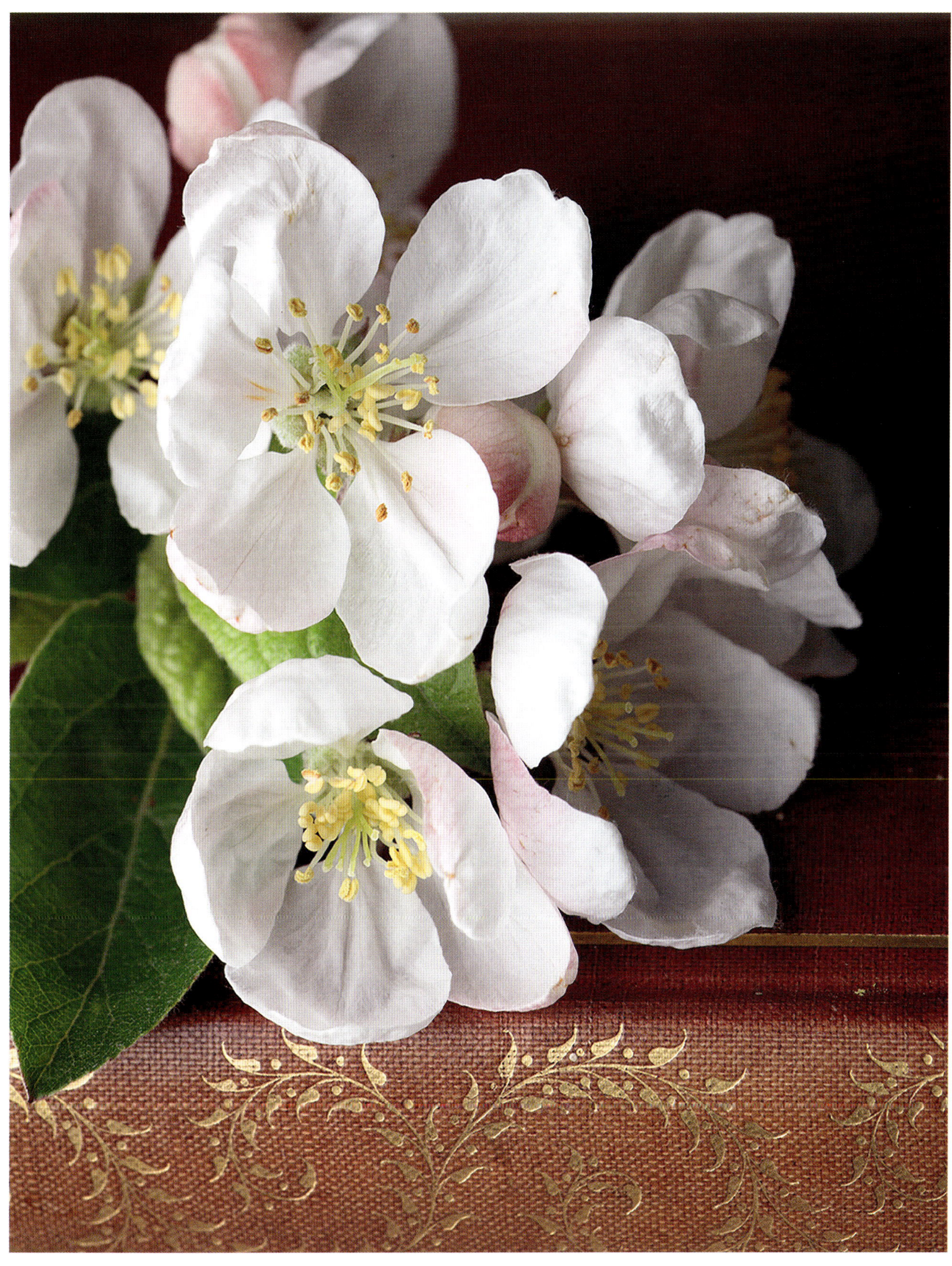

LEFT: Crab apple blossoms, *Malus* 'Evereste', Skagit Valley, Washington, USA. April 2013. ABOVE: Crab apple blossoms, Hillhaven Garden, Shoreline, Washington, USA. April 2013. OVERLEAF: *Magnolia × loebneri* 'Ballerina', Washington Park Arboretum, USA. April 2009.

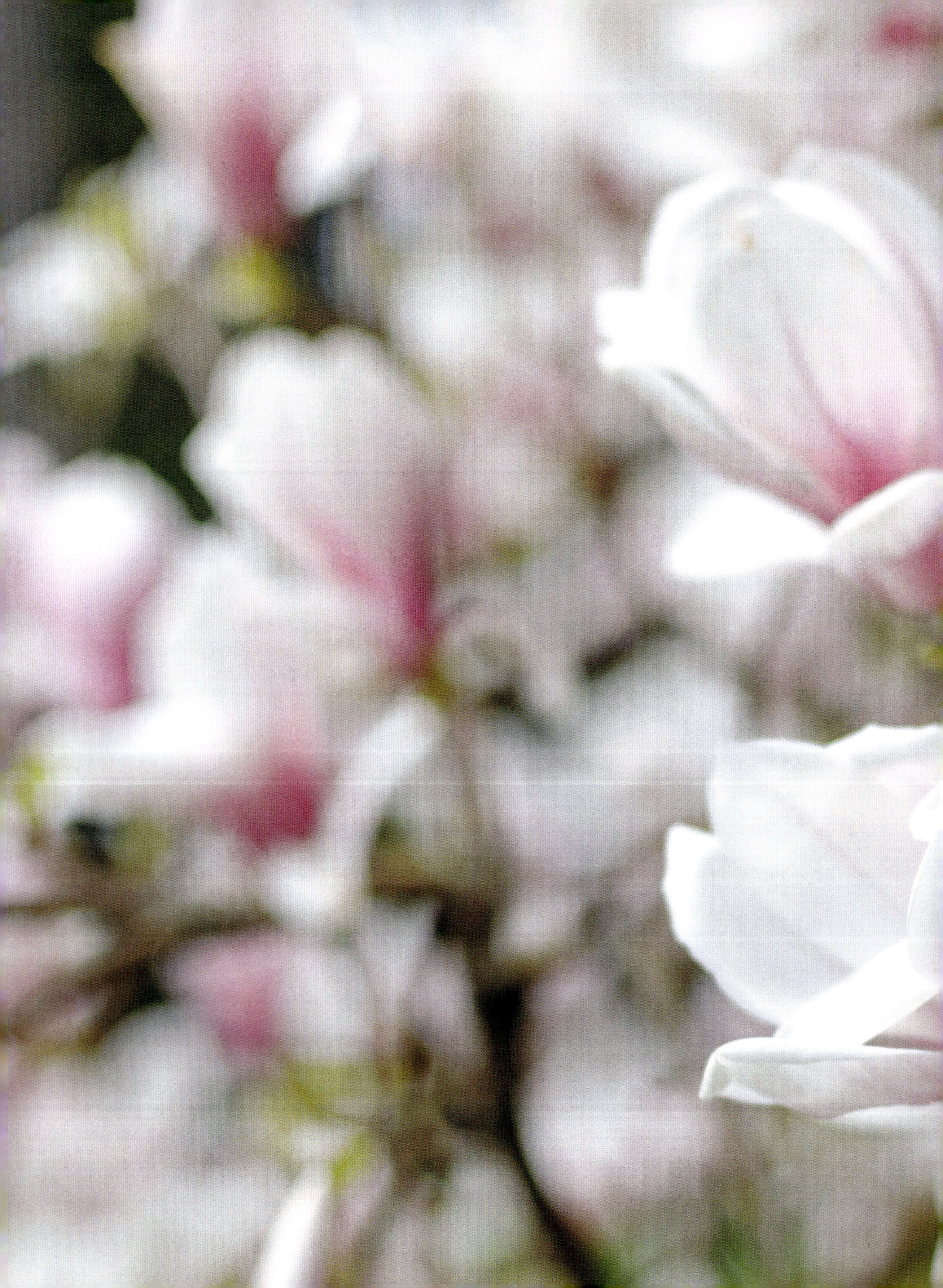

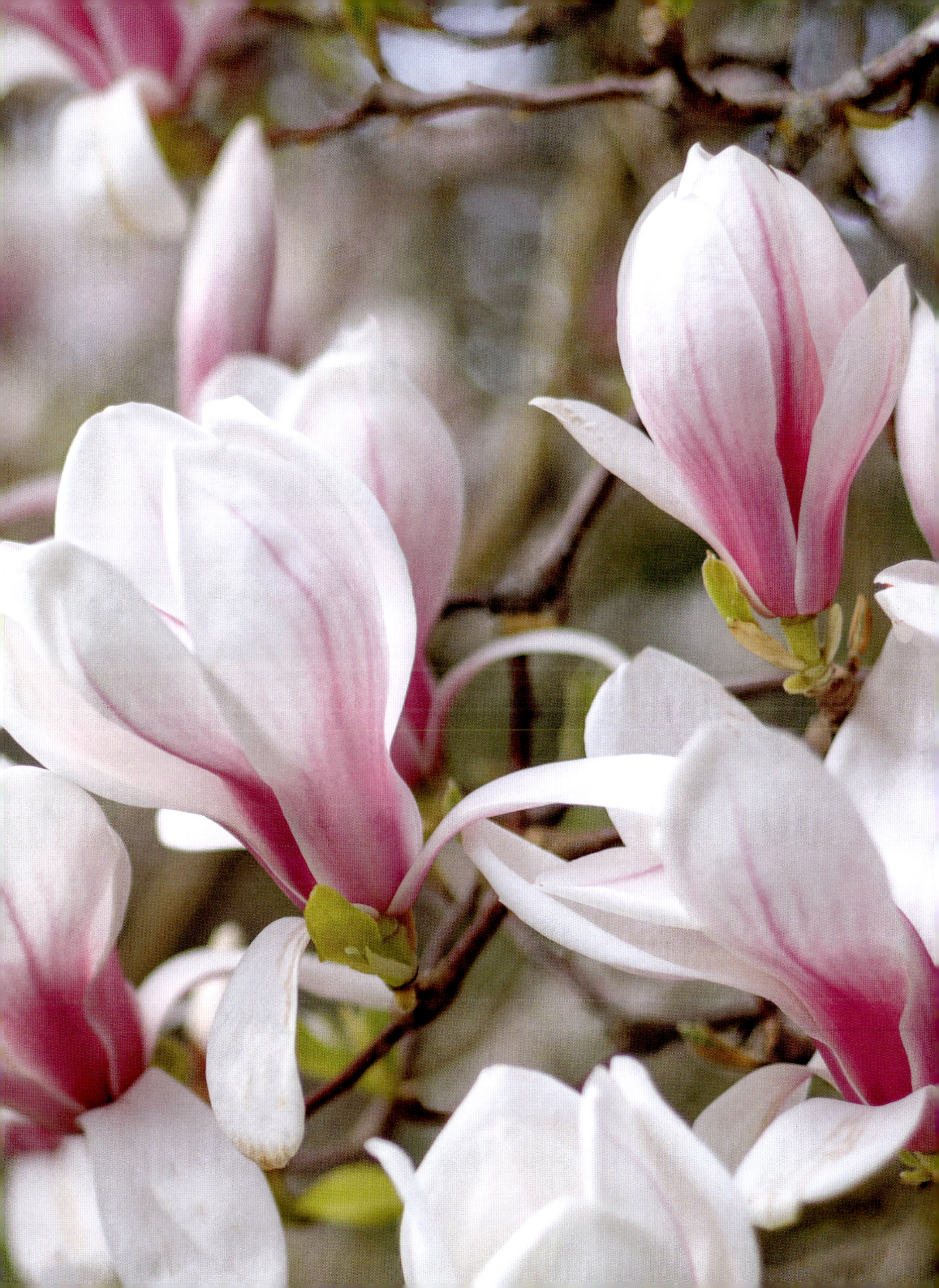

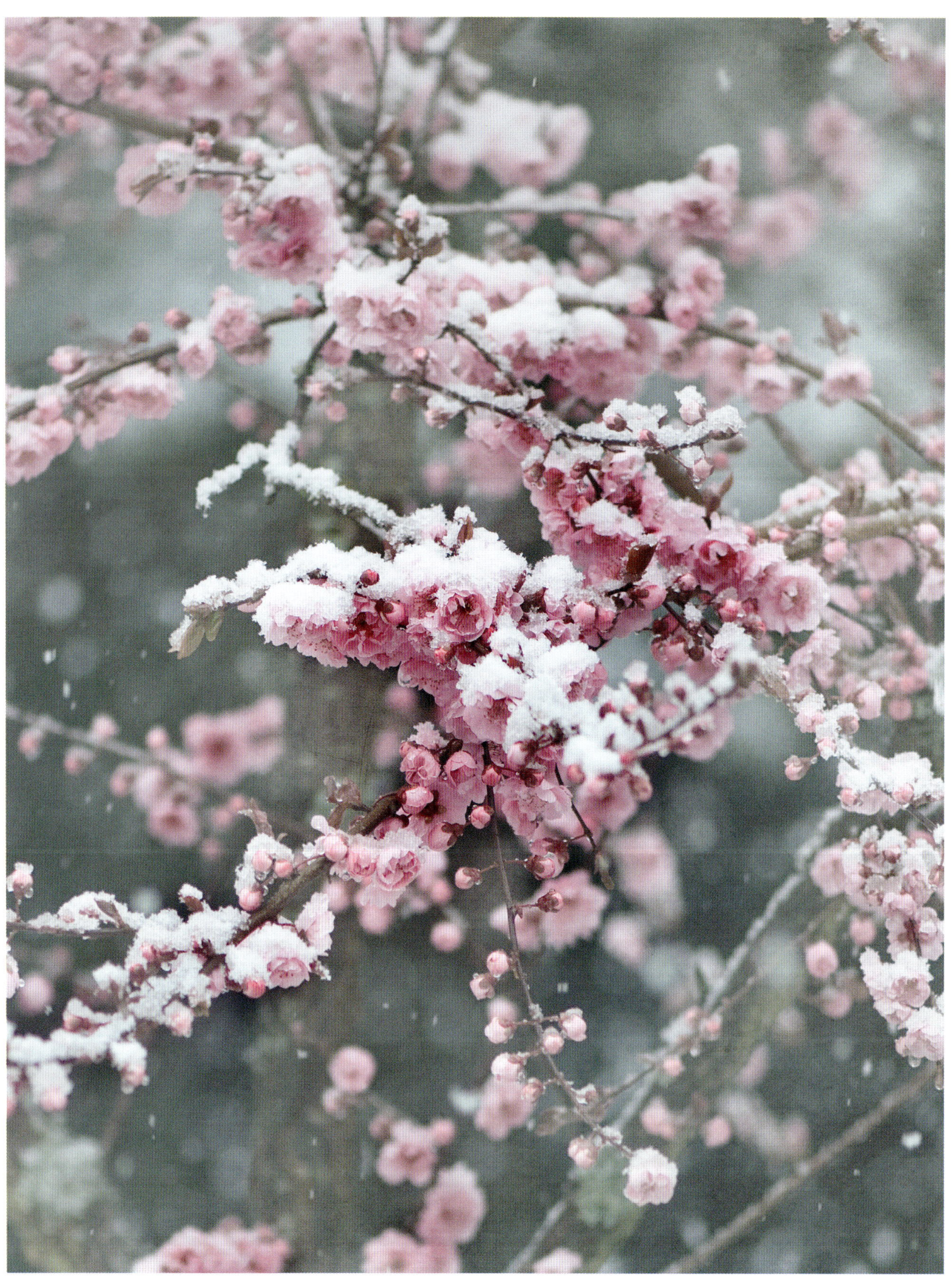

ABOVE: Blireiana plum blossoms in snow (*Prunus × blireiana*), Hillhaven Garden, Shoreline, Washington, USA. March 2008. RIGHT: Blireiana plum blossoms in vintage French enamel pitchers, Hillhaven. March 2013. OVERLEAF: Blireiana plum blossoms floating in water, Hillhaven. April 2019.

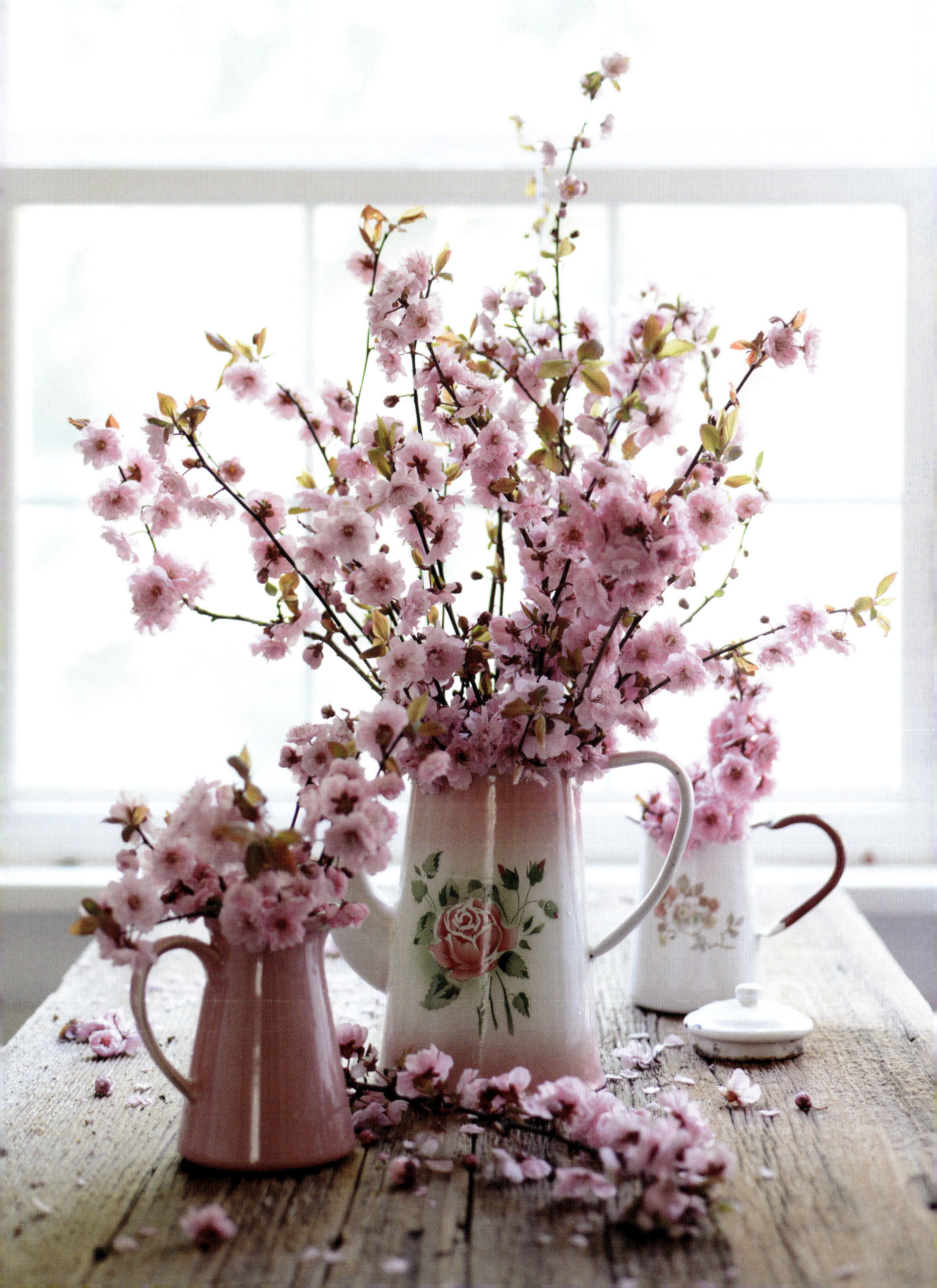

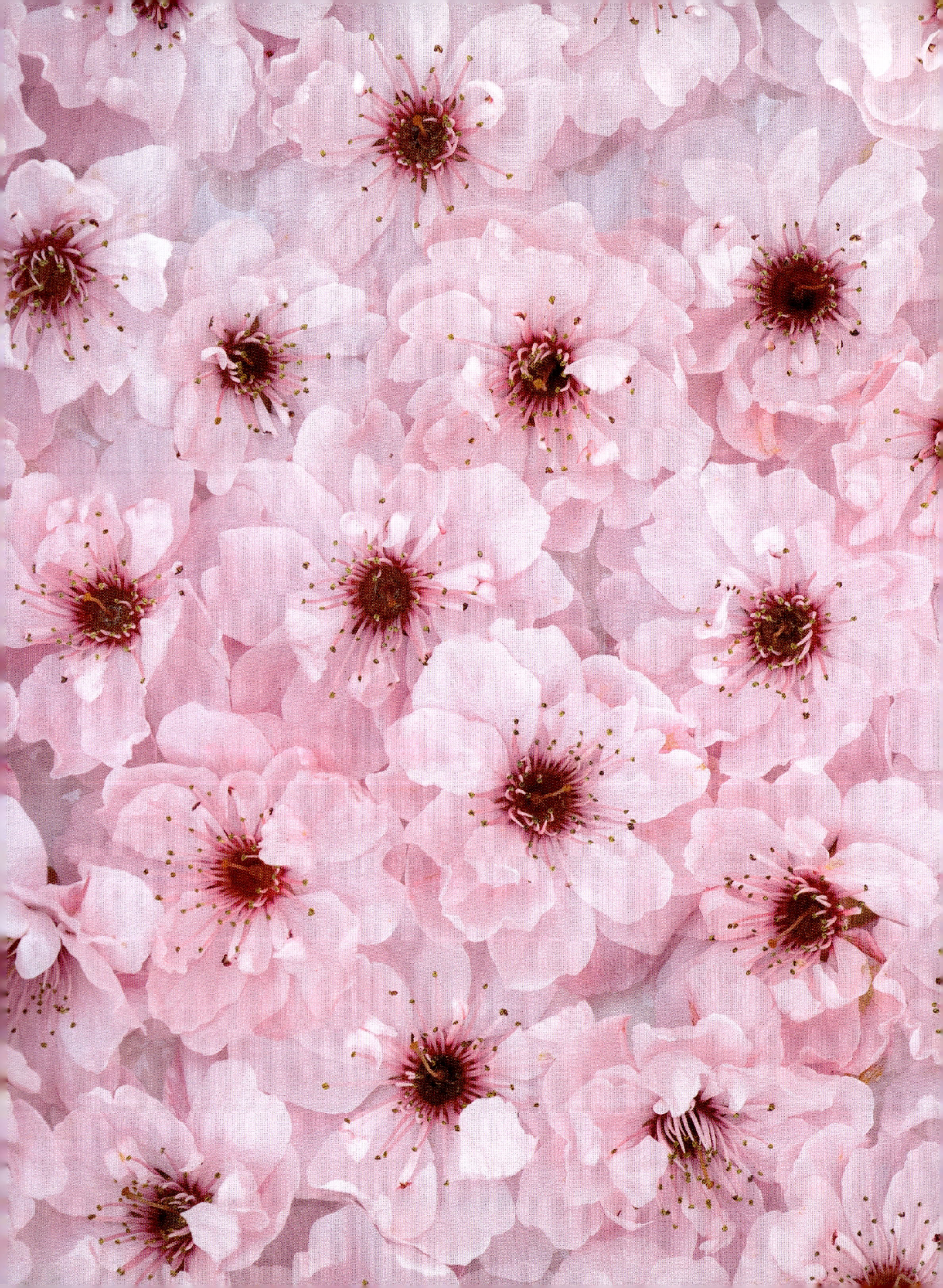

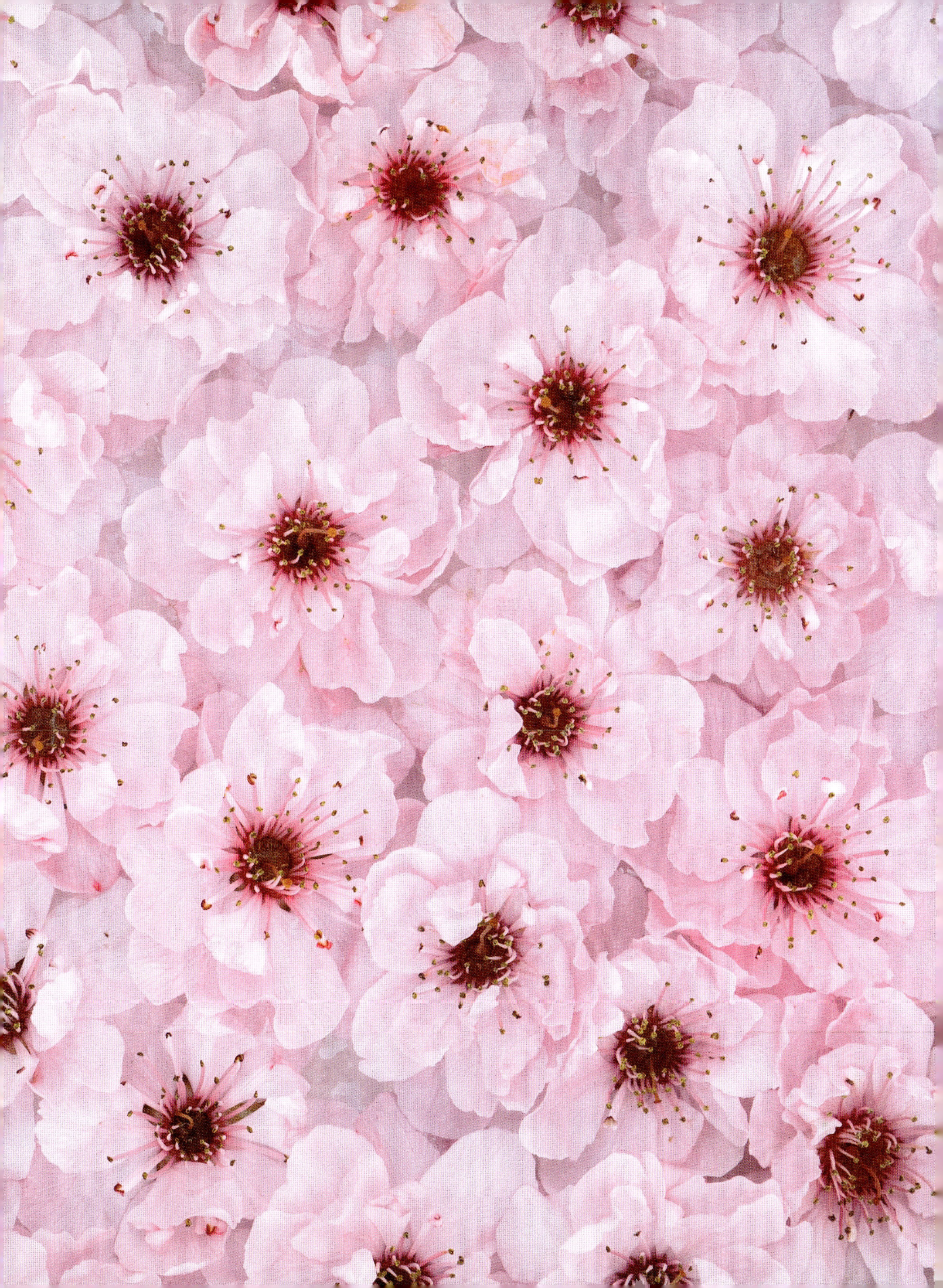

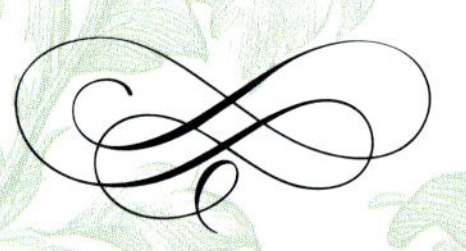

AN EVENING AT PALAIS ROYAL

Paris, France
May 2022

Although the caprices of spring can affect the timely appearance of cherry or wisteria or chestnut blossoms, the roses at the Jardin du Palais Royal, as if by decree, reliably bloom in the third week of May. Most days, I walk from my Left Bank apartment across Pont du Carrousel and past the Pyramide du Louvre to reach the Jardin. All distractions are ignored and nothing tempts me from this pilgrimage. One evening, when most had departed the grounds, I arrived as the sky darkened, not yet threatening but with a hint of menace. The hanging lanterns between the soaring columns, already lit against the gloom, swayed slightly in the strengthening breeze. The namesake 'Palais Royal' roses lifted and fell, and the storm light played over the petals, illuminating them like pearls.

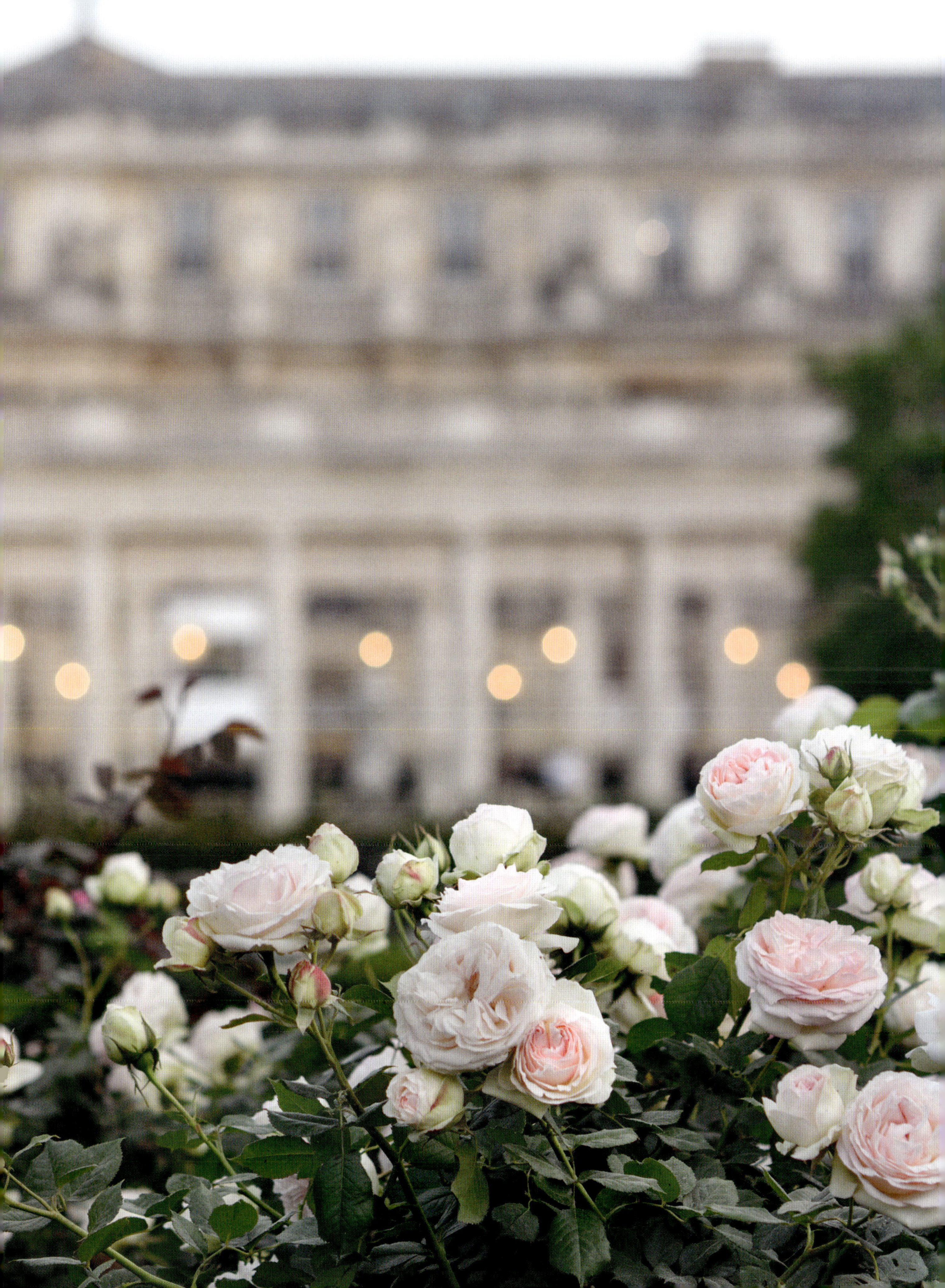

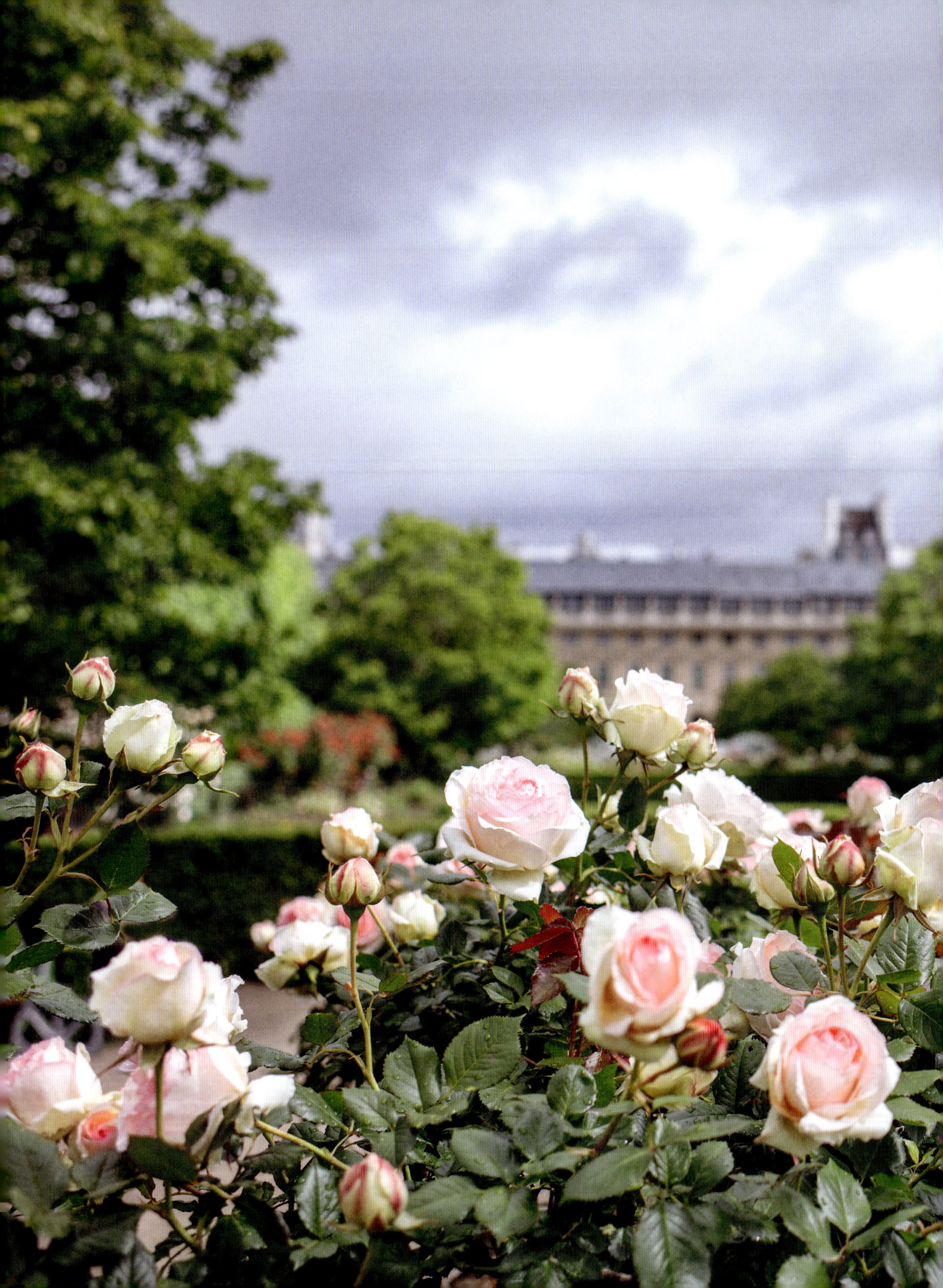

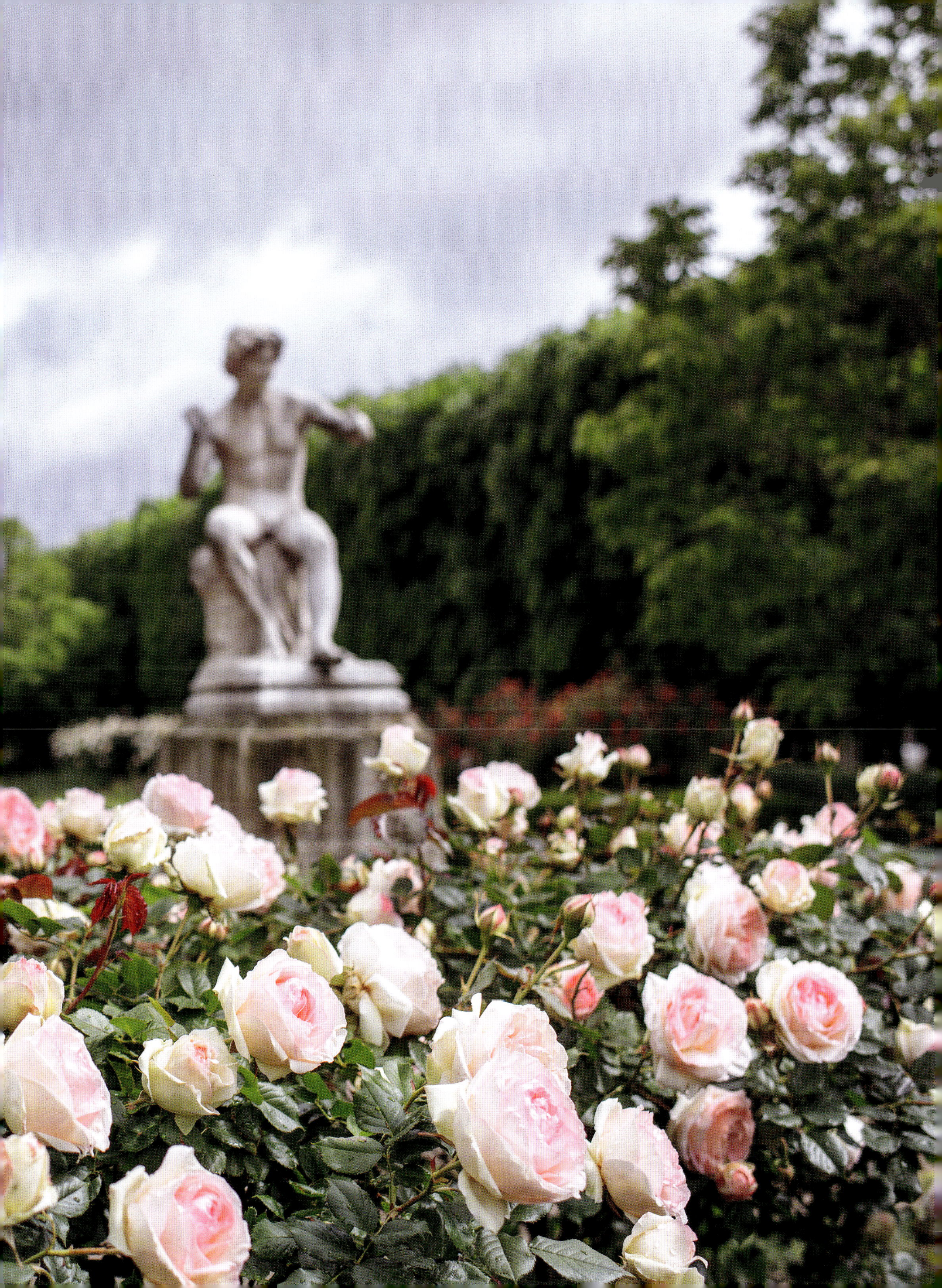

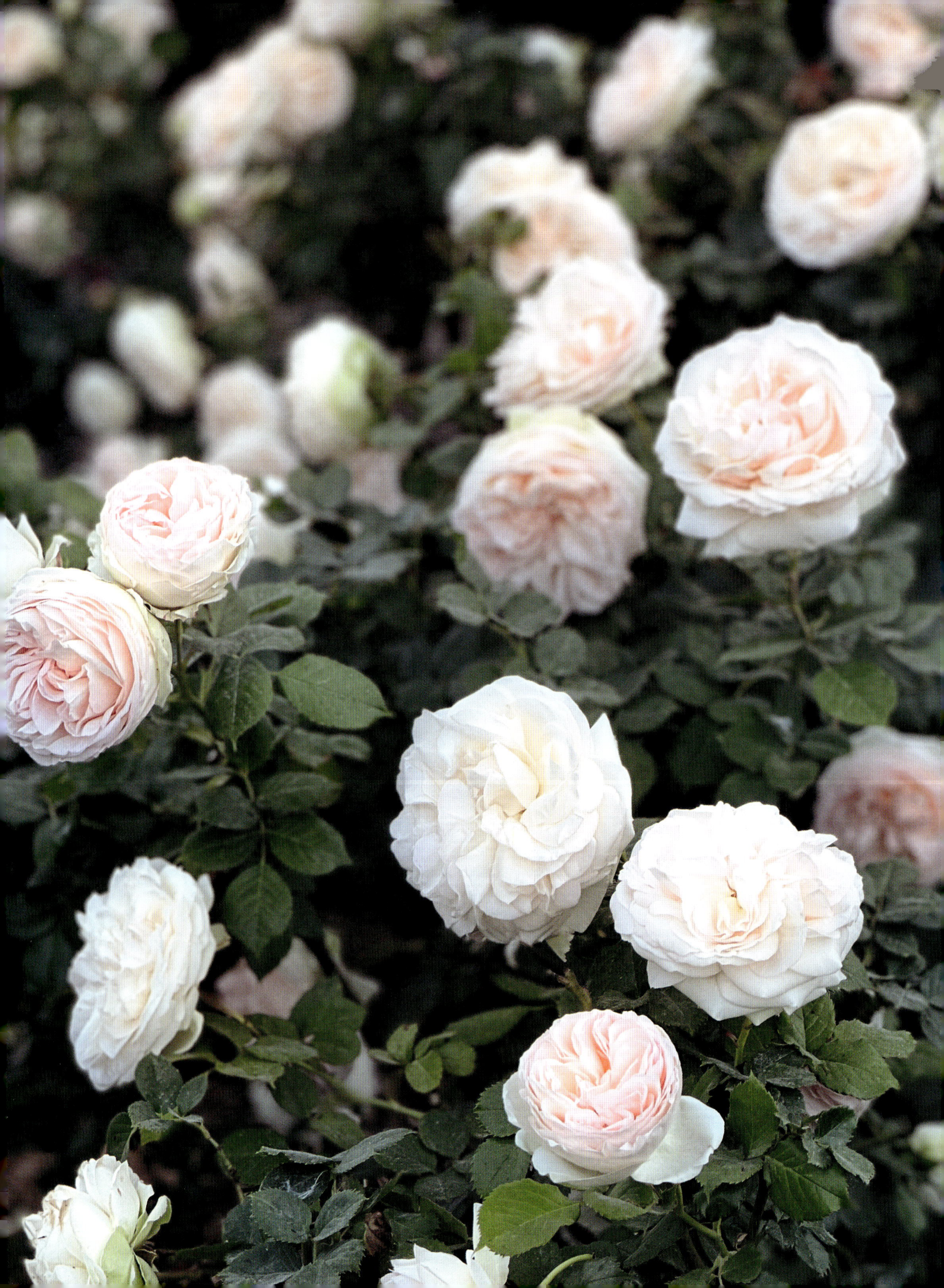

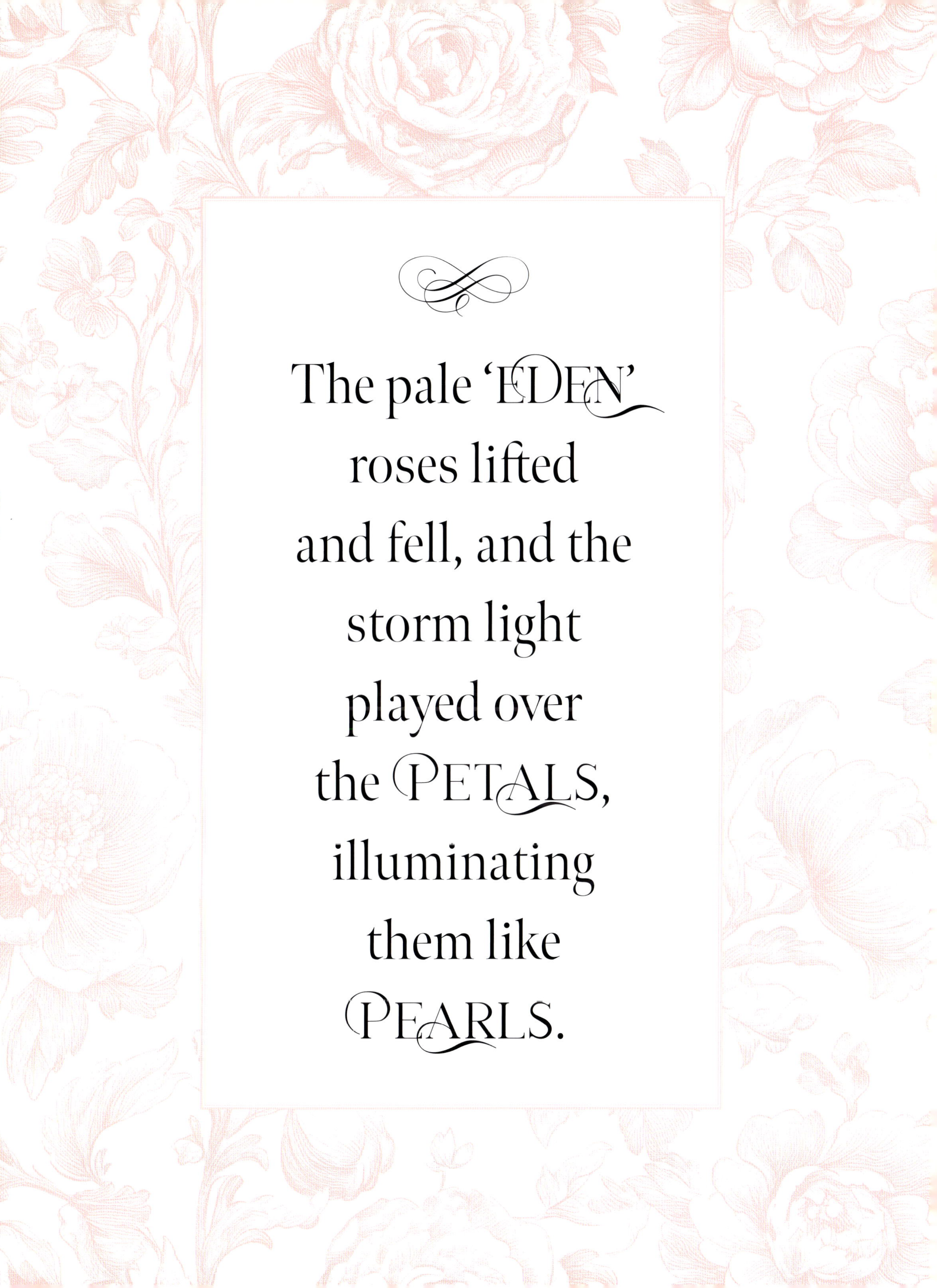
The pale 'EDEN'
roses lifted
and fell, and the
storm light
played over
the PETALS,
illuminating
them like
PEARLS.

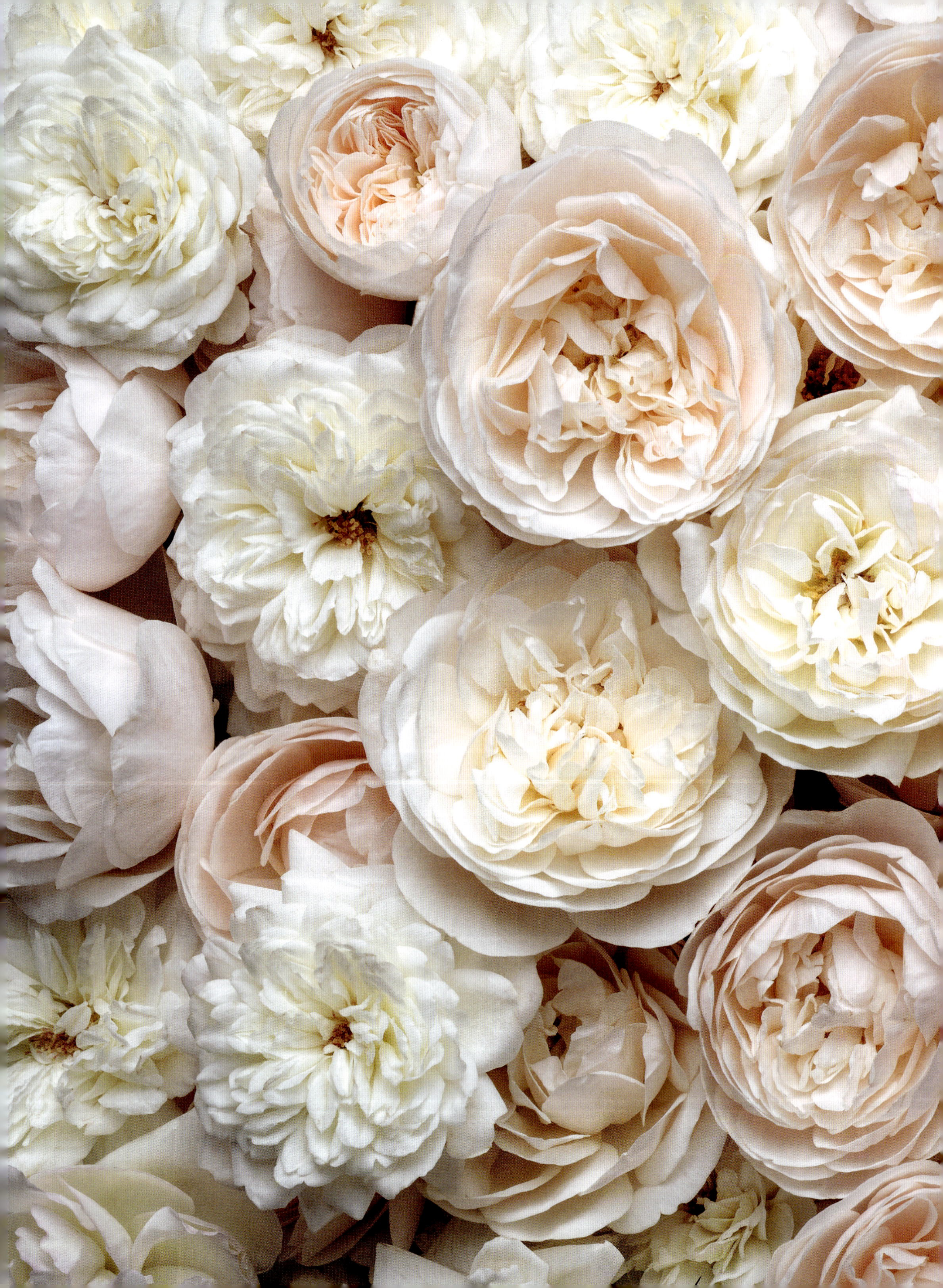

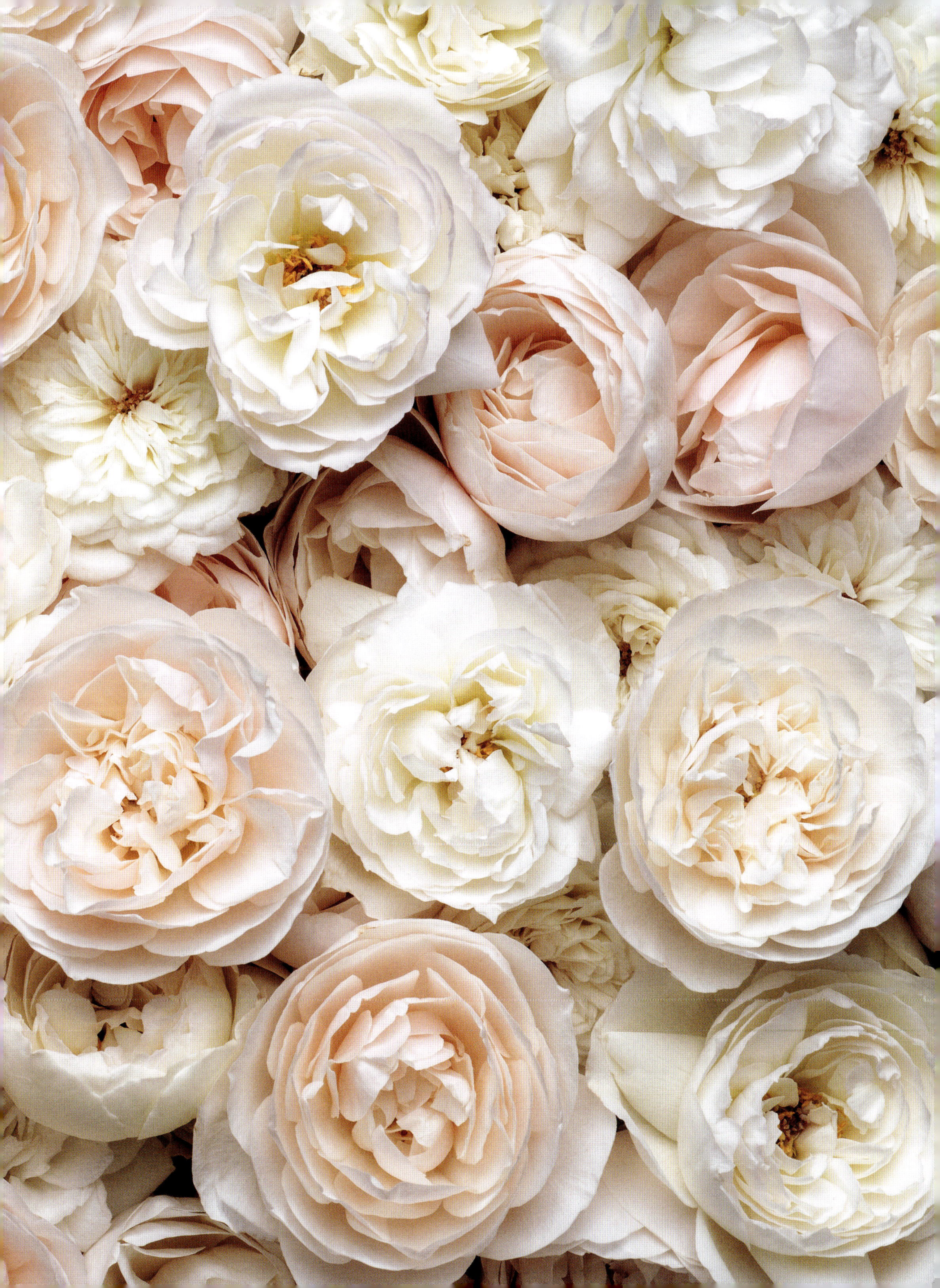

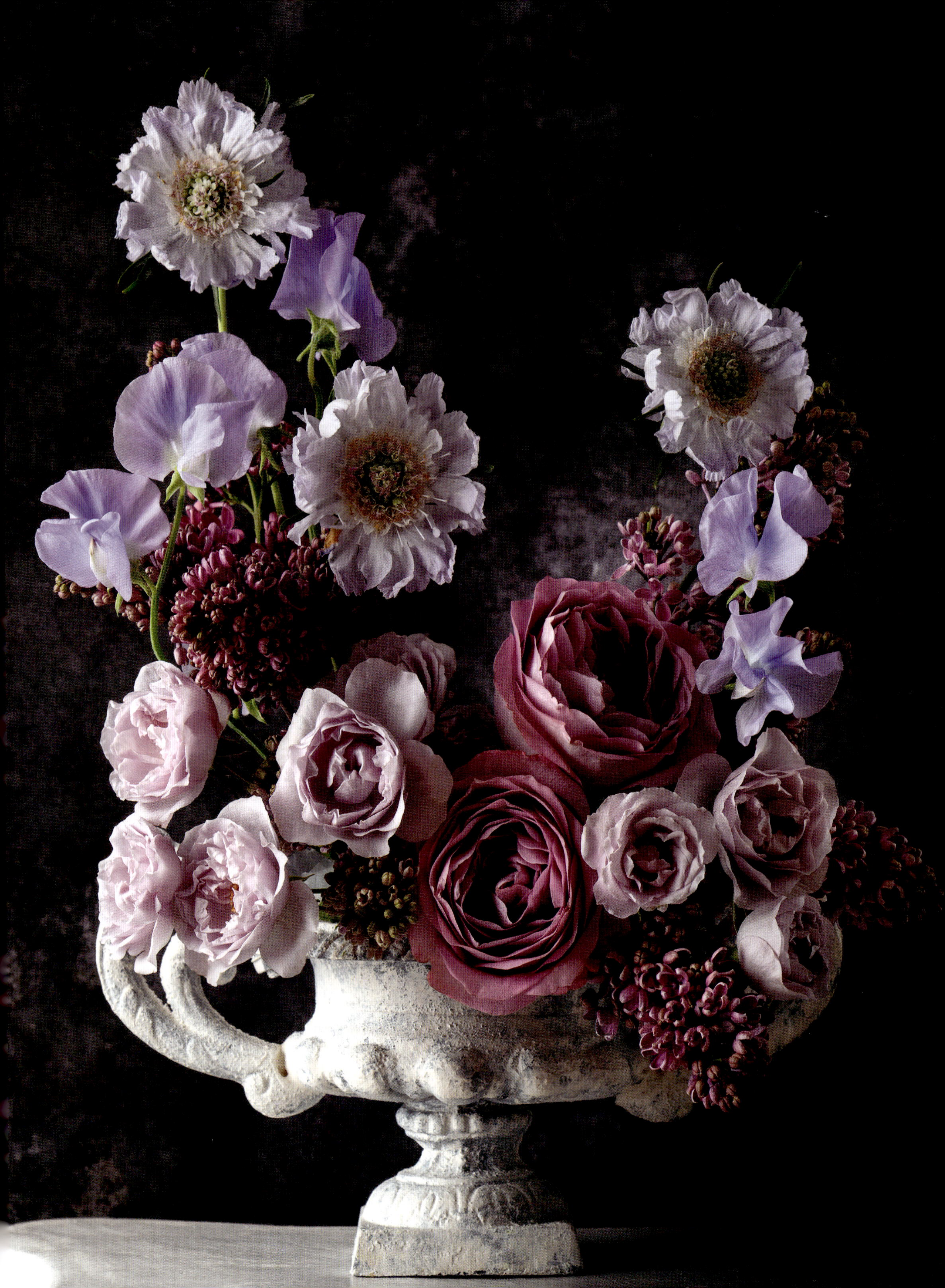

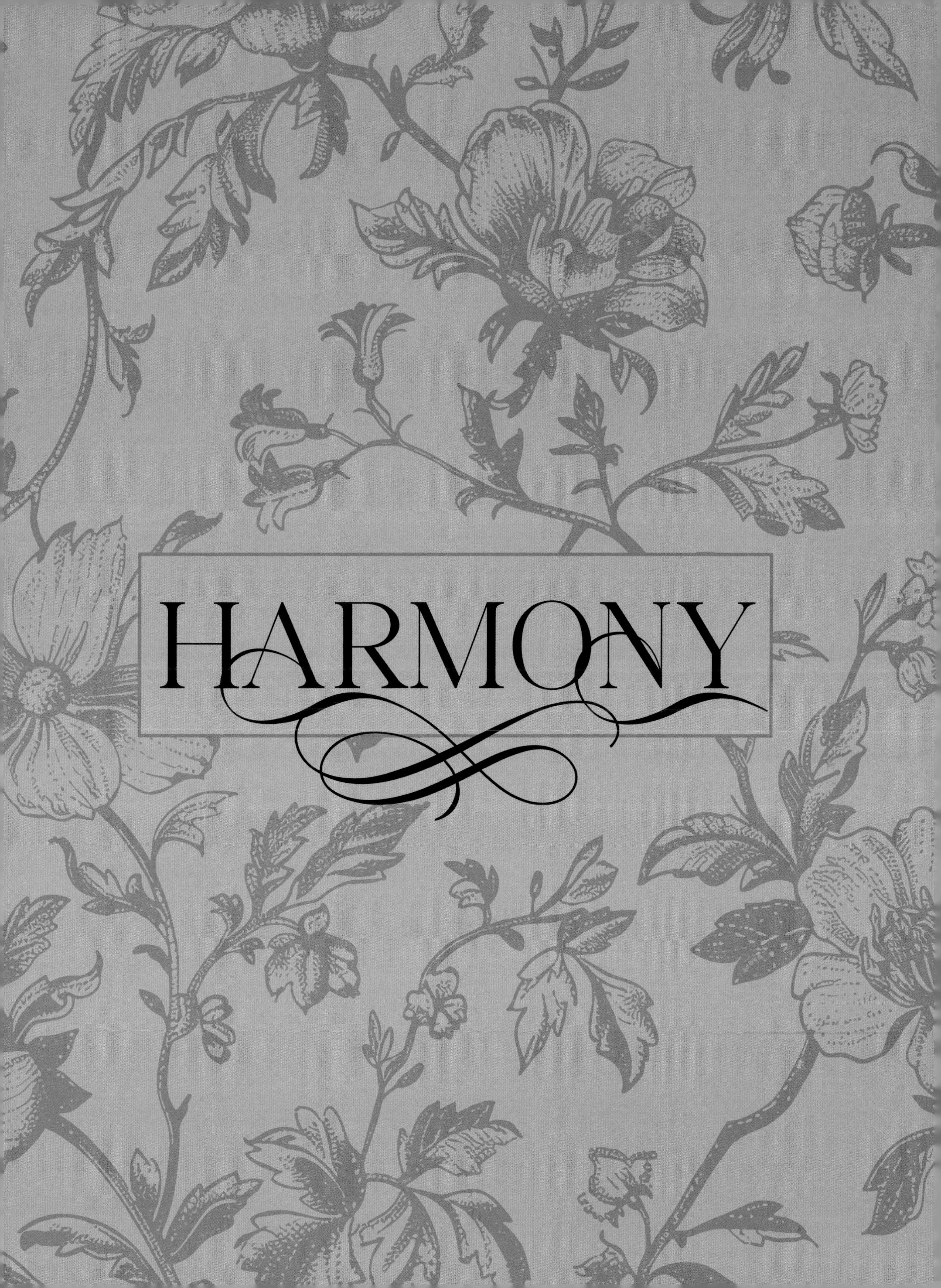

HARMONY

Harmony:

Coherence, compatibility, empathy, affinity; in agreement or accord, balance, symmetry, unity.

The contemplations of *Reverie* progress naturally to a greater understanding of *Harmony*, the observation of elements that align, that are in tune, that fit together like notes within a musical chord.

In the opening images here, the roses, sweet peas, scabiosa, lilacs and *Campanula* – in purple, mauve and gold – are complementary on the color wheel, demonstrating that harmony can be a pleasing contrast of opposites.

The influence of the natural world leads one to notice coincidences or serendipitous happenstance. The singular blue of the Himalayan blue poppy, a species valued for its rarity, is uncannily similar to that of a common bluebell, which spreads freely across huge swathes of countryside.

The distinctive speckles on a Kuchibeni lily closely resemble those inside the bell-shaped flowers of foxglove, which are designed to alert pollinators where to alight.

A lone, stray yellow tulip in the Skagit Valley, Washington, resides quite companionably in a field of purples, no matter what accident of fate brought them together.

The veining of the pollen-dusted purple *Trillium* and rain-soaked iris petals echo each other not only in color and texture, but in mood and message.

A strategic benefit of living in Europe is proximity to important garden and botanical destinations vital to my work. Within a few hours I can be on location in the UK, the Netherlands, Italy, Belgium and, of course, my adopted home country of France.

For my book *Daffodils*, I traveled north of Amsterdam to a beautiful farm, Flying Colors Daffodils, owned by a most enthusiastic and kind person. As well as being a dedicated daffodil breeder, Michiel de Waard is a commercial pilot who uniquely shares aerial views of his own golden fields as the jet he is flying takes off from Schiphol airport – a delightful convergence of his two careers. Michiel gave me full access to his immaculate fields, where I gathered pristine blooms for the

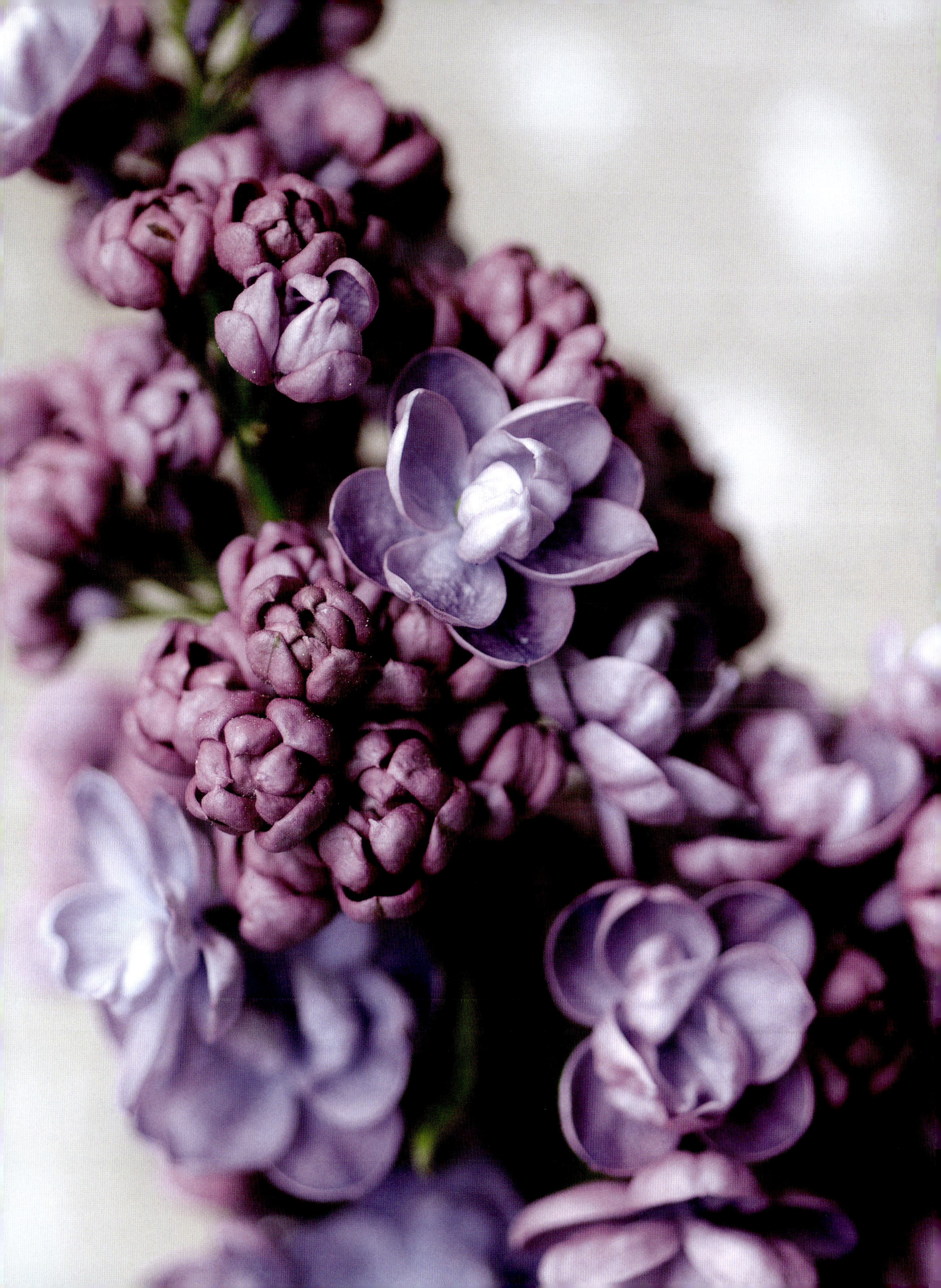

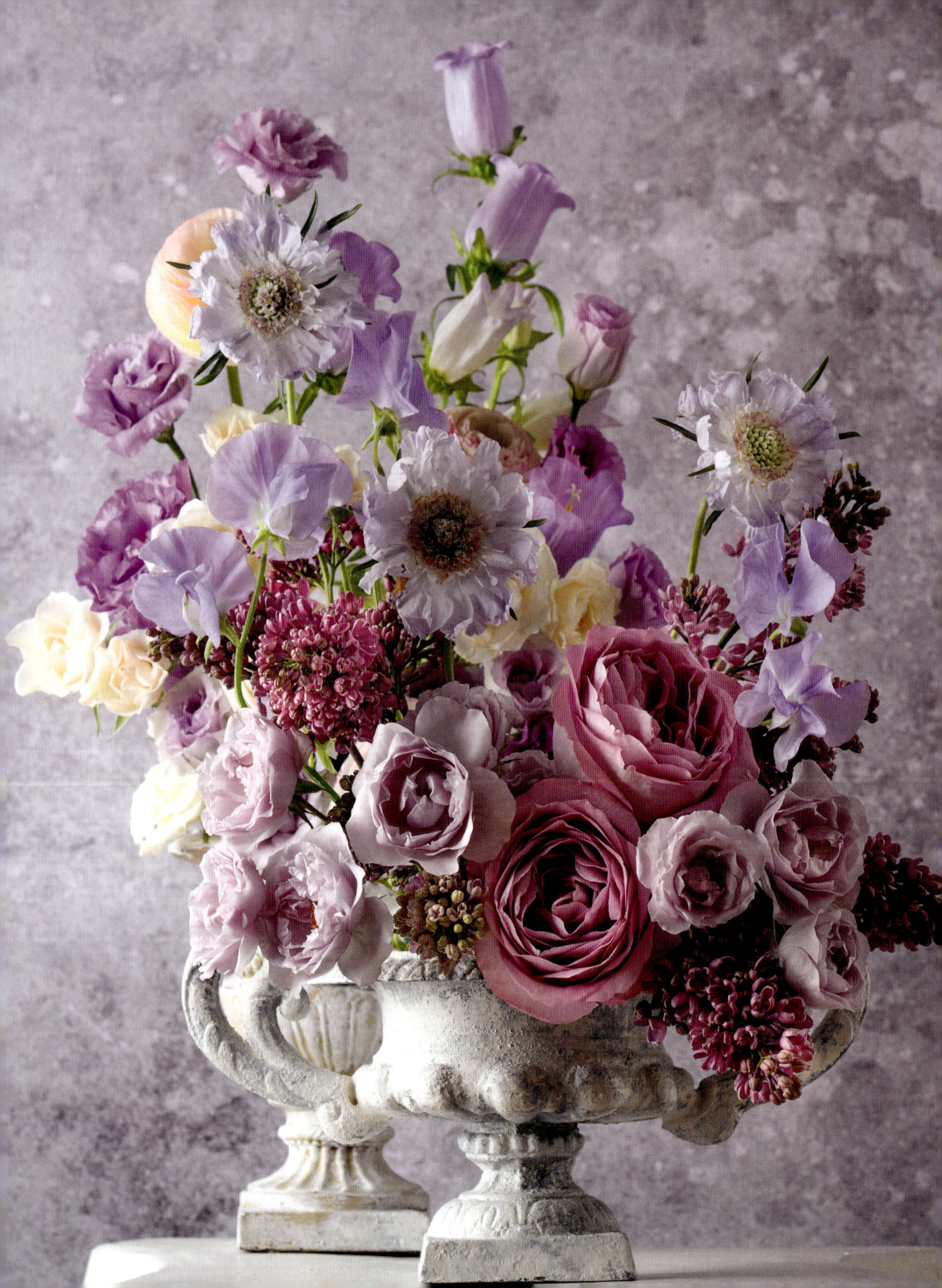

book cover and interior pages. He then helped me load the precious cargo into my rental car and I drove carefully back to Amsterdam, where I photographed them in the historic seventeenth-century canal house home of my dear friend Natasja Sadi. Within an hour of arriving there, a massive squall tore through the region, decimating many of the area's flower fields. As it raged, I safely captured the flowers in Natasja's beautiful studio. As with so many of my location shoots, timing proved critical. I am ever mindful of the vagaries of weather and, hence, continually monitor meteorological reports and have become an amateur forecaster myself. The image of monochromatic *Narcissus* did not appear in *Daffodils* but happily makes its debut here.

In my book *Hydrangeas,* I included many of our much-loved varieties. What a great privilege it is to grow in one's own garden an absolute jewel of nature, admiringly sheltering and protecting its fleeting beauty. Whatever hydrangeas lack in fragrance, they more than compensate for with exquisitely-formed petals, heavenly shades and the way they soften the contours of a garden.

In *Hydrangeas,* I was also able to include an internationally notable location. A scenic train ride from Paris brought me to the pretty seaport and harbor of Dieppe, in Normandy. From there, I took the short drive to Jardin Shamrock, home of the French National Collection of Hydrangeas.

Dedicated to the preservation and understanding of *Hortensia*, Shamrock attracts gardening enthusiasts, botanists and horticulturists from all over the world.

Founded by Corinne Mallet in 1984, and designated a 'Jardin Remarkable', Shamrock is acknowledged as the world's premier hydrangea collection, with over 1,500 varieties on two hectares. It was a great pleasure and privilege to meet with her husband, Robert Mallet, who generously took the time to tour me around the garden, sharing his vast expertise and passion.

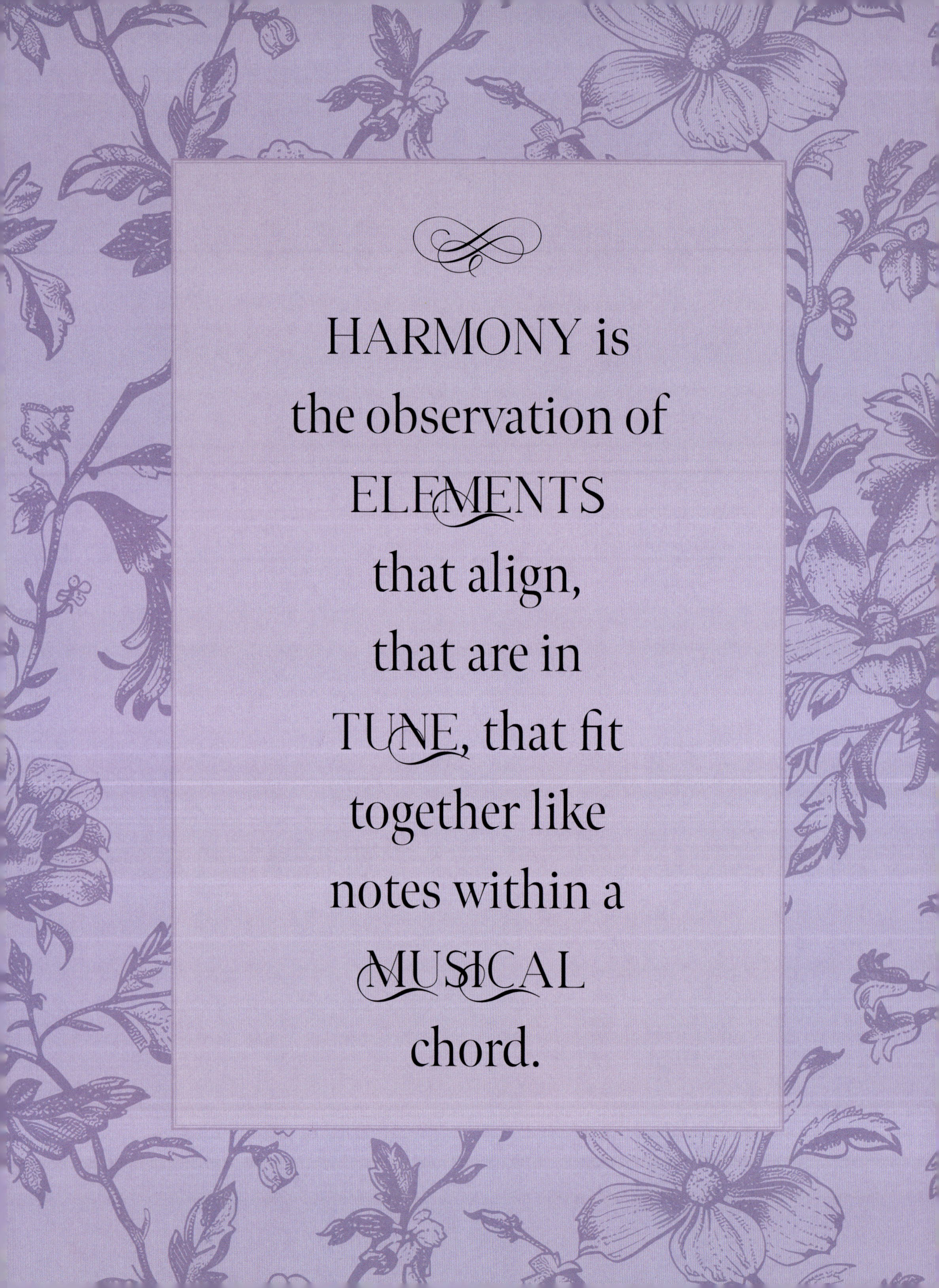
HARMONY is
the observation of
ELEMENTS
that align,
that are in
TUNE, that fit
together like
notes within a
MUSICAL
chord.

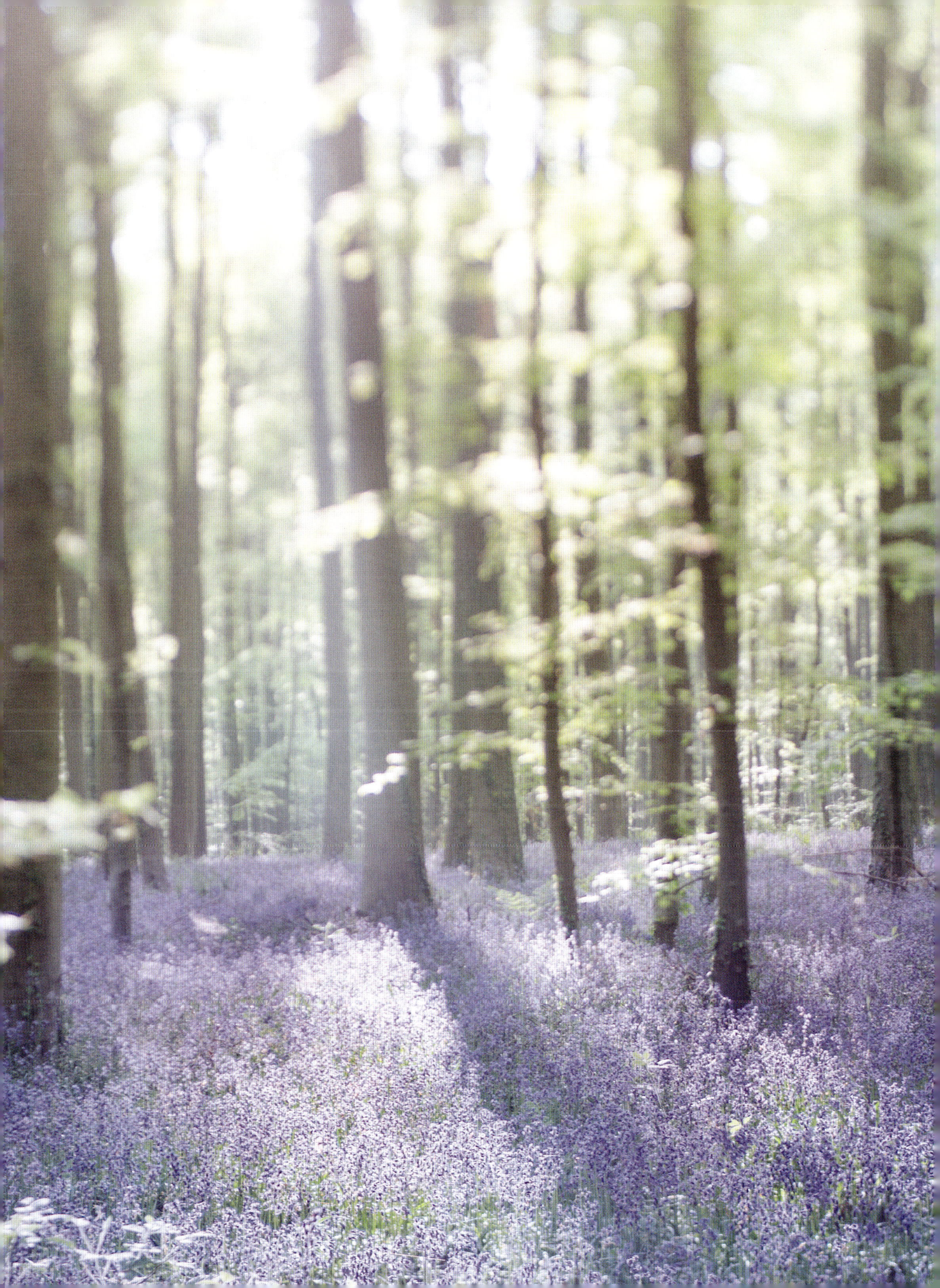

We strolled for some hours, inspecting each meticulously cared-for and labeled plant. Photographing the garden was a significant honor and I was very lucky to visit on two occasions, once when the hydrangeas were at their summer peak, and a few months later as autumn's coolness had subdued the bright blues and pinks to shades of faded teal and mauve.

Each visit ended with a congenial French country lunch in excellent company, a reminder of how felicitous it is to undertake these floral adventures amongst such purposeful and generous people.

We close with nostalgic lilacs. As with hydrangeas, they inhabit the cooler end of the color spectrum, and in such a narrow range that an array of every variety known would visually create a harmonious whole without a single discordant or clashing note.

RIGHT: *Iris versicolor,* Flag iris. June 2008.

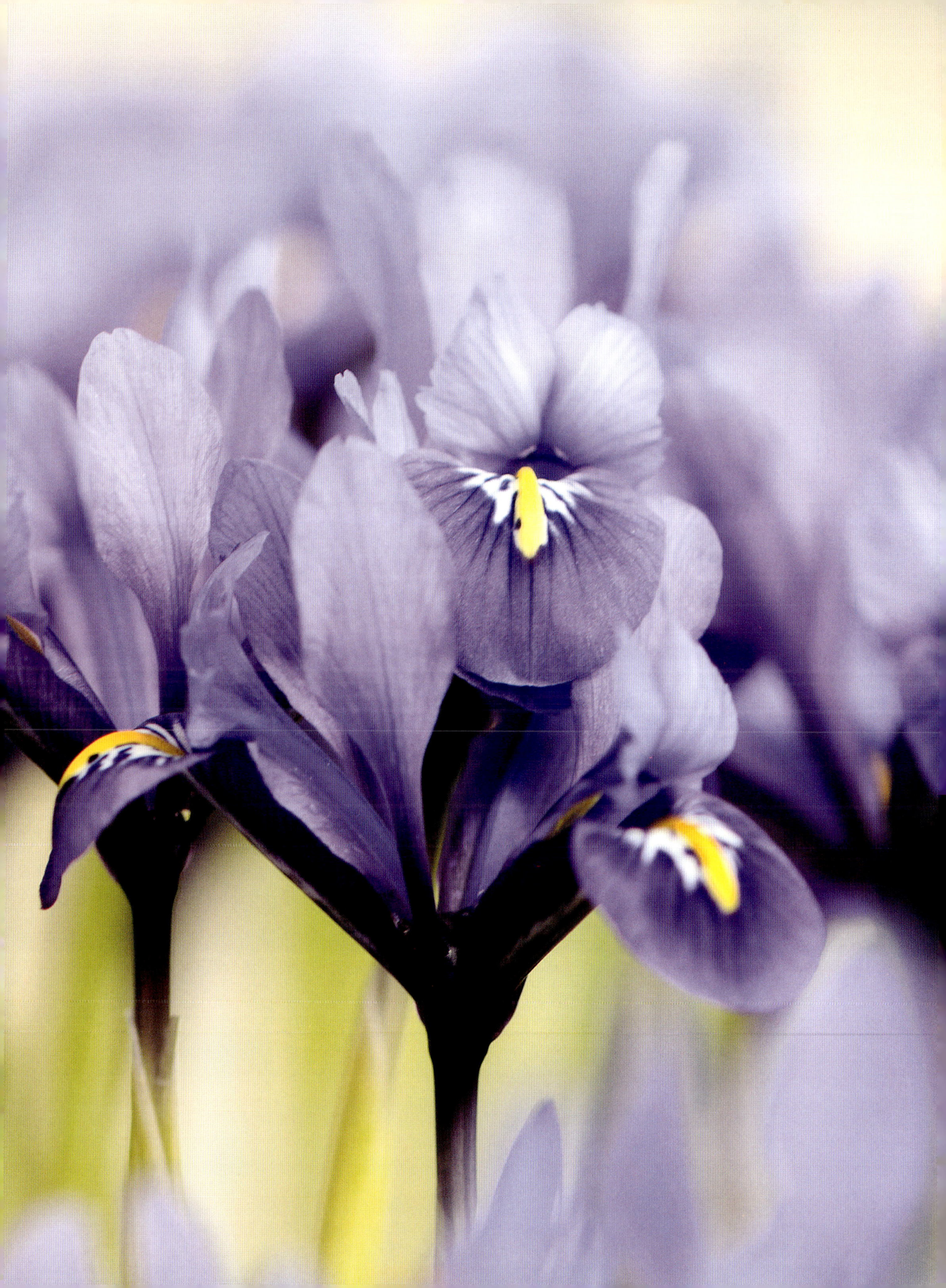

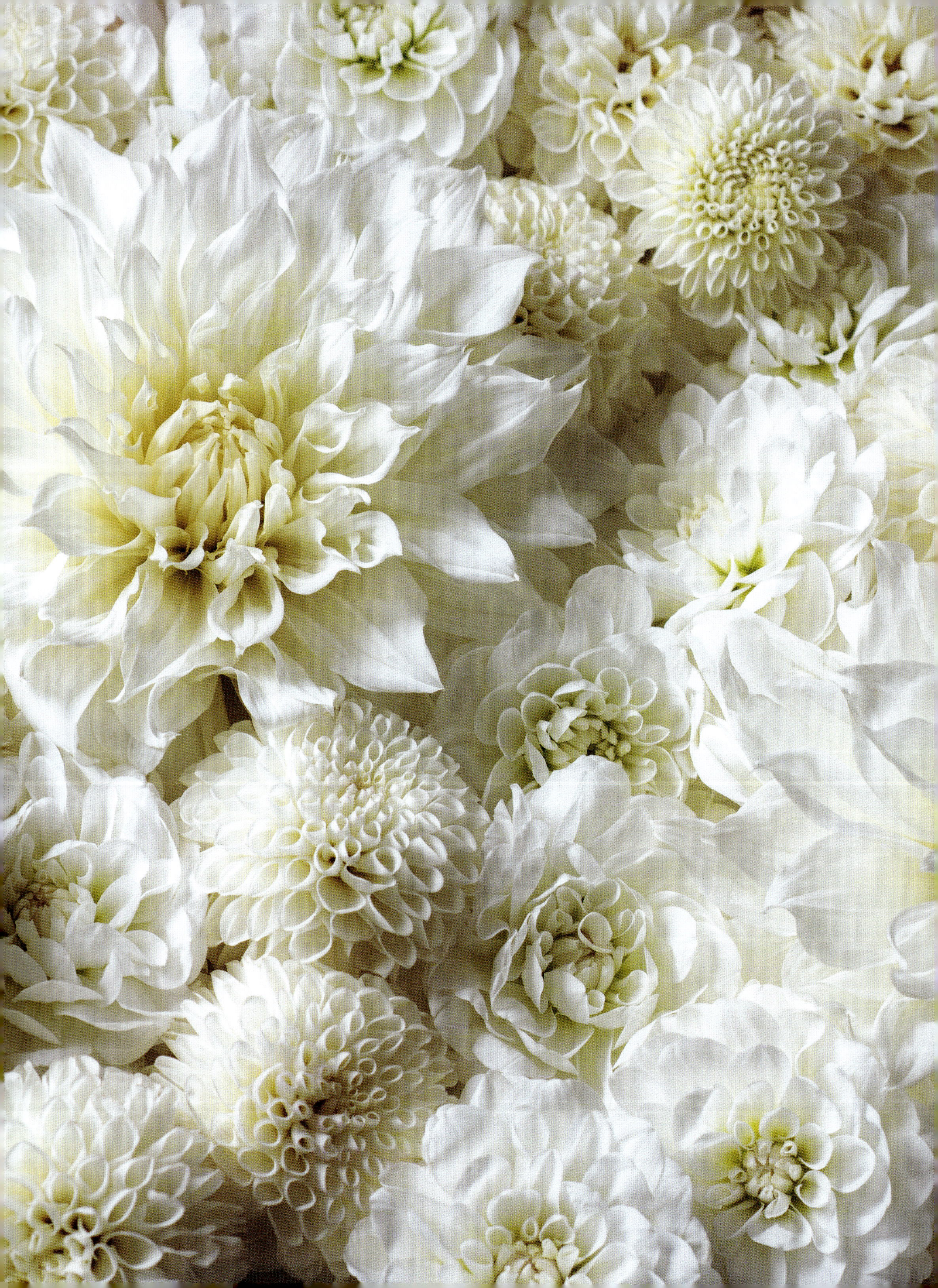

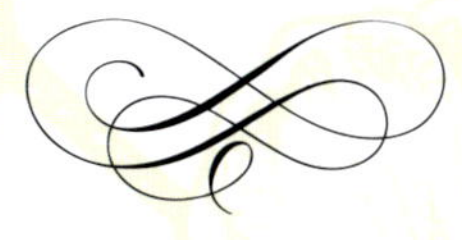

HARMONY OF SHAPE AND SHADE

When working with many varieties of flowers, I look for connections and relationships that suggest how best to weave their stories together. Such alignments result in a more visually satisfying image – distinct, but still open to a viewer's interpretation.

The moonlit tones of these creamy dahlias and their pillowy shapes – all individual but very much belonging together – made me think of a pastoral hideaway where fairy Queen Titania might repose in cushiony comfort, in between nocturnal mischiefing and cases of mistaken identity. A leap of imagination?

Perhaps. But Titania's tale very much involves the (mostly humorous) disruption, and ultimate restoration, of the order and harmony of the natural world, and mankind's as well. Moonlight revels, indeed.

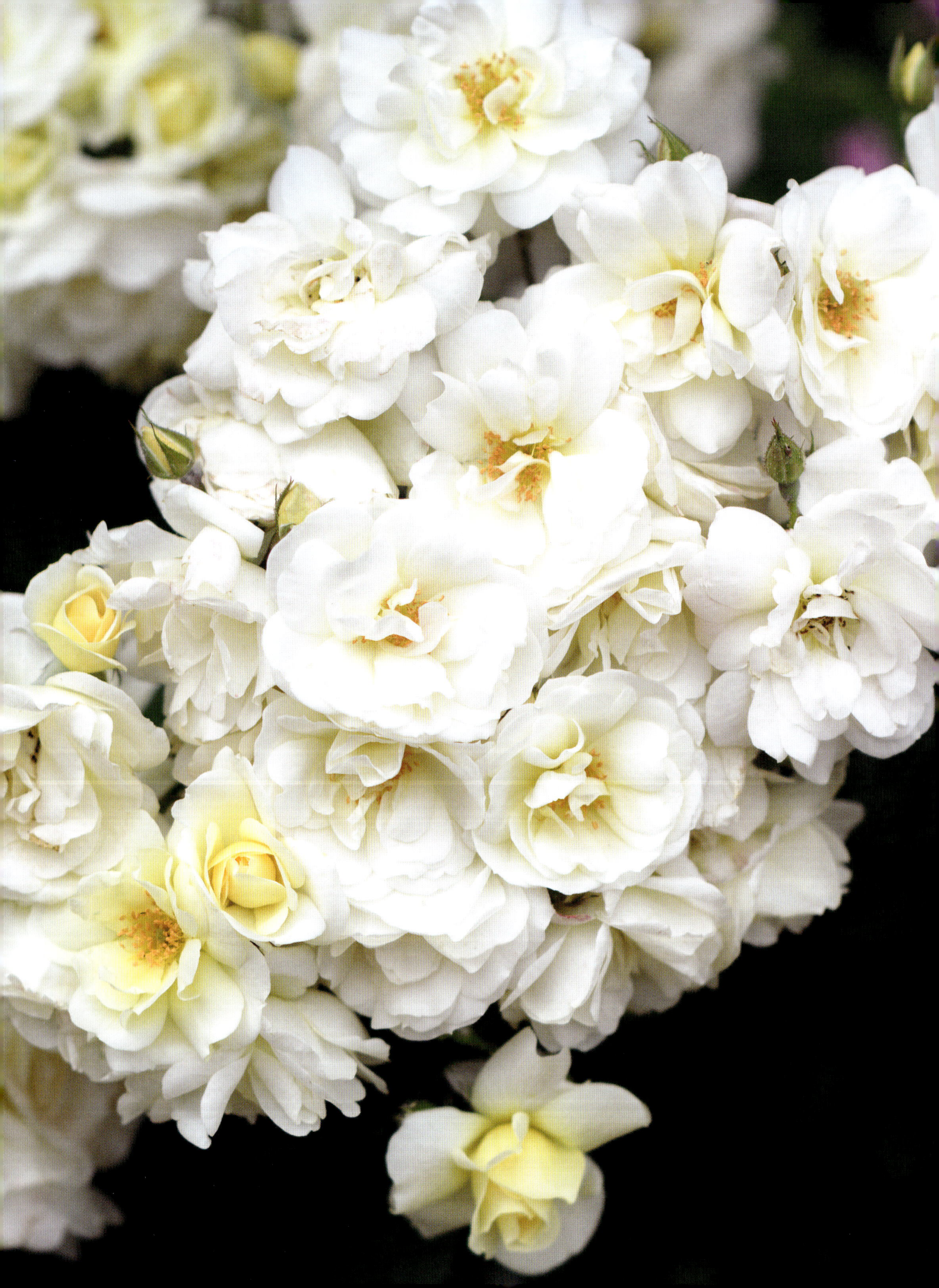

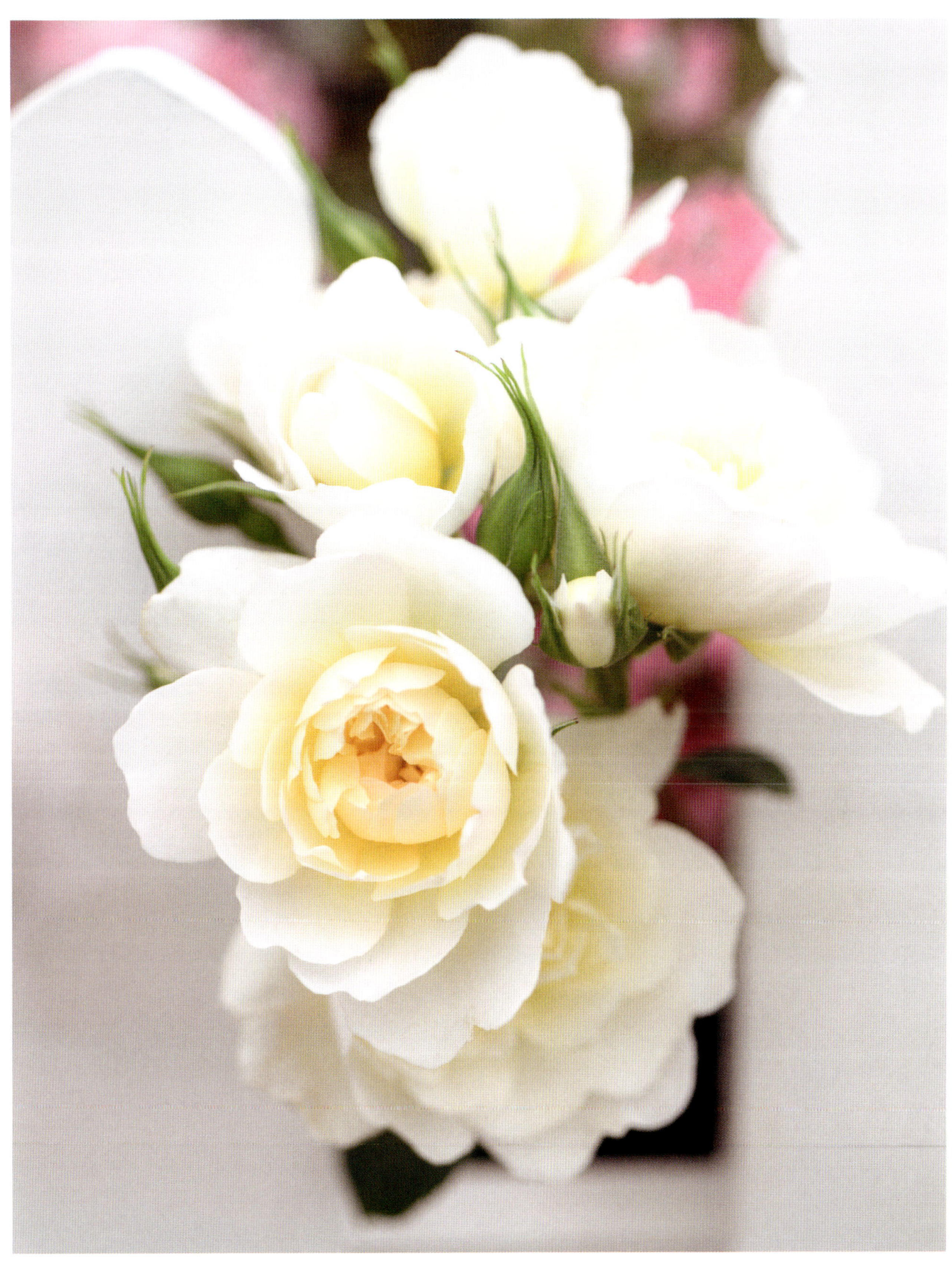

LEFT: White roses, Hyde Park Rose Garden, London, England. May 2018. ABOVE: David Austin white roses, RHS Chelsea Flower Show, London, England. May 2022.

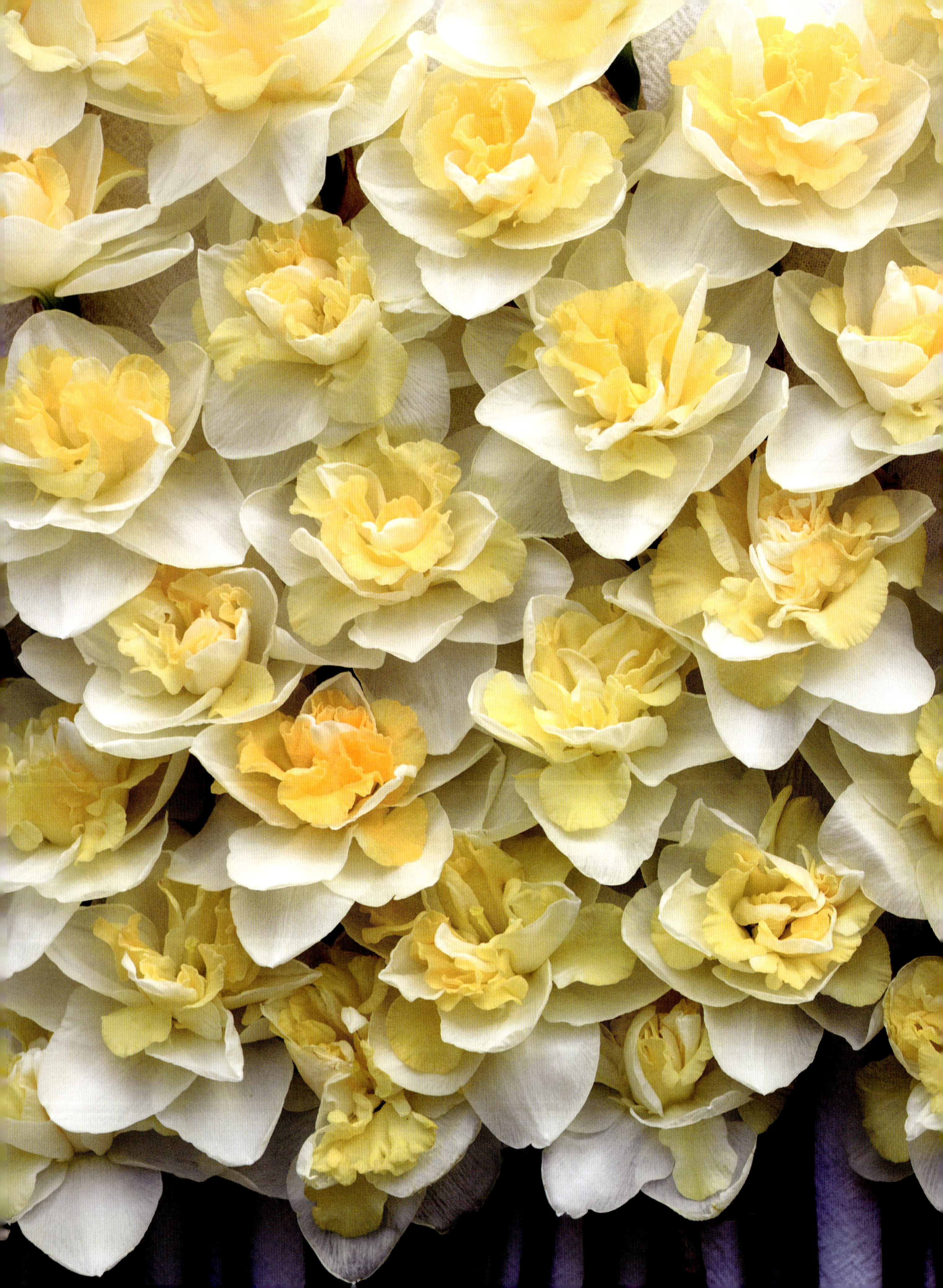

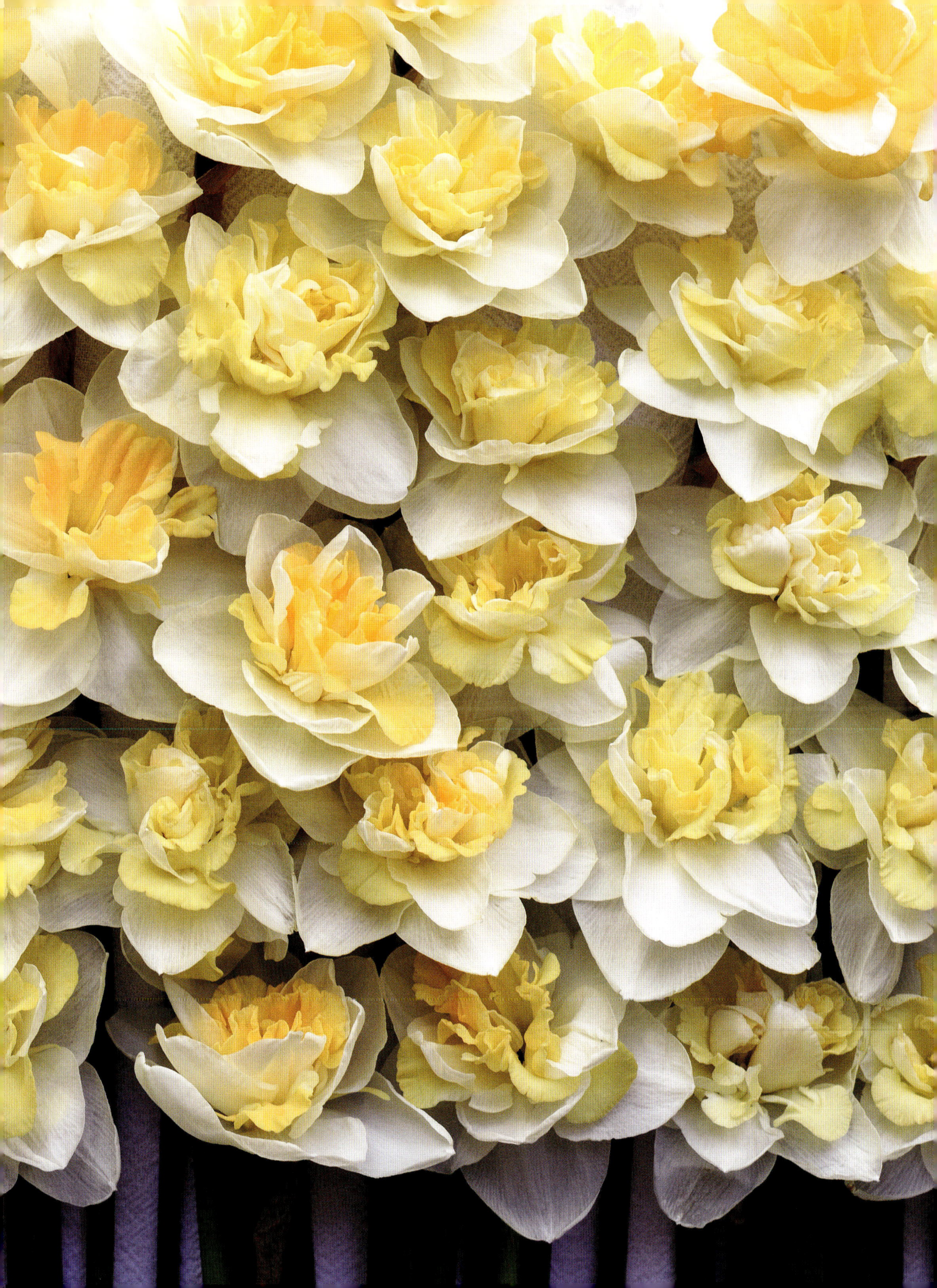

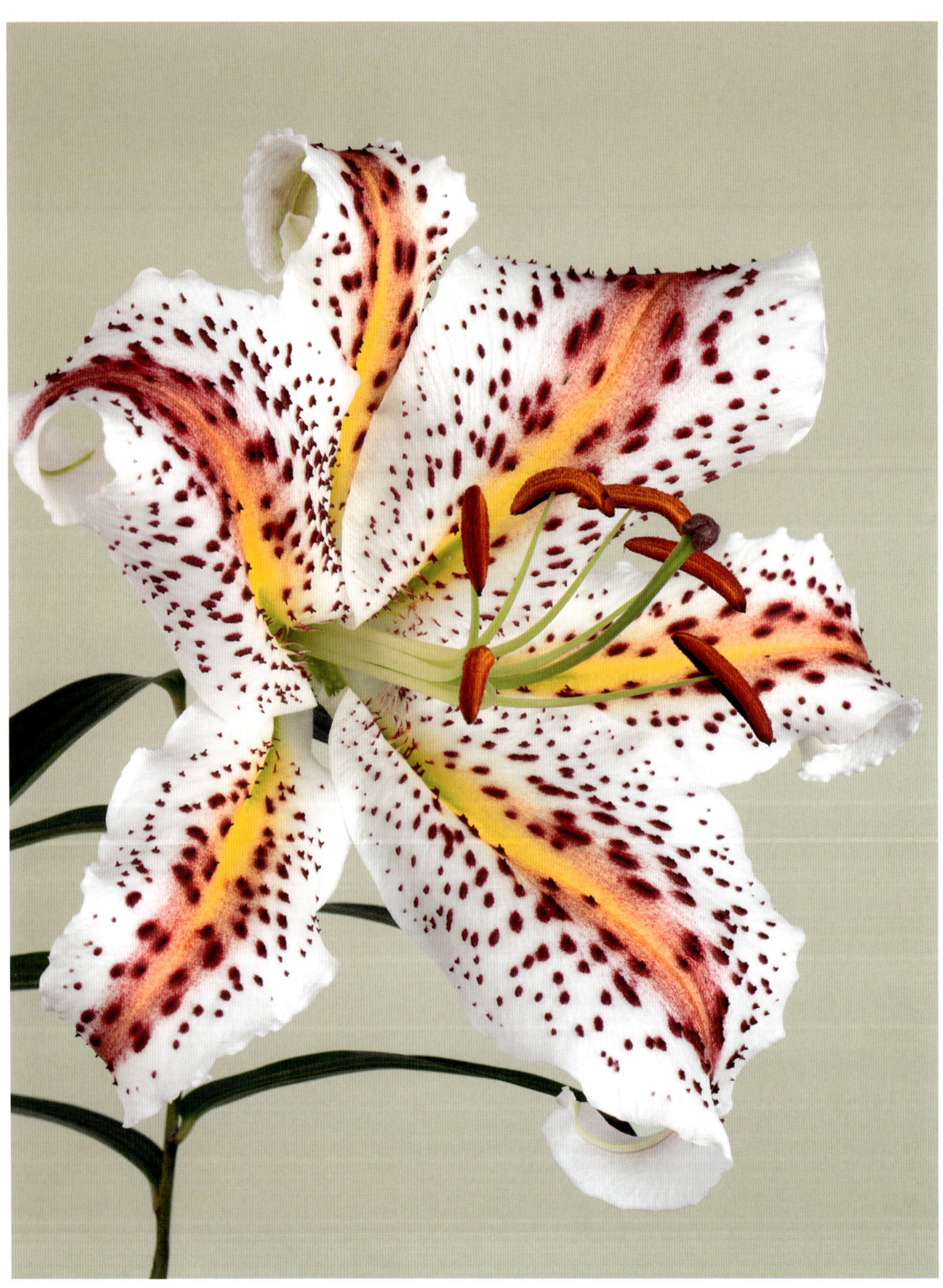

ABOVE: Lily 'Kuchibeni' (*Lilium auratum* 'Kuchibeni'), USA. July 2020. RIGHT: Foxglove (*Digitalis purpurea*), USA. May 2018.

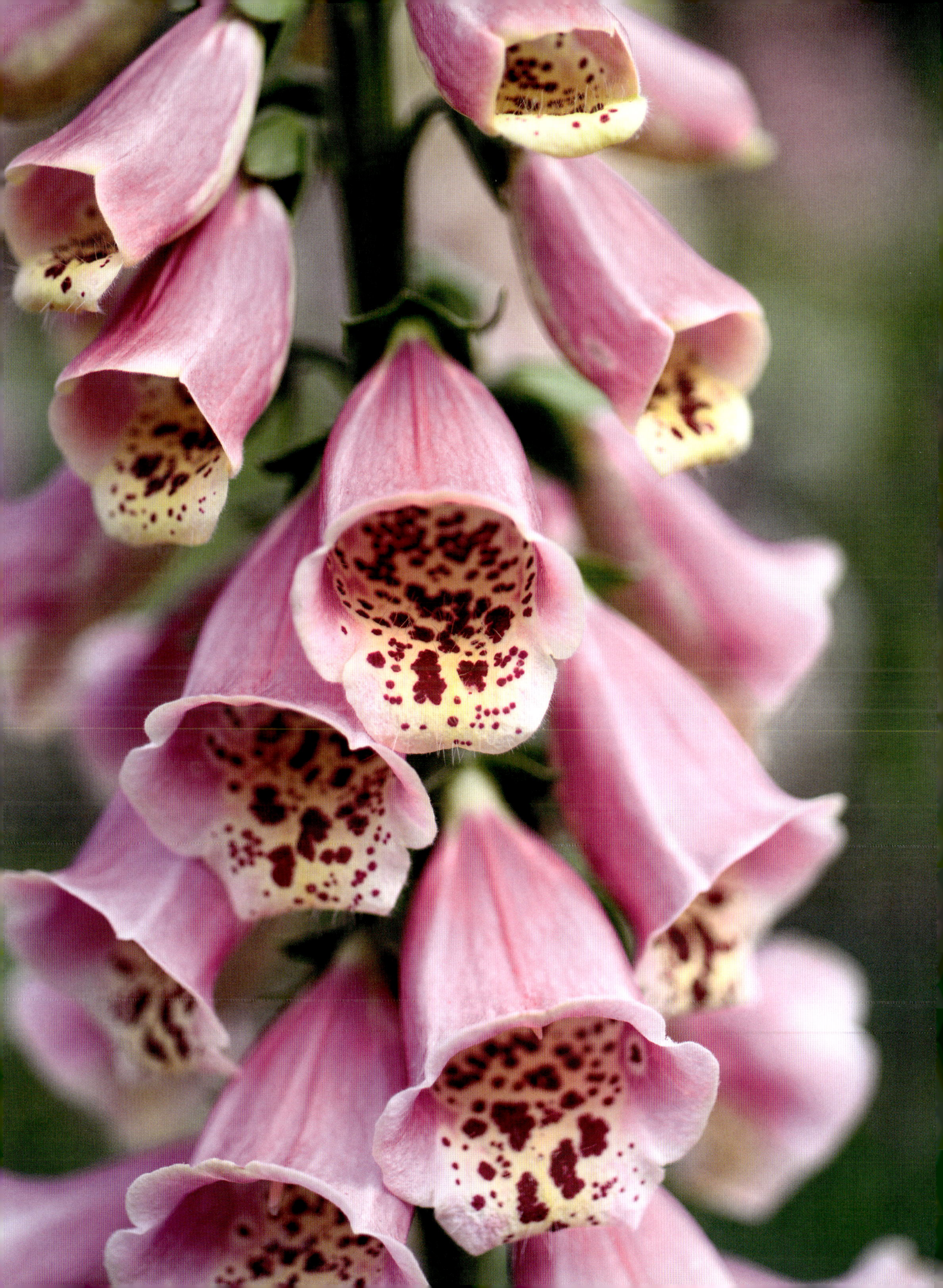

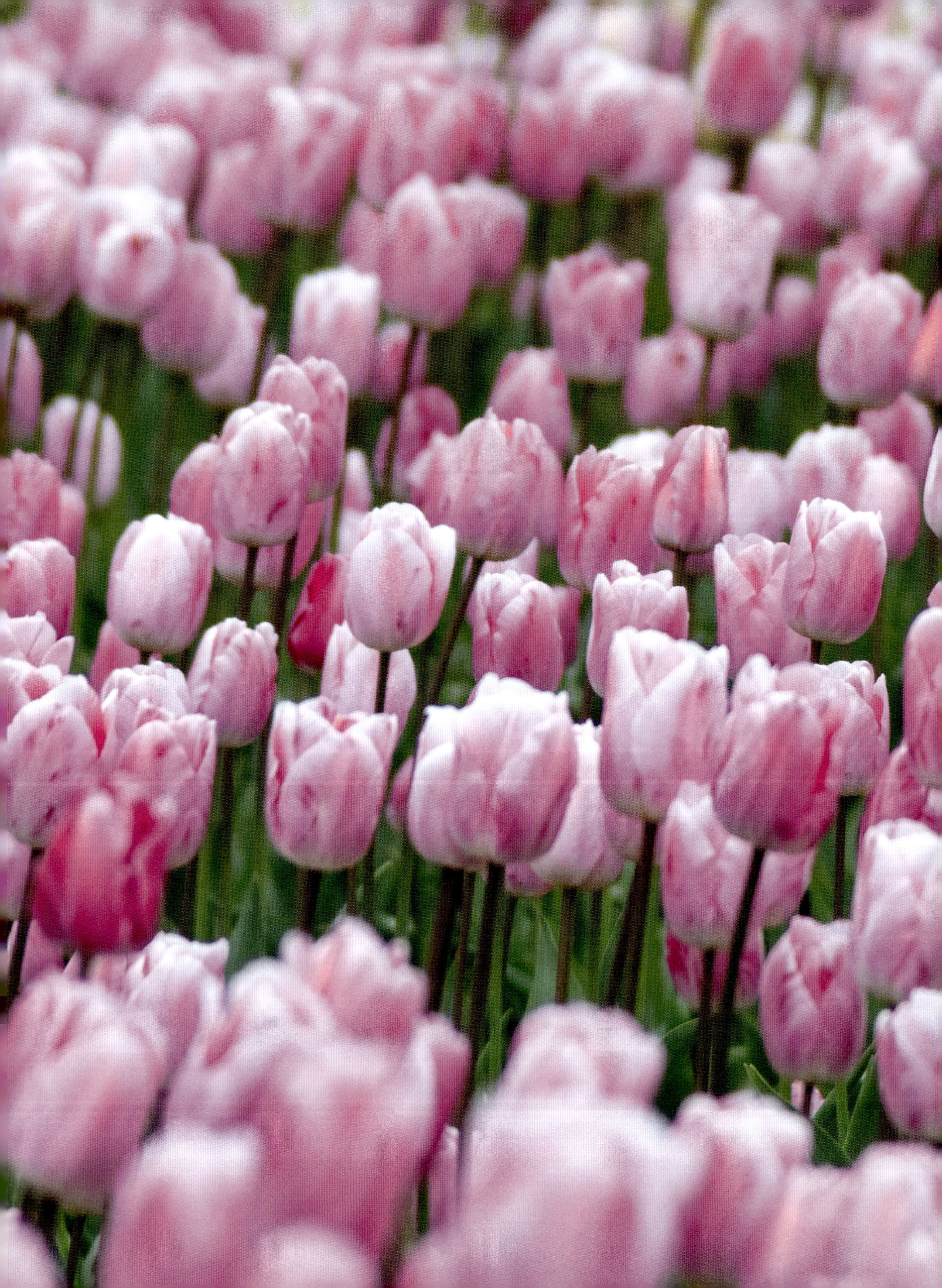

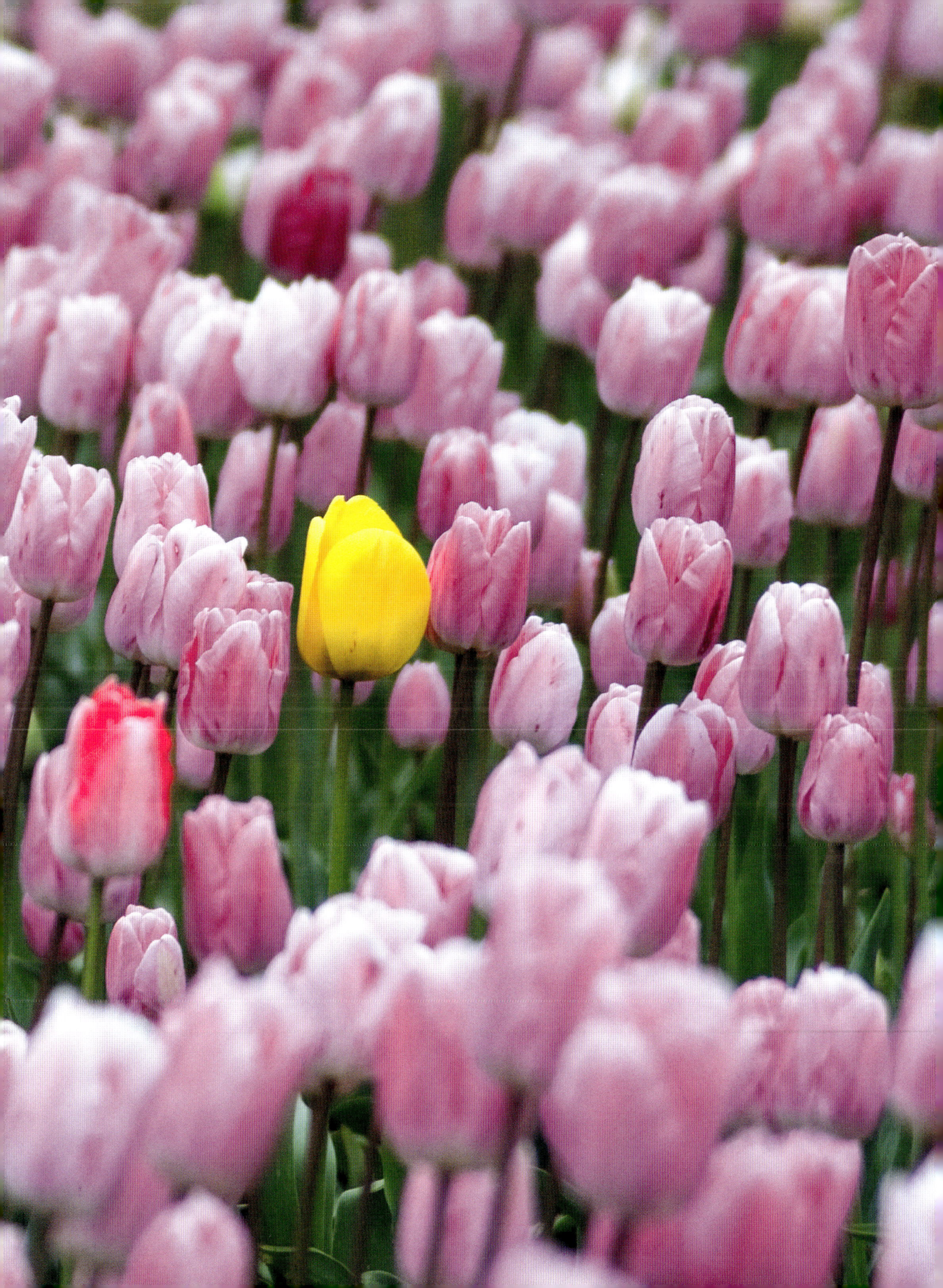

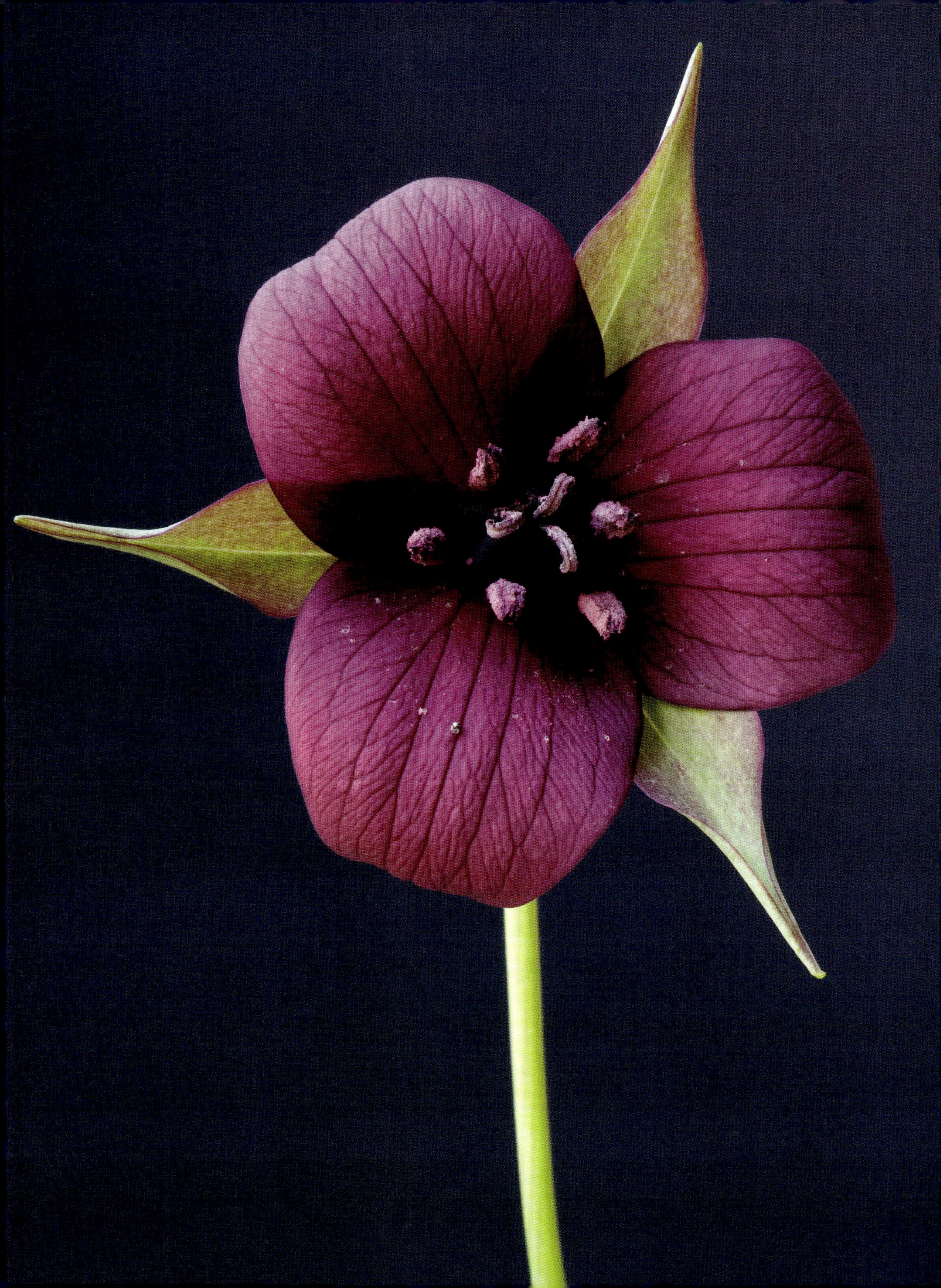

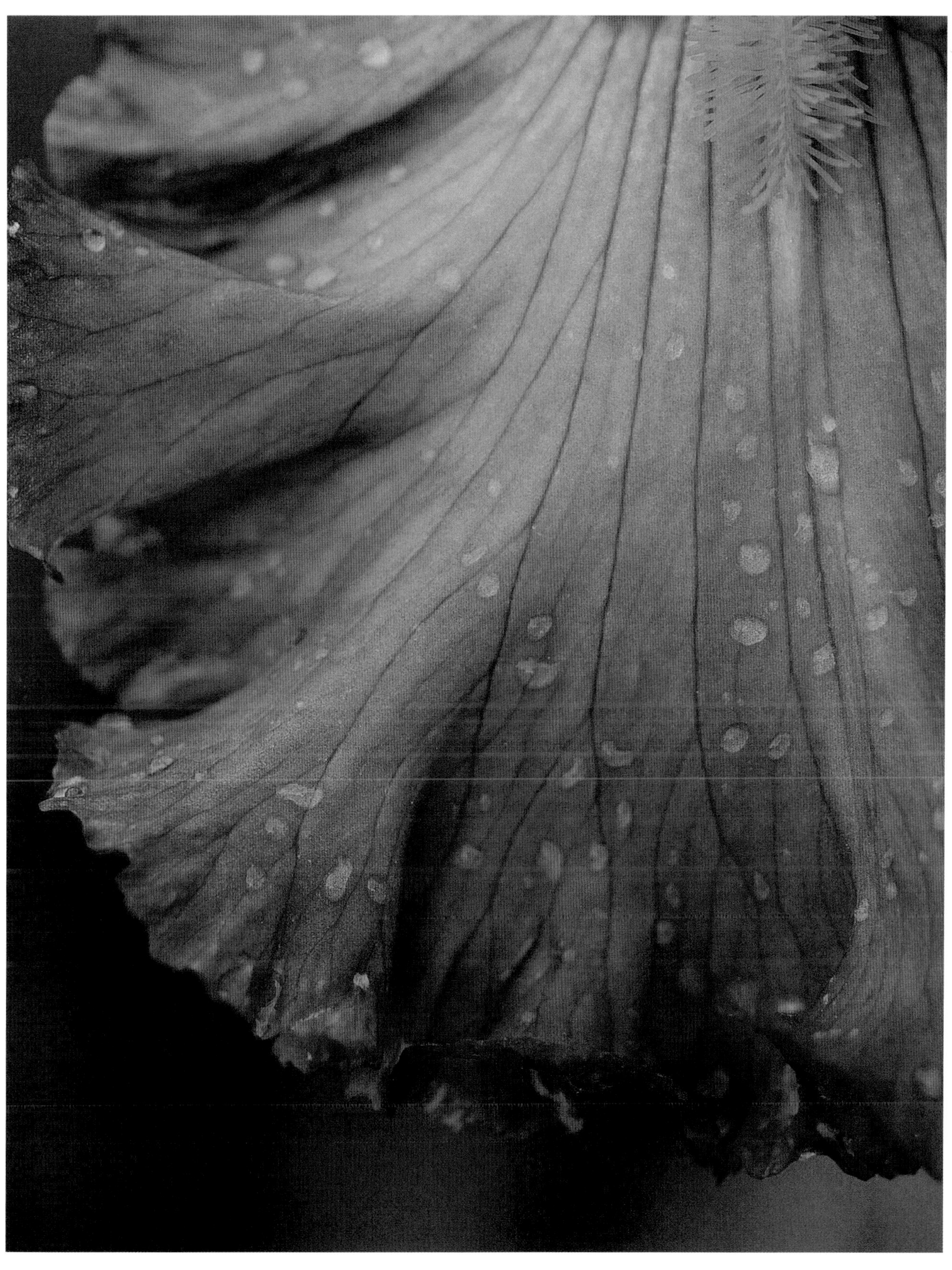

LEFT: Purple *Trillium*, Hillhaven Garden, Shoreline, Washington, USA. May 2009. ABOVE: Petal of *Iris* 'Enchanted Memory', Schreiner's Iris Garden, Salem, Oregon, USA. May 2010.

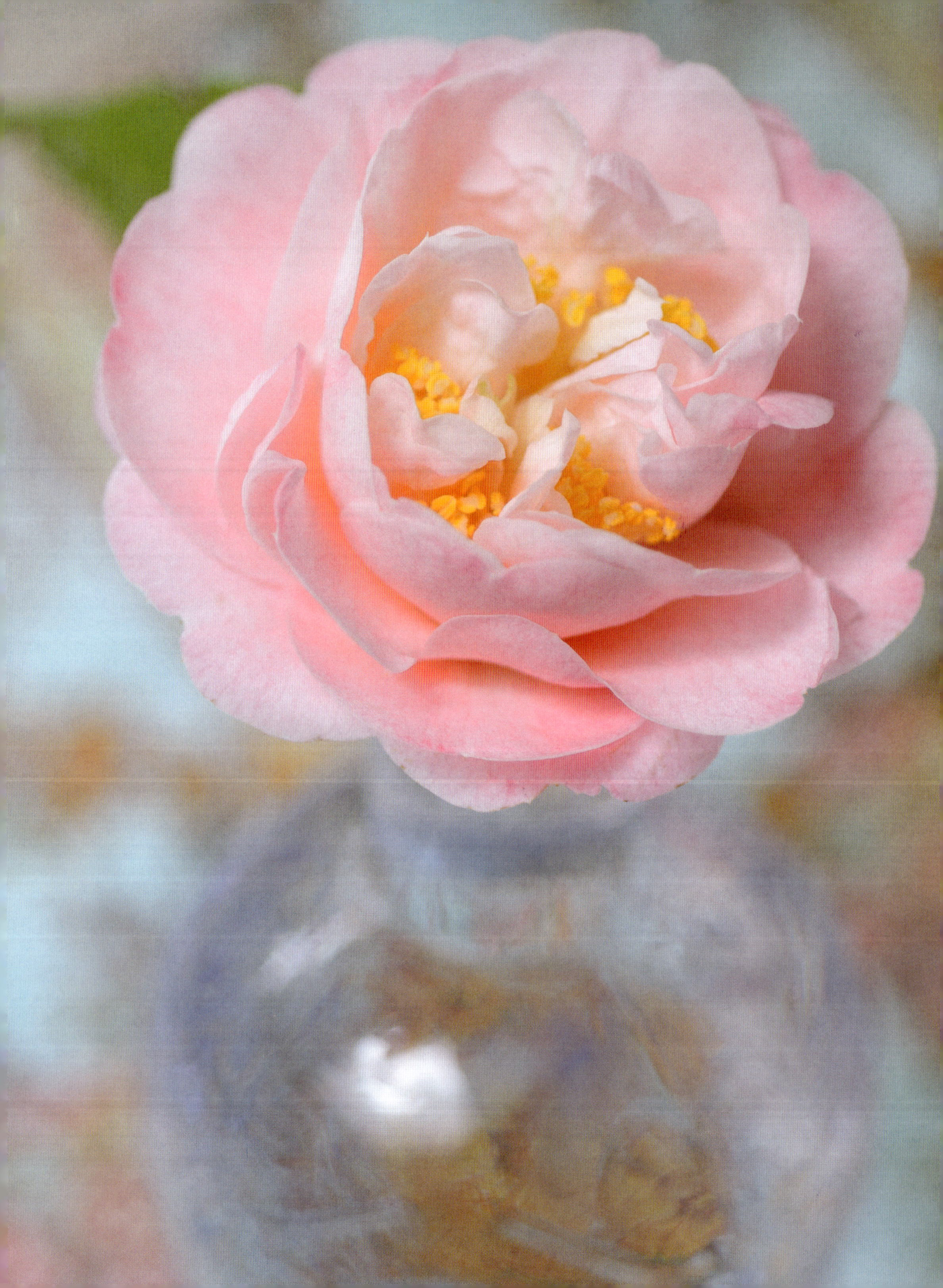

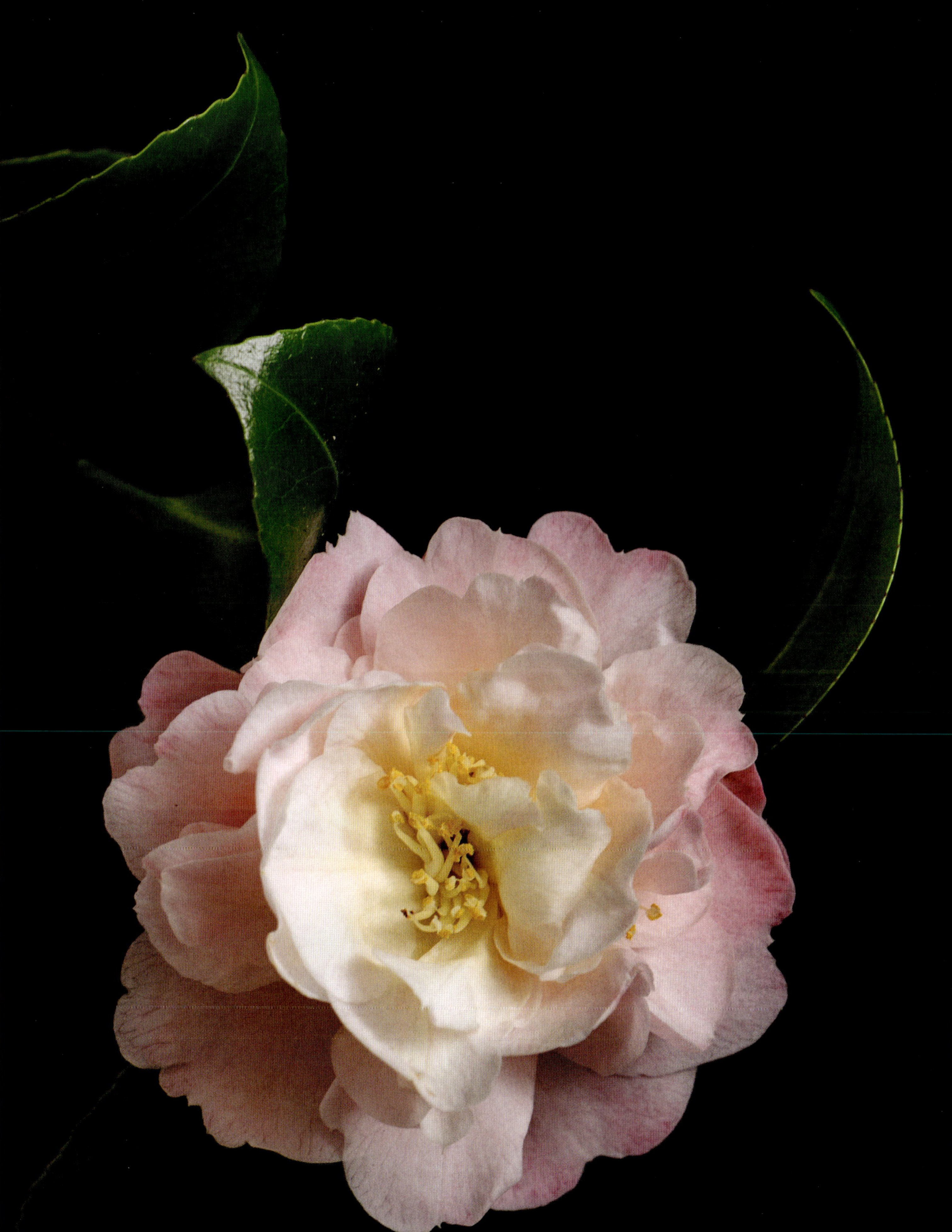

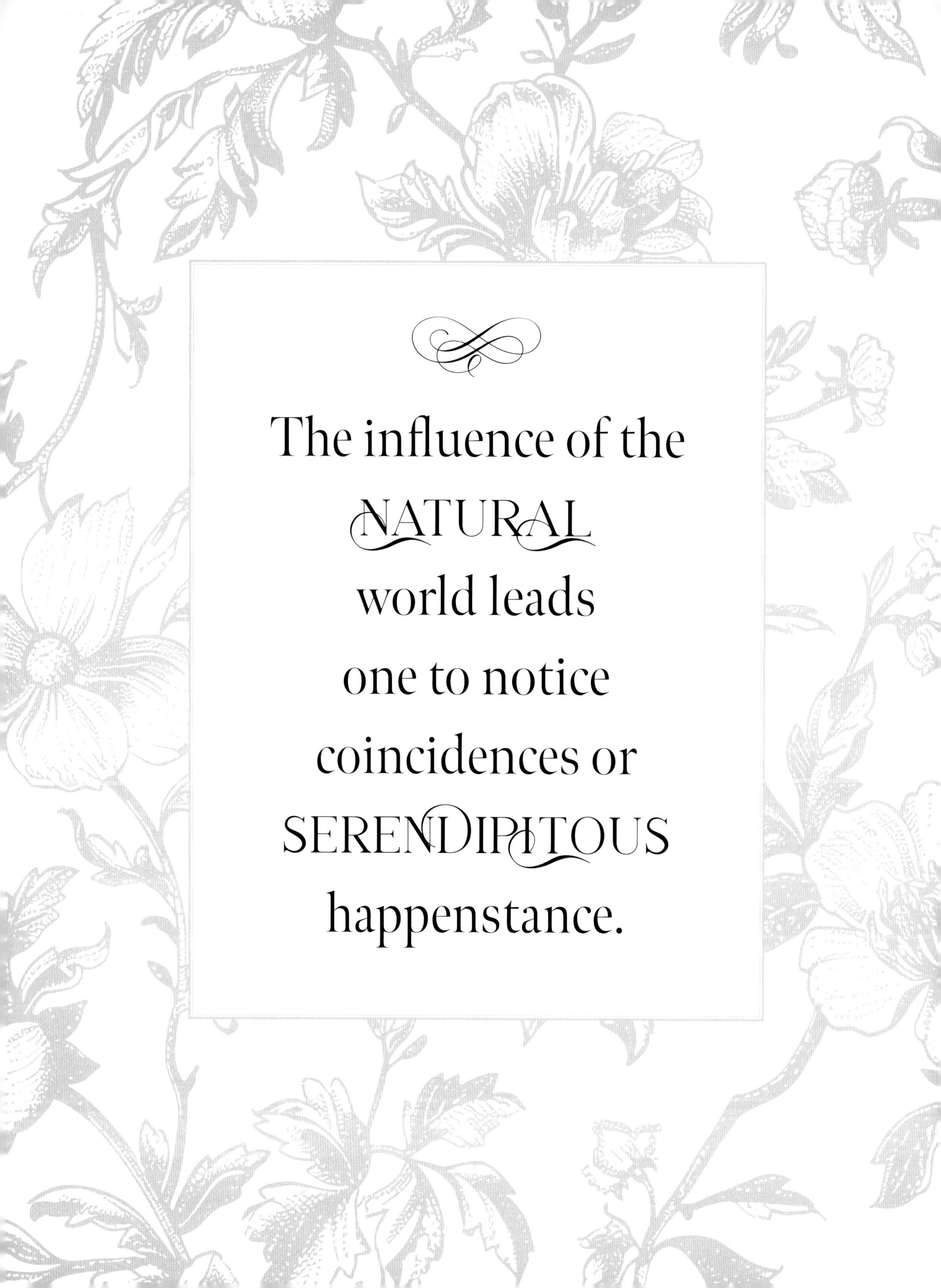

The influence of the NATURAL world leads one to notice coincidences or SERENDIPITOUS happenstance.

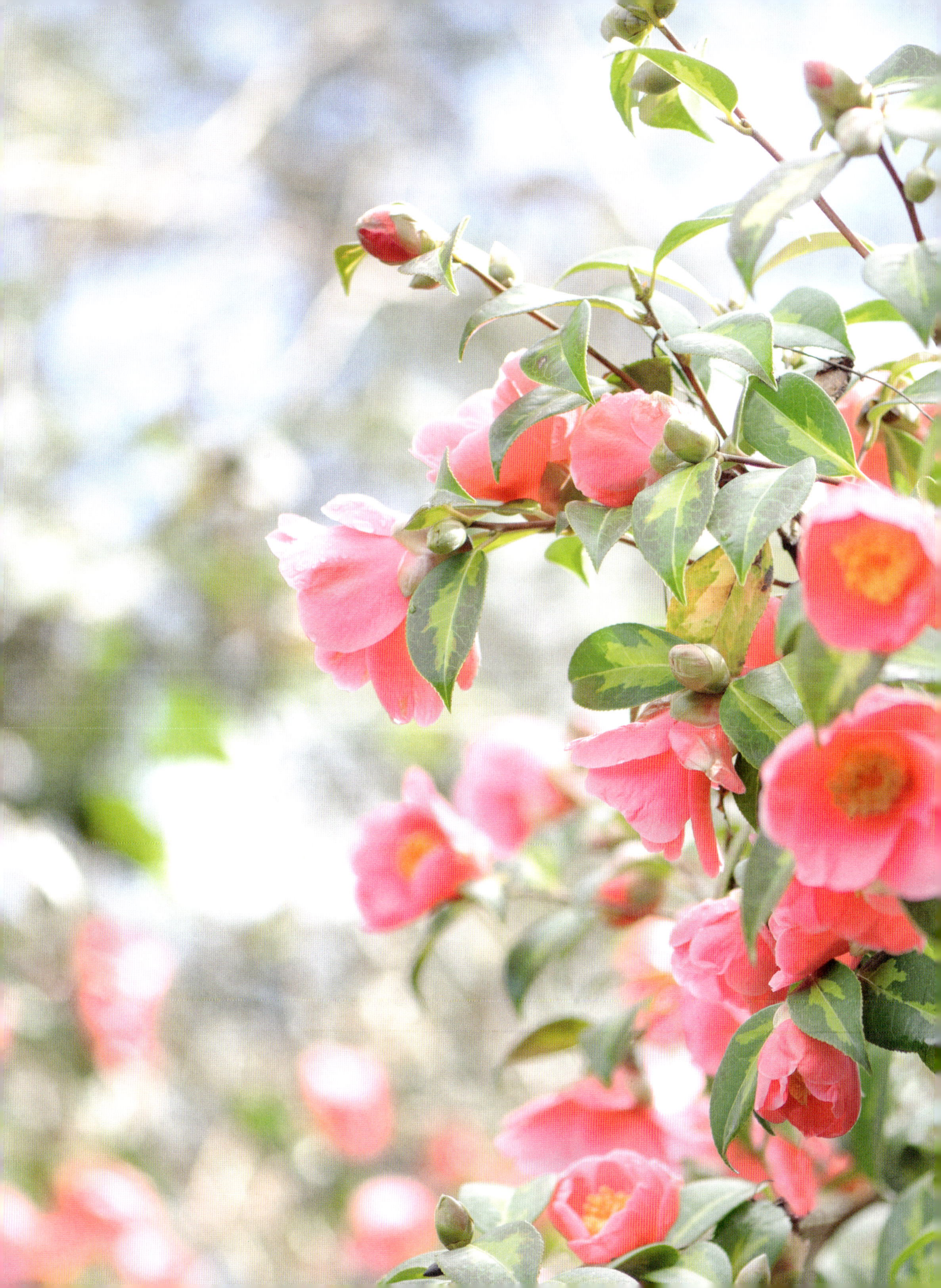

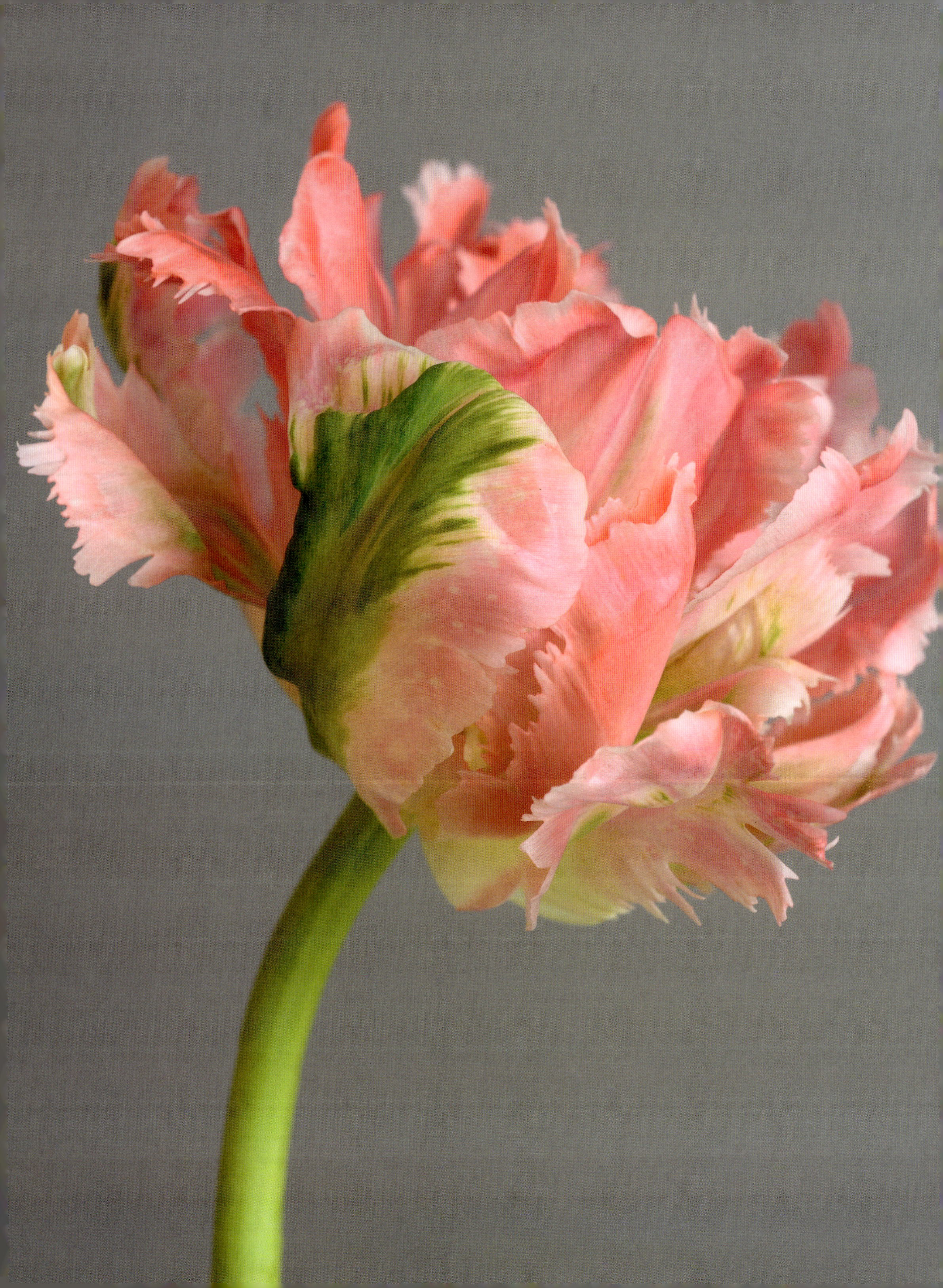

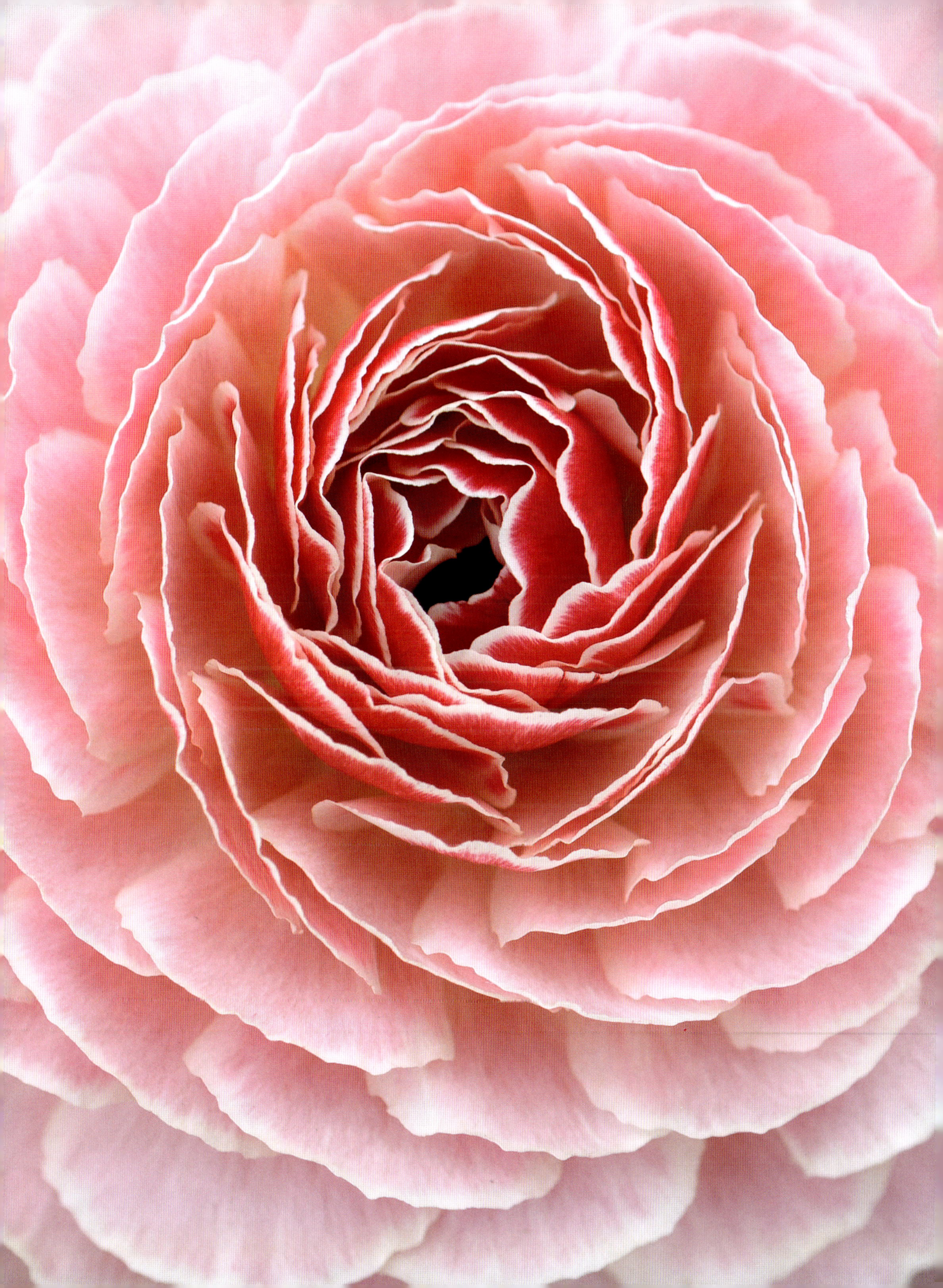

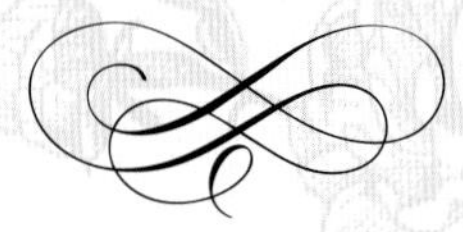

ON THE COAST OF FRANCE

Jardin Shamrock, Varengeville-sur-Mer, France
July–September 2019

Hydrangeas love shade, and Jardin Shamrock provides the ideal setting, under mature trees, caressed by sea breezes. As a lover of hydrangeas in all colors and forms, spending time at Shamrock with M. Mallet was an experience that I would bottle up and carry with me always. I am grateful every day to do the work I do, but even more so when circumstances bring me to such a place of quiet harmony. Especially, the cool palette of pinks, mauves, blues, whites and greens, with nary a red or orange in sight, was something to revel in. In all their multitude of varieties and characteristics, a garden of only hydrangeas might be the ultimate in harmonious presentation. That such places exist is always a wonder to me, and that there are dedicated souls who devote themselves to their continuance for others to enjoy.

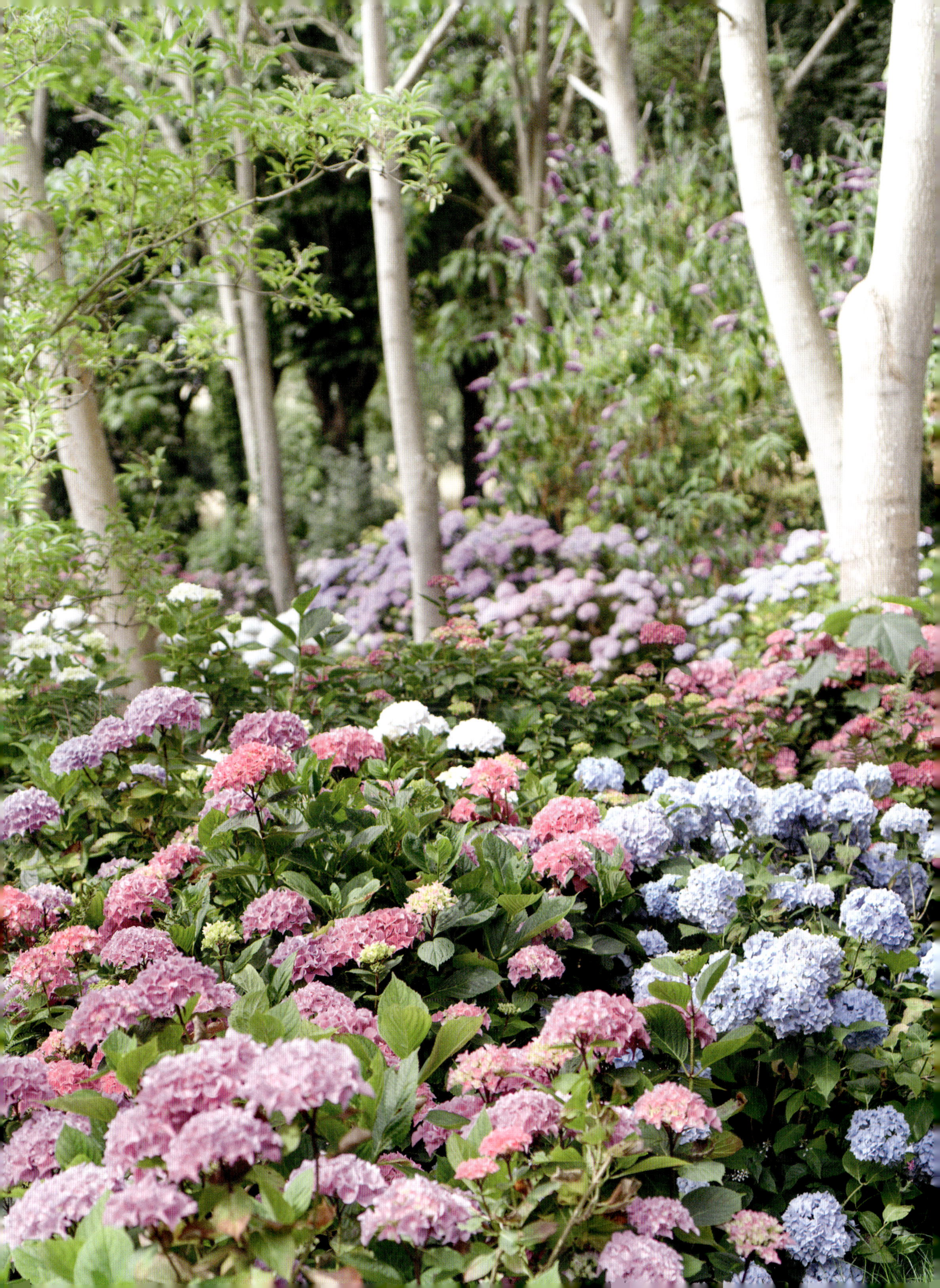

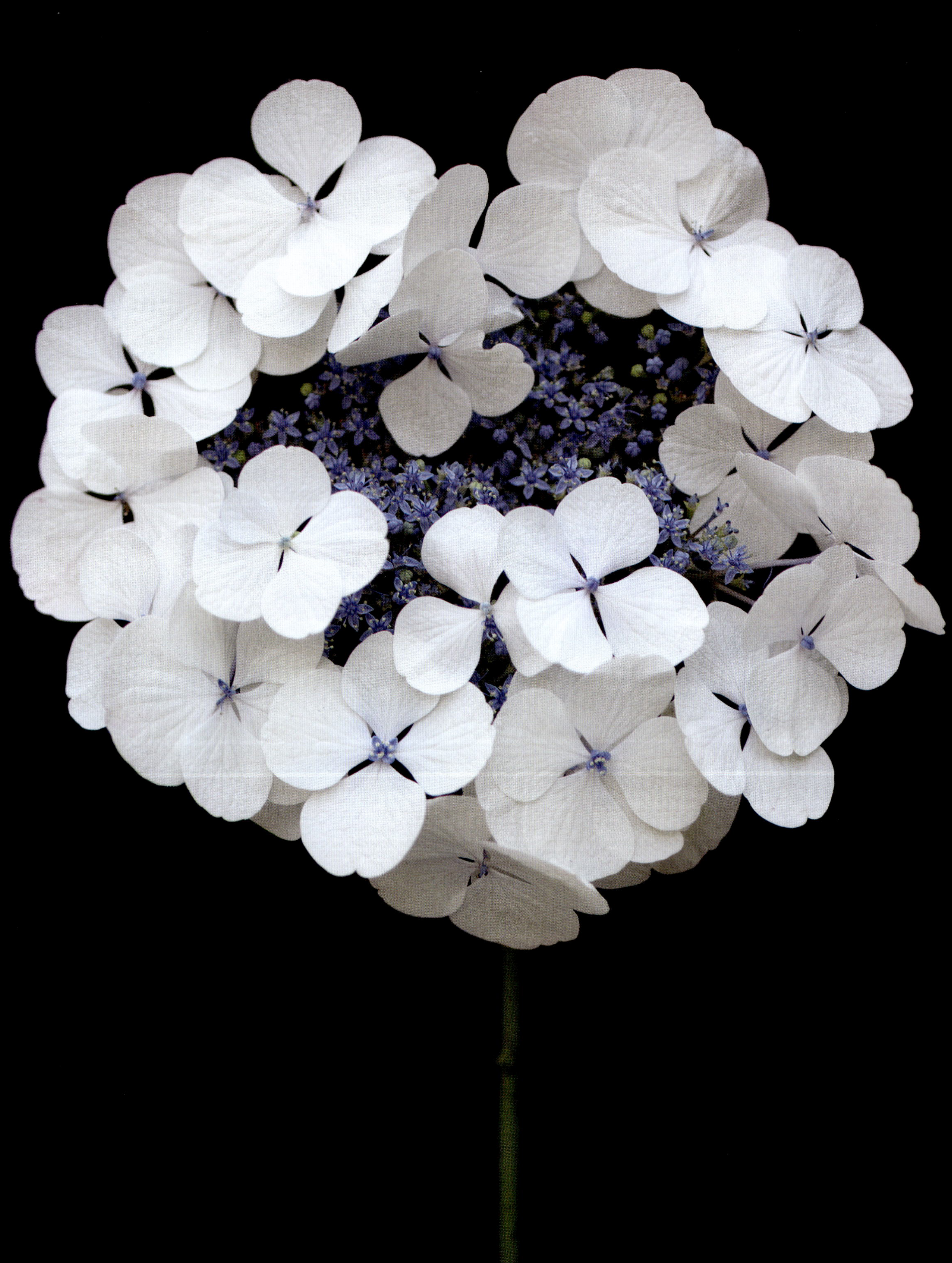

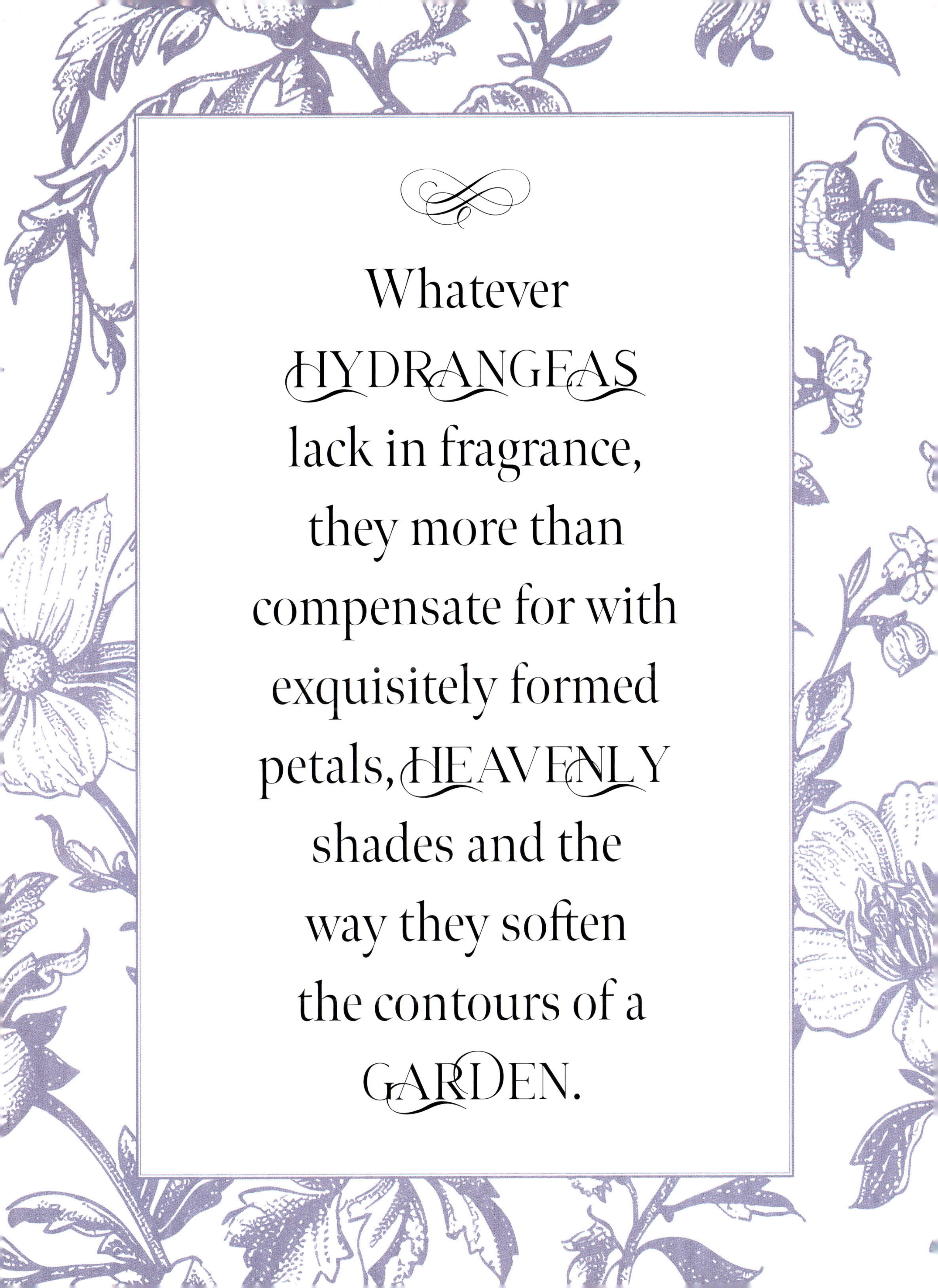

Whatever HYDRANGEAS lack in fragrance, they more than compensate for with exquisitely formed petals, HEAVENLY shades and the way they soften the contours of a GARDEN.

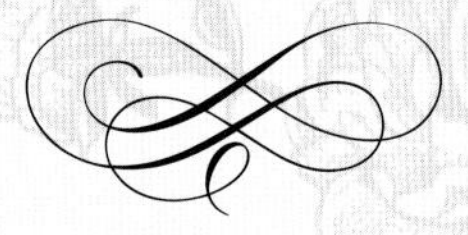

Hydrangea Petals

Hillhaven Garden, Shoreline, Washington, USA
August 2019

The interplay of the varying shapes and shades of these hydrangea petals from our garden resemble perfectly fitting pieces of a puzzle. No two are alike, yet they present a unified whole when grouped together, without a single point of dissonance. This image is a small section of the much larger arrangement, spread over the surface of a great marble table that I used for such projects. Snipping individual petals from our dozens of hydrangeas, I was struck, as I so often am, by grand designs in nature, symbolically representing broader abstract ideas or principles.

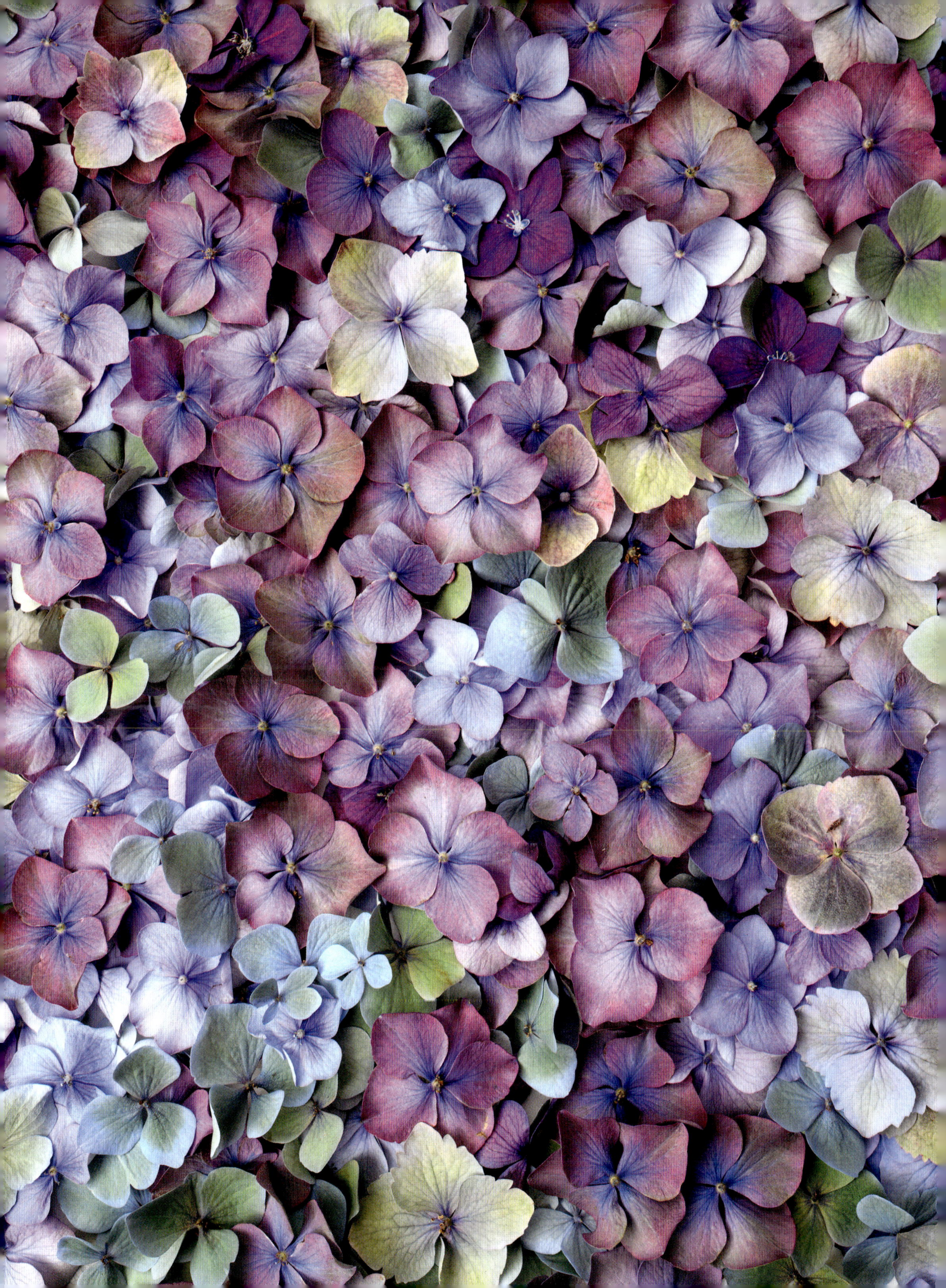

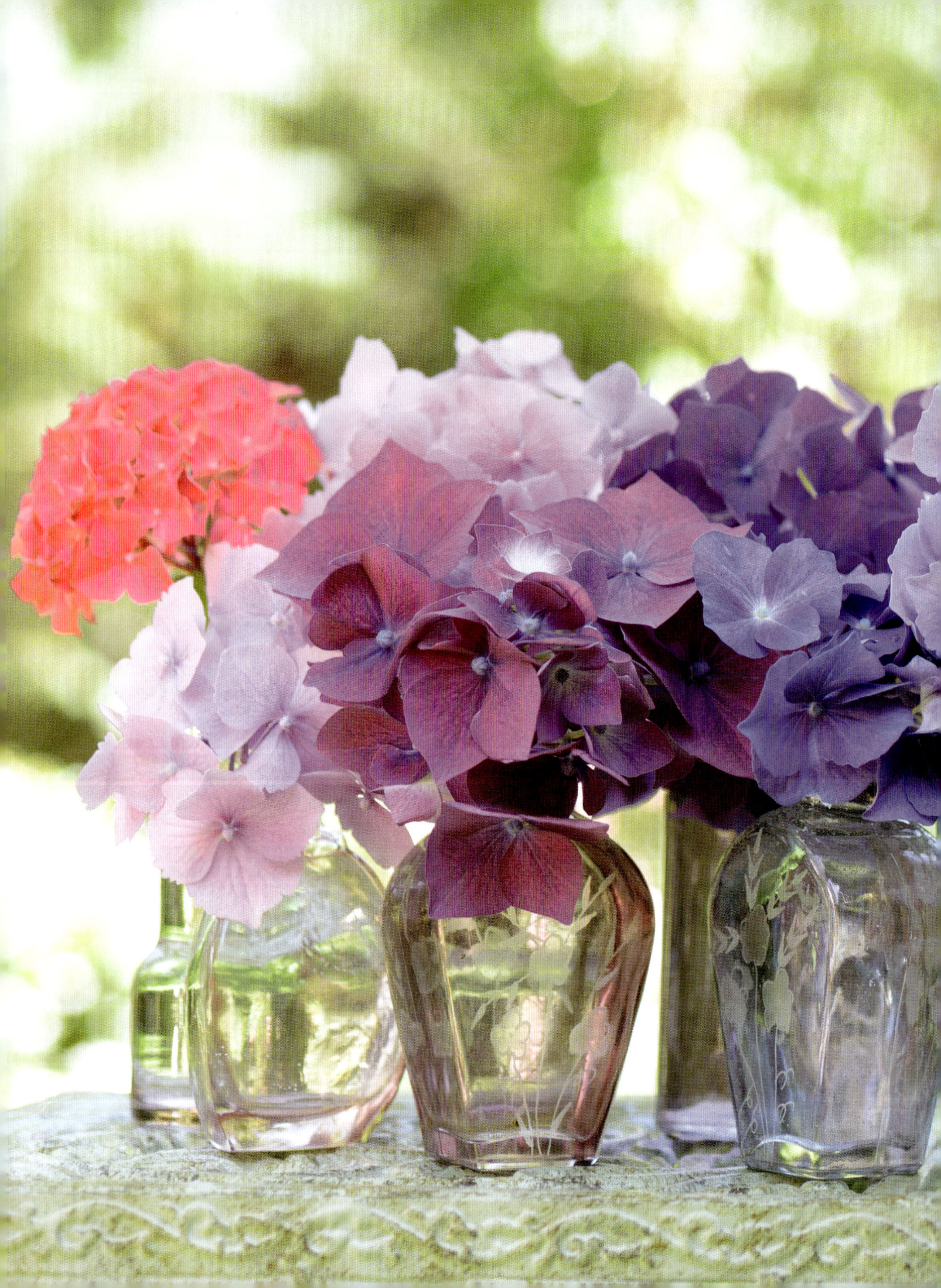

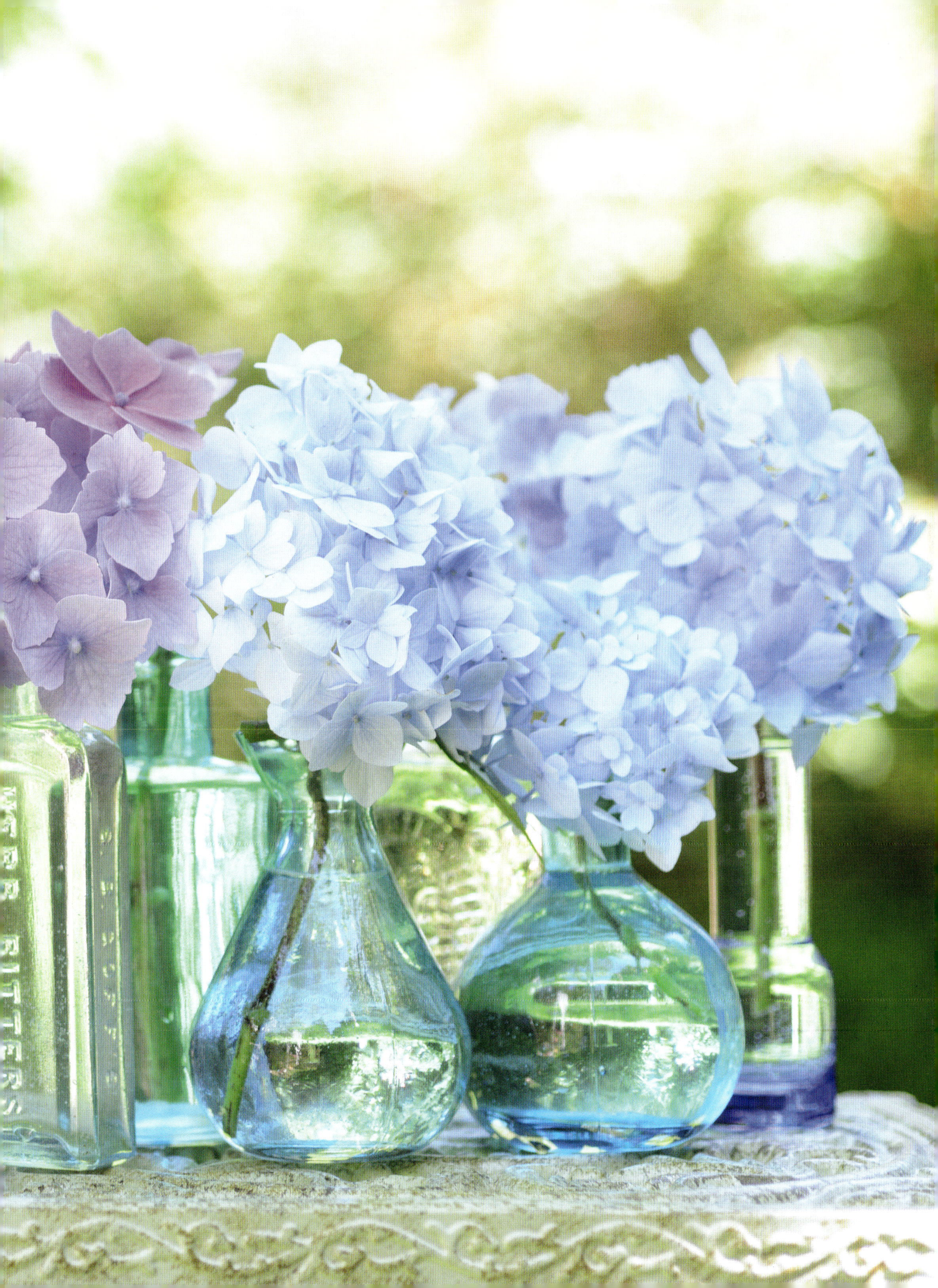

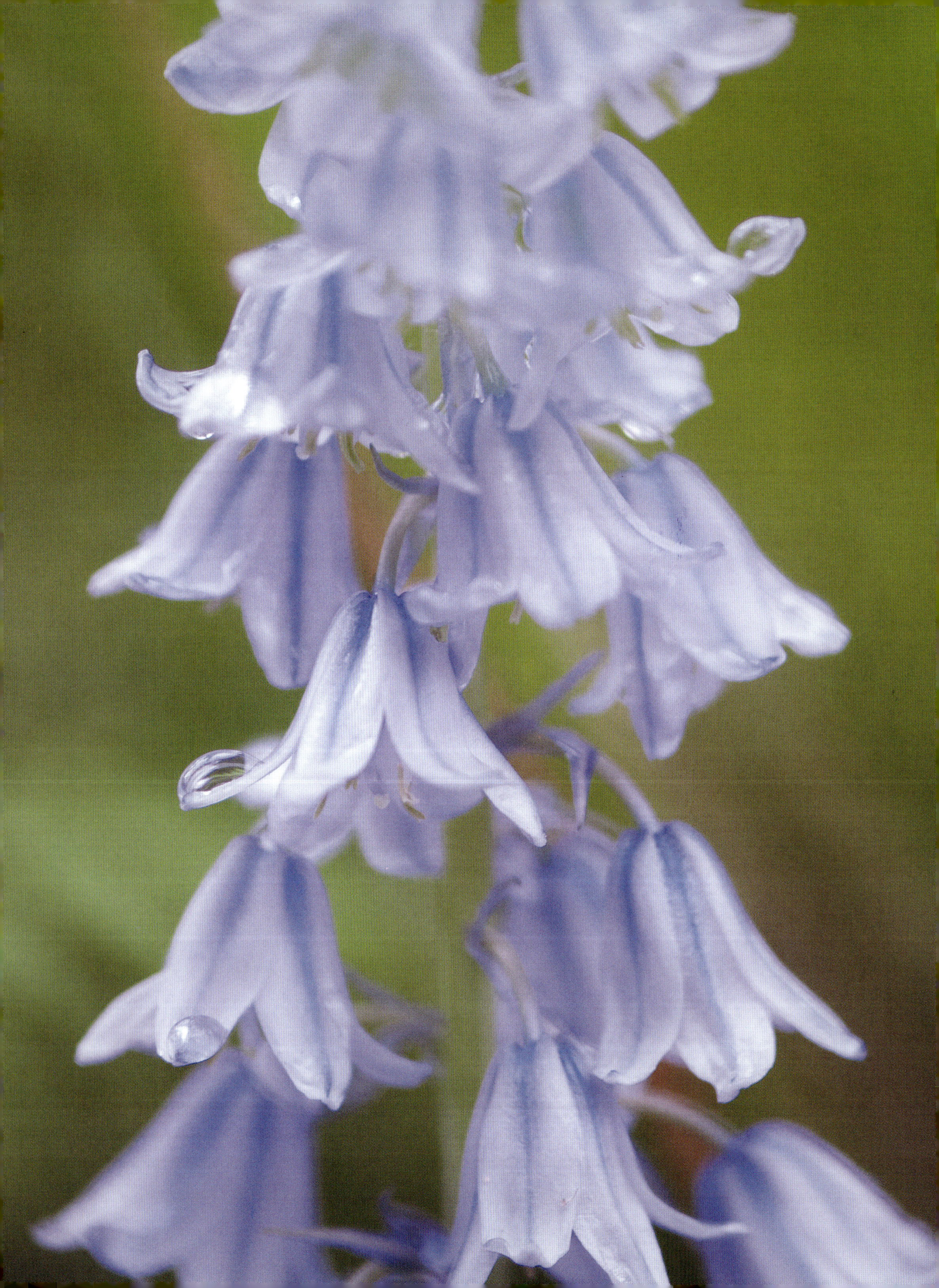

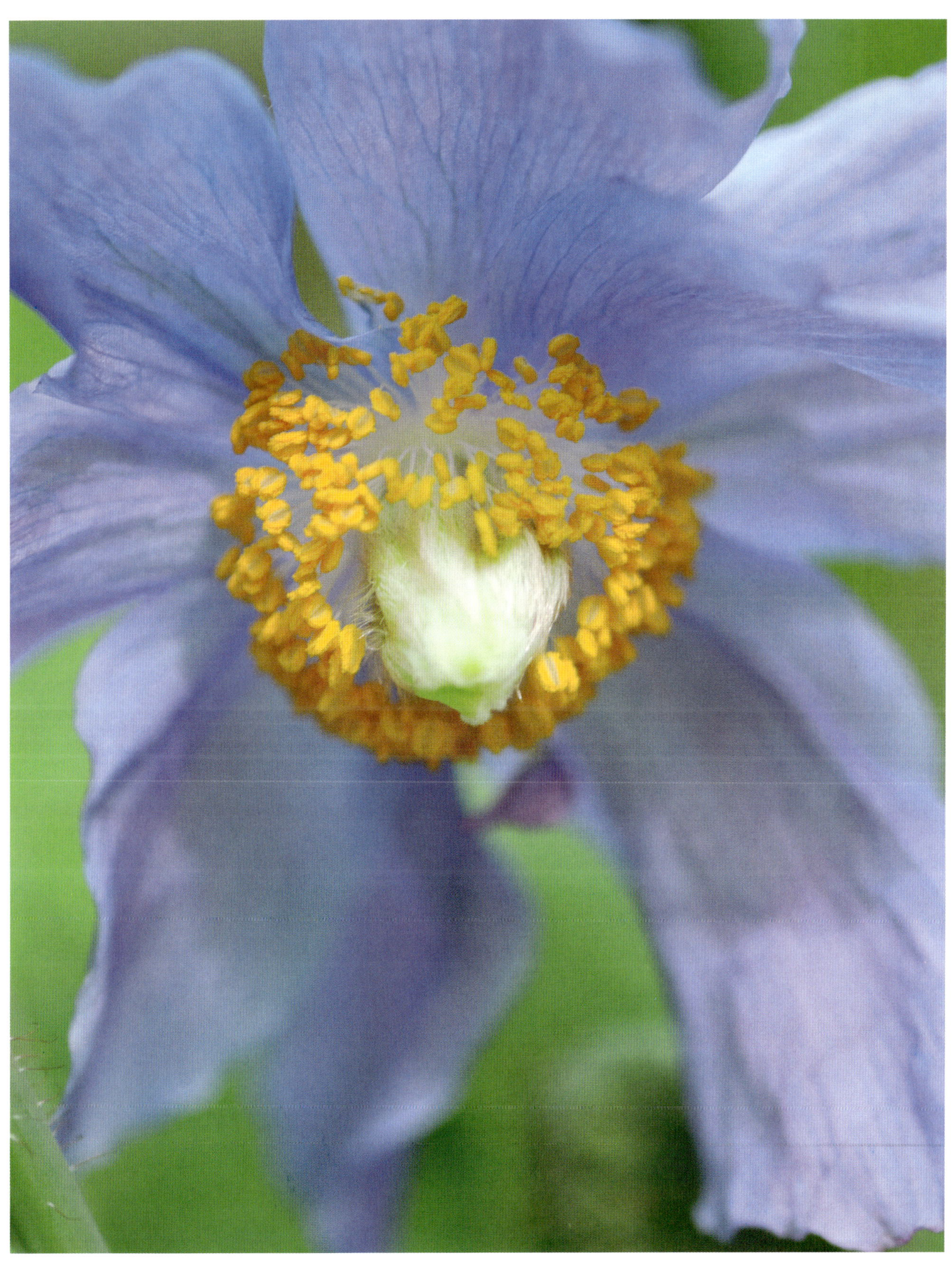

LEFT: Common bluebell (*Hyacinthoides hispanica*), Washington, USA. May 2008. ABOVE: Himalayan Blue Poppy (*Meconopsis betonicifolia*), The Butchart Gardens, Canada. May 2008.

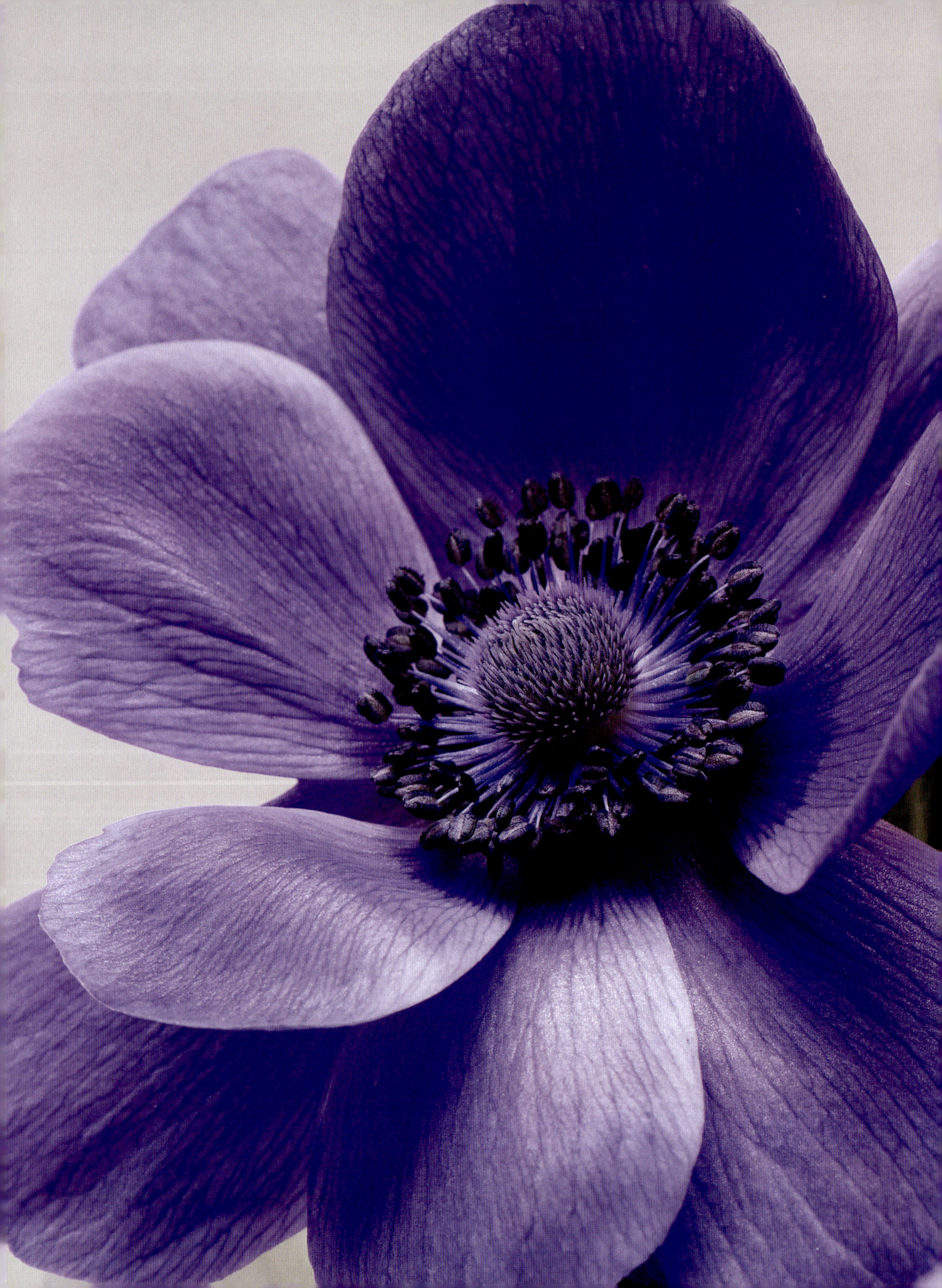

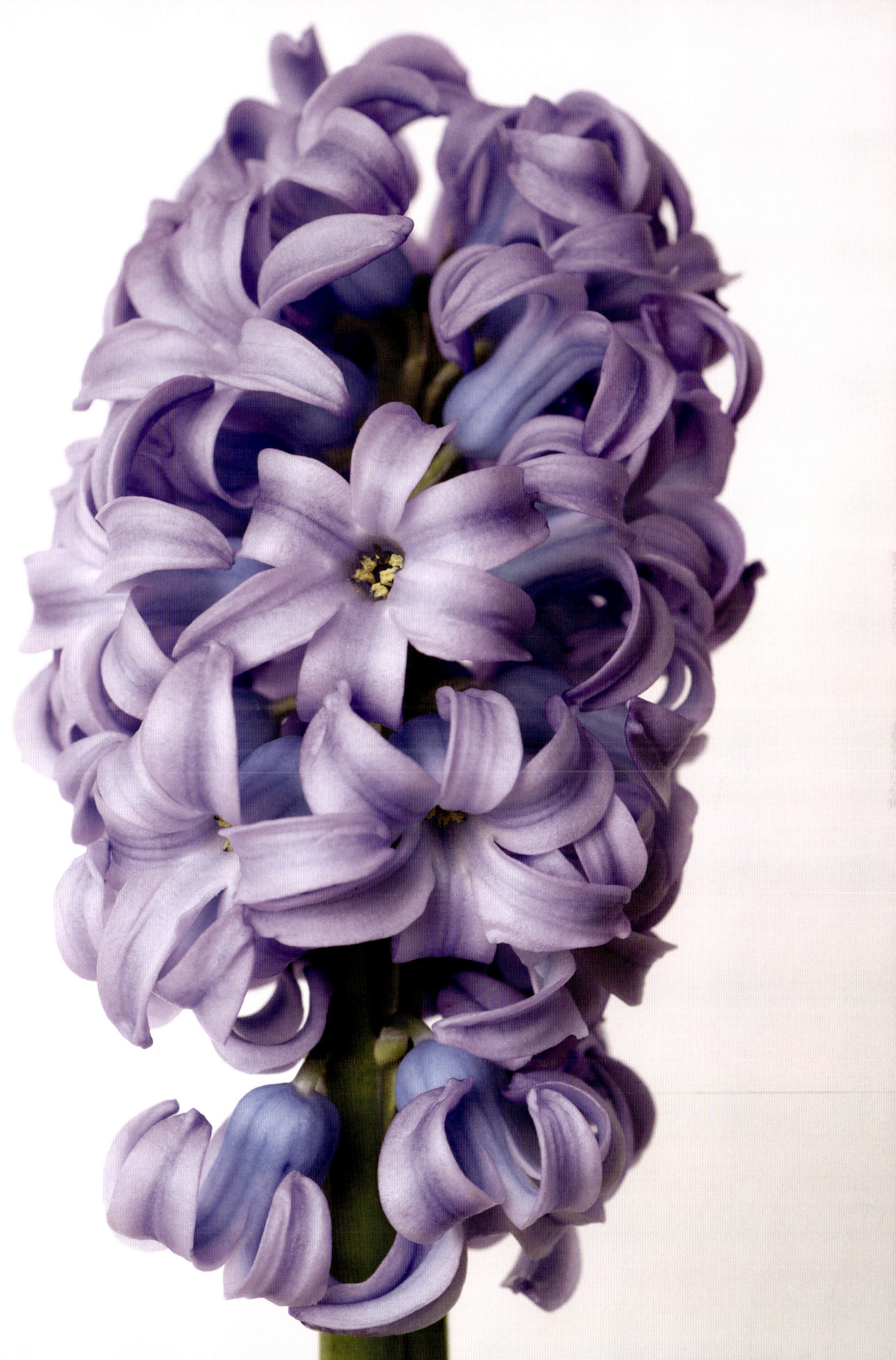

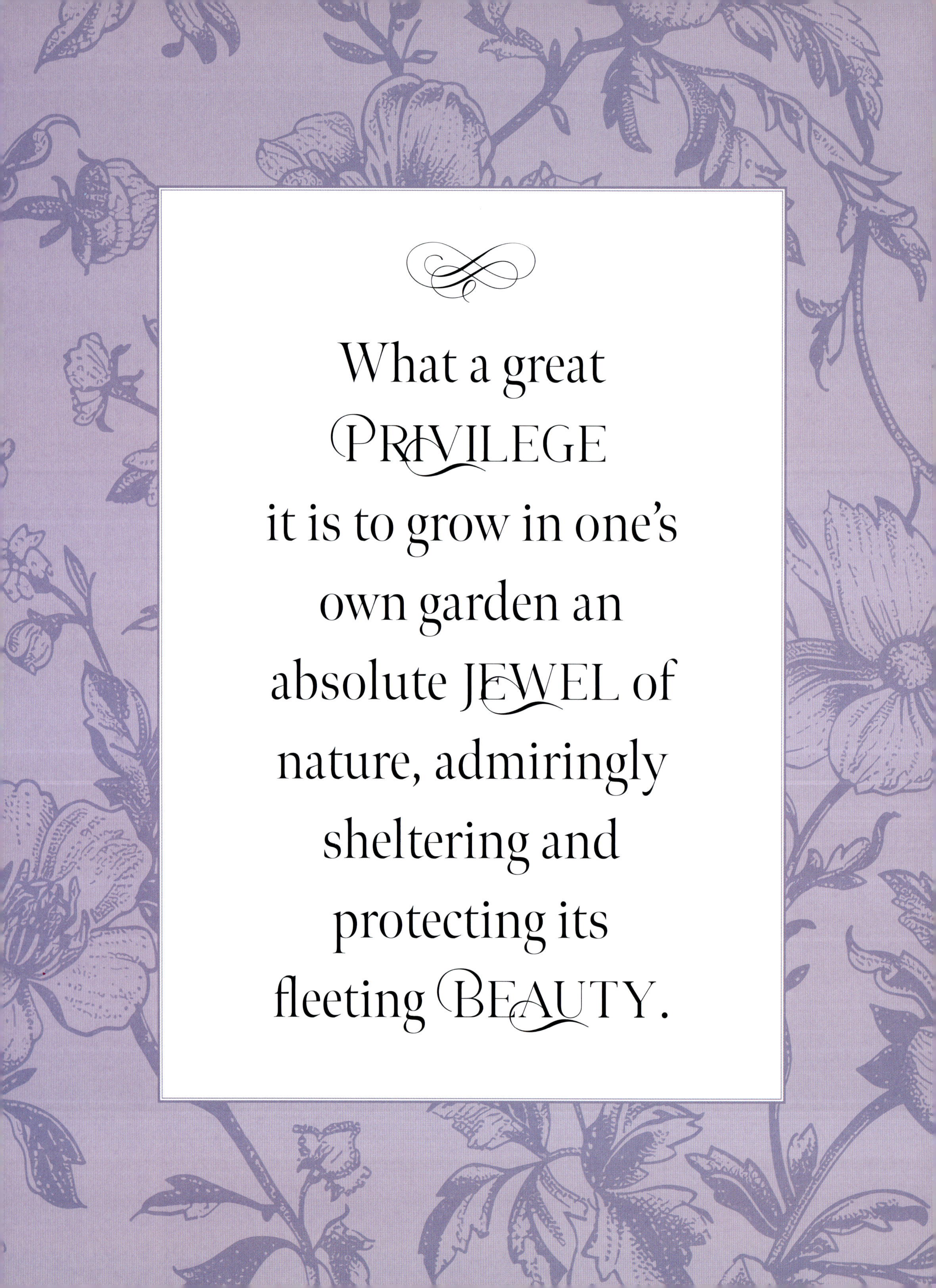
What a great
PRIVILEGE
it is to grow in one's
own garden an
absolute JEWEL of
nature, admiringly
sheltering and
protecting its
fleeting BEAUTY.

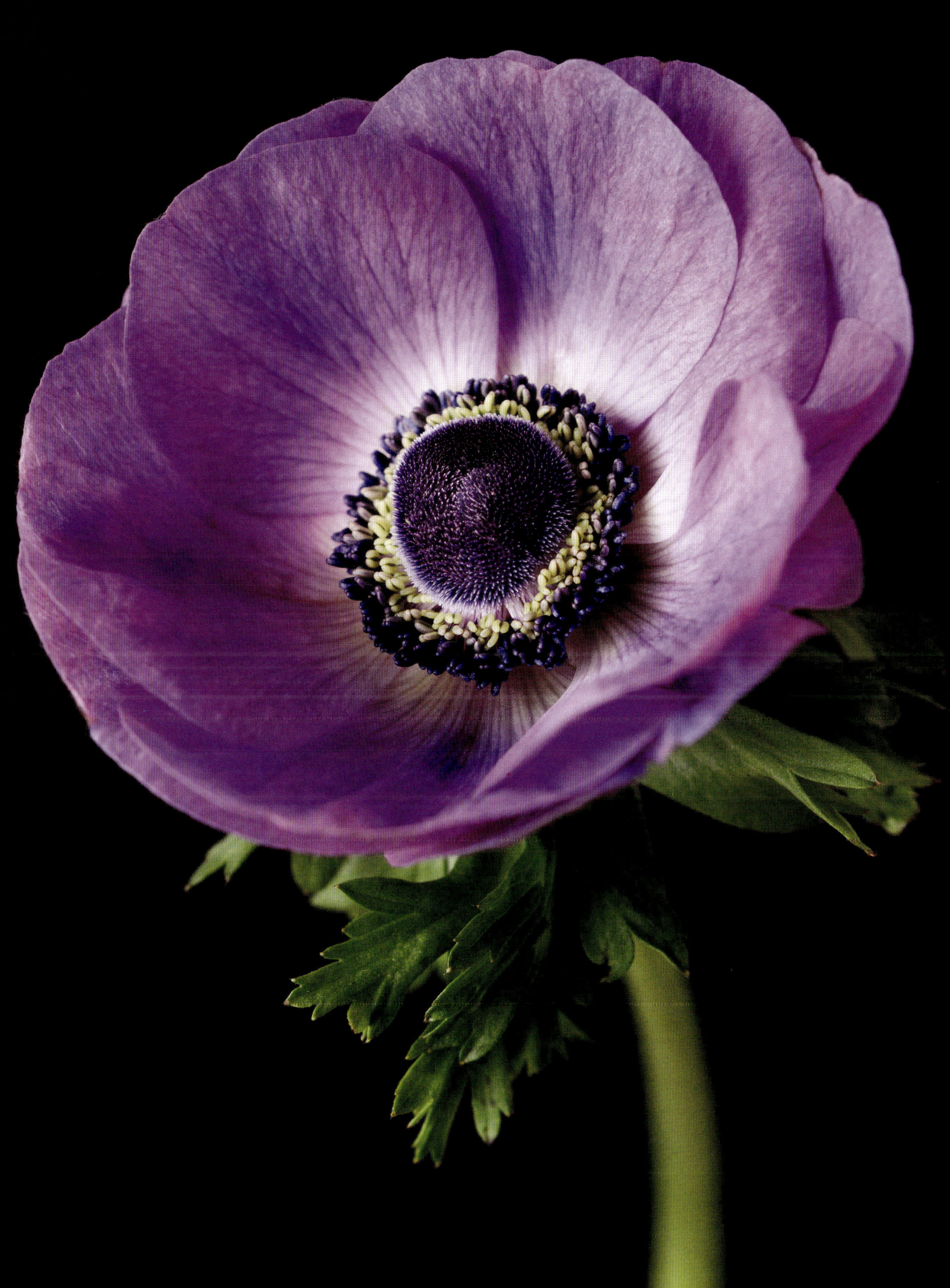

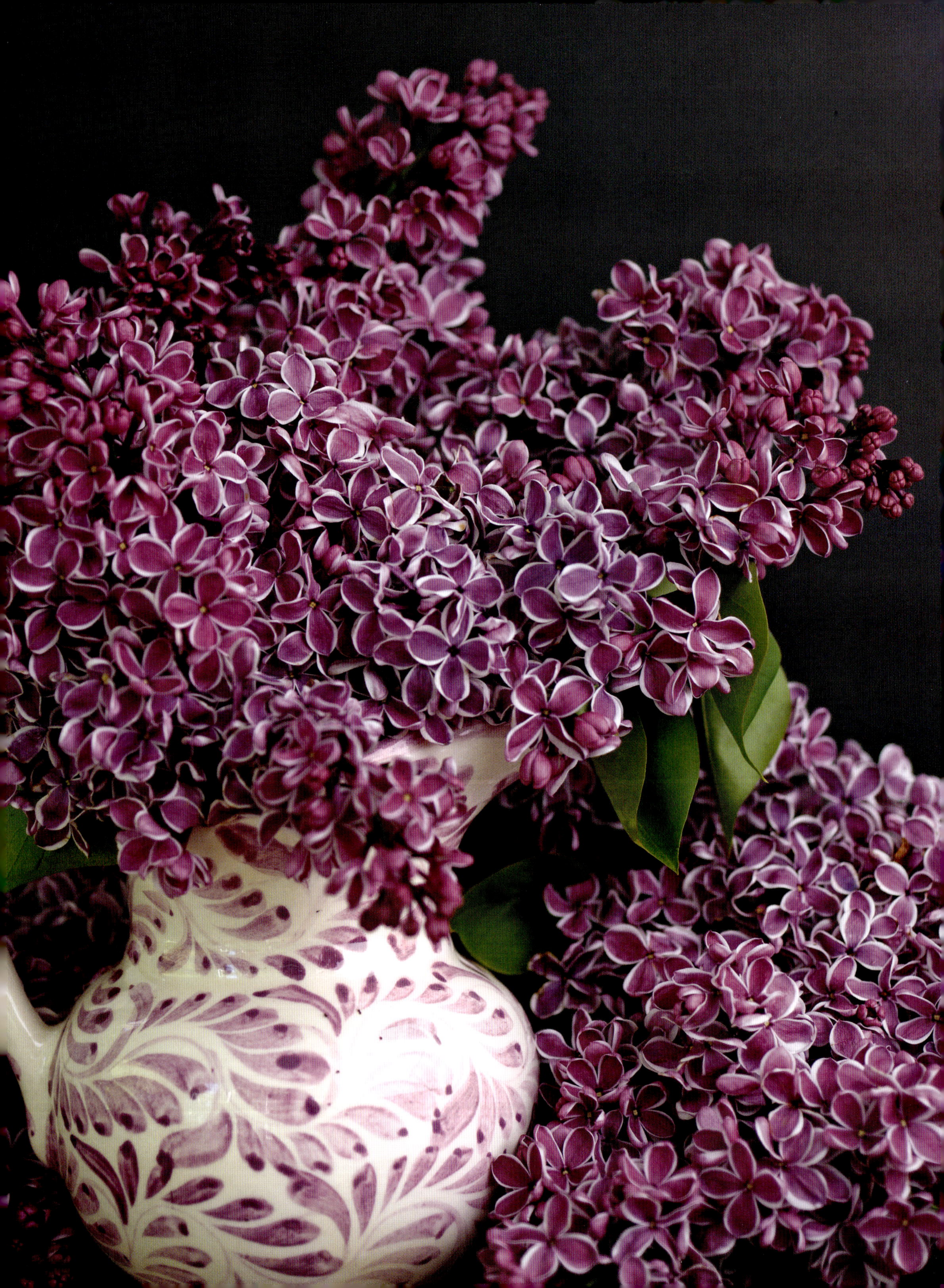

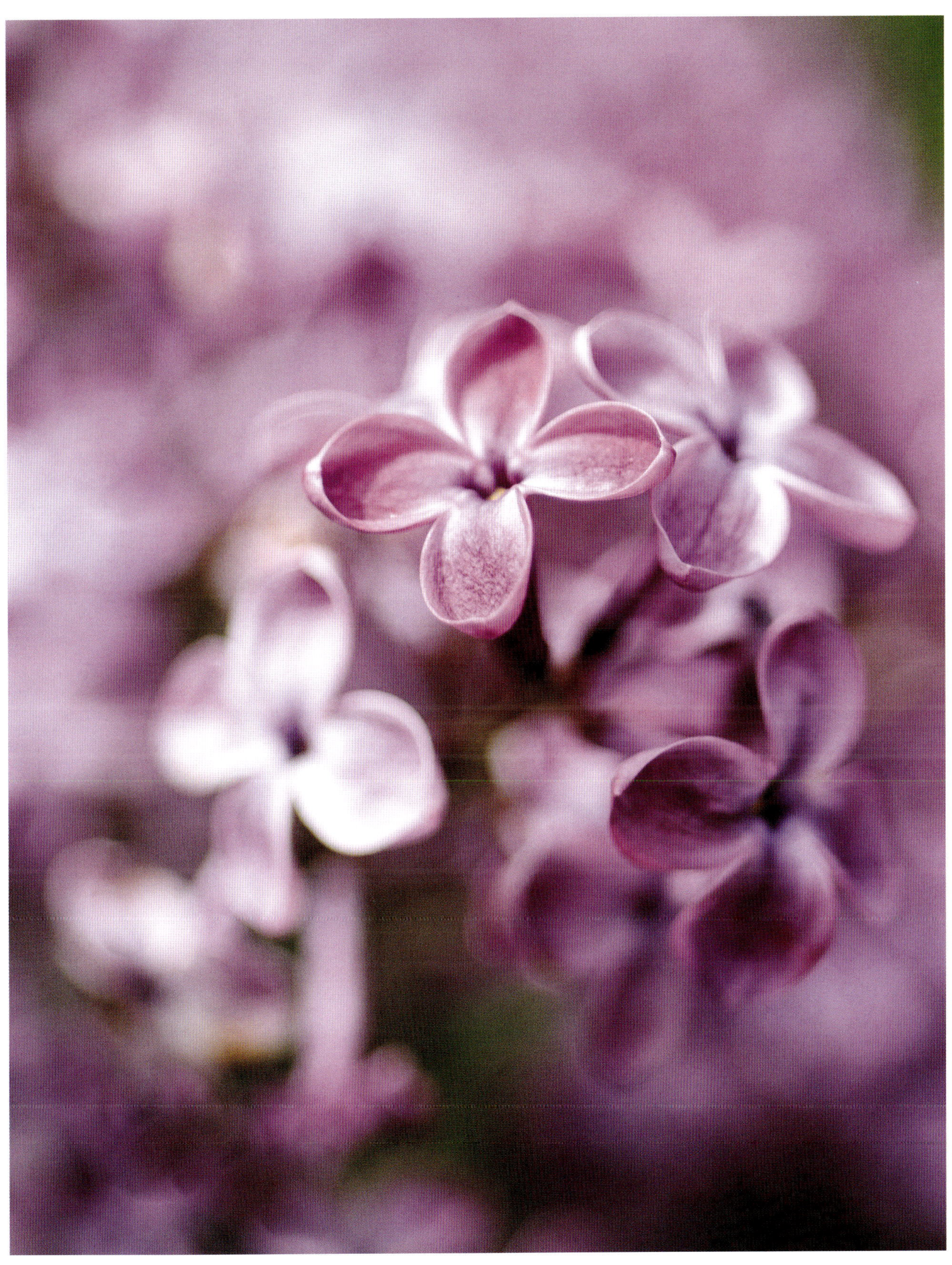

LEFT: Lilac 'Sensation' (*Syringa vulgaris*), Washington, USA. April 2015. ABOVE: Lilac 'Pocahontas', Washington, USA. May 2010.

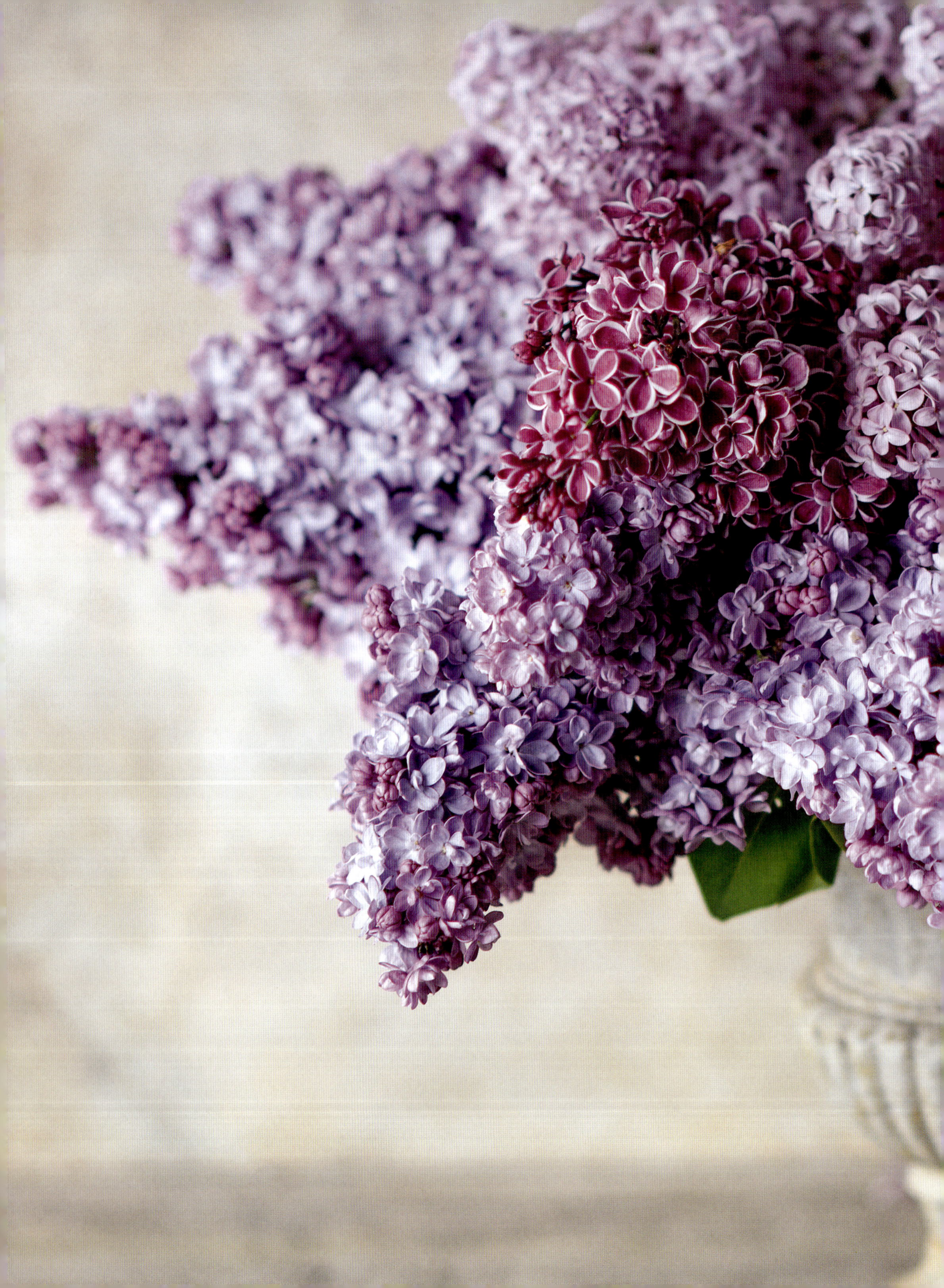

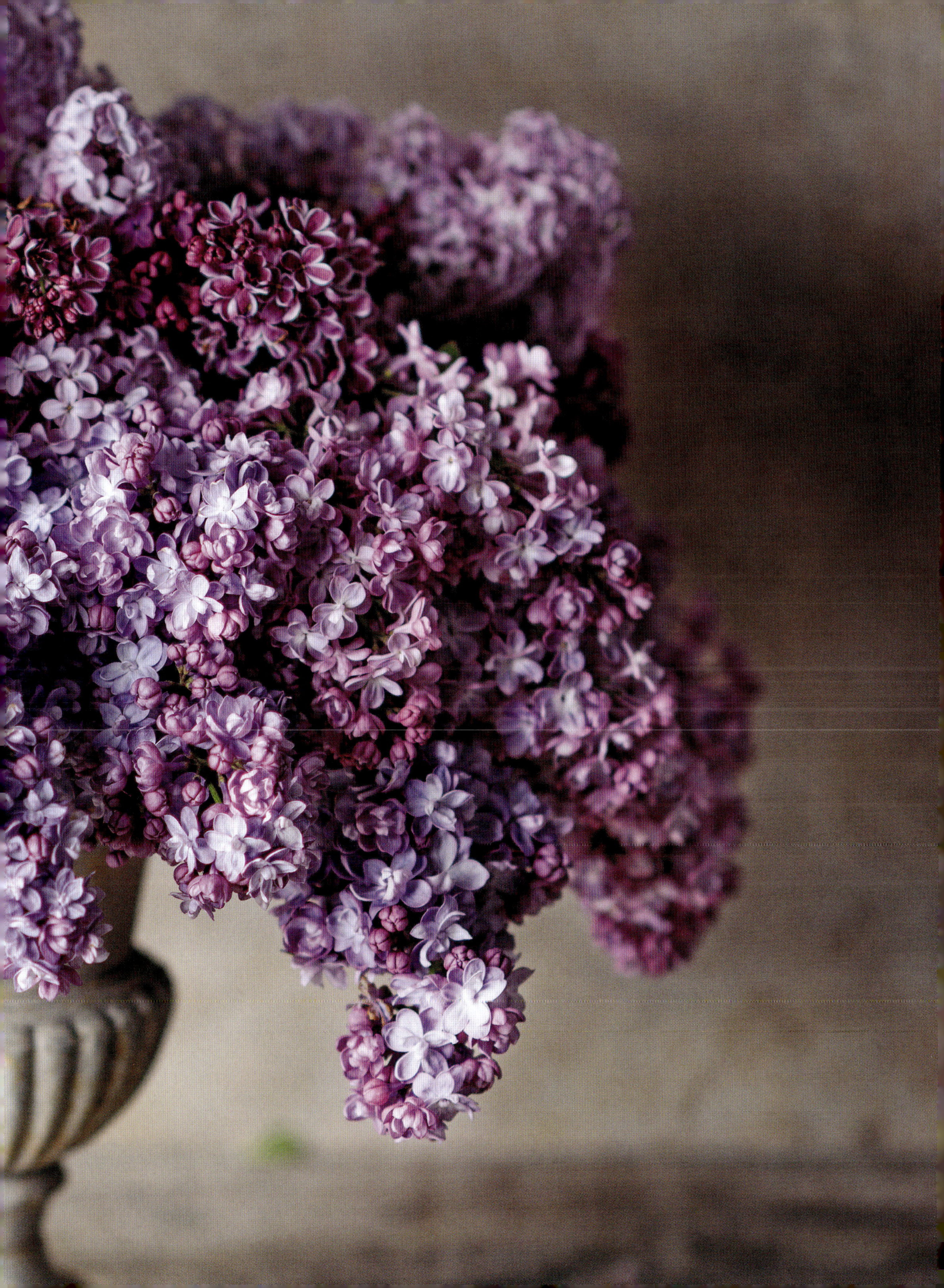

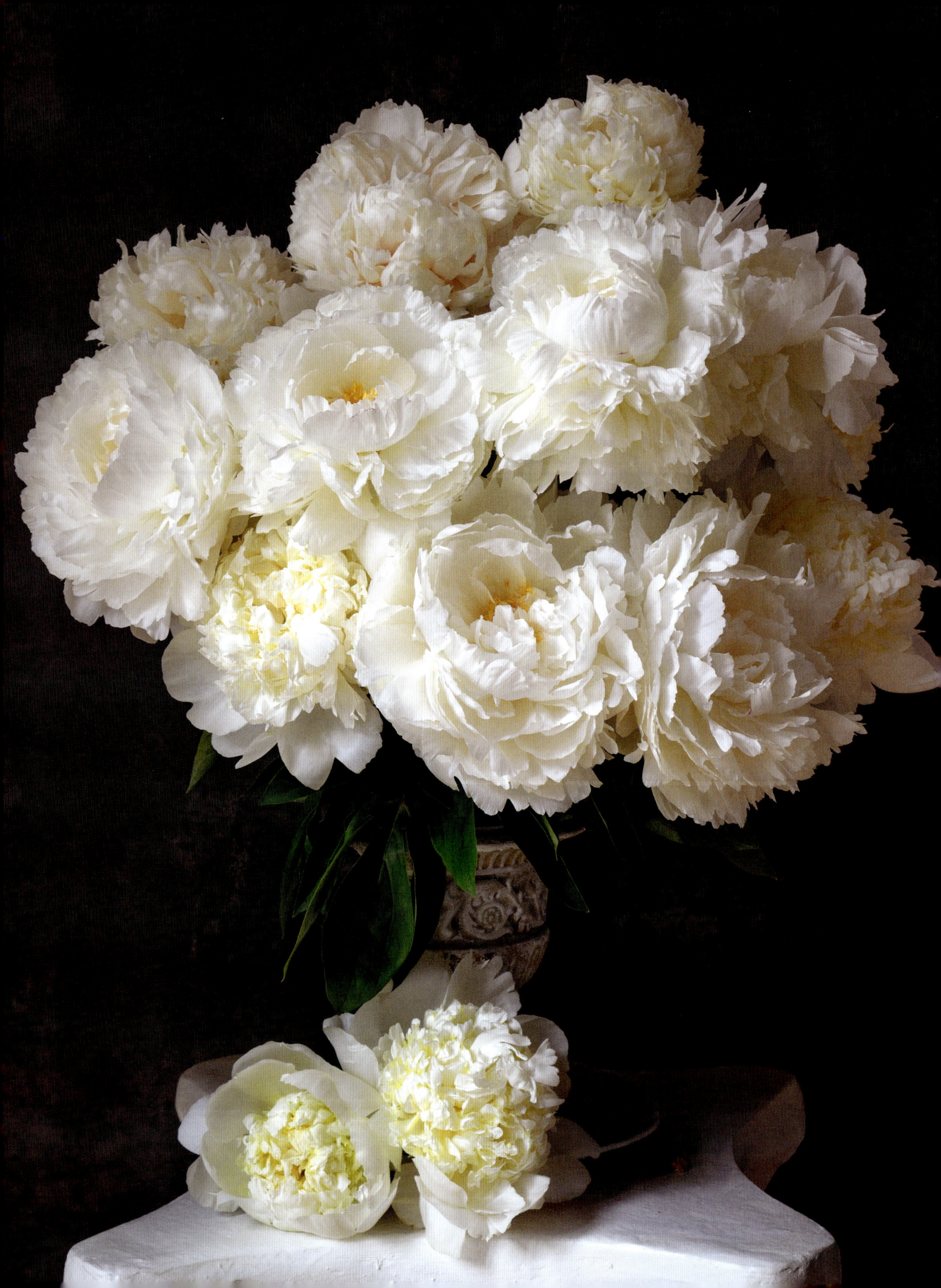

SERENITY

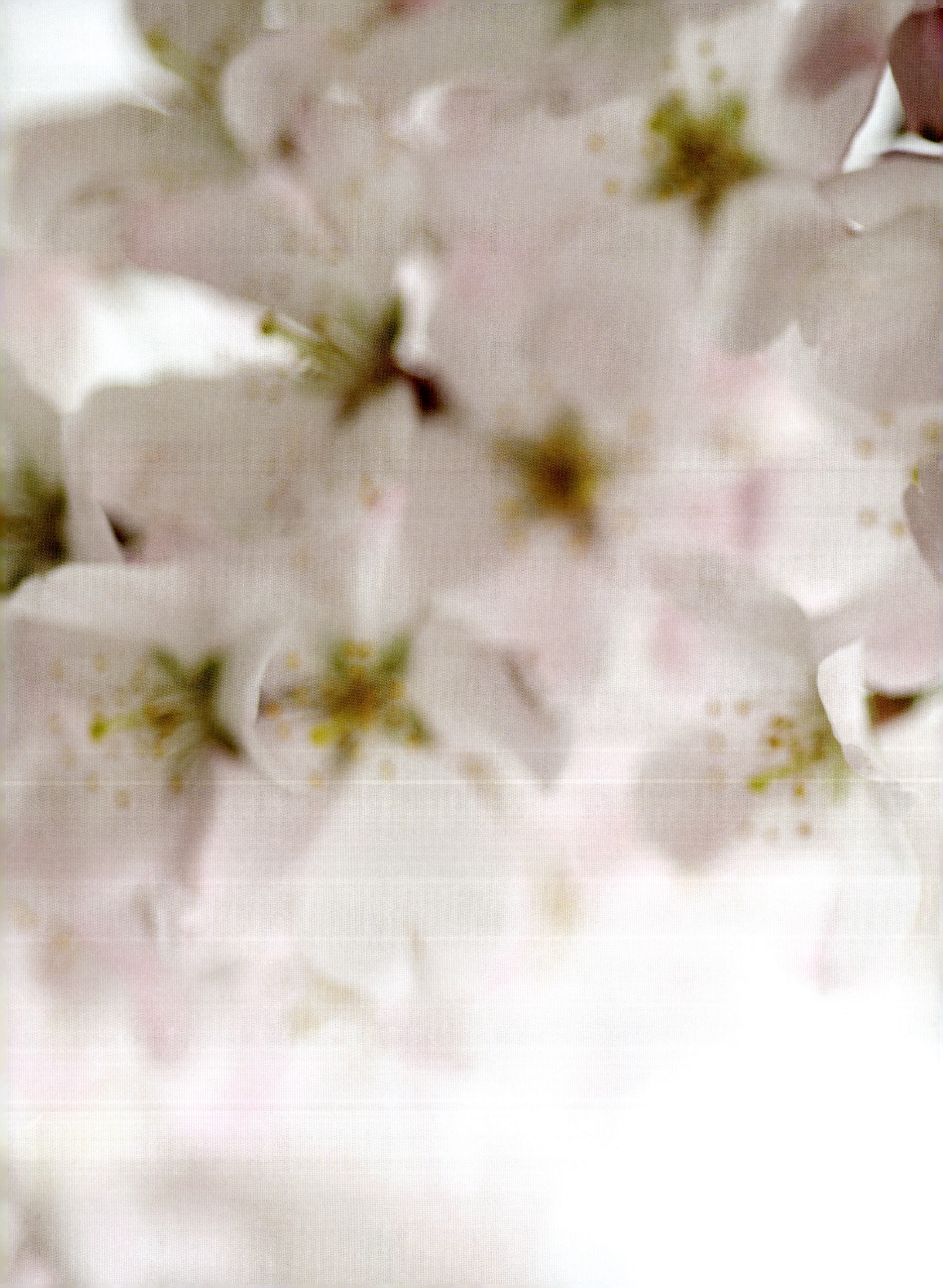

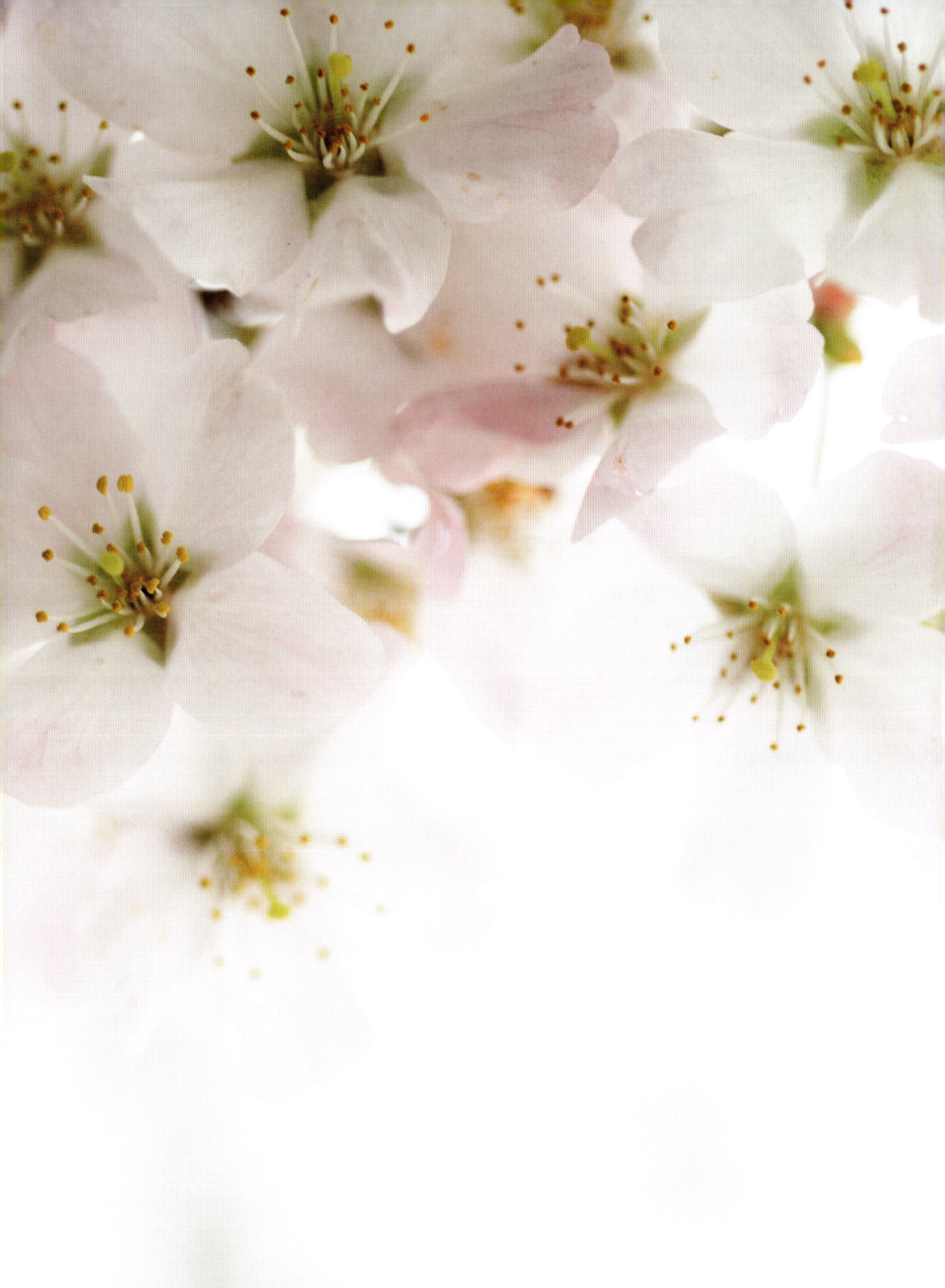

Serenity:
A state of supreme tranquility and unruffled repose or quietude.

We have progressed from awe-struck *Wonder*, through lighthearted *Joy*, dreamlike *Reverie*, balanced *Harmony* and now we have arrived at a state of *Serenity*.

To me, serenity is much more than calmness. It is a point of equilibrium, of unshakable certainty of one's position on an elevated and higher plane of existence, as if upon a figurative mountaintop, where passing storms create little effect and one's vision is far-reaching and pure. There is a centeredness and peacefulness of gentle and steady breathing. It is not by chance that serenity is near the culmination of this journey.

I have always had as an artistic goal for my work to produce such a state in my viewers, that an image I created might lift someone up from their daily entanglement of distractions, worries and anxiety to a place miles above the turbulent clouds of modern life, and there, view the whole from a lofty and unencumbered plateau.

My hope has been that, seeing my work, one could feel, at least for some moments, that state of serenity, a return to a more native and blissful plane of existence, and if I achieved that, I would feel that I had been successful, that I had done my job.

Here, my vision of this exalted place is a spring oasis of fresh greens and pristine whites, tinged with pale gold, the faintest dusting of purple and a dash of that piquant chartreuse green particular to unfolding new life.

I've opened with a recent image of the purest of white 'Bridal Shower' and 'Duchesse de Nemours' peonies, brushed ever so slightly with a faint yellow that fades away as they mature. Introduced in 1856, and still one of the most popular varieties, the luscious blooms of 'Duchesse' have been painted by French masters Claude Monet and Henri Fantin-Latour, whose style inspired my photograph, taken here in Paris. Interestingly, Fantin-Latour frequented the Louvre early in his career, where he spent time copying Old Masters, just a few blocks from my apartment.

RIGHT: *Trillium*, Hillhaven Garden, Shoreline, Washington, USA. March 2013.

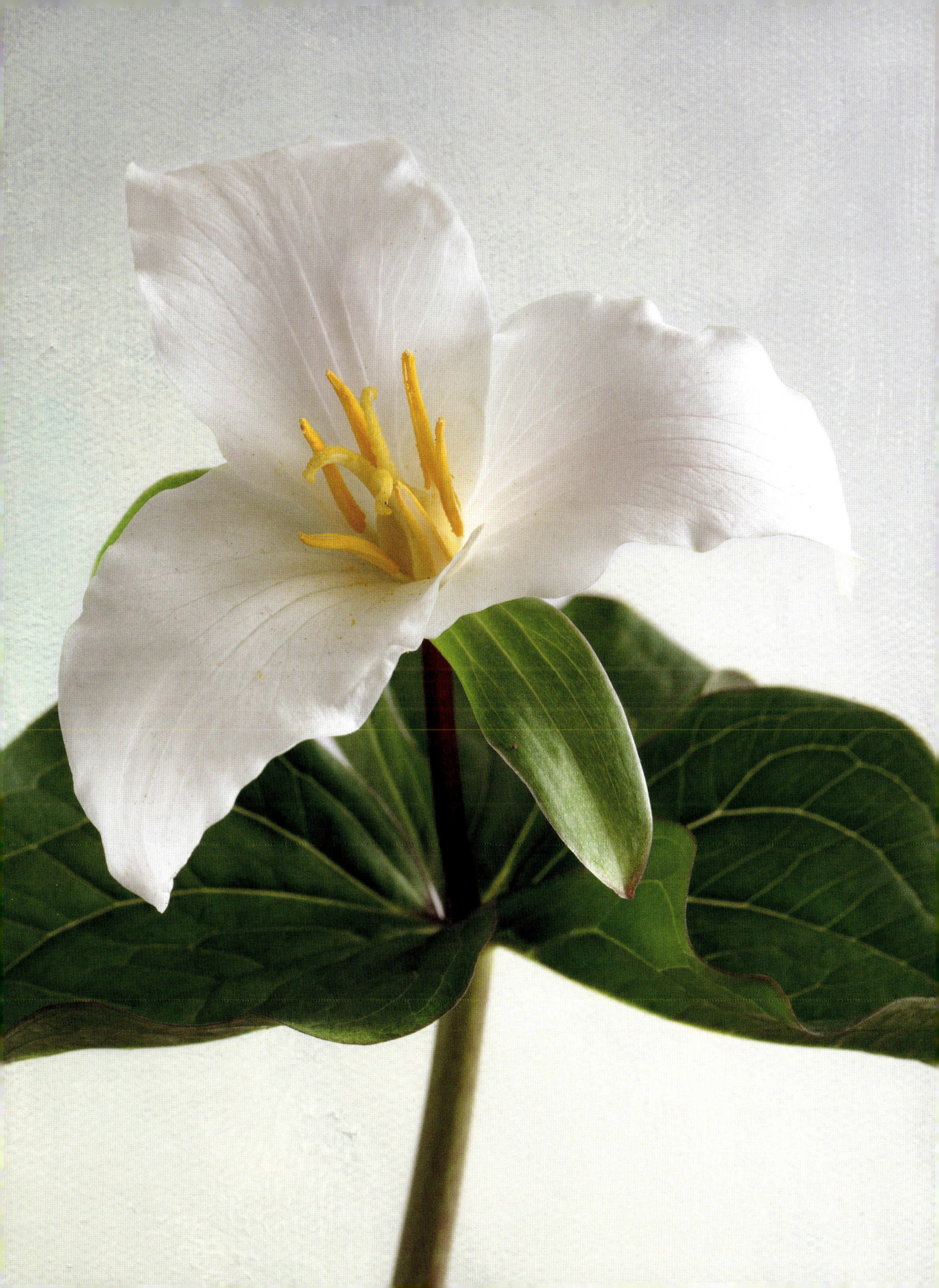

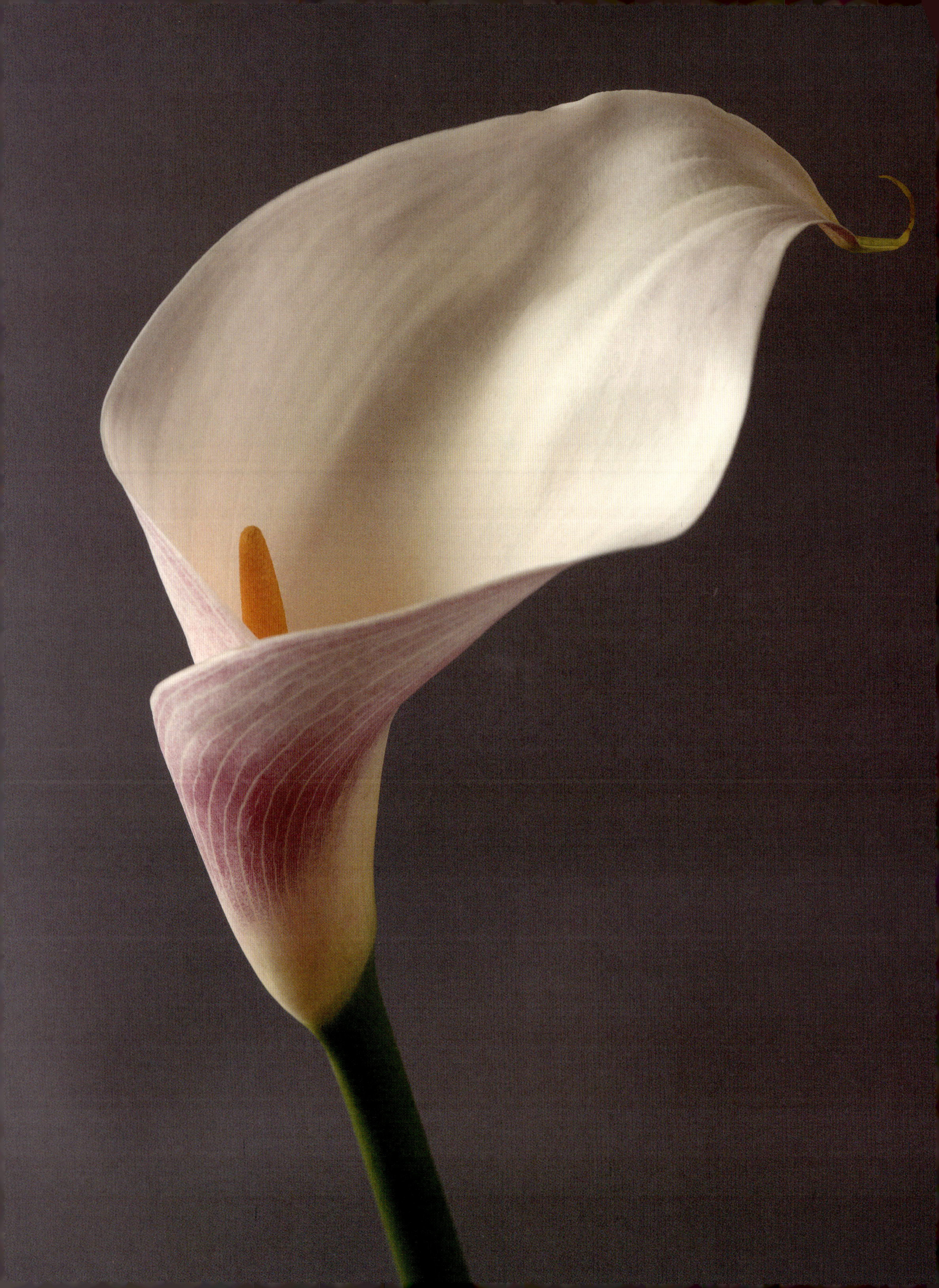

All gardens emit a restful atmosphere, but I believe none are so serene as the woodland in spring. Under the shade of deciduous or evergreen trees, a hushed peace is palpable, as ferns soften the path and the most charismatic of flowers begin to emerge.

Woodland plants are amongst my favorites and I've gathered a selection in this chapter, along with a few tropicals of similar personality. You'll find hellebores, lily of the valley, dogwood, *Enkianthus*, peonies, tulips, calla lily, white cherry blossom, orchids and one of the dearest to me – *Trillium*.

Sacred to Native Americans and often considered to be a symbol of the Holy Trinity due to their three petals, three stamens and three leaves, *Trillium* plants are indigenous to North America and Asia. Some species are legally protected in forests, as damage to parts of the plant can cause its demise. But nurtured in the garden, they are tough and resilient, returning faithfully in late March or early April. Ours, both the white and the maroon varieties, grew in the shade of a stone wall where I loved photographing them each year.

The enduring allure of lily of the valley is inherent in the tiny bell-shaped blooms, true elven flowers exuding the scent of fairyland. A favorite for nuptials and elegant celebrations, it is emblematic of the month of May.

In France, the first of May, called *La Fête du Muguet*, or Festival of the Lily of the Valley, is a highlight of the calendar for me. On this day, a centuries-old tradition is carried out: to present friends and loved ones with a sprig or bouquet of *muguet* as a token of affection, fortune and good luck. Begun in 1560 by King Charles IX, the custom endures throughout the country. All over Paris, flower markets, shops and street vendors set out abundant displays, and the day is filled with sweet scenes of Parisians of all ages carefully choosing the most fragrant bunches to give. I love to visit the flower markets to witness heartwarming scenes of the bestowing of these gifts to loved ones. And I am always encouraged that this long and gracious practice is still deeply respected in this modern age.

LEFT: Calla lily (*Zantedeschia*), Paris, France. April 2025.

I am known for my images of spring in Paris, and each year I revisit my favorite cherry and magnolia trees, old friends by now, in a treasured ritual. The species that I've not found plentiful in the city, however, is dogwood, another woodland staple with arching branches laden with pale green, white or pink blooms. The actual flowers are miniature, but the surrounding bracts create the impressive display. On the East and West Coasts of the United States, the appearance of the flowering dogwood in April is a comforting reminder that spring is well and truly on its way. I simply love the tapered shape of the bracts, framed by the sturdy, glossy leaves. A few branches in a vase make a full and dramatic arrangement.

One June, we rented a cottage and spent a number of weeks in a deep immersion of the glorious English gardens of Kent and East Sussex, indulging ourselves with almost daily visits to the renowned gardens at Sissinghurst and Great Dixter. What a treat it was to have the luxury of time to linger until sunset at Sissinghurst and to view the famous White Garden as the shadows lengthened and the flowers began to glow. Designed by Vita Sackville-West, its refreshing palette is limited to white, gray, green and silver, including the white calla lilies featured in this chapter.

The spring-themed floral heart was created in Paris in 2016 for my book *Paris in Bloom,* but it was never published. The design featured anemones, ranunculus, lilacs, hellebores, pussy willows, tulips, hydrangeas and roses, all elevated above the floor, which was covered in black velvet. Keeping it all in place was an engineering feat I was quite proud of, so I am happy that it is finally making its debut here.

RIGHT: Orchids (*Orchidaceae*), Keukenhof. April 2014.
OVERLEAF: *Magnolia stellata* 'Alba', white star magnolia.

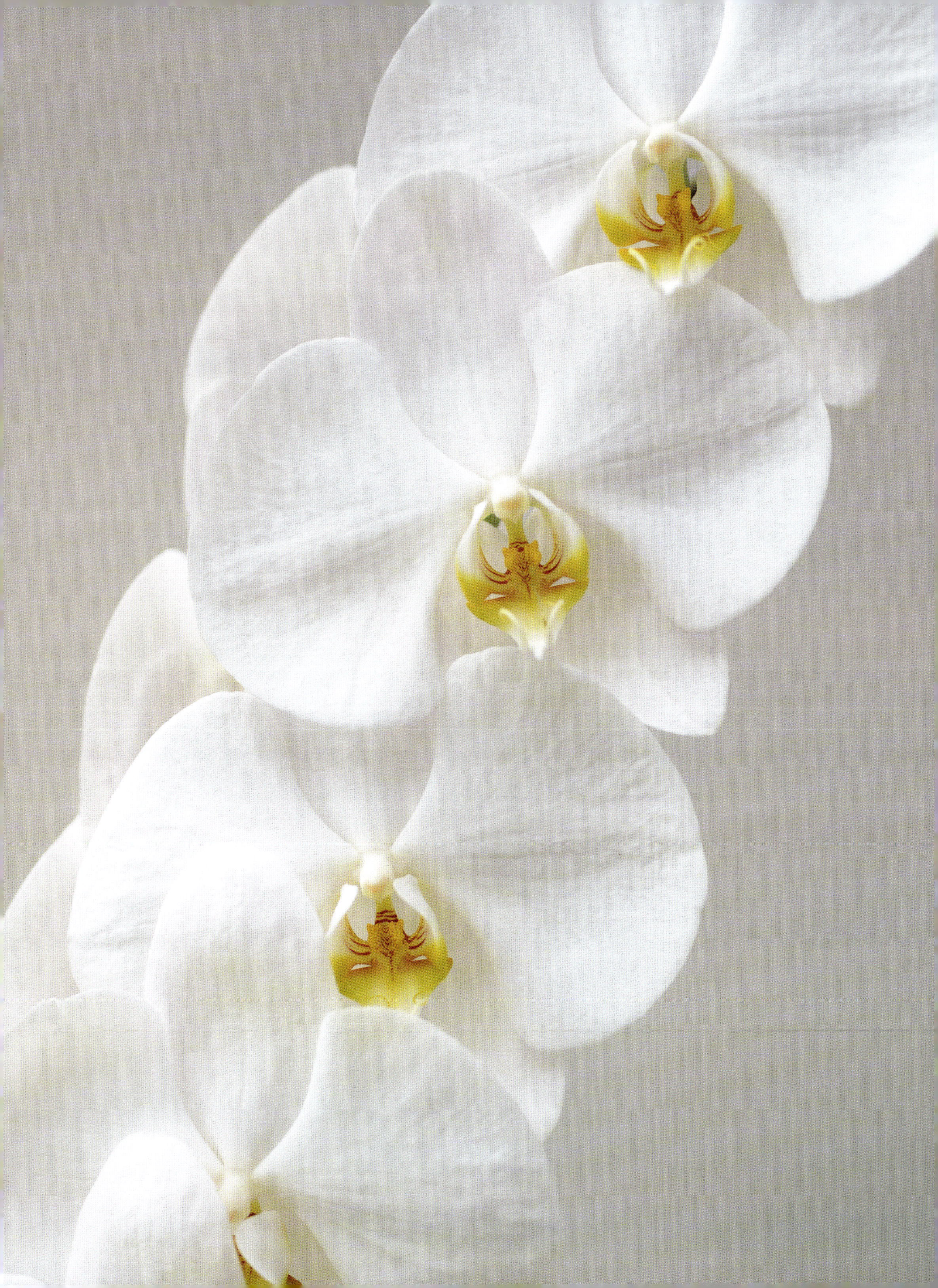

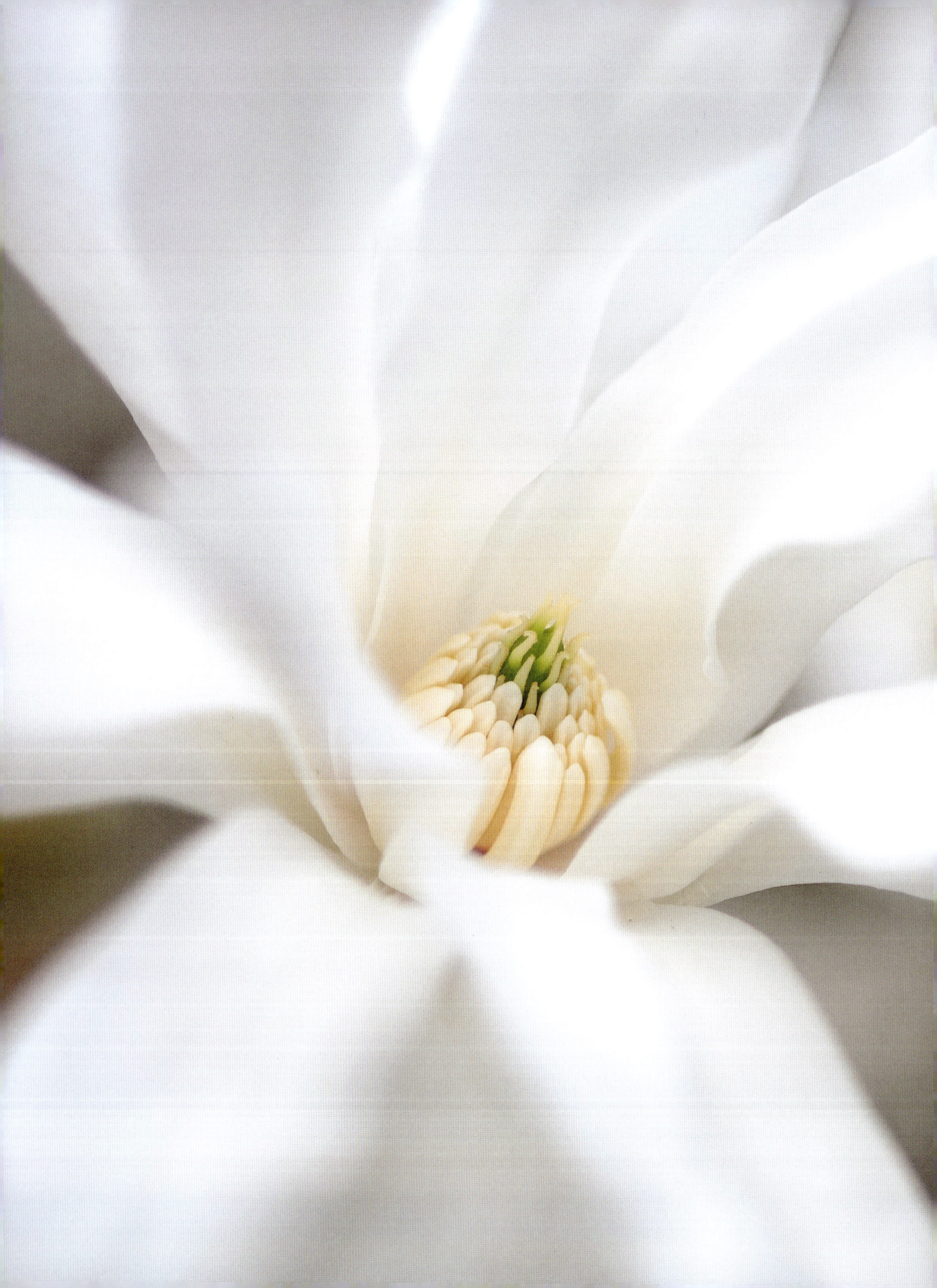

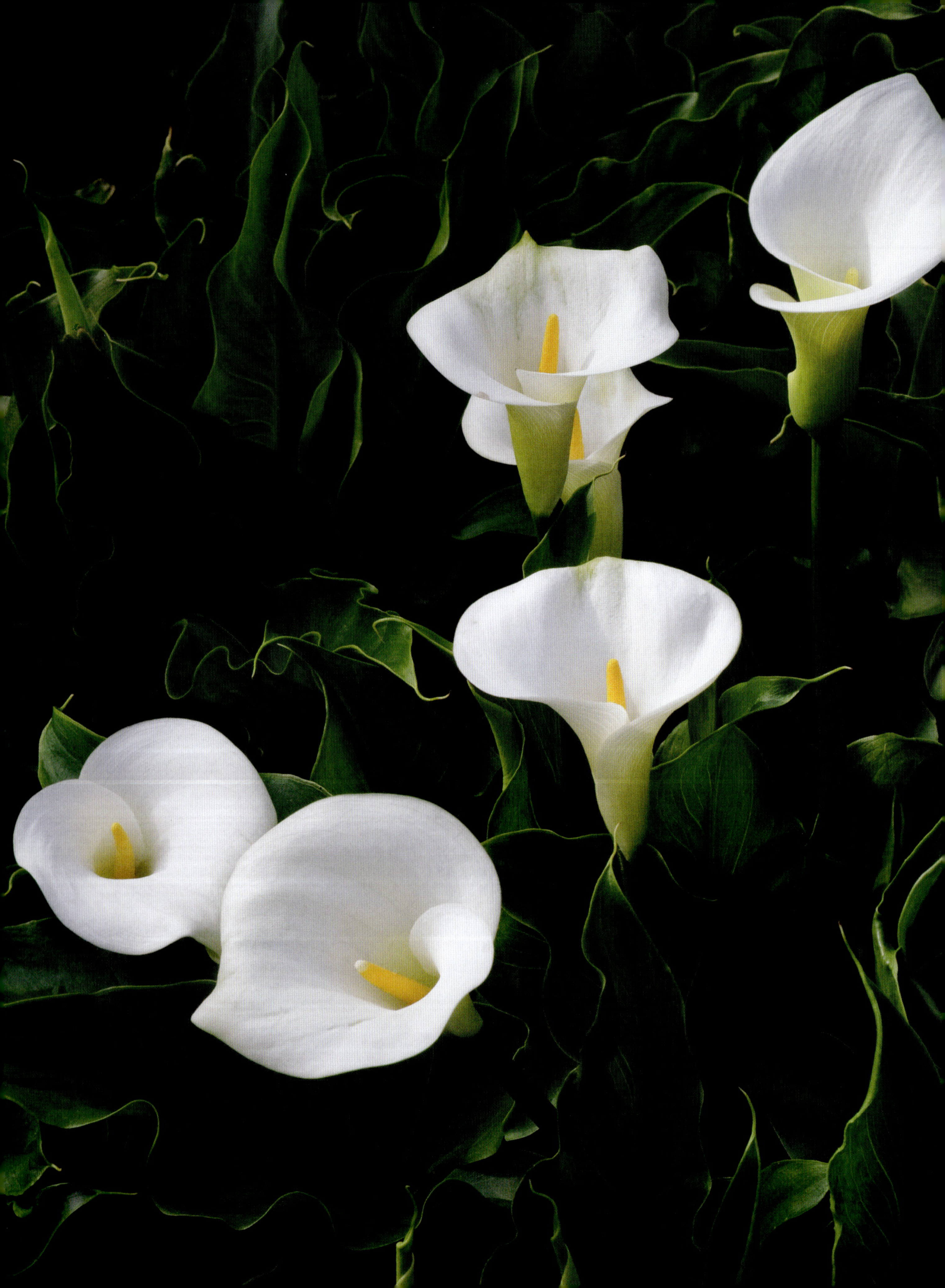

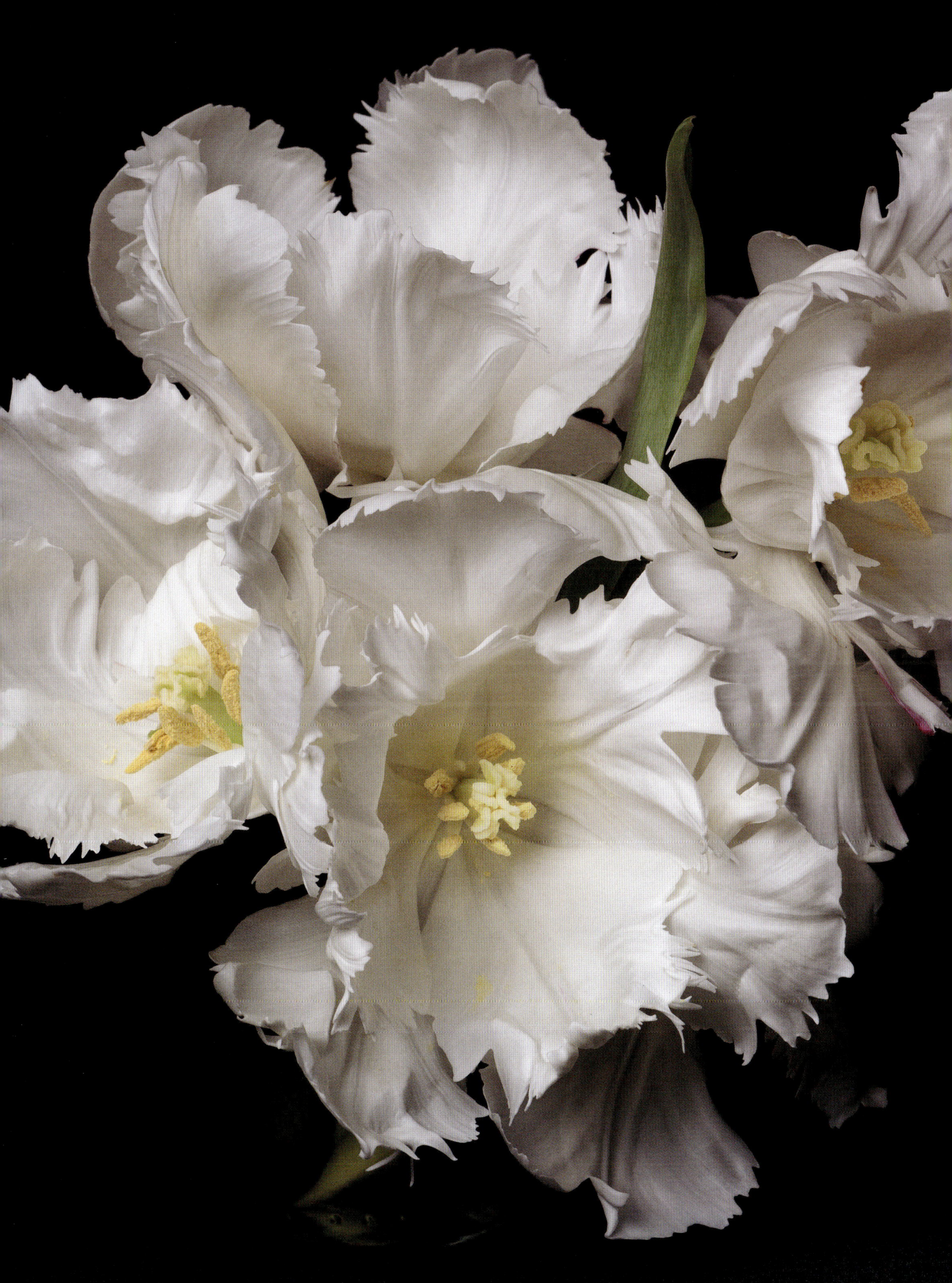

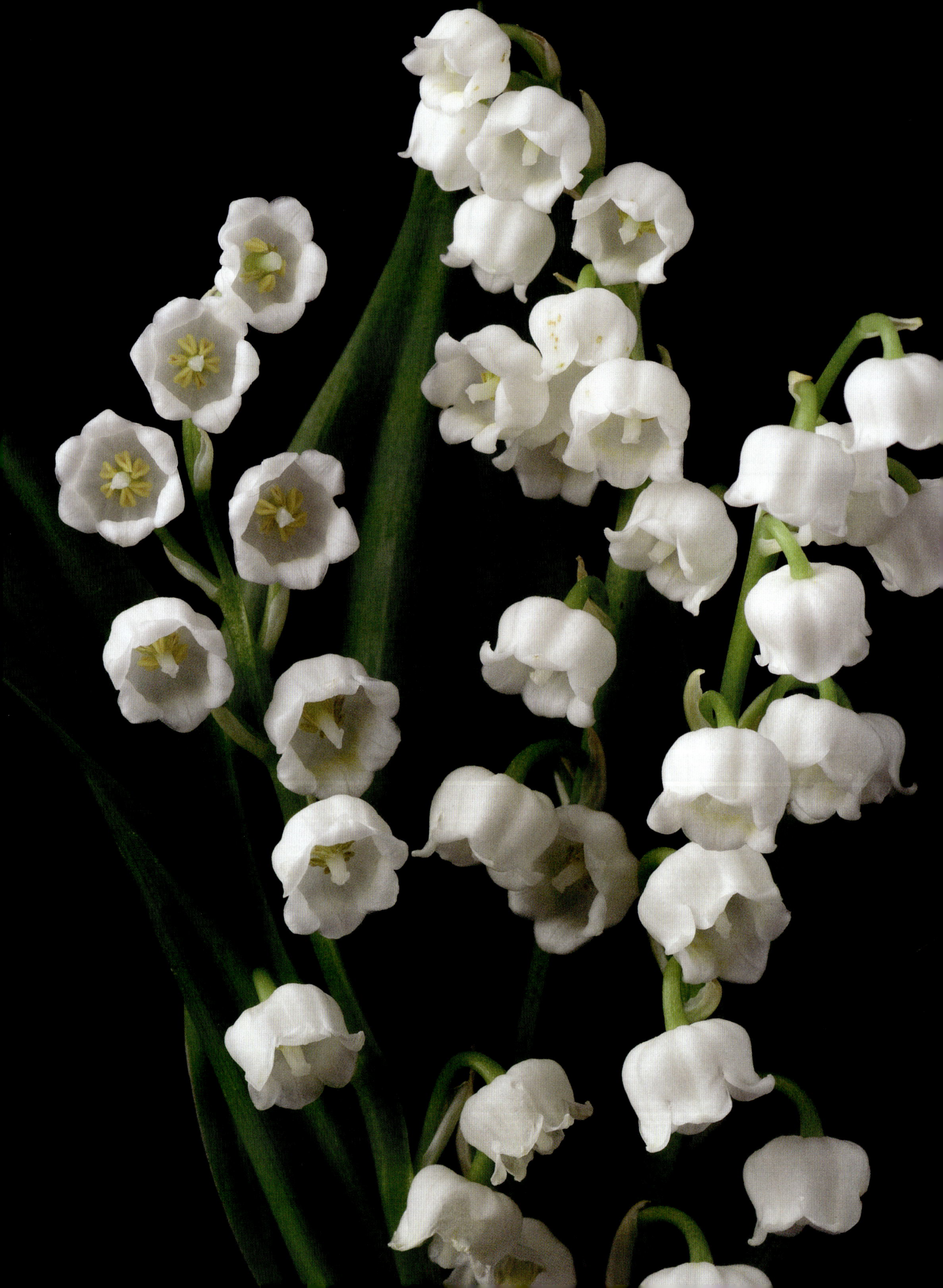

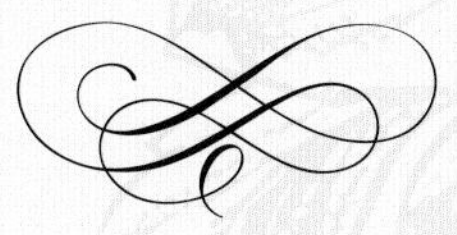

LILY OF THE VALLEY

Hillhaven Garden, Shoreline, Washington, USA
April 2015

Lily of the valley, representing sweetness, humility and a return of happiness, produces one of the most evocative scents of any flower.

In my former garden, Hillhaven, lily of the valley grew wildly and abundantly. Each May, I cut extravagant bouquets for inside the house and to photograph in my studio. Many have become some of my most enduring images, including one of an antique Limoges bowl with hundreds of stems, representing a small fortune if I'd purchased them through a florist. After a photo shoot, my "models" would sit on my desk, perfuming the entire room.

In my Paris apartment, I celebrate La Fête du Muguet with a display of small arrangements and potted plants under cloches, arrayed on one of our marble fireplace mantels.

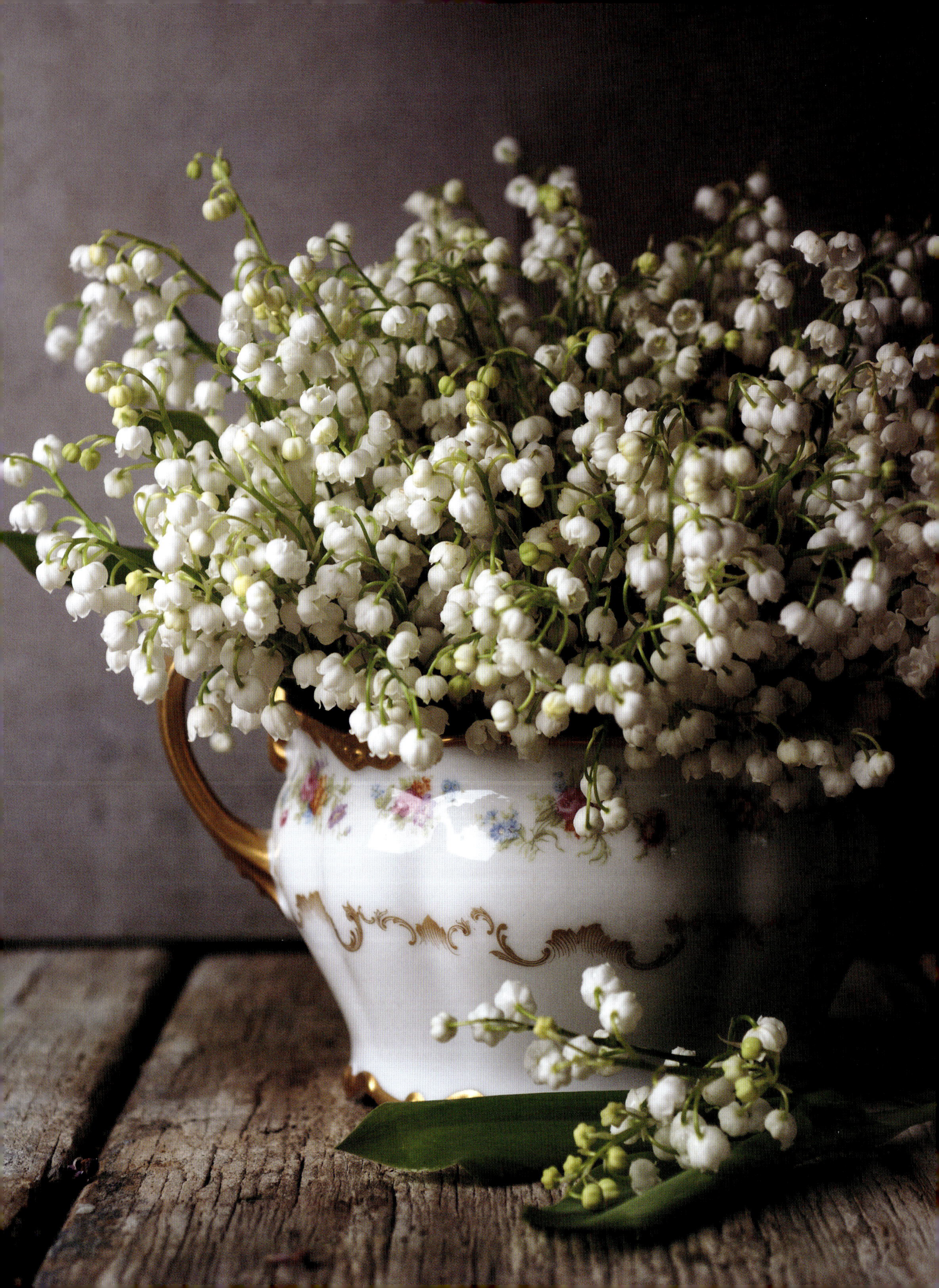

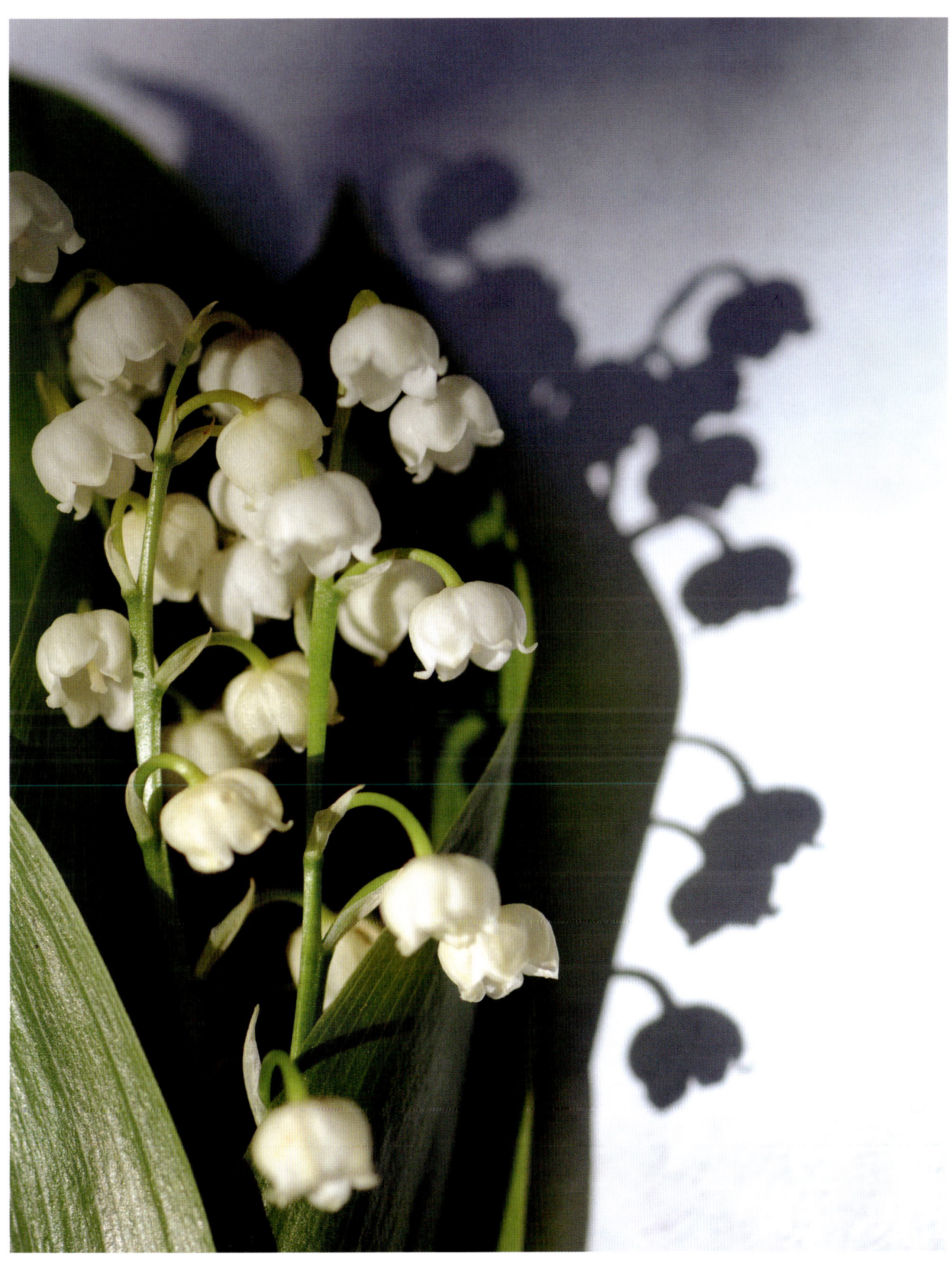

LEFT: Lily of the Valley (*Convallaria majalis*), Hillhaven Garden, Shoreline, Washington, USA. May 2015. ABOVE: Lily of the Valley, Hillhaven. May. 2009. OVERLEAF: Display of Lily of the Valley, Paris, France. May 2022.

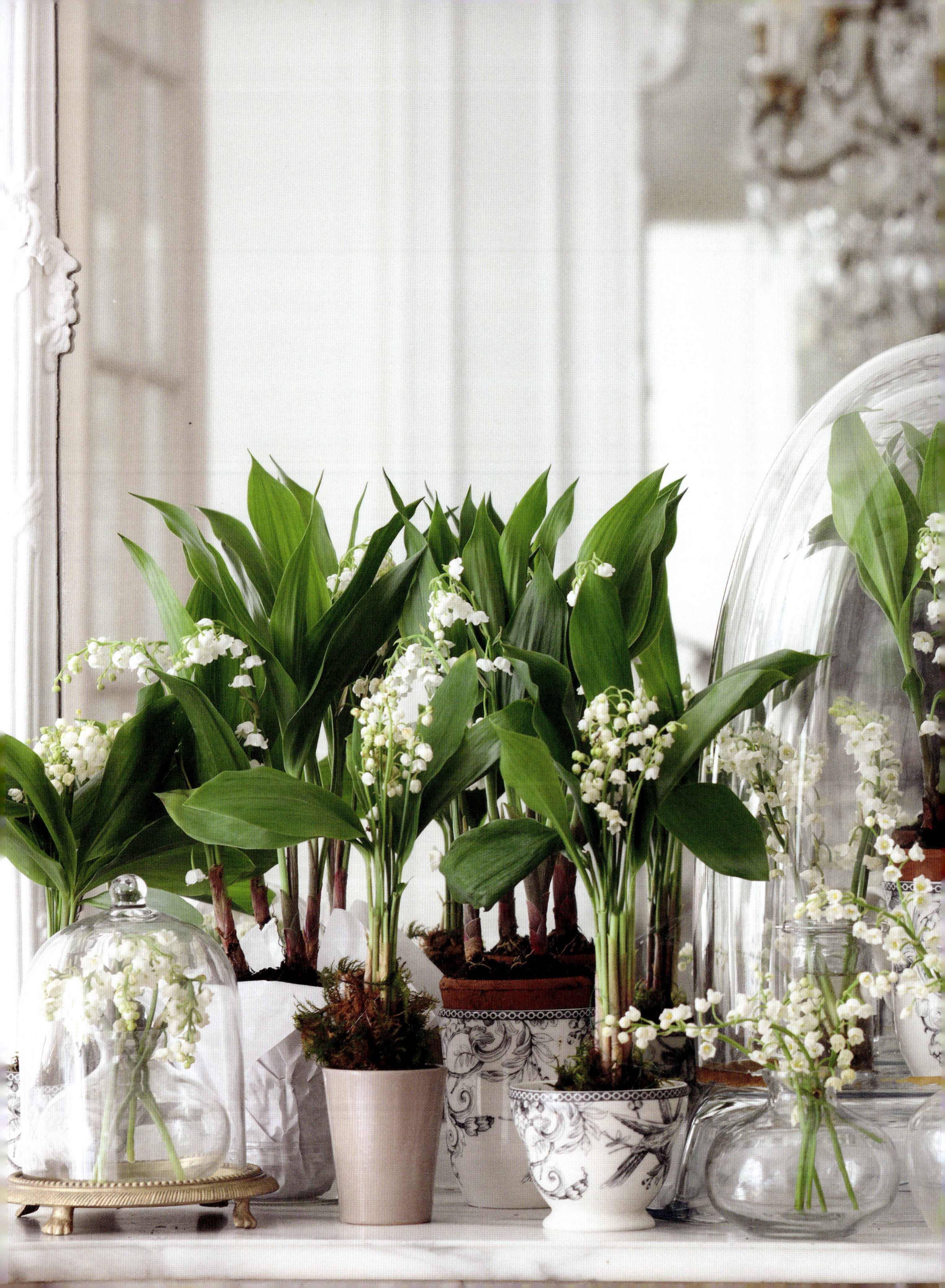

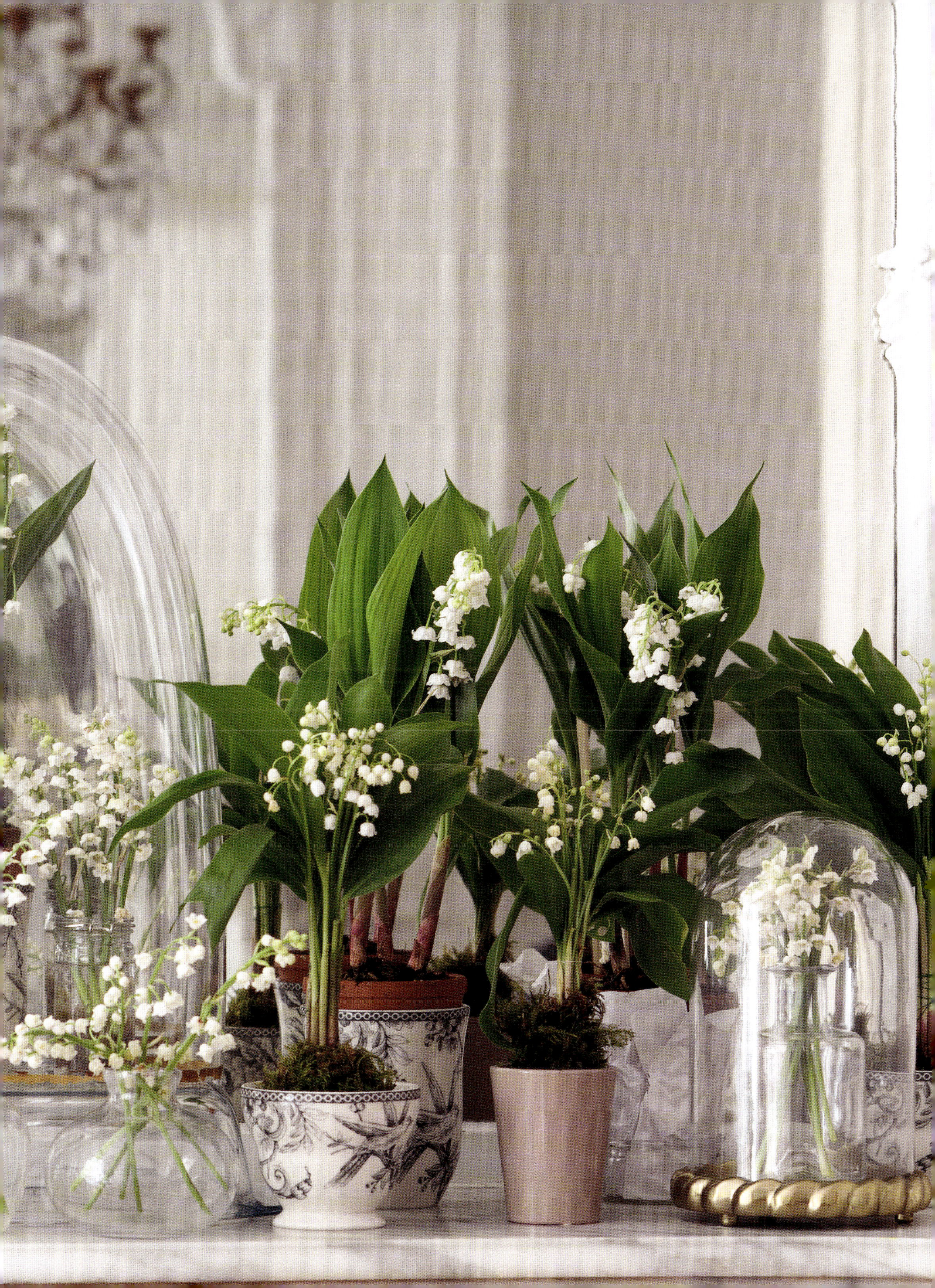

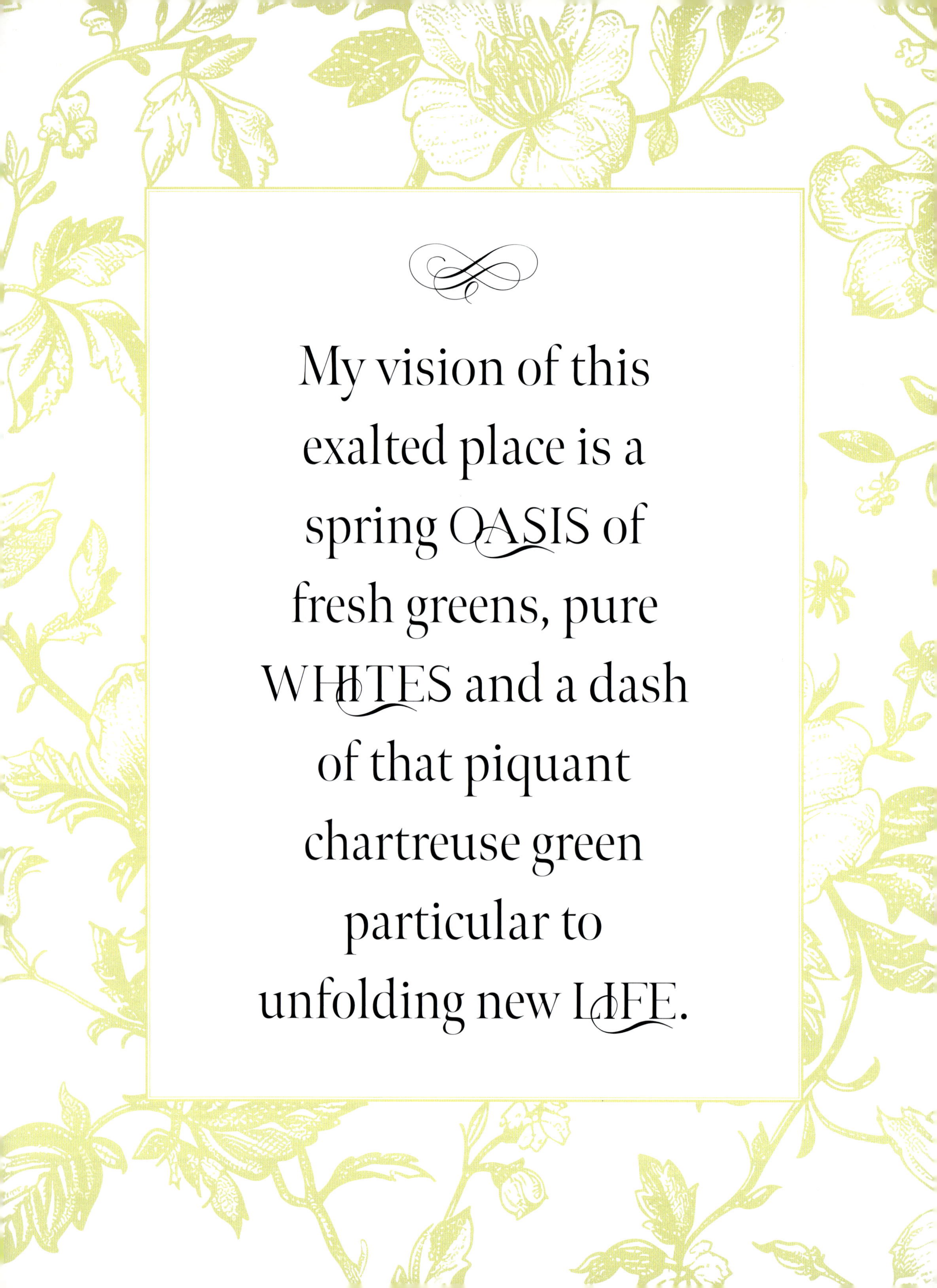

My vision of this exalted place is a spring OASIS of fresh greens, pure WHITES and a dash of that piquant chartreuse green particular to unfolding new LIFE.

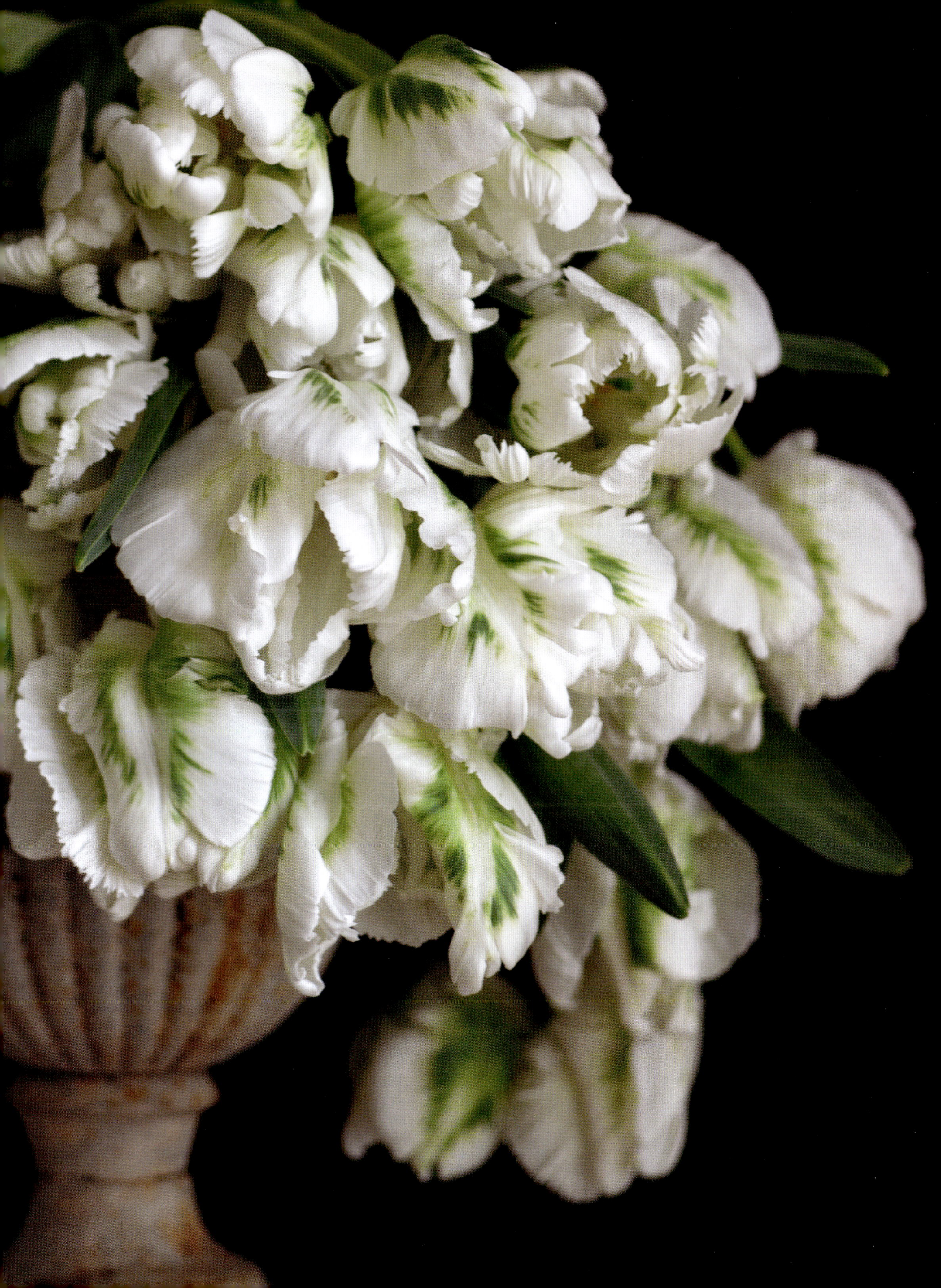

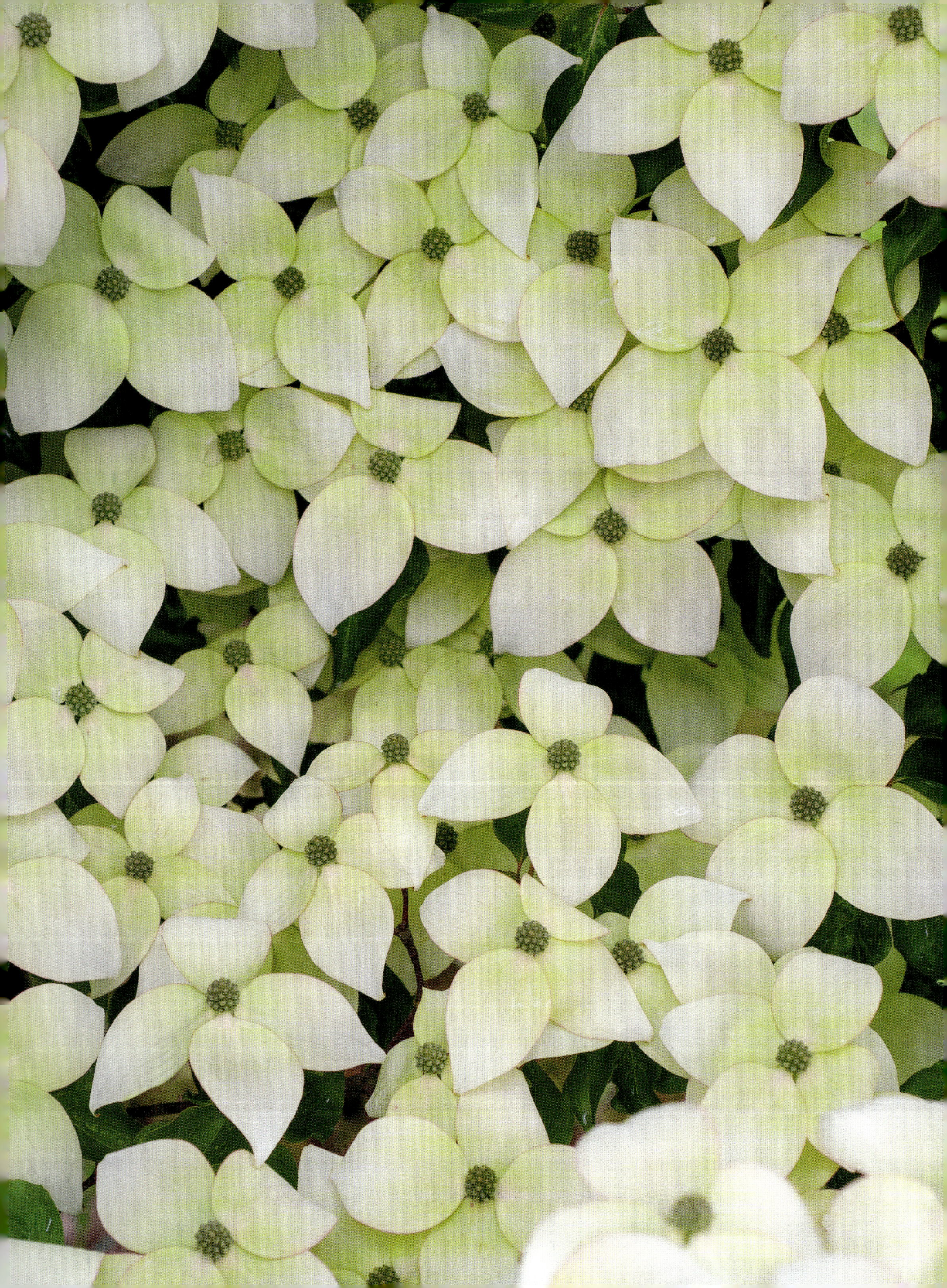

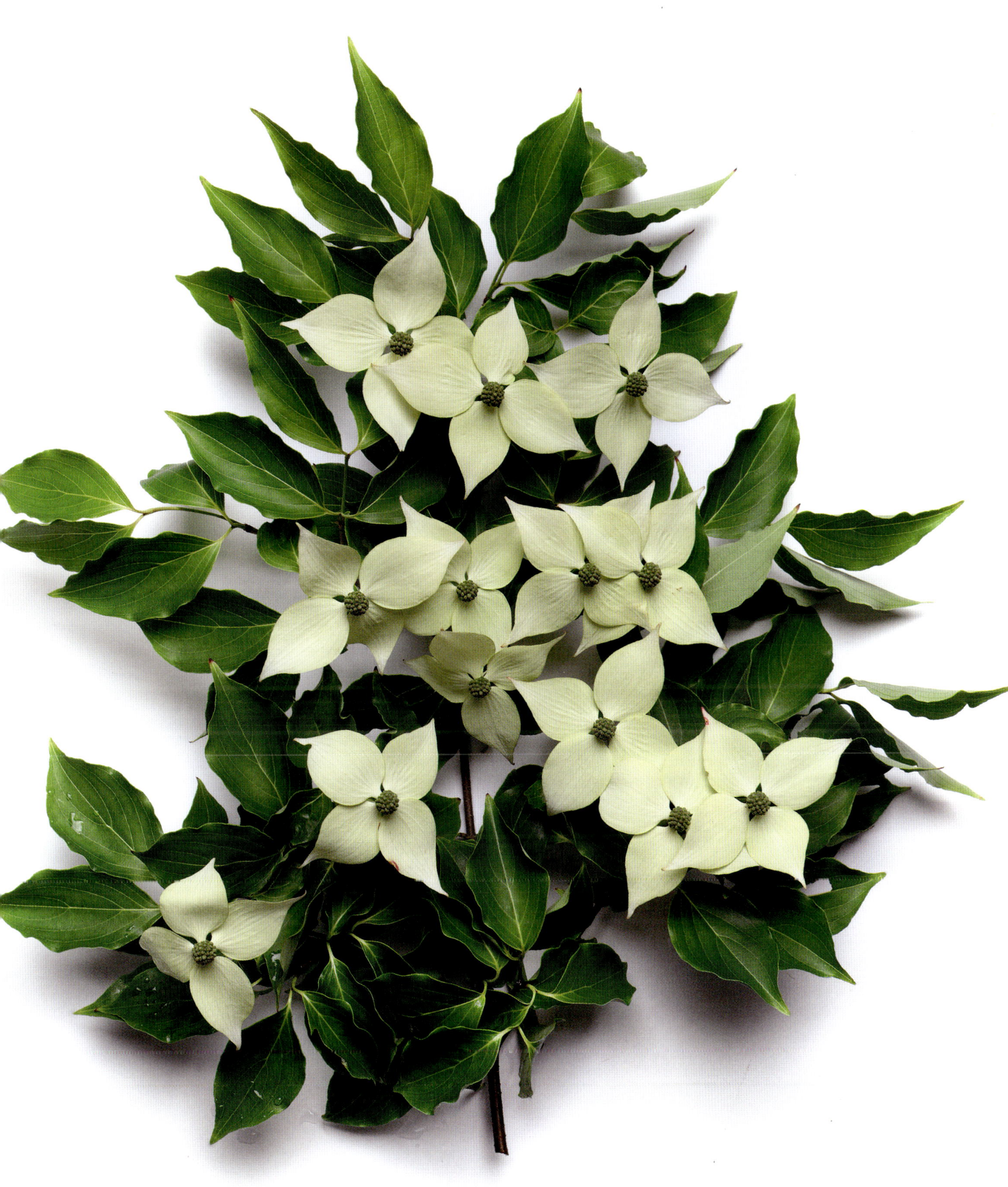

LEFT and ABOVE: Branches of dogwood blossoms (*Cornus kousa* 'Greensleeves'), Washington, USA. May 2007 and June 2017.

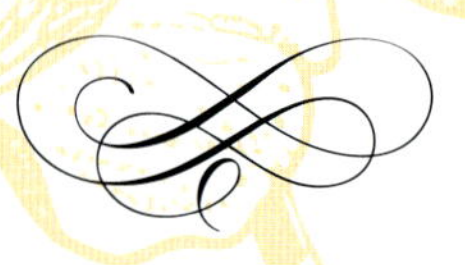

FROM THE SPRING GARDEN

Hillhaven Garden, Shoreline, Washington, USA
April 2015

Freshness and hope are qualities exemplified in a garden in spring. The bell-like flowers of these spring snowflake blooms (Leucojum vernum)*, echoing the shape of lily of the valley, are like sweet heralds, ringing in a welcome season of growth.*

Equally charming are the pink-tinged flowers of Enkianthus campanulatus *and multi-petaled hellebores, both bearing an amiable and gentle demeanor that seems to say "take your time, linger awhile and discover our delights."*

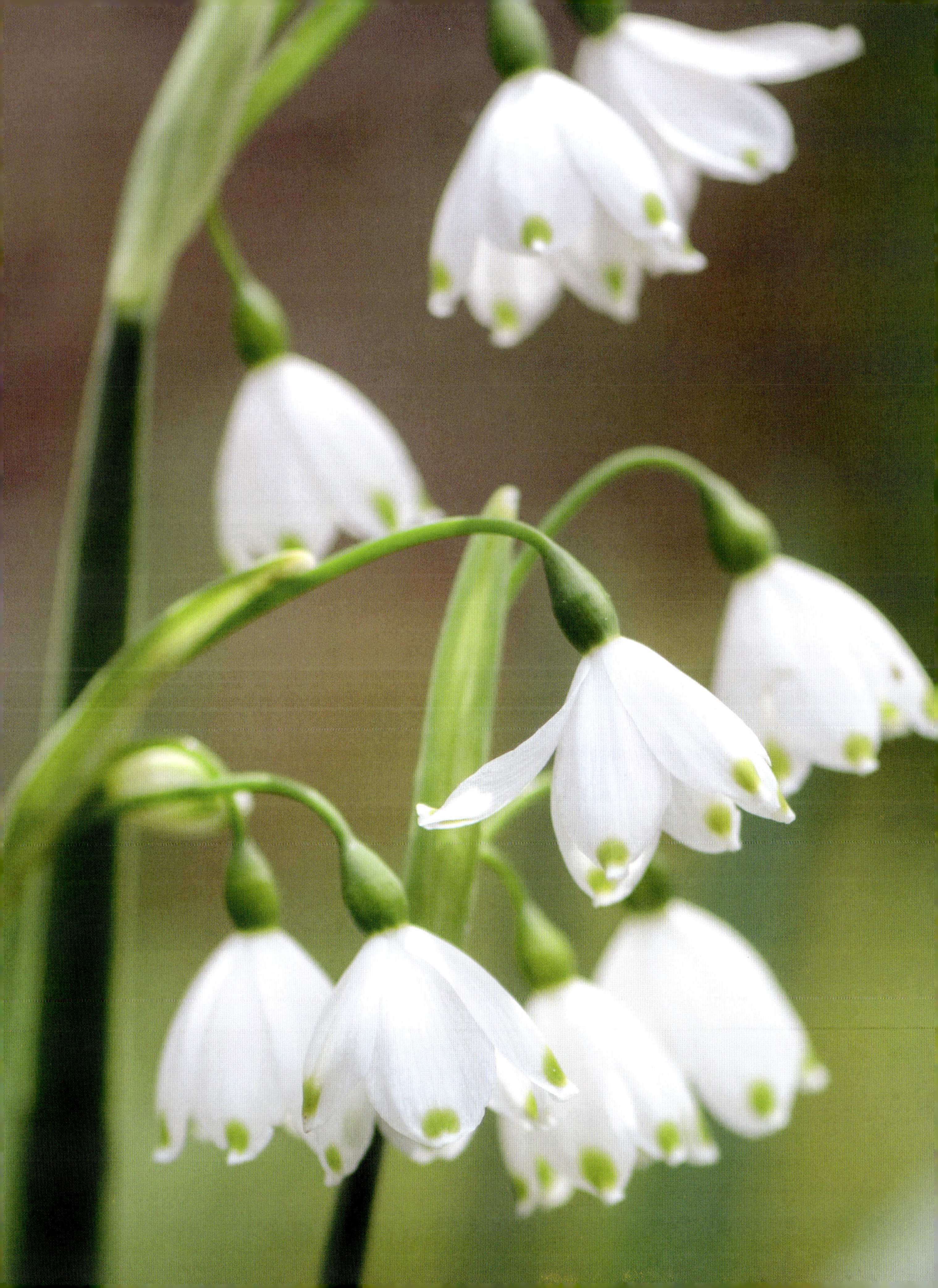

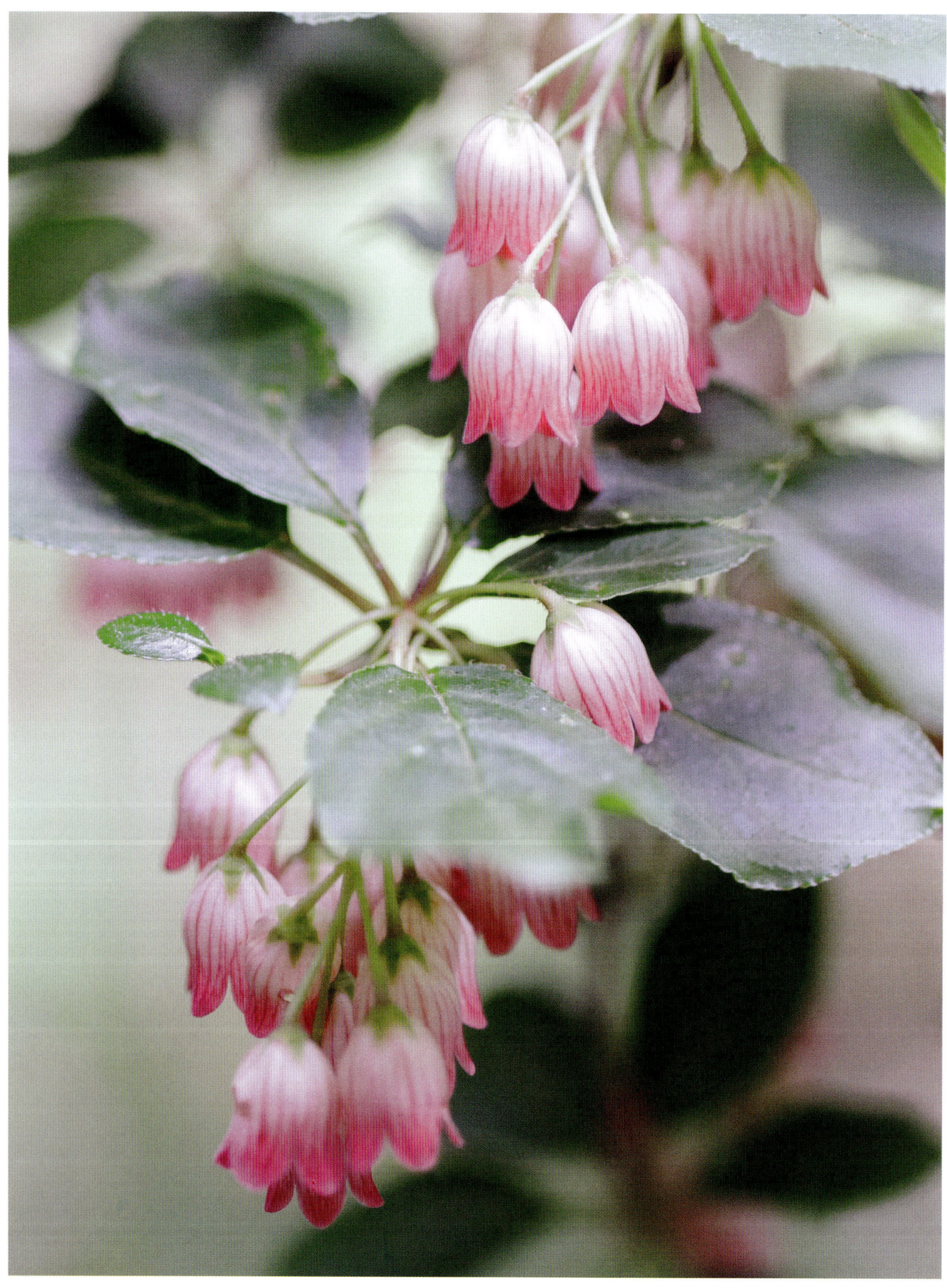

ABOVE: Branch of flowering *Enkianthus campanulatus*, Washington, USA. May 2019. RIGHT: Close-up of a field tulip, Washington, USA. April 2008.

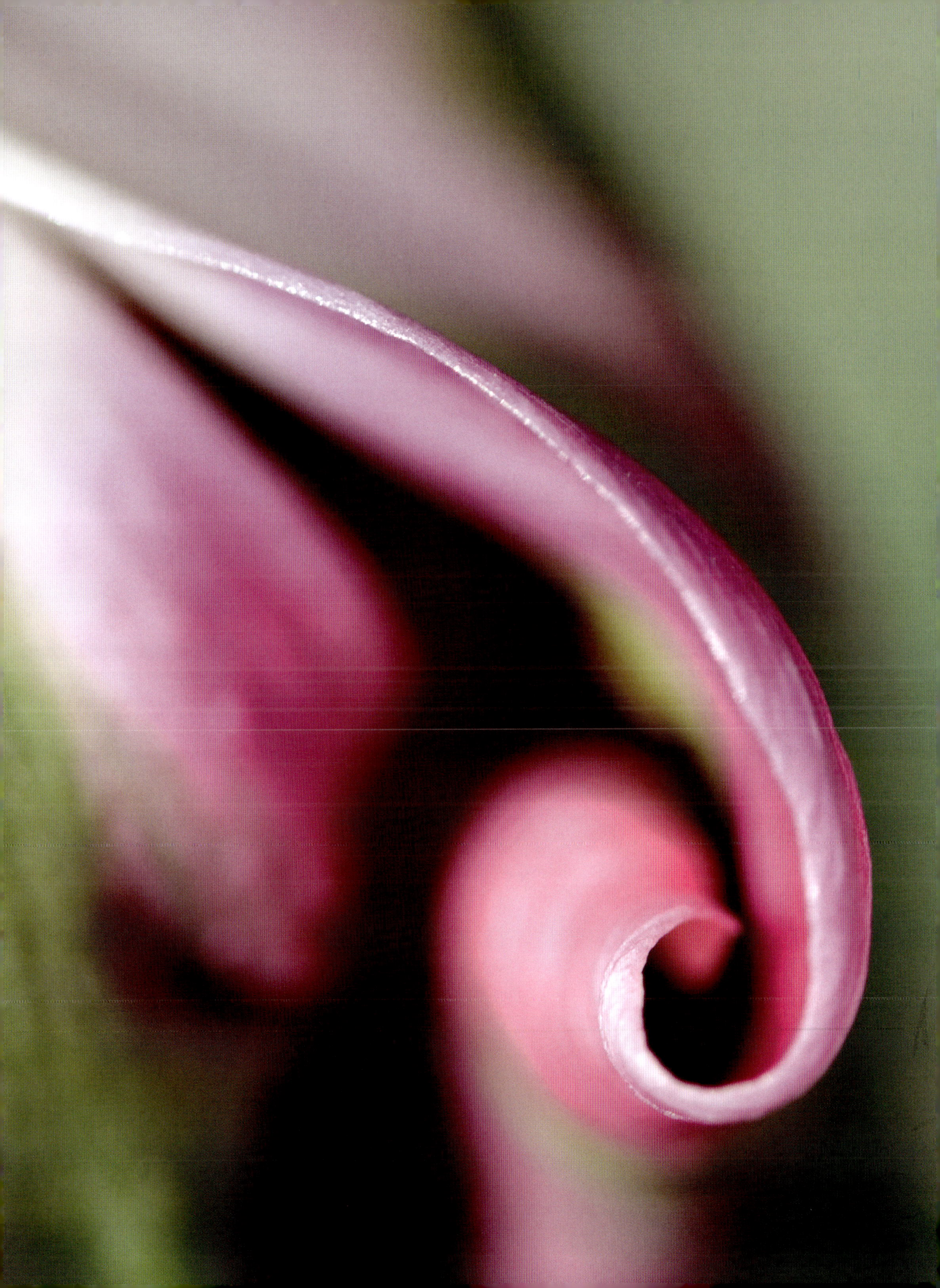

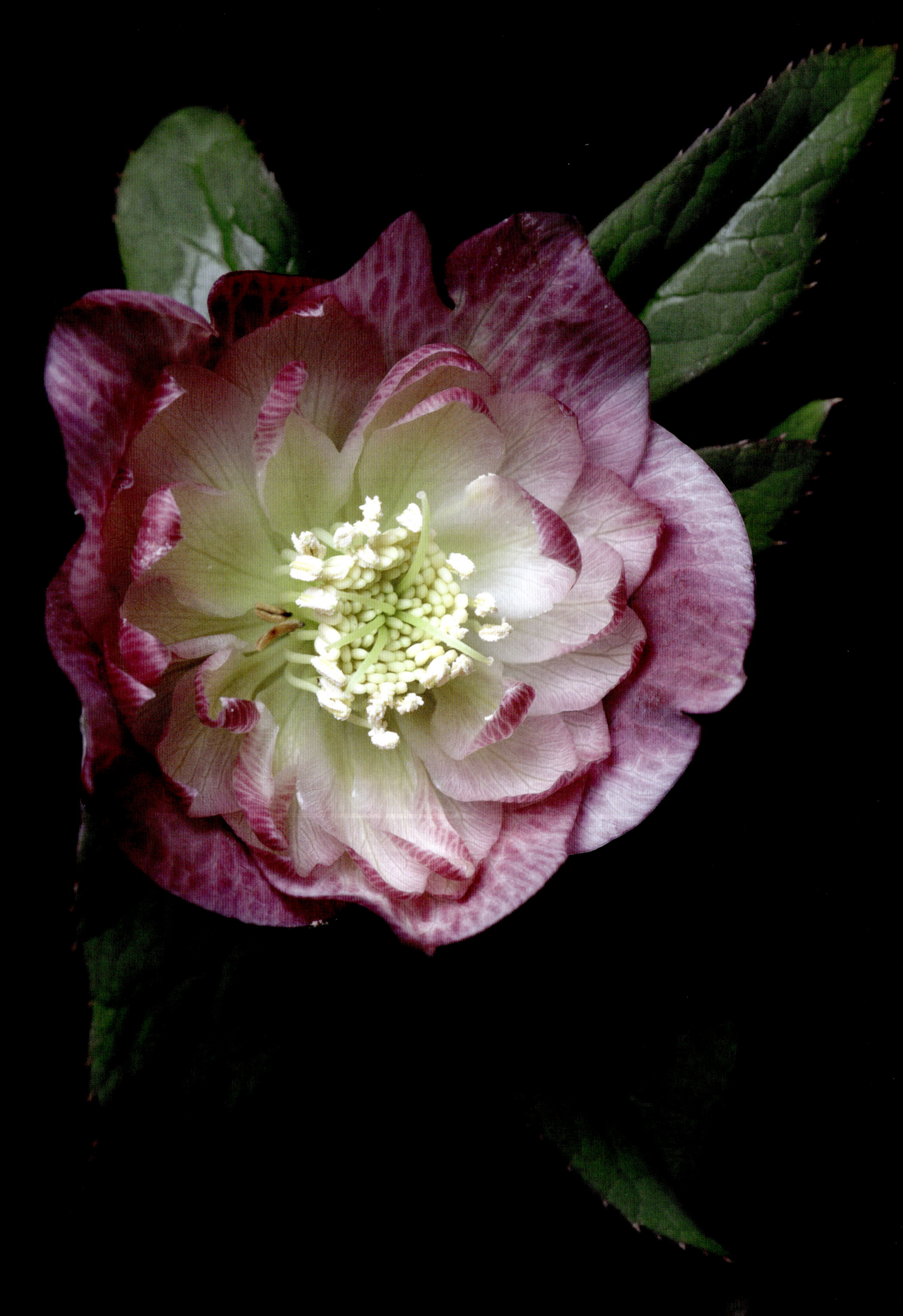

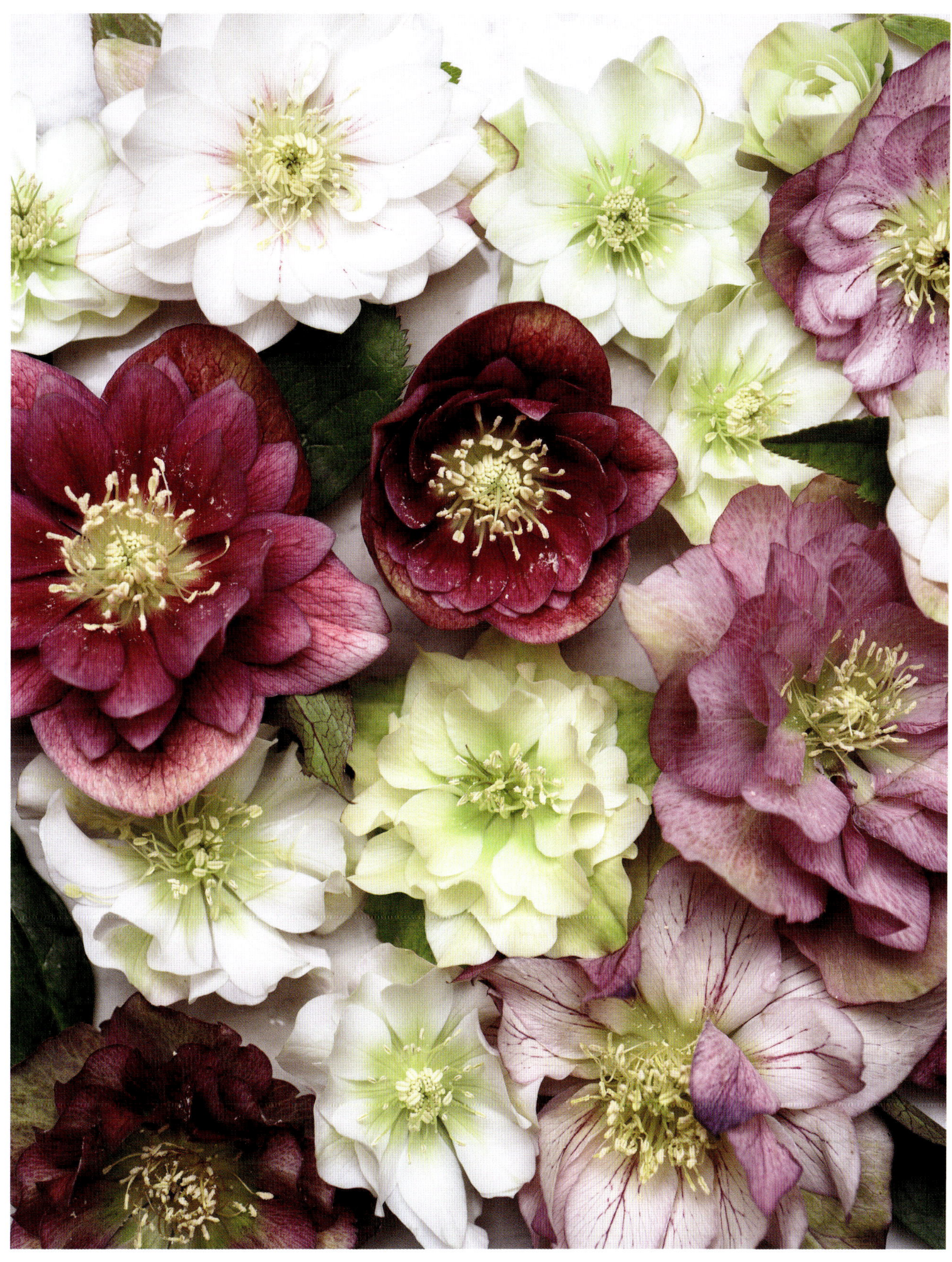

LEFT and ABOVE: *Helleborus*, Paris, France. March 2016. OVERLEAF: Floral heart with roses, tulips, hydrangea, anemone, ranunculus, pussy willow, lilac, hellebore, Paris, France. March 2016.

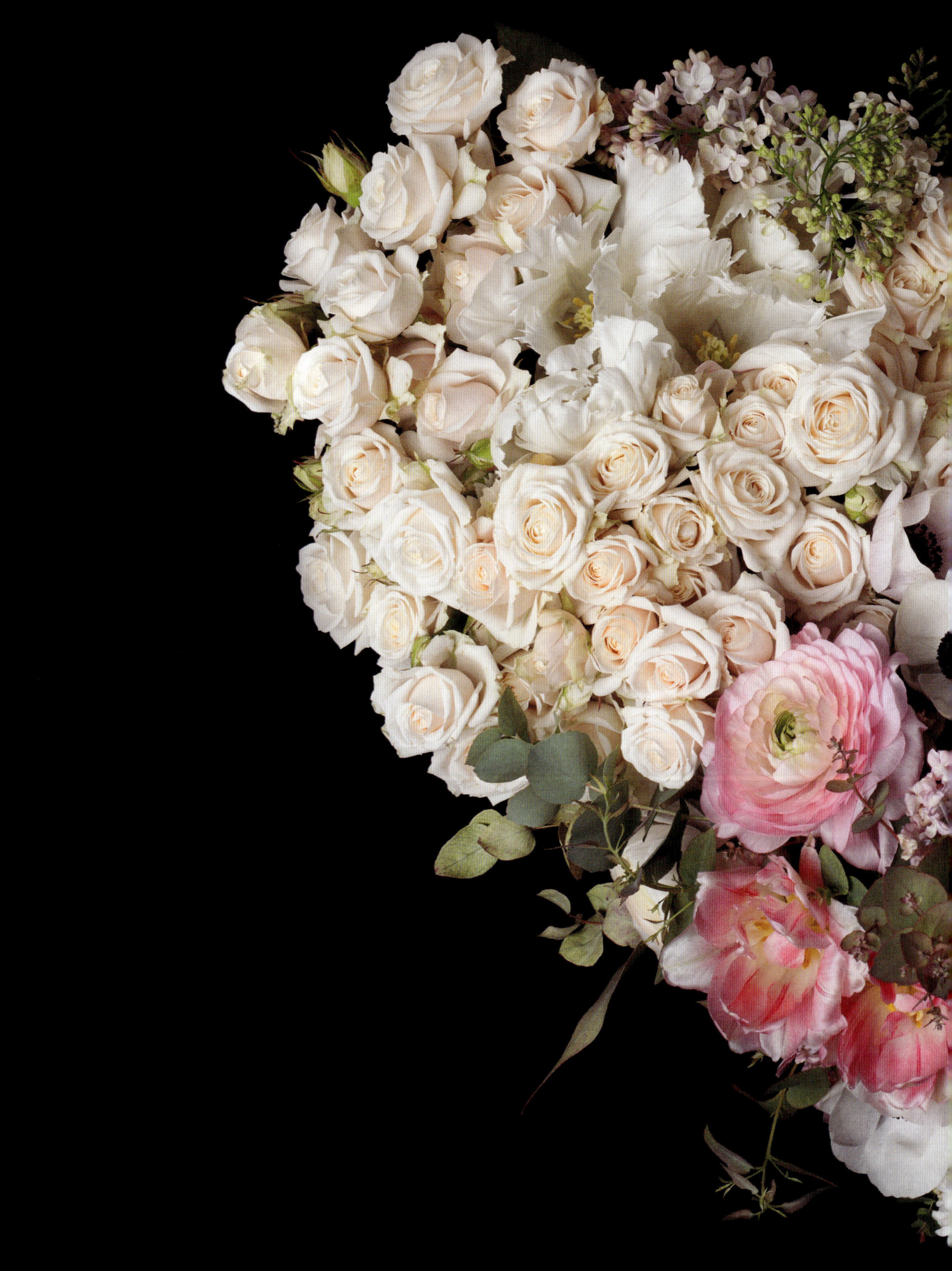

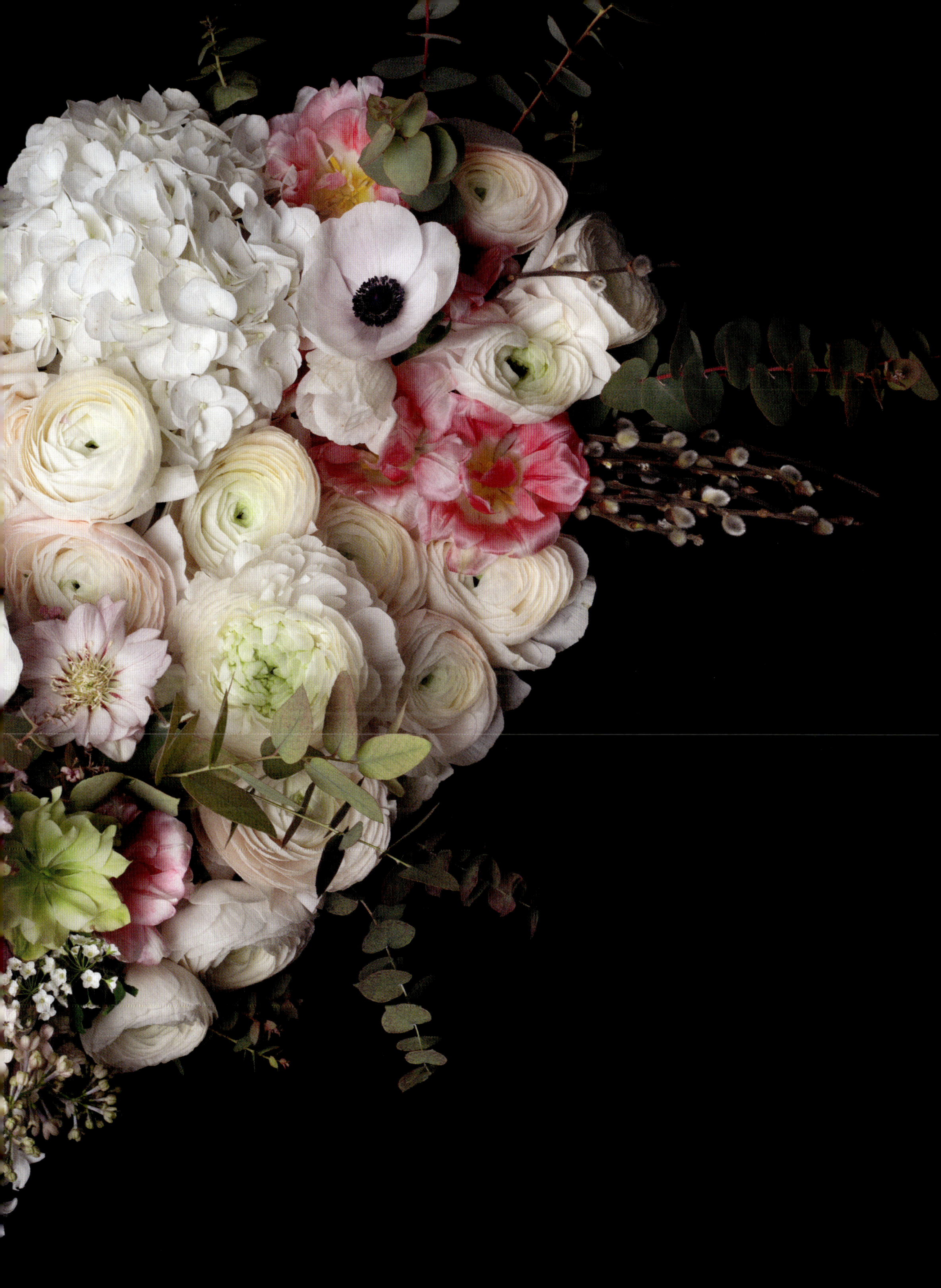

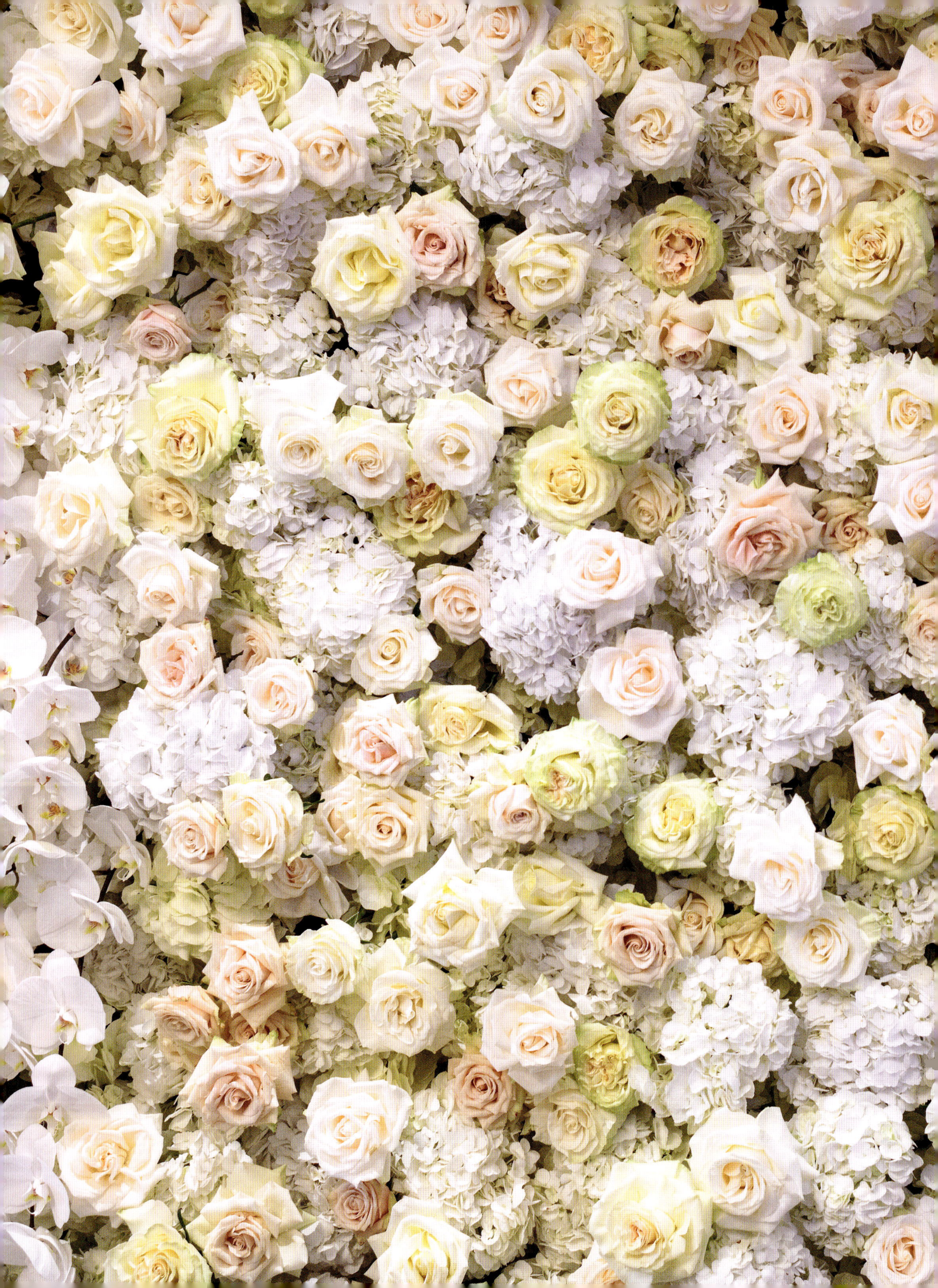

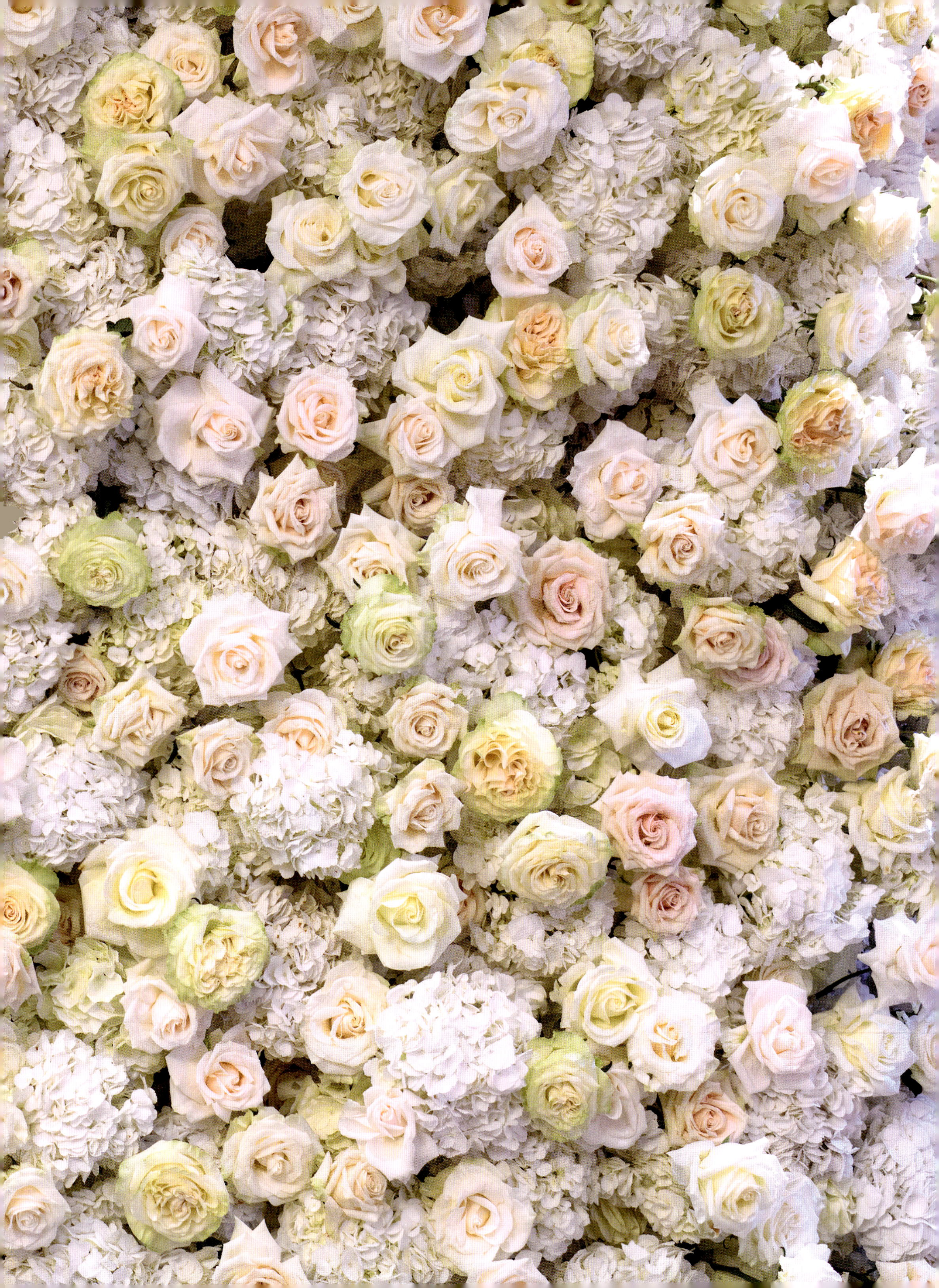

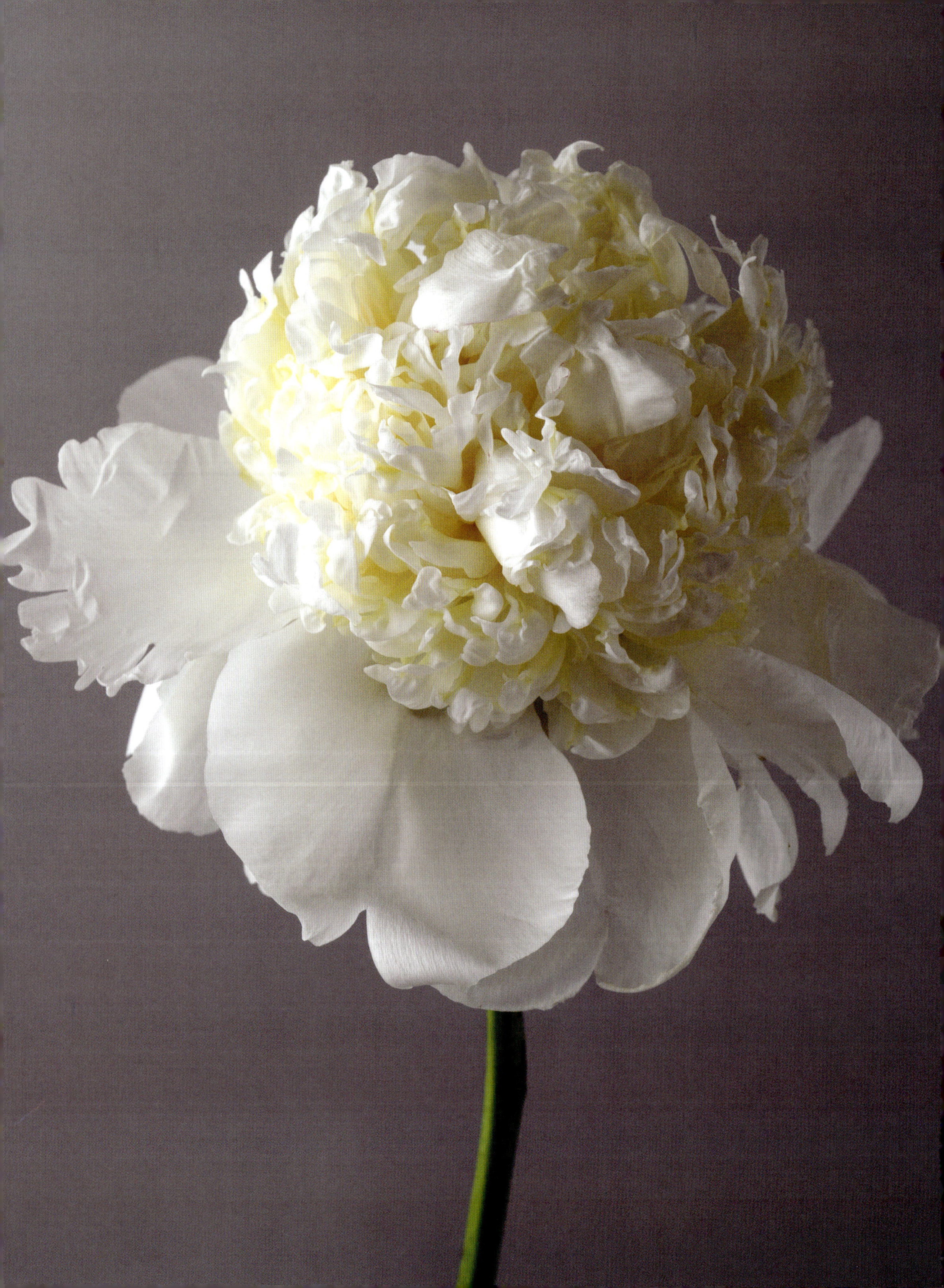

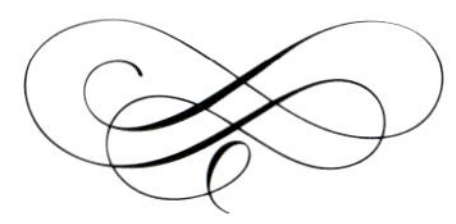

I cherish deep
CONVERSATIONS
with the flowers,
gently coaxing out
their ENIGMATIC
secrets and the private
MYSTERIES
tucked between
their petals.

LEFT: *Paeonia lactiflora* 'Bridal Shower', Paris, France. May 2025.

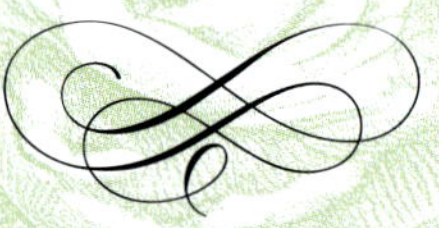

THE PEONY CHÂTEAU

Conservatoire de la Pivoine, Château de Sourches, Saint-Symphorien, France

For any lover of peonies, allow me to show the way to a heaven on Earth. Not far from the historic city of Le Mans, about two hours west of Paris in the Pays de la Loire, lies the grand mid-eighteenth century, neoclassical Château de Sourches.

Within its massive, deep moat, the owner, my friend Bénédicte de Foucaud, has created the world's largest collection of peonies, passionately searching the globe for every rare and heirloom variety to be included. The Conservatoire de la Pivoine is open to the public during the blooming season, at which time one can amble through the garden, sit in pretty iron chairs to admire the bounty and be immersed in its unparalleled surroundings. I have been most appreciative to visit and photograph Sourches on numerous occasions, and selected varieties from Bénédicte's collection grace the pages of my book Peonies.

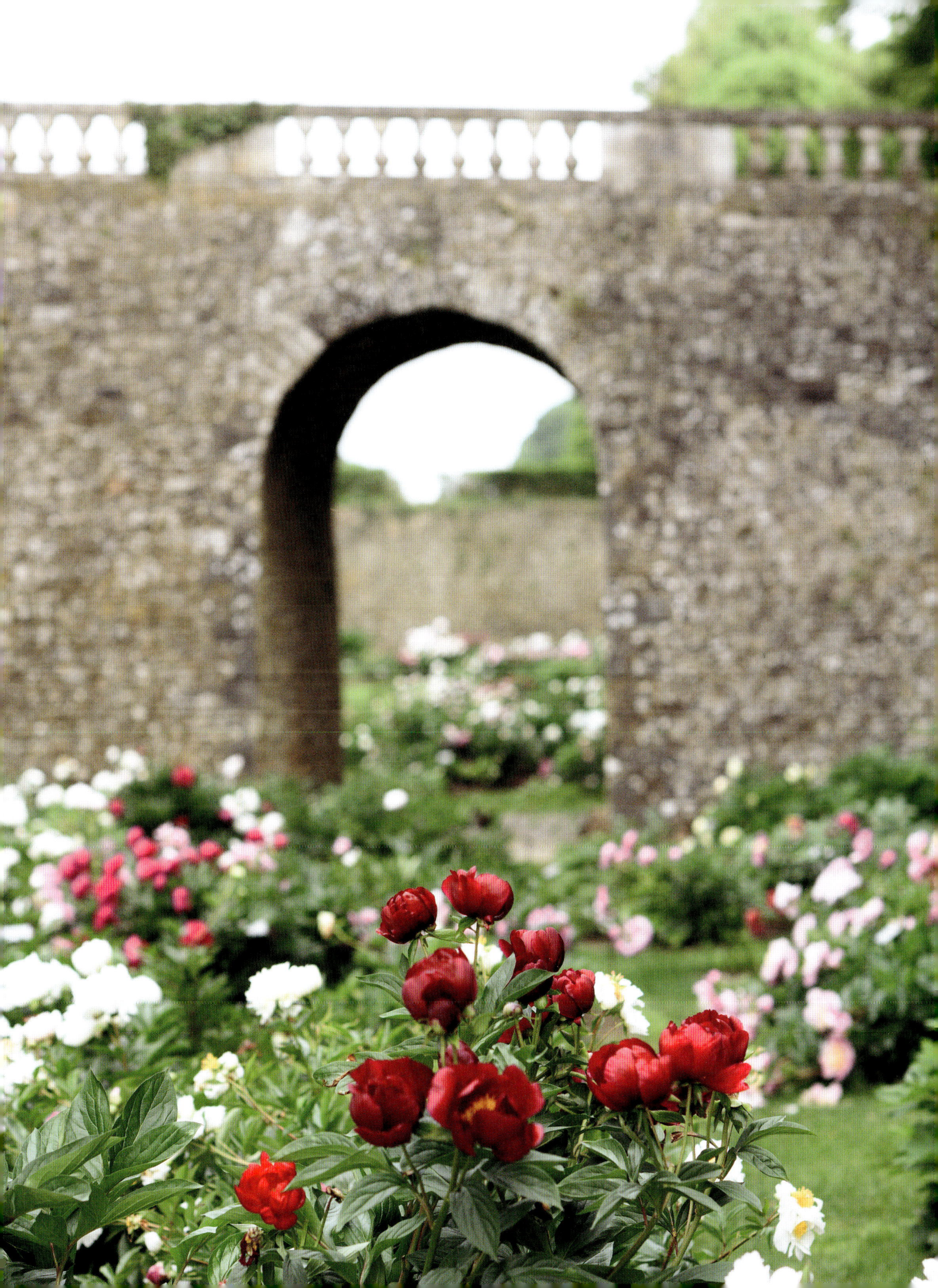

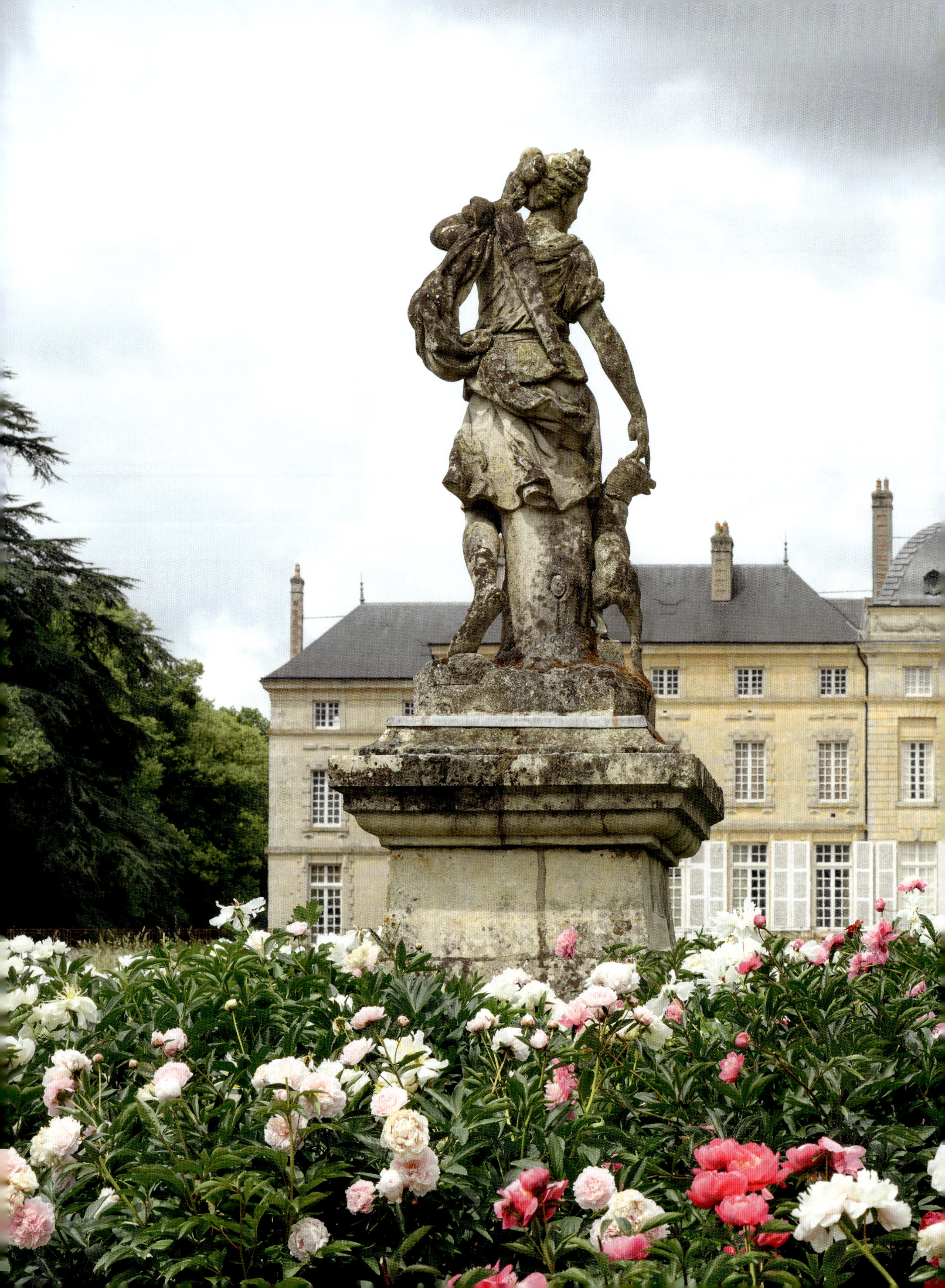

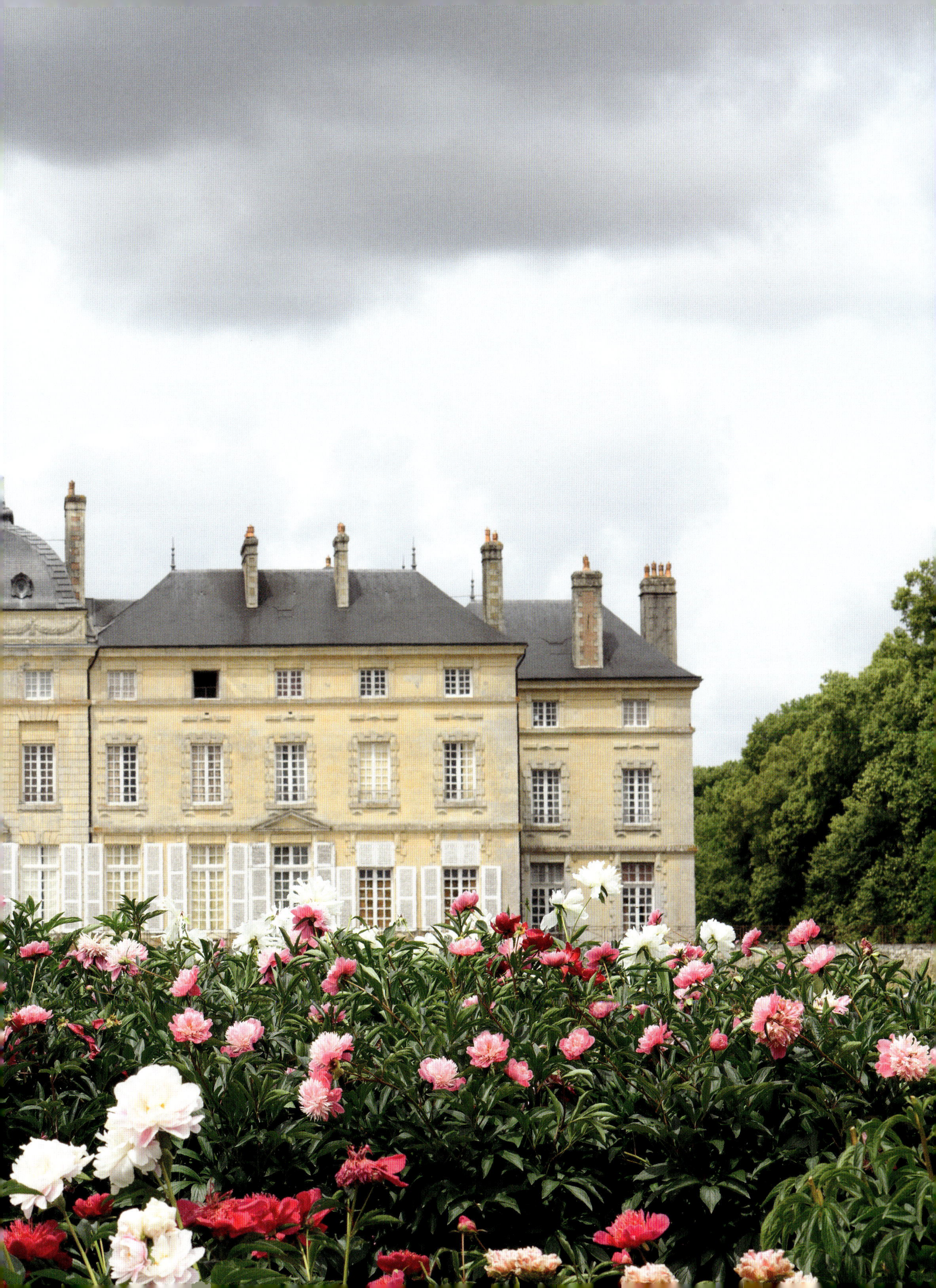

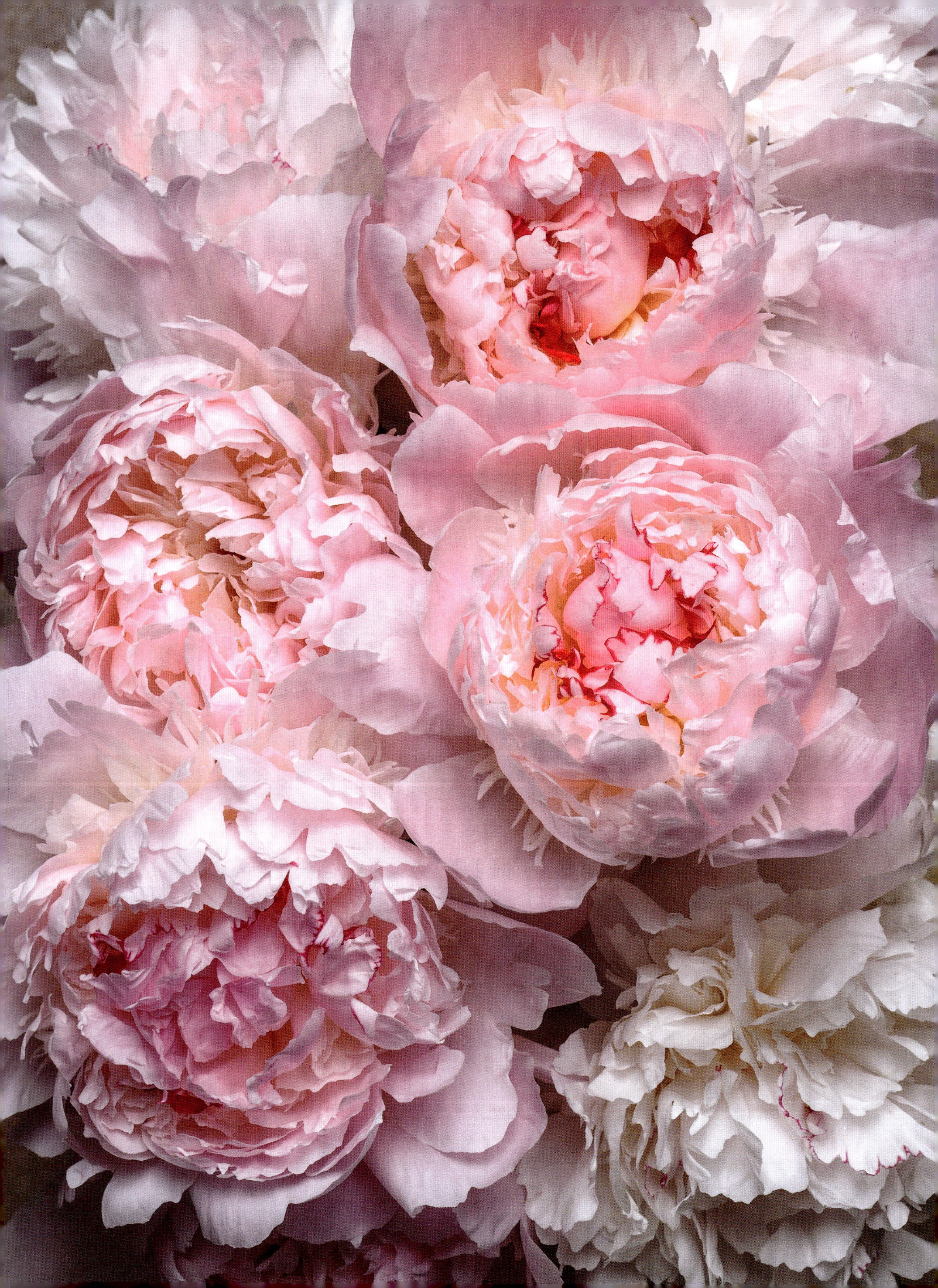

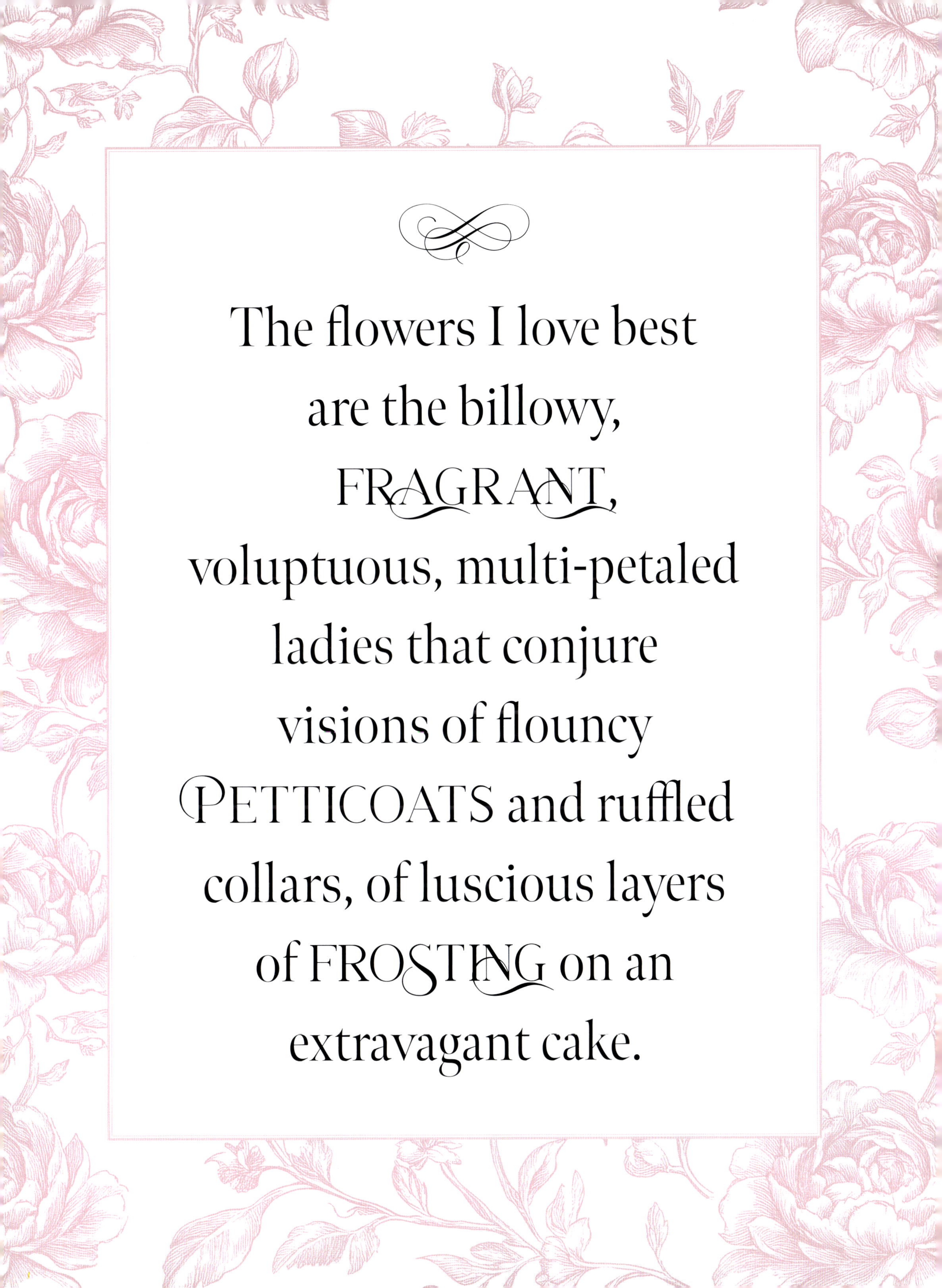

The flowers I love best
are the billowy,
FRAGRANT,
voluptuous, multi-petaled
ladies that conjure
visions of flouncy
PETTICOATS and ruffled
collars, of luscious layers
of FROSTING on an
extravagant cake.

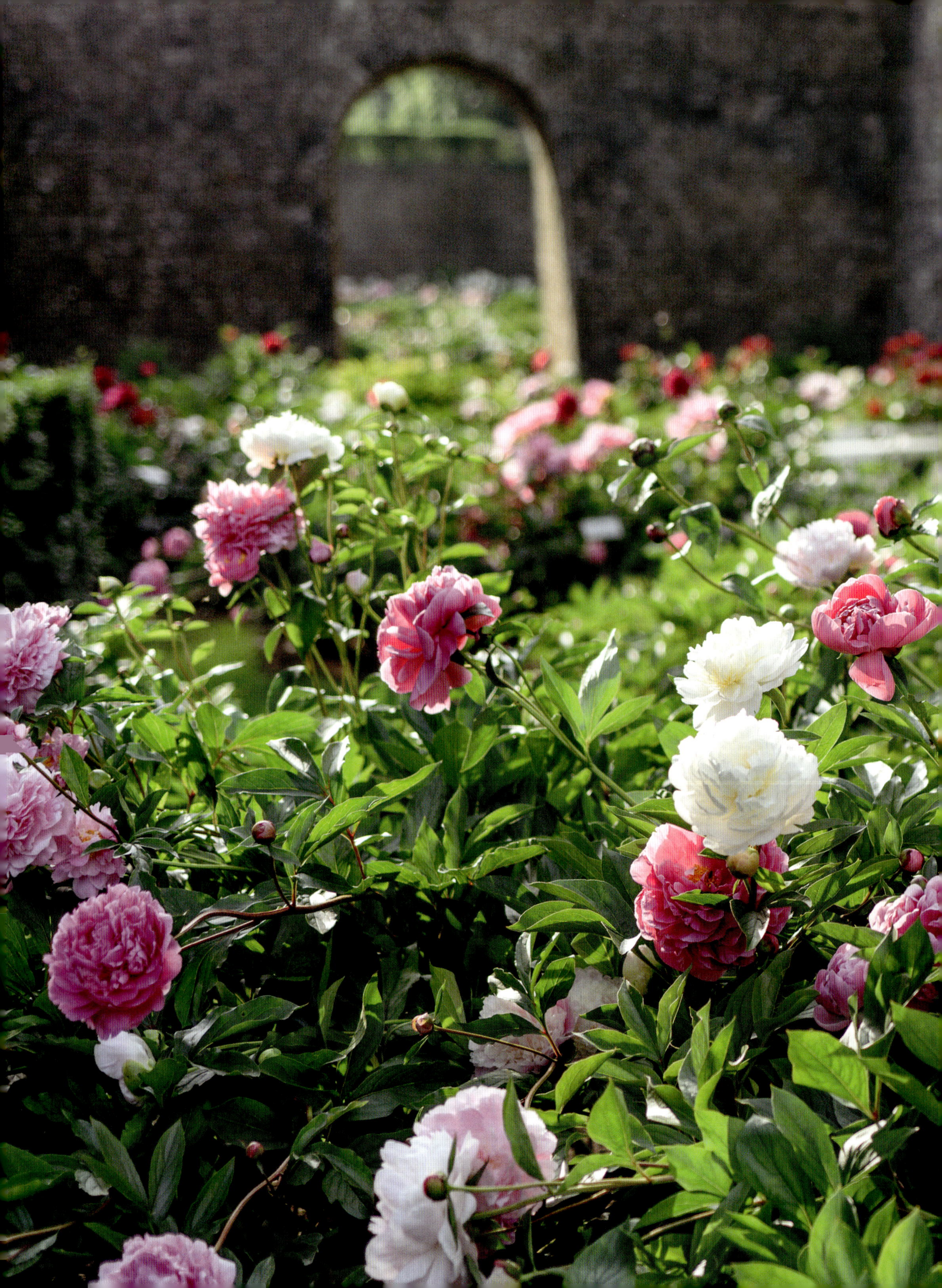

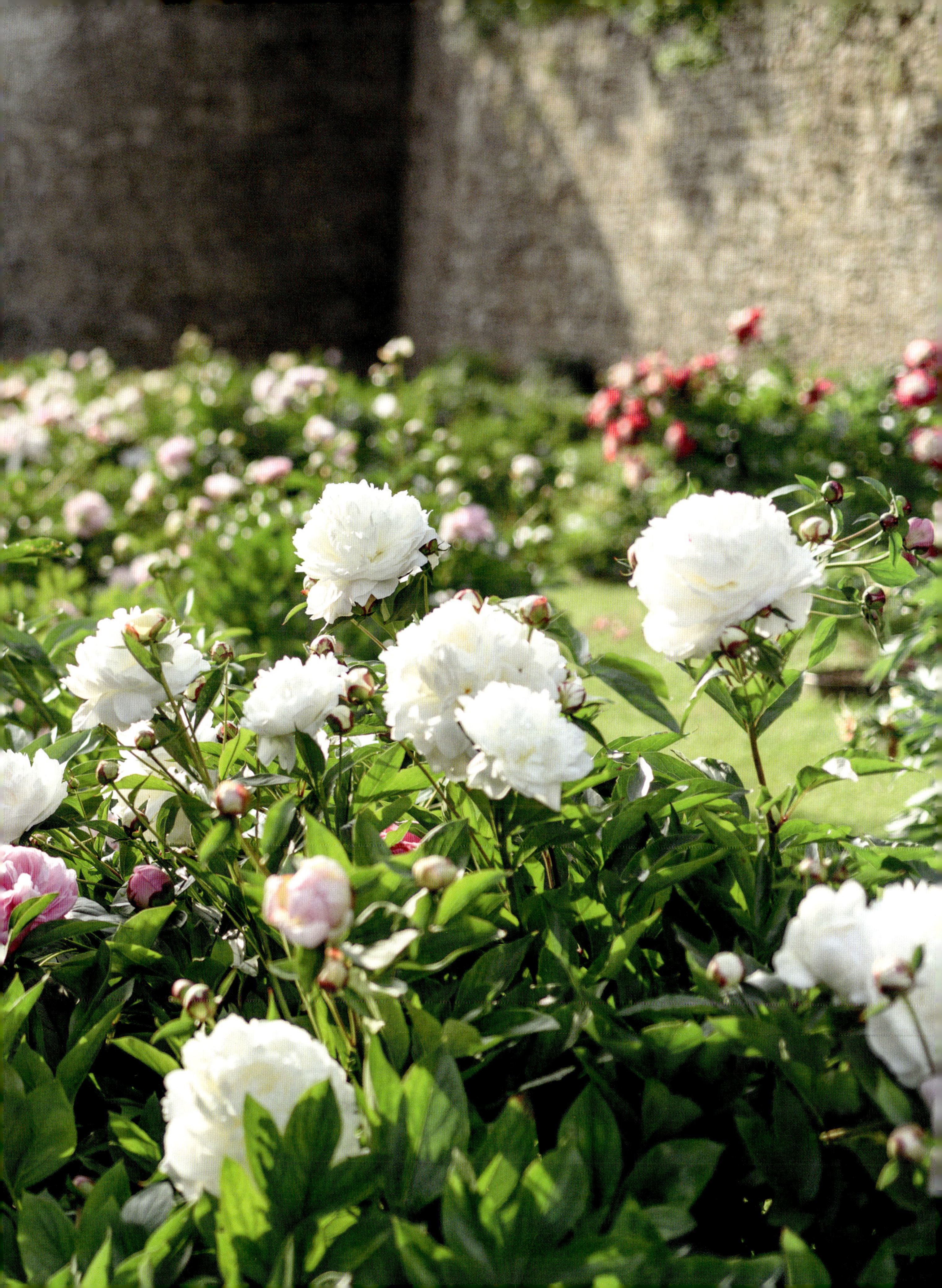

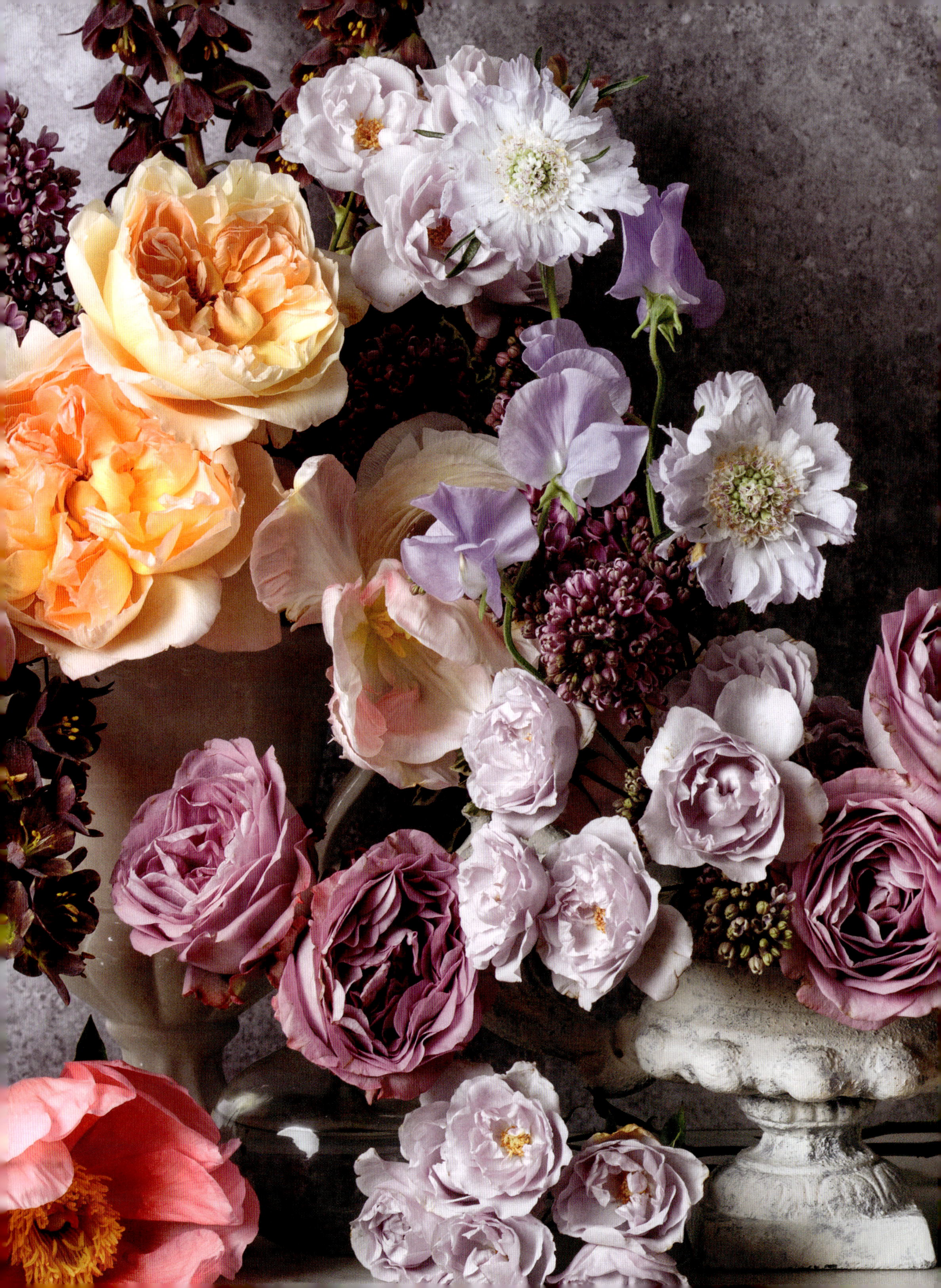

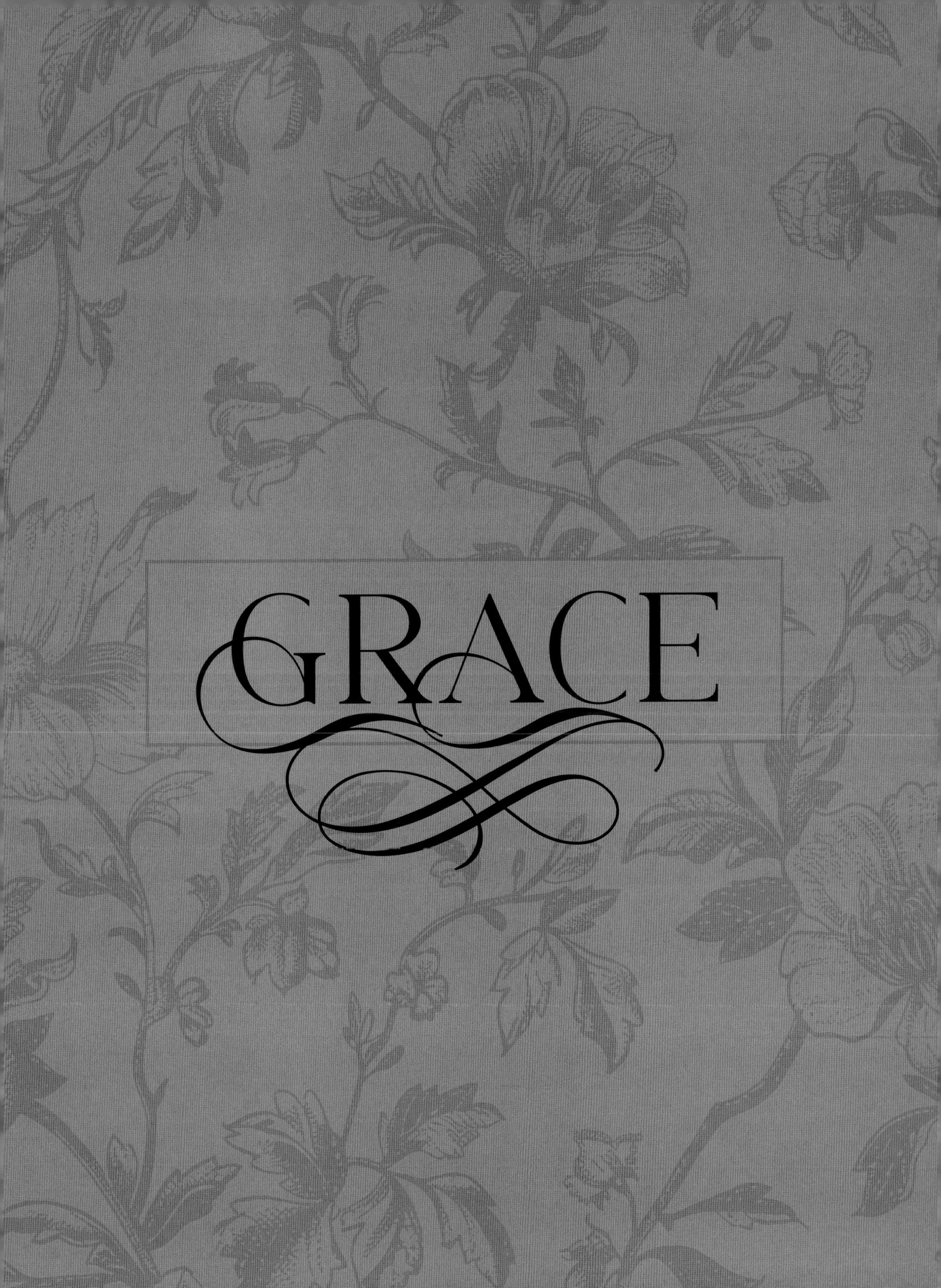
GRACE

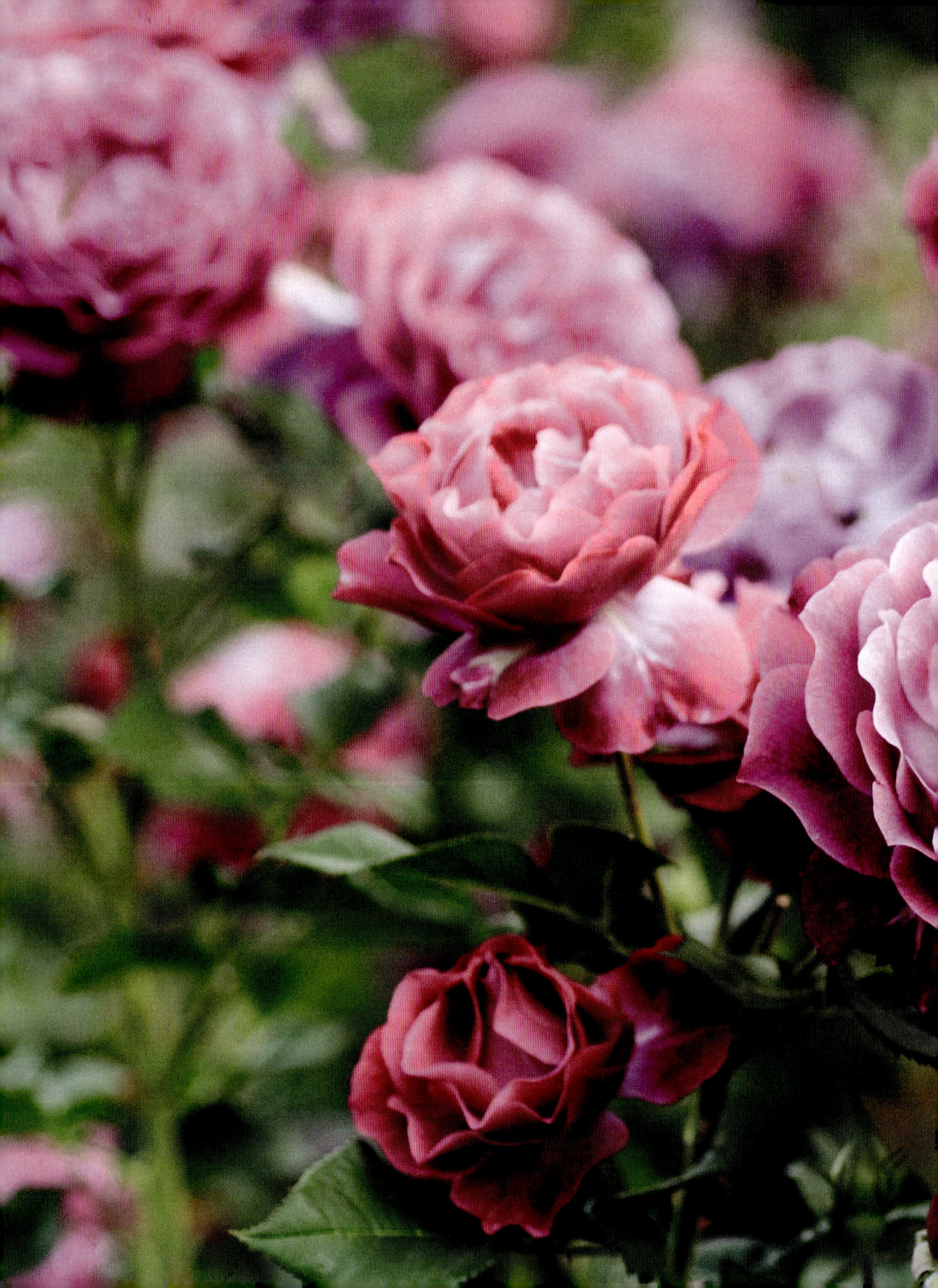

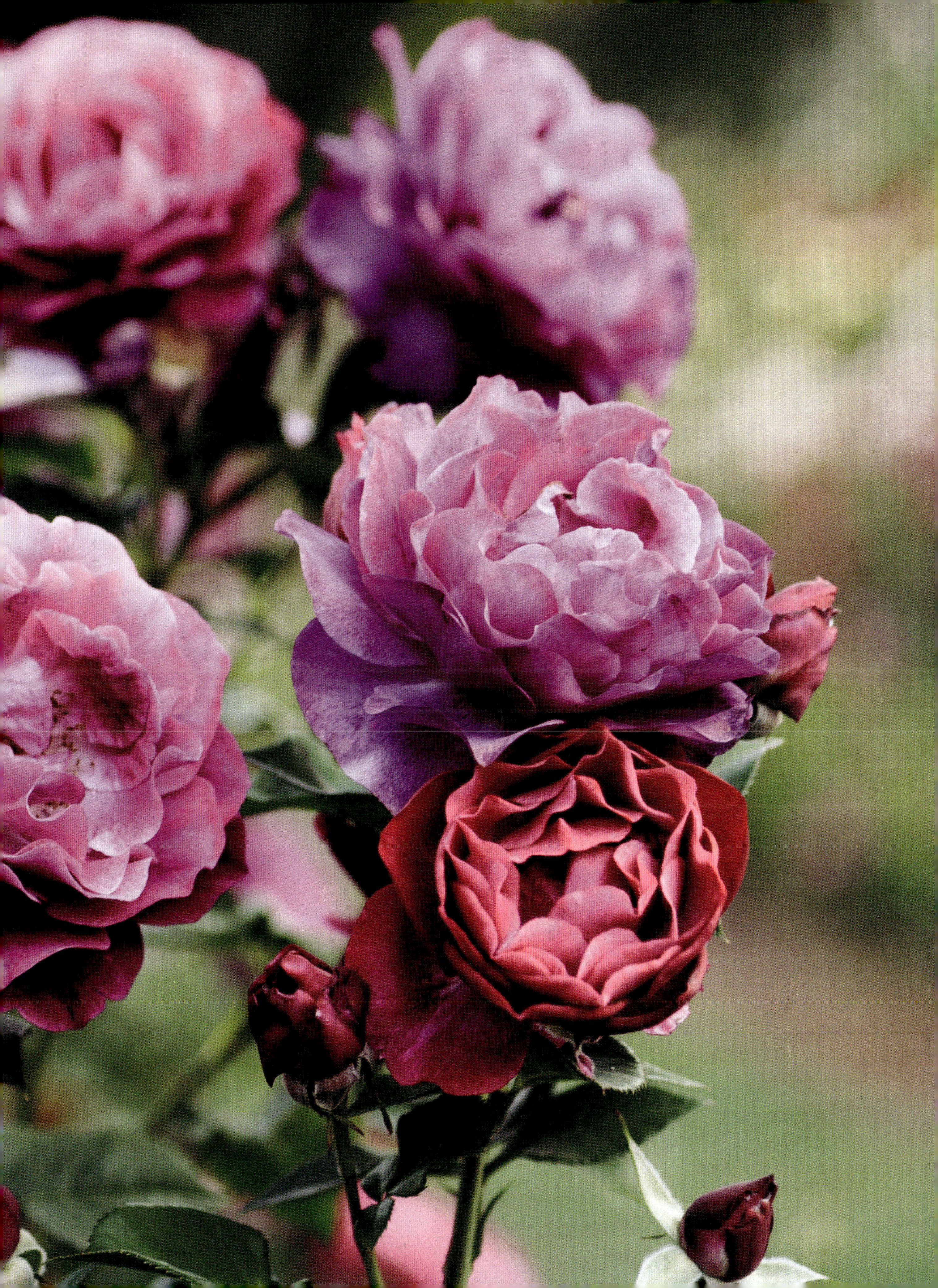

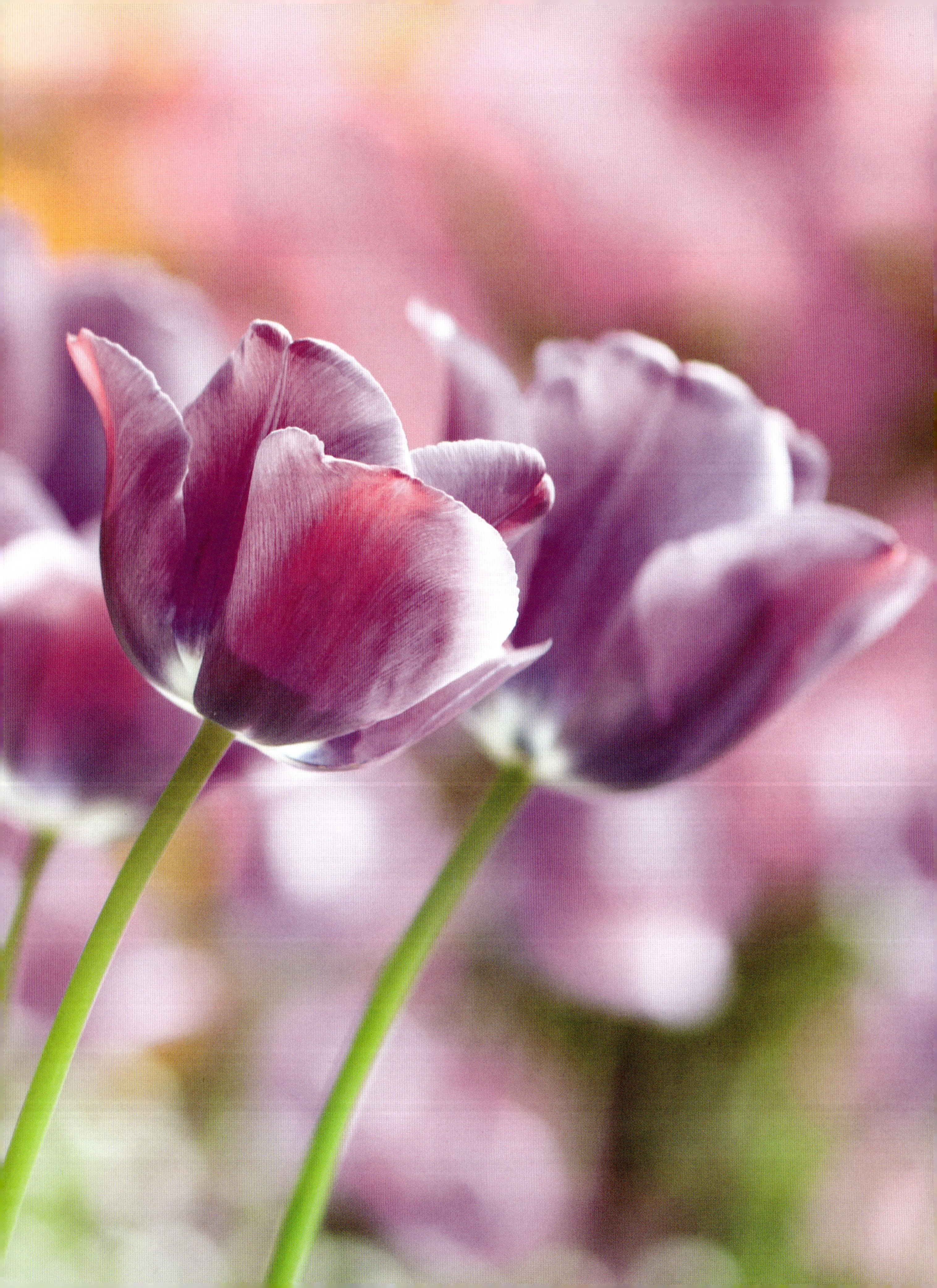

Grace:
An act of goodwill, dignity of bearing, kind consideration.

And so we arrive at *Grace*, a benevolent place of understanding and generosity of spirit. Grace is bestowed compassion, a state of living that radiates understanding and offers a safe haven.

Here, I have envisaged grace as the end of a glorious day, rendered in sunset hues of golds, purples, peaches and orange, shifting in a metamorphosis of light.

The sun is a powerful symbol of grace, as is the spiral – continuous, everlasting, eternal. Thus it could be interpreted that grace is endings and beginnings, folding one into another, as sunset gives way to sunrise and, in its turn, again to sunset.

The opening scene for this chapter features urns filled with golden roses, lavender, scabious and sweet peas, stems of lilac, mauve roses, *Fritillaria persica*, pale-pink parrot tulips and an 'Etched Salmon' peony, all photographed in my Paris studio.

The theme continues with a showcase of an expansive scene of purple and mauve 'Wild Blue Yonder' roses, taken at the International Rose Test Garden in Portland, Oregon. The home of over 10,000 rose bushes, representing over 600 varieties, it is the oldest continuously operating test garden in the United States. And its unique origins make it well suited for inclusion here.

The garden was instituted to serve as a refuge for European heirloom roses during World War I. It was feared by rosarians that those priceless varieties could be lost forever if they were destroyed in bombings. By early 1918, hybridizers from England and other locations were sending specimens to be nurtured and preserved.

A perennially popular destination, and, on each of my visits, quite crowded, it is not the spot for a bit of alone time. But it is well worth any effort required in order to witness this historic place and to be utterly surrounded by roses of all types.

On a more *petit* scale, a lovely setting in which to spend a thoughtful morning or afternoon is another Pacific Northwest rose garden, at Woodland Park in Seattle, Washington. Rarely crowded, its 2.5 acres of formal landscaped park feature a reflecting pool, gazebo and more than 3,000 roses. Opened in 1924, the garden is also notable for being pesticide-free since 2006. I photographed the golden, pink-edged *Rosa* 'Dream Come True' and the ethereal amethyst *Rosa* 'Sweetness' (page 262) there on one of my many visits. Amethyst, both the stone and the color, can represent wisdom, clarity and inner strength.

To me, the most appealing style of arrangement is loose and relaxed, with the flowers providing their own wreath of foliage, and half-opened buds punctuating the whole. And midsummer's bounty is unmatched for romantic offerings. I present, as a quintessential example, the David Austin rose bouquet in this chapter, composed of stems freshly cut from the field, arranged without artifice in an antique pitcher and nestled in a bed of lavender in the cottage garden where I was staying that summer. This setting then inspired the inclusion here of the picturesque field of purple and white lavender, layered into the distance, resembling clouds rippling through a violet evening sky.

I mentioned in the introduction to this book my penchant for – in addition to soft pastels – regal, jewel-like colorings. The ruby, coral, citrine, garnet and tourmaline-pink peonies in a tangle on a mottled gray marble window seat at Château de Sourches are like a cluster of fancy rings. Neither bashful nor discreet, they command attention. The crowning gem, though, is the riveting *Paeonia* 'Red Charm', a ball of upright petals cinched with a twirly skirt. I can attest to the intensity of the color, and the challenge in photographing it. No camera encompasses the range or nuances discernible by the human eye, and reds are especially tricky to get right. As often as possible, I will edit an image while I still have the model to hand. I may never match it precisely, but achieving a true rendition is always the goal. I feel a responsibility to aim for this, and though the ebb and flow of fashionable photos may favor, for a period, desaturated colors and murky backgrounds, for a timeless portrait, exactitude is the standard.

RIGHT: *Rosa* 'Dream Come True', Washington, USA. July 2008.

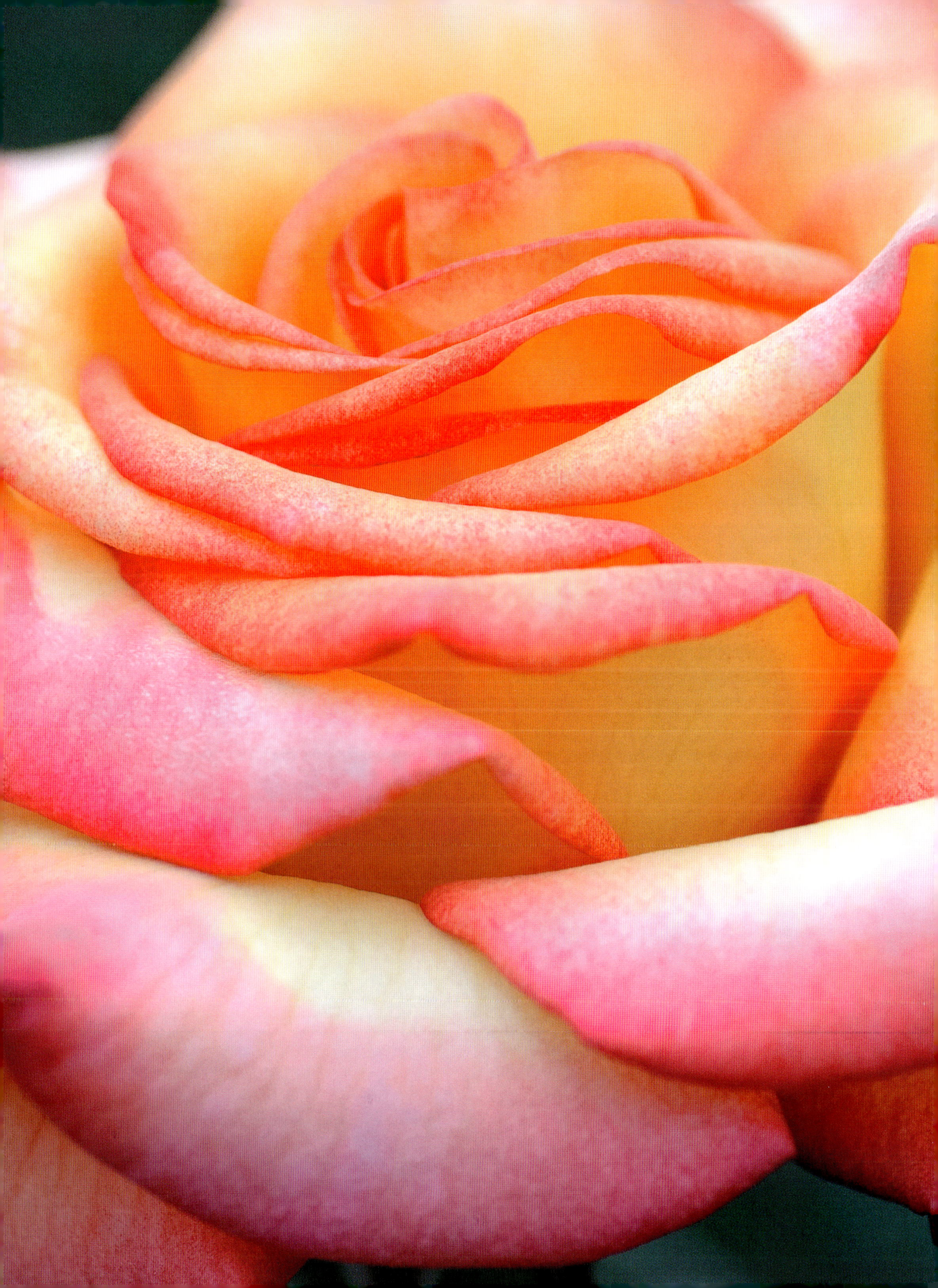

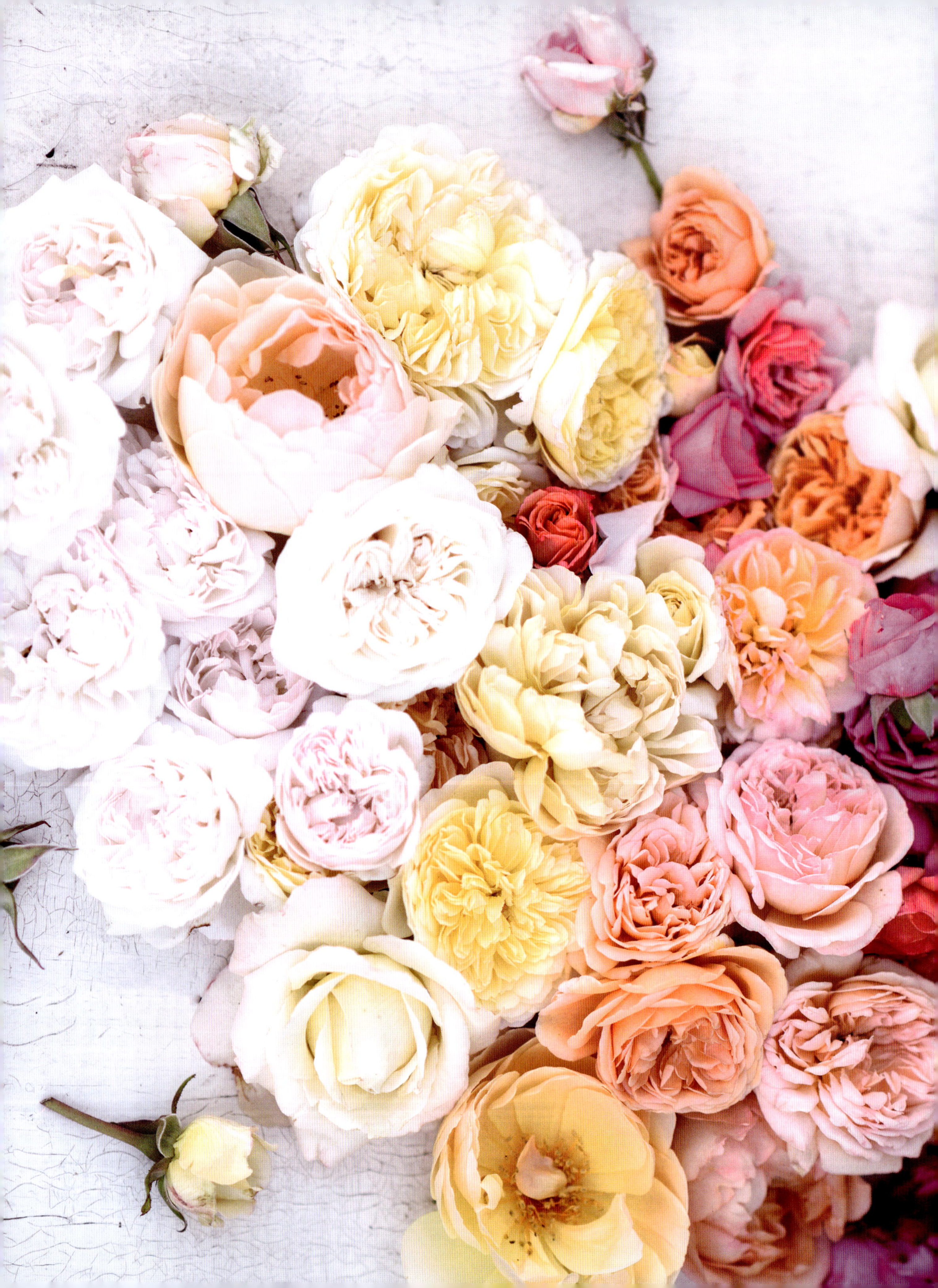

In sourcing the freshest blooms in Paris, I have collaborated for years with several floral designers and local flower shops, but I most often will visit my organic weekend market, where I know the vendors who grow and harvest their own. One summer, not long ago, I discovered and immediately purchased several dozen such home-grown finds – peachy-salmon roses with saucy waves of petals that became much-photographed subjects that week. Uncharacteristically, I didn't note the name, so I may never find them again, but they live on in cheery photographs.

PIONEERING FLOWER CARPETS

Well before it became a floral trend, I regularly experimented with carefully arranged large-scale "flower carpets," composed of hundreds of blooms, laid out with precision on my hands and knees, and photographed with a wide-angle lens from directly above. Several of this type of image appear throughout this book and, in this chapter, I've included one featuring mixed David Austin roses, salvaged from an afternoon of deadheading at a friend's rose farm (pages 270–71). The blooms, although wilting on the shrub, still were full of life, enough to warrant one last opportunity to document them.

Perhaps the state of grace cannot be measured or brought into existence at will but, assuredly, it permeates our enduring empathy with flowers.

OVERLEAF: David Austin rose bouquet, including *Rosa* 'Darcy Bussell', 'Thomas à Becket', 'Desdemona', 'Grace', 'Port Sunlight' and 'Tranquillity', Shropshire, England. July 2015.

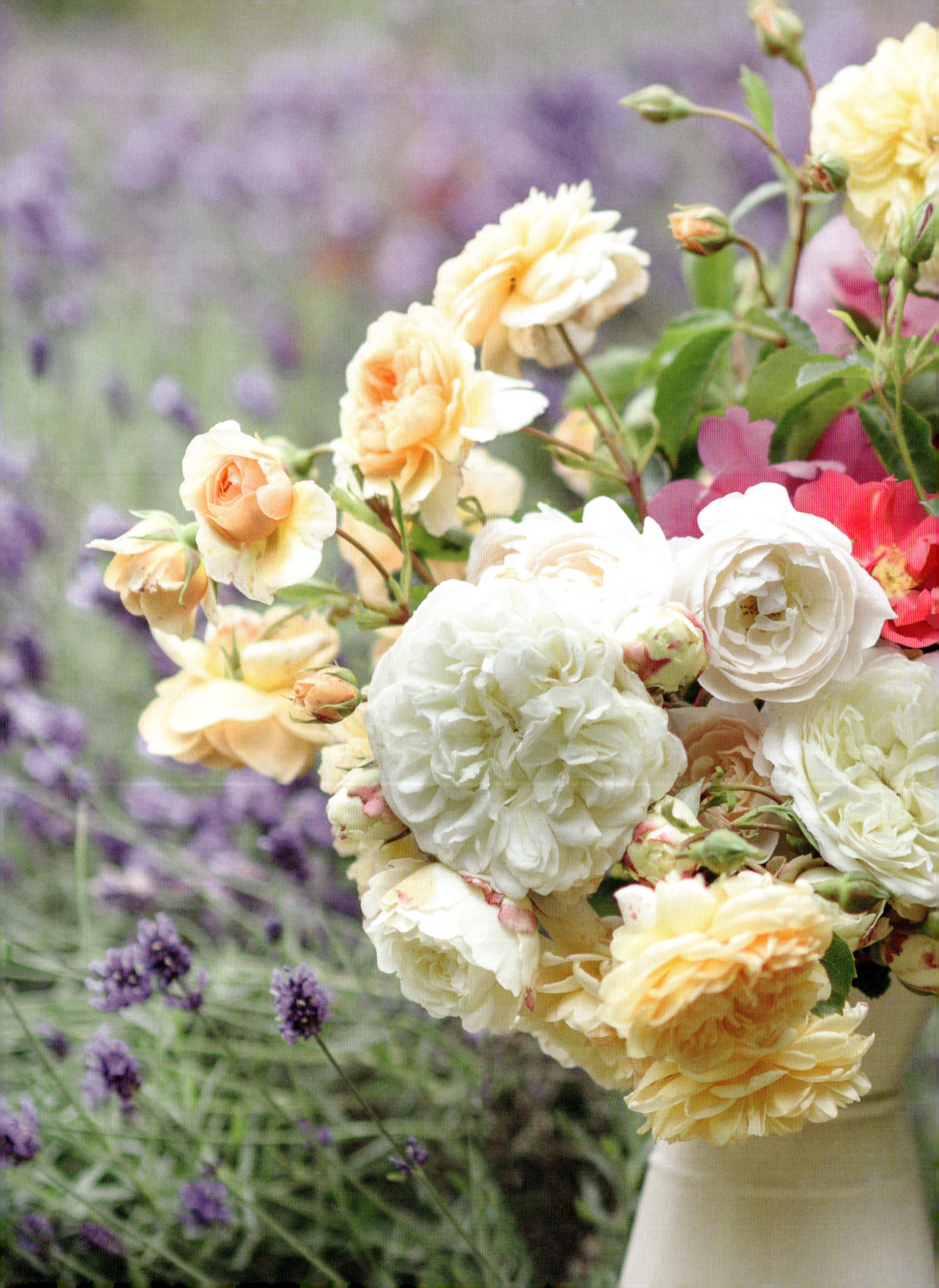

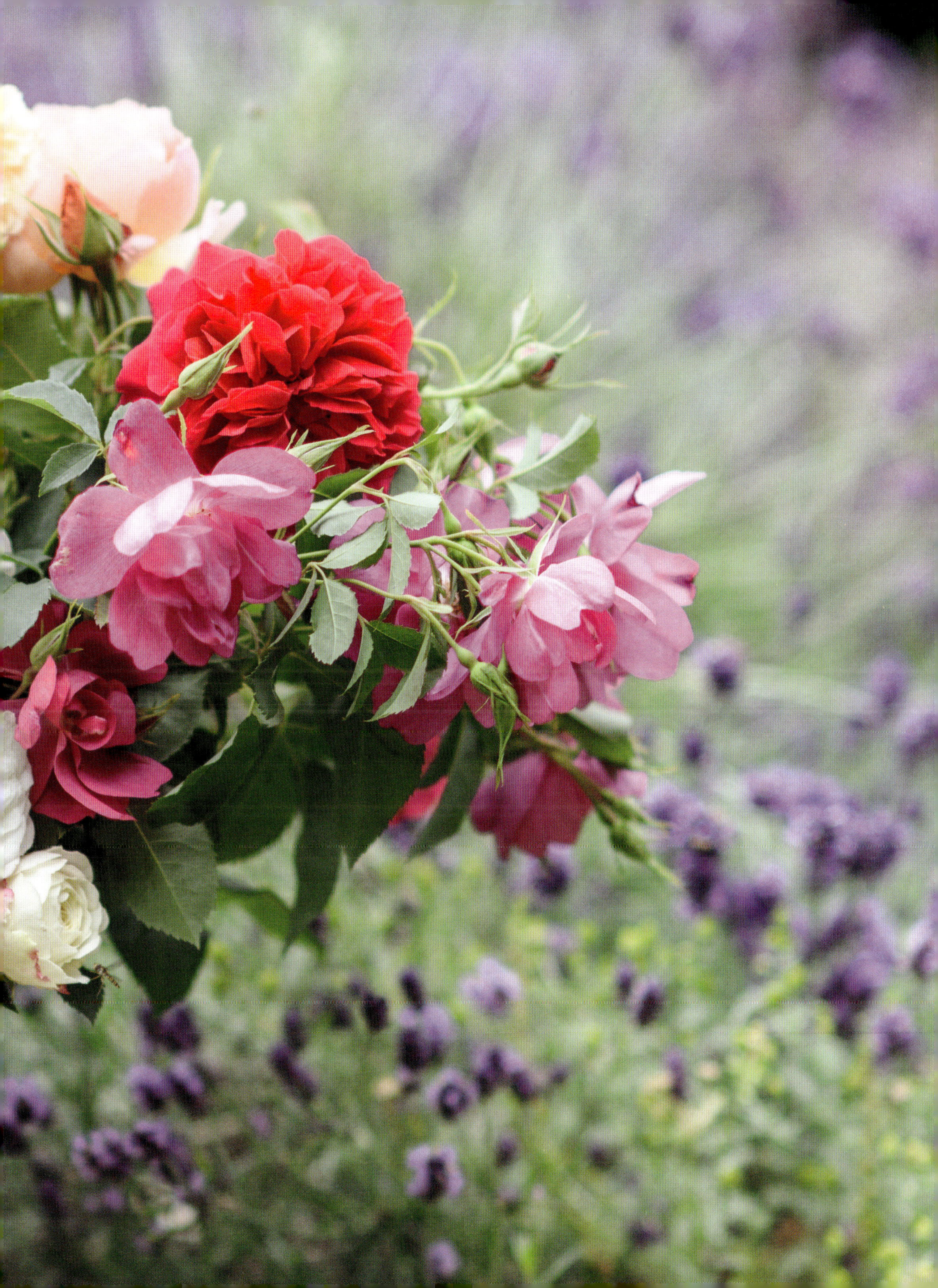

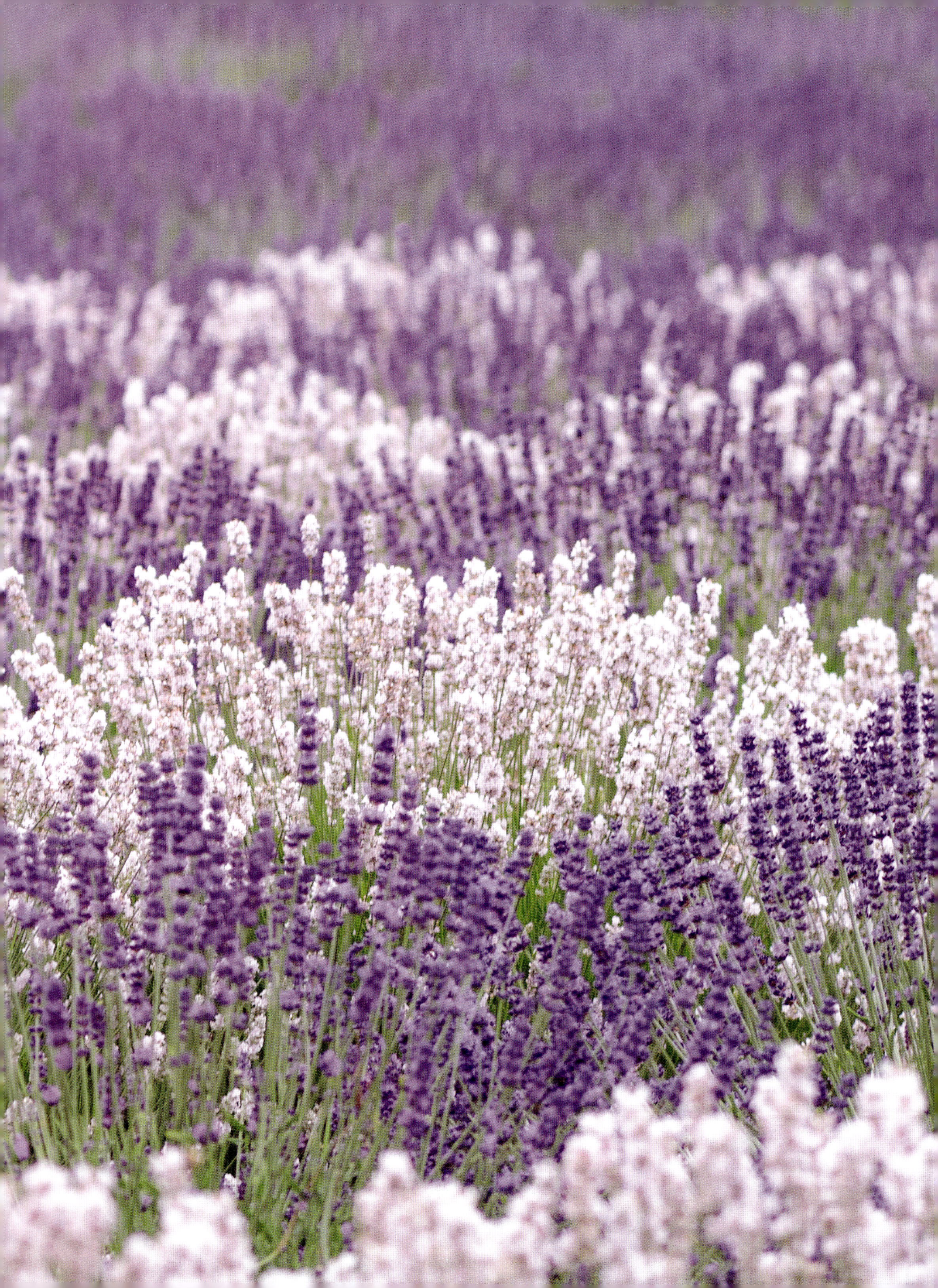

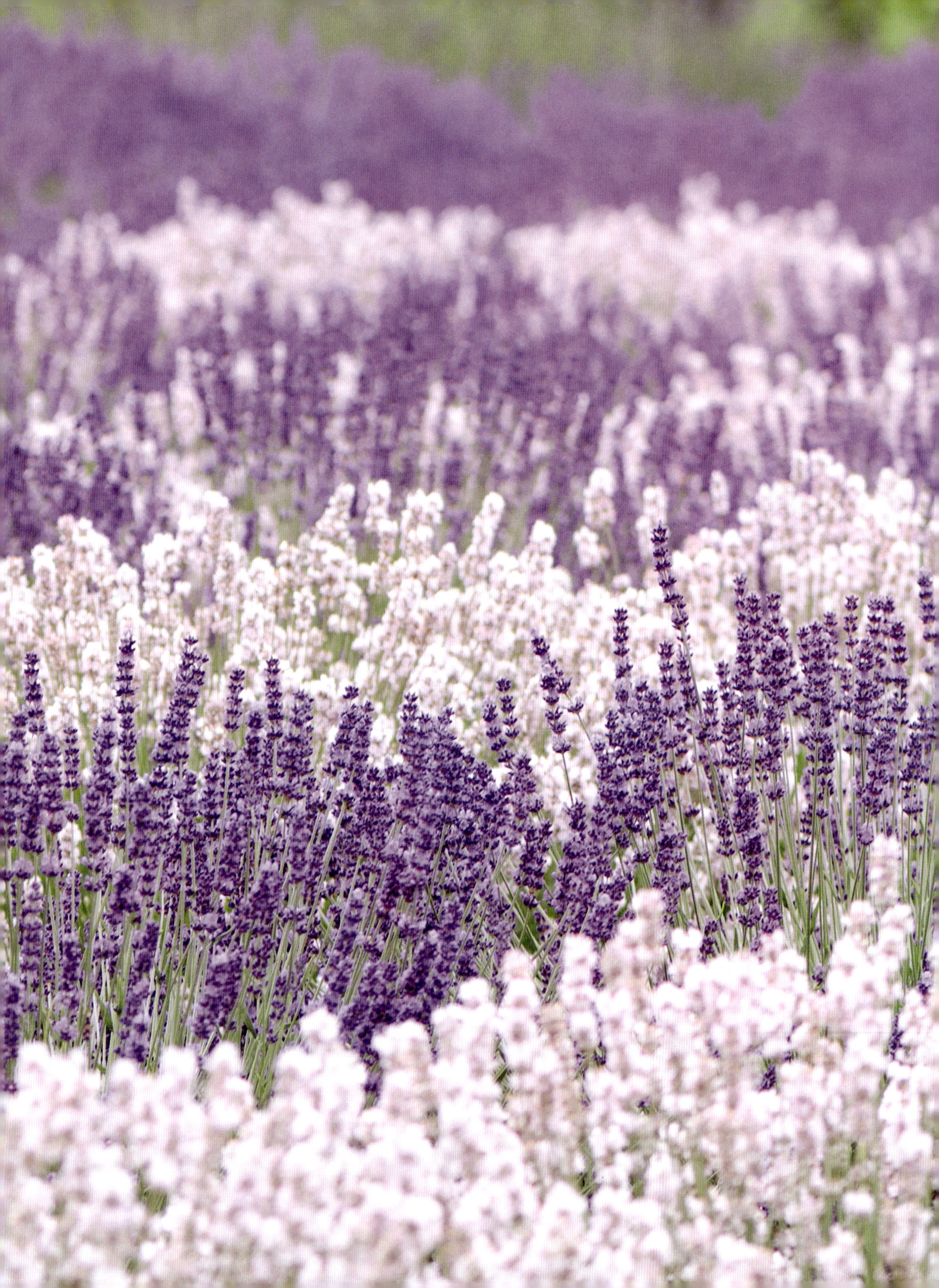

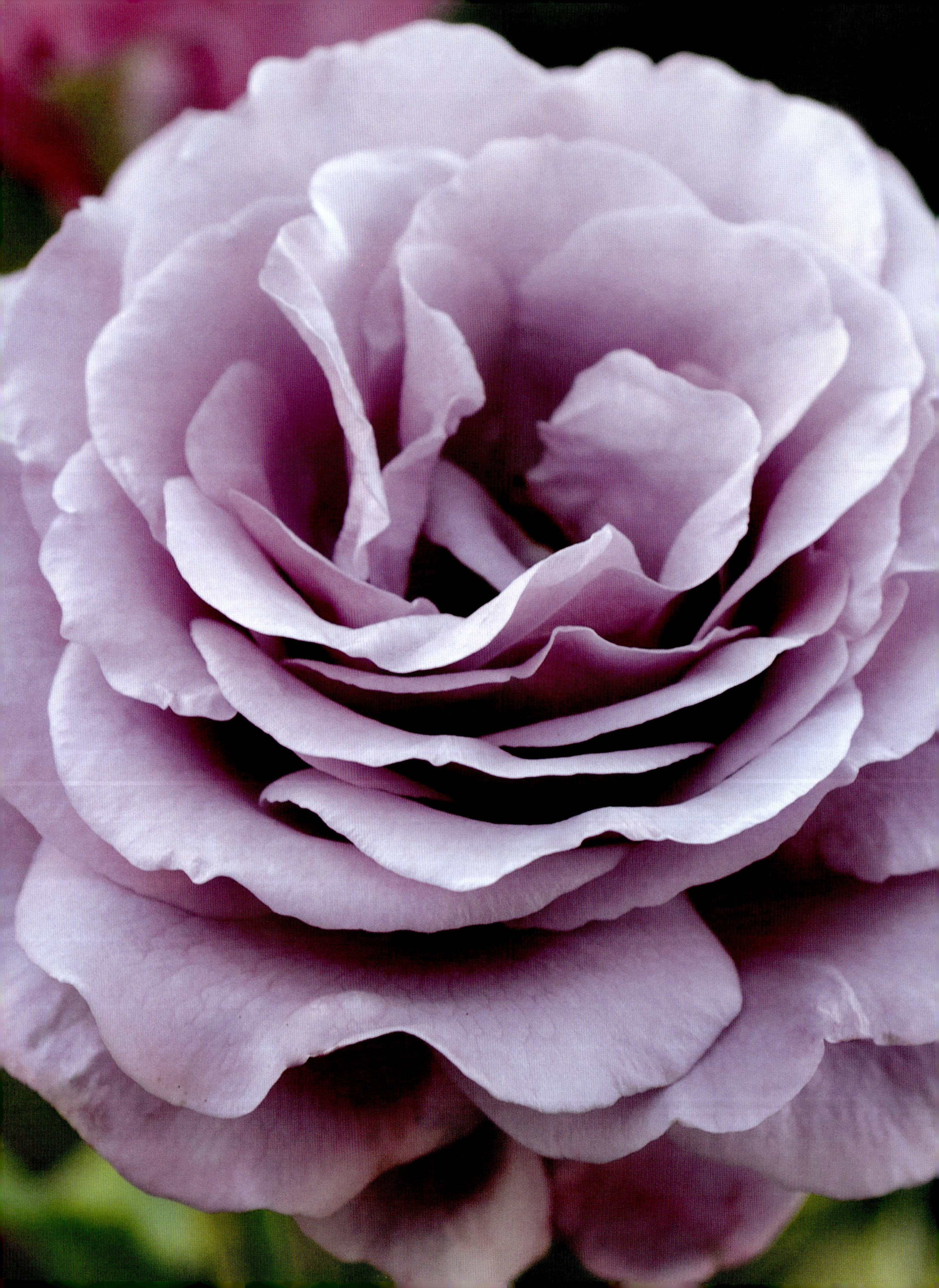

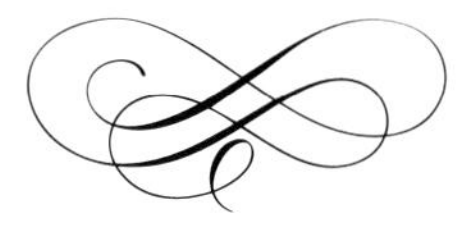

AMETHYST,
both the stone
and the color,
can represent
WISDOM,
clarity and inner
STRENGTH.

Rosa 'Sweetness', Seattle, Washington, USA. August 2010.

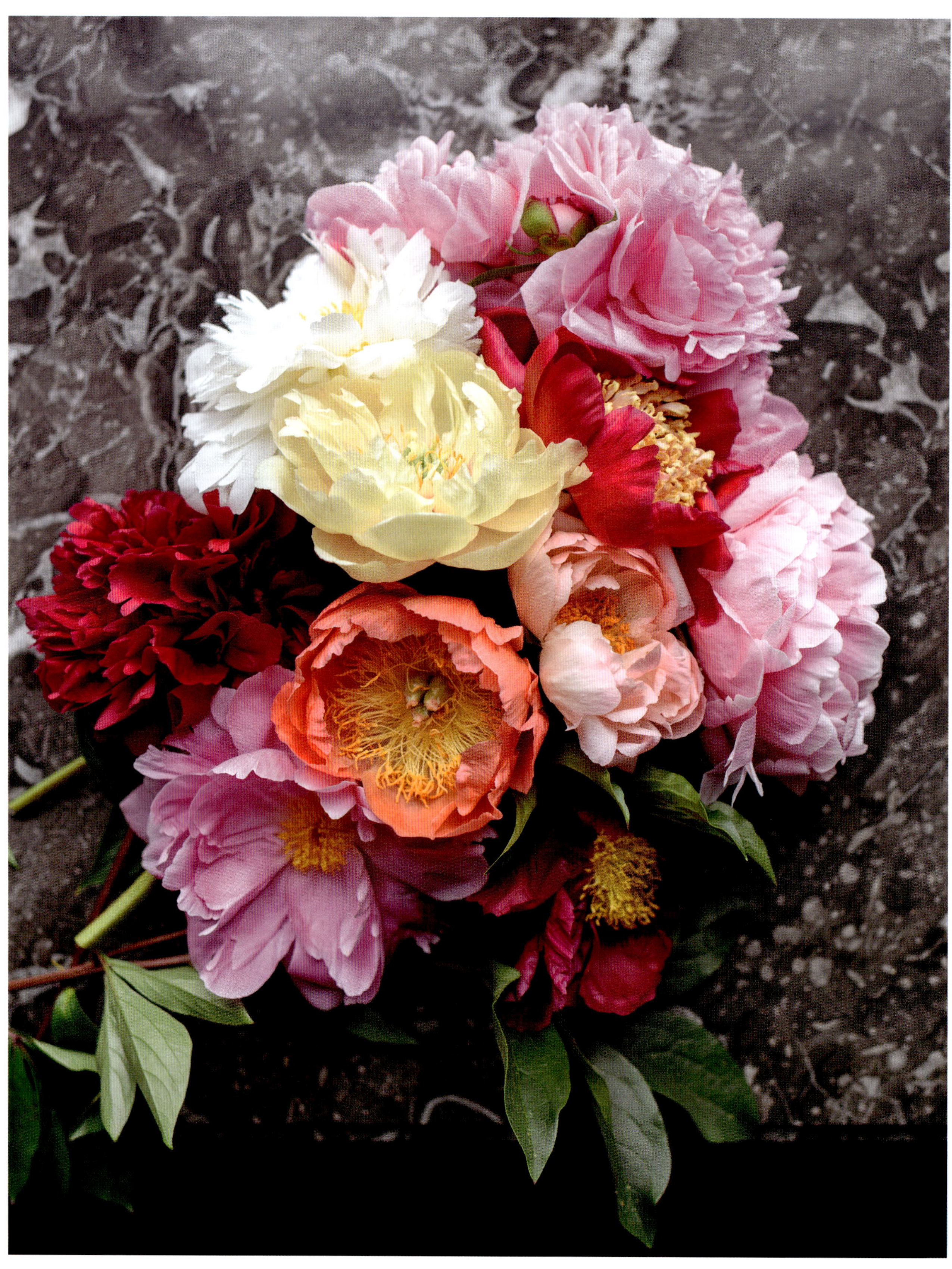

ABOVE: Mixed peonies including *Paeonia* 'Coral Charm', 'Dr. Alexander Fleming', 'Red Charm' and 'Sarah Bernhardt', Château de Sourches, Saint-Symphorien, France. May 2017. RIGHT: *Paeonia* 'Red Charm', Washington, USA. May 2015.

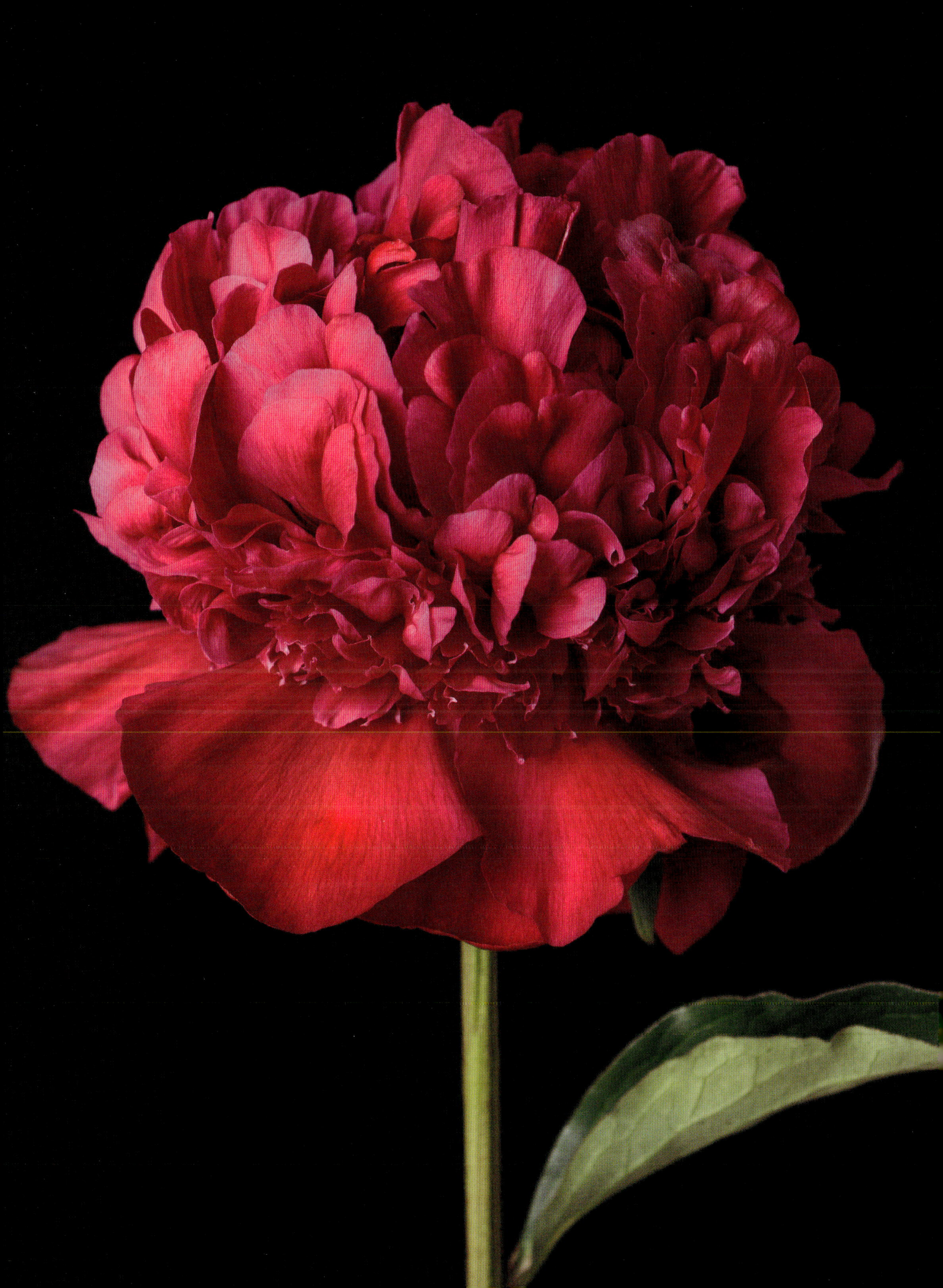

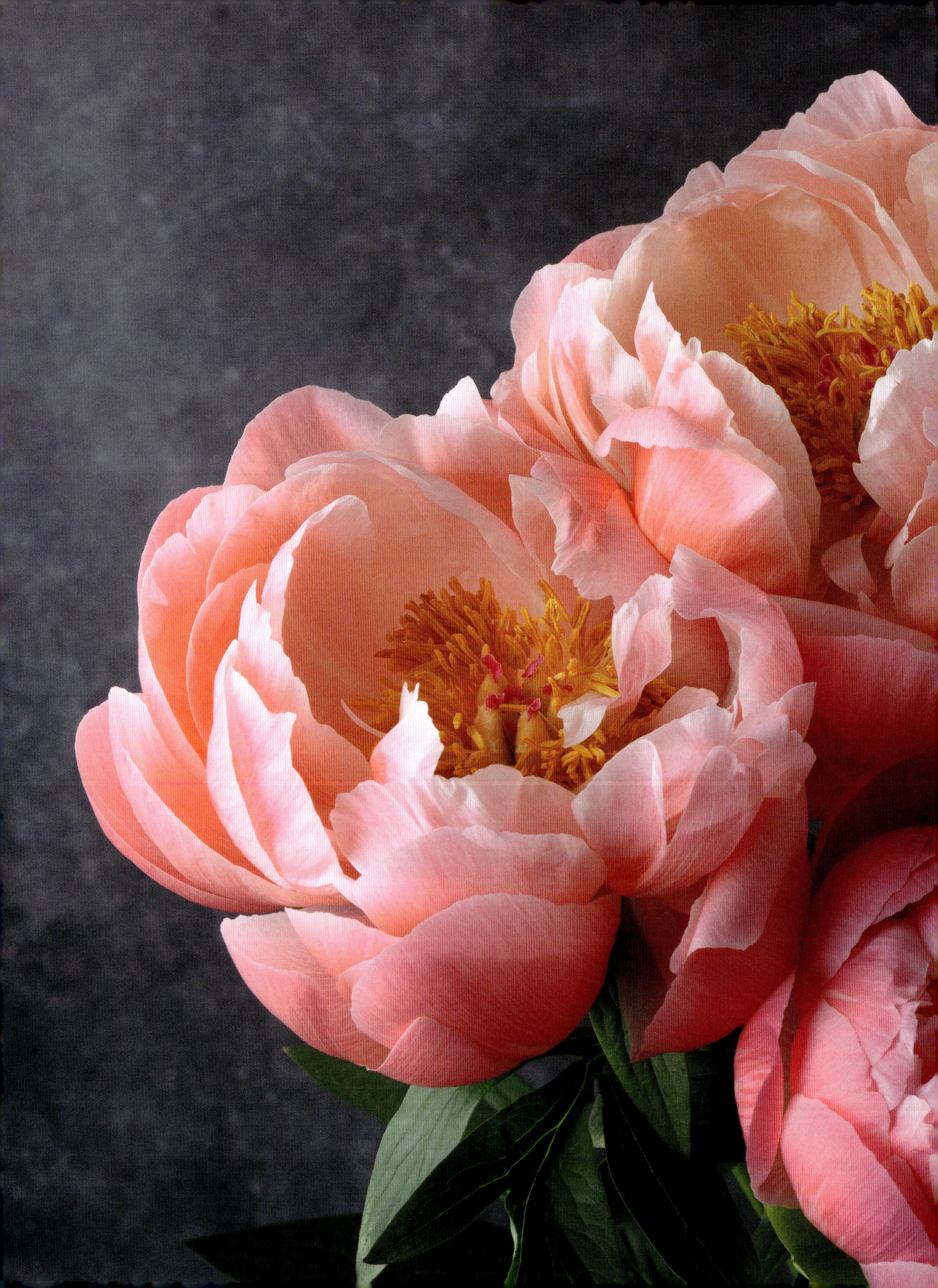

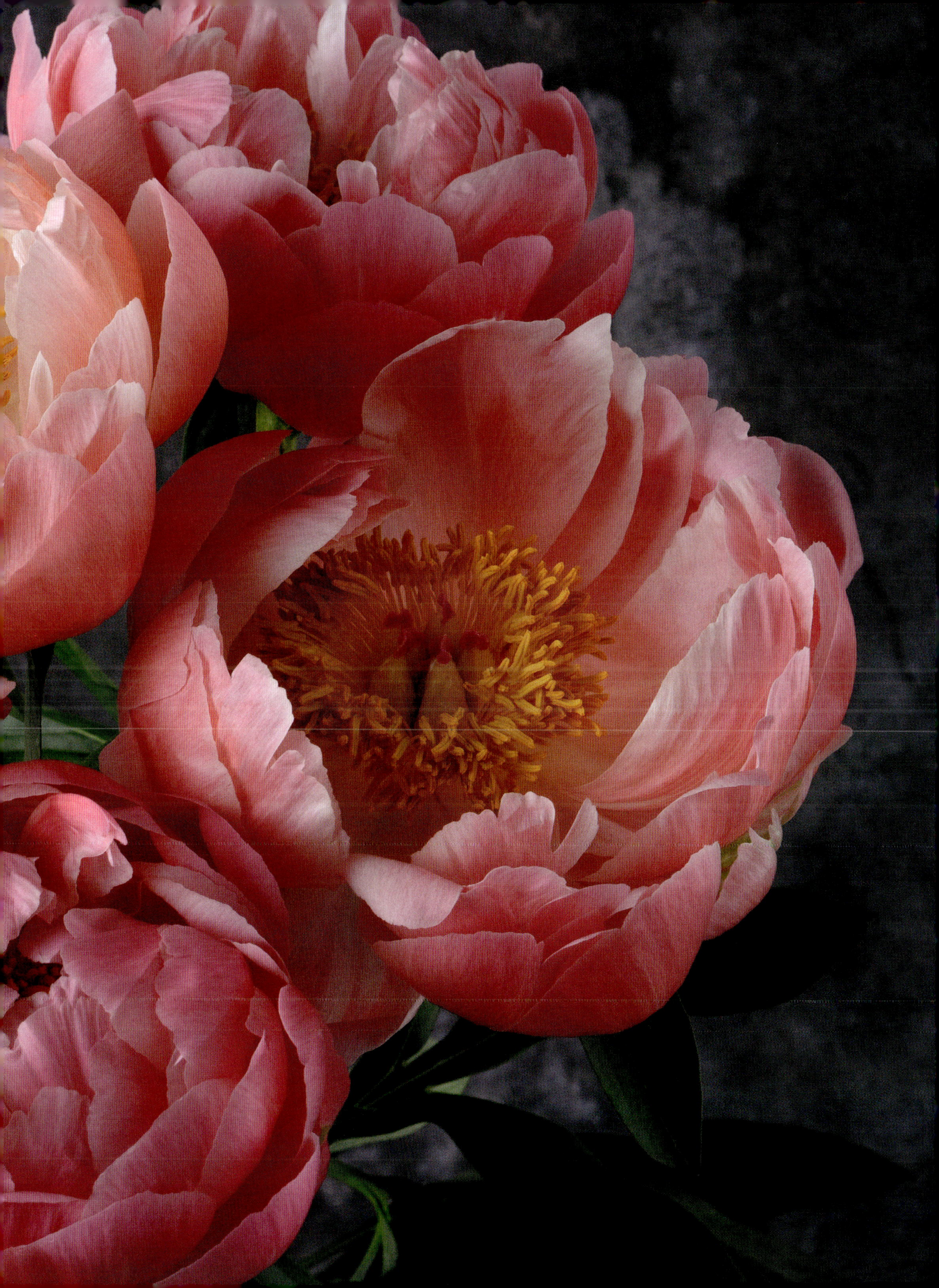

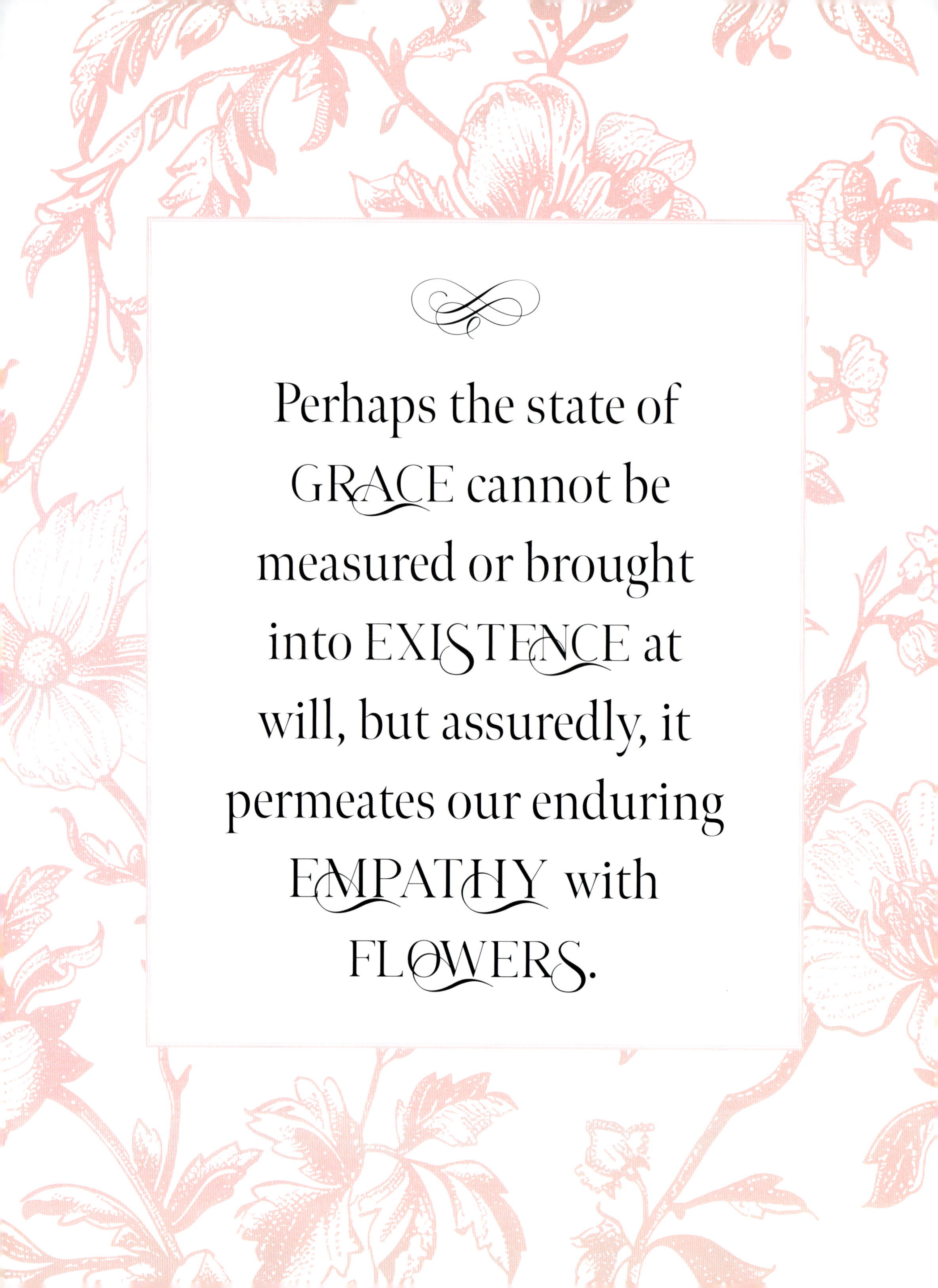
Perhaps the state of GRACE cannot be measured or brought into EXISTENCE at will, but assuredly, it permeates our enduring EMPATHY with FLOWERS.

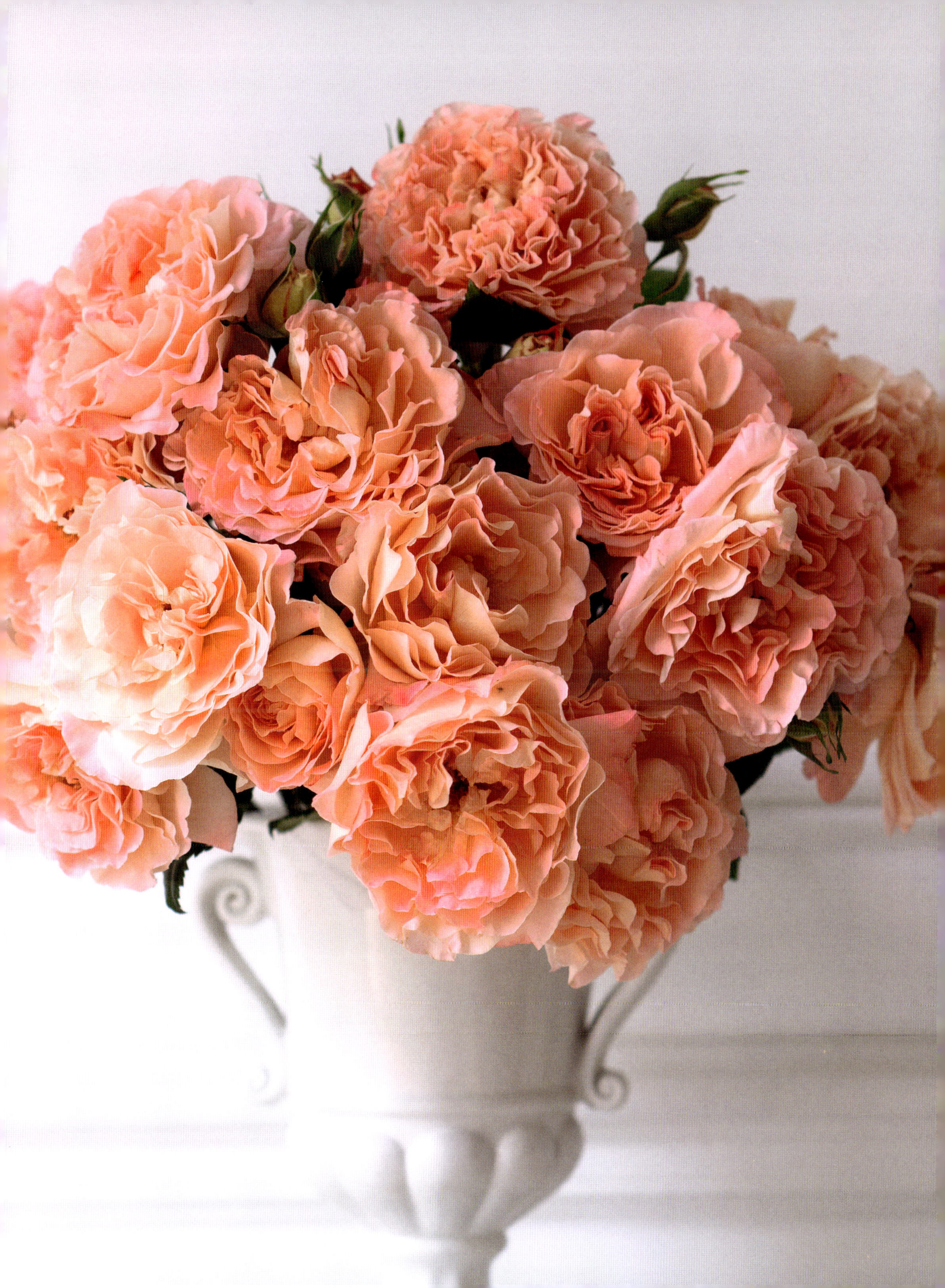

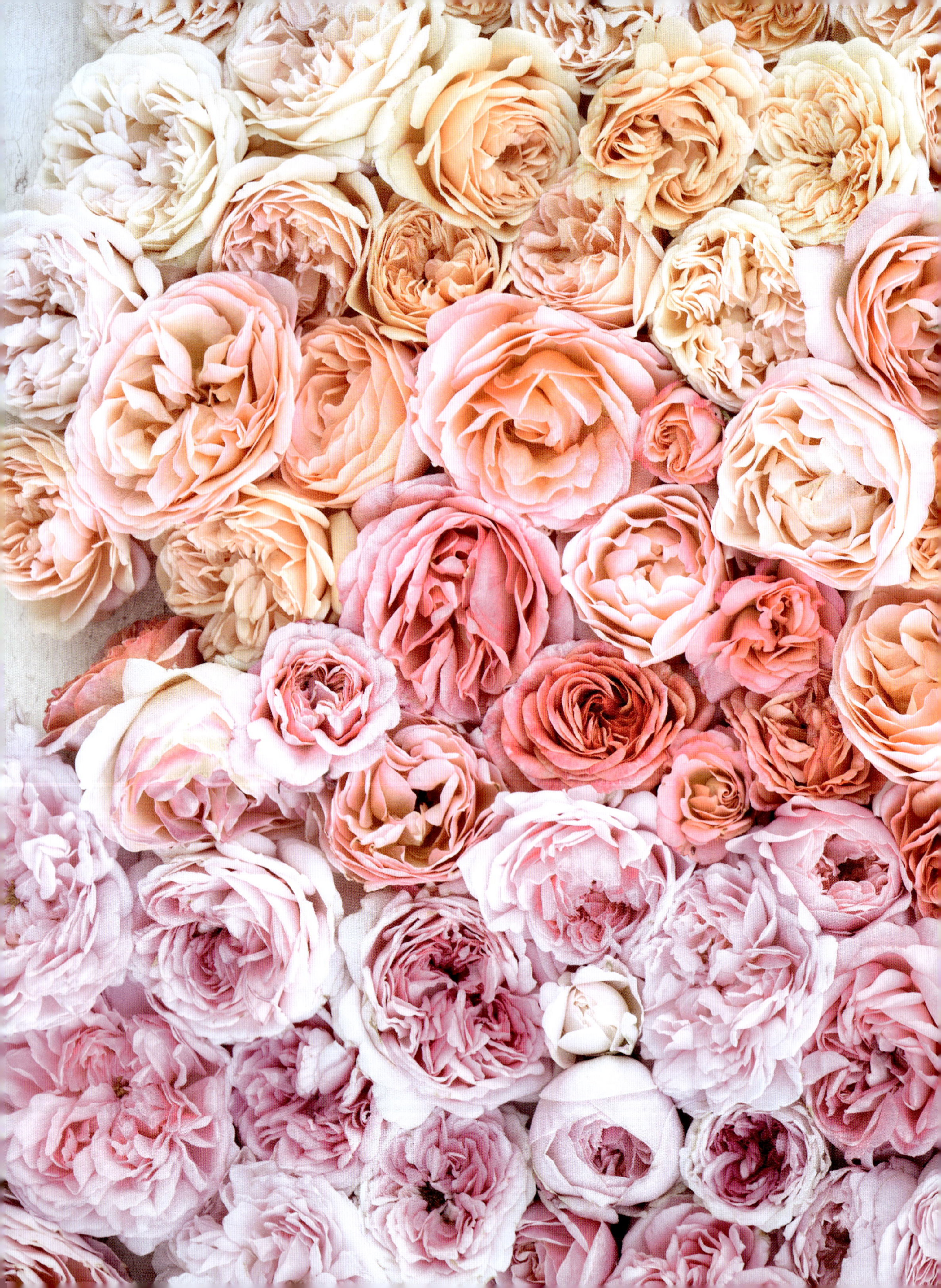

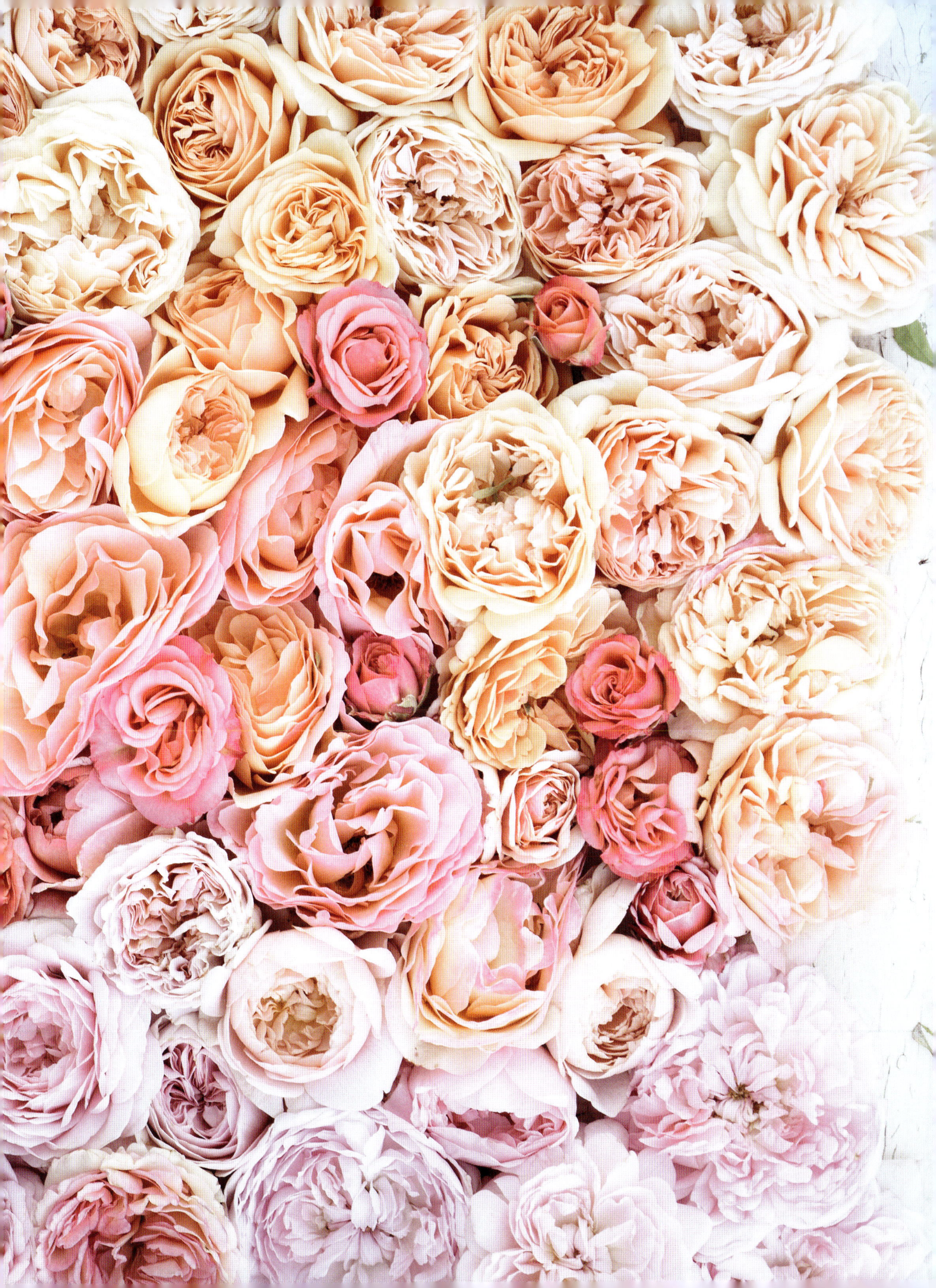

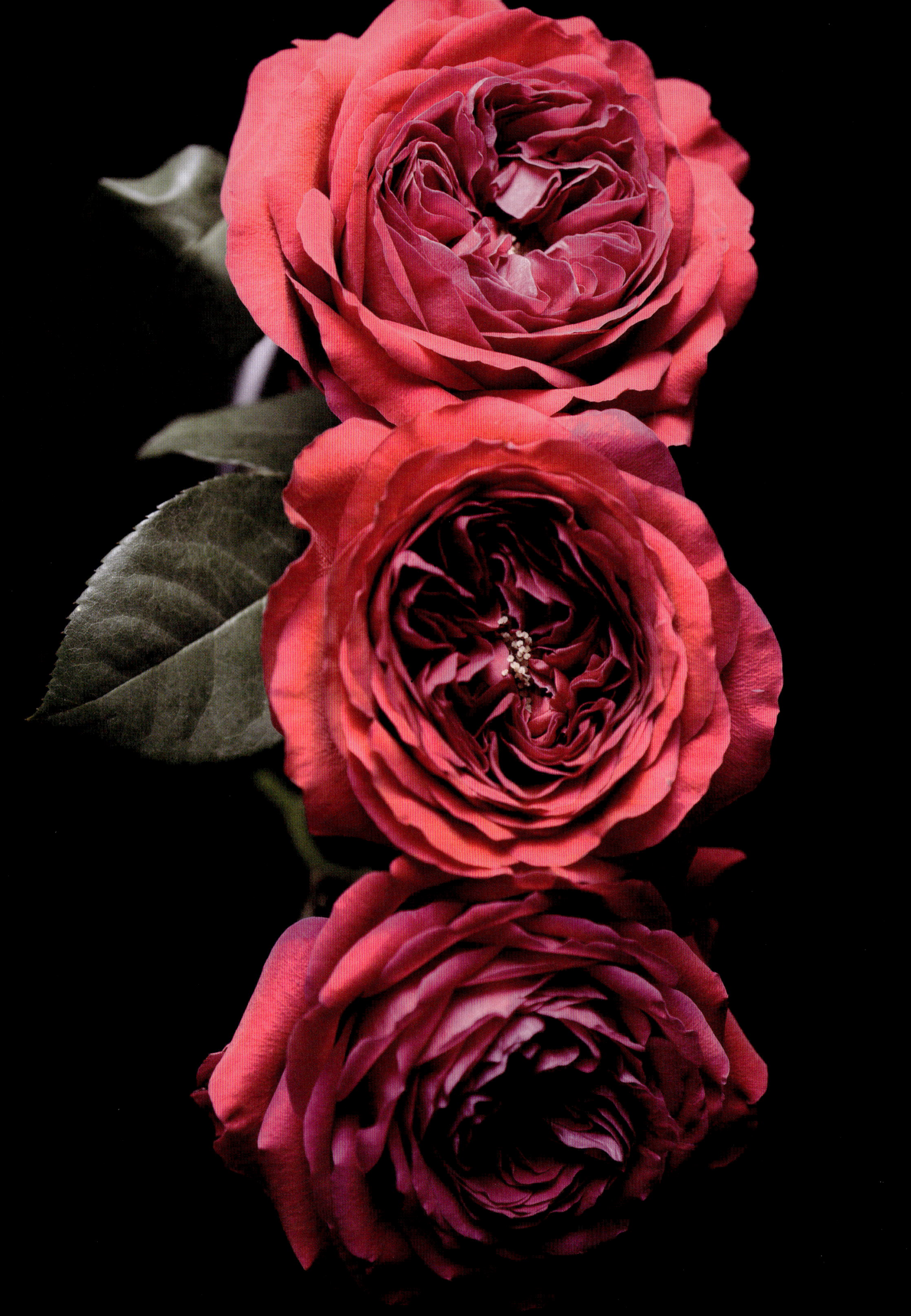

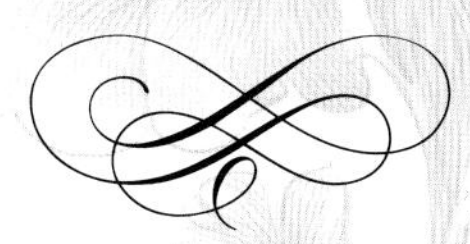

AN UNASSUMING GRACE

Hillhaven Garden, Shoreline, Washington, USA
April–June 2015

Often in flower photography, simplicity of presentation is more eloquent than an elaborately staged arrangement. An unadorned portrayal of a bloom focuses attention on its quietly dignified bearing and majestic form.

Such images allow the viewer to study each in breathtaking clarity, delving into minute details that celebrate the individuality of every unique specimen.

And it is no secret that these portraits are amongst my favored methods of floral photographic expression.

Here, the David Austin rose 'Darcey Bussell' *astonishes one with swirls of crimson and raspberry in more than 100 densely packed petals. And on the following pages, the David Austin rose* 'Fighting Temeraire' *(whose name was inspired by J. M. W. Turner's renowned, sunset-hued painting) and peachy-coral sweet peas require no embellishment in order for one to appreciate their marvelous perfection.*

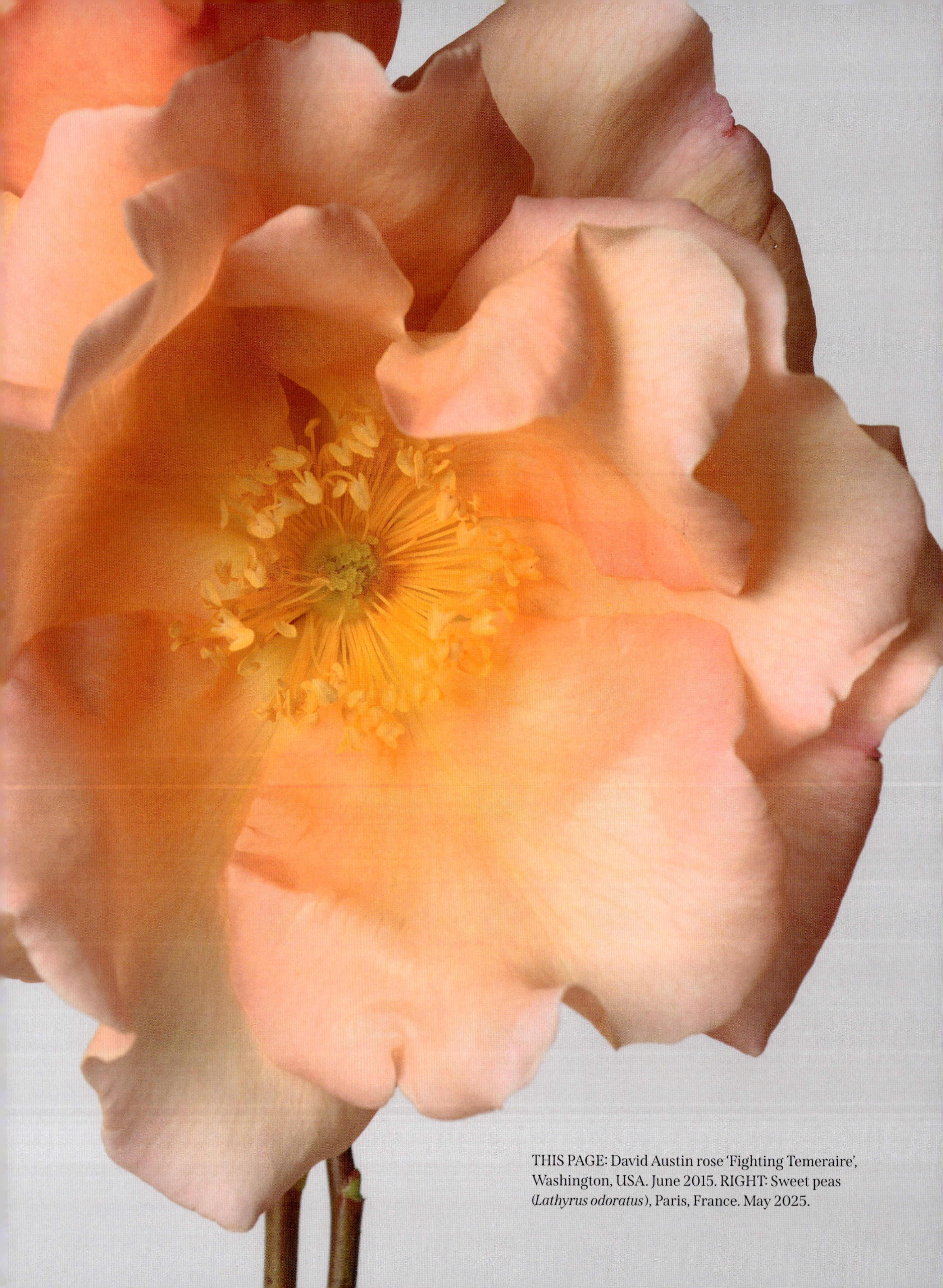

THIS PAGE: David Austin rose 'Fighting Temeraire', Washington, USA. June 2015. RIGHT: Sweet peas (*Lathyrus odoratus*), Paris, France. May 2025.

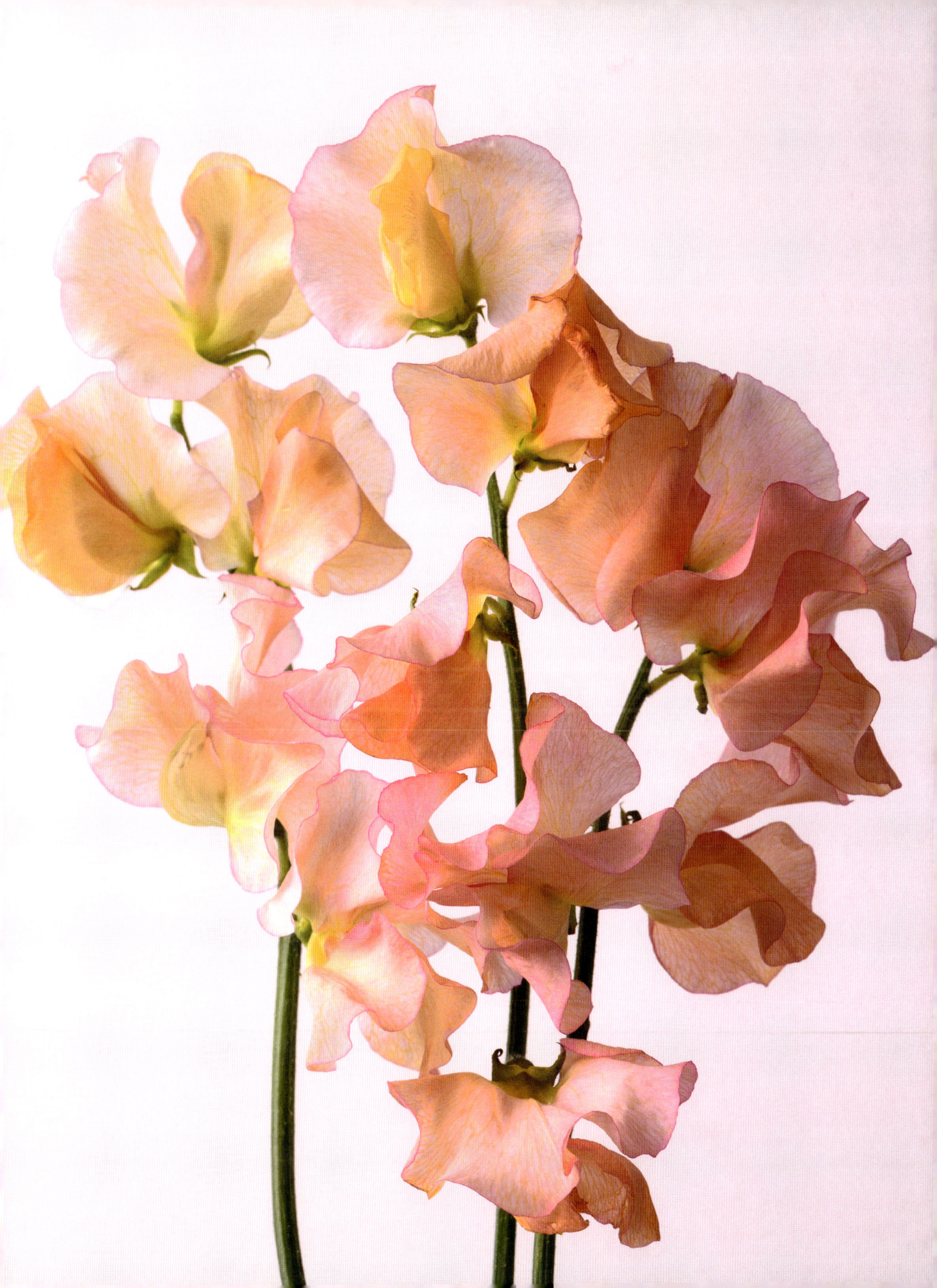

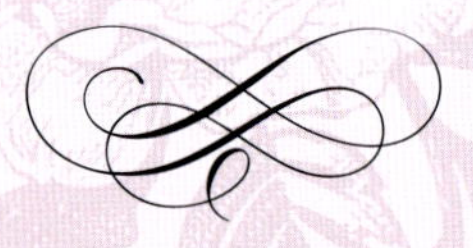

TULIPS

A ubiquitous fixture of spring gardens and flower shops, tulips nonetheless remain worthy artistic subjects, as irresistible to photographers now as they were to the Dutch painters in the seventeenth and eighteenth centuries. Their sumptuous colors, coupled with a romantic droopiness, ensure that the intrigue of capturing them will never wane for me.

Mimicking the brilliant shades of the tropical bird, parrot tulips possess an undeniable wow factor. They boast wavy-edged, wayward petals in a rainbow-range of colors, from the striking and nearly gaudy Tulipa *'Blumex', shown here, to the more delicate apricot and pink, to dramatic greens and almost black. I photograph the paler varieties lit from behind, making them appear to be undulating, as if under water.*

And the more sedate multi-petaled double tulips, with rose- or peony-like fullness, catch and reflect light with a shimmering iridescence. A flower that truly ages gracefully, to me, faded tulip petals resemble the texture of fine silk.

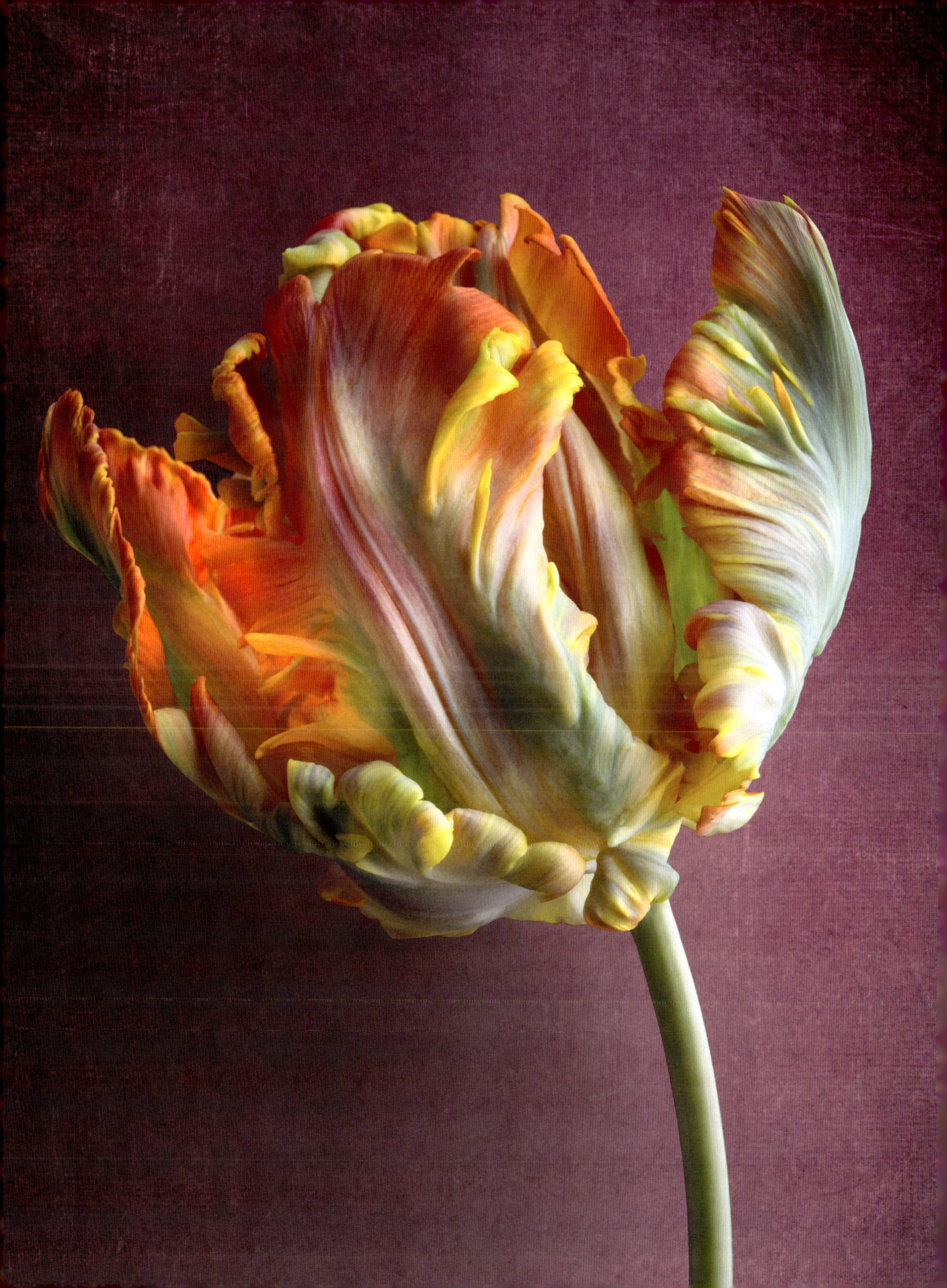

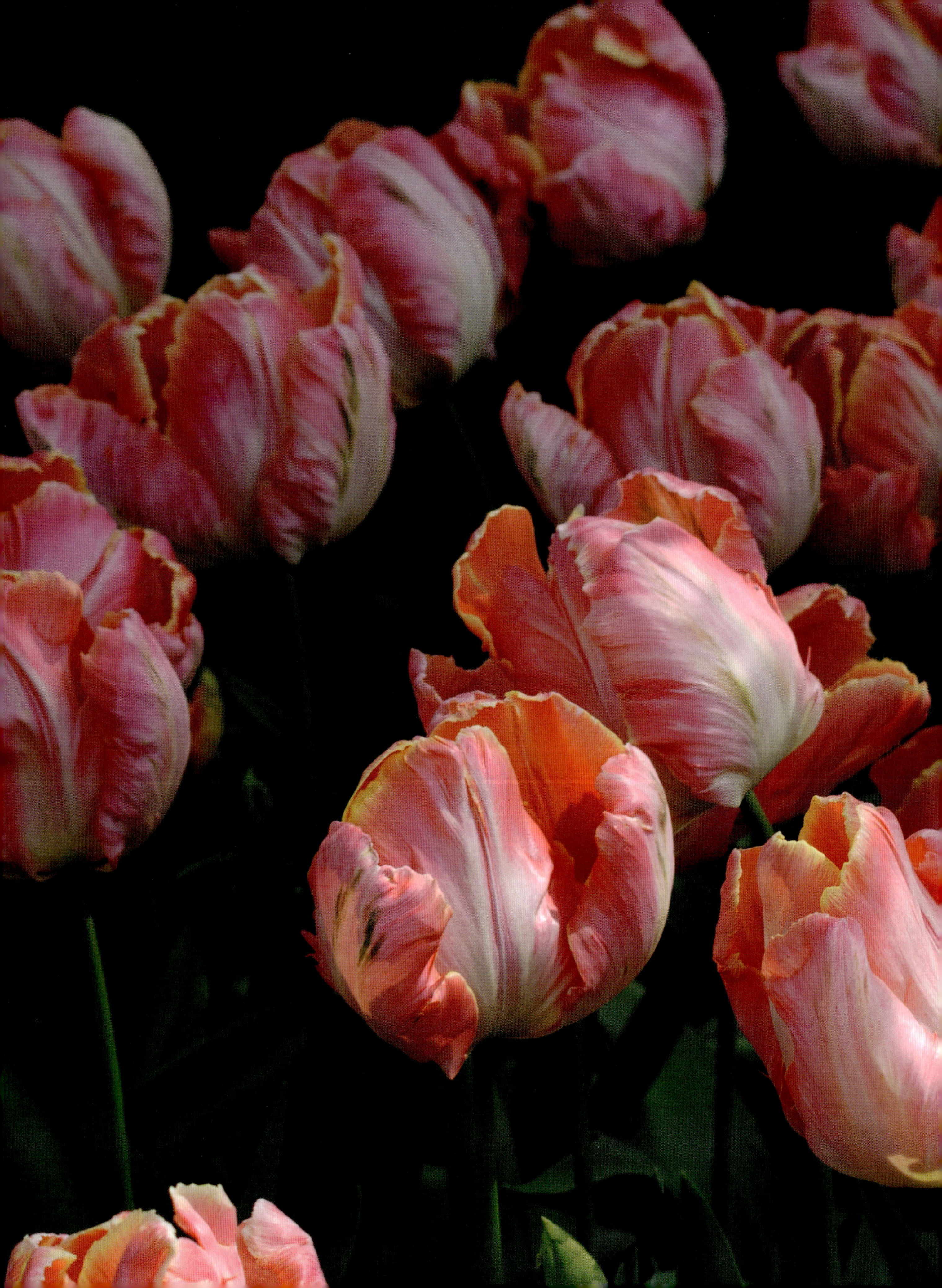

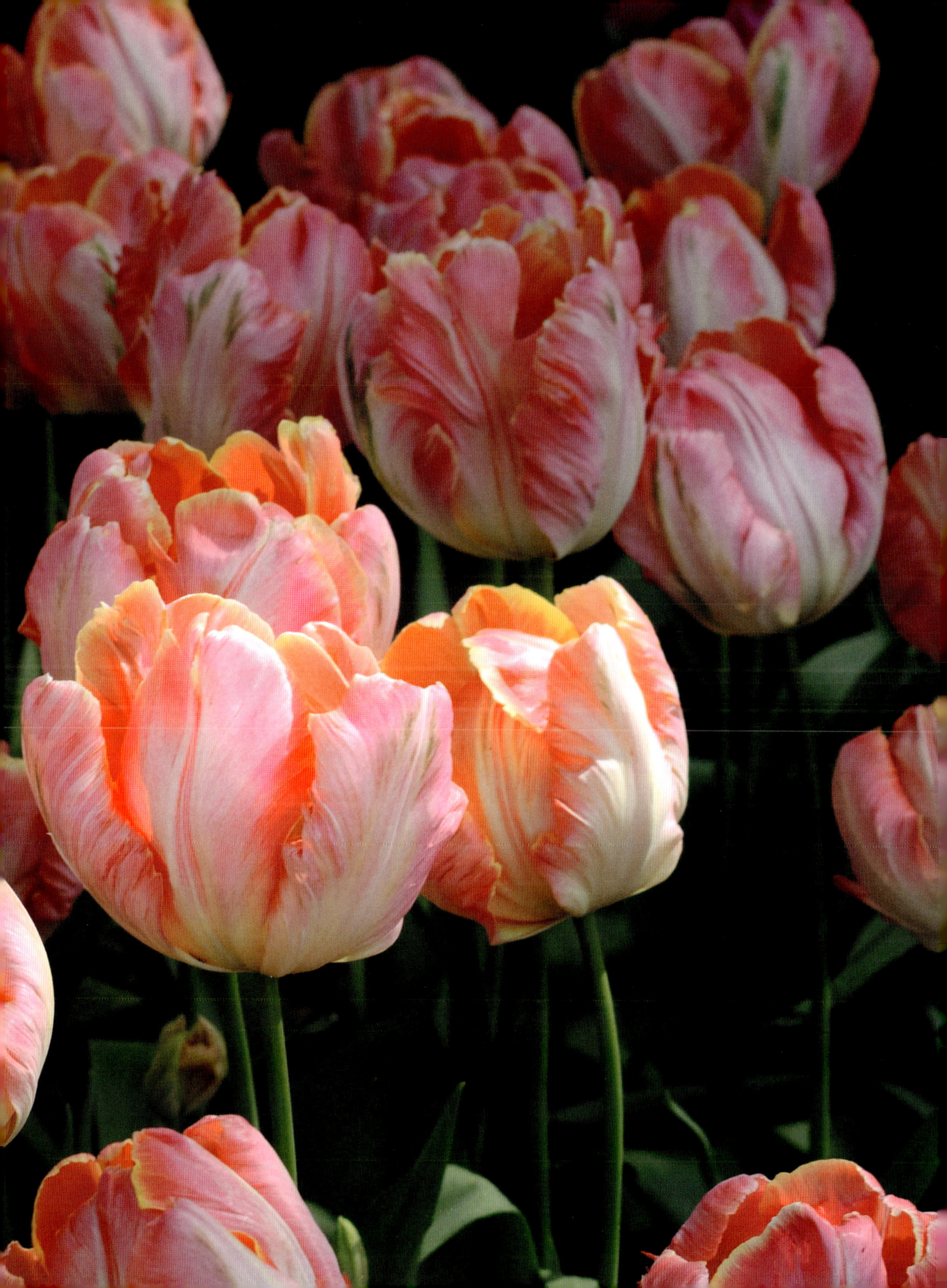

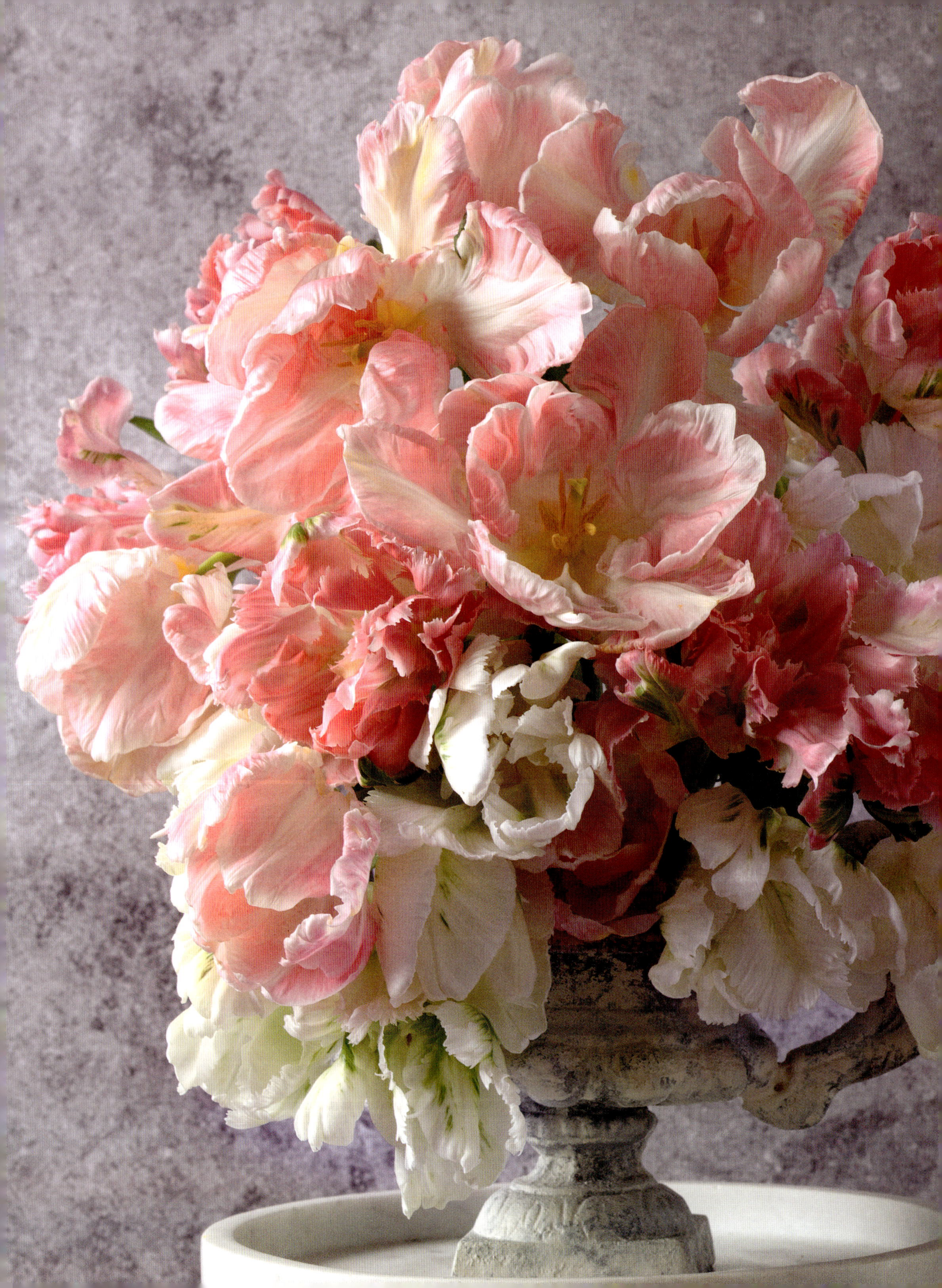

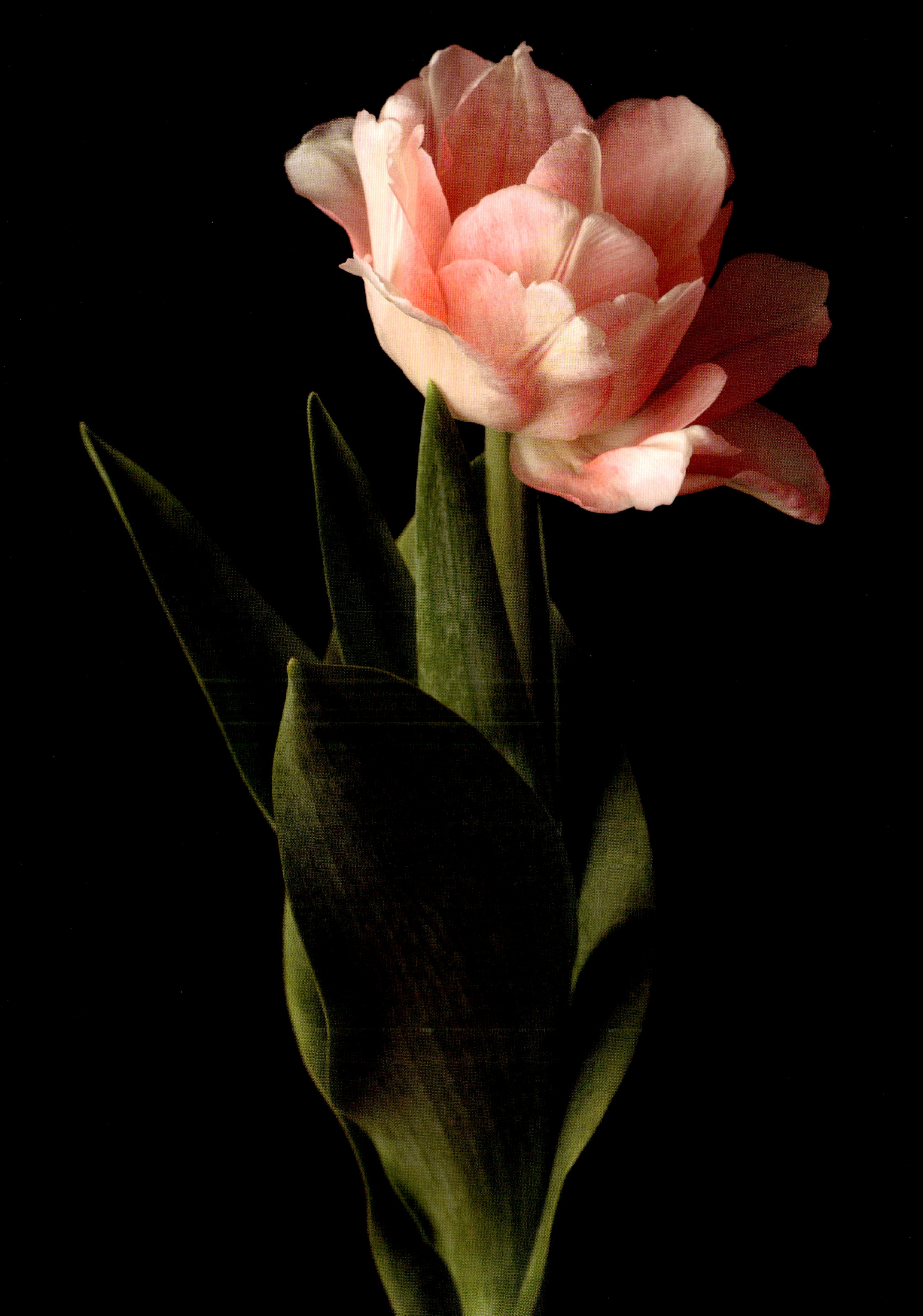

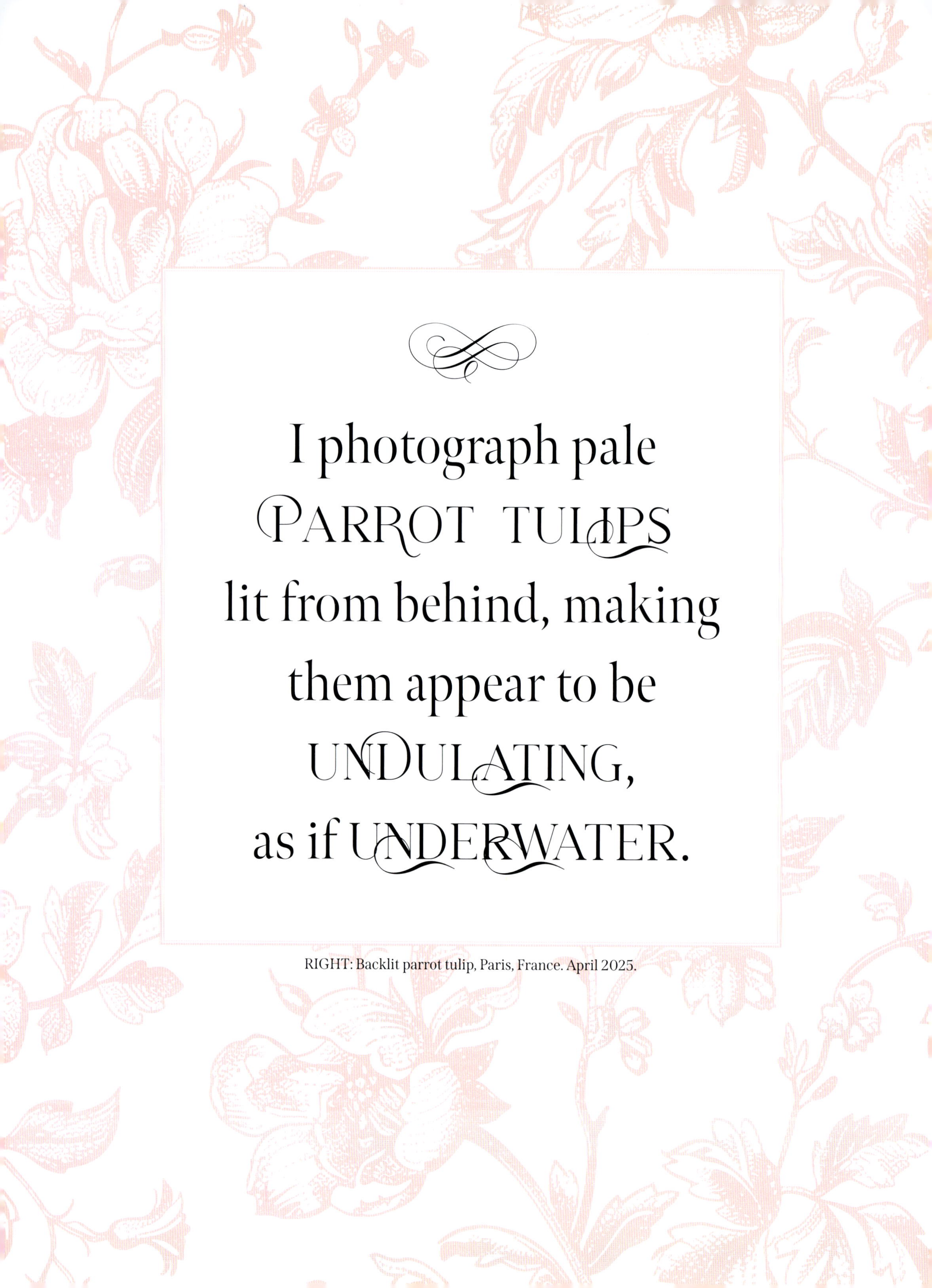

I photograph pale PARROT TULIPS lit from behind, making them appear to be UNDULATING, as if UNDERWATER.

RIGHT: Backlit parrot tulip, Paris, France. April 2025.

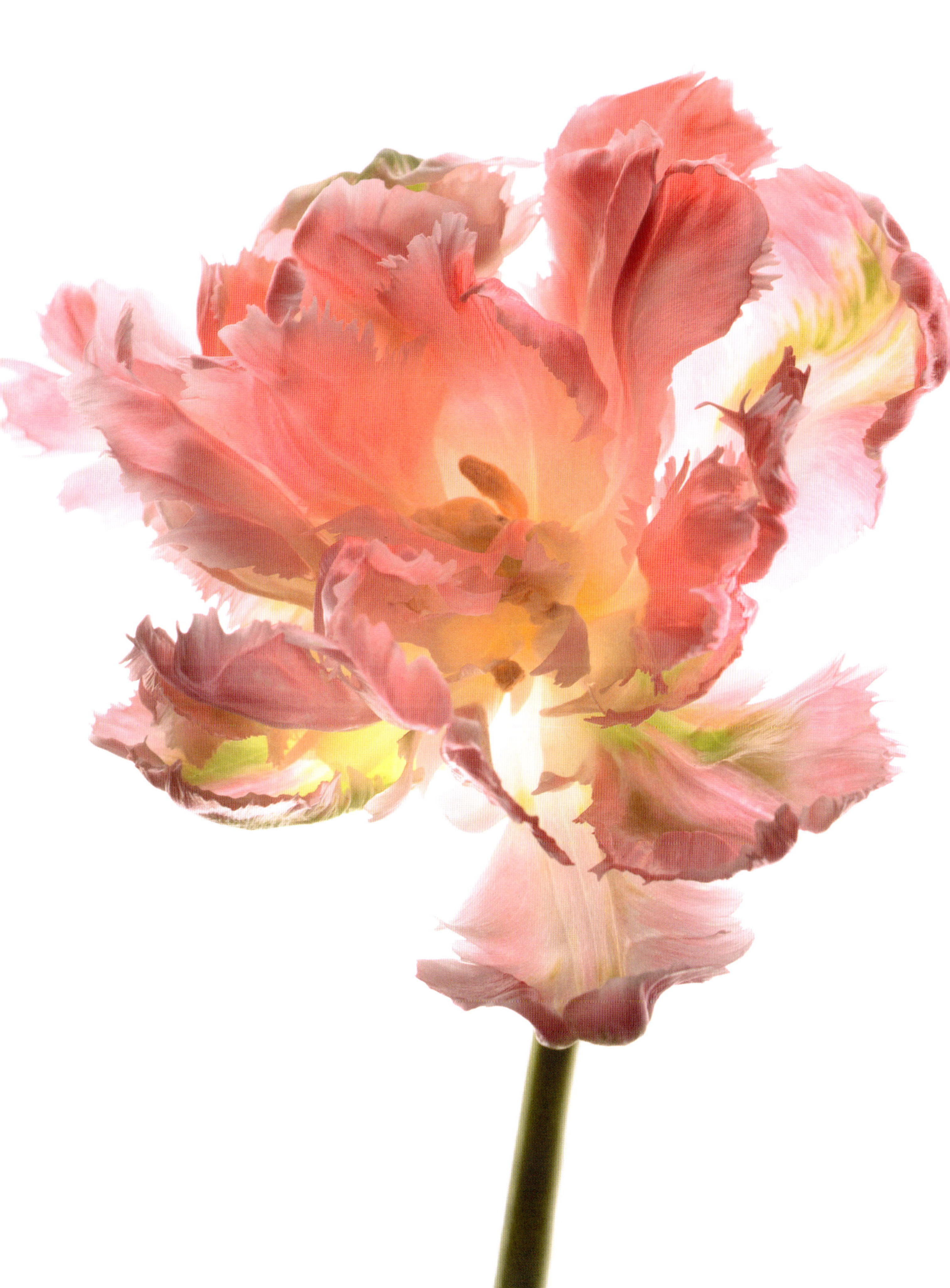

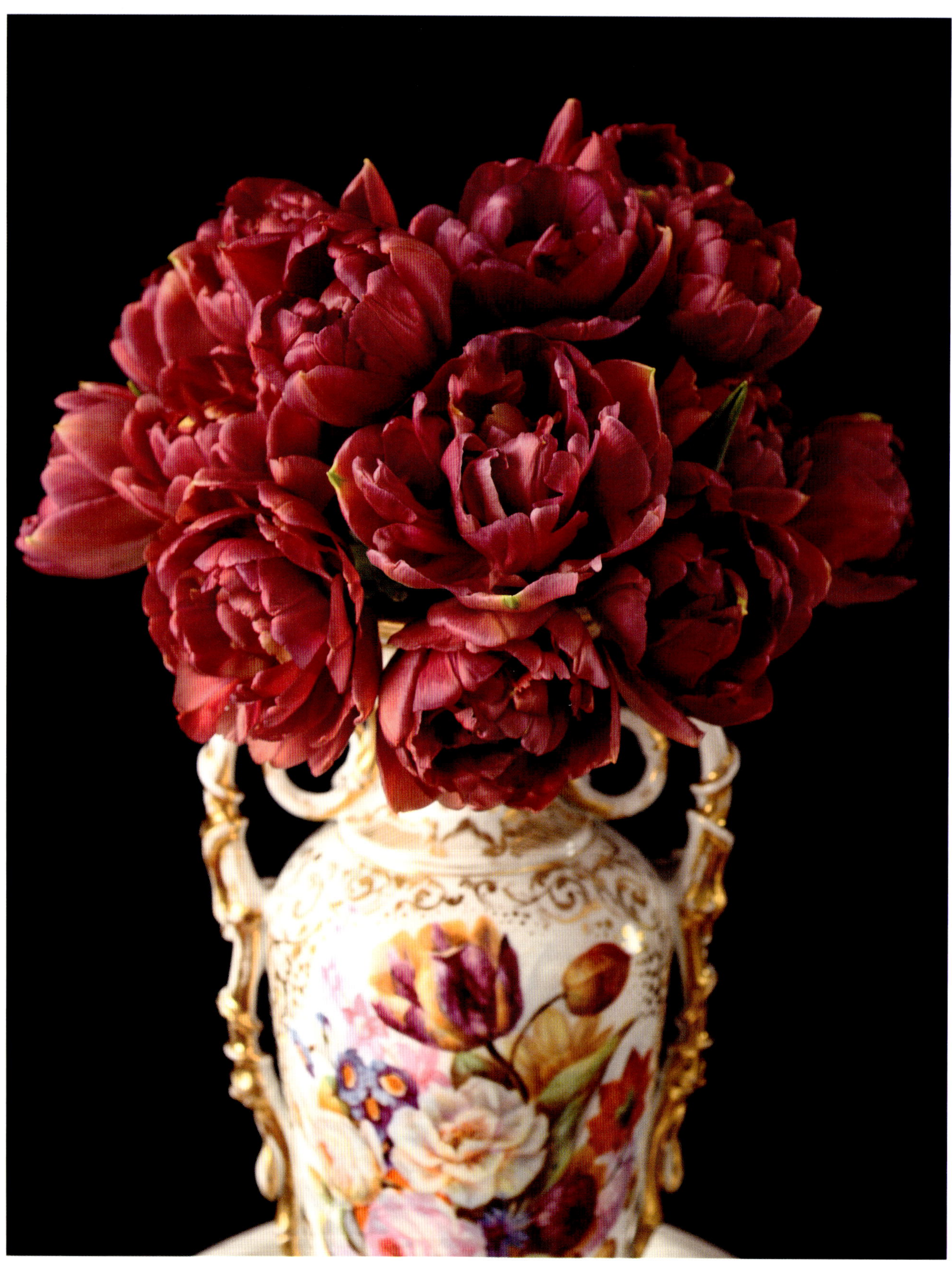

ABOVE and RIGHT: Double tulips, Paris, France. April 2025.

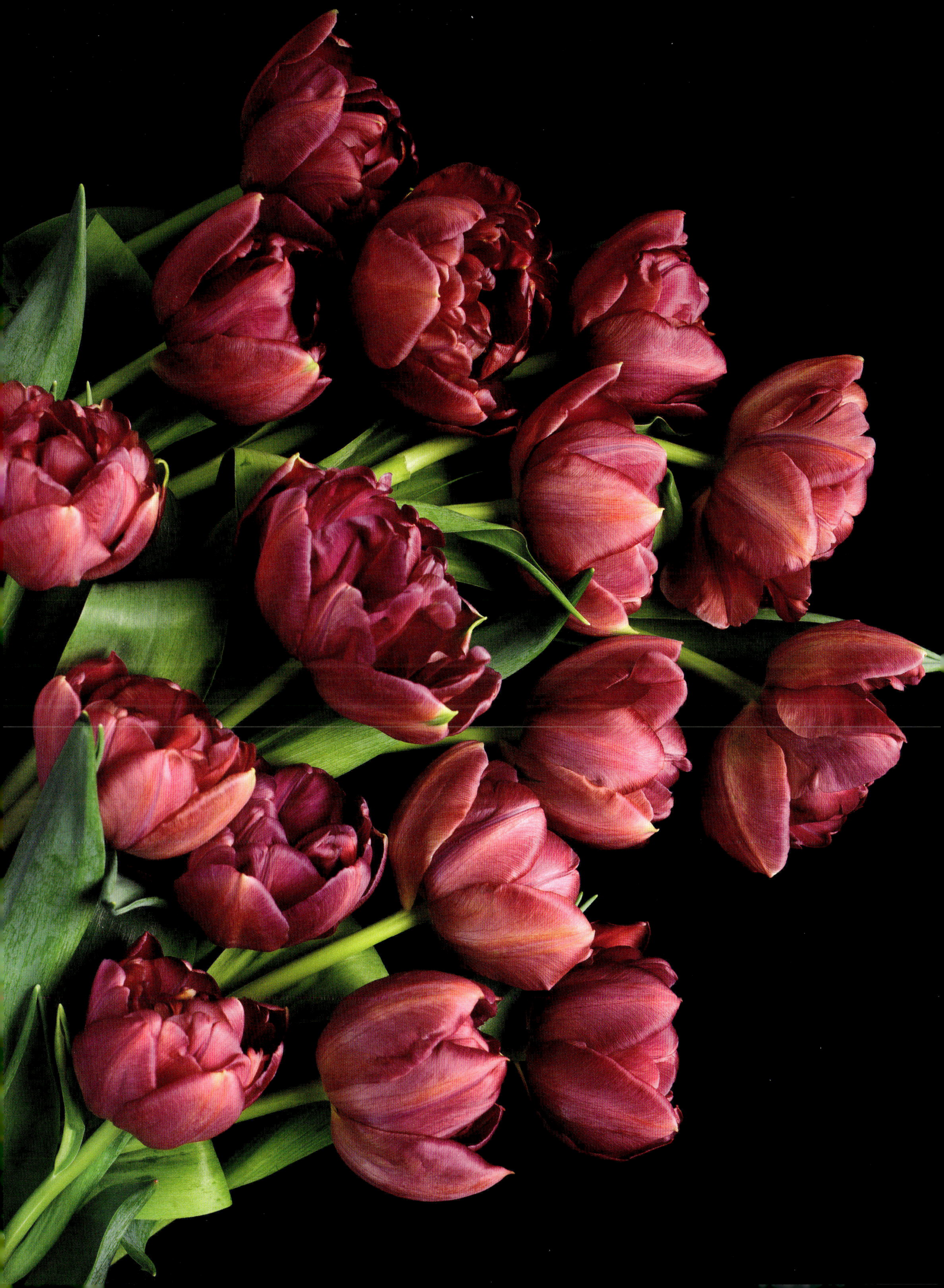

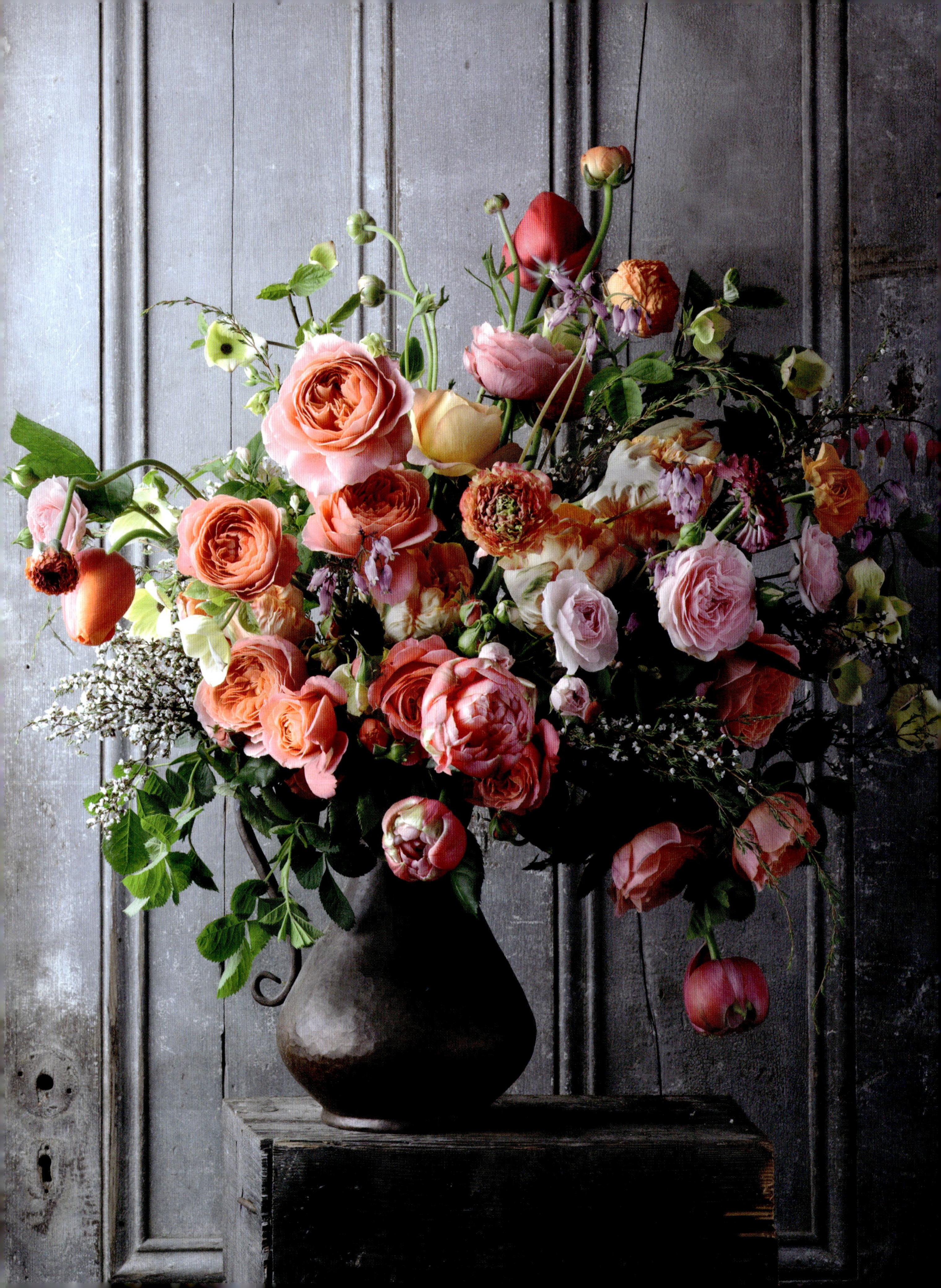

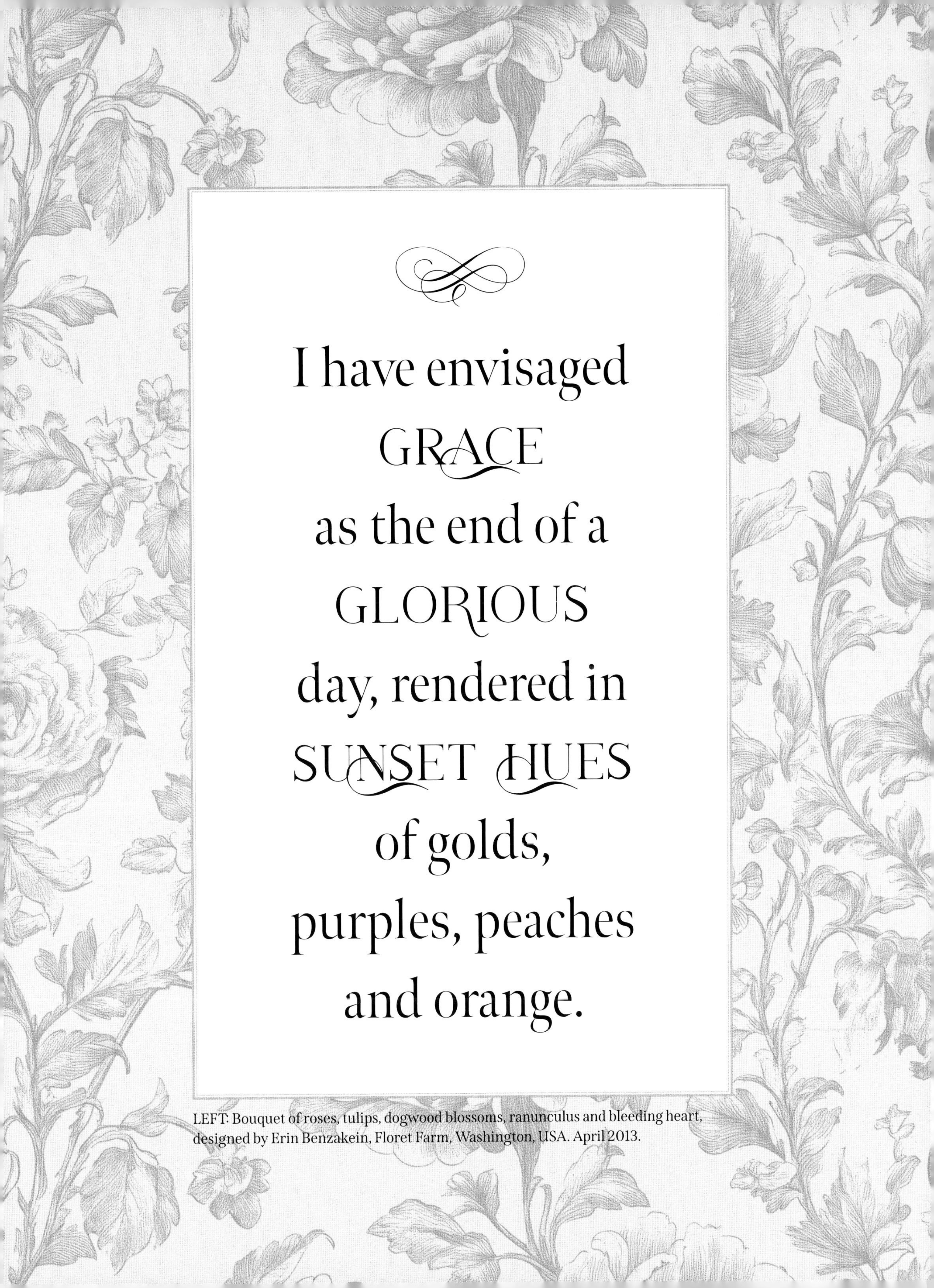

I have envisaged
GRACE
as the end of a
GLORIOUS
day, rendered in
SUNSET HUES
of golds,
purples, peaches
and orange.

LEFT: Bouquet of roses, tulips, dogwood blossoms, ranunculus and bleeding heart, designed by Erin Benzakein, Floret Farm, Washington, USA. April 2013.

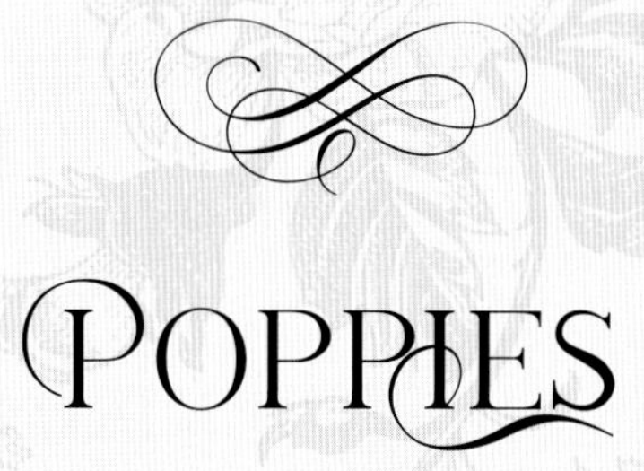

POPPIES

Hillhaven Garden, Washington, Shoreline, Washington, USA
Normandy, France

Iconic and richly symbolic with allegory and cultural significance, delicate poppies make a dramatic statement, either singly or spicing up an impromptu bucket of freshly cut spring blooms. With their crinkled, papery petals, creating graphic portraits of their unique silhouettes is one of the most interesting ways to portray them.

But en masse *they have a more profound effect. Driving through the peaceful French countryside in Normandy one June, we unexpectedly came upon a silent, endless field of poppies.*

Stirred slightly by the early summer breeze, under a lowering sky, their sombre presence was powerfully moving. My images from that encounter always affect me emotionally, forever associated with remembrance, and with grace personified.

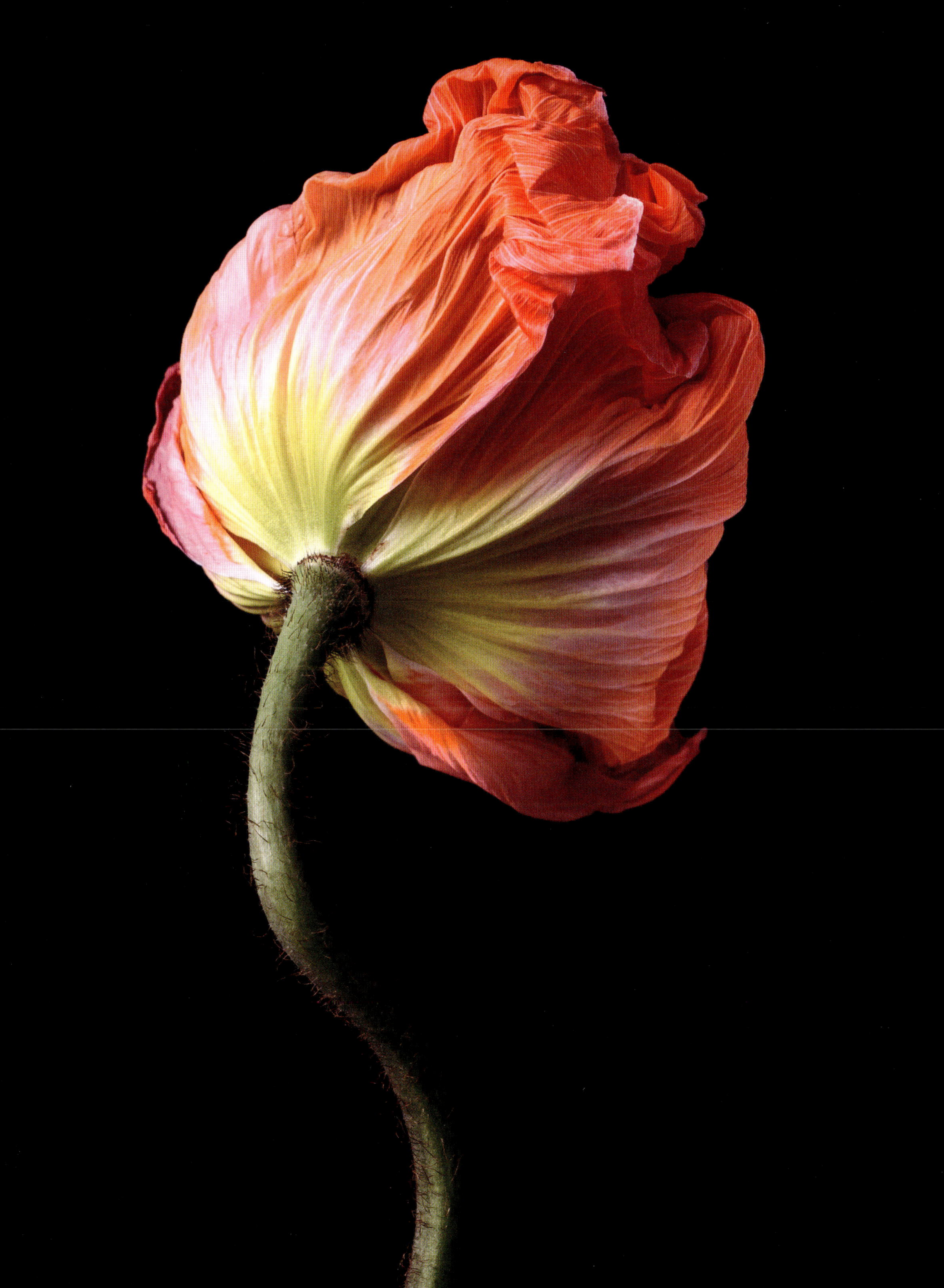

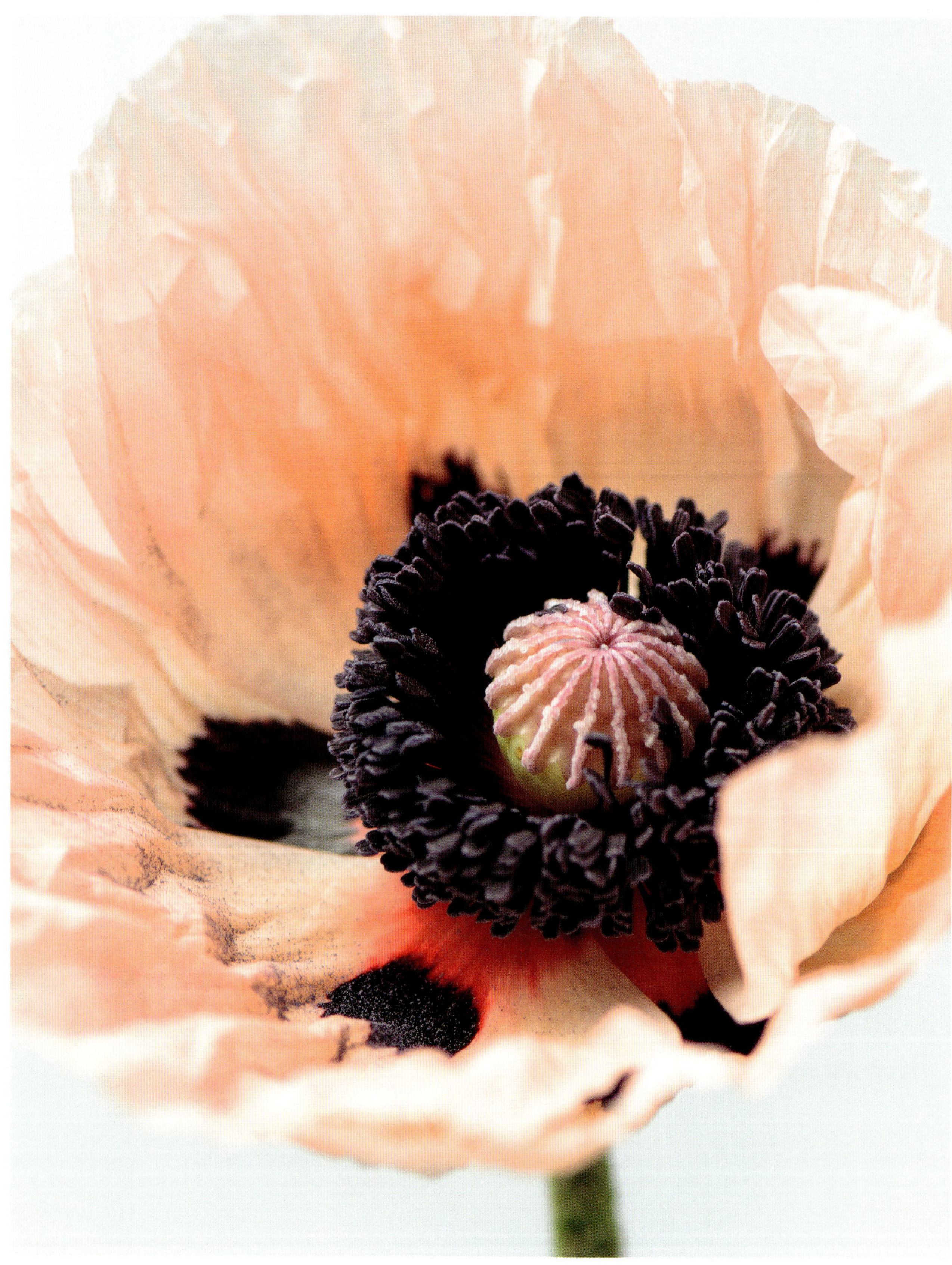

ABOVE: Close-up of poppy (*Papaver orientale*), Washington, USA. June 2013. RIGHT: Arrangement of poppies, peonies, ranunculus and variegated Italian buckthorn, Washington, USA. June 2015. OVERLEAF: Field of poppies, Normandy, France. June 2011.

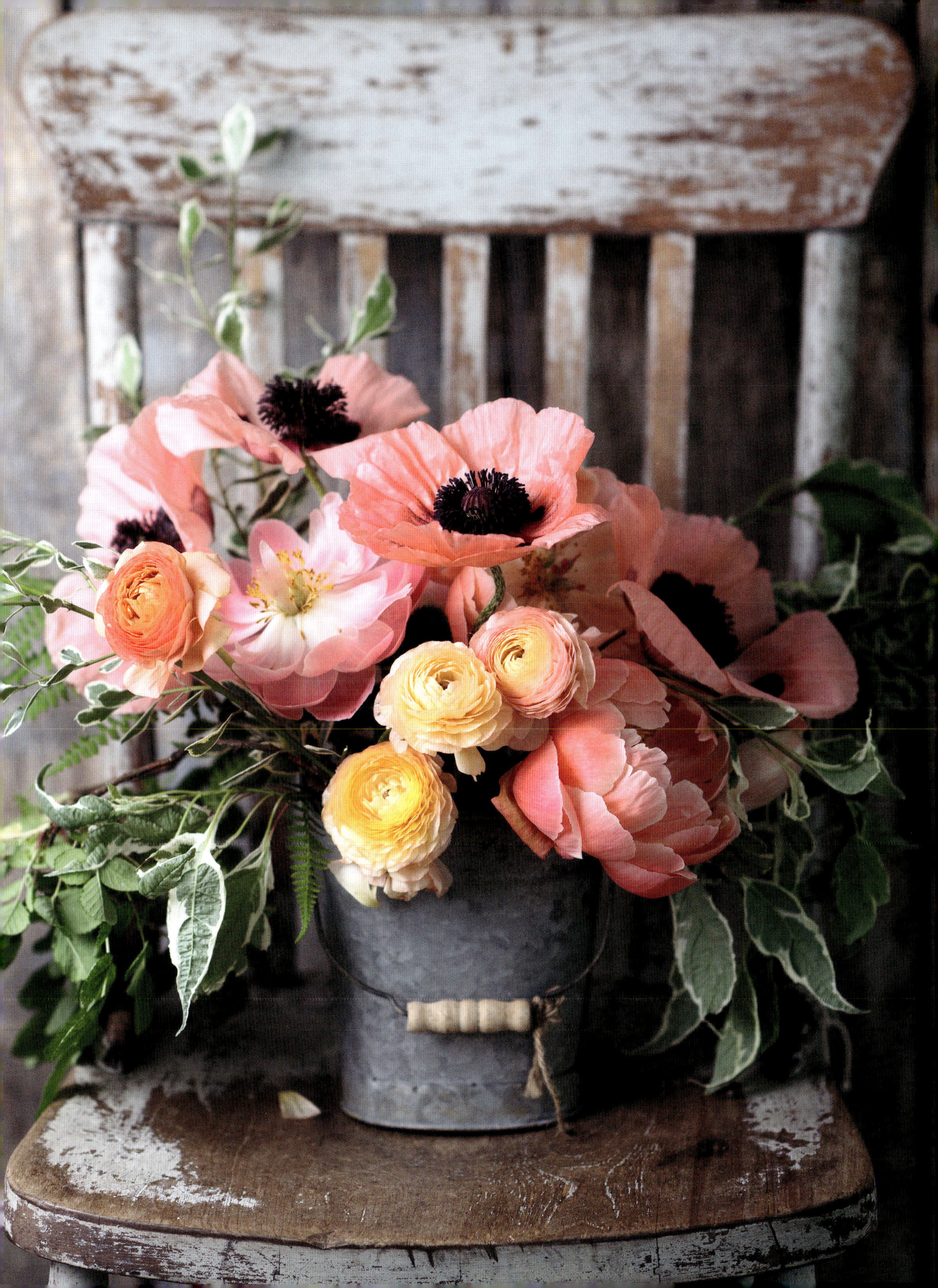

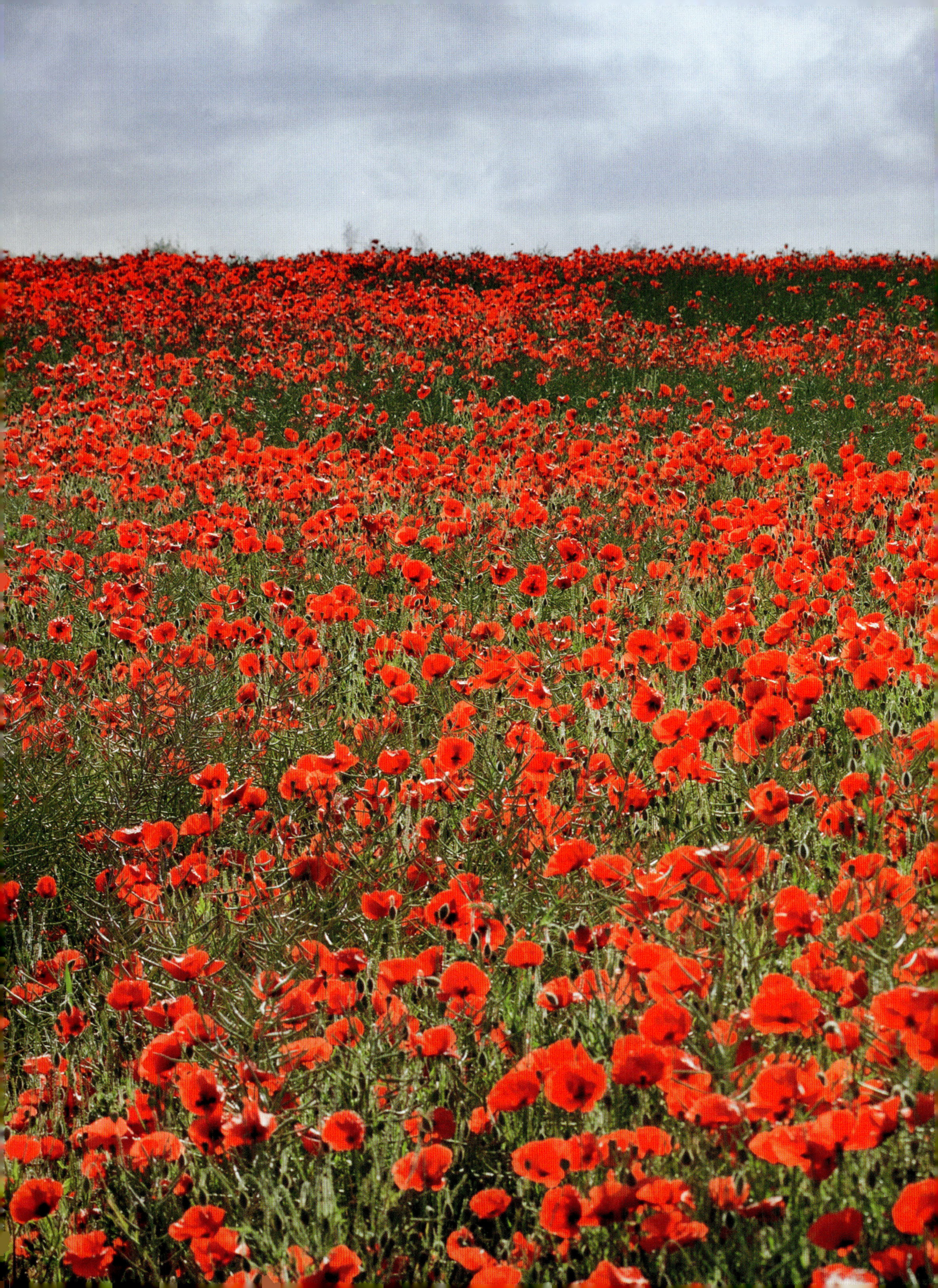

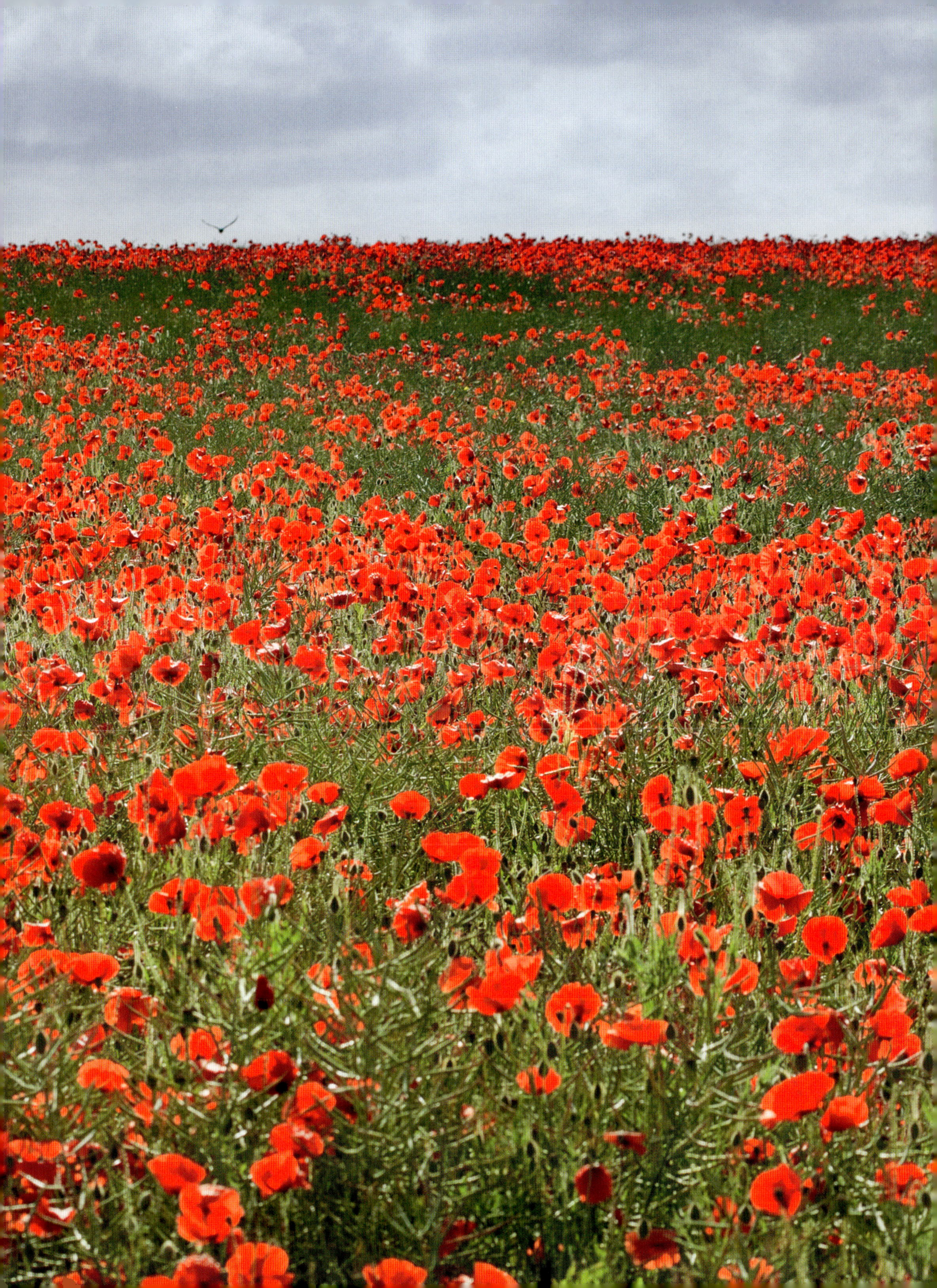

A BRIEF GUIDE TO PHOTOGRAPHING FLOWERS

The most rewarding aspect of floral photography is being connected to nature in an intimate manner, whether out in a garden or working with a single bloom indoors. Take advantage of the opportunity to slow down, observe and deepen your connection with the natural world.

This is by no means a comprehensive instruction manual, but these guidelines will offer a basic approach to the endlessly enjoyable world of flower photography.

Please note: The information herein applies most directly to SLR, DSLR or mirrorless equipment with interchangeable lenses. I have always used exclusively Nikon SLR and DSLR equipment, and all images in this book were taken with this system. However, with a few exceptions, the basics outlined here also apply to phone photography, which has advanced tremendously.

LOCATION

Don't think that you have to travel to a world-class garden or commercial flower field to capture exceptional floral images. Your own backyard or neighborhood can be excellent sources of worthy subjects. Garden centers, plant nurseries, roadside meadows, even the car park of your local shopping center can have pretty plantings.

If you choose to shoot indoors, gorgeous images can be obtained with a simple setup of a single bloom or bouquet next to a window. Or a favorite of mine is through the open door of a barn or shed, which casts a wide swathe of light.

EQUIPMENT

You will have the most creative freedom with a camera that has interchangeable lenses and that you can fully control as to exposure (shutter speed, aperture, light sensitivity). However, you do not need, at least initially, to shoot in manual mode. While that is something to strive for, cameras now are very sophisticated, and the automatic modes produce excellent results. There is no shame in using them, and sometimes they can be expedient in catching a shot you might otherwise miss.

Using a macro lens or macro setting will allow you to get very close to the flower and record details of its structure and form. Alternatively, a wide-angle lens will capture an overall landscape scene and enhance the feeling of space.

Becoming good friends with your tripod will open up a world of possibilities for flower photography. To ensure perfect sharpness, a tripod is vital.

For indoor photography, small backdrops in a selection of textures or colors are handy ways to give variety to your images. Foam core boards in black and white should be part of your basic setup.

SUBJECT AND MESSAGE

Begin with the vision of what you'd like to create. When starting out it can be helpful to have a visual reference library of images that you've seen and would like to emulate.

In deciding upon your subject, you can choose a single bloom or a cluster of flowers that might have interesting repeating patterns or textures.

Choose a specimen that is representative of that specific flower but is also photogenic, and one that is fresh and firm with minimal flaws and no petal or leaf damage. Examine it from all angles and visualize how you feel it would best be shown. Determine its unique features – the shapes of the petals, their color, the center detail or the way its features catch the light. What do you most want to share about this bloom with others? What mood or message does it suggest to you?

COMPOSITION

Decide how tight you want to frame the image and how much of the flower you want in focus. Most flowers lend themselves to close-ups with a shallow depth of field, where only a small section of the image is in sharp focus. Having one area of sharp focus, usually the center of the flower and its stamens, will give the viewer a focal point and entrance point to the image. The eye is always seeking something to land upon in a scene.

Be aware of the background. Simplify. Avoid clutter, hot spots of light or conflicting colors. Move around your subject until you have a background that is not distracting.

Try different perspectives and heights. Get down low on the same level as the flower, or even beneath it. Or try getting directly above it. Practice capturing different angles and see which is most effective to you.

All basic photography composition rules apply, including the rule of thirds, symmetry, filling the frame, foreground interest, etc.

LIGHTING

Lighting is your most important aspect to consider.

You can instantly improve much outdoor flower photography by avoiding direct sunlight. That high-contrast light creates dark shadows on the subject and burns out highlights, so you lose the detail in a flower. The eye is distracted by the extreme shifts of light and shadow.

A slightly overcast day is perfect, with a soft, even light that will illuminate the beauty of the flower and allow all its features to be seen. If you can't avoid the sun, you can block it with an umbrella or diffuser.

If I'm shooting outdoors on location, I'm particular about the light, and if it's too bright or contrasty, I simply won't shoot or will go out with diffusers to try to soften it. But I'd rather just shoot when the sky is cloudy and the light is gentle and uniform. That is the best way to capture all the detail and nuances of color in a flower. Early morning and late afternoon/golden hour, when the sun is low, are also excellent times. A greenhouse, such as in a garden center, offers near-perfect light conditions.

Backlighting can be dramatic and give flowers a glowing radiance, but make sure you don't lose detail by overexposure. Window lighting gives a classic look to an image. It's likely you will need a tripod, though, for more control.

Artificial lighting, when used correctly, can give you much more freedom, such as shooting late at night or on gloomy days. I don't recommend using an on-camera flash, but a reasonably priced, simple strobe system is a very useful tool. These are designed to match the color temperature of sunlight and, when used correctly, can help you create extremely sharp portraits without the need for a tripod. And since they replicate sunlight, it can be virtually impossible to tell if the image was created with natural or artificial light. This may seem a bold claim, but I have tested the theory many times and viewers really cannot tell the difference.

CHALLENGES

Most challenges are seasonal or weather-related. I am constantly consulting weather reports, climate charts, sunset and sunrise timetables. I pore over images from locations to try to accurately determine bloom times. It can be frustrating, so patience is required! Wind is always challenging and truly annoying, but these considerations do not need to concern you when you are starting out. Just be aware that when dealing with nature there are always variables to take into account.

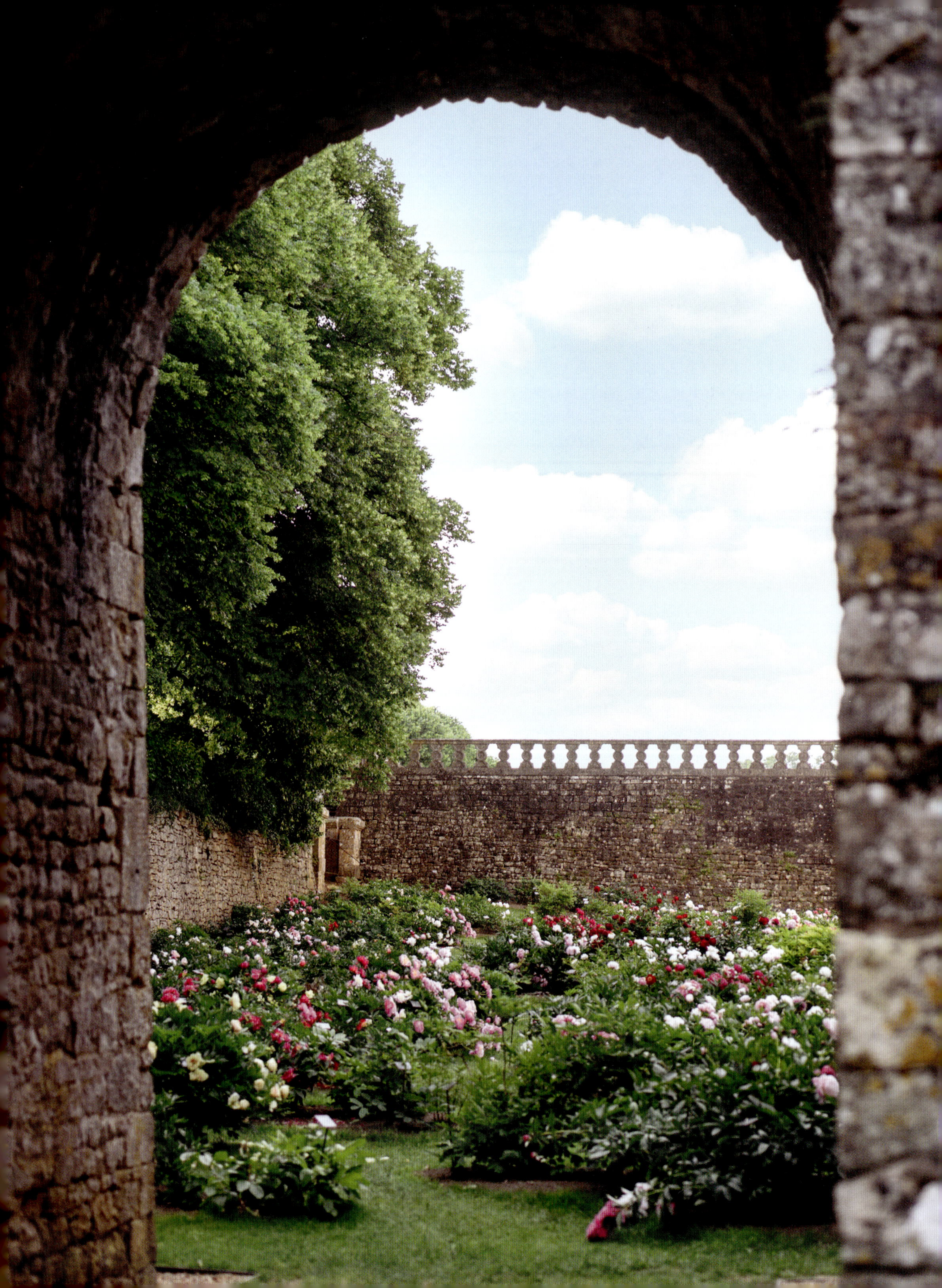

GARDEN INDEX

USA

Hillhaven Garden
Shoreline, Washington
Private garden, closed to the public

RoozenGaarde Tulips
15867 Beaver Marsh Rd
Mount Vernon, Washington 98273
www.tulips.com

Schreiner's Iris Gardens
3625 Quinaby Rd NE
Salem, Oregon 97303
www.schreinersgardens.com

Washington Park – International Rose Test Garden
400 SW Kingston Avenue
Portland, Oregon 97205
www.portland.gov/parks/washington-park-international-rose-test-garden

Woodland Park Rose Garden
750 N 50th Street
Seattle, Washington 98103
www.zoo.org/roses

CANADA

The Butchart Gardens
800 Benvenuto Avenue
Brentwood Bay
British Columbia V8M 1J8
butchartgardens.com

UNITED KINGDOM

David Austin Roses
Bowling Green Lane
Albrighton, Shropshire WV7 3HB
www.davidaustinroses.co.uk

The Regent's Park
The Royal Parks
London NW1 4NR
www.royalparks.org.uk/visit/parks/regents-park-primrose-hill

UK National Dahlia Collection
Kehelland Trust
Kehelland, Camborne TR14 0DD

EUROPE

Château de Brécy
8 rue du Château
14480 Creully sur Seulles, France
www.parcsetjardins.fr/jardins/84-jardins-du-chateau-de-brecy

Château de Sourches
Conservatoire de la Pivoine
72240 Saint-Symphorien, France
www.chateaudesourches.com

Jardin des Plantes
57 rue Cuvier
75005 Paris, France
www.jardindesplantesdeparis.fr

Jardin du Palais Royal
8 rue de Monpensier
75001 Paris, France
www.domaine-palais-royal.fr/en

The Tuileries Garden
Jardin des Tuileries
113 rue de Rivoli
75001 Paris, France
www.louvre.fr/decouvrir/les-jardins#le-jardin-des-tuileries

Jardin Shamrock
Route de la Cayenne
76119 Varengeville-sur-Mer
France
www.shamrock-varengeville.com/gb-accueil

Keukenhof
Stationsweg 166A
2161 AM Lisse
Netherlands
keukenhof.nl/en

Flying Colours Daffodils
Zomerdijkje 15
1934CT Egmond aan den Hoef
Netherlands
www.flyingcoloursdaffodils.com

SOUTH AMERICA

Maria Cécelia's Garden
El Arrayán, Chile
Private garden, closed to the public

TRADEMARK NOTICES FOR REGISTERED PLANTS

DAVID AUSTIN® ROSES

Throughout this book each David Austin® rose variety is referred to by its commercial name (e.g., 'Heritage'™). The variety denomination in relation to worldwide Plant Variety Rights (e.g., Austiger) and any trademark around the world relating to the commercial name has been omitted for ease of reading. The list below gives variety denominations and the trademark status of the commercial names.

Rosa 'Queen of Sweden'® Austiger
Rosa 'Boscobel'® Auscousin
Rosa 'Grace'® Auskeppy
Rosa 'A Shropshire Lad'® Ausled
Rosa 'Lady Emma Hamilton' Ausbrother
Rosa 'Gentle Hermione'® Ausrumba
Rosa 'Eglantyne'® Ausmak
Rosa 'Graham Thomas'® Ausmas
Rosa 'Port Sunlight'® Auslofty
Rosa 'Desdemona'® Auskindling
Rosa 'Kew Gardens', Ausfence
Rosa 'Golden Celebration'® Ausgold
Rosa 'Tranquillity'® Ausnoble
Rosa 'James Galway'® Auscrystal
Rosa 'Fighting Temeraire', Austrava
Rosa 'Charles Rennie Mackintosh', Ausren

MEILLAND®

Rosa 'Eden Rose'® (aka 'Pierre de Ronsard'®), Meiviolin

WALBERTON'S®

Scabiosa 'Butterfly Blue'®

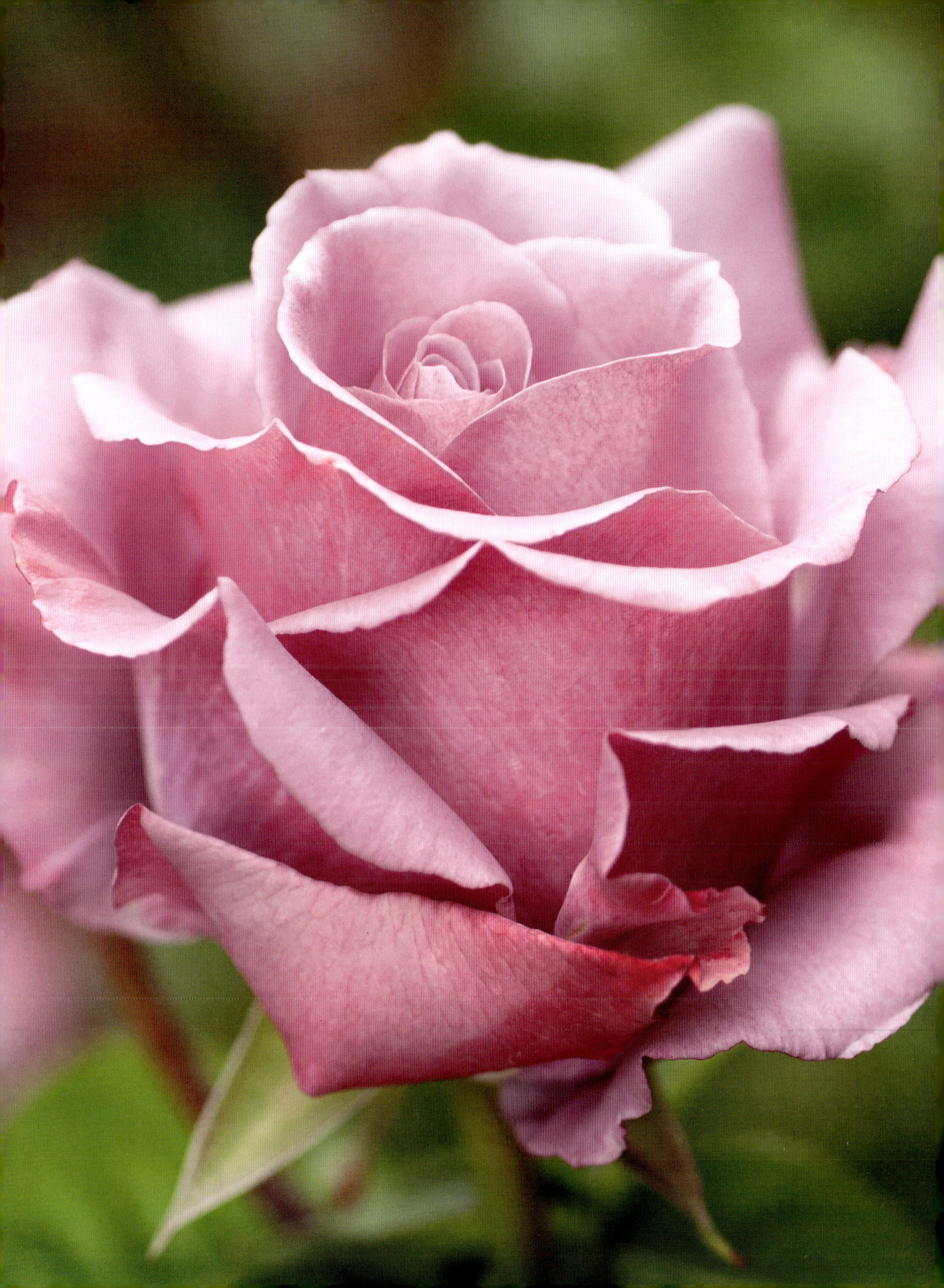

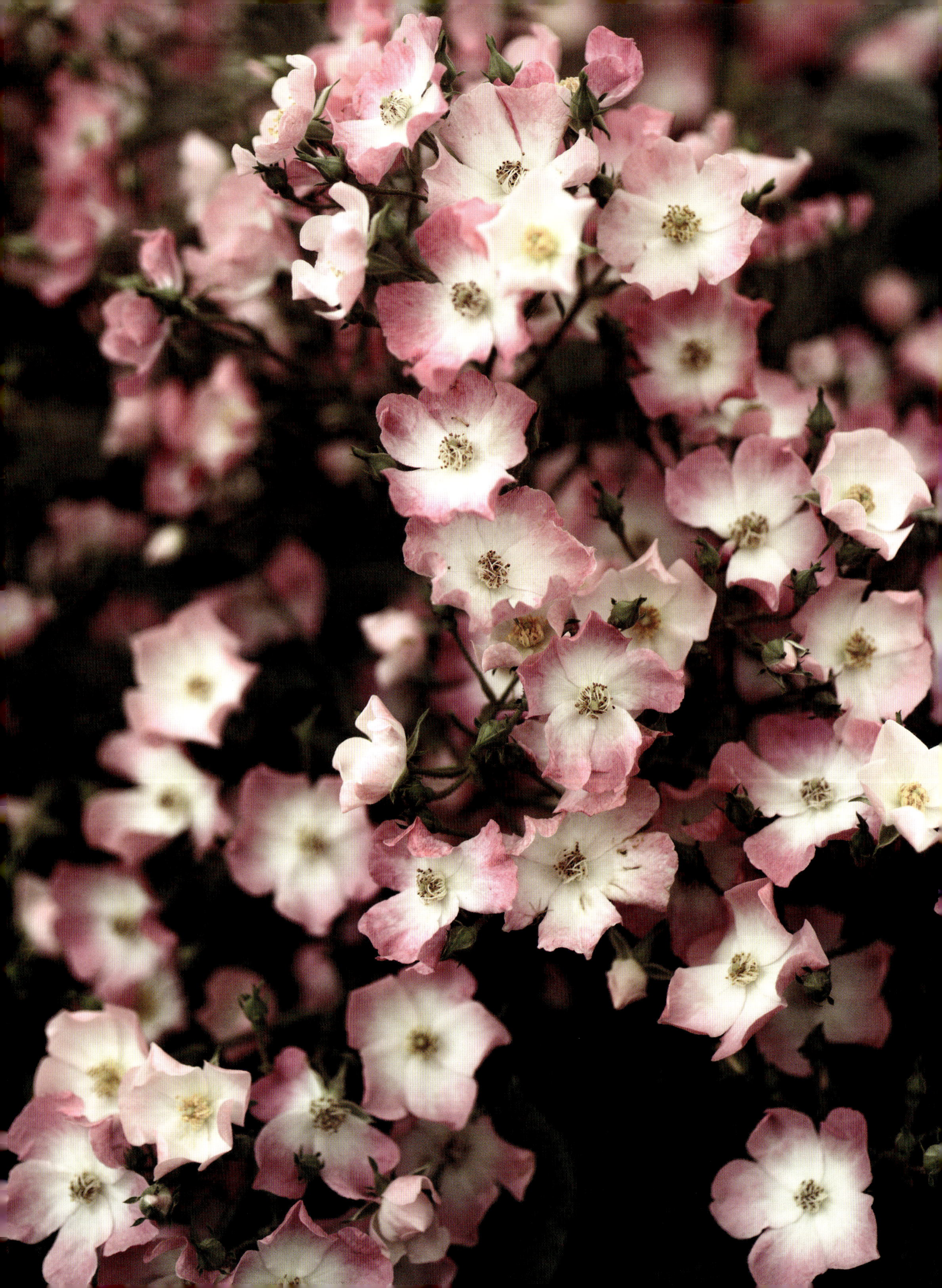

Dedicated to my sister, Leslie, with infinite love and gratitude for making so much possible.

ACKNOWLEDGMENTS

My heartfelt thanks to Managing Director and Publisher Lisa Milton, Publishing Director Laura Russell, Commissioning Editor Lucy Smith and Design Manager Alice Kennedy-Owen at Pavilion/HarperCollins UK for steadfastly guiding the creation of this book.

At Gibbs Smith, my gratitude to Senior Acquisitions Editor Madge Baird, who has long championed my work and who proposed the initial concept for this volume; and to the dedicated team there who are so integral to the continued success of my books.

Thank you to Laetitia Mayor of Floresie for her lavish floral installations over many years, and especially the recently created arrangements for the cover and chapter openings of this book.

Merci infiniment to my friends Bénédicte, Jean, Anne and Alexandre de Foucaud at Conservatoire de la Pivoine, Château de Sourches, France, and to Robert and Corinne Mallet at Shamrock Garden, Normandy, France.

Nothing herein would have been possible without the enthusiastic contributions of the hundreds of growers, breeders, farmers, florists, garden owners and flower friends I have been fortunate to know, who love, grow and share all these beautiful blooms. My deep appreciation to:

– David C. H. Austin, OBE, founder and breeder of David Austin Roses, and to Master Rosarian Michael Marriott.

– The owners, administrators and staff of RoozenGaarde Gardens and the Woodland Park Rose Garden, Washington, USA; The Portland Rose Garden and Schreiner's Iris Garden, Oregon, USA; The Butchart Gardens, Canada; Keukenhof Gardens, The Netherlands; Jardin d'Argences and Jardin de Brécy, Normandy, France; Jardin des Plantes, Jardin des Tuileries and Jardin du Palais Royal, Paris, France.

– The following Washington, USA–based flower farmers for supplying me with gorgeous blooms over many years: Dawn Severin of All My Thyme Farm, Geraldine Kildow of North Field Farm, and Erin Benzakein of Floret Flower Farm, whose beautiful arrangements appear on pages 60 and 286.

– My fellow passionate rose-loving friend Gracie at Grace Rose Farm for the dreamy Stephen Rulo roses, and my dear friend Maria Cecilia Lorca Mateluna for sharing her Chilean rose haven with me.

– As ever, endless gratitude to my family for their unfailing patience and support.

AUTHOR'S BIO

With a prominent international career spanning two decades, Georgianna Lane is recognized as one of the world's leading floral photographers.

She is the author and photographer of the bestselling *Cities in Bloom* trilogy (*Paris in Bloom*, *London in Bloom* and *New York in Bloom*) published by Abrams Books.

For ten years she has photographed the popular *Beautiful Varieties* floral book series, published by Pavilion Books and Gibbs Smith, which includes *Vintage Roses*, *Peonies*, *Dahlias*, *Lilies*, *Hydrangeas*, *Lilacs*, *Ranunculus*, *Chrysanthemums* and *Daffodils*.

Her romantic, light-infused images have appeared in hundreds of books, magazines and lifestyle products including calendars, stationery, wall decor and giftware, with her licensed greetings cards selling over 400,000 copies worldwide.

Additional publishing clients and licensing partners include Random House, HarperCollins US, American Greetings, Papyrus/Recycled Greetings, Hoffman Media and Graphique de France.

Publications featuring her work include *The New Yorker*, *Country Living*, *House Beautiful*, *National Geographic Traveler*, *ArtNEWS*, *Victoria*, *Garden Design*, *Garden Gate*, *The English Garden*, *Horticulture*, *Flower magazine*, *BBC Gardens Illustrated*, *Britain*, *Romantic Homes*, *Nikon Owner* and *Gardener's World*.

She lives in the beautiful 7th arrondissement of Paris.

AUTHOR WEBSITE AND JOURNAL:
GEORGIANNALANE.COM

PARIS LIFESTYLE BRAND:
GEORGIANNALANEPARIS.COM

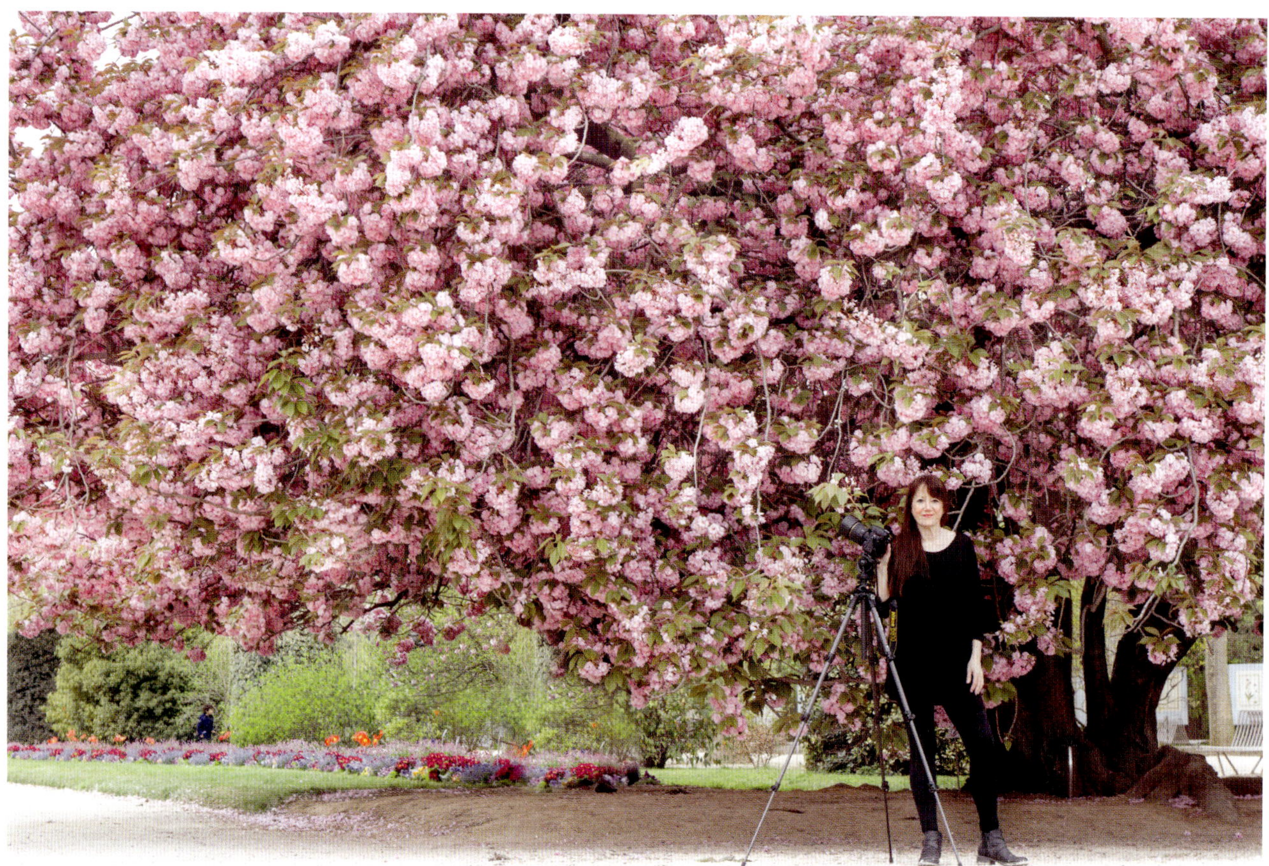

Georgianna with her favorite tree in Paris at Jardin des Plantes. Photograph by Julia Willard.

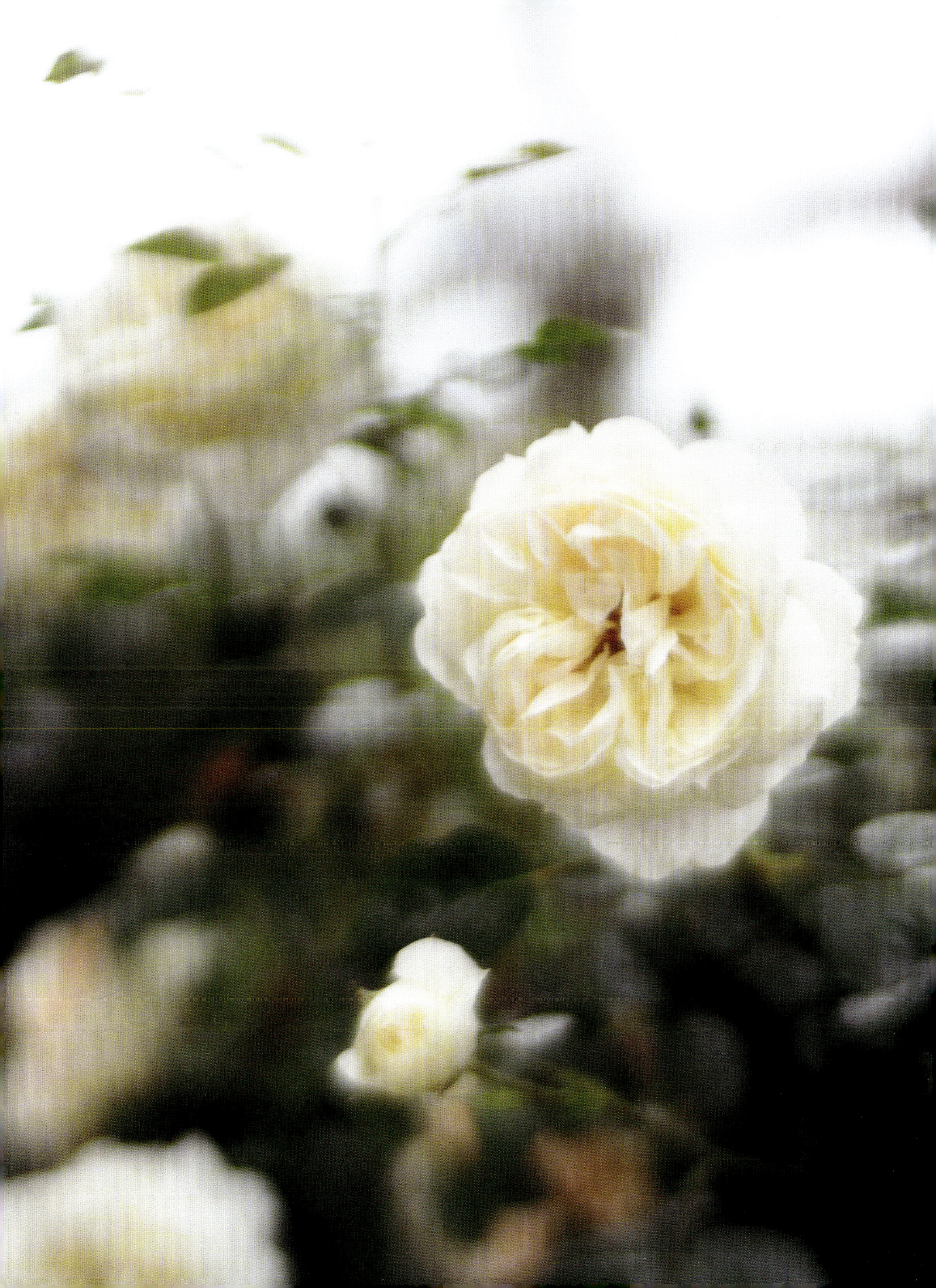

30 29 28 27 26 10 9 8 7 6 5 4 3 2 1

Published in the United States of America
by Gibbs Smith
570 N. Sportsplex Dr.
Kaysville, Utah 84037
www.gibbs-smith.com

Published by arrangement with HarperCollins
Publishers Ltd

The authorized representative in the EEA is Simon and Schuster Netherlands BV, Herculesplein 96 3584 AA Utrecht, Netherlands, info@simonandschuster.nl

Library of Congress Control Number: 2025937453
ISBN 978-1-4236-6966-1

Publishing Director: Laura Russell
Commissioning Editor: Lucy Smith
Editorial Assistant: Daisy Gudmunsen
Design Manager: Alice Kennedy-Owen
Designer: Sophie Yamamoto
Production Controller: Emma Hatlen
Copyeditor: Helena Caldon
Proofreader: Corinne Colvin
Senior Production Controller: Louis Harvey

Reproduction: Rival Colour Ltd, UK

Printed and Bound in China by RR Donnelley, APS

This product is made of FSC®-certified and other controlled material.